ORGANIZATIONS
THEORY AND DESIGN

ARTHUR G. BEDEIAN
Louisiana State University
RAYMOND F. ZAMMUTO
University of Colorado at Denver

THE DRYDEN PRESS
Chicago   Fort Worth   San Francisco   Philadelphia
Montreal   Toronto   London   Sydney   Tokyo

Acquisitions Editor: Robert Gemin
Developmental Editor: Judy Sarwark
Project Editor: Teresa Chartos
Design Manager: Alan Wendt
Production Manager: Barb Bahnsen
Permissions Editor: Doris Milligan
Director of Editing, Design, and Production: Jane Perkins

Cover Designer: C. J. Petlick, Hunter Graphics
Copy Editor: Maggie Jarpey
Indexer: David Talley
Text Type: 10/12 Palatino

Library of Congress Cataloging-in-Publication Data

Bedeian, Arthur G.
    Organizations—theory and design / Arthur G. Bedeian, Raymond F.
Zammuto. — 1st ed.
      p.   cm.
    ISBN 0-03-012583-9
     1. Organizational behavior.   2. Organizational change.
    3. Organizational effectiveness.   I. Zammuto, Raymond F.
    II. Title
    HD58.7.B415   1991
    658.4—dc20   90-3102
                                                                       CIP

Printed in the United States of America
012-015-987654321
Copyright © 1991 by The Dryden Press, a division of
Holt, Rinehart and Winston, Inc.

Address orders:
The Dryden Press
Orlando, FL 32887

Address editorial correspondence:
The Dryden Press
908 N. Elm St.
Hinsdale, IL 60521

The Dryden Press
Holt, Rinehart and Winston
Saunders College Publishing

Cover Source: J. A. Kraulis/Masterfile.

To Varsenick and Arthur Bedeian
for reasons lost to history

and

to Lynda, Katherine, and Tab
for every reason

Arthur G. Bedeian

In memory of Louis R. Pondy—
friend, teacher, and scholar

and

to Marilyn, Jackie, and Rachel
for their love, support, and patience

Raymond F. Zammuto

PREFACE

As modern society's most dominant institution, organizations—the subject of this book—exert a tremendous influence on our lives. To provide information that will help current and aspiring managers, the authors apply more than three decades of combined teaching experience in explaining the foundations and implications of organization theory based on major research findings. Each chapter aims to bridge the gap between theory and practice, using real-world examples to illustrate how organizations are influenced by structure, design, and the environment. The intent is not to present an exhaustive review of research studies but, rather, to create the most current, challenging, readable, and exciting survey of organization knowledge that has yet to appear.

CONTENT

Organizations: Theory and Design is divided into four major sections. Chapters 1 through 3 (Part I) explain how organizations function as goal-seeking systems. After an overview presented in Chapter 1, Chapter 2 examines more closely the role of goals in organizations, the kinds of goals, the purposes they serve, and how they change. Chapter 3 explores the concept of organizational effectiveness within the context of three different evaluative approaches—the goal-based, the systems, and the stakeholder models. Each approach highlights a different aspect of an organization's input–output relationships.

Chapters 4 through 7 (Part II) examine how managers structure their organizations for effective performance. Chapter 4 describes a number of basic design concepts, including job specialization, formalization, and centralization. Chapter 5 examines how individuals and jobs are grouped into work units and how different structuring patterns affect an organization's ability to accomplish different ends. This chapter also looks at the techniques that managers use to overcome the shortcomings of the particular structure they have chosen. Chapter 6 focuses on the relationship between an organization's technology (along with its coordination and control needs) and its structure. Also examined in this context are advanced information technologies and computer-integrated manufacturing systems. Finally,

Chapter 7 looks at organization design in a global economy that has created new coordination and control needs, requiring different types of structures.

Chapters 8 through 10 (Part III) discuss the relationship between an organization and its environment, focusing on how environmental conditions affect strategy and structure. Chapter 8 examines the three major streams of contemporary thought on this subject—contingency theory, strategic choice, and population ecology, historically considered competing views. Chapters 9 and 10 present an integrative model of the complementary aspects of these approaches. Chapter 9 specifically considers strategy in this context; Chapter 10, structure.

Chapters 11 through 14 (Part IV) examine the transitions, dynamics, and processes common in organizations as they are redesigned. Chapter 11 deals with organizational growth, whereas Chapter 12 focuses on the special challenges of managing a declining organization, and discusses the design implications of turning such an organization around. Chapters 13 and 14 look at, respectively, two fundamental organizational processes that have to be managed in both growing and declining organizations: decision making/learning and organizational change. Techniques for overcoming resistance to change are included in the discussion.

LEARNING-ORIENTED FEATURES

An effort has been made throughout *Organizations: Theory and Design* to combine both a theoretical and a practical perspective, in the belief that neither is sufficient alone. Thus, the following learning-oriented features have been incorporated into each chapter in order to tie organization theory together with its application.

Learning Objectives

Each chapter begins with a set of learning objectives keyed to main topics, intended to serve as study guidelines.

Opening Vignettes

Chapter-opening vignettes capture reader interest by applying ensuing material to a real-world situation. They also provide relevant examples for discussion.

Focus on Design

The boxed items that appear in each chapter are carefully crafted to present real-world examples showing the application of key organization design concepts.

Summaries

Each chapter concludes with a summary that repeats and answers the "Learning Objectives," thus reiterating main topics in a logical and thorough manner.

Discussion Questions

Every chapter is supplemented with relevant questions to assess student understanding of the main topics examined. Each question calls for an analysis or practical application of what has been learned, thereby serving as a mechanism for self-teaching.

Key Terms and Glossary

Key terms are set in boldface type within each chapter when introduced. They are arranged in alphabetical order in the glossary at the back of the book to provide a handy reference for the reader.

Design Audits

Each chapter closes with a unique design audit exercise, developed by Ray Zammuto, that walks the student, step by step, through the application of important organization design concepts. Using the design audits is an extremely effective way to learn about organization design because they are the closest approximation possible of "hands-on" experience. Complete teaching notes describe how to integrate the design audit exercises into your course.

Part Cases

Comprehensive cases demonstrating an actual organization design challenge appear at the end of each part. Analysis of these cases requires integrating relevant material drawn from the chapters and parts. The cases have been drawn from various sources in the popular press (for example, *Business Week, Fortune, The Wall Street Journal*), and *illustrate* selected design concepts, showing how actual organizations deal with the challenges and issues presented in each part. Suggestions for using the cases with specific chapters and integrating part cases are included in the *Instructor's Manual*.

INSTRUCTOR'S MANUAL

Co-authored with John E. Gould and Shelly C. Whittington, the *Instructor's Manual* contains learning objectives, chapter outlines, responses to discussion questions, multiple-choice test items, and 35 transparency masters taken from key figures in the text. Ray Zammuto has developed the teaching notes and suggestions for design audits and part cases.

ACKNOWLEDGMENTS

No book, fact or fiction, is ever exclusively the product of the individuals whose names appear on its title page. Inevitably, authors are influenced by interactions with others. We would like to thank the following professors who reviewed the book and provided many useful comments and suggestions:

Jeff Alexander, *University of Michigan*

Gordon E. Dehler, *University of Dayton*

Bruce H. Drake, *University of Portland*

Thomas C. Head, *DePaul University*

Y. Paul Huo, *Washington State University*

Alan Meyer, *University of Oregon*

William Moore, *Drake University*

Luke Novelli, Jr., *University of North Carolina—Greensboro*

Brad Shrader, *Iowa State University*

The Louisiana State University College of Business Administration has continued to provide a unique setting in which to work. Research support and release time were provided by the Ralph and Kacoo Olinde Distinguished Professorship. Special thanks go to Dean James B. Henry for giving me the autonomy to continue my work. Appreciation is also due Brenda M. Gatlin and Patti J. Gunter for their excellent secretarial support. The efforts of Syed F. Hoda, Susan M. Moniotte, Ravindran Adimoolam, Antoinette S. Phillips, Rebecca G. Long, and Andrew Ferguson, graduate assistants over the past four-plus years, were indispensable. Special thanks are due John E. Gould and Shelly C. Whittington for their assistance in preparing the accompanying *Instructor's Manual*. It was a privilege to work with this entire group.

Thanks are due to the more than 200 graduate and undergraduate students at the University of Colorado at Denver who used the manuscript in draft form. Their comments on the chapters, cases, and design audits significantly improved the quality of the book. Appreciation is also due to Mike Hayes, University of Colorado at Denver; Edward J. O'Connor, University of Colorado at Denver; and Stephen Shortell, Northwestern University, whose comments were very helpful. Special thanks to Mary Waller for her efforts in preparing the chapter-opening vignettes.

At The Dryden Press, Robert Gemin, Judy Sarwark, and Penny Gaffney were a pleasure to work with on this project. Teresa Chartos and Barb Bahnsen cheerfully saw the project through the various stages of production. Doris Milligan skillfully obtained necessary permissions. Designer Alan

Wendt applied his creative talent to integrate the text type and graphics, resulting in a visual presentation that captures the dynamic spirit of the text's topic. Maggie Jarpey's copyediting skills added greatly to the clarity of the text, and David Talley has prepared a complete, detailed index.

Finally, on the home front, our families provided encouragement and inspiration. Our expressions of gratitude are long overdue.

Arthur G. Bedeian
Raymond F. Zammuto

October 1990

ABOUT THE AUTHORS

Arthur G. Bedeian is the Ralph and Kacoo Olinde Distinguished Professor, and Chairman of the Department of Management at Louisiana State University. He is a past president of the Academy of Management, the Foundation for Administrative Research, the Allied Southern Business Association, the Southern Management Association, and the Southeastern Institute for Decision Sciences.

A former editor of the *Journal of Management*, Professor Bedeian has authored more than 150 articles, monographs, and papers. His work has appeared in the *Academy of Management Journal, Journal of Applied Psychology, Journal of Management, Journal of Vocational Behavior, Academy of Management Review, Behavioral Science, Personnel Psychology,* and *Organizational Behavior and Human Decision Processes.* In addition to *Organizations: Theory and Design,* Professor Bedeian is the author of *Management* (2d ed., The Dryden Press, 1989).

Professor Bedeian has taught management, organization theory, organizational behavior, and the development of management thought. He has been involved in management development and consulting for the Veterans Administration, Booz Allen & Hamilton, CBS, and the United States Air Force.

Raymond F. Zammuto is an Associate Professor of Management at the University of Colorado at Denver. He is an officer in the Organization and Management Theory division of the Academy of Management and an Associate Editor of the Academy's *Executive.* He also has been a member of the Organizational Behavior Teaching Society board.

Professor Zammuto has served on the editorial boards of *Administrative Science Quarterly,* the *Academy of Management Journal,* and the *Organizational Behavior Teaching Review.* His research has appeared in the *Academy of Management Review, Research in Organizational Behavior, Journal of Management Studies, Journal of Applied Psychology, Research in Organizational Change and Development, Personnel Psychology,* and in several other journals. He has authored one other book, *Assessing Organizational Effectiveness: Systems Change, Adaptation, and Strategy* (SUNY Press, 1982).

CONTENTS IN BRIEF

CONTENTS

Contents

Contents

Contents

Contents

Why Organization Design Is Important

Organizations and Organization Design

Learning Objectives

Upon completing this chapter, you should be able to

1. Understand how, as the dominant institution in modern society, organizations exert a tremendous influence on our lives.
2. Explain why it is worthwhile to study organizations.
3. Define what is meant by an "organization."
4. Discuss organizations as open systems.
5. Explain why it is worthwhile to study organization theory and design.
6. Understand why organizations are continually being redesigned.

HOW THE COOKIE CRUMBLES

It is not unusual in California's Silicon Valley to hear about entrepreneurs who have suddenly become multimillionaires. Although most have become wealthy by designing computer chips, cookie baker Debbi Fields has proven that chocolate chips can be just as lucrative.

The story of how Debbi Fields turned into Mrs. Fields "The Cookie Lady" is now a legend in U.S. business history.[1] In 1977, at the ripe old age of 20, Debbi opened the first Mrs. Fields Chocolate Chippery (as it was then called) in a downtown Palo Alto grocery near Stanford University. Since opening her second store one year later at the Pier 39 shopping mall in San Francisco, Mrs. Fields Cookies has become a chain of over 700 outlets, including international stores in Hong Kong, Japan, Australia, Canada, and England. By 1987, this family of stores included 122 La Petite Boulangeries, a chain of bakery/cafes; 129 Jessica's Cookies and Famous Chocolate units; two Jenessa's retail stores offering handmade gifts in Park City, Utah, and Santa Ana, California; Jenny's Swingset, selling children's playwear in Park City; a Mrs. Fields Dessert Store for ice cream, cookies, cakes, and pies in west Los Angeles; and a Mrs. Fields Candy Factory and Cookie College in Park City, the latter to provide week-long training sessions for store managers. Finally, since Mrs. Fields uses 10 percent of the world's macadamia nut crop, it owns a farm in Hawaii to assure a continuous supply.

Over one decade, Mrs. Fields Cookies grew from an exceedingly simple idea into a highly successful organization. Beginning with a $50,000 bank loan, Debbi now heads an international company whose shares are traded on the London Stock Exchange. The story of how Mrs. Fields Cookies evolved from a one-person adventure into a worldwide food empire offers a classic example of the need for understanding organization design.

Originally Debbi had wanted only one small store where she could personally serve each customer. However, as her first store became more successful, several of her employees wanted to manage their own Mrs. Fields. So, Debbi opened another store.

While at her first store, she had to literally stand out front and give cookies away, her second store at Pier 39 was an almost immediate success. A few weeks after opening, she received a call from the Pier 39 management. They yelled, "You've got long lines. Get rid of the lines—you're driving us crazy!" The line of customers waiting to buy cookies stretched out the door and wrapped around the building, jamming up the doorways of other shops. Debbi had to expand the store and hire more employees.

Soon Debbi found that she was 22 years old and working 16 hours a day, rushing frantically from store to store, trying desperately to keep everything under control. Mrs. Fields Cookies was taking every ounce of her energy. She clearly needed help. It had become increasingly clear that the now three stores did not require three times the effort of one store, they required ten times the effort.

5

Debbi was learning what the managers of every expanding organization ulti-
mately learn. The means by which one person produces a few dozen chocolate chip
cookies is soon no longer efficient for making some 15 different kinds of cookies, served
at over 700 stores in 39 states and 5 foreign countries. Such a far-flung empire,
generating over $87 million in annual sales in 1987, requires clearly communicated
goals, a coordinated structure, and dedicated employees with specific duties. Employ-
ees performing similar tasks had to be grouped together into departments. Additional
levels of management were required to coordinate various departmental functions.
Staff specialists were needed to introduce policies, procedures, and rules for account-
ing, sales, personnel, and marketing activities.

Mrs. Fields Cookies success was as much a result of having developed a sound
organization structure as it was of having outstanding products. As it began to
expand nationally and internationally, Debbi wisely realized that a congruence
must exist between the company's philosophy and its structure. In this respect,
however, Mrs. Fields Cookies is not unique. The successful management of any
undertaking requires a carefully designed organization structure. As the follow-
ing chapters will demonstrate, a thorough understanding of organization theory
and design greatly enhances an organization's ability to achieve its goals in an
efficient and effective manner.

WHY STUDY ORGANIZATIONS?

AS modern society's most dominant institution, organizations exert a
tremendous influence on our lives. Whether by choice or necessity, we
obtain a large measure of our cultural, material, and social satisfaction from
organizations. Modern organizations include factories, offices, hospitals,
prisons, churches, schools, armies, newspapers, health agencies, voluntary
associations, labor unions, public agencies, farmers' cooperatives, and universities. These and other organizations influence virtually every aspect of
our existence. We are born in hospitals and educated in schools. A typical
workday finds most of us on our jobs in organizations for half our waking
hours. When not at work, we participate in organized recreational activities.
Politics, community activities, and religious observances are also typically
carried out in organized settings. As Robert Roy notes, "In human society
almost everyone, save the few who live in hermit-like seclusion, belongs to
more than one organization and most belong to many. Organizations are as
familiar and ubiquitous as people."[2] In this respect, organization is as old as
human society itself.

Organizations were first created to reach goals beyond the capacity of a
single person's hands and brain. In today's world, only organizations can
produce and distribute the multiplicity of goods and services that for many
are an indispensable part of modern life. Goods such as Boeing 747 airplanes,

TV sets, and heating and air-conditioning systems could not be produced efficiently by a single individual. Services such as electrical power for homes and offices, cable TV, accident insurance, and international investments in currencies and real estate can rarely be performed single-handedly. The intricacies of producing modern goods and services call for the joint efforts of many people. Organizations are thus the principal mechanism in today's modern world by which humans join together to satisfy many important needs.

The reasons for studying organizations can be summarized as follows:

1. *Organizations are the bedrock of modern civilization.* Not only are organizations a dominant and inescapable feature of contemporary society, they have largely redefined modern civilization. As an "action medium," organizations "have been, and remain, the instrumental means through which man has harnessed and controlled nature."[3] Indeed, as Edward Mason contends, "to suggest a drastic change in the scope or character of [their] activity is to suggest a drastic alteration in the structure of society."[4]

Decisions made in organizations—particularly business firms—affect, among other things, the availability and allocation of goods and services, the distribution of wealth and privilege, and the opportunity for meaningful work, growth, and self-expression. In short, organizations shape the conditions whereby we live and work, that is, our very conditions of existence, our life chances. They pervade every aspect of modern society, making all of us, for good or bad, dependent on them. No matter where we turn, we are subject to their influence. This alone is justification for their study.

2. *Organizations have immense power.* The power that the largest organizations, the multinational industrial corporations, wield is mind-boggling. The world's 50 biggest industrial corporations employ 8.8 million people, more than the population of Sweden. They generated 1987 sales of $1.5 trillion. Their profits totaled over $56.7 billion, nearly twice the gross national product of Ireland. The mainstays of this elite—General Motors, Royal Dutch/Shell, Exxon, Ford, Toyota, DuPont, Unilever—set styles, invest money, and build plants that alter national economies.[5]

In addition to tremendous financial power, the world's multinational industrial corporations have tremendous social power. Consider the fact that in 1987 the 500 largest U.S. industrial corporations took in two-thirds of the profits of the whole American corporate universe, providing payroll for some 12 percent of the nation's employees, and perhaps more importantly, their physical and intellectual environment for 40 hours or more a week.[6] These same 500 not only produce half the goods and services that we consume, but the advertising that affects the way we think about these products and, in many instances, our lifestyles and the way we think about ourselves as well. Even further, they provide the financial support for commercial television, clearly the most important influence on our culture for the last 50 years.[7]

3. *Studying organizations has great practical value.* Most of us work in organizations. In the United States, there has been a steady trend away from self-employment, almost without interruption, for at least three-quarters of this century. By 1970 less than 10 percent of the U.S. workforce was self-employed; over 90 percent being employees of an organization.[8] This pattern is quite likely to continue and become increasingly relevant to more individuals throughout the world. Understanding how organizations function is thus not only important so that we can help make them more effective, but also so that they will be better workplaces.

Furthermore, understanding how organizations function is helpful for anticipating the challenges typically encountered at work. After all, people must more or less conform to the requirements of their roles as organization members. Whatever your current or planned vocation, whether in business, government, education, or health care, the study of organizations offers an important opportunity to form relevant insights that will serve as a vital supplement to actual work experience—and increase the probability of your career success. As Peter F. Drucker observes, "Young people today will have to learn organizations the way their forefathers learned farming."[9] To the extent that all organizations are in some sense managed, the study of organizations is increasingly necessary.

4. *Organizations are potential agents for economic and social change, playing several public-policy roles.* In many quarters, the growth of society is viewed as dependent on the functioning of organizations. From the perspective of civil rights activists, corporations are vehicles that can create work for unemployed minorities, as well as provide necessary job training. In the international realm, these same corporations may be called upon to be instruments of development, assisting in the pursuit and implementation of collective social goals. In today's world, such social services as health, education, and welfare are largely the responsibility of organizations.

As potential agents for both economic and social change, organizations play several important public-policy roles.[10] First, they are most often the means by which public policy is *implemented.* Government agencies such as police departments and public hospitals are consciously formed as policy implementers. Likewise, private-sector organizations such as defense contractors and research laboratories implement public policy as they receive contracts and grants.

In addition to being the typical means for implementing policy, organizations are also typically the forum in which public policy is *formulated.* Besides legislative bodies, public policy is formulated in innumerable legislative, judicial, and administrative government agencies. Perhaps more subtly, public policy is also formed when private-sector organizations such as trade associations (National Association of Manufacturers), professional alliances (American Medical Association), and coordinating groups (Tobacco Institute) lobby for direct cash subsidies, tax credits, rate increases, and trade barriers.

Finally, organizations are often the *object* of public policy. For example, nearly every department of an average business firm has a counterpart in one or more government agency. The scope of regulations enforced by these agencies range from an organization's activities obtaining resources (including regulations of employment practices and energy consumption), to conditions in production (including employee safety and health, and environmental pollution), to the nature of goods and services they produce (product safety and warranty regulations). On overview, our ability to overcome the challenges addressed by these regulations depends on our society's "organizational potential."[11] Without understatement, the study of organizations provides a key to understanding modern society and its prospects for needed economic and social change. Moreover, in a very real way, the future success of our society rests on our ability to manage organizations effectively.

WHY STUDY ORGANIZATION DESIGN?

What Are Organizations?

Organizations have been viewed from many perspectives. Depending on the background and interests of the investigators, the dimensions and characteristics of organizations that are emphasized vary greatly. Agreement exists, however, that organizations generally develop as instruments for attaining specific goals, and that they are likely to emerge in situations where people recognize a common or complementary advantage that can be best served through collective, as opposed to individual, action. Thus, by their very nature, organizations imply an integrating and structuring of activities directed toward goal accomplishment.

Features common to most organizations are as follows:

1. *Organizations develop to achieve goals.* The behavior of organizations is ideally goal-directed rather than purely reflexive or random.

2. *Organizations are social entities composed of sets of interacting positions.* By social entity we mean that an organization is the outcome of collaborative actions of individuals in pursuit of some common or complementary goals. It is these individual interactions that give rise to organized activities.

3. *Organizations are deliberately structured and consciously coordinated.* Activities are segmented or departmentalized, and connections are established within and among departments according to some logical pattern. It is this patterning that is known as **organization structure**. **Organization design** is the activity of developing or modifying an organization's structure.

4. *Organizations exist as part of the larger social environment.* Organizations do not exist in isolation. They acquire resources (e.g., people, materials,

Figure 1.1
Basic Open-Systems Model

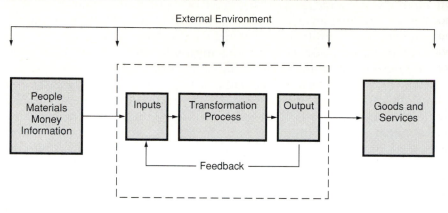

money, information) from the larger social environment, and they return finished goods or services to it.

Thus, when we speak of organizations in this book, we refer to social entities that (1) are developed to achieve specific goals; (2) are composed of interacting positions that have been deliberately structured and consciously coordinated; and (3) exist within the larger social environment.

Organizations as Open Systems

Almost all organization theory and research for the past three decades has assumed that organizations are open systems.[12] For our purpose, a **system** may be defined as a set of interdependent parts that relate in the accomplishment of some purpose. By **open system** we mean that organizations must exist in a continuous exchange with their environment in order to survive. As open systems, organizations transform inputs into outputs, which are subsequently discharged into their external environment in the form of goods and services. Inputs may take the form of people, materials, money, or information. For example, a steel mill transforms iron ore and other raw materials into industrial and consumer goods. Colleges and universities transform uneducated students into educated graduates. Hospitals transform sick patients into healthy individuals. Feedback is necessary for a system to function in a goal-directed manner and to maintain a steady state. Information concerning a system's output is fed back from the environment as an input leading, as required, to changes in the system's transformation process and future outputs.

As illustrated in Figure 1.1, this cycle of inputs, transformations, outputs, and feedback is continuous. The goods and services produced by an organization are exchanged for the resources necessary to secure further required inputs. Hence, an organization can survive only if it is capable of producing some output that can be exchanged for the resources necessary to not only obtain new inputs but also maintain itself in operating order. In a business setting, this means that a firm must make a profit or at least live within its budget to survive. If excess profits exist, they can be held in reserve for hard times or used to finance growth.

If an organization cannot maintain a favorable ratio of inputs to outputs, it must receive other funds to exist. This is why organizations that do not sell their goods or services in the marketplace (e.g., public television, city schools, free museums, nonsubscription libraries) require other sources of funding (e.g., government and foundation grants, donations) to endure. Without the continual infusion of new resources, organizations-as-systems are subject to **entropy**, in that they tend to deteriorate, eventually failing. Table 1.1 illustrates the universal nature of the input-transformation-output-feedback cycle. Thus, most organizations can survive only as long as they are capable of producing some output that can be exchanged in the larger environment.

Managing the Organization-as-an-Open System

The concept of organizations-as-systems sounds simple and straightforward until you realize that the larger systems within which organizations exist continually change. The availability and cost of people, materials, money, and information (inputs) change over time as do consumer preferences for goods and services (outputs). The means by which organizations convert (transformation processes) people, materials, money, and information into finished goods and services also change over time. Such changes require that organizations be redesigned in order to perform effectively over the long run. The end result is that organizations are continually redesigning themselves, trying to find ways to best coordinate and control activities so as to produce goods and services that can be exchanged for additional resources.

Let's return to Mrs. Fields Cookies. When we left Mrs. Fields in 1987, it had just earned a net income of $17.7 million on sales of $87 million. In contrast, the company lost $15.1 million in the first six months of 1988 despite a 26 percent increase in sales. Why, you might ask, did this highly successful organization suddenly experience such a problem. Analysts attribute Mrs. Fields' downturn to two factors: changing market conditions and a flawed organization structure. With respect to changing market conditions, Mrs. Fields' dependence on cookie sales—a relatively limited and fickle market—left it vulnerable to a number of uncontrollable factors, such as soaring rents and increased competition. One competitor, who runs a competing cookie chain that diversified into ice cream and wholesale food products several years earlier noted, "I saw the handwriting on the wall that just selling cookies was the way to go quickly broke."[13] Mrs. Fields began diversifying in 1987 by buying the La Petite Boulangerie bakery chain from PepsiCo, Inc.

Table 1.1
Examples of Open Systems

	Inputs	Transformation Process	Outputs

General Motors	Steel
	Rubber
	Plastic
	Equipment
	Labor
	Capital
		Fabricate
		Assemble
		Paint
			Automobiles
			Trucks
			Automotive
			  products
			Diesel engines
			Turbine aircraft
			  engines

*Mount Sinai
  Hospital*
	Patients
	Physicians
	Nurses
	Equipment
	Support staff
	Insurance
	  payments
	Fees
		Diagnose
		Ameliorate
		Cure
		Prevent
			Healthy people

Folsom Prison	Convicts State/federal funds	Therapy Rehabilitation	Productive citizens

*Louisiana
  State University*
	Students
	Faculty
	Support staff
	Tuition
	Grants
	Contracts
		Teaching
		Research
		Public service
			Graduates
			Books/mono-
			  graphs
			Articles/reports
			Extension activities

Washington National Cathedral	Communicants Penitents Clergy Tithings	Divine worship Hymns Prayer Communion	Spiritual salvation

But diversification, rapid growth, and international expansion strained Mrs. Fields' ability to coordinate and control its operations.

During 1988 Mrs. Fields began restructuring its management system and operations. It closed, or made provisions to close, 95 cookie stores, and began converting existing operations from cookie stores to full-line bakeries/cafes. Mrs. Fields also entered into a joint venture with a French company to operate its European stores, and it retained consultants to help devise a new management system.[14]

Stories such as Mrs. Fields' are common. Organizations that survive their first few years do so because they successfully sell a good or service. But then they often experience difficulties because of internal management problems or because of changing environmental conditions. Most often it is a combination of the two. Mrs. Fields' problems were caused both by an outgrown organization structure and by increased competition and uncertainties in the marketplace. Rapid growth placed new demands for coordination and control that needed to be addressed by redesigning its structure. And changing market conditions required a shift in strategy that also required a change in structure. In other words, successfully managing an organization over time requires that managers pay attention to whether the existing structure meets current coordination and control needs, and to how changes in its external environment affect both its strategy and, subsequently, its structure. The implication is that long-term success requires the continual redesign of an organization's structure as its environment and strategy change.

PURPOSE AND PLAN OF THE BOOK

The general purpose of this book is to provide information that will help current and aspiring managers better design organizations. We do not present an exhaustive review of research studies; rather, the major findings upon which current organization theory is based have been integrated and explained.

Focus

The book's focus is primarily at the level of the organization and its subunits, as opposed to the individual or group levels of analysis. Stated differently, "organizations can be viewed either in terms of their structure ('anatomy') or their processes ('physiology')."[15] While individuals and their interactions comprise what might be considered the players of an organization, the intent of this book is to deal specifically with the field on which these interactions take place—an organization's structure. Therefore, it focuses primarily on organizations as the unit of analysis, and not on individuals or groups. Of course, behavior of individuals and groups will also be discussed. The extent to which individual and group behavior affects, or in turn is affected by, organization structure is a legitimate concern of all organization theorists. For example, job design is usually examined in organizational behavior courses focusing on the individual level of analysis. At the same time, job design plays an important role in organization theory because the way that individual jobs are designed has significant implications for coordination and control within an organization's structure.

Plan of the Book

The preceding sections provide a general introduction for the following chapters. The book is divided into four major sections. Chapters 1 through 3 (Part I) look at organizations as goal-seeking systems. Chapter 2 examines the role of goals in organizations: what kinds of goals organizations have; what purposes they serve; and how they change. Chapter 3 examines the concept of organizational effectiveness within the context of three different evaluative approaches—the goal-based, systems, and stakeholder models. Each presents a different view of effective performance. The *goal-based* approach focuses on goal attainment; the *systems* approach on an organization's ability to obtain resources from its surrounding environment; and the *stakeholder* approach on an organization's ability to satisfy the needs and preferences of participating stakeholders, such as employees, shareholders, customers, creditors, and so on. Each approach highlights a different aspect of an organization's input-output relationships.

Chapters 4 through 7 (Part II) examine how managers structure their organizations for effective performance. Chapter 4 looks at a number of basic design concepts—how jobs are designed (specialization), mechanisms of coordination and control (formalization), and extent to which decision-making authority is delegated within an organization (centralization). Chapter 5 examines how individuals and jobs are grouped into work units, and shows how different structuring patterns affect an organization's ability to accomplish different ends. This chapter also looks at the techniques that managers use to overcome the shortcomings of the particular structure they have chosen. Chapter 6 focuses on the relationship between an organization's technology and its structure. It shows that different technologies present different coordination and control needs that, in turn, require different kinds of structures to operate effectively. Also examined is how advanced information technologies and computer-integrated manufacturing systems change an organization's coordination and control needs, and the changes in structure that are required to effectively implement them. Chapter 7 looks at organization design in a global economy. Research shows that globalization has created new coordination and control needs that require different types of structures than have been common in the past. Two relatively new trends in organization design that address these needs, globally integrated designs and interorganizational designs, are examined.

Chapters 8 through 10 (Part III) focus on the relationship between an organization and its environment. The underlying issue addressed in these chapters is the relationship between environmental conditions, an organization's strategy and structure, and the subsequent effectiveness of organizational performance. Chapter 8 examines the three major streams of contemporary thought on this subject—contingency theory, strategic choice, and population ecology—which have historically been viewed as competing views. Chapters 9 and 10 present an integrative model that shows how these approaches actually provide complementary insights about the organization-environment relationship. Chapter 9 looks at how different types of changing environmental conditions affect the relative success of different organizational strategies. Chapter 10 then discusses the relationship between organization structure and strategy, showing how different strategies require different structures to be effectively implemented. It also explains why adapting to changing environmental conditions is more difficult for some organizations than others.

Chapters 11 through 14 (Part IV) examine the transitions, dynamics, and processes common in organizations as they are redesigned. Chapter 11 looks at the transitions and design problems associated with organizational growth. Chapter 12 focuses on the other side of the equation—managing a declining organization—and discusses the design implications of turning around declining operations. Chapters 13 and 14 look at two fundamental organizational processes that have to be managed in both growing and declining organizations—decision making and organizational change. Long-term effectiveness requires that managers perceive, interpret, act on, and learn from information about changing environmental conditions, which is the focus of Chapter 13. Chapter 14 examines change processes, important to all managers attempting to redesign their organizations. Barriers to innovation and factors that cause resistance to change are identified, and techniques for overcoming these problems are discussed.

Each chapter closes with a design audit that will aid the reader in learning how to apply important organization design concepts. The design audits will help you *apply* the concepts to an organization you have chosen to analyze. These design audits walk you through the concepts, step-by-step, showing you how to apply them and understand their implications. Using the design audits is perhaps the best way to learn about organization design because they provide a format for gaining a "hands-on" understanding of design principles and implications. Each of the book's four parts closes with several case studies. The cases *illustrate* selected design concepts, showing how actual organizations deal with the challenges and issues presented in each chapter.

Overall, this book will help you understand why organization design is an important topic for managers, and how this understanding can be used to manage effectively. It also should give you a clear understanding of the often overlooked fact that organizations aren't simply designed, they are continually redesigned as the world changes around them. Managing for effective performance over the long run requires an appreciation of this simple truth, and a willingness and ability to apply one's understanding of design principles and tools.

SUMMARY

Learning Objective 1: Understand how, as the dominant institution in modern society, organizations exert a tremendous influence on our lives. As the dominant institution in modern society, organizations exert a tremendous influence on our lives, since, whether by choice or necessity, we obtain a large measure of our cultural, material, and social satisfaction from them.

Learning Objective 2: Explain why it is worthwhile to study organizations. There are several reasons for studying organizations: (1) organizations are the backbone of modern civilization; (2) organizations have immense power; (3) studying organizations has great practical value; and (4) organizations are potential agents for economic and social change, playing several public-policy roles.

Learning Objective 3: Define what is meant by an "organization." Organizations are social entities that (1) are developed to achieve specific goals; (2) are composed of interacting positions that have been deliberately structured and consciously coordinated; and (3) exist within a larger social environment.

Learning Objective 4: Discuss organizations as open systems. As open systems, organizations, procure and transform inputs (people, materials, money, and information) into outputs that are subsequently discharged into their surrounding environment in the form of goods and services. Feedback is necessary for a system to function in a goal-directed manner, particularly as the larger environment changes. Information concerning a system's output is fed back as an input into the system, leading, as required, to changes in its transformation process and future outputs. This cycle of inputs-transformation-outputs-feedback is continuous. The goods and services produced by an organization are exchanged for the resources necessary to secure further required inputs. An organization can thus survive only if it is capable of producing some output that can be exchanged for the resources necessary to not only obtain new inputs but also maintain itself in operating order.

Learning Objective 5: Explain why it is worthwhile to study organization theory and design. Studying organization theory and design provides an understanding of the principles and techniques managers can use in structuring their organizations for effective performance. Different objectives often require that different design principles be applied.

Learning Objective 6: Understand why organizations are continually being redesigned. Successfully managing an organization over time requires that managers continually be aware of the need for redesign, because the outcomes of past organizational actions, such as growth, and changes in an organization's environment can alter the effectiveness of its existing structure. Both factors can change organizational coordination and control needs, which often require different structuring methods for continued effective performance. The implication is that long-term organizational success requires the continual redesign of an organization's structure as coordination and control needs change.

Discussion Questions

1. "Our primitive ancestors, before history began to be written, felt both the urge and the necessity to band together. By day, this awkward Man, with his new-found weapons in his clumsy hands, could stand alone and hold his enemy at bay by the power of his growing cunning. But when night fell, his helplessness weighed upon him and he fled in terror to the retreats where others of his kind were congregated, and sought them with a mutual solace of the fears that beset them all. Here these earliest men drew strength, courage, and inspiration from the simple fact of their presence together. They saw, with their dawning intelligence, that in battle with life they could not stand alone."[16] Does the very universality of organization furnish sufficient evidence of its necessity in the general scheme of life? Explain. (Hint: How has human experience demonstrated the practical necessity of organization for the attainment of all group purposes?)

2. "Organizations pervade our lives, and we tend to take their existence for granted. Consider, however, that much of an individual's biography could be written in terms of encounters with organizations: born in a hospital, educated in a school system, licensed to drive by a state agency, loaned money by a financial institution, employed by a corporation, cared for by a hospital and/or nursing home, and at death served by as many as five organizations—a law firm, a probate court, a religious organization, a mortician, and a florist. Even one's use of leisure time is constrained by the options offered by certain organizations."[17] Write the biography of your life in terms of your encounters with organizations.

3. "Organizations exist to enable ordinary people to do extraordinary things."[18] Cite several examples to demonstrate the truth of this quote.

4. According to Intel Corporation President Andrew S. Grove, "Our society has become what Peter Drucker calls a society of organizations."[19] Comment on how our society's standard of living largely depends on how well these organizations perform.

5. "'Organization' comes to English from the Latin word for 'instrument.' Considering this origin, one might think of an object made up of many parts that, when played, produces harmonious sounds. Or one might think of a tool the parts of which are subordinate to the whole. Certainly both connotations are valid extensions of the word."[20] Reflecting on both connotations, how has business and organization (as an abstract force) physically shaped the lives of workers and their managers?

6. According to former Quaker Oats President Kenneth Mason, "A good case can be made that . . . the large corporation is the central institution of our age—as the Church was in the Middle Ages, the army in Roman times, the courts of the princes, and the great university have been at various epochs on history." While Mason acknowledges several reasons for this, notably the sheer quantity of physical, financial, and human assets that they have at their disposal, he contends what truly makes corporations the central institution of our age is "the rich and varied career opportunities they offer young people to work with superb financial, physical, intellectual, and human assets, all brought together by these corporations. Because the corporation cannot keep the skills its teaches or the information it collects, young people can obtain skills and knowledge which they may take with them into other areas of life and work."[21] Discuss Mason's contention, using as an example your own career or that of a relative or friend with whom you are familiar.

7. Recognizing the nature of international business competition, industrialist Henry C. Frick (1849–1919) once commented: "Without great, powerful organizations, America cannot hope to compete successfully in the world."[22] Do you agree? Why? Why not?

8. "Organizational America is something of a paradox. On the one hand, the efficiencies of large-scale organizations have made possible the unprecedented material growth of the twentieth century; on the other hand, the scope of their power and influence has come to threaten our basic social and political values, particularly individual freedom."[23] Discuss this paradox.

9. Testifying before the U.S. Senate Armed Services Committee, former General Motors President Charles E. Wilson commented, "What is good for General Motors is good for the country and what is good for the country is good for General Motors."[24] Do you agree? Why or why not?

DESIGN AUDIT #1

Selecting an Organization for Study

The Design Audits included at the end of each chapter show you how to apply the ideas contained in this book, as well as their implications for organization design. When you complete the following chapters and corresponding design audits, you will have a much better understanding of how organization design can be used to improve both an organization's efficiency and effectiveness and, consequently, its performance.

To use the Design Audits, you will have to select an organization to study. Talk with people in the organization, dig through its archives, and do library research. Sift through the information you obtain from people in this organization and compare it with your own observations and research findings. In many instances, you'll find that problems people identify are the same you observe. In others, you may find that your analysis leads you to a different set of insights about the organization's problems and recommended future courses of action. In short, completing these Design Audits will teach you about a different way of seeing organizations—through the lens of organization design.

Selecting an Organization

For many people, selecting an organization to study is easy: they simply choose their employer. Some people might manage their own organizations, which they'll want to study. Others may choose to study a relative's or friend's employer. Other options include voluntary organizations in which you are interested (i.e., a church, a fraternal association, a civic group). And still other people may want to find an organization that they would like to have contact with in the future, perhaps as their employer. Any organization—large or small—can be studied within the framework of these Design Audits.

Selecting one organization over another is more of a personal choice than anything else. The organization you choose will influence the kinds of information you can obtain. For example, there is likely to be more public information available about a large, publicly held corporation and its operations than about a small, privately held company. On the other hand, you may have access to people at all levels of a small organization. If you choose a very large organization, you'll probably find it necessary to focus your analysis on some part of its operations, such as a division. The Design Audits will advise you when it is more appropriate to focus on an entire organization versus a smaller unit.

The most critical factor in selecting an organization to study is access. Virtually any organization will work within the context of the Design Audits as long as you have reasonable access to people within it, or through public sources. Past experience shows that most managers are willing to let students study their organizations, provided that the information they provide remains confidential. (The issue of confidentiality should be discussed with your instructor.)

Perhaps the only kind of organization to avoid for the purpose of completing the Design Audits is one with fewer than 15 employees. Such organizations tend to have very rudimentary structures that provide you with relatively little information for the Design Audits. The exception is if you are the owner/manager of a small enterprise. In this situation, the Design Audits can help make you aware of some of the decisions you'll need to make as your organization grows—and thus increase the probability that your organization successfully makes it through some common "growing pains." Take some time over the next few days to think about what organization you would like to study. Check your access to people within it. When you've selected an organization, complete the section on the following page.

Preliminary Information

1. Name of organization_____

2. How many people does this organization employ?_____

3. If this is a large organization, do you plan to study all or part of it?

    _____ Entire organization

    _____ Part of the organization (Describe what part of the organization
    you propose studying in the space below.)

4. How do you plan to obtain information about the organization's
    operations?

5. On separate sheets of paper, please provide a brief description of the organization you've selected, including:
   a. A short history of the organization (when founded, original mission, major transformations that have occurred since its founding).
   b. A brief description of the organization's current operations (What goods/services does it provide? What is the scope of its operations [local, regional, national, international]? Where are its primary facilities located?)

Notes

1. Debra J. Fields with Alan Furst, *One Smart Cookie* (New York: Simon and Schuster, 1987).

2. Robert H. Roy, *The Cultures of Management* (Baltimore: Johns Hopkins University Press, 1977), 3.

3. Douglas Pitt and Simon Booth, "Paradigms Lost? Reflections in the Coming Organizational 'Revolution,'" *Futures* 15 (1983): 193.

4. Edward S. Mason, ed., *The Corporation in Modern Society* (Cambridge, Mass.: Harvard University Press, 1966), 1.

5. Frederick H. Katauama and William Bellis, "The World's 50 Biggest Industrial Corporations," *Fortune*, August 1, 1988, D1.

6. Walter Guzzardi, "Big Can Still Be Beautiful," *Fortune*, April 25, 1988, 50; Mark Alpert and Sandra L. Kirsch, "The *Fortune* 500 Largest U.S. Industrial Corporations," *Fortune*, April 25, 1987, D1.

7. Kenneth Mason, "The Multinational Corporation: Central Institution of Our Age," in *Corporations and the Common Good*, ed. Robert B. Dickie and Leroy S. Rouner (Notre Dame: University of Notre Dame Press, 1986), 79.

8. Arthur G. Bedeian, *Organizations: Theory and Analysis*, 2d ed. (Hinsdale, Ill.: The Dryden Press, 1983), 6.

9. Peter F. Drucker, quoted in W. Richard Scott, *Organizations: Rational, Natural, and Open Systems*, 2d ed. (Englewood Cliffs, N.J.: Prentice-Hall, 1987), 1.

10. The following discussion draws heavily on Richard H. Hall and Robert E. Quinn, "Question: Is There a Connection Between Organizational Theory and Public Policy," in *Organizational Theory and Public Policy*, ed. Richard H. Hall and Robert E. Quinn (Beverly Hills: Sage, 1983), 7–8.

11. Amitai Etzioni and Edward W. Lehman (comp.), *A Sociological Reader on Complex Organizations*, 3d ed. (New York: Holt, Rinehart and Winston, 1980), v.

12. For an extensive discussion of the open systems approach to organizations, see Daniel Katz and Robert L. Kahn, *The Social Psychology of Organizations*, 2d ed. (New York: Wiley, 1978): 18–34.

13. Buck Brown, "How the Cookie Crumbled at Mrs. Fields," *The Wall Street Journal*, January 26, 1989, B1.

14. Brown, "How the Cookie Crumbled at Mrs. Fields," B1; "Tough Cookies?" *Fortune,* February 13, 1989, 112; Don Steinberg, "Crumbling Mrs. Fields Puts Its Chips on PCs in Bakeries," *PC Week,* February 21, 1989, 1, 59, 61.

15. Herbert A. Simon, foreward to Arlyn J. Melcher, *Structure and Process of Organizations: A Systems Approach* (Englewood Cliffs, N.J.: Prentice-Hall, 1976), xi.

16. James D. Mooney and Alan C. Reiley, *The Principles of Organization* (New York: Harper, 1939), ix.

17. Howard Aldrich and Peter V. Mardsen, "Environments and Organizations," in *Handbook of Sociology,* ed. Neil J. Smelser (Beverly Hills: Sage, 1988), 362.

18. Theodore Levitt, "The Innovating Organization," *Harvard Business Review* 66, no. 1 (1988): 7.

19. Andrew S. Grove, "Keeping Favoritism and Prejudice Out of Evaluations," *The Wall Street Journal,* February 2, 1984, 26.

20. Charles Burden, Elke Burden, Sterling Eisminger, and Lynn Ganim, eds., *Business in Literature* (New York: McKay, 1977), 1.

21. Mason, "The Multinational Corporation," 78–79.

22. Henry C. Frick, quoted in *The Wit and Wisdom of Wall Street,* Bill Adler with Bill Adler, Jr. (Homewood, Ill.: Dow Jones-Irwin, 1985), 44.

23. Frank Fischer and Carmen Sirianni, "Organization Theory and Bureaucracy: A Critical Introduction," in *Critical Studies in Organization and Bureaucracy,* ed. Frank Fischer and Carmen Sirianni (Philadelphia: Temple University Press, 1984), 3.

24. Charles E. Wilson, quoted in Adler and Adler, *Wit and Wisdom,* 44.

Organizational Goals

Learning Objectives

Upon completing this chapter, you should be able to

1. Identify two essential characteristics of a goal.
2. Distinguish between official and operative goals.
3. Explain why official goals may differ from operative goals.
4. Detail the benefits goals provide.
5. Name the key result areas in which all organizations should establish goals.
6. Understand the meaning of *reification* as it applies to an organization.
7. Define the term *coalition*.
8. Discuss how organizational goals are determined.
9. Know what is meant by a side payment.
10. Define the term *organizational slack*.
11. Describe the means-ends hierarchy.
12. Differentiate between goal succession and goal displacement.

3M'S GOALS FOR THE FAST TRACK

It was 1922. Minnesota Mining & Manufacturing inventor Francis G. Okie was dreaming up ways to boost sales of sandpaper, then the company's premiere product, when a novel thought struck him. Why not sell sandpaper to men as a replacement for razor blades? Why would they risk the nicks of a sharp instrument when they could rub their cheeks smooth instead? The idea never caught on, of course. The surprise is that Okie, who continued to sand his own face, could champion such a patently wacky scheme and keep his job. But unlike most companies then—or now—3M Company demonstrated a wide tolerance for new ideas, believing that unfettered creative thinking would pay off in the end. 3M is now considered one of the world's most innovative companies.

Corporate goals help promote the innovative environment at 3M. A prime one is the 25 percent rule, which requires that a quarter of a division's sales come from products introduced within the past five years. Meeting the 25 percent test is a crucial yardstick at bonus time, so managers take it seriously. Then there's the 15 percent rule, which allows 3M employees to spend up to 15 percent of the workweek on anything they want to, as long as it's product-related. The practice is called bootlegging, *and its most famous innovation is the ubiquitous yellow Post-it note.*

Obviously, for 3M to achieve such innovative success, its official goals must be clearly communicated and translated into day-to-day, or operative, goals. Chapter 2 shows how official and operative goals can play an important role in guiding an organization into its future.

Source: "Masters of Innovation—How 3M Keeps Its New Products Coming," *Business Week,* April 10, 1989, 58.

As stressed in Chapter 1, organizations are goal-setting social systems likely to be created when people recognize a common or complementary advantage that can be best served through collective as opposed to individual action. Goals are thus an essential part of the everyday language of organizations and a cornerstone of traditional organization theory.[1] Indeed, Gross suggests that goals are the central factor in the study of modern organizations.[2] Interest in goal accomplishment may be easily traced to the work of such turn-of-the-century theorists as Henri Fayol and Max Weber. Building upon this legacy, as well as on the work of more recent theorists, the position taken in this chapter is that organizations are structural devices for accomplishing specific goals and that to understand them fully one must understand these goals.

Thus, the primary purpose of this chapter is to explore the nature of organizational goals. After defining the term *goal* and differentiating between official and operative goals, we will explore the numerous benefits of organizational goals and discuss the "key result areas" in which all organizations should establish goals. Next, we will consider individual versus organizational goals, the various influences on goal formulation, the structural process (means-ends hierarchy) whereby organizational goals are made operational, and, finally, the ways goals are adapted and occasionally replaced as a result of various internal and external pressures.

GOALS DEFINED

In spite of the fact that the goal concept is central to the study of organizations, few serious attempts have been made to develop a clear definition of the term *organizational goal*. Etzioni, probably the most frequently quoted authority on this point, defines an organizational goal as "a desired state of affairs which the organization attempts to realize" and as "that future state of affairs which the organization as a collectivity is trying to bring about."[3] Warner, in another often quoted definition, suggests that an organizational goal is "a state of affairs or situation which does not exist at present but is intended to be brought into existence in the future by the activities of the organization."[4] Stated more directly, **organizational goals** are those ends that an organization seeks to achieve by its existence and operation.

Effective managers have long recognized that before initiating any course of action, goals should be clearly determined, understood, and stated. This requirement underscores two essential characteristics of goals:

1. Goals are predetermined, that is, stated in advance.
2. Goals describe *future* desired results toward which *present* efforts are directed.

At the outset, we should state that although some authors distinguish goals from objectives, these terms are generally used interchangeably in academic and business circles, and this book will follow suit.

OFFICIAL VERSUS OPERATIVE GOALS

Official goals are the general aims of an organization as expressed in its corporate charter, annual reports, and the public statements of its top managers (see Focus on Design 2.1). **Operative goals** reflect the actual intentions of an organization as disclosed by its operating policies, and they may not correspond with the organization's officially professed aims.[5]

FOCUS ON DESIGN 2.1

Official Goals: Two Examples

Official goals are the general aims of an organization as expressed in its corporate charter, annual reports, and public statements. J. C. Penney closely adheres to the time-honored goals formulated by its founder some 75 years ago. The Limited, a company that first opened its doors in 1963, offers a statement of its official goals that is as sassy as the fashions it sells.

The Penney Idea

---

1. To serve the public, as nearly as we can, to its complete satisfaction.
2. To expect for the service we render a fair remuneration and not all the profit the traffic will bear.
3. To do all in our power to pack the customer's dollar full of value, quality, and satisfaction.
4. To continue to train ourselves and our associates so that the service we give will be more and more intelligently performed.
5. To improve constantly the human factor in our business.
6. To reward men and women in our organization through participation in what the business produces.
7. To test our every policy, method, and act in this wise: "Does it square with what is right and just?"

Adopted 1913

(continued)

This distinction between the professed and the actual goals of an organization has long been a major problem in the study of organizations. One of the most documented observations in organization theory is, "Organizations are rarely what they pretend to be."[6] Consider:

• A state employment agency found that the official, or declared, goals of providing the best service possible to "workers seeking employment and employers seeking workers" was secondary to the goal of maximizing the proportion of interviews resulting in referrals, because the performance of

---

FOCUS ON DESIGN 2.1 *(continued)*

The Limited, Inc.

**Limited
Goal:**   To be one of the world's major forces in apparel retailing.

**Limited
Policy:**   Most of the measures that we—and others—put on our business
                       are quantitative, but we believe that in retailing, as in
                       other endeavors, quantity is derived from quality. It is the quality
                       of our thought and execution and the quality of our critique—that
                       produces quantity.

**Limited
Principles:**   To offer the absolute best customer shopping experience
                       anywhere—the best store—the best merchandise—the best
                       merchandise presentation—the best customer service—the
                       best "everything" that a customer sees and experiences;

                       To become the world's foremost retailer of life-style fashions;

                       To be known as a high quality business with an unquestioned
                       reputation for integrity and respect for all people;

                       To maintain a revolutionary and restless, a bold and daring
                       business spirit noted for innovation and cutting-edge style;

                       To maintain a management culture which is action oriented,
                       always flexible and never bureaucratic;

                       To be tough-minded, disciplined, demanding, self-critical and
                       yet supportive of each other and of our team;

                       To never be satisfied or content—to advance a leading, aggressive,
                       and creative vision of the future.

---

agency interviewers was primarily measured by this and similar quantitative rather than qualitative indices.[7]

• A study of prisons and a study of correctional institutions for delinquents found that despite the announced aim of such organizations to rehabilitate, in reality they spent very little time or effort in this area, instead providing primarily custodial care.[8] This would suggest that the real, or operative, goal of the institutions investigated was custodial care, not rehabilitation.

• A study of community service clubs found that community service is often an "incidental" part of the activities of such groups (as measured in terms of time and money spent) and that generating funds for club benefit via community service projects, such as the sale of products made by the handicapped, is often their operative, or true, goal.[9]

•   In the business world, the statement of goals in a company's annual report is often suspected to differ drastically from its unpublicized objectives as top management understands them. IBM, for example, says its goals are to increase revenues by 15 percent a year and to head off competition from Japanese computer manufacturers. Some industry analysts, however, think the real goal behind IBM's highly aggressive marketing tactics is to force domestic competitors from the market.

An organization's official goals, even if they disagree with its true, or operative goals, nevertheless perform a necessary role. By giving an organization a favorable public image, official goals often provide a source of legitimacy, justifying its activities. (This point will be further developed in the following section.) The reasons that operative goals may differ from official goals include the following:

1. Participants may disagree on an organization's actual goals. Consider the following example:

> The university president may describe the purpose of the institution as one of turning out national leaders; the academic dean sees it as imparting the cultural heritage of the past; the academic vice-president as enabling students to move toward self-actualization and development, the graduate dean as creating new knowledge, [and] the dean of [students] as training young people in technical and professional skills which will enable them to earn their living.[10]

2. Perceptions about how best to accomplish official goals may differ.

3. Official goals may be unrealistic for financial or other reasons. Thus, to avoid failure, they are adapted to available alternatives.

4. As we will discuss in a later section, operative goals are typically the outcome of continuous bargaining among groups or coalitions who are attempting to ensure that their interests are represented. Thus, although an organization's official goals may remain unchanged, its operative goals may vary over time because of such bargaining. In this connection, Quinn has made the interesting observation that some organizations purposely avoid stating specific goals so as not to attract potential competition or become a focus of opposition groups. Rather, they announce only general (official) goals that are unlikely to attract competitors or contain significant points of controversy.[11]

As this discussion suggests, an organization's verbal or other pronouncements are insufficient for determining its real goals. Both research and experience suggest that one can determine an organization's true (operative) goals not by reading its corporate charter, but by examining its resource-allocation process.[12] Despite claims to the contrary, it is the allocation of resources for certain activities and the withholding of them from others that operationally defines an organization's goals. To paraphrase

Figure 2.1
The Benefits of Goals

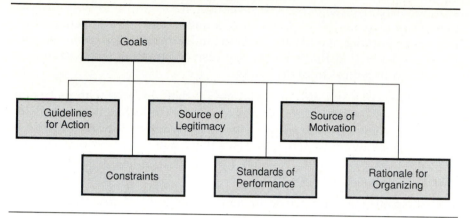

Buck, an organization must put its resources where its mouth is if something is to be accepted by others as a goal.[13]

BENEFITS OF ORGANIZATIONAL GOALS

As the reader may begin to suspect, "the concept of organizational goal is among the most slippery and treacherous of all those employed by the analyst of organizations."[14] The prime reason for this complexity is that goals serve a variety of functions. Consequently, the goals stressed in one instance (social and employee welfare, for example) may not be the same as those emphasized in another (productivity and profit maximization, for example). In fact, they may conflict. Viewed in broad perspective, goals provide several important benefits that vary according to time and circumstance. As illustrated in Figure 2.1, these benefits are as follows.

1. *Guidelines for action.* By describing future desired results, goals serve as guidelines for action, directing and channeling employee efforts. In this way, they provide focus and direction for employees by prescribing what "should be" done. Consequently, goals provide parameters for strategic planning, allocating resources, and identifying new product–development opportunities. They tell employees how and where to direct their strongest efforts. In brief, by identifying what an organization wants to succeed in, goals help it keep on track.

2. *Constraints.* To the extent that goals prescribe what "should be" done, they also serve to prescribe what "should not be" done. An organization that commits itself to certain goals reduces its discretion to pursue other goals. For example, an organization that commits itself to maximizing immediate stockholder dividends in effect reduces the amount of financial resources it has available for expanding production or investing in the development of new products. Thus, by their nature, goals also function to constrain employee activities.

3. *Source of legitimacy.* Goals also serve as a source of legitimacy by justifying an organization's activities and, indeed, its very existence to such stakeholder groups as customers, politicians, employees, owners, and society-at-large. **Legitimacy** is a global or summary belief that "this organization is good," or "this organization has a legitimate right to continue its operations." The goals that lend legitimacy, for example, to hospitals would include the provision of medical services aimed at curing, ameliorating, and preventing disease. Prisons and mental hospitals gain public approval by espousing such objectives as therapy and rehabilitation, and churches by offering opportunities for divine worship and spiritual salvation. Imagine how differently we would feel about a hospital if its stated objective was to keep its occupancy rate up by doing as much surgery as possible, or about a church whose avowed objective was to amass funds through the collection plate to finance the opulent lifestyles of its top ministers.

An organization whose goals are deemed legitimate enjoys a greatly enhanced ability to obtain resources and other support from its environment. This largely explains the fund-raising success of organizations such as the Girl Scouts, Salvation Army, and the United Way. Each has achieved acceptance through the recognized legitimacy of its goals. Some two decades ago, the weight-reduction business was seen as a collection of gimmicks engineered by charlatans to take advantage of people in need. Then Weight Watchers International was able to establish the industry's legitimacy by justifying its goals. Currently, massage therapy, dating services, singles bars, and singles-oriented adult education companies are among the many organizations trying to establish the legitimacy of their goals.

4. *Standards of performance.* To the extent that goals are clearly understood and stated, they offer direct standards for evaluating an organization's performance. Once an organization establishes goals in quantifiable areas such as sales, market share, and profit, the degree to which they have been attained should be easily verifiable.

5. *Source of motivation.* An organization's goals can also serve as an important source of employee motivation. By presenting a challenge, they tell what characterizes success and prescribe how to achieve or maintain it. Thus, in a very real sense, organizational goals are often incentives for employees. This phenomenon is perhaps clearest in organizations that offer their employees awards for achieving specified sales levels. Consider Domino's Pizza. One of its prime goals is to increase sales. It pursues this goal with a wide-ranging incentive program. Every manager who tops $10,000 in weekly sales gets a special $70 Hermes brand tie. When a store tops the company's weekly sales record (it now exceeds $60,000), founder Tom Monaghan takes the $16,000 Swiss-made gold watch off his wrist and gives it to the store's manager. Other incentive awards for accomplishing different goals include trophies, bonuses, trips, outings on Domino's million-dollar yacht, and vacations at its exclusive lodge in northern Michigan. Such victories mean continued success for Domino's and satisfaction for its employees.

6. *Rationale for organizing.* Stated simply, organizational goals provide a basis for organization design. Organizational goals and organization structure interact in that the actions necessary for goal accomplishment may impose unavoidable restrictions on employee activities and resource utilization patterns, necessitating implementation of a variety of organization design elements: communication patterns, control mechanisms, departmental structures, and so on. For instance, the more the goals of a functionally structured organization call for diversification, the greater will be its need to evaluate alternative structural arrangements such as product or matrix departmentalization. The various bases for arranging an organization's activities will be discussed at length in Chapter 5.

KEY RESULT AREAS

Many attempts have been made to identify **key result areas** in which all organizations should establish goals. The most widely accepted are those of Peter F. Drucker,[15] presented in Figure 2.2. It is Drucker's contention that an organization should establish goals in each area vital to its existence. Although principally applicable to profit-oriented organizations, Drucker's eight key result areas also are relevant for public-sector and other not-for-profit ventures.

Market Share

Simply stated, every organization should establish goals relative to its competition. Sales figures are meaningless until they are compared against market potential. Thus, Kellogg, which already dominates the U.S. cereal business with 41 percent of the market, has as its long-range goal a towering 50 percent share. Market share also has intrinsic importance in that a business that holds less than a certain share becomes a marginal supplier. The prices it can charge for its products then become dependent on the decisions of its larger competitors. And in a market downturn, it runs the chance of being squeezed out altogether. When competition becomes intense, distributors tend to favor the most popular products. In the soft-drink industry, for instance, every time a bottler loses a fraction of a percentage point of market

Figure 2.2
Drucker's Eight Key Result Areas

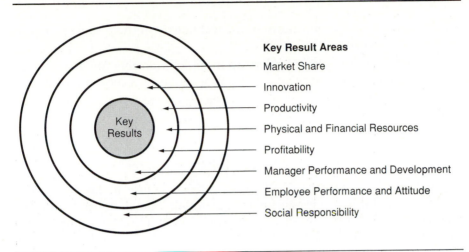

share, it is likely to lose a little supermarket display space as well, since grocers generally allocate space on the basis of sales per square foot. Furthermore, if a business's market share becomes too low, it may be unable to provide necessary customer service. Finally, having a substantial market share, as do Eastman Kodak and Gillette, is helpful in establishing brand loyalty, simply because many people are most comfortable buying something that a lot of other people buy.

Market share goals might include

- Increasing market share from 15 percent to 25 percent within five years.
- Increasing military sales 12 percent over the next 12 months.
- Achieving total sales of 50,000 units a year by 1995.
- Increasing overall company dollar sales 7 percent annually, and for each product at least 5 percent annually.

Innovation

The message is quite clear in today's technology-driven world: Innovate or evaporate. In their analysis of America's best-run companies, Thomas J. Peters and Robert H. Waterman, Jr., found that excellent companies possess an almost radical preoccupation with innovation.[16] A major case in point is 3M Co., which adds more than 100 new products each year to a catalog that already boasts 60,000 items. An ironclad requirement of 3M's 40-plus divisions is that at least 25 percent of their sales be from products less than five years old. This requirement clearly recognizes that 3M's continued existence depends on its ability to develop innovations. Innovation goals might include

- Being the leading contributor to the technology of the plastics industry within ten years.
- Achieving technological leadership in digital transmission and switching systems for ordering voice communications by a certain year.
- By decade's end, developing a fail-safe means for moving a gene from one living organism to another.

Productivity

Productivity is a measure of an organization's ability to produce more goods/services with less inputs (people, materials, money, information) and thus less cost. At companies such as General Electric, Texas Instruments, and General Motors, productivity is a basic, primary goal. General Electric (GE), for example, calculates that a single percentage point increase in productivity translates into an extra $300 million of pretax income. In this respect, productivity is crucial to GE's ability to control its destiny. The higher it is, the more cushion GE has to cut prices and go for market share. Increasing productivity, thereby decreasing costs, is thus one of management's most important jobs. Productivity goals might include

- Increasing sales per sales representative from $750,000 to $1 million within the next 18 months.
- Decreasing production costs per unit of output by 5 percent in the next year.
- Increasing quarterly output per hour by 5 percent with a less than 5 percent increase in expenses.
- Decreasing labor costs as a proportion of total product costs by 3 percent over the next 6 months.

Physical and Financial Resources

An organization should establish goals for the use of all resources—equipment, buildings, inventory, and funds. Every organization needs both physical and financial resources to produce the goods/services that justify its existence. Goals for physical and financial resources should be the result of carefully prepared policies. The costs of using obsolete equipment and patching up old buildings are often hidden—indeed, such old equipment and buildings may appear very profitable when standard methods of depreciation are used. If they have been written down to zero, they will appear to involve no cost at all, which, of course, is a pure fallacy.

Financial resources are generally considered so important that large companies, such as AT&T, have entire departments that attend to nothing else. Physical and financial resource goals might include

- Increasing plant floor space by 500,000 square feet by 1995.
- Maintaining equipment and tools at existing levels of readiness until further notice.
- Increasing monthly cash flow by 6 percent over the next 9 months.
- Maintaining a minimum working capital balance of $1.5 million at all times.

Profitability

A minimum acceptable goal for profitability should be specified. At Rubbermaid this minimum is a 15 percent average annual increase in profits and earnings per share. *Note that profit can be broadly interpreted as the gain resulting from an activity and is thus universal to all managerial situations.* While it is true that a business must earn a profit to continue to exist in the long run, profit need not be thought of only in the narrow sense of money left over after the bills are paid. The director of an art gallery may define profit as the increased recognition of the artists he represents, gained by exhibiting in a charity art show. To the dean of a university, profit may be thought of as the number of new National Merit Scholars on campus. Profitability goals might include

- Achieving an 18 percent pretax rate of return on investment in the next three years.
- Increasing profit from an annual rate of 8 percent to 14 percent in two years.
- Increasing annual United Fund contributions by 12 percent.
- Increasing annual student Scholastic Achievement Test scores to the national mean.

Manager Performance and Development

Good management is the key to organization success. To accomplish its goals in an efficient fashion, an organization principally depends on its managers. Thus, goals dealing with continued development of managerial talent, for the future as well as the present, are essential. Recognizing this, companies such as Walt Disney Productions, with its Disney U., and McDonald's, with its Hamburger U., invest heavily in training. At IBM, every employee, regardless of seniority, spends an estimated 15 days a year in formal training. Bechtel Corporation intentionally takes on small, economically unprofitable projects to provide new managers with on-the-job training. Manager-performance-and-development goals might include

- Establishing a career-counseling office within two years to assist every manager in designing a personal career plan.
- Annually sponsoring at least four separate in-house training programs for each level of management.
- Beginning a tuition-reimbursement program for all levels of management by year's end.
- Initiating a "fast-track" top-management training program by the end of 1995.

Employee Performance and Attitude

As repeatedly suggested, an organization's employees are its most important asset. In their study of America's leading companies, Peters and Waterman found a pervasive theme of respect for the individual. These successful companies treat people like adults, like partners. This is reflected in the very language the companies use. Employees are called "crew members" at McDonald's, "hosts" at Disney Productions, and "associates" at J. C. Penney. At Delta Airlines, it's the "Family Feeling." At Hewlett-Packard, its "the HP way." Employee-performance-and-attitude goals might include

- Maintaining current levels of employee satisfaction through 1995.
- Establishing an apprenticeship training program by year's end.
- Decreasing time lost due to accidents by 50 percent over the next 12 months.
- Reducing absenteeism to a steady level of no more than 3 percent a year.

Social Responsibility

The idea of social responsibility is that in addition to an organization's economic and legal obligations, it must respond to society in general. Social-responsibility goals might include

- Hiring and training at least ten handicapped persons every year.
- Sponsoring an annual Junior Olympics for local handicapped children.
- Being a 100-percent contributor to the United Fund.
- Supporting local youth baseball by sponsoring at least two teams.

Four Points Regarding Key Result Areas

The following four conclusions may be drawn from our discussion of key result areas.

1. Conceptions of organizations as having one or two goals do not reflect the real world. Organizations must almost always pursue a multiplicity of goals to assure their long-term survival.

2. Virtually all organizations have potentially conflicting goals. For example, consider the case of a common pair of goals for a business: (a) increased market share and (b) increased profit. Market share can be ordinarily increased by decreasing price. The effect of a price decrease on profit, however, would have to be carefully considered. Unless care is taken, these goals could be logically inconsistent, with one being satisfied only at the expense of the other.

Organizations resolve conflict among goals, in part, by attending to different goals at different times. Just as a political candidate is likely to resolve conflicting pressures to "go left" and "go right" by first doing one and then the other, a business organization is likely to resolve conflicting goals to "increase market share" and "increase profit" by first doing one and then the other: Differences in the time frames in which goals are to be achieved make this course of action possible. Thus, in the short range, an organization might strive to increase market share while maintaining a long-range goal of increasing profit.

3. Organizational goals are not mutually exclusive. What is viewed by one group as a social-responsibility goal may well be seen by another as an employee-performance-and-attitude goal. Affirmative action guidelines are a case in point. For many people, increasing the number of women and minority group members in top-management positions is undoubtedly a social-responsibility goal. To others, it may be a manager-performance-and-development goal.

4. The fact that organizational goals are not mutually exclusive contributes to the general impossibility of formulating a single, completely adequate goal function. A measure of conflict consequently accompanies the selection of organizational goals. Quinn's observation that some organizations purposely avoid articulating specific goals in order to avoid opposition thus seems politically astute.

GOAL FORMULATION

Individual Preferences and Organizational Goals

Having discussed the nature and benefits of organizational goals, we now turn to the more specific topic of how goals are selected. In this chapter's introduction, organizations were defined as goal-seeking social systems. Perusing a copy of *The Wall Street Journal*, we are likely to see this definition reflected in headlines such as:

- "Intel Dominates Microprocessor Market"
- "Campbell Soup Introduces New Product"
- "GE to Build New Plant"
- "American Airlines Invests $20 Million"

Each of these headlines treats the organization in question as a rational actor. It is extremely important to realize that, since they can act only through their members, organizations as such cannot have goals except in a purely metaphorical or figurative sense. Attributing such things as goals and needs to an organization amounts to attributing the power of thought and action to a social construct and places us in a position of *reifying* the organization; that is, granting it human characteristics.

In reality, organizations are mental abstractions. They have no existence independent of their members. People have goals; organizations do not. Yet one cannot equate the goals of an organization with the sum total of those of its individual members, since, in fact, the two often differ. As Barnard points out:

> We have clearly to distinguish between organization purpose and individual motive. It is frequently assumed in reasoning about organizations that common purpose and individual motive are or should be identical. With the exception noted below, this is never the case; and under modern conditions it rarely even appears to be the case. Individual motive is necessarily an internal, personal, subjective thing; common purpose is necessarily an external, impersonal, objective thing even though the individual interpretation of it is subjective. The one exception to this general rule, an important one, is that the accomplishment of an organization purpose becomes itself a source of personal satisfaction and a motive for many individuals in many organizations. It is rare, however, if ever, and then I think only in connection with family, patriotic, and religious organizations under special conditions, that organization purpose becomes or can become the *only* or even the major individual motive.[17]

The issue being addressed is thus much more complex than might initially be assumed. If organizations per se cannot be said to set and pursue goals, and if the goals of an organization are more than the simple sum of the personal goals of its members, how then are the goals of an organization formulated? An answer that avoids both extremes is provided by the work of Cyert and March.

Coalitions and Organizational Goals

In an effort to deal with this apparent goal-setting dilemma, Cyert and March postulate the presence of **coalitions**, which can be construed as the agents for formulating an organization's goals.[18] The coalition concept avoids both the reification of an organization as a rational actor and the notion that an organization's goals are the sum total of the purposes of its individual members. Rather, it suggests that organizations adopt goals that are the result of negotiations among internal and external interest groups making competing claims on an organization's resources.

As traditionally defined, a coalition is an alliance of individuals or groups who believe they can attain something they value through an organization. Members can be either internal or external to the organization's boundaries.

Their interests need not be the same, just not competing. This more sophisticated approach for explaining goal formulation has gained widespread support as organizations have increasingly been shown to be comprised of sets of subgroups that have divergent interests and views regarding what organizations are and what they should be. According to this view, organizational goals are determined by continued bargaining among coalitions attempting to ensure that their differing interests are represented. For example, stockholders bargain with employees over the relative division of profits, and departmental units bargain with one another for increased resources. As a consequence of such bargaining, organizational goals represent compromises reflecting the relative power of various organizational coalitions. Power, and thus influence, is achieved through control over critical events and essential resources.

In brief, this alternative approach emphasizes that the impact of organizational goals on organizational action is mediated by a continual process of bargaining in which various coalitions attempt to protect and advance their special interests. The suggestion is that organizations do not necessarily formulate goals and, subsequently, allocate resources based on rational criteria, but rather on political influence, since political behavior is necessary to safeguard and promote coalition interests.

The impact of coalitions is, of course, not equal. Hickson and his colleagues suggest that a coalition's or subgroup's political position and power in the bargaining process largely depend on the **nonsubstitutability** of its activities and the **centrality** of its work flows.[19] Substitutability is a function of the replaceability of a group's activities. Centrality refers to a group's importance and degree of connectivity of its assigned tasks. For instance, an accounting department (subgroup) typically performs a set of activities that are essential to the normal operation of a firm, exemplifying low substitutability. Likewise, the tasks it performs generally have substantive ramifications for such other departments as credit, sales, production scheduling, and shipping, illustrating high centrality. In most instances, the greater a group's nonsubstitutability and centrality, the more secure its political position and power are. In this respect, Hickson and his colleagues note that nonsubstitutability and centrality interact such that both have to be present for a group to be influential.

Perhaps the most well-known study in this area provides an example that is quite consistent with the Cyert and March coalition perspective. Analyzing the historical development of a general hospital over a 74-year period, Perrow showed how shifts in goal emphasis (from financial through technical training and research to stability-efficiency goals) corresponded across time with the relative bargaining positions of trustees, physicians, and administrators.[20] The coalition of participants that controlled the authority structure and resources of the hospital at a given point in time likewise controlled major operating strategies and thus hospital goals. Based on his findings, Perrow concluded (consistent with Hickson and his colleagues) that over the long run an organization will be controlled by those individuals who perform the most difficult (nonsubstitutable) and critical (central) tasks.

As the Perrow study suggests, establishing the boundaries of a coalition once and for all is impossible. Changing interests will give rise to changing coalitions. Thus, as Gillespie has observed, in a social welfare agency "one might find . . . staff and clients forming a coalition in opposition to the administration with respect to monetary support for paraprofessionals or assistants; administrators and clients forming a coalition against staff with regard to work evaluations; staff and administrators united to resist the clients' quest for direct representation in agency policymaking."[21]

Side Payments

A fundamental part of Cyert and March's approach to goal formulation centers around the idea of **side payments**. As described, coalitions are formed through a process of continuous bargaining. Throughout the tug and pull of bargaining, side payments are employed by coalitions to induce other groups to join with them in the pursuit of common interests (goals). Side payments can take any number of forms: money, private commitments, authority, position, and so on. They are, in a sense, the price participants require for their cooperation with the demands of other participants or groups of participants. Thus, in exchange for wages, employees agree to produce. Similarly, in exchange for dividends, shareholders agree to invest. *Note that what is a goal for one participant is simultaneously a side payment for another participant, and vice versa.*

The reciprocal nature of coalition formation can perhaps be best appreciated through a simple example. Consider an organization composed of these participants: an entrepreneur, one employee, and one customer. The system of inducements (side payments) and return contributions may be represented as follows:

Participant	Inducement	Contribution
Entrepreneur	Revenue	Production costs
Employee	Wages	Labor
Customer	Goods	Purchase price

As indicated, each *participant* is offered an *inducement* to secure cooperation in return for making a *contribution* to the organization.

> The customer's contribution of the purchase price is used to provide inducements to the entrepreneur in the form of revenue. The entrepreneur's contribution provides the employee's wages. The employee's contribution is transformed into goods that provide the customer's inducement.[22]

While this example is obviously an oversimplification, including only the most explicit inducements and contributions, it does illustrate the fundamentally symmetrical nature of coalition bargaining. Organizations rest on reciprocal relations among various participants. In this sense, each participant powerful enough to force attention to its preferences helps to determine the courses of action (or goals) that will be considered by an organization. For this reason, it is perhaps more accurate to view goals as complex statements that summarize the multiple requirements (or constraints) that an acceptable course of action must satisfy.[23]

In this respect, as open systems, organizations can survive and grow only so long as they are able to distribute enough inducements, produced out of the contributions they receive, to maintain a reciprocal flow of contributions. That is, an organization must receive enough revenue from customer sales to pay its employees' wages; it must receive enough labor from its employees to produce goods adequate to maintain a steady stream of money from customers; and, finally, on balance there must be enough revenue remaining (over and above any remaining residual costs of production) to meet the entrepreneur's demand for an acceptable level of revenue. Individuals participate in organizations for a host of reasons—money, prestige, the need to belong to something. These inducements (benefits)—current or anticipated—must be sufficient to warrant their continued contributions (burdens). This principle applies to all participants—investors, employees, and customers.

The idea of inducements and contributions can be expanded to incorporate significant outsiders or special-interest groups who influence the goals of an organization. Suppliers, tax collectors, regulatory agencies, political parties, and other nonmembers may seek better prices, tax code revisions, safer products, donations, and so on, in return for their support and approval.

Organizational Slack

Under favorable conditions, organizations sometimes accumulate resources in excess of those necessary to meet their required side payments (that is, inducements). The resulting difference between the total resources thus available to an organization and the total side payments necessary to maintain participant contributions comprises what has been termed **organizational slack**.[24]

Slack may take many forms. In general, it is a cushion of unused or convertible resources that enables an organization to successfully adjust to various internal and external pressures as well as to initiate required changes in strategic posture. Liquid financial assets such as cash, marketable securities, and current accounts receivable are perhaps the most utilitarian form of slack. Other forms of slack include dividends in excess of those required to ensure continued stockholder investment, wages paid at a level above that necessary to attract an acceptable labor force, perquisites and personal treatments provided to executives in excess of those necessary to keep them, uncommitted capital assets such as under-utilized plant capacity or technologies, and even surplus managerial resources and capabilities.

Some degree of slack is unquestionably necessary to allow organizations to maintain stability through intermittently good and bad times and adapt to variations in work flow and in environmental influences. Organizations with little or no slack will find it difficult to take advantage of emerging marketplace opportunities. Slack provides time and resources for developing product innovations, initiating changes, and testing new goals.

With regard to the present discussion, slack is of special significance to the coalition process of goal formation. The structuring of coalitions and the intensity of their bargaining are directly related to the availability of resources. It is much easier to satisfy the demands of competing coalitions in a growth situation, provided that the growth is not obtained at the expense of other returns or by incurring disproportionate expenses. Scott has diagnosed this type of situation well:

> The fierceness with which coalitions bargain is clearly affected by the state of the organization as a whole. If times are good and the organization is fat with resources, the several groups can afford to be generous in the bargains they strike; competing and even conflicting goals may be simultaneously pursued. However, in those lean times when the organization is forced to struggle for its very survival, hard bargaining takes place with the result that the desires of weaker groups are sacrificed.[25]

The Cyert-March Approach Summarized

The Cyert-March approach essentially views organizations as political systems in which goals are formulated through a complex process of bargaining among various coalitions with different, and possibly competing, expectations. This view refutes the notions that (1) organizations are distinct entities that rationally establish their own objectives and that (2) the goals of an organization can be determined simply by totaling the preferences of all members. Rather, goals are established through a process of bargaining involving interdependent participants who, to borrow Thompson's phrase, "collectively have sufficient control of organizational resources to commit them in certain directions and to withhold them from others."[26]

THE MEANS-ENDS HIERARCHY

Given that an organization has multiple goals, it is imperative that a logical relationship exist among them. Hence, in most organizations, goals normally exist in a hierarchy. That is, objectives at one hierarchical level typically serve as the means for accomplishing goals at the next higher level. Except for the broadest, most encompassing goal, each goal within an organization can be considered an end in itself as well as a means for achieving a higher-level goal. Accordingly, an organization's overall goals can be viewed as being divided into second-, third-, and *n*th-order goals, and as forming what is called a *means-ends hierarchy*, illustrated in Figure 2.3.

The overall goal of the organization in the example in Figure 2.3 is "to remain a leader in developing and applying technological innovations." As depicted, two *means* (at the middle-management level) are available for accomplishing this goal: (1) developmental research and (2) applied research. Each of these means can in turn be considered top management's *subobjectives*. Following the first alternative, we see that at the first-line management level there are two (compatible) means for conducting developmental research: "create second- and future-generation technologies" and "maintain an active patent-filing program." If generating second- and future-generation technologies is selected as means for developmental research, it becomes a goal itself and in turn can be pursued at the operative level by such means as (1) "pioneering in semiconductor research and development" and (2) "pioneering in lightwave research and development."

This example could easily be extended to include goals that are more and more specific in nature, each being an appropriate means for fulfilling a more general goal. In this manner we would eventually come to include all means necessary for accomplishing the organization's overall goal: "to remain a leader in developing and applying technological innovations."

By dividing goals into subgoals for lower-level employees, the means-ends hierarchy directs the activities of each employee and each department toward the accomplishment of an organization's overall goal. It is through the translation of successive means-ends chains that broad organizational goals are eventually translated into specific task assignments. As a by-product, as means become ends for each subsequent hierarchical level, the degree of freedom in decision making becomes increasingly limited in lower-level positions. It is true, of course, that if lower-level employees do not fulfill their goals, the full realization of an organization's overall goal will be impossible.

GOAL ADAPTATION AND CHANGE

It is important to remember that goal adaptation and change occur more or less continuously in response to environmental and internal changes. For instance, as the set of members within an organization changes, and the character of its surrounding environment fluctuates, organizational (operative) goals appropriate at one point in time may become either irrelevant or impractical. Two basic forms of goal change can be identified: goal succession and goal displacement.

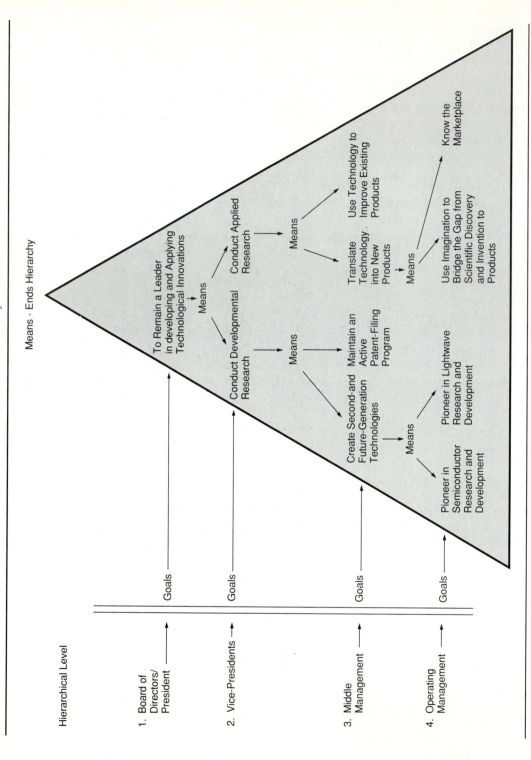

Figure 2.3
A Means-Ends Hierarchy

Goal Succession

As a basic form of goal change, **goal succession** refers to the deliberate replacement of an organization's primary goal, once it has been achieved, with a new goal.[27] Goal succession takes on special significance when it is realized that goal achievement and survival are sometimes at odds. Yet few organizations with this conflict acknowledge it. One exception is the Cystic Fibrosis (CF) Foundation, a group dedicated to finding a cure for the fatal genetic disease of the same name. Says CF Foundation CEO Robert Dressing, "My objective is to get out of business. The day that happens, we will have found a cure."[28]

A classic example of goal succession is the National Foundation for Infantile Paralysis, widely known for its annual March of Dimes Campaign.[29] Established in 1938, the foundation was initially formed to gather public support for medical research into the prevention and treatment of polio. With the successful development of the foundation-sponsored Salk vaccine (1952–1954), it became clear that its primary purpose was about to be realized and its reason for existence thus extinguished. The organization was faced with the choice of either disbanding or developing a new goal or goals. It chose a new goal, combating arthritis and birth defects, and subsequently changed its name to simply the National Foundation. In this case, goal succession was the only alternative to liquidation.

Goal Displacement

The second basic form of goal change, **goal displacement**, "arises when an organization displaces its goal—that is, substitutes for its legitimate goal some other goal for which it was not created, for which resources were not allocated to it, and for which it is not known to serve."[30] An example of this phenomenon is presented in Focus on Design 2.2. Goal displacement is particularly characteristic of organizations such as research and development laboratories and social service agencies that seek goals that are intangible. The more ambiguous and less visible an organization's goals, the less they provide a workable basis for achieving goal consensus and subsequent group action, and the more likely there is to be disagreement over goal interpretation. In this regard, goal *tangibility* is a function of (1) the precision with which goals can be described, (2) the clarity with which they can be identified, and (3) the extent to which they can be made operational (that is, be observed and measured).[31]

Three principal causes of goal displacement can be cited. Perhaps the most frequent cause is the substitution of means (the methods of doing work) for ends (output), or what is referred to as **means-ends inversion**. As Cyert and MacCrimmon explain, "At any point in the organization's means-ends chain, the activities performed may become divorced from the higher-level

FOCUS ON DESIGN 2.2

Orphanages: Goal Displacement in Action

Goal displacement is a form of goal change in which an organization substitutes some other goal for its original goal. Perhaps the most frequent cause of goal displacement is the substitution of means (the methods of doing work) for ends (output), or what is referred to as *means-ends inversion.* Orphanages, which are supposed to exist for their clients, are theoretically interested in placing as many children as possible in good homes. However, often orphanages surround themselves with so many rules concerning adoption that it is nearly impossible to pry a child out of the place. Orphanages may deny adoption unless the applicants are a married couple, both of the same religion as the child, without history of emotional or vocational instability, with a specified minimum income, a private room for the child, and on and on.

If the primary goal is to place children in good homes, then the rules ought to constitute means toward that goal. Goal displacement results when these means become ends-in-themselves that displace the original goal.

To some extent these rules are required by law. But the influence of the reward system on the orphanage's management should not be ignored. Consider, for example, that

1. The number of children enrolled often is the most important determinant of the size of the allocated budget.
2. The number of children under the director's care also will affect the size of his staff.
3. The total size of the organization will determine largely the director's prestige at the annual conventions, in the community, etc.

Therefore, to the extent that staff size, total budget, and personal prestige are valued by the orphanage's executive personnel, it becomes rational for them to make it difficult for children to be adopted. After all, who wants to be the director of the smallest orphanage in the state?

Source: Adapted from Steven Kerr, "On the Folly of Rewarding A, While Hoping for B," *Academy of Management Journal* 18 (1975): 769–783.

goals they were directed toward . . . . Under such circumstances means may easily become ends in themselves."[32] Renault Robinson, a Chicago policeman, interviewed in Studs Terkel's book *Working,* in which "people talk about what they do all day and how they feel about what they do," cites a classic example of means-ends inversion. In the excerpt that follows, note how the behavior ordered by Officer Robinson's supervisor (originally intended as a means to an end—the reduction of vice) becomes transformed into an end in itself, shifting or displacing effort away from the original goal.

My supervisor would say, "We need two policy arrests, so we can be equal with the other areas." So we go out and hunt for a policy operator . . . .

A vice officer spends quite a bit of time in court. You learn the judges, the things they look for. You become proficient in testifying. You change your testimony, you change the facts. You switch things around 'cause you're trying to get convictions . . . .

Certain units in the task force have developed a science around stopping your automobile. These men know it's impossible to drive three blocks without committing a traffic violation. We've got so many rules on the books. These police officers use these things to get points and also hustle for money. The traffic law is a fat book. He knows if you don't have two lights on your license plates, that's a violation. If you have a crack in your windshield, that's a violation. If your muffler's dragging, that's a violation. He knows all these little things . . . .

So many points for a robbery, so many points for a man having a gun. When they go to the scene and the man with the gun has gone, they'll lock up somebody anyway, knowing he's not the one. The record says, "Locked up two people for UUW"—unlawful use of weapons. The report will say, "When we got there, we saw these guys and they looked suspicious." They'll get a point even if the case is thrown out of court. The arrest is all that counts.[33]

A second principal cause of goal displacement is associated with what Etzioni calls **over-measurement** and Gross labels **number magic**.[34] Both terms refer to the tendency to attach an artificial importance to goals that are easy to quantify and hence readily measurable. Such distortion can result in the overemphasis of quantitative and measurable goals at the expense of nonquantitative goals. As a consequence, the more qualitative a goal, the more likely it is to become displaced. Familiar examples of the phenomenon include:

- Emphasizing production output with little regard for product quality.
- Compensating university faculty on the basis of number of courses taught rather than on the quality of their classroom performance.
- Looking at profit rather than customer goodwill.
- Determining promotions on the basis of seniority rather than job knowledge.

A final principal cause for the displacement of goals is the tendency within many, if not most, complex organizations to **suboptimize**, or to function at less than an optimum level because subunit goals take on an importance greater than that of overall organizational goals. As Mintzberg notes, "Units are naturally inclined to pursue narrow goals that pertain to their own function at the expense of the broad or formal goals that pertain to the overall organization."[35] Thus, prior to Chrysler's resurgence as a growing organization, "the production people had wanted to build cars. They did not care if they were sold; they were built to inventory. The engineering people wanted to design state-of-the-art automobiles, and were unconcerned if the marketing people could or could not sell them."[36] In brief, Chrysler was led to the brink of bankruptcy because subunit goals had taken on an importance greater than overall organizational goals.

A second example of suboptimization results from the unfortunate rivalry among the military services. While the overall (official) goal of the Defense Department is to provide adequate defense for the United States at the lowest possible cost, the evidence indicates otherwise. Consider:

> Several years ago, the Joint Chiefs of Staff attempted to form a single military command to facilitate rapid deployment of troops and equipment to needed areas. This command unit would expedite transportation over land and sea; thus it would require both the army and the navy to forsake some control of resources toward a common end. After numerous studies and negotiations, the idea was dropped. The two services would not surrender their individually optimal, but collectively suboptimal, goals for the sake of improved national defense.[37]

SUMMARY

The primary purpose of this chapter has been to explore the nature of organizational goals. As defined, goals are those ends that an organization seeks to achieve by its existence and operation.

Learning Objective 1: Identify two essential characteristics of a goal. First, goals are predetermined—that is, stated in advance. Second, goals describe *future* desired results toward which *present* efforts are directed.

Learning Objective 2: Distinguish between official and operative goals. Official goals are the general aims of an organization as expressed in its corporate charter, annual reports, and public statements of its top managers. Operative goals reflect the actual intentions of an organization as disclosed by its operating policies. They represent what an enterprise is actually trying to do, regardless of its officially professed aims.

Learning Objective 3: Explain why official goals may differ from operative goals. There are several reasons why official and operative goals may differ: (1) participants may disagree on an organization's actual goals; (2) perceptions about how best to accomplish official goals may differ; (3) official goals may be unrealistic for financial or other reasons; and (4) operative goals are typically the outcome of continuous bargaining among groups or coalitions attempting to ensure that their interests are represented. Thus, although an enterprise's official goals may remain unchanged, its operating goals may vary over time as a consequence of such bargaining.

Learning Objective 4: Detail the benefits goals provide. Goals serve as (1) guidelines for action, (2) constraints, (3) a source of legitimacy, (4) standards of performance, (5) a source of motivation, and (6) a rationale for organizing.

Learning Objective 5: Name the key result areas in which all organizations should establish goals. The eight key result areas are (1) market share, (2) innovation, (3) productivity, (4) physical and financial resources, (5) profitability, (6) manager performance and development, (7) employee performance and attitude, and (8) social responsibility.

Learning Objective 6: Understand the meaning of *reification* as it applies to an organization. Reification in the present context means granting an organization human characteristics it does not possess.

Learning Objective 7: Define the term *coalition*. An alliance of individuals or groups who believe they can attain something they value through an organization constitutes a coalition.

Learning Objective 8: Discuss how organizational goals are determined. Organizational goals are determined by continued bargaining among groups or coalitions attempting to ensure that their differing interests are represented.

Learning Objective 9: Know what is meant by a side payment. A side payment is the price participants (for example, investors, employees, customers) require for their cooperation with the demands of other participants or groups of participants.

Learning Objective 10: Define the term *organizational slack*. Organizational slack is the difference between the total resources available to an organization and the total side payments necessary to maintain participant contributions.

Learning Objective 11: Describe the means-ends hierarchy. Goals normally exist in a hierarchy. That is, goals at one hierarchical level typically serve as the means for accomplishing goals at the next higher level. Except for the broadest, most encompassing goal, each goal within an organization can be considered an end in itself as well as a means for achieving a higher-level goal. Accordingly, an organization's overall goal can be viewed as being divided into second-, third-, and nth-order goals, and as forming a hierarchy of means and ends.

Learning Objective 12: Differentiate between goal succession and goal displacement. Goal succession is the deliberate replacement of an organization's primary goal, once it has been achieved, with a new goal. Goal displacement refers to instances in which an organization substitutes some other goal for its original goal.

Discussion Questions

1. As the successful head coach of a nationally recognized university football program, explain what your goals will be for the upcoming season. Of what benefit are these goals to you and your team?

2. Some two decades ago, the weight-reduction business was seen as a collection of gimmicks engineered by charlatans to take advantage of people in need. Founded in 1963 by Jean Nidetch, Weight Watchers International (now an H. J. Heinz subsidiary) was able to establish the industry's legitimacy by justifying its goals. Discuss how organizations such as the Girl Scouts, Salvation Army, and United Way have established the legitimacy of their activities.

3. Recognizing that goals tend to be abstractions, comment on the following quote as it relates to the difference between official goals and operative goals. "Organizational goals are elusive. You may identify them, write them down, and publish them next to the corporate logo, but there will remain a lingering doubt if these are the *real* organizational goals."[38]

4. Imagine that you are the CEO of a *Fortune* 500 company testifying before a Select Committee of the U.S. House of Representatives investigating alleged price-fixing violations. You have been asked why the company's goals as stated in its corporate charter bear so little resemblance to its actions. How would you respond?

5. Select any enterprise you wish as an example and explain the importance of the enterprise establishing goals in each of the so-called key result areas.

6. Imagine that you are the CEO of a major chemical company, and cite an example where your company's multiple goals might possibly conflict.

7. Prepare a means-ends hierarchy depicting how you plan to achieve your overall career goal.

8. Imagine that you are the chairperson of an all-volunteer citizen committee in your hometown. The committee's charge is to develop a set of goals to guide future neighborhood and commercial zoning decisions. How do you suppose the committee will establish the requested goals? What forces do you suppose will influence its deliberations?

9. It could be argued that goals are best understood as a source of movement—a push against inertia. In this respect, Nobel laureate Herbert A. Simon has stated that the real function of goals is "to motivate activity which in turn will generate new goals."[39] Comment.

10. Taken together, the material presented in this chapter implies that (1) the setting of organizational goals is a dynamic rather than a static process, and (2) organizations do not possess unlimited goal-setting discretion; factors from without and interest groups from within each impose conflicting and competing priorities. In this respect, goals appear to be a function of the interaction within an organization and between an organization and its surrounding environment. Using the National Foundation or another organization with which you are familiar as an example, illustrate these two implications.

DESIGN AUDIT #2

Analyzing Your Organization's Goals

This design audit will help you analyze your organization's goals by applying the concepts from Chapter 2.

1. In the spaces below identify the official and operative goals that your organization has in each key result area (KRA).

    Hint: *Remember that official goals are the general aims of an organization as expressed in its charter, annual reports, strategic plans, and public statements of top managers. Operative goals are actual intentions as disclosed by an organization's operating policies.*

    Large organizations often have official goals; many small organizations do not. If you are studying a small, privately held organization, it may be difficult to find statements of official goals. In this case, concentrate on its operative goals. If your organization does not have explicit official goals or implicit operative goals for a specific KRA, leave that space blank. Also remember that some key result areas may be more applicable than others, depending on the type of organization you are studying.

Key Result Area	Official Goals	Operative Goals
Market Share	(a) _____	(a) _____
	(b) _____	(b) _____
		(c) _____
Innovation	(a) _____	(a) _____
	(b) _____	(b) _____
		(c) _____
Productivity	(a) _____	(a) _____
	(b) _____	(b) _____
		(c) _____
Physical and Financial Resources	(a) _____	(a) _____
	(b) _____	(b) _____
		(c) _____

Profitability

(a) _____

(b) _____

    (a) _____

    (b) _____

    (c) _____

Manager Performance
and Development

(a) _____

(b) _____

    (a) _____

    (b) _____

    (c) _____

Employee Performance
and Development

(a) _____

(b) _____

    (a) _____

    (b) _____

    (c) _____

Social Responsibility

(a) _____

(b) _____

    (a) _____

    (b) _____

    (c) _____

2. Are there any KRAs in which your organization doesn't have goals and you think it should? Write those goals using a different color pencil or ink, and explain below why you think it should adopt these goals.

Notes

1. Steven Maynard-Moody and Charles McClintock, "Weeding an Old Garden: Toward a New Understanding of Organizational Goals," *Administration & Society* 19 (1987): 126.

2. Edward Gross, "The Definition of Organizational Goals," *British Journal of Sociology* 20 (1969): 277–294.

3. Amitai Etzioni, *Modern Organizations* (Englewood Cliffs, N.J.: Prentice-Hall, 1964), 6.

4. W. Keith Warner, "Problems in Measuring the Goal Attainment of Voluntary Organizations," *Adult Education* 19 (1967): 4.

5. Charles Perrow, "The Analysis of Goals in Complex Organizations," *American Sociological Review* 26 (1961): 855.

6. Leonard Deutscher, "Toward Avoiding the Goal-Trap in Evaluation Research," in *Readings in Evaluation Research,* ed. Frances G. Caro (New York: Russell Sage, 1977), 221.

7. Peter M. Blau, *The Dynamics of Bureaucracy* (Chicago: University of Chicago Press, 1955).

8. Donald Cressey, "Achievement of an Unstated Goal," *Pacific Sociological Review* 1, no. 2 (1958): 43–49; Mayer N. Zald, "Comparative Analysis and Measurement of Goals: The Case of Correctional Institutions for Delinquents," *Sociological Quarterly* 4 (1963): 206–230.

9. Charles K. Warriner, "The Problem of Organizational Purpose," *Sociological Quarterly* 6 (1965): 139–146.

10. Daniel Katz and Robert L. Kahn, *The Social Psychology of Organizations,* 2d ed. (New York: Wiley, 1978), 19.

11. J. Brian Quinn, "Strategic Goals: Process and Politics," *Sloan Management Review* 19 (Fall 1977): 21–37.

12. Michael J. Stahl and Adrian M. Harrell, "Identifying Operative Goals by Modeling Project Selection Decisions in Research and Development," *IEEE Transactions on Engineering Management* 30 (1983): 223–226.

13. Vernon Buck, "The Organization as a System of Constraints," in *Approaches to Organizational Design,* ed. James D. Thompson (Pittsburgh: University of Pittsburgh Press, 1966), 109.

14. Sanford M. Dornbusch and W. Richard Scott, *Evaluation and the Exercise of Authority: A Theory of Control Applied to Diverse Organizations* (San Francisco: Jossey-Bass, 1975), 65.

15. Peter F. Drucker, *The Practice of Management* (New York: Harper & Row, 1954), 62-87.

16. Thomas J. Peters and Robert H. Waterman, Jr., *In Search of Excellence: Lessons from America's Best-Run Companies* (New York: Harper & Row, 1982).

17. Chester I. Barnard, *The Functions of the Executive* (Cambridge, Mass.: Harvard University Press, 1938), 88–89.

18. Richard M. Cyert and James C. March, *A Behavioral Theory of the Firm* (Englewood Cliffs, N.J.: Prentice-Hall, 1963), 26–43.

19. David J. Hickson, C. Robert Hinings, Charles A. Lee, Rodney H. Schneck, and Johannes M. Pennings, "A Strategic Contingencies' Theory of Intraorganizational Power," *Administrative Science Quarterly* 16 (1971): 216–229.

20. Charles Perrow, "Goals and Power Structures: A Historical Case Study," in *The Hospital in Modern Society,* ed. Eliot Friedson (New York: Free Press of Glencoe, 1963), 112–146.

21. David F. Gillespie, "Discovering and Describing Organizational Goal Conflict," *Administration in Social Work* 1 (1977): 401–402.

22. Herbert A. Simon, "A Comparison of Organization Theories," *Review of Economic Studies* 20 (1952–1953): 42.

23. Herbert A. Simon, "On the Concept of Organizational Goals," *Administrative Science Quarterly* 9 (1964): 1–22.

24. Richard M. Cyert and James G. March, "Organizational Factors in the Theory of Oligopoly," *Quarterly Journal of Economics* 70 (1956): 44–64.

25. W. Richard Scott, "Some Implications of Organization Theory for Research on Health Services," *Milbank Memorial Fund Quarterly* 44, pt. 2 (October 1966): 37.

26. James D. Thompson, *Organizations in Action* (New York: McGraw-Hill, 1967), 128.

27. Blau, *Dynamics of Bureaucracy,* 195.

28. Mark Alpert, "Sweet Charity," *Fortune,* February 13, 1989, 113.

29. David L. Sills, *The Volunteers: Means and Ends in a National Organization* (Glencoe, Ill.: Free Press, 1957).

30. Etzioni, *Modern Organizations,* 10.

31. W. Keith Warner and A. Eugene Havens, "Goal Displacement and the Intangibility of Organizational Goals," *Administrative Science Quarterly* 12 (1968): 539–555.

32. Richard M. Cyert and Kenneth R. MacCrimmon, "Organizations," in *Handbook of Social Psychology,* 2d ed., vol. 1, ed. Gardner Lindzey and Elliot Aronson (Reading, Mass.: Addison-Wesley, 1968), 575.

33. Studs Terkel, *Working* (New York: Pantheon, 1974), 137–140.

34. Etzioni, *Modern Organizations,* 8; Bertram M. Gross, *Organizations and Their Managing* (New York: Free Press, 1968), 293.

35. Henry Mintzberg, "Organizational Power and Goals: A Skeletal Theory," in *Strategic Management: A New View of Business and Policy Planning,* ed. Dan Schendel and Charles W. Hofer (Boston: Little, Brown, 1979), 71.

36. Rick Molz, "How Leaders Use Goals," *Long Range Planning* 20, no. 5 (1987): 99.

37. Molz, "How Leaders Use Goals," 97.

38. Ibid., 92.

39. Herbert A. Simon, *The Sciences of the Artificial,* 2d ed. (Cambridge, Mass.: Massachusetts Institute of Technology Press, 1981), 186.

Organizational Effectiveness

Learning Objectives

Upon completing this chapter, you should be able to

1. Distinguish between efficiency and effectiveness.
2. Explain and critique the goal approach to assessing organizational effectiveness.
3. Explain and critique the system-resource approach to assessing organizational effectiveness.
4. Explain and critique the stakeholder approach to assessing organizational effectiveness.
5. State why organizational effectiveness is a value-based concept.
6. Know six critical questions that should guide assessments of organizational effectiveness.

SHAREHOLDER PRESSURES AT GM

General Motors Corp.'s market share is way down, its stock price listless, and its productivity on the assembly line the poorest of any Detroit carmaker. But GM's president vows to "stay the course." That's about the last thing some of GM's largest stockholders wanted to hear, and they're letting GM know.

In an unusual public challenge, California's and New York's public employee pension funds, both of which own large amounts of GM stock, are demanding that GM's board detail how it will choose a successor to its current CEO, who is about to step down. As GM stock declines, so may the value of the pension funds, and their managers obviously want to see GM take a new, more profitable direction. But GM board members aren't saying whom they've considered to replace the CEO—and they don't think they should. "Some guy wants to know how they select management, and the inference is that this board, which is an outstanding board, doesn't know how to do it," one director argues. "Are fund managers going to be consultants now?"

Directors are supposed to be watching out for shareholder interests, but it's possible that too many shareholder demands would only serve to hog-tie executives and prevent them from getting on with the task of managing. As Chapter 3 explains, methods other than shareholder opinion exist to evaluate an organization's effectiveness.

Source: James Treece, with Judith Dobrzynski, "Can GM's Big Investors Get It to Change Lanes?" *Business Week,* January 22, 1990, 30.

EFFECTIVENESS is one of the most frequently referenced concepts in organization theory. Indeed, much of the literature about organizations has been a by-product of the quest for improved organizational effectiveness. This search, however, has not led to the development of a universally accepted theory or methodology for assessing an organization's overall effectiveness. Rather, divergent definitions of effectiveness abound, along with the identification of many different explanatory variables and equally diverse schemes for measuring effectiveness.

Early management theorists defined effectiveness as the meeting or surpassing of organizational goals. For example, Chester Barnard—one of the earliest management theorists—viewed it in terms of goal attainment. "When a specific desired end is attained we shall say that the action is 'effective.'"[1] This perspective has been labeled the *goal approach* to the study of organizational effectiveness, since it views organizations as principally concerned with the attainment of specific outcomes or goals.

Two recent alternative views of organizational effectiveness have emerged that are particularly relevant to our present discussion. The first, the so-called *system-resource approach*, views organizations as social systems operating in environments of scarce resources. Incorporating an open-systems viewpoint, it defines effectiveness as the degree to which an organization is successful in acquiring scarce and valued resources. Thus, considering the whole of an organization and not just its end products or goals, effectiveness (according to this approach) relates to the nature of the interaction between an organization and its surrounding environment.

A second, even more recent viewpoint on organizational effectiveness, the *stakeholder approach,* focuses on the satisfaction of an organization's "stakeholders"—that is, the various groups, both external and internal, that can either affect or be affected by an organization's performance. These groups each have a "stake" in an organization's continued survival, and at the same time, play a vital role in its success. Examples of a typical organization's major stakeholders include owners, employees, customers, suppliers, government at various levels, and society-at-large.

This chapter explores the nature of organizational effectiveness and its implications for managers. In doing so, our discussion naturally builds on that of the previous chapter, in which we dealt with the nature and establishment of organizational goals. After pausing briefly to comment on the relationship between effectiveness and its companion concept, efficiency, we will analyze more completely the goal, system-resource, and stakeholder models as three major approaches to organizational effectiveness. In further explaining the operation of these approaches, we will stress their complementary nature, and attempt to at least partially reconcile their differences. The balance of the chapter will then be devoted to discussing their managerial implications.

EFFICIENCY AND EFFECTIVENESS

When discussing various approaches for assessing organizational effectiveness, it is helpful to distinguish between efficiency and effectiveness. **Efficiency** is generally defined as the ratio of some output (good or service) to some input (e.g., labor, capital, raw materials, information). It indicates how much of an organization's inputs emerge as outputs and how much is absorbed in internal processing and thus is concerned with the better use of resources, as opposed to resource acquisition. In economic terms, the concept of efficiency can be reformulated as a basic optimization problem: What is the least-cost combination of inputs that will produce a given level of output?

An organization is judged efficient if, when compared to similar organizations, its output of goods or services is relatively high in comparison to the costs of producing them. Thus, as Steers observes: "If two companies making the same product finish the fiscal year with equal production levels but one attained the level with fewer invested resources than the other, that company [other things being equal] would be described as being more efficient. It achieved the same level of output with fewer inputs."[2]

Effectiveness is a more ambiguous concept. Depending on the approach taken (goal, system-resource, or stakeholder), it can be defined in several equally valid ways. In a very general sense, however, effectiveness may be thought of as "doing the right things," whereas efficiency involves "doing things right." The important point to note is that, while effectiveness and efficiency are complementary, they are not interchangeable. That is, an organization could easily be judged effective without being efficient, just as it could be judged efficient without being effective. Neither condition is a necessary prerequisite of the other.

For example, following the goal approach, a firm may set 250,000 units as a production goal. Subsequently, due to material shortages, only 200,000 units may be produced, but with near 100 percent efficiency. The firm would be judged ineffective but highly efficient. In contrast, 250,000 units may be produced as scheduled, but with considerable waste of capital, labor, and raw materials. This time the firm would be judged effective but inefficient.

Ideally, an organization would seek to be both efficient and effective. This aside, however, effectiveness is typically viewed as being more important than efficiency. While low efficiency can harm an organization, no amount of efficiency can save an organization that is doing the wrong things, such as efficiently producing a good or service no one wants. Buggy whip manufacturers went out of business not because they were inefficient, but because they failed to "do the right things."

THE GOAL APPROACH

Originating in traditional measures of performance used in accounting, the goal model—including both operative and official goals—is unquestionably the most commonly used and widely discussed approach for assessing organizational effectiveness. As noted earlier, its distinctive feature is that it defines effectiveness in terms of goal attainment. That is, the greater the extent to which an organization's goals are met or surpassed, the greater its effectiveness.

The goal model assumes that the goals of an organization can be clearly established and that the necessary human and material resources can be manipulated for the attainment of those goals. It follows (according to this approach) that the way to assess an organization's effectiveness would be to establish measures of how well its goals are being achieved, as shown in Table 3.1. A typical proponent of this position would argue that this is the only definition of organizational effectiveness. Effectiveness is the extent to which an organization attains its goals.[3]

Accordingly, if the goal is a 10 percent return on sales, then the Tupperware division of Dart and Kraft (with an average 30 percent annual

Table 3.1
Examples of Goals and Evaluative Criteria

Goal	Evaluative Criteria	Type of Organization
Productivity	Units produced per hour of labor	Manufacturer
	Scrap rate	Manufacturer
	400 occupied beds/day	Hospital
	75% billable hours	Consulting firm
Innovation	Implement new MIS system	Government agency
	Develop new product by . . .	Consumer products firm
	Decentralize management to facilities managers	Nursing home chain
	Develop new customer service procedures by . . .	Service firm
Employee performance and attitude	Reduce absenteeism rate to 10 days per employee	Manufacturer
	Reduce annual nursing turnover rate to 25%	Hospital
	Increase training to 40 hours per year per employee	Insurance company
Social responsibility	Increase United Way participation to 75% of employees	Retail chain
	Increase volunteer hours by 25% over last year	Computer firm
	Participate in carpooling campaign	Bank
	Promote public transportation	Oil company

rate of return) is highly effective. If it is a 30 percent market share, then Budweiser and Coca-Cola are effective organizations. If it is 50 new products annually, then 3M, with more than 100 new product offerings each year, is clearly effective.

In the following section, we outline the case of Reserve Mining Company to demonstrate the logic of the goal approach to organizational effectiveness. We also will use this same case to illustrate the differences between the goal, system-resource, and stakeholder approaches in later sections.

An Example: Reserve Mining Company

In 1947 Reserve Mining Company was opened in Silver Bay, Minnesota, as a wholly owned subsidiary of Armco and Republic Steel Corporations.[4] Reserve's goal was to profitably mine and process taconite—a low-grade iron ore—and supply its parent companies with a steady supply of raw material. Between 1947 and 1976 Reserve Mining was an effective organization from the perspective of the goal approach because it met these objectives. Reserve provided a steady supply of raw material to its parent companies, while making a profit—$1 million per month during the early 1970s.

This situation changed when, in 1977, after six years of lawsuits, federal authorities required that Reserve modify its waste disposal methods. It had to stop dumping taconite tailings (the waste product from processing taconite) into Lake Superior and devise and implement a land-based disposal system, and it was required to control emissions of dust from its taconite-processing operations. These changes cost Reserve $370 million, more than the $350 million spent to build its physical plant. In part, these expenditures were made possible by the rising price of iron ore in the late 1970s, and by IRS approval for Reserve to issue $167 million in tax-exempt pollution control bonds. Overall, servicing the debt and operating the pollution control system added over $50 million in annual costs to Reserve's operating expenses, and reduced productivity by 3.4 percent. These added costs substantially reduced profitability and made Reserve one of the industry's high-cost producers.

In the early 1980s demand for U.S.–produced steel declined as the economy went into a recession and foreign competitors grabbed large parts of the remaining market. In turn, iron ore demand plummeted over 50 percent between 1979 and 1986. In 1983 Reserve was closed for several months, then reopened in 1984 at less than half capacity. Demand continued to drop, and Reserve filed for bankruptcy, closing its doors on July 21, 1986. Viewed through the lense of the goal approach, Reserve's effectiveness declined from 1977 through 1986 because of reduced profitability and lowered productivity.

Limitations of the Goal Approach

On the surface, the goal model appears to be a valid and reliable approach to the measurement of organizational effectiveness. Comparing actual performance to official and operative goals sounds easy enough. But closer inspection reveals some difficulties.

Goals as Ideal States. Goal attainment may be an unrealistic standard of organizational effectiveness.[5] Goals, as norms or targets, are ideal states. Organizations, as systems of coordinated activity, are social systems, and as such, tend to be less consistent and less perfect in actual performance than anticipated. Some discrepancy between goals (an ideal state) and performance (a real state) is almost inevitable, so to judge effectiveness solely in terms of complete, or even substantial, goal attainment is to virtually assure a disappointing conclusion in many cases. Moreover, an organization may in reality be ineffective even when substantially accomplishing its goals if the goals are too low, harmful, or otherwise misplaced.

This point can be best illustrated by a hypothetical example. Suppose two similar companies are in competition with each other. The first sets its goal in terms of annual profit at $1 million and the second at $10 million. If the first attains its goal of a $1 million profit and the second makes a $9 million profit ($1 million short of its goal), the goal approach would deem the first company more effective than the second. In short, comparison of goal-based judgments of effectiveness among companies with different goals can lead to erroneous conclusions.[6]

Multiplicity of Goals. Most organizations, particularly large ones, have multiple goals that they seek to accomplish at the same time (see Focus on Design 3.1). Sometimes, though, the realization of one goal inhibits the attainment of another. For instance, a high rate of return on investment may well be achieved at the expense of long-term organization growth or long-term research and development. In this case, it may be impossible for an organization to perform effectively in all areas at the same time. Trade-offs in the attainment of any such conflicting goals should be dealt with in the goal-setting process.[7]

Generally, organizations tend to be effective in a limited number of domains and downright ineffective in others. For example, Liggett & Myers (now Liggett Group) has been largely ineffective in terms of cigarette product innovation. It has yet to introduce a successful filter or low-tar brand. Yet, at the same time, it has been the most effective "Big Six" tobacco firm at diversifying into nontobacco products, acquiring Paddington Corporation, Atlantic soft drinks, and Diversified Products, among other companies.

Ambiguity of Criteria. Another limitation of the goal model is the difficulty of establishing unambiguous criteria for measuring effectiveness. Many profit-making organizations have vaguely stated goals at best, and many nonprofit and public-sector organizations, such as voluntary associations and social welfare agencies, have largely unmeasurable goals.[8] Social action groups, for instance, sponsor "broad-aim programs" that are targeted at the achievement of nonspecific forms of change-for-the-better, and the relationship between cause and effect is unclear. For example, do youth camps reduce the threat of neighborhood delinquency? Do consumer education classes result in increased buying skills? In such instances, an organization's goals typically specify an area of activity rather than specific objectives. Therefore, the interpretation of exactly what constitutes goal attainment is subject to wide differences. Needless to say, the lack of agreed upon or measurable goals also is likely to result in disagreements over tasks to be performed, personnel to be hired, resources to be allocated, and so on.

Despite such limitations, the goal model remains a dominant approach to the study of organizational effectiveness. "Its dominance," Hall suggests, "is linked to the fact that organizations do in fact utilize goals, as witnessed by annual reports and planning documents." Hall further points out that

FOCUS ON DESIGN 3.1

Multiple Goals—A Survey

Application of the goal approach to assessing organizational effectiveness is complicated by the problem that most organizations have multiple goals. Since these goals often conflict, effectiveness cannot be assessed by single outcomes. Effectiveness in attaining one goal may be inversely related to effectiveness in attaining other goals. Nevertheless, multiple goals must somehow be considered simultaneously.

One example of multiple goals is from a survey of 82 of the largest U.S. corporations. The 12 goals they reported as being most important follow. The number of objectives per corporation ranged from 1 to 18 with an average of 5 to 6. The most common goals were profitability, growth, and market share. Following close behind were social responsibility, employee welfare, and product quality/service.

Most Frequently Cited Objectives of 82 U.S. Corporations

Objective	Percent Mentioning Objective
Profitability	89
Growth	82
Market share	66
Social responsibility	65
Employee welfare	62
Product quality and service	60
Research and development	54
Diversification	51
Efficiency	50
Financial stability	49
Resource conservation	39
Management development	35

Source: Adapted from Yermal K. Shetty, "A New Look at Corporate Goals," *California Management Review* 22 (Winter 1979): 73.

"while these can be labeled as rationalizations for past actions, goals remain a central component of most theories of organizations and of organizational effectiveness."[9]

THE SYSTEM-RESOURCE APPROACH

The **system-resource approach** was proposed as an alternative to the goal model in the late 1950s, and attracted considerable attention from organizational researchers during the 1960s and 1970s.[10] Defining effectiveness as the degree to which an organization is successful in acquiring scarce and valued resources, the system-resource approach focuses on the interaction between an organization and its environment. In contrast to the goal model, inputs replace outputs as the primary consideration. Organizations are viewed as being involved in a bargaining relationship with their environments, acquiring various scarce resources (e.g., physical facilities, ideas, raw materials, personnel) to be transformed and returned to the environment as goods and services. Clearly, an organization will survive only if it can maintain a greater intake than is required to produce its output. That is, an organization's long-run success hinges upon its ability to establish and maintain a favorable input-output ratio. Thus, the procurement and transformation of inputs and their subsequent distribution serve as the system-resource approach's focal frame of reference. Accordingly, this approach proposes that an organization is most effective when it "maximizes its bargaining position and optimizes its resource procurement."[11]

Most applications of the system-resource approach appear to be in situations where the causal linkages between inputs and outputs is unclear. For example, college and university accreditation procedures are implicitly based on the system-resource approach. The American Assembly of Colleges and Schools of Business is the national accrediting body for colleges and schools of business. Accreditation criteria such as student/faculty ratios, travel budgets, student credit hours taught per full-time faculty member, library resources, and so on, focus on a business school's ability to obtain resources from its larger university community. An implicit *assumption* of such evaluations is that if sufficient resources are available, the desired ends will be attained. Little, if any, attention is paid to examining outcomes.[12]

Reserve Mining Revisited

The system-resource approach can be used to draw another picture of Reserve Mining's effectiveness. Most of the high-grade iron ore in Minnesota's Mesabi Range had been mined out by the late 1940s, and U.S. steelmakers were faced with either importing iron ore or finding another way of producing it. The solution for Armco and Republic Steel Corporations was to create Reserve Mining, which would use an experimental process to produce high-grade iron ore pellets from taconite, a low-grade iron ore. The process involved pulverizing taconite, removing iron oxide magnetically, and forming it into pellets for shipment. But the technique had not been used yet in high-volume production, so there was a risk. The extraction process worked, and Reserve delivered a steady supply of taconite pellets to its parent companies through the early 1980s. From the system-resource approach, Reserve was an effective organization because it was able to exploit its environment for a scarce and valued resource. Then in the early 1980s the demand for iron ore decreased as a result of recessions and import competition. Thus, the supply of taconite pellets became less critical to the parent companies, and Reserve's effectiveness declined.

Comparing this system-resource interpretation of Reserve's effectiveness to the earlier assessment using the goal approach, we find that both result in similar evaluations of effectiveness through 1977. Both approaches evaluate the organization as performing effectively. But then their assessments diverge through the late 1970s and early 1980s. The goal approach portrays effectiveness as declining from 1977, when profitability disappeared with the cost of pollution controls. The system-resource approach, in contrast, continues to yield a positive assessment of effectiveness through the early 1980s because the organization has continued to obtain a scarce resource for its parent companies, although less efficiently. But in the end, both judge the organization as being ineffective since it ceased operating in 1986.

Limitations of the System-Resource Approach

Despite the appeal of the system-resource approach's emphasis on organization-environment transactions, it has a number of recognizable limitations.

Difficulty of Operationalization. While the system-resource approach takes into account that organizations are dependent on their surrounding environment for resources, it provides little guidance as to what constitutes optimum resource exploitation. By drawing too heavily upon its environment, an organization can endanger its long-run effectiveness, not only potentially depleting its resource base, but also running the risk of stimulating countervailing forces (such as government regulation). Thus, without some optimization criterion or principle, the system-resource approach is difficult to operationalize and apply to actual organizations. We are thus left with an unanswered question: "How does one know when a system has reached a point of optimal input or exploitation?" Furthermore, Cameron argues that organizations "may prove to be effective even when inputs are not optimal and when a competitive advantage in the resource marketplace does not exist."[13] To illustrate this point, he cites the case of the New York Yankees organization during the late 1970s: Widespread bickering, player turnover, accusations, limited trust, and at the same time, World Series championships in 1977 and 1978, and considerable profits.

Identifying Relevant Resources. A second limitation of the system-resource approach is that it provides little guidance in determining which scarce and valued resources are relevant as a basis for the absolute or comparative assessment of an organization's effectiveness.[14] Without reference to specific output goals, the definition of a resource becomes ambiguous. Moreover, while the system-resource approach focuses on an organization's ability to obtain needed resources, it does not elaborate on their internal allocation. Yet, unless resources are unlimited, the rate of resource flow and the allocation of resources over time are likely to be even more important to an organization's effectiveness than sheer ability to garner resources. Although advocates of the system-resource approach have recognized the need for general measures of resource efficiency that address these issues, they have seldom been used.[15]

Overemphasis on Resource Acquisition. A final limitation of the system-resource approach is that it focuses on resource acquisition and ignores resource use. As a consequence, organized crime, terrorist groups, or drug cartels could conceivably be judged effective. Indeed, some proponents of the approach have noted this kind of effectiveness with seeming admiration.

As a result of these limitations, academic interest in the system-resource approach has declined since the 1970s, and few organizations use it today. But while it has fallen by the wayside in terms of research and practical application, it serves an important role in providing a contrast to the goal approach, and it has been valuable in directing attention toward the interplay of an organization and its environment in determining effectiveness.

THE STAKEHOLDER APPROACH

An alternative to the goal and system-resource views, known as the **stakeholder**, or **multiple-constituency approach**, began attracting attention in the late 1970s.[16] Like the system-resource approach, it directs attention to an organization's relationship with its larger environment; and like the goal approach, it directs attention to the outcomes of an organization's performance. The basic logic of the stakeholder approach is easily understood. Individuals or groups become involved with organizations for various reasons. As would be anticipated, these reasons are reflected in their preferences and expectations for an organization's performance. Employees want high wages and good working conditions; customers want high-quality products at low prices; and shareholders want high dividends and rapid growth in stock value. The stakeholder approach defines effectiveness as the extent to which these *multiple constituencies,* or *stakeholders,* are satisfied with an organization's performance. It focuses on the various groups—both internal and external—that can either affect or be affected by an organization's performance. Since an organization could not exist without the support or resources provided by each of these groups, they play a vital role in its success.

As generally portrayed, a typical organization's stakeholders include owners, employees, customers, suppliers, governments (local, state, and federal), and society-at-large. A short list of stakeholder-effectiveness criteria is presented in Table 3.2. As is evident, each stakeholder group tends to have its own peculiar performance preferences related to the nature of its exchange

Table 3.2
Examples of Stakeholder-Effectiveness Criteria

Stakeholder	Effectiveness Criteria
Owners	Dividends, share price
Employees	Pay, interesting work, opportunities for advancement
Customers	Quality, service, price
Suppliers	Timely payments, future sales potential
Government	Adhering to laws, paying taxes
Society	Providing employment, support of community activities

relationship with an organization. These differences highlight an often over-looked aspect of the effectiveness construct: *organizational effectiveness is an inherently value-based concept.*[17] Effectiveness lies in the eyes of the beholder, because different people have different preferences and expectations for an organization's performance. What one person might judge effective may be ineffective to another because of their differing perceptions. As a result, it may be more useful to think in terms of organizational *effectivenesses* (plural) because an organization is typically evaluated on a number of fronts by different stakeholders using different evaluative criteria, as opposed to thinking in terms of some single standard of overall organizational effectiveness.[18]

The explicitly value-based orientation of the stakeholder approach gives rise to three rather complicated issues:

1. Any and all aspects of an organization's performance will doubtlessly be viewed in terms of self-interest by each of the stakeholders.

2. Despite claims to the contrary, an organization's performance is unlikely to be viewed impartially. Assessments of effectiveness do not take place in a neutral vacuum. Each aspect of an organization's performance is likely to benefit some stakeholders more than others.

3. Given differences in stakeholder preferences and expectations, maximizing the satisfaction of some stakeholders is likely to result in the increased dissatisfaction of others.

The essential questions for managers using the stakeholder approach are: "Who wants what, and how important is it that the demand be satisfied? And what are the implications of the satisfaction of one demand for the satisfaction of other demands?"[19] Managers, in other words, engage in a balancing act, trying to at least minimally satisfy diverse preferences for performance in order to ensure a continued supply of scarce and valued resources from various stakeholders.

The Goal and System-Resource Approaches
from a Stakeholder Perspective

Although not as obvious as in the stakeholder approach, values are the foundation of the goal and system-resource approaches as well. The difference is that the latter two approaches present a single, internally consistent value perspective. The **goal approach** represents the interests of managers (and usually an organization's owners). Goals are ranked according to these interests, and alternative means for reaching them reflect the preferences and interests of an organization's managers.

We can see how sharp differences concerning the state of an organization's goals and effectiveness could (and frequently do) develop within the context of the stakeholder approach. As Hall and Clark note, "It is possible to conceive of effectiveness on a particular goal or set of goals from the standpoint of the organization itself and its professional staff, from the standpoint of the community-at-large, and from the standpoint of individuals being served or processed by the organizations." The implication, they add, is that "effectiveness from one of these standpoints could well be gross ineffectiveness from another standpoint."[20]

The stakeholder approach also explains why organizations have diverse goals, as reflected by the key result areas discussed in Chapter 2. Moreover, it acknowledges the role that stakeholder preferences play in an organization's survival, and acts as a reminder that an organization's performance is judged across many areas.

The ramifications of varying stakeholder perspectives for the system-resource approach are just as complex. Both internal and external stakeholders are links to important resources and must be at least minimally satisfied before scarce resources can be acquired. Consequently, the demands of suppliers, employees, customers, and other groups, whose cooperation is essential for an organization's survival, must be met. Two recent trends in business—the increased emphasis on output quality and the rising number of hostile takeovers—clearly illustrate this point. In the first case, managers have found that consumer preferences for high-quality goods and services must be met, or consumers will abandon their organization's products for those of competitors. Focus on Design 3.2 shows how these stakeholder preferences can become embedded in an organization's own goals. In the latter case, managers are under intense pressure to comply with shareholders' demands for high profitability and rates of return or face the possibility of a hostile takeover.

Overall, the stakeholder approach incorporates the underlying logic of both the goal and system-resource approaches. Goals are evident within the stakeholder approach, both management's and those of stakeholders that management may or may not acknowledge. And the importance of the environment is clearly acknowledged by the necessity of satisfying stakeholders to obtain needed resources.

FOCUS ON DESIGN 3.2

The Customer Counts

Storage Technology Corporation, the largest manufacturer of IBM-plug compatible storage devices and a *Fortune* 500 firm, went into bankruptcy in 1984 and struggled for two years to turn itself around. Part of its problem was customers abandoning it because of unreliable equipment. As part of its turnaround effort, Storage-Tek reformulated its goals as quality, accountability, people, action, and practices. Each goal shows how an organization can accept the preferences and expectations of major stakeholders as its own. Steve Jerritts, President and Chief Operating Officer, explains:

> The principle states that "our standards of *quality* will ensure our competitiveness. We will sacrifice short-term gain for reliability and excellence in serving our

customers' needs." In other words, the level of quality and service of the products we produce will determine our competitiveness and the long-term viability of our corporation. Meeting deadlines at the expense of reliability is no longer acceptable because quality is a necessary ingredient for success in our marketplace.

Our definition of quality is conformance to customer requirements. This conformance to customer requirements includes more than quality products. It is the total relationship we have with our customers from order entry through field service. It is the contribution *each* of us makes, in the performance of our tasks, to customer satisfaction.

Source: Steve Jerritts, "Editorial: Quality," *StorageTek Dialog,* (May 1986).

Reserve Mining: A Final Visit

When Reserve Mining began operations in 1947, it was seen as something of a corporate hero. Jobs had evaporated in the Mesabi Range region of Minnesota as high-grade iron ore deposits were mined out. Many stakeholders benefited from Reserve's operations—employees had new, well-paying jobs, the tax-base of state and local governments increased, and Reserve's parent companies—Armco and Republic Steel received a steady supply of iron ore and profits. Through the early 1960s Reserve's major stakeholders were reasonably satisfied with its performance.

During the 1960s, however, public concern about the environment began to grow, and the passage of the federal Water Quality Act of 1965 marked a turning point in public sentiment about water pollution and about Reserve's operations. Reserve's production process generated about 10 million tons of solid waste annually in the form of taconite tailings, and it required 130,000 gallons of water per minute for its operations. The taconite tailings were discharged in a slurry form into Lake Superior, under a series of permits issued by various regulatory agencies in the late 1940s. Changing public sentiment about pollution led the federal government to conduct a series of studies on Lake Superior's water quality between 1966 and 1969. These studies concluded that Reserve's taconite-tailing discharges were polluting the lake, and recommendations for on-land disposal were made. Reserve filed suit against the Minnesota Pollution Control Agency in 1969 to test the validity of new pollution-control laws, beginning a series of legal actions that would last for most of the next decade. At the same time, public sentiment about Reserve's operations became more negative as environmental concerns increased.

A turning point was reached in 1973, when scientific studies revealed that asbestos fibers were a likely cancer threat, and that the fibers in Reserve's smokestack emissions and taconite-tailing discharges were asbestos-form fibers. Legal action immediately heated up as concerns grew that the health of communities in three states (Minnesota, Wisconsin, and Michigan) drawing water supplies from Lake Superior was being endangered by Reserve's discharges. The situation became even more complex when the court discovered that Reserve had introduced misleading evidence designed to prolong the trial while it made $1 million a month in profits.

In April 1974 a court issued an injunction halting Reserve's operations, which Reserve immediately appealed. Court battles seesawed back and forth for the next two years, when a federal court imposed fines of more than $1 million in May 1976. Later that month the Minnesota Pollution Control Agency rejected Reserve's disposal plan, and a federal judge ordered operations shut down. Reserve appealed the decision, and it was not until April 1977 that the Minnesota Supreme Court upheld the lower court ruling and required land-based disposal of the taconite tailings.

Reserve continued disposing taconite tailings into Lake Superior under court supervision until 1980, when its land-based disposal system was ready for operation. But by that time the taconite-pellet market began to soften. While the concerns of regulatory agencies, the communities bordering Lake Superior, and society-at-large were being met, the interests of Reserve's employees and its parent companies began to suffer as iron-ore demand declined. Between 1983 and 1986, Reserve laid off hundreds of employees, never operating at more than 40 percent of capacity. Finally, all Reserve's employees lost their jobs when it filed for bankruptcy in 1986, and Minnesota lost a major tax-paying employer.

Table 3.3 presents a summary of stakeholder judgments of Reserve's effectiveness at different points in time. Four important observations can be made:

1. The number of different stakeholders Reserve faced increased over time. When Reserve began operations in 1947, its major stakeholders were the parent companies, its employees, the State of Minnesota and its regulatory

Table 3.3
Changes in Reserve Mining's Major Stakeholders and Their
Evaluations of Effectiveness over Time

Late 1940s	Late 1960s	Mid 1970s	Early 1980s
Parent companies +	Parent companies +	Parent companies +	Parent companies –
Employees +	Employees +	Employees +	Employees –
State of Minnesota +	State of Minnesota +	State of Minnesota +	State of Minnesota –
Various state regulatory agencies +	Various state regulatory agencies +	Various state regulatory agencies +	Various state regulatory agencies +
	Federal regulatory agencies –	Federal regulatory agencies –	Federal regulatory agencies +
	Courts (neutral)	Courts –	
	Environmentalists –	Environmentalists –	Environmentalists +
		Wisconsin and Michigan –	Wisconsin and Michigan +

+   Positive evaluation

–   Negative evaluation

agencies. Thirty years later, several other states, environmentalists, federal agencies, several courts, and society-at-large had entered the fray.

2. Changing stakeholder preferences resulted in changing evaluations of Reserve's performance over time. The rise of environmentalism in the United States, improved scientific information about water and air quality, and information about the relationship of asbestos fibers to cancer changed the criteria that many stakeholders used to evaluate Reserve's performance.

3. Stakeholder evaluations of Reserve's performance changed over time—from positive to negative—even though Reserve continued operating in the same way between 1947 and 1977.

4. In many instances, satisfying the preferences and expectations of some stakeholders led to the dissatisfaction of other stakeholders.

In summary, the case of Reserve Mining shows that the stakeholder approach provides a much more complex rendering of how an organization's performance is evaluated relative to the goal or system-resource approaches. We also see that, in this case, viewing organizational effectiveness from the stakeholder approach yields significantly different results than evaluations using the goal and system-resource models. At some points in time, the different approaches' assessments were similar, but at others they diverged widely.

Limitations of the Stakeholder Approach

While the stakeholder approach presents a richer picture of organizational effectiveness, it is not without its shortcomings. One aspect of the approach that has received considerable attention focuses on the question of whose preferences should an organization attempt to satisfy? Some have argued that organizations should attempt to satisfy the preferences and expectations of their most powerful stakeholders since they control resources most necessary for an organization's survival.[21] Others argue from a social-justice perspective that organizations should focus on satisfying the needs and expectations of their most disadvantaged stakeholders.[22] In Reserve's case, this would have meant operating in a manner that satisfied the interests of society-at-large rather than maximizing the interests of its parent companies. Still others suggest that organizations should act in a manner that maximizes their ability to survive in the long run, which operationally means acting in an organization's long-term interests.[23] Finally, some suggest that there is no way to choose among different stakeholders.[24]

The value-based nature of the organizational effectiveness construct, and the issue of "who gets what," are brought to the forefront by the stakeholder approach. In the final analysis, the stakeholder approach indicates that determinations of organizational effectiveness are as much a matter of philosophical beliefs as they are of any "science" of management.

ISSUES IN MANAGING EFFECTIVENESS

While issues of organizational effectiveness may not have "scientific" answers, they are extremely important to managers and their organizations. Almost daily, we each make judgments about the effectiveness of organizations as we choose where to invest, where to seek medical care, where to send our children to school, where to have our car repaired, where to seek employment, and so on. These judgments determine the extent to which an organization's various stakeholders will participate with an organization, and that participation determines whether an organization will survive over the long run. Thus, messy as the concept of organizational effectiveness might be, it is a central one with which managers must deal. The examination of the goal, system-resource, and stakeholder approaches, and the discussion of Reserve Mining, point to a number of practical issues that managers should keep in mind when evaluating their organization's effectiveness.

Effectiveness over Time

As the case of Reserve Mining shows, judgments about an organization's effectiveness change over time, even if its performance remains the same. Stakeholders' judgments of effectiveness as well as their preferences can change for three major reasons.

First, an organization's past performance can change stakeholder preferences. Consider, for example, employee preferences for high wages. Employee definitions of what constitutes high wages change over time due to increased living costs and changes in the wages an organization currently offers, among other factors. The general trend is toward rising expectations. Thus, satisfying employees' wage preferences at one point in time can change their future preferences.

Second, the social context in which performance is evaluated changes over time. Consider the case of Reserve Mining. When Reserve opened in the late 1940s, dumping taconite tailings into Lake Superior was an acceptable practice allowed under government permits. But as society's concerns with environmental quality began to grow, the practice became unacceptable, and stakeholder evaluations of Reserve's effectiveness changed from positive to negative. Similarly, the civil rights movement resulted in changing definitions of acceptable employment practices. No longer could employers discriminate on the basis of race, religion, national origin, gender, or age, all of which had been allowable practices in earlier times. Those that continued such discriminatory practices often ran afoul of both their immediate stakeholders and the law. In much the same way, the consumer movement and foreign competition heightened pressures on manufacturers to increase product quality and safety, and to design products that directly fit consumer needs. Organizations that did not respond accordingly often found themselves losing customers and, frequently, going out of business.

Third, who an organization's stakeholders are can change over time, modifying the preferences that it has to satisfy, as happened in Reserve's case. New stakeholder groups may bring new expectations and preferences for performance that affect an organization's operations. Sometimes new stakeholders appear unexpectedly. For example, could the tobacco companies picture in the 1960s that *nonsmokers* would become one of their most important stakeholders?

The implication of changing stakeholders and changing preferences for managers and their organizations is that they must remain aware of what is happening in the world. It is exceedingly difficult to satisfy demands you know nothing about. Also, an organization's goals should be periodically examined to see whether they fit an organization's existing social environment. Do its goals provide guidance for maintaining satisfactory relationships with the stakeholders who provide resources necessary for its survival both now and in the future? Or do those goals reflect past stakeholder preferences that may no longer be relevant? Moreover, as we will show in the following chapters, an organization's design has a major impact on its ability to sense changing preferences and respond to them. In short, managers must be aware that their task is one of continually *becoming* effective, rather than *being* effective, because the definition of effective performance changes over time.[25]

Table 3.4

Six Critical Questions in Assessing Organizational Effectiveness

---

- What is the domain of activity for the evaluation?

- Whose perspective is being considered in the evaluation?

- What level of analysis is appropriate for the domain of activity and perspective being used in the evaluation?

- What information should be used?

- What referent should be used in interpreting the information?

- What time frame should be employed?

Six Critical Questions

Because of the complex nature of organizational effectiveness, most evaluations are necessarily limited in scope. Managers can nevertheless conduct meaningful assessments of effectiveness if they keep the following six questions (Table 3.4) in mind.[26] These questions help focus an assessment and remind managers of the limits of any particular evaluation.

1. *What is the domain of activity for the evaluation?* Evaluations of organizational effectiveness are typically limited in scope because most organizations do many different things. They provide jobs for their employees, goods or services for their customers, dividends for their shareholders, and so on. Thus, managers rarely try to answer the question, "What is the overall effectiveness of my organization?" (And, as the discussion above suggests, this question itself may be meaningless.) So managers need to ask instead, "What is the domain of activity that is being evaluated? Is it employment, goods and services, financial performance (etc.)?"

2. *Whose perspective is being considered in the evaluation?* Almost any activity can be evaluated from different stakeholder points of view. For example, should we look at an organization's performance as an employer from its employees' perspective, from its management's perspective, from its community's perspective (etc.)? Whose perspective is being employed makes a difference in the evaluation criteria that should be used, as well as in interpreting results. Being aware that there are different perspectives for evaluating a given domain of activity also increases managers' awareness of the trade-offs inherent in satisfying divergent stakeholder interests.

3. *What level of analysis is appropriate for the domain of activity and perspective being used in the evaluation?* The level of analysis refers to the level of the organization that is being evaluated. For example, are you evaluating performance at the individual level (e.g., performance appraisal), at the subunit level (e.g., effectiveness of the production unit, the sales unit, etc.), or the organizational level (e.g., the organization as a whole). Different levels of analysis are conducive to evaluating different aspects of performance. For example, if an organization wants to examine the effectiveness of customer service, there are a number of different approaches that could be employed, each focusing on a different level of analysis. If, for example, an organization's managers wanted to examine employee effectiveness in delivering services, they would focus on the individual level of analysis. If they were interested in how well customers perceived the service provided by its sales, production, and customer service departments, they would approach the assessment on a subunit level. If they were curious about customers' overall perceptions of service, compared to other organizations, they would conduct the assessment at the organization level of analysis.

4. *What information should be used?* The relevant domain of activity, the perspective employed, and the level of analysis of interest will influence the type of information that should be used in an evaluation. For example, evaluations of productivity or profitability are usually conducted using archival data available from an organization's accounting and financial records. On the other hand, if the organization is interested in customer perceptions of service quality, questionnaire and interview data collected from customers would be more appropriate. Given time and resource constraints, managers should try to use multiple data sources (e.g., archival, questionnaire, interview). The broader the range of data sources used in an evaluation, the more likely it is to be accurate.

5. *What referent should be used in interpreting the information?* A commonly used referent against which evaluative information can be compared is an organization's goals. This is, in essence, goal-based evaluation, wherein actual performance is compared to an organization's goals. Other potential referents include other organizations (comparative evaluation), an organization's own performance at an earlier point in time (improvement evaluation), or against some ideal (normative evaluation). Each type of referent presents a different evaluative perspective on an organization's performance. It is important to choose a referent that fits an evaluation's purpose. For example, if managers want to assess their organization's effectiveness relative to others in their industry, comparative referents are appropriate. But if they want to assess relative improvements in their organization's performance over time, comparative referents are irrelevant.

6. *What time frame should be employed?* Choice of a time frame is important because long-term and short-term effectiveness may be incompatible. For example, long-term success in changing product markets requires that an organization invest in research and development. But investment in research and development reduces short-term profitability. Similarly, investments enhancing customer service may be expensive in the short run but profitable over the longer term.

Consciously addressing the time frame for an assessment can make managers more aware of the performance trade-offs organizations face. Some of these trade-offs are of the short-term efficiency/long-term effectiveness nature just discussed. Others have to do with an organization's ability to satisfy the interests of different stakeholders over time. Some stakeholders may want their preferences satisfied "now," such as customers purchasing a service. Others may have a longer-term perspective, such as when employees working to build a company are willing to forgo pay raises in the short term for more substantial long-term profit sharing. Understanding stakeholder time frames can aid managers in setting priorities for "who gets what when."

SUMMARY

Learning Objective 1: Distinguish between efficiency and effectiveness. Efficiency is generally defined as the ratio of some output (goods and services) to some input (e.g., labor, capital, raw materials). Effectiveness is a more ambiguous concept. Depending on the approach taken (goal, system-resource, or stakeholder), it can be viewed from several distinct perspectives. In a very general sense, however, effectiveness may be thought of as "doing the right things," as compared to efficiency, which involves "doing things right."

Learning Objective 2: Explain and critique the goal approach to assessing organizational effectiveness. The goal approach to assessing organizational effectiveness views organizations as principally concerned with the attainment of specific end states or goals. It defines effectiveness in terms of goal attainment. That is, the greater the extent to which an organization's goals are met or surpassed, the greater its effectiveness. Critics feel it is unrealistic to use goal attainment as the single standard of organizational effectiveness. Their reasons are as follows: (1) because organizations are social systems they will almost always be less consistent and less perfect than anticipated; (2) organizations have multiple, often conflicting, goals that they seek to accomplish at the same time; (3) goals are often ambiguous, making the establishment of criteria for measuring effectiveness difficult or impossible.

Learning Objective 3: Explain and critique the system-resource approach to assessing organizational effectiveness. The system-resource approach to assessing organizational effectiveness views organizations as social systems operating in environments of scarce resources. It defines effectiveness as the degree to which an organization is successful in acquiring scarce and valued resources. It has been criticized for (1) providing little guidance as to what constitutes optimum environmental exploitation, a key concept in the approach; (2) failing to develop general measures of resource effectiveness to be used in determining which scarce and valued resources are relevant as a basis of assessment; (3) focusing on resource acquisition and ignoring resource use.

Learning Objective 4: Explain and critique the stakeholder approach to assessing organizational effectiveness. The stakeholder approach to organizational effectiveness examines the extent to which an organization's stakeholders are at least minimally satisfied. It focuses on the various groups—both internal and external—that can either affect or be affected by an organization's performance. It has been criticized for not resolving the issue of which stakeholder's preferences are most important for an organization to satisfy.

Learning Objective 5: State why organizational effectiveness is a value-based concept. Organizational effectiveness is a value-based concept because all criteria for assessing effectiveness reflect a valued outcome to someone. The result is that effectiveness lies in the eye of the beholder; what may be effective to one person may be ineffective to another who values the outcomes of an organization's performance differently.

Learning Objective 6: Know six critical questions that should guide assessments of organizational effectiveness. Because of the complex nature of organizational effectiveness, most evaluations are necessarily limited in scope. Managers can conduct meaningful assessments of effectiveness by keeping six questions in mind: (1) What is the domain of activity for the evaluation? (2) Whose perspective is being considered in the evaluation? (3) What level of analysis is appropriate for the domain of activity and perspective being used in the evaluation? (4) What information should be used? (5) What referent should be used in interpreting the information? (6) What time frame should be employed?

Discussion Questions

1. You have just returned from an open lecture given by a CEO for a major aircraft manufacturer as part of the College of Business's Executive-in-Residence Program. During his address, the CEO commented, "All aspects of management have effectiveness at their core." Explain what he meant.

2. Imagine that your cardiologist has just informed you that you must undergo triple-bypass heart surgery within the next 24 hours. Two surgeons are available to perform the operation. Dr. X is described as "efficient." In contrast, Dr. Y is described as "effective." Reflecting on the old line that "the operation was a success, but the patient died," and this chapter's claim that "effectiveness is typically viewed as more important than efficiency," to which surgeon would you entrust your life? Why?

3. Imagine that you are the last of 35 students remaining in the final exam for this course. You have one item to complete within ten minutes. The item reads, "In one page or less, compare and contrast the goal and system-resource approaches to assessing organizational effectiveness." How would you respond?

4. Suppose that you are sitting in your organization theory professor's office. You are upset. Despite having studied for two days for the last exam, you made a C. Even more infuriating is the fact that your roommate spent less than an hour studying for the same exam and made an A. You tell the professor that you deserve a higher grade than your roommate since you studied so much harder. Your professor replies that it's results, not effort, that counts in assigning grades. Is your professor using a goal or system-resource approach? How would the basis for your grade differ under each approach?

5. The question, "How well is organization X performing?" seems simple enough to answer. As an organization theorist, however, you realize that the answer to this question is inevitably contingent on whom one is asking. With this in mind, explain how "the evaluative criteria required to transform a descriptive into an evaluative statement flow from the individuals or groups to whom we refer as 'stakeholders,' not from some abstract, value-free theory of organizations."[27]

6. A noted organization theorist contends that "stakeholders are . . . the claimants of organizational effectiveness—it is they who are the judges of organizational effectiveness." He goes on to claim that "to be effective, an organization has first to determine who its stakeholders are, and then to determine the outputs desired by its stakeholders."[28] Considering what you have learned about different approaches to assessing organizational effectiveness, do you agree with such an absolute contention? Why or why not?

7. As a principal in a major management consulting firm, you have been asked to assist in your alma mater's ten-year self-study. More specifically, you have been asked to chair a committee to assess the university's performance. What approach for measuring its effectiveness would you recommend? Why?

8. Organization theorists have devoted increasing attention to similarities and differences between public and private organizations. Explain why certain effectiveness criteria (for example, market share) may be relevant for certain types of organizations (business firms and other sales-oriented undertakings), but have little applicability for others (voluntary associations such as churches, and service organizations such as juvenile courts and social welfare programs).

DESIGN AUDIT #3

Analyzing Your Organization's Effectiveness

This design audit will help you analyze the effectiveness of your organization's performance using the goal and stakeholder approaches.

Goal Attainment

1. Using the goals you identified in the Chapter 2 design audit, rate your organization on how well it has attained its official and operative goals. Indicate your rating of its performance by circling the appropriate number, where 4 = excellent, 3 = good, 2 = poor, 1 = not at all.

Key Result Area	Official Goals	Rating
Market Share (MS)	(a) _____	4 3 2 1
	(b) _____	4 3 2 1
Innovation (INN)	(a) _____	4 3 2 1
	(b) _____	4 3 2 1
Productivity (PRD)	(a) _____	4 3 2 1
	(b) _____	4 3 2 1
Physical and Financial Resources (PFR)	(a) _____	4 3 2 1
	(b) _____	4 3 2 1
Profitability (PRFT)	(a) _____	4 3 2 1
	(b) _____	4 3 2 1
Manager Performance and Development (MPD)	(a) _____	4 3 2 1
	(b) _____	4 3 2 1

Employee
Performance
and Development   (a) _____   4 3 2 1
(EPD)
      (b) _____   4 3 2 1

Social
Responsibility   (a) _____   4 3 2 1
(SR)
      (b) _____   4 3 2 1

Key Result Area	Operative Goals		Rating
Market Share (MS)	(a)	_____	4 3 2 1
	(b)	_____	4 3 2 1
	(c)	_____	4 3 2 1
Innovation (INN)	(a)	_____	4 3 2 1
	(b)	_____	4 3 2 1
	(c)	_____	4 3 2 1
Productivity (PRD)	(a)	_____	4 3 2 1
	(b)	_____	4 3 2 1
	(c)	_____	4 3 2 1
Physical and Financial Resources (PFR)	(a)	_____	4 3 2 1
	(b)	_____	4 3 2 1
	(c)	_____	4 3 2 1
Profitability (PRFT)	(a)	_____	4 3 2 1
	(b)	_____	4 3 2 1
	(c)	_____	4 3 2 1

Manager Performance and Development (MPD)	(a) _____	4 3 2 1
	(b) _____	4 3 2 1
	(c) _____	4 3 2 1

Employee Performance and Development (EPD)	(a) _____	4 3 2 1
	(b) _____	4 3 2 1
	(c) _____	4 3 2 1

Social Responsibility (SR)	(a) _____	4 3 2 1
	(b) _____	4 3 2 1
	(c) _____	4 3 2 1

2. Average the scores for the official goals and for the operative goals within each key result area. On the following chart, plot the mean scores and connect the dots to get a profile of your organization's performance. How much variation is there in your evaluation of performance across key result areas?

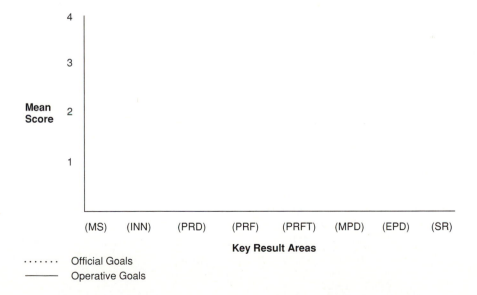

Key Result Areas: (MS) (INN) (PRD) (PRF) (PRFT) (MPD) (EPD) (SR)

Mean Score

· · · · · · · Official Goals
———— Operative Goals

Stakeholder Assessments

3. This section examines your organization's effectiveness from the perspective of its stakeholders. They may or may not have similar performance expectations. First, list five major stakeholders in the spaces below (e.g., customers, employees, shareholders). List up to three major performance preferences for each stakeholder (e.g., customers = high-quality products, low prices, fast service). Then rate the extent to which your organization's performance satisfies those preferences, where 4 = excellent, 3 = good, 2 = poor, and 1 = not at all.

Stakeholder	Performance Preferences	Rating
1. _____	(a) _____	4 3 2 1
	(b) _____	4 3 2 1
	(c) _____	4 3 2 1
2. _____	(a) _____	4 3 2 1
	(b) _____	4 3 2 1
	(c) _____	4 3 2 1
3. _____	(a) _____	4 3 2 1
	(b) _____	4 3 2 1
	(c) _____	4 3 2 1
4. _____	(a) _____	4 3 2 1
	(b) _____	4 3 2 1
	(c) _____	4 3 2 1
5. _____	(a) _____	4 3 2 1
	(b) _____	4 3 2 1
	(c) _____	4 3 2 1

4. Stakeholders often have conflicting preferences for an organization's performance, and satisfying one stakeholder's preferences may affect its ability to satisfy others'. Think about the preferences you listed earlier. Does, for example, what Stakeholder 1 want from your organization conflict with what Stakeholder 2 wants? Write the name of a stakeholder in each box below. Then place a +, −, or 0 on each line connecting the boxes to indicate the extent to which these stakeholder preferences are compatible. Use + to indicate compatibility, − for incompatibility, and 0 when satisfying one stakeholder doesn't affect your organization's ability to satisfy the other. Finally, explain the incompatible relationships in the space below.

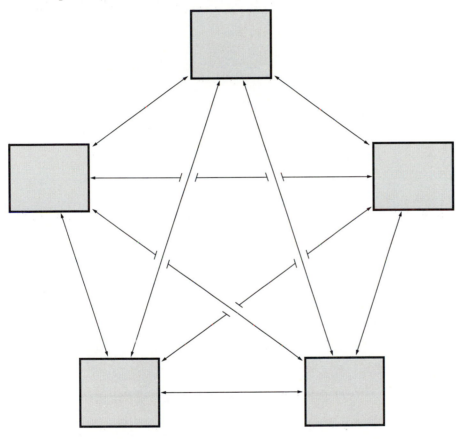

5. How does this pattern of preferences affect the management of your organization? Is there any difference when you look at preference compatibility in the short run versus the long run? Look at the goals listed in the Chapter 2 design audit. Do you now think there are any other goals your organization should include in its statement of official goals? What are they? How would they help?

Notes

1. Chester I. Barnard, *The Functions of the Executive* (Cambridge, Mass.: Harvard University, 1938), 19.

2. Richard M. Steers, *Organizational Effectiveness: A Behavioral View* (Santa Monica: Goodyear, 1977), 51.

3. William J. Reddin, *Managerial Effectiveness* (New York: McGraw-Hill, 1970), 3.

4. Information for this case study was drawn from James E. Post, *Corporate Behavior and Social Change* (Reston, Va.: Reston Publishing Company, 1978), 168–184; Ralph E. Winter, "Balancing Act: Reserve Mining Project Illustrates the Dilemma of Jobs vs. Ecology," *The Wall Street Journal,* November 15, 1977, 1, 20; Ralph E. Winter, "Reserve Mining's Polution Control Will Go Ahead," *The Wall Street Journal,* July 10, 1978, 5; J. Ernest Beazley, "Armco Closes Mine Venture with LTV," *The Wall Street Journal,* July 23, 1986, 9; Ralph E. Winter, "Iron Ore Industry's Best Efforts Fail to Halt Its Decline," *The Wall Street Journal,* November 19, 1986, 6.

5. Amitai Etzioni, "Two Approaches to Organizational Analysis: A Critique and a Suggestion," *Administrative Science Quarterly* 5 (1960): 257–277.

6. This example is paraphrased from Roger Mansfield, *Company Strategy and Organizational Design* (New York: St. Martin's Press, 1986), 27.

7. Kim S. Cameron, "Measuring Organizational Effectiveness in Higher Education," *Administrative Science Quarterly* 23 (1978): 604–632.

8. William C. Birdsall, "When Benefits Are Difficult to Measure," *Evaluation and Program Planning* 10 (1987): 109–118.

9. Richard H. Hall, "Effectiveness Theory and Organizational Effectiveness," *Journal of Applied Behavioral Science* 16 (1980): 538.

10. Basil S. Georgopoulos and Arnold S. Tannebaum, "A Study of Organizational Effectiveness," *American Sociological Review* 22 (1957): 535–540.

11. Ephraim Yuchtman and Stanley E. Seashore, "A System Resource Approach to Organizational Effectiveness," *American Sociological Review* 32 (1967): 898.

12. In the case of public colleges and universities, this situation is rapidly changing as state legislatures mandate student-outcomes assessment as a requirement for future funding.

13. Kim S. Cameron, "Critical Questions in Assessing Organizational Effectiveness," *Organizational Dynamics* 9, no. 2 (1980): 69.

14. Lawrence B. Mohr, "The Concept of Organizational Goal," *American Political Science Review* 67 (1973): 470–481.

15. William M. Evan, "Organization Theory and Organizational Effectiveness: A Preliminary Analysis," in *Organizational Effectiveness: Theory, Research, and Application,* ed. S. Lee Spray (Kent: Kent State University Press, 1976), 15–28.

16. Terry Connolly, Edward M. Conlon, and Stuart J. Deutsch, "Organizational Effectiveness: A Multiple Constituency Approach," *Academy of Management Review* 5 (1980): 211–218; Michael Keeley, "A Social Justice Approach to Organizational Effectiveness," *Administrative Science Quarterly* 22 (1978): 272–292; Johannes M. Pennings and Paul S. Goodman, "Toward a Workable Framework," in *New Perspectives on Organizational Effectiveness,* ed. Paul S. Goodman and Johannes M. Pennings (San

Francisco: Jossey-Bass, 1977), 146–184; Jeffrey Pfeffer and Gerald R. Salancik, *The External Control of Organizations* (New York: Harper & Row, 1978); Raymond F. Zammuto, *Assessing Organizational Effectiveness: Systems Change, Adaptation, and Strategy* (Albany, N.Y.: State University of New York Press, 1982).

17. For detailed discussions of the value-based nature of organizational effectiveness, see Zammuto, *Assessing Organizational Effectiveness*, 31–46; Raymond F. Zammuto, "A Comparison of Multiple Constituency Models of Organizational Effectiveness," *Academy of Management Review* 9 (1984): 606–616.

18. Lawrence J. Hrebiniak, *Complex Organizations* (St. Paul, Minn.: West, 1978), 326.

19. Pfeffer and Salancik, *The External Control of Organizations*, 87.

20. Richard H. Hall and John P. Clark, "Organizational Effectiveness: Some Conceptual, Methodological and Moral Issues" (Paper presented at the annual American Sociological Association meeting, Chicago, September, 1977), 17.

21. Pennings and Goodman, "Toward a Workable Framework," 154–157; Pfeffer and Salancik, *The External Control of Organizations*, 84–88.

22. Keeley, "A Social Justice Approach to Organizational Effectiveness," 285–286; Michael Keeley, "Impartiality and Participant-Interest Theories of Organizational Effectiveness," *Administrative Science Quarterly* 29 (1984), 10–13; Ernest R. House, *Evaluating with Validity* (Beverly Hills: Sage, 1980).

23. Zammuto, *Assessing Organizational Effectiveness*, 78–84.

24. Connolly, Conlon, and Deutsch, "Organizational Effectiveness: A Multiple Constituency Approach," 212–213.

25. Zammuto, *Assessing Organizational Effectiveness*, 161.

26. This section is adapted from Kim S. Cameron, "Critical Questions in Assessing Organizational Effectiveness," *Organizational Dynamics* 9, no. 2 (1980): 66–80; Kim S. Cameron, "The Enigma of Organizational Effectiveness" in *New Directions in Program Effectiveness: Measuring Effectiveness*, ed. D. Baugher (San Francisco: Jossey-Bass, 1981), 1–13.

27. Quote adapted from Connolly, Conlon, and Deutsch, "Organizational Effectiveness: A Multiple Constituency Approach," 212.

28. Aubrey L. Mendelow, "Setting Corporate Goals and Measuring Organizational Effectiveness—A Practical Approach," *Long Range Planning* 16, no. 1 (1983): 70.

C A S E 1

The Turnaround

You can find JoAnn's Expressway Lounge on the West Chestnut Expressway in Springfield, Mo. It's located in a yellow cinder-block bunker, fringed along the roof with blue shingles. Inside, there are two pool tables and a pinball machine, a juke-box, a bar, and assorted tables. For most of any given day, it is exactly what it appears to be: another juke joint along another midwestern highway. But around 4:30 every afternoon, JoAnn's is transformed into a kind of true-grit tabernacle, when the regulars begin to arrive from Springfield Remanufacturing Center Corp. (SRC).

At the moment, about 25 of them are scattered around the bar, playing and talking as the jukebox pleads, "I want to bebop with you, baby, ALL NIGHT LONG." They range from assembly-line workers to senior managers, the latter indistinguishable except for an occasional loosened tie. Here, for example, are Pam Smith and Verna Mae Ross, who assemble fuel-injection nozzles, as well as general foremen Steve Choate and Joe Loeber. Over there, pounding on a pinball machine called Memory Lane, is Doug Rothert, the production manager, and the guy trying to bank the nine ball is executive-vice president Mike Carrigan.

It's an odd assortment of people, defying the normal stratification of corporate society—a fact of which they are all aware. "The barriers between management and employees just don't exist here," says Pam, the nozzle assembler, to which Verna Mae adds, "Here I am, pretty low in seniority, and I can sit here and bullshit with Jack over there."

"Jack" is John P. Stack, SRC's president and largest shareholder, who is presently lost in thought, calculating the more esoteric geometries of pool. He is 37 years old, slightly under six feet tall, thin, and lanky, with thick brown hair and a boyish face. Of all JoAnn's regulars, he is the most regular. On any

Source: "The Turnaround" by Lucien Rhodes with Patricia Amend. Reprinted with permission, *Inc*. magazine, August, 1986, pp. 42–48. Copyright © 1986 by Goldhirsh Group, Inc., 38 Commercial Wharf, Boston, MA 02110.

day, Stack can be found here from roughly 4:30 to 6:00 p.m., just in case someone should want to talk through a problem in less formal surroundings. Right now, however, he is more intent on making his next shot.

Standing there, leaning on his pool cue, blowing cigarette smoke over the green felt, he hardly seems like a man with a mission. And yet he is just that, for Stack has come about as close as anyone to solving one of the more perplexing business puzzles of our time.

The problem dates back to the early 1960s, when the idea took hold in boardrooms and business schools across the country that the secret of effective management lay in the numbers: first, in collecting the raw data on sales, profit margins, inventory levels, and countless other statistics; then, in arranging them into various pie charts and bar graphs; and finally, in conforming business strategies to their mathematical authority. Aided by the advance of computer technology, "quantitative" management soon became the shibboleth of the executive suite. Unfortunately, this preoccupation with numbers all too often reduced employees to the status of mere ciphers, thereby isolating the company from the creative energies of its work force.

It was a dangerous balance: too many statistics could prove toxic to humans, and too few could just as easily murder a business. To this day, the proper mixture of dismal science and effervescent humanity is the subject of heated debate, not to mention a number of best-selling books. What Stack and some 360 of his colleagues seem to have demonstrated is that a rigorous, even obsessive, quantitative regimen can still produce a strikingly people-oriented enterprise. Indeed, Stack is convinced that his number-crunching works so well *because* his people are so involved.

Ironically, all this has happened in a company that, up until three years ago, was a division of International Harvester Co.—the industrial giant that grew out of Cyrus McCormick's original reaper company. A rebuilder of engines and engine components, SRC was losing $2 million a year on sales of $26 million when Stack arrived in 1979 to turn things around. In 1983, he and 12 other employees bought the business from Harvester and struck out on their own. Carrying a crushing debt load, and facing potential ruin, they developed a meticulously detailed reporting system that at one point had them calculating a full-blown income statement every day.

The results have been impressive. Since the leveraged buyout, SRC's sales have grown 40% per year and are expected to reach $42 million in fiscal 1986; net operating income has risen to 11%; the debt-to-equity ratio has been cut from 89-to-1 to 5.1-to-1; and the appraised value of a share in the company's employee stock ownership plan has increased from 10 cents to $8.45. Meanwhile, absenteeism and employee turnover, once high, have all but disappeared, and the frequency of recordable accidents in the plant has fallen dramatically. To hear Stack tell it, this turnaround owes much to SRC's exacting quantitative controls, but even more to its almost evangelical insistence on giving human potential its due. "Look, we're appealing to the highest level of thinking we can in every employee in our company," he says between pool shots at JoAnn's. "Why hire a guy and only use his brain to grind crankshafts?"

It is 11:15 on a weekday morning, and—in the company cafeteria—SRC is appealing to the highest level of thinking of the workers on the first shift. They are sitting at long Formica tables, talking, laughing, eating their lunch from brown bags and Tupperware containers. There is just one thing out of the ordinary: high on the wall above the microwave oven sits a red, electronic message board, quietly flashing the words, "FUEL INJECTION LABOR UTILIZATION 98%."

What the message means, as any of the lunching laborers can tell you, is that the fuel-injection pump assemblers spent 98% of their work time on direct labor (rather than overhead) during the first half of their shift. If they keep it up, they become eligible for a sizable bonus under an SRC plan known as STP-GUTR, an acronym for "Stop the Praise—Give Us the Raise." The electronic ticker tells them how they're doing.

"It's like the big red board at Caesars Palace," says Stack. "You know, the one with 10 or 15 games on it, for any sport you want to bet on. The odds are constantly changing, and the action is fantastic. Well, it's the same thing here. When you walk through this factory, you hear numbers everywhere you go. It's like you're in the middle of a bingo tournament."

SRC certainly does have more than its share of numbers. Those numbers guide its operational and financial reporting system, which is as elaborate, and as rigorous, as any in American business. What sets it apart is the level of employee involvement. Springfield's workers all play active roles in it; they are all directly responsible for helping to make it work.

The cafeteria ticker is part of that system, and—like most of the other parts—it is something Stack dreamed up as he went along. "I had no education," he says. "I had no master plan. My feelings were more basic. I just felt that, if you were going to spend a majority of your time doing a job, why couldn't you have fun at it? For me, fun was action, excitement, a good game. If there's one thing common to everybody, it's that we love to play a good game."

Gamesmanship lies at the heart of Stack's approach to management. Virtually everything that happens at SRC is based on the premise that business is essentially a game—one, moreover, that almost anyone can learn to play. As with most games, however, people won't bother to learn it unless they "get" it. That means, first, they must understand the rules; second, they must receive enough information to let them follow the action; and third, they must have the opportunity to win or lose.

It is hard to exaggerate the lengths to which Stack has gone to get everyone at SRC involved in the Great Game of Business. For openers, he has set up an extraordinary education program, designed to teach employees how the Game is played. At one point, he even went so far as to have every worker in the plant take a series of courses covering most elements of a business curriculum, from accounting to warehousing.

More recently, the company has organized an ongoing management training program, aimed at opening up opportunities for employee advancement. At SRC, those opportunities are real. General foremen Steve Choate and Joe Loeber started out as janitors; director of safety and training Lee Shaefer began as a "gofer"; Wendall Wade, the 29-year-old supervisor of engine disassembly, was a shipping clerk. Inspired by such examples, some 80% of SRC's employees have taken courses under the program.

But promotion is just one of the possible rewards for playing the Game well. More important, perhaps, are those offered by the STP-GUTR bonus program. Here, too, the approach is unusual. Instead of funneling a predetermined percentage of profits into a bonus pool, as is common, SRC ties its bonuses to the achievement of specific goals. In fiscal 1985, for example, there were two such goals: to control costs (specifically, to reduce the plant's overhead charge-out rate from $39 to $32 per hour), and to increase operating income from 6% to 15% of sales. Although the charge-out rate was eventually cut to $23 per hour, the company missed its operating-income objective. As a result, employees received bonuses amounting to 7.8% of gross salary, rather than the 10% they would have earned had the company met both goals.

Additional rewards are offered to employees whose ideas improve the company's operations—up to $500 per idea. Such programs are not uncommon in business, but SRC's works better than most. Thirty-two-year-old engine disassembler Freeman Tracy, for one, has turned in some 50 ideas, earning him $7,500 and saving the company almost $2 million in production costs—and that's just since the buyout. Before, says Tracy, he "wasn't in a thinking mood, but now you know you're helping yourself as well as the company."

Then, of course, there is the long-term reward of stock accumulation. Stack had originally planned to offer direct ownership to everyone as part of the leveraged buyout, but he ran afoul of a Missouri state law that limits the number of owners in a privately held corporation. Instead, he set up the ESOP. "To me," Stack says, "giving ownership to the people who do the work has always seemed like the simplest way to run a business. It frees you to concentrate on productivity.

If the education program teaches employees the rules of the Game, and the compensation program allows them to participate in the risks and rewards, everything else is geared toward playing the Game as well as it can be played. Like any successful team in any sport, SRC concentrates on the fundamentals, on doing the thousand and one little things that separate a champion from an also-ran; turning the double play, hitting the cutoff man, covering the bag, advancing the runner. In the sport of remanufacturing, the fundamentals include such things as using hand tools correctly, watching the labor utilization rate, figuring out better ways to make spare parts. To a certain extent, SRC works on its fundamentals through its education program and its system of rewards. Mainly, however, SRC keeps employees focused on the basics by giving them all the information they need to follow the flow of the Game.

To begin with, everyone—managers, supervisors, administrative personnel, production workers—has access to the company's monthly financial
report, a weighty tome often running to 90 pages. In small group sessions,
supervisors or department heads go over the figures, encouraging questions.
In addition, there are the daily printouts from the cost-accounting department, detailing the progress of every job in each supervisor's area.

But perhaps the most extraordinary aspect of SRC's information flow
involves its use of the income statement. Granted, every business concerns
itself with the income statement at some point. Seldom, however, does a
company do so as frequently, as intensely, or with as broad participation as
SRC. "If you picture this organization," says Stack, "it's like a continuous
Dow Jones ticker tape. For almost every single hour of every single day, there
is a new number about the business crossing my desk. For us, the income
statement is the same as the daily racing form is to a guy handicapping a race,
or the same as the tape is to a guy betting on the market. I mean, it's addictive
because it's fun, it's action."

The action begins every Tuesday morning, when some 25 managers
and supervisors get together in a conference room near Stack's office.
Everyone comes armed with a detailed, preprinted, projected income
statement. The first column of figures lists the income and expense figures
for the previous month. The next column gives the projections for the
current month as they appeared in the budget at the start of the fiscal year.
The following three columns are blank. Every week, one of the columns
is filled in with adjusted projections, based on the reports given at the
meeting.

Today, for example, quality supervisor Steve Shadwick notes a drop in
the "average monthly deficiency rate" on General Motors diesel engines for
the year to date—from 26% to 9%. What this means, chimes in executive
vice-president Mike Carrigan, is that the company has saved between three
and four "equivalent men" in extra labor costs because fewer parts have to
be reworked. Production scheduler Ron Maus reports unexpected problems
with a spare-parts supplier. Engine disassembly supervisor Wendall Wade
confesses that his department has gone $268 over budget on protective
gloves. And so it goes.

In about 45 minutes, the morning's work is done. Stack, who has been
recording the variances on a board in the front of the room, works the income
statement down to a net operating income figure that is well above the 15%
of net sales needed to trigger a bonus distribution for the quarter. Everyone
appears pleased.

That same afternoon, the supervisors and managers carry the news to
hourly workers all over the plant. In one lecture room, Wendall Wade stands
before 17 engine disassemblers sitting expectantly around two long conference tables. Most are dressed in grease-stained T-shirts and jeans, and several
wear caps embellished with the logos of brand-name beers, whiskeys, or
chewing tobacco.

First, production manager Doug Rothert presents a brief review of the income statement, with heavy emphasis on the bonus distribution. Wade follows with a solemn soliloquy on the virtues of conserving protective gloves. Then comes 19-year-old Bobby Voelker, the department's safety representative, who reports that there have been nine recordable accidents and 14 days lost as a result. "We've got to do better than that," he says, adding self-consciously, "you've got to wear your safety glasses to and from lunch." Wade asks if there is anyone who does not understand the income statement. Two people raise their hands, and Wade offers to tutor them after work.

Meanwhile, in another room, general foreman Steve Choate is addressing the fuel-injection pump department. The pump has long been the most profitable item in SRC's product line, he is saying, but now it is threatened by aggressive domestic competition and cheap foreign imports. If the department could reduce the cost of remanufacturing the pump by 25%, SRC would still reign supreme for quality and price.

After the meeting, 30-year-old supervisor Tim McVeigh explains that the department has already begun shooting for this reduction. For the past month, a four-worker task force has been studying the possibilities and will eventually enlist the other pump assemblers in the effort. "You've got to get people involved," McVeigh says.

That is, indeed, a theme heard constantly around the plant. There are no spectators in the Great Game of Business, at least as it is played at SRC. Everybody is encouraged to get involved, to take responsibility. As for the top executives of the company, they work diligently, and often ingeniously, to keep raising the level of participation.

Consider, for example, how executive vice-president Mike Carrigan went about getting managers and supervisors, and ultimately employees, more involved in planning the company's future results. He selected operating expenses as the place to start. After working up his own projections in some 20 areas—welding supplies, abrasive materials, hand tools, and so on—he asked every manager and supervisor to take personal responsibility for one account, and to report back in a month as to whether his projections were realistic.

Over the next few weeks, each of them went around asking employees about their needs, researching past expenditures, testing the production scheduler's assumptions, checking with the various buyers, forcing Carrigan to defend his calculations. When the group reconvened at the end of the month, the managers and supervisors were surprised to learn that henceforth their findings would be accepted as the budget figures for the coming fiscal year.

"You see, what happened here," says Carrigan, "is that now these people were in effect running their own small businesses. They had set their own budgets, and they had to live with them. If they wanted to complain, they had to complain to themselves. This is above all an awareness program. Every little bit counts, and only the people here can make the numbers work."

Getting people to make the numbers work is, of course, a major goal of the Great Game of Business. It is one, moreover, that the employees of SRC routinely achieve. Day in, day out, they run their drills so smartly, so effortlessly, so smoothly that an outsider is tempted to think of them as natural athletes, participating in a sport they were born to play. Watching them, it is difficult to imagine that, a few years ago, SRC was teetering on the brink of disaster.

But Stack remembers.

It was January 1979, and Stack, then 30 years old, had just arrived as the new plant manager. SRC was foundering badly. Opened by International Harvester in 1974 to remanufacture diesel engines and engine components for its truck and agricultural and construction equipment dealers, the plant had lost $2 million in the most recent fiscal year, and the big question was whether the employees, previously nonunion, would vote to join the Teamsters or the United Auto Workers in an election scheduled for March.

Stack had been given six months to determine whether the plant should be scrapped or saved. On his first day, he held a meeting in the cafeteria for all 140 plant employees. "I was giving them this Knute Rockne routine," he recalls, "and when I looked out over the crowd, I felt like I was looking into an aquarium. Totally immobile faces." At the end of his remarks, he asked for questions. There was a pause; then someone in the back hollered, "How old are you anyhow?"

"That was the only question I got," says Stack. "I knew then it wasn't going to be easy."

But Stack was not without experience in such matters. Four years earlier, at the age of 26, he had been named superintendent of the machining division of Harvester's Melrose Park, Ill., plant. There he had found himself in charge of five general foremen, all more than 50 years old; roughly 400 employees; and a division that ranked last in productivity out of seven divisions in the plant. Hoping to stimulate their competitive juices, Stack had hit on the idea of giving each foreman a copy of the division's daily productivity figures, broken down by foreman and then compared in total with the other six divisions. Productivity began to soar. The first time the foremen beat the previous high score, Stack bought them coffee; the second time, he bought them coffee and doughnuts; the third time, he invited them all to his house for poker, pizza, and beer. Within three months, Stack's division had risen from last to first place in the plant's productivity rankings. Thus was born the Great Game of Business.

By the time Stack got to Springfield, he had refined the concept somewhat, but he could not yet apply it to SRC. The place was in a shambles. Thanks to a critical shortage of parts, production had nearly stopped. "But the people wanted to work," says Stack. "Most of them had come off the farms. They were dedicated, hardworking people, and they were disgusted because they didn't have the tools to work with. The only reason they wanted the union was that they thought it might get them the tools they needed."

Stack convinced them otherwise. "It was very sophisticated," he says. "Me and the other managers got down on our hands and knees out on the shop floor and begged them to give us a shot."

"At least he was talking to us," says 27-year-old Randy Rossner, now a fuel-injection pump assembler. "Before, we didn't see much of anybody out here. It was as if nobody cared. Jack looked like somebody we could work with." Most of Rossner's colleagues evidently agreed. The union proposal was defeated by a 75% margin. Meanwhile, Stack managed to finagle a supply of spare parts from his erstwhile cronies in Melrose Park. So SRC's production line went back up to speed. "Now," says Stack, "we had to start winning."

Before they could start winning, however, they had to create the Game. Stack began by choosing three modest goals, which he called "accountabilities": product quality, safety, and housekeeping (meaning the organization and cleanliness of each work area). In addition, management cobbled together some production goals. Stack's purpose in all this was to focus attention on common objectives, and to suggest in some small way that performance could be measured. "Things were in such disarray," he says, "you had to start with something. We needed something to celebrate."

And celebrate they did. On the afternoon marking 100,000 hours without a recordable accident, the plant closed down for a beer bust. The theme song from *Rocky* played over the loudspeaker system, and members of the safety committee marched around, handing out fire extinguishers. Forklift trucks festooned with crepe paper were driven in a parade through the plant as onlookers cheered.

The celebrating continued as departments began exceeding their production goals. The department that won by the highest percentage was given an award—the "Traveling Trophy," a huge confection in marble and brass, topped off by a winged goddess holding a torch. Whenever the award changed hands, the winning department would strut en masse to the ex-winners' department and carry off the trophy amid much self-congratulatory brouhaha.

Stack's approach to quality control was no less dramatic. If, say, a transmission broke down in service, he would fly the hapless reassembler to the job site. One poor fellow spent a weekend repairing such a transmission in Kentucky, before the customer calmed down enough to let him go home. "I can tell you," says Stack, "when the guy gets back here, the word gets around fast that you don't ever want to experience that kind of pressure."

The effect of all this was soon apparent. Within four months, SRC had earned its reprieve. "Harvester was very happy," says Stack. "They left us alone and told us to keep going." At the end of nine months, the company recorded a profit of $250,000.

But encouraging as this start was, the Game was still quite primitive. There were no training programs, no financial controls, no systems for monitoring costs. As for the goals and rewards, they served to motivate people in a general way, but they were not targeted to SRC's specific business objectives, notably improved productivity.

Part of the problem, Stack realized, was that the plant operated under a system that measured labor, overhead, and materials by their actual costs, rather than their standard costs. As a result, he and his managers could not figure out what should be used (as opposed to what was used), nor could they accurately gauge their progress in using resources more efficiently.

So in February 1980, they organized a new cost department, which was given the task of taking SRC from an actual cost system to a standard cost system. This move—critical to the quantitative analysis SRC adopted after the leveraged buyout—sent a small army of engineers and accountants swarming over the shop floor. Measuring costs with the precision of diamond cutters, they were soon able to calculate, for example, the portion of the plant's heating and electrical expenses that should be allocated to a fuel-injection pump. When the cost commanders presented their findings to Stack, he nearly disappeared behind the mounds of data.

"Now I had all these numbers," Stack recalls, "and what was I going to do with them? Only the people could make them work. And how were they going to do that if they didn't know what the hell the numbers meant?" His solution was to educate the entire population, some 200 people.

Thus began SRC's Great Leap Forward. In the first three weeks of March 1980, groups of 10 to 15 employees rotated, during working hours, through a full range of business courses: production scheduling, purchasing, accounting, plant audit, standard cost, industrial engineering, inspection and warehousing, and so on. Most of the sessions, which lasted 1 or 2 hours, were taught by SRC supervisors, but occasionally outside instructors were brought in. All told, 96 hours of training were offered, involving more than 1,300 hours of student instruction and preparation.

The courses were immensely popular, and Stack was thrilled. He immediately set out to expand his list of "accountabilities," devising an intricate method of evaluating each manager's individual performance. The system seemed to be working well enough until two managers showed up in Stack's office one afternoon, each with a hand on the other's lapel. It turned out that one manager had reached his goal by cutting inventory—a move that prevented the other from meeting one of his. "The whole thing blew up in my face," says Stack. "These guys wanted to duke it out right there in the office." With customary flair, Stack ended the experiment by gathering up all the rating sheets and setting them on fire in a small picnic area in back of the plant.

"It served its purpose though," says Gary Brown, manager of human resources, "because it showed us some of the dangers in statistics."

Despite this setback, the Great Leap Forward reached a splendid crescendo in October 1980, with an extravaganza billed as "Employee Awareness Day." The plant closed and reconvened in the ballroom of the local Hilton Inn. The employees lunched and suppered and listened to speakers. They also watched a documentary about Japanese business, which warned that—unless the United States improved its productivity—the next generation of Americans would be the first to experience a declining standard of living.

After the film, Stack stood up to speak. "Do you want this responsibility?" he asked. "Do you want to be the ones who started this decline? We've got to do something about it, don't we?" The audience rose as one, cheering and raising their arms, soldiers now in a great holy war. "I was standing there," says Wendall Wade, the engine disassembly supervisor, "and everyone was all around me, and I never knew working could be anything like this. It was great. It was simply great."

Little did any of them suspect how close they were to losing what they had just begun to build.

By February 1981, SRC could report that profits had climbed to $1.1 million, the highest in its history; return on sales had risen from .9% in 1979 to 8.0% in 1980; and productivity had increased 53%. The next month, Stack and six of his managers were called to a meeting at Harvester headquarters. Because of precarious economic conditions, they were told, SRC could not exceed 33% of its capacity for the next three years. "That was the handwriting on the wall," Stack says. "If you're not going to increase your sales, you're just going to die."

The United States had entered a recession. Farm income had fallen sharply, creating severe overcapacity in International Harvester's largest operations—the truck, agricultural equipment, and construction equipment divisions. The company was in trouble, meaning SRC was in trouble, too.

Stack returned to Springfield and held a meeting with his managers. They saw three possible scenarios: Harvester would reduce its capital commitment to SRC, causing the plant to deteriorate in an agonizing process of layoffs and cutbacks; the plant would be closed; or the plant would be sold. "Then the light came on," Stack says. "I thought, 'Why don't we ask Harvester to sell the plant to us?'"

Stack took the idea to the vice-president and the controller of Harvester's construction equipment division, to which SRC reported. Both men asked to participate as investors and operating officers. With Stack, they submitted a proposal to buy the plant for $6 million. While Harvester was considering the plan, Stack set about selling the idea to other potential investors. "I went to one of the biggest venture capital firms in Chicago," he recalls, "and the guy says, 'It's got no schmazzle. Redo the plan.' Hell, I was a grease monkey, and I produced a grease-monkey plan. But from all those rejections, I got better at it."

In the meantime, business conditions continued to deteriorate. By 1982, Harvester, burdened with close to $4 billion in debt, was desperately trying to stave off bankruptcy, and all signs pointed to the imminent liquidation of SRC. Seventy-six employees were laid off, and wages remained frozen at the November 1980 level. SRC's shining esprit de corps had descended to fretful paranoia. "There was a lot of uneasiness," says SRC manager Robert A. Bigos.

"Employees here would ask me if they should get married, if they should have a kid, if they should buy a car. I mean, it's pretty strange when someone asks you if they should get married."

To no one's surprise, Harvester soon began encouraging bids for sizable chunks of its business, including its five remanufacturing centers, which it preferred to sell as a group. As a result, Stack found himself in the uncomfortable position of describing SRC's merits to potential purchasers. "I did everything I could to help them," Stack says, "but they always wanted to know if the existing management team would stay on. I'd say I didn't know. I mean I honestly didn't know. On the other hand, now they weren't sure about their bid either."

Such niggling uncertainties did not deter Dresser Industries Inc., which bid on SRC in late 1982. At the last moment, however, the deal fell through. On the day before Christmas, Harvester informed Stack that it wanted to proceed with his earlier proposal—but only if they could reach an agreement in one week. Stack nearly burst a major artery. How was he going to arrange financing and hire lawyers and incorporate and do everything else in one week? He absolutely had to have another month. Harvester agreed.

Stack described the opportunity before a meeting of his 12 managers, who reacted with tentative enthusiasm. "You know you want to do it," says executive vice-president Mike Carrigan, "but at times like that, you can't help thinking about what will happen if you lose your job." Nonetheless, they agreed to go for it.

Somehow, in the next month, all of the pieces fell into place. "No one remembers the Christmas of 1982," says Stack. The managers put up $100,000; the Bank of America lent them $6 million; and Harvester took back a note for $1 million. It was an all-out, mad rush to meet the deadline.

On the afternoon of Monday, January 31, human-resources manager Brown sat anxiously by his phone, waiting for a call from Stack, who was negotiating with Harvester at his lawyer's office in downtown Springfield. Since SRC did not want to assume Harvester's liabilities to employees for sick pay and vacation time, everyone in the plant had to be terminated as soon as the buyout was completed. Finally, Brown decided he could wait no longer, and fired everybody, including himself and Stack.

The negotiations dragged on into the afternoon of February 1. At 2:30 p.m., Stack called Brown. "It's done. We own it." That evening, the managers and their wives celebrated in a second-floor room above a local restaurant. "It was probably one of the most fantastic moments you could ever have in your life," says Stack. "It was total euphoria. We knew that if we started thinking about tomorrow, we might get scared."

In the next few weeks, the business literally had to be founded all over again. New stationery had to be printed, a name adopted, a corporate logo designed. More important, all of SRC's outstanding contracts had to be renegotiated, including several with Dresser Industries, which had purchased Harvester's construction equipment business and now represented

60% of SRC's annual volume. Of the 171 terminated employees, 115 were immediately rehired as fast as the paperwork could be processed—about 30 per day.

Most important, the company had to choose a marketing strategy. According to industry observers, it chose wisely. Instead of selling through wholesalers to the thousands of job shops and assorted distributors—the common industry practice—SRC decided to sell only to original equipment manufacturers under private-label arrangements. With this stroke, the company spared itself a host of uncertain receivables and avoided the need to establish an extensive and costly distribution network. At the same time, SRC set out to diversify its market structure, eventually moving into four market segments: trucks, tractors and farm equipment, construction equipment, and automotive.

Meanwhile, the stakes had risen in the Game of Business, and Stack was not entirely sure the players understood the new rules. "I was frustrated because I couldn't get some people to see that it was a matter of survival," Stack says. "The question wasn't whether the johns were going to get cleaned or not. If things got down and dirty, we were going to have to come in and turn wrenches ourselves. This wasn't going to be any kind of administrative takeover."

To some extent, Stack realized, they all were victims of their environment, even the 13 managers. "All of us came from huge corporations," Stack says. "There was still this mentality that we had an endless supply of cash. Probably half the people here didn't realize that this was it—that there was no turning back."

So now Stack had to revamp the Great Game of Business to conform with SRC's new reality as a freestanding corporation. "We had to set up a game," he says, "where we couldn't make a $10,000 mistake—or at least where we would know how to correct it right away. And we had to do this without establishing a dictatorship. Systems don't run companies, people do."

The solution, he decided, lay in the income statement. It could be a versatile tool, he thought; it could emphasize the urgency of SRC's position, transcend individual preoccupations, and measure performance. Once he set up the ESOP, moreover, the income statement could be used to encourage employee participation as well.

But the use of income statements would also require a much higher level of business sophistication. Again, Stack attacked the problem with mass education. SRC's managers and supervisors attended a series of in-house courses on income statement construction and analysis. Then supervisors returned to the shop floor and held abbreviated versions for the hourly employees in their departments. "And then they began to see," says Stack. "Their scope was no longer one of emotional protection of fiefdoms. It became one of logic and sequence. You can't live like a king. Most kings inherit their wealth. We had to scratch ours out. We had no time to lose. If we stumbled once, it was all over. So what we had to do is go by the numbers."

Thus did Jack Stack repair the rift between quantitative management and people-oriented enterprise, thereby solving the puzzle that had baffled so many for so long.

There is an ironic story about Stack, one that he tells with some amusement. It seems that, in the summer of 1968, when he was 19, Stack and a bunch of his pals from suburban Elmhurst, Ill., piled into four or five cars and headed for Chicago to sample the commotion surrounding the Democratic National Convention. Grant Park was Stack's favorite haunt. There he would jostle his way to a spot up front, close enough to hear full blast the rants and raves of assorted political activists railing against the profiteers of corporate America.

Stack shared their resentment of corporate profit, but that was not why he had come. The engine of history, usually so distant and remote, had stopped near home that summer, and for once a kid from the suburbs could get close enough to feel its heat. Of course, he had his own opinions about Vietnam and politics, but they were often swamped in a churning sea of more conventional teenage concerns. He had no expectations then of making any meaningful contribution to the disposition of weighty national issues.

So today, leaning on his pool cue here in JoAnn's Expressway Lounge, Stack must find it endlessly curious how fate has worked its will on him, bringing him, in its own good time, to this point where his accomplishments illuminate a subject of persistent national interest—namely, the way people live and work in corporations.

He has time to ponder such questions these days, if only because SRC seems healthier than ever. Last year, it signed a new contract to remanufacture diesel engines for General Motors, allowing it to diversify into yet another market. The deal also promises to add $75 million to SRC's top line over the life of the agreement. To accommodate the increasing volume, SRC has opened two new plants.

So much has happened so fast that even Stack sometimes worries about the dream turning a little sour. In a recent edition of the company's newsletter, he pledged himself to shoring up the retained-earnings account against the "off chance that the company runs into hard times." No, there is no specific reason. He is just the type to fret that, with so much going right, something is surely about to go wrong.

Perhaps his caution is reasonable. Paradoxically, SRC now must face the challenge of its own success. During the past few years, the company has been a close-knit family, whose daily life in the home could be more easily influenced. Now, with new plants, more people, and more business, the company has to see if its management philosophy can accommodate a substantially larger, and probably less personal, enterprise. Some, like materials manager Dave LaHay, already feel the strain. "If I see one more person at the copier that I don't know," he says, "I'm going to freak out."

But here in JoAnn's, such vague and nameless threats could hardly seem more distant or more irrelevant. Pam Smith has just stunned the crowd with an account of a recent Frozen Carp Throwing Contest to benefit the visually impaired youth of southwestern Missouri. She explains how she herself came up a winner by pitching a 10-pound specimen of the frozen fish a full 21 feet. And Steve Choate has just sunk three balls with one shot—a feat that has set him to whooping and gyrating. And Jack Stack, leaning on his pool cue, must find it endlessly curious how fate has worked its will.

Questions

1. What are the basic premises of "the game" played at Springfield Remanufacturing Center (SRC)?

2. What were the "game's" essential components? What did SRC do to make the "game" work?

3. What evidence is there that the "game" worked at SRC?

4. Based on your reading of Chapter 2, explain under what conditions or in what situations SRC's "game," or any other very explicit set of goals, could work to an organization's disadvantage.

Rocky Flats: A Big Mistake from Day One

The small crowd gathered at the gate of the Rocky Flats Nuclear Munitions Plant near Denver early last June 6 was unlike any other seen at the plant in its 18-year history. There had been dozens of protests at the weapons complex, but these were not demonstrators. Most wore suits and ties. Many carried briefcases.

They entered the facility followed by a convoy of about three dozen cars, trucks, and vans. Some 75 people piled out and began searching the 6,550-acre complex, their mission hinted at by the initials on the back of the overalls some were wearing: FBI. The plant's Energy Department managers and contractors became bystanders as the FBI agents began a three-week search for evidence of deliberate violations of environmental laws.

The search marked public disclosure of the first probe of criminal violations of environmental laws at any of the federal government's 17 major nuclear weapons installations. And Rocky Flats is central to the country's nuclear weapons production chain. It manufactures the plutonium fission bombs that "trigger" thermonuclear weapons and is often described in an oversimplified way as making "triggers for nuclear warheads."

Dubbed Operation Desert Glow, the FBI investigation lent credibility to the environmental mismanagement charges leveled against Rocky Flats since the early 1970s. Other studies released after the raid documented more problems. One said the plant's environmental protection efforts were hampered by poor communications and planning, and that sample collection and laboratory analyses were inadequate.[1] Another, made public in early October,

Source: "Rocky Flats: A Big Mistake from Day One" by Bryan Abas. Reprinted by permission of the BULLETIN OF THE ATOMIC SCIENTISTS, a magazine of science and world affairs, December 1989, pp. 18–24. Copyright © 1989 by the Educational Foundation for Nuclear Science, 6042 South Kimbark Avenue, Chicago, IL 60637, USA.

found that several kilograms of plutonium had lodged in one of the plant's ventilation pipes beyond the reach of one of two sets of filters intended to keep the toxic material from entering the atmosphere.[2]

Soon after the raid, federal Energy Secretary James Watkins acknowledged Rocky Flat's poor environmental track record. "I am certainly not proud or pleased with what I have seen over my first few months in office," Watkins told a congressional panel. "I am making decisions today on a crisis basis, and I don't like that."[3] Within four months Rockwell International, the facility's contract manager since 1975, had been replaced by EG&G, Inc., a Wellesley, Massachusetts, engineering firm that operates the department's Idaho National Engineering Laboratory among other facilities.

The raid came at a time when Congress has begun focusing on the operations of nuclear weapons plants nationwide. Watkins has asked Congress for $17 billion over five years to launch an overhaul of management of all nuclear weapons plants to insure stricter compliance with environmental laws.[4] But the biggest mistake at Rocky Flats does not concern the haphazard disposal of hazardous waste, on which the FBI focused, but the decision nearly four decades ago to locate the plant so near a major population center.

The full-scale nuclear weapons production program launched by President Harry Truman in the early 1950s required new bomb-manufacturing plants. The task of finding a place to manufacture the plutonium triggers to detonate the new generation of bombs was code-named Project Apple. The Atomic Energy Commission (AEC) site-selection team was assigned in January 1951 to have a plant built and operating by the end of the year. The team quickly hired a site-selection consulting firm, the Austin Company of Cleveland, Ohio.

Under the wartime Manhattan Project, Lt. Gen. Leslie Groves set guidelines requiring that plutonium processing facilities be located at least 20 miles from any city of more than 1,000 people.[5] But such guidelines apparently were no longer in effect in 1951. The Project Apple principals decided that the site they were seeking had to be no fewer than five and no more than 25 miles from a city of at least 25,000 in order to be able to attract top-quality scientists and researchers. Denver was "the one location that can combine nationally known recreational facilities and services of a large metropolitan center," Austin officials wrote.

Their surveyors identified seven possible sites near Denver. To distinguish among them, the site-selection team looked in part to wind patterns. They had been told to look for a site downwind from Denver so that if plutonium was accidentally released, it would at least blow away from the city. Partly because prevailing winds were from the south, five sites south of Denver were eliminated from consideration.

The two remaining sites were Rocky Flats and a site just north of the Rocky Mountain Arsenal, a U.S. Army nerve gas manufacturing depot built nine years earlier northeast of the city. The arsenal site was close to civilian commercial operations, however, and Austin officials warned that if the plant's neighbors learned of the new secret project there might be an "undesirable reaction of the public."[6] Rocky Flats, on the other hand, seemed at a safe distance. This mesa at the foot of the Rockies was located about 16 miles northwest of Denver, which had a population of 567,000 at the time. And there was little in between except brush.

But the team members were using a map that showed wind patterns at Stapleton Airport northeast of Denver and about 27 miles from the foot of the Rockies.[7] It did not occur to them that the winds might be different at Rocky Flats. "There was no real discussion of wind patterns," team member Francis Langell of Dow Chemical, which originally managed the plant, said in an interview last year. "It wasn't a serious consideration."

Had they tested the winds at Rocky Flats the team would have discovered that winds rush down the mountain canyons and usually blow east or southeast—toward Denver. But, on March 27, 1951, just two months after they had started the search, Austin recommended the site to the AEC. Operations began in 1952.

Rocky Flats manufactures the plutonium parts of nuclear warhead cores and various other fission bomb components. It receives fissile material from Energy Department weapons plants in Hanford, Washington, and Savannah River, South Carolina, and machines it into "triggers"—fission bombs used in hydrogen bombs to generate a sufficiently high temperature and density to set off a fusion reaction. Plutonium is the core of the operation and of the controversy surrounding Rocky Flats. This radioactive element is hazardous in minute quantities and loses its toxicity slowly. The half-life of the plutonium 239 isotope is 24,110 years.

Plant workers were the first victims of breakdowns in Rocky Flats safety procedures. Spills, accidents, and fires resulted in repeated reports of contamination and illness. A study published in the *American Journal of Epidemiology* found that the deaths of plant workers from cancers of the blood and lymph tissues were at a higher rate than in the normal population.[8] Complete health statistics are not available because federal managers have refused to release medical records of plant workers.

By the 1980s, several retired Rocky Flats workers were trying to prove that their cancers were caused by exposure to radiation. They wanted benefits from the state's worker compensation program. The widow of one Rocky Flats worker won a $45,000 award in 1983 after establishing that the 1974 death of her husband was due to colon cancer he probably contracted as a result of working at Rocky Flats for 15 years.[9]

That case was the first successful worker's compensation claim in the country in which the cancer of a nuclear weapons plant employee was found to have been caused by exposure to levels of radiation the government considered safe. Two other cases have been settled; six are pending. But most claimants end up frustrated because of the difficulty of proving that radiation exposure during their employment at Rocky Flats, rather than smoking or family predisposition, caused their cancers. According to one government lawyer, six cases have been dismissed on that basis and no new cases have been filed in four years. Lawyer Bruce Deboskey, who has represented most of the Rocky Flats workers, is also frustrated. "I never thought when I began these cases that by 1989 we'd be close to where we started," he said recently.[10]

Dozens of fires occurred at the plant during its first two decades of operation. One of the biggest broke out on September 11, 1957, when filters over the glove boxes that were designed to prevent plutonium from escaping the building caught fire. They had been manufactured with flammable materials and, since many of them had not been changed in four years, there was plenty of plutonium in them. Fire-fighters turned on the ventilation fans, which spread the fire. The blaze was not contained for 13 hours.[11]

Plant officials did not know how much plutonium escaped. Smokestack monitors were not turned on until seven days after the blaze, when they showed that emissions contained levels of radioactive elements 16,000 times greater than the standards.[12] Soil samples showed similarly high concentrations of plutonium. Nevertheless, Rocky Flats officials did not warn local residents, cities, or health agencies. No emergency action was taken to protect the public.

Fires were not the only problem. Between 500 and 2,000 curies of tritium were released accidentally in 1973.[13] Beginning in 1958, more than 3,000 barrels leaking plutonium-contaminated oil were stored in an open area at the plant. Dow Co. managers did not remove the barrels until 1967, even though they knew of the leaks as early as 1959. The contaminated soil was not completely capped until 1969, and during the cleanup, more plutonium was scattered into the wind.[14]

In 1971, nuclear chemists at the National Center for Atmospheric Research in Boulder conducted soil tests around Rocky Flats and found that plutonium contamination two miles east of the plant was up to 250 times higher than the levels attributable to fallout from nuclear tests worldwide. Eight miles east of the plant, in Westminster—which had become one of Denver's largest suburbs—the levels were 10 times those accepted as normal.[15]

The amount of radioactivity released from Rocky Flats is a small fraction of that released by atmospheric nuclear tests. But much of the bomb test radioactivity dispersed into the upper atmosphere, while the Rocky Flats releases stayed much closer to the surface. In 1974, the land downwind from Rocky Flats was said to have the highest level of plutonium of any area in the country.[16]

But the major difference between Rocky Flats and other sources of plutonium contamination is that about 1.4 million people live within 50 miles of the plant—and downwind. Every time the wind blows at Rocky Flats, plutonium in the soil is resuspended over the Denver area. In late 1986, environmentalists began calling it "creeping Chernobyl."

The first attempt to project the health impact of the contamination was a study in 1974 by Carl Johnson, the chief health officer for Jefferson County, where Rocky Flats is located. Two years earlier, the state of Colorado had become the first public agency to adopt a plutonium soil contamination standard, two disintegrations per minute per gram of dry soil to a depth of one-eighth inch. Johnson found that soil on some of the land to be developed for homes for 10,000 people exceeded the standard by a factor of seven.[17] He launched a series of soil tests and checked death records to see if there was a correlation between plutonium-contaminated soil and cancer.

Johnson's controversial findings, released in two studies in the late 1970s and early 1980s suggested that Denver's overall cancer rates were higher than expected, and higher still in residential areas near Rocky Flats. Another study by Johnson also found higher infant mortality rates that corresponded with proximity to the plant.[18] He recommended evacuating all residents within four miles of the plant.

Federal housing officials directed realtors to distribute a notice to prospective home buyers near Rocky Flats who sought federally backed loans, warning them about possible adverse health consequences. And Colorado health officials declared that industrial uses were more appropriate than residential uses for land within four miles of the plant because evacuation would be easier.

But several researchers challenged Johnson's findings, and the impact of his warnings eventually dissipated.[19] In 1981, Johnson was fired from his Jefferson County public health position. In 1982, federal housing officials cancelled the order to distribute warnings.

In 1985, landowners who had sued Rocky Flats, alleging that plutonium contamination had made their land worthless, settled for about $9 million and a court ruling assuring them their land was safe.[20] As part of the settlement, the landowners agreed not to call any witnesses and to allow the defense's expert witnesses to testify unchallenged. This one-sided trial satisfied both sides. "Our basic intention was to have the federal judge bless our land," landowner Charles McKay conceded in 1987.

Another part of the settlement called for Jefferson County to purchase 800 acres of the affected property for $2 million, half its appraised value, for use as a park. County officials assured residents it was safe for recreational use, but some residents were skeptical. "We don't think it will ever be safe," park activist Carol Karlin said in 1987. "We're sorry so much money was spent on a useless piece of land. I'm going to call it Poison Park."[21]

Early this year, city council members of the Denver suburb of Arvada agreed to annex land for the first phase of a 20,000-acre residential, commercial, and industrial development adjoining Rocky Flats on its southern boundary, ignoring the 1979 state health department recommendation against residential development within four miles of the plant.[22] The brush land the site surveyors saw between Rocky Flats and Denver in 1951 is about to become a continuous stream of office buildings, businesses, and homes. Each year, dozens of families move closer to Rocky Flats without any idea of the health hazards they may face.

Plutonium pollution is not the only hazard at Rocky Flats. The plant produces about 16,000 tons of waste a year.[23] While the radioactive waste has typically been shipped away, most of the chemical waste is disposed of on site; since 1986, this requires permits from the Colorado Health Department. Pending approval of permit applications, Rockwell obtained interim permits. Although state and federal regulators knew as early as 1983 of several violations of these interim permits, they asked only that new and more detailed permit applications be submitted.[24]

Colorado Health Department officials cited Rocky Flats in 1988 for nine violations of hazardous waste disposal laws, but a year later they had not determined the amount of the fine—it could have been $25,000 a day for each violation—let alone collected any money.[25] And Environmental Protection Agency officials, responsible for enforcing groundwater protection laws, had only fined Rockwell for the improper storage of PCBs.[26] Hefty fines would not have been much of a financial threat, since the Energy Department reimburses contractors for any fines levied. But fines would have sent a message that violations of environmental laws would not be tolerated.

Rocky Flats was proposed for inclusion on the EPA's Superfund list of the dirtiest sites in the country in 1985 and was added to the list in September 1989, about four months after the FBI raid. Last year, the congressional Government Accounting Office ranked groundwater contamination at Rocky Flats the most serious environmental threat at any of the country's nuclear weapons facilities—primarily because the contaminated groundwater may affect reservoirs supplying drinking water to Denver suburbs. The report noted the inadequacy of monitoring equipment in use.[27]

Despite this record, no politicians elected to statewide or federal office in Colorado have called for closing Rocky Flats. A task force appointed by Gov. Richard Lamm and congressman (now senator) Timothy Wirt, a Democrat whose district encompassed the plant, recommended in 1975 that federal officials consider relocating the plant. It stayed put, Lamm left office in 1987, and Wirth did not call for relocating Rocky Flats until later that year, and then it was not out of concern for public health but because of the cost of a major renovation project.

Leaders of the Colorado Medical Society called in 1979 for the plant to be relocated. Dozens of demonstrations and protests were held at the plant over the years. Finally, early this year, Energy officials unveiled plans to phase out Rocky Flats. They cited public opposition, but recommended a phase-out timetable that will keep the plant operating until 2010.[28]

The June FBI raid was partly the result of persistent efforts by Jim Stone, a six-year Rocky Flats engineer who had been laid off in 1986. He was convinced he had been fired because for years he had been pestering plant managers about safety concerns. Stone sued, but he looked for another way to pursue the safety problem. He found it in the person of FBI agent Jon Lipsky, who had been trained in the enforcement of environmental laws.

Stone showed Lipsky a copy of a 1986 Energy Department memo acknowledging that some of the hazardous waste treatment facilities at Rocky Flats were "patently illegal," that the facility was "in poor condition generally in terms of environmental compliance," and that "some of its permit applications are grossly deficient."[29] Rockwell and federal officials had been maintaining at the time that the facility was in "full compliance" with all environmental laws.[30]

Lipsky found evidence of numerous violations of hazardous waste laws in EPA and state files on Rocky Flats. With the help of the criminal enforcement division of the EPA, the FBI did some of its own research. It took water samples from streams that crossed Rocky Flats, and these, the agency concluded, indicated that toxic wastes were being dumped illegally at night. A surveillance plane picked up evidence that convinced the FBI that an incinerator was being used in a building plant managers had said was temporarily shut down.[31]

The 1986 memo, the files, and the research provided Lipsky with more than enough evidence to establish probable cause. He secured a search warrant and led the 75 agents on the plant search. A special grand jury was impaneled; indictments are expected late next year.

A few days after the raid, 12 national groups, including Physicians for Social Responsibility, along with 15 local groups called for an immediate shutdown of Rocky Flats. Leaders of the Denver and Colorado Medical Society called for a halt in production until independent oversight is established.

Colorado Gov. Roy Romer was angry that he had not been told of the undercover probe, and that laws were possibly being broken with impunity.[32] But some environmentalists criticize Romer for making environmental enforcement a low priority for fear it would undermine his efforts to attract new industry to the state. The Colorado Health Department and the regional EPA office "act as boosters" for the largest polluters in the Denver area, charges Adrienne Anderson of the National Toxics Campaign.

Romer persuaded Watkins to provide $700,000 for a health impact study, $730,000 for monitoring equipment, and $1.8 million a year for a beefed-up inspection program to be led by state health officials.[33] That was enough for the medical society leaders, who withdrew their call for a production halt at Rocky Flats.

Watkins has also promised to release records on plant workers and plutonium mishaps that would allow for a thorough study of the plant's health impact.[34] The department's inspector general released a report calling for a review of the policy that allows weapons plant contractors to pass the cost of fines to the government.

In September, Watkins and Rockwell officials agreed to terminate Rockwell's management contract, the first time a weapons plant contract was terminated before expiration.[35] The decision was made the day after Rockwell sued the department, alleging it was being forced to violate hazardous waste laws because the government had failed to provide a permanent storage site for liquid wastes contaminated by both radioactive and nonradioactive toxins.

Environmentalists welcomed the move, but one congressman doubted that it would improve plant management. The contractors who manage nuclear plants "play a game of musical chairs," Tom Luken, an Ohio Democrat who chairs a hazardous materials subcommittee, said in September. "When the pressure is on to clean up past pollution and comply with the law, [Energy Department] contractors pack up and move on. But these so-called house cleanings are an illusion, because the same personnel continue to run the plants, and contaminate the environment, under a new corporate name."[36]

At Rocky Flats there are signs of business as usual. A month after the raid, Energy Department officials found 10 radiation safety problems during a one-week inspection, including one involving leaking boxes of radioactive waste. "The radiological protection program at Rocky Flats continues to be inadequate," one inspector wrote.[37] But Watkins was satisfied. A month later, he declared that the plant is "operating safely."[38]

Then in October, the department released the report documenting the presence of plutonium in the ventilation pipes. Plant managers had said there was no plutonium in the pipes, but it was discovered by a team of inspectors under contract to Scientech, Inc., a Rockville, Maryland, firm hired by the department to review part of the plant's safety record. The team reported evidence of plutonium in other pipes, too, and noted that former plant engineer Jim Stone had suggested that the pipes were a probable place for plutonium to collect.[39]

The Scientech team said Rocky Flats managers lack "inquisitiveness" about safety. "Until safety is given appropriate priority relative to production and until [the Energy Department] instills a healthy, questioning attitude about nuclear safety in all of the people who work there, Rocky Flats Plant will not operate as safely as it can and should."

Notes

1. U.S. Department of Energy Special Assignment Environmental Team, "Assessment of Environmental Conditions at the Rocky Flats Plant" (Aug. 1989).

2. Scientech, Inc., "An Assessment of Criticality Safety at the Department of Energy Rocky Flats Plant" (Oct. 1989).

3. Gary Schmitz, "Energy Boss Raps Nuclear Plant Policies," *Denver Post*, June 28, 1989.

4. Thomas Lippman, "Bomb Plant Cleanup Plan Set," *Washington Post*, July 31, 1989, p. 1.

5. Leslie Groves, *Now It Can Be Told: The Story of the Manhattan Project* (New York: Harper & Row, 1962), p. 70.

6. The Austin Company, "Engineering and Survey Report" (March 27, 1951), pp. 1–3.

7. Ibid., pp. 4-6.

8. Gregg Wilkinson et al., "Mortality among Plutonium and Other Radiation Workers at a Plutonium Weapons Facility," *American Journal of Epidemiology*, vol. 125, no. 2 (Feb. 1987), pp. 231–50.

9. Colorado Workmen's Compensation claim no. 29239-74.

10. Marianne Lavell, "Woes Mounting for Rocky Flats Nuclear Plant," *National Law Journal* (July 4, 1989), p. 34.

11. Dow Chemical Co., "The Report of Serious Incident in Building 71 on September 11, 1957" (Oct. 7, 1957).

12. Carl Johnson, "Comments on the 1957 Fire at the Rocky Flats Plant, in Jefferson County, Colorado," paper delivered to the Conference on the Relation of Environmental Pollution to the Cancer Problem in Colorado, Lakewood, Colorado, Sept. 26, 1980. Johnson cites an unpublished Rocky Flats report dated March 13, 1958.

13. "The Final Report of the Lamm-Wirth Task Force on Rocky Flats" (Denver, Oct. 1, 1975, pp. 45–46.

14. S. Poet and E. Martell, "Plutonium-239 and Americium-241 Contamination in the Denver Area," *Health Physics*, vol. 23 (Oct. 1972), pp. 537–48.

15. Ibid.

16. McDonald Wren, "Environmental Levels of Plutonium and the Transplutonium Elements," *Proceedings of Public Hearings: Plutonium and the Other Transuranium Elements*, EPA ORP-CSD-75-1 (Washington, D.C.: Environmental Protection Agency, Dec. 10-11, 1974), table 5, p. 112.

17. Letter from Carl Johnson to Jefferson County commissioner Joanne Paterson, Dec. 30, 1974.

18. Carl Johnson, "Cancer Incidence in an Area Contaminated with Radionuclides near a Nuclear Installation," *Ambio*, vol. 10 (Aug. 1981), pp. 176–82; Carl Johnson et al., "Cancer Incidence and Mortality, 1957–1981, in the Denver Standard Metropolitan Area Downwind from the Rocky Flats Nuclear Plant," paper presented to the epidemiological section of the annual meeting of the American Public Health Association (Nov. 11, 1983).

19. See, for example, L. Hamilton, "Alternative Interpretation of Statistics on Health Effects of Low Level Radiation," *The American Statistician*, vol. 37 (Nov. 1983), pp. 422–58.

20. Richard Matsch, Findings of Fact and Conclusion of Law, 75-M-1162, Federal District Court for the District of Colorado, July 3, 1985.

21. Alan Prendergast, "Pardon Our Dust," *Westword* (March 4, 1987), pp. 10–14.

22. Renate Robey, "Arvada Annexes 4,400 Acres," *Denver Post*, July 11, 1989.

23. Part A, hazardous waste disposal permit application filed by Energy Department and Rockwell with EPA, Nov. 8, 1985.

24. Affidavit and application for search warrant by FBI agent Jon Lipsky, case no. 89–730M, Federal District Court for the District of Colorado, June 6, 1989, p. 32.

25. Janet Day, "Flats Operator Faces Fine over Waste Violations," *Rocky Mountain News*, June 12, 1989, p. 7.

26. Chance Conner, "Rocky Flats Fined over PCB Violations," *Rocky Mountain News*, Aug. 7, 1986.

27. Government Accounting Office, "Nuclear Health and Safety: Summary of Major Problems at DOE's Rocky Flats Plant," RCED-89-53-BR (Oct. 1988) p. 15.

28. Joan Lowy, "DOE Cites Public Opposition in Plan to Close Flats," *Rocky Mountain News*, Jan. 13, 1989, p. 6.

29. "Briefing Paper for DOE Assistant Secretary for Environment Safety and Health Mary L. Walker," attached to July 14, 1986, memorandum from Walker to Assistant Secretary of Defense S. R. Foley, Jr., J. Michael Farrell of the Office of General Counsel, and R. G. Romatowski, manager of the DOE Albuquerque Operations Office.

30. Environment, Safety and Health Division of DOE Albuquerque Operations Office, "Comprehensive Environmental Assessment and Response Program, Phase I: Installation Assessment, Rocky Flats Plant," (April 1986).

31. Search warrant affidavit, p. 83.

32. "Romer Angry State Kept in Dark about Probe," *Denver Post*, June 7, 1989.

33. Thomas Graf, "Safety Pact Reached on Rocky Flats," *Denver Post*, June 17, 1989.

34. "Risks to Nuclear Workers Admitted," *Denver Post*, June 17, 1989.

35. Thomas Graf and Beth Ferking, "Rockwell Out as Flats Contractor," *Denver Post*, Sept. 23, 1989, p. 1.

36. Office of Thomas Luken, press release, Sept. 27, 1989.

37. Thomas Graf, "Flats Safety Problems Cited One Month after FBI Raid," *Denver Post*, Aug. 12, 1989.

38. Gary Schmitz and Mark Obmasick, "Energy Chief: Flats Now Safe," *Denver Post*, Aug. 2, 1989.

39. See note 2.

Questions

It is December 31, 1989, and in a couple of days you will assume your responsibilities as EG&G's plant manager at the Rocky Flats Nuclear Munitions Plant. On your first day you will head an open meeting for all interested parties to discuss their concerns about Rocky Flat's future operations. You have followed stories in the newspapers about the plant over the past year, and you are aware of the controversy surrounding the plant's operation. "Before the meeting," you think, "I should develop lists of who the interested parties (stakeholders) are, what they want, and what my options are. What will your lists look like? Construct lists of the following:

1. Identify seven stakeholder groups involved in the Rocky Flats controversy.

2. What do you think each of these stakeholders wants?

3. To what extent are the preferences of these stakeholders compatible or incompatible? (*Hint:* You will find that some stakeholders' own preferences conflict, such as employees wanting high-paying jobs without health threats, as well as conflicting preferences across stakeholder groups.)

4. What are your options? How do you think the different stakeholders would react to each option?

Designing Organizations

Basic Components of Organization Design: Specialization, Formalization, and Centralization

Learning Objectives

Upon completing this chapter, you should be able to

1. Identify three design components that managers can manipulate to assure effective organizational performance.
2. Differentiate between horizontal and vertical job specialization.
3. Describe the problems associated with job specialization.
4. Distinguish between job enlargement and job enrichment.
5. Identify five core job dimensions used to horizontally enlarge and vertically enrich jobs.
6. Understand the role of rules, policies, and procedures as coordination and control mechanisms.
7. Recognize the role of professional training as a coordination and control mechanism.
8. Outline the importance of socialization to both individuals and organizations.
9. Appreciate how the use of job specialization, rules/policies/procedures, and socialization can vary by hierarchical level and functional area within an organization.
10. Explain centralization.
11. Detail the advantages and disadvantages of decentralization.

WORKERS TEAM UP FOR SUCCESS

Employees of Aid Association for Lutherans (AAL)—an 84-year-old fraternal society that operates a huge insurance business—speak reverently of AAL's three-year "transformation." The climax occurred at precisely 12 noon on "D-Day," when AAL's entire insurance staff of 500 clerks, technicians, and managers piled their personal belongings on office chairs and said good-bye to fellow employees. Pushing the chairs along corridors, all 500 made their way to newly assigned work areas.

The purpose of this "organized chaos" was to reorganize AAL's insurance operations. Within two hours, its home-office employees had converted the cumbersome, centralized, functionally organized bureaucracy into streamlined, all-purpose teams that could operate without several managerial layers. AAL's overall goal of operating entirely with "self-directed" teams in a highly participative work culture has produced remarkable results: a 20 percent increase in productivity and a reduction in case-processing time by as much as 75 percent.

AAL switched to teamwork mainly to speed up the processing of insurance cases and thus provide better service to its field agents and policyholders. For team members, the abrupt switch brought mixed feelings. "There was uncertainty and a lot of broken friendships when we moved to the new system, and personally I feel more tension," remarked one employee. But most workers now like the team approach because it enables them to manage themselves. According to one clerk, "The team idea lets you grow, and you don't always have a supervisor sitting over you."

Despite the growing interest, only a few service organizations have actually adopted teamwork. As you'll see in Chapter 4, a wide array of design options is available to organizations, but choosing the appropriate design can be a complex task.

Source: John Hoerr, "Work Teams Can Rev Up Paper-Pushers, Too, *Business Week,* November 28, 1988, p. 64.

IN the last two chapters, we indicated that organizations are created for the purpose of achieving goals, and that their effectiveness can be judged using goal-attainment, systems-resource, or stakeholder approaches. The question examined in the next three chapters is, how do organizations coordinate and control the activities of their members in order to assure effective performance? For example, how should the activities of individuals and work units in a semiconductor firm be coordinated so that desired output is produced efficiently while new-product development is encouraged? Similarly, how should the activities of nurses in a public health department be coordinated so that client needs are served in a timely manner while minimizing associated costs?

The answer to this general question is intimately tied to the twin concepts of organization structure and design. An **organization's structure** can be defined as the patterns of coordination and control, workflows, authority, and communication that channel the activity of its members. **Organization design** is the managerial activity of creating and modifying these patterns.

Organization structure provides the arena within which human activity occurs. Like buildings, different organization structures are designed to serve different purposes.

> The idea of structure is basically simple. Buildings have structures in the form of beams, interior walls, passageways, roofs, and so on. The structure of a building is a major determinant of the movements and activities of the people within it. Buildings are supposed to have structures that fit the activities that go on within them. An office building is different from a factory. Factories where automobiles are produced are different than those where computers are manufactured. Architects design buildings to fit the needs of the activities that are to be carried on within them. They are designed to accommodate populations of various sizes (no architect would design a huge cathedral for a small congregation) and to withstand the environment in which they are located. Buildings in Minnesota are different from those in Arizona. While the size, the major activity or technology to be used, and the environment are all important in building design, so too is the element of choice—decor, color, and so on. Buildings also reflect the ideologies of the persons in control—corporate headquarters and state capitols do not take the form they do by accident.[1]

Thus, an organization's structure reflects choices managers make about how to best coordinate and control necessary activities—the workflows, communications, and activities of its members. These choices are not fixed. An organization's structure is dynamic, changing over time. Managers can design an initial structure, but changing circumstances may make it unworkable as operating technologies advance, new goods and services are developed, goals change, and markets evolve. As a result, organizations are continually being redesigned to meet changing coordination and control needs.[2]

To continue with the preceding analogy, it may be more appropriate to view managers as engaging in a continuous process of redesigning organizations, rather than as architects designing them anew. Managers continually rearrange an organization's walls, add and subtract rooms—and in some cases, may simply decide to move the organization to a new locale.

What are the building blocks of organization structure—the design components that managers can manipulate in their effort to coordinate and control necessary activities These are the subject of this chapter: job specialization, formalization, and centralization.

JOB SPECIALIZATION

Job specialization reflects the choices managers make about the division of labor within an organization. It is an important design component because, as we'll see later in this chapter, the way that jobs are structured can have a major effect on other design components. There are two types of job special-ization: horizontal and vertical.

Horizontal Specialization

Horizontal specialization refers to the scope of a job, or the degree to which an employee performs a complete job. The smaller the employee's part is of an overall task or project, the more horizontally specialized his or her job. The concept of horizontal specialization was introduced into modern orga-nizations by engineers such as Frederick W. Taylor, the "Father of Scientific Management" (see Module 1: Early History of Organization Design). The premise underlying this early form of job design was that efficiency would increase by simplifying jobs—breaking them down into smaller sets of tasks—and training employees to perform just one or the other set. Higher levels of efficiency were, of course, expected to increase the financial rewards reaped by both management and labor.

The concept applies well to simple and repetitive jobs. As Figure 4.1 shows, the jobs of three employees—one who assembles a component, an-other who tests it, and another who packages it—are simpler and more horizontally specialized than the job of an employee who performs all three tasks. As Sexton notes, there are several benefits to horizontal specialization.

> There is time saved in training, due to the simplicity of the assignment, and in operation, since the worker need not change tasks nor equipment. In addition, it provides the opportunity for utilizing the dominant talents of each individual worker. Naturally, the consequent repetition leads to a degree of expertise that leads to efficiency.[3]

Horizontal specialization is common in professional jobs as well, since many professionals have highly specialized areas of expertise. For example, engineers specialize in various areas—such as electrical, mechanical, struc-tural, materials, and civil engineering. Completing a complex engineering design usually requires the efforts of several engineers with different special-ties. A single engineer would be unlikely to have the expertise to design a jet aircraft. In such situations, specialization is demanded by the complex knowledge needed to complete the project. In other instances, a task's sim-plicity might call for horizontally specialized jobs. Simple and complex jobs that are highly specialized differ in the degree to which employees control decisions about how a job should be performed.

Vertical Specialization (and Its Relationship to Horizontal Specialization)

Vertical specialization refers to the degree of control an employee has over a job. The more decisions an employee makes about how and when to perform tasks, and the less the employee's behaviors are dictated by rules,

Figure 4.1
Horizontal Job Specialization

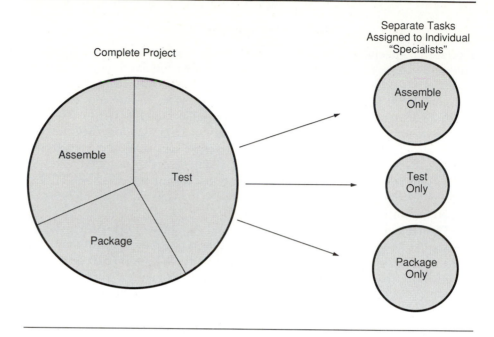

policies and procedures, direct supervision, or by the prevailing technology, the less vertically specialized his or her job is. When a job is simple and repetitive, there is a positive relationship between horizontal and vertical specialization: the smaller a job's scope, the less control an employee is likely to have over it. For example, employees on an assembly line have jobs that are horizontally specialized; they complete only a small part of an overall assembly task. In addition, their jobs are vertically specialized, since they have little control over how the work is performed—the method and pace of job performance are dictated by first-line supervisors, rules, policies and procedures, and by the relevant production technology. Similarly, a clerical employee in an insurance company whose job is to type policyholder correspondence that a supervisor writes, assigns, and checks has a job that is both horizontally and vertically specialized. The horizontal specialization in such jobs, by limiting an employee's perspective of the overall task, creates a need for vertical specialization (a supervisor—or set of preestablished instructions—must coordinate the various jobs).

When jobs are complex, vertical specialization usually does not accompany horizontal specialization. Complex tasks require that an employee retain discretion to make decisions about how a job will be done.[4] When seeing a patient, for example, a physician needs discretion to determine what

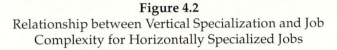

Figure 4.2
Relationship between Vertical Specialization and Job
Complexity for Horizontally Specialized Jobs

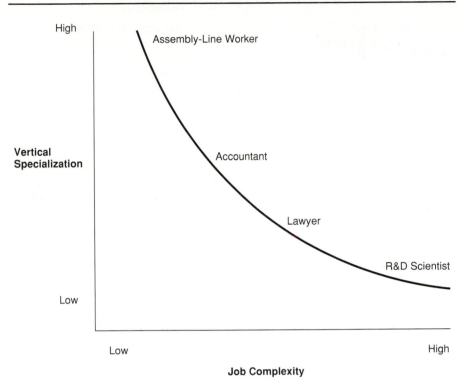

tests will be ordered, whether a patient will be treated on an inpatient or outpatient basis, what medications are required, and so on. The task's complexity makes it difficult to use formal rules, policies, and procedures or direct supervision to standardize performance.

Thus, the degree of vertical specialization in a horizontally specialized job decreases as its complexity increases. As Figure 4.2 indicates, an assembly-line worker has relatively little discretion in job performance; most activities are controlled by others. In contrast, relatively few activities of a R&D scientist are controlled by others; most are left to the individual's discretion.

Drawbacks of Job Specialization

The benefits of job specialization are obvious, but over the past two decades drawbacks associated with high levels of both horizontal and vertical specialization have triggered increasing concern. (The benefits and drawbacks

Table 4.1
Job Specialization—Benefits and Drawbacks

Benefits	Drawbacks
Time saved in training	Reduced job satisfaction
Simplicity of assignment	Lower employee commitment
Simplicity in operation	Increased employee alienation
Utilization of dominant talents	Decreased worker involvement
Expertise from repetition of performance	
Dependence upon particular individuals or special skills minimized	

of job specialization are summarized in Table 4.1.) It has become more and more evident that the price of highly specialized jobs includes reduced job satisfaction, worker alienation, decreased employee involvement with and commitment to an organization. As a U.S. Department of Health, Education, and Welfare-commissioned study noted, "Significant numbers of American workers are dissatisfied with the quality of their working lives. Dull, repetitive, seemingly meaningless tasks, offering little challenge or autonomy, are causing discontent among workers at all occupational levels."[5] Or as one employee explained, "Most of us, like the assembly-line worker, have jobs that are too small for our spirit. Jobs are not big enough for people."[6] As a result, much attention has been paid in recent years to alternative ways of designing jobs to ameliorate these problems.

ALTERNATIVE JOB DESIGN STRATEGIES

As a job design strategy, job specialization operates on the theory that employees will be motivated by the idea of increasing their efficiency (through specialization) in order to obtain higher pay—or some other such extrinsic motivator. More recent job design strategies have focused on intrinsic motivators (such as job characteristics that make work itself inherently more satisfying) in an attempt to eliminate the drawbacks of job specialization.

Beginning in the early 1970s, organizations began experimenting with alternative work designs (e.g., job enrichment, cross-training and job rotation, autonomous work groups, project teams), alternative work schedules (e.g., flextime, compressed work week, job sharing), and participative decision strategies (e.g., joint labor-management committees, quality circles, problem-solving teams, work councils) under the label of *quality of work life (QWL)* programs.[7] Two of the earliest concepts associated with QWL efforts were job enlargement and job enrichment.

Figure 4.3
Job Enlargement and Job Enrichment

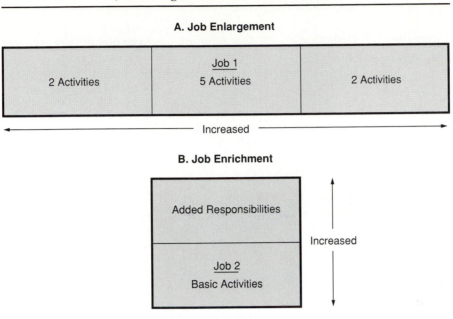

A. Job Enlargement

| 2 Activities | Job 1
5 Activities | 2 Activities |

← Increased →

B. Job Enrichment

Added Responsibilities

Job 2
Basic Activities

↕ Increased

Job enlargement decreases horizontal job specialization by extending the *scope,* or *range,* of a job by increasing the number of activities an employee performs. For example, in Figure 4.3 (Panel A), Job 1 consists of five activities. To enlarge its scope or range, four activities could be added, two from the preceding job in the workflow and two from the following job.

Job enrichment decreases vertical job specialization by extending the *depth* of a job so that employee discretion or control is increased. For example, in Figure 4.3 (Panel B), Job 2 consists of certain basic activities. To enrich its depth, employee discretion or control can be expanded by adding new responsibilities such as ordering materials or quality control. The overall effect of both job enlargement and job enrichment is to make simple jobs more complex and thus more challenging.

Core Job Dimensions

The theoretical basis for many current job redesign strategies rests on the work of Hackman and Oldham.[8] They identified five core dimensions that can be modified to horizontally enlarge and vertically enrich jobs, and suggest that managers can determine the quantity and quality of the different dimensions present in the jobs they supervise. These core job dimensions are skill variety, task identity, task significance, autonomy, and performance feedback (Table 4.2):

Table 4.2
Hackman and Oldham's Core Job Dimensions

Dimension	Definition	Examples of Low Amount	Examples of High Amount
Skill Variety	Number of skills used in performing a job	One insurance clerk interviews claimants, another checks the paperwork, and still another processes the claims	Each insurance clerk performs all three duties for a subset of claimants (A greater number of skills are used in performing the job)
Task Identity	Extent to which employees can identify with the outcome of their work	One dressmaker cuts patterns, another assembles them, and a third sews the garments	Each dressmaker cuts, assembles, and sews a complete garment (Employees are more likely to identify with the results of the completed work)
Task Significance	Employees' perception that they have made a significant contribution to others through their job performance	Nurses working on a team-care nursing unit, where one administers medications, another checks vital signs, and another bathes and feeds patients	Nurses working on a primary care unit, where each nurse provides all the services for a subset of the unit's patients (Employees are more likely to feel that have made a significant contribution to health and well-being of their patients)
Autonomy	Extent to which employees are free to schedule their own activities, decide procedures, select needed equipment, etc.	Salespersons whose routes and appointments are set by a scheduling manager	Salespersons who set their own routes within an assigned territory and schedule their own calls. (Employees are more likely to feel that they have control over their jobs)
Performance Feedback	Extent to which employees receive information about their job performance from supervisors, co-workers, or personal feelings about the job itself	Production employees on an assembly line who receive broad, annual performance evaluations	Employees on an assembly line with weekly posted quality control information on units produced, defect rates, and changes over time (Employees have greater control over their jobs, and are more likely to take corrective actions to solve problems)

- **Skill variety** refers to the number of skills that employees use on their job. Increasing skill variety decreases horizontal specialization.
- **Task identity** is the extent to which a job allows employees to perform a whole piece of work and to clearly identify with the outcome of their efforts. Horizontally specialized jobs are low in task identity because employees perform only a small segment of an entire job, and they often have difficulty seeing how their part of the task fits into the whole.
- **Task significance** refers to employees' perceptions that their job performance makes a significant contribution to the lives or work of others, either within or outside their organization. A feeling of having made significant contribution through their jobs is an important motivator for many employees.
- **Autonomy** refers to the extent that employees are free to schedule their own activities, decide procedures, and select required equipment. Some jobs allow employees to decide what to do and when to do it, as long as the necessary work is completed within cost and quality limits. This way, the employees control their own job pace, tool usage, and other factors.
- **Performance feedback** refers to the extent to which employees are provided with information about how well they are doing their jobs. It may come from co-workers, immediate supervisors, subordinates, or from the job itself. Other possible sources include performance appraisals, awards, and promotions, and even personal evaluations of their own feelings and ideas. A lack of feedback can create ambiguity and stress for employees.

The general thrust of Hackman and Oldham's work is that the more a job contains these core dimensions, the more likely an employee will experience feelings of satisfaction and be motivated by the job itself. While Hackman and Oldham warn that not all employees desire horizontally enlarged or vertically enriched jobs, they hold that enough employees do appreciate such changes that four beneficial effects will likely result from a well-formulated job redesign program:

1. Higher work motivation.
2. Higher quality performance.
3. Higher job satisfaction.
4. Lower absenteeism and turnover.

New Approaches to Job Design

During the 1970s managers experimented with many different job enlargement and enrichment techniques. *Flextime,* for example, was an early effort to increase job autonomy by increasing workers' control over when they were at the workplace. *Job rotation* was used to increase skill variety and task identity by rotating workers through different jobs or positions on an assembly line. *Quality circles* were employed by many organizations as a first step in increasing autonomy by bringing employees into decision-making processes. Some organizations experimented with *autonomous work groups,* which are employee teams that produce a complete good or service. These work groups often assume many of the responsibilities typically associated with first-level supervisors, including job assignment, quality control, purchasing, and, in some cases, employee selection, hiring, and performance appraisal. Thus, autonomous work groups are designed to have high levels of all five core job dimensions.

In the 1980s the *team approach*—essentially another name for autonomous work groups—attracted much interest in both service and manufacturing organizations. For example, the 22 employees in B.F. Goodrich's Tire Group Billing Department, who had specialized jobs verifying, editing, and entering billing data on a computerized system, were reorganized into work teams. The result was a 21 percent increase in the number of billing documents processed daily, and a 15 percent increase in the number of documents processed per employee-hour. Cost per employee hour dropped 9.4 percent and the cost of each bill produced by 11 percent. Absenteeism also dropped by 40 percent.[9]

Digital Equipment Corporation redesigned its Enfield, Connecticut, plant using highly autonomous work teams that were responsible for their own support work, materials handling, purchasing, quality inspections, interviewing, and hiring. Five years after this approach was implemented, productivity had increased 40 percent and product yields had doubled.[10] The important point for our discussion is that managers can make choices about how to design jobs and, as will be discussed, there are trade-offs among the different approaches.

Example: Different Approaches to Engine Assembly

Figure 4.4 illustrates how different approaches to assembling an automobile engine vary in horizontal and vertical specialization. Point A in Figure 4.4 reflects a traditional assembly-line job where employees are assigned to a position on the line. This job is both horizontally and vertically specialized. Point B also represents assembly-line production, but employees are rotated across positions on the line. This technique decreases horizontal specialization by increasing skill variety and task identity, but these jobs still have a relatively high degree of vertical specialization. Point C represents engine assembly using a team approach, where a work team assembles entire engines. The team decides on job assignments, performs its own quality control checks, and evaluates team member performance. Point D represents assembly of a complete engine by a single employee, such as done at Ford Motor Company's Aston-Martin Lagonda plant in England. Each engine is handmade and autographed by a single craftsman.

Each approach has benefits and drawbacks. For example, the traditional assembly-line method is very efficient but is prone to the dysfunctional

Figure 4.4
Alternative Designs for Assembling an Engine

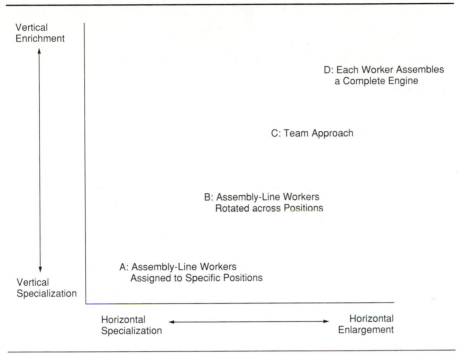

consequences described earlier that can reduce productivity and product quality. The assembly line with job rotation maintains many of the benefits of job specialization while decreasing some of its dysfunctional consequences. The team approach can have productivity as high or higher than traditional assembly lines without any of the dysfunctions of job specialization. But whether these benefits can be gained depends on the successful implementation of the team concept, a topic we look at in Chapter 4. (Focus on Design 4.1 introduces some of the problems in making the team approach work.) Hand-building an engine, on the other hand, is relatively inefficient but high on the core job dimensions that result in motivated and satisfied employees. In short, there are advantages and disadvantages to any job design approach.

CHOOSING A JOB DESIGN STRATEGY

Managers need to choose a job design strategy that best suits their organization's and employees' needs. Many factors will influence this selection, including

FOCUS ON DESIGN 4.1

What Makes Work Teams Succeed?

Work teams came to this country from the English coal mines and, for the most part, have not transplanted well. Quality circles, imported from Japan, are still only tenuously grafted onto American business methods. The failure of these and other participative movements to catch on widely in this country has little to do with results. When quality circles and autonomous work groups work, they show impressive results. Why, then, is there so much resistance to the notion of letting employees work smarter?

Experts such as Raymond E. Miles, dean of the University of California's business school at Berkeley, believe that "the problem with participative management is that it works."

General Electric has initiated almost 90 work teams in the past 20 years. Though the teams made productivity gains in nearly all instances, most have disappeared or dwindled. A survey of former team members found that they did not want to see the teams end but believed that general foremen, top management, and nonteam members did. "The most important condition for the success of work teams," says management consultant Billie Alban, "is that the management above the plant understands and buys into the philosophy and values that are involved."

In addition, she points out, top management must demonstrate its commitment to a number of difficult changes: in work design, in organizational structure, and in information and measurement systems, to name just a few. There must be a reward system that recognizes team effort and values people's input to the team, and there must be performance appraisal of the team as a team.

It is the complexity and difficulty of achieving such changes that sink most work teams. Among the survivors, most started from scratch at new sites like Digital's Enfield plant or Exxon's Venetia refinery. TRW and Proctor & Gamble have also had success with work teams at new plant sites.

Bill Byham, whose firm Development Dimensions International trains managers and others in participative skills, believes that work teams offer their members a strong psychological incentive to participate and benefit from the energy of group process techniques. But his chief condition for success is plenty of training for the workers and their supervisors. In a work team setting, both groups need particular skills. Workers may need training in taking initiative while supervisors need to learn nonmanagement leadership.

Wilson Learning Corporation recently surveyed 20 companies on the design of high-peformance work teams. Vice president for curriculum development, Steve Buchholtz, summarizes the following ingredients for success:

authentic participation;

wide scope of activities (many problems to solve or many solutions to deal with);

ideas consistent with organization's culture;

perception of trust;

rewards for participants spelled out clearly.

For Steve Cohen, CEO of Wilson Learning's Interactive Technology Group, the key to success is empowerment. "Participative management only works if individuals are empowered to make decisions, to contribute, and to act without the encumbrance of an organizational structure that prevents risk-taking."

Source: Patricia Galagan, "Work Teams That Work," *Training and Development Journal* (November 1986): 35.

- *An organization's production technology.* Sunk costs in an existing production technology may limit a manager's job design options. For example, a traditional assembly-line system may preclude the use of a team approach. In many respects, it is easier to develop a production technology and design jobs at the same time.

- *Managers' beliefs about human nature.* If managers believe that employees are inherently lazy or irresponsible, they are likely to use job design approaches that give them more control over the employees' behavior. Conversely, if managers believe that employees are responsible and willing to use their own initiative, they are more likely to use alternative job design approaches.

- *Employees' needs and beliefs.* Some employees do not desire jobs that give them more responsibility, or that require a greater investment of energy and effort in their work. Alternative job designs are difficult to implement in this case.

- *Competitive pressures.* The need for greater productivity and product quality in order to survive in an increasingly competitive global economy often overrides other concerns. Since alternative job design approaches have been proven largely successful in increasing both productivity and product quality, organizations in the automotive, steel, and other global industries have begun using them in spite of other, limiting factors.

The selection of a job design approach also has implications for other aspects of an organization's design (and vice versa). As we will see in the following sections, job design is related to the type of coordination and control mechanisms used in an organization, and to the extent to which decision making is centralized or decentralized. In Chapter 5, we show that job design also is related to the manner in which people are grouped into work units, and to the necessity of creating mechanisms to coordinate the efforts of employees across work unit boundaries. And, in Chapter 6, we show how job design and the choice of a production technology are related.

FORMALIZATION

Formalization refers to the extent to which rules, policies, procedures, formal training, norms, and traditions standardize behavior in an organization. Standardizing behavior is a primary method for coordinating and controlling employee activities. It reduces the need for direct supervision by specifying, in advance, appropriate behaviors or actions under a given set of circumstances: if x occurs, do y. Formalization has been narrowly defined as the extent to which written rules, policies, and procedures govern behavior.[11] Our position, however, is that unwritten rules, norms, and traditions can be as effective as formal rules, policies, and procedures in standardizing behavior.[12] Mintzberg discusses three types of mechanisms that are used to standardize behavior in organizations: (1) written rules, procedures, and policies, (2) training, and (3) socialization, all of which we include under the label of *formalization*.[13]

Rules, Procedures, and Policies (RPPs)

Virtually every organization has written rules, procedures, and policies (RPPs) that standardize behavior by telling individuals what is expected. While rules, procedures, and policies have been combined here, they vary in the amount that they limit individual discretion. *Rules* are the most restrictive. They prescribe or prohibit actions by specifying what an individual may or may not do: "Employees will report to the workplace by 8:00 a.m." *Procedures* are less restrictive. They specify a series of steps to achieve a given purpose: "Assemble parts A, B, and C. When assembly is completed, deliver the assembled unit to the packing station." *Policies* are the least restrictive. They are general statements that guide decision making: "Preference will be given to hiring the handicapped." Their important shared characteristic is that, to one degree or another, RPPs standardize behavior by constraining employee behavior.

Functions and Dysfunctions of RPPs. There are two important intended outcomes of RPPs. First, standardizing behavior reduces variability in performance across employees and thereby promotes control. For example, McDonald's uses extensive RPPs to ensure that employees prepare hamburgers that taste the same in Denver as in London. In essence, RPPs program human behavior much like a computer programmer does a computer. It is possible to do this for simple, repetitive tasks because the most efficient process for completing a job can generally be predetermined.

Second, RPPs promote coordination, which is particularly important when there is a high degree of horizontal job specialization. When simple, repetitive jobs are horizontally specialized, employees may not have a good sense of how their small task fits into a larger whole. Horizontal job specialization thus increases the need for coordination, which RPPs resolve, because they instruct employees on how to do their jobs. Ideally, extensive RPPs provide all the instructions necessary to coordinate employees' activities across horizontally specialized jobs. Of course, by definition, their use also increases vertical job specialization and therefore limits employee discretion.

Research shows that excessive use of RPPs can be dysfunctional for both individuals and their organizations. The extreme limitation of discretion in the workplace can result in what has been described as the *bureaucratic personality*, where following rules and regulations becomes more important than achieving an organization's goals.[14] Rules become ends in themselves, which is the means-ends inversion discussed in Chapter 2. In turn, heavy use of RPPs creates a reliance on an organization's past experience to interpret and respond to current organizational and market conditions, even as conditions change over time. As we'll show in Chapter 12, "living in the past" is a major reason that many organizations experience decline. Overuse of RPPs also can destroy individual initiative, eliminate risk-taking behavior, decrease job satisfaction, and lead to high levels of employee cynicism and worker alienation.[15]

Why Organizations Have Extensive RPPs. Given the trade-offs between coordination and control on one hand, and the negative effects of RPPs on the other, an important question emerges: "Why do some organizations become overly dependent on RPPs?" There are four major reasons. First, as an organization ages, there is a natural tendency for managers to codify the solutions to problems they have solved in the past. As a result, RPPs accumulate over time. Everyone has heard of municipal laws that are out of place in current society. There are, for example, some communities that still prohibit horse racing on city streets. A law that was appropriate at one time has become outdated.

Second, RPPs tend to increase as an organization grows larger. As the number of hierarchical levels in an organization increases, there is a tendency for top management to delegate decision-making authority to lower levels,[16] a topic discussed in more detail later in this chapter. As decision-making authority is delegated to lower-level managers, their superiors use RPPs to create boundaries within which decisions can be made. In this way, upper-level managers retain a degree of control over lower-level decision making.

Third, external demands from regulatory bodies, majority shareholders, and so on, can lead to extensive use of RPPs as top managers attempt to ensure that lower-level employees conform to the standards for which they are held responsible.[17] For example, government contractors usually have voluminous policy and procedure manuals because the federal government imposes a wide variety of regulations concerning the use of public funds. These policies and procedures can cover many areas of an organization's operations, from employment practices, environmental protection, workplace safety, to reporting and accounting standards, travel, employee conduct, and the like. For small government contractors, the number of pages of RPPs often exceeds their number of employees. In a small, federally funded research organization that one of the authors was affiliated with there were approximately ten pages of RPPs per employee.

Finally, the use of RPPs is related, in part, to managers' beliefs about human nature, as captured in McGregor's work on Theory X and Theory Y management.[18] Theory X managers assume that employees are fundamentally lazy and irresponsible, unwilling to display initiative or ambition. Managers with Theory X assumptions believe that employees must be controlled, and they are likely to use extensive RPPs for that purpose. In contrast, Theory Y managers view employees as responsible, willing to exerciseself-direction and self-control, and that they have the ability to make good decisions on their own. Thus, Theory Y managers are less likely to use extensive RPPs to control behavior than their Theory X counterparts.

Focus on Design 4.2 is a report detailing the use of RPPs at a McDonald's franchise.

Training

It is generally difficult to standardize work processes using RPPs when jobs are complex and nonrepetitive. In such situations, organizations often rely on the standardization of employee skills (rather than work processes) to control and coordinate behavior. This standardization means that the knowledge, skills, and abilities required to perform a complex job can be specified and acquired through formal training.[19] Such training is usually, though not always, acquired prior to organizational entry. For example, engineers, accountants, physicians, social workers, and so on, bring the basic skills needed for job performance to their employing organization from their professional training programs, which are usually conducted at colleges and universities. In some cases, training is done inside an organization, as in the case of police officers and soldiers. The important point is that training provides an individual with the knowledge, skills, and abilities required to decide what to do and when.

Cardiovascular surgeon Frank Spencer's description of "surgical cookbooks" is a clear example of the complex, standardized skills acquired through professional training.

> The jargon term "cookbook" evolved from my loyal office staff, as this essentially describes "How I do this operation," somewhat analogous to "How I bake a cake." . . .
>
> The components of a complex operation, such as repair of the tetralogy of Fallot, may be divided into 10 to 15 sequential steps, with two to five essential features in each step. If each feature is symbolized by a single word, essential steps of an operation can be reduced to a series of chains of symbols, varying from six to ten chains containing 30 to 40 symbols. These are committed to memory, with review frequent enough so that the essential 30 to 40 symbols representing key features of an operation can be reviewed mentally in 60 to 120 seconds at some time during the day preceding the operation. The sheer memorization feature is crucial, as opposed to simply scanning one's notes, with the ability to envision the chain of symbols rapidly, like quoting the alphabet. With these basic features firmly memorized, decision-making, especially with unexpected events, is greatly augmented.[20]

In short, professional training provides employees with the knowledge, skills, and abilities needed to perform complex tasks. It standardizes employee behavior by defining the decisions and actions required under different

FOCUS ON DESIGN 4.2

Formalization: Under the Golden Arches

McDonald's has raised the use of RPPs to a fine art. Indeed, in some ways a McDonald's franchise resembles a machine because each position requires a rigid set of tasks, and every task is divided into the smallest of steps.

A McDonald's trainee must become familiar with an entire manual of RPPs, which specifies absolutely everything one needs to know about operating a franchise. The manual outlines a task for every day of the year. McDonald's potato peelers are cleaned on July 25 all over the world; snow-removal contracts are verified on November 2; and parking lots are repainted on April 7.

New McDonald's crew members are first given a guided tour of their employing franchise then they are shown videotapes that explain how typical jobs are done. The videotape on preparing French fries begins by showing cartons of frozen fries being unloaded from a delivery truck. The cartons are stacked exactly six boxes high in a freezer and precisely one inch apart, with two inches between the stacks and freezer walls. The actual cooking and bagging of the fries are explained in 19 steps.

Before moving to a new station or assignment, crew members are evaluated on their efficiency, manner, grooming, and so forth. When a crew member has learned all the stations— the counter station, the condiment station, the bun station, and the like—the next rung on the ladder to manager is crew trainer. Crew chief comes next, then part-time manager, then manager trainee.

McDonald's franchises operate as precisely as Swiss watches. Little is left to chance. RPPs detail how many servings of Big Mac sauce should come from a jar (170 to 180), how many sandwiches should be dressed per pound of lettuce (24 to 28), and how many pickle slices to expect per pound of pickles (111 to 135). Mustard is doled out in five perfect drops. Ketchup is one big shot. A quarter ounce of onions and two pickles— three if they're small—are used per sandwich. Drink cups are filled with ice up to a point just below the arches on their sides. Take-out bags are folded exactly twice. RPPs go so far as to prescribe what color nail polish female crew members can wear.

While almost every organization has RPPs, few go as far with them as McDonald's does. The two intended outcomes of RPPs—standardized behavior from employees to promote control and improved coordination— are readily evident with a visit to any McDonald's from Moscow, Idaho, to Moscow, U.S.S.R.

Sources: Kathleen Deveny, "Bag Those Fries, Squirt that Ketchup, Fry that Fish," *Business Week,* October 13, 1986, 86; Gareth Morgan, *Creative Organization Theory: A Resourcebook* (Newburg Park, Calif.: Sage, 1989), 271–273.

circumstances. Just as important, training provides professional employees with the wherewithal to identify the circumstances when a specific set of decisions and actions should be applied.

Socialization

Organizational socialization refers to the manner in which individuals learn what behaviors are and are not acceptable within a work setting.[21] It reduces variability in behavior by imbuing employees with a sense of "what's expected" and "how things are done here." When employees share a common frame of reference, they are more likely to act in a similar manner. In other words, socialization standardizes behavior by giving employees an internalized sense of how they should behave.

Importance of Socialization. Socialization is important from both an individual and an organizational perspective. Entering an organization as a new hire is an anxiety-provoking experience. We ask a lot of questions of ourselves in this situation: "What am I supposed to do?" "How am I expected to behave?" "How do I fit in?" As employees learn the answers to these questions, they become functioning organization members. For organizations, socialization is important because new employees are not fully functioning members until they "learn the ropes." And until they internalize an organization's behavioral norms and its way of looking at the world, they are potentially disruptive influences. Or, as Van Maanen and Schein bluntly note, "New members must be taught to see the organizational world as do their more experienced colleagues if the traditions of the organization are to survive."[22]

Socialization becomes more important as a coordination and control mechanism when jobs are remote or sensitive.[23] It is important that individuals with jobs distant from an organization's primary location have a strong internal sense of the organization's interests because there are few, if any, external controls to ensure compliance with organizational mandates. For example, missionaries, spies, and managers of foreign subsidiaries have to act alone in the interests of their organizations. A vivid example of the coordinating and controlling role of socialization is provided by Anthony Jay in his book, *Management and Machiavelli*.

> St. Augustine once gave as the only rule for Christian conduct, "Love God and do what you like." The implication is, of course, that if you truly love God, then you will only ever want to do things which are acceptable to Him. Equally, Jesuit priests are not constantly being rung up, or sent memos, by the head office of the Society. The long, intensive training over many years in Rome is a guarantee that wherever they go afterwards, and however long it may be before they even see another Jesuit, they will be able to do their work in accordance with the standards of the Society.[24]

Socialization also is important in managerial jobs. Managers often have technically simple jobs that require the exercise of discretion. As a result, the use of extensive RPPs and professional training have limited value in coordinating and controlling their behavior. Rather, socialization is the primary mechanism for managerial coordination and control.

Moreover, the extent to which an individual has internalized an organization's norms and values is an important determinant of career advancement. Individuals who show that they share an organization's values and norms, and understand what is important and what is not, are likely to advance through an organization's ranks because they can be trusted to act in its best interest.[25]

Methods of Socialization. Organizations and professions socialize their members in many ways, including formal training programs. Focus on Design 4.3 describes how General Electric and Motorola are using corporate training programs to socialize managers and other employees to new corporate philosophies. Public-sector organizations rely on formal socialization techniques as well. The U.S. Army socializes its new members in boot camp. Police departments socialize new members in police academies.

Socialization is sometimes informal, such as through on-the-job training, where new hires are socialized by their peers within an organization. It can occur in a short period of time, such as a week-long corporate orientation program. Or, it can take place over a much longer period, such as the years of socialization experienced by an aspiring physician through premed, medical school, then an internship and a residency. The shared characteristic of these socialization methods is that they provide individuals with a sense of organizational or professional norms as well as with the training required to perform in their occupational roles.

RELATIONSHIPS BETWEEN JOB SPECIALIZATION AND FORMALIZATION

Research has shown that there are regular patterns in the way that organizations use specialization and formalization. Simple, routine jobs tend to be both horizontally and vertically specialized, with vertical specialization accomplished through the use of extensive RPPs. Training and socialization usually play only a small role in these jobs. On the other hand, as simple, routine jobs are horizontally enlarged and vertically enriched (such as by adopting a team approach to job design), RPPs become less effective and training and socialization more useful.

Complex jobs are usually horizontally but not vertically specialized. There are fewer RPPs and greater use of training to control and coordinate behavior, because complex jobs require employee discretion for effective performance.[26]

Given that these coordination and control mechanisms differ in their situational appropriateness, it should be apparent that their use will vary by hierarchical level and functional area within an organization. For example, RPPs are more likely to be used to standardize behavior in production and staff units when jobs are relatively simple and repetitive (i.e., horizontally

FOCUS ON DESIGN 4.3

Socialization and Corporate Training Programs

When Jack Welch took over as chief executive at General Electric (GE) in 1981, he found a business that had grown fat and lost its competitive edge. His mission since then has been to revitalize GE by redesigning its organization structure and changing its culture. These changes can be characterized as moving GE from being "formal, stable, and gentlemanly" to "tough and aggressive." The key to these changes is nurturing a new breed of managers who understand and accept Welch's "new" management philosophy. GE has expanded management training programs at its Management Development Institute in Croton-on-Hudson (New York) as its best bet for getting the new philosophy across. Over 5,000 GE employees attend the institute each year, including every new manager and every new college recruit. Experienced managers and senior executives are rotated through the institute, too, to learn about the new management philosophy.

A similar story is being written at Motorola. In 1982 it vied with Texas Instruments as the world's largest maker of semiconductors. By 1988 it had slipped to fourth place, and its other businesses were under siege by foreign competitors. To regain its position, Motorola is radically overhauling the way it operates. "Motorola's fall resulted from uneven quality of products and delays in deliveries to customers, who found the company unresponsive to their needs. 'It used to be like dealing with the federal government,' complained one large customer. 'You had trouble getting the simplest questions answered.'" Motorola is trying to improve this situation by changing its corporate culture to emphasize "total customer satisfaction." Since 1984 both managerial and nonmanagerial employees have spent more than 3.2 million man-hours in company-run classes that last from half a day to eight weeks, where they study such subjects as just-in-time inventory and design-for-assembly as well as risk taking and managing change. The message: *Quality and customer satisfaction is what counts.* And the program is beginning to show signs of success. Defect rates have fallen dramatically in some units, others have reached high on-time delivery goals, and in others production costs are falling.

Source: "Jack Welch: How Good a Manager?" *Business Week,* December 14, 1987, 92–103; and "Motorola Sends Its Workforce Back to School," *Business Week,* June 6, 1988, 80–81.

specialized). A greater reliance on training and socialization to standardize behavior will be found in production and other units where jobs are complex and require professional expertise for successful performance, or where simple, repetitive jobs have been horizontally enlarged or vertically enriched. Finally, at higher hierarchical levels, socialization plays an important role in standardizing behavior while RPPs and training become less prominent. These relationships are summarized in Figure 4.5.

Figure 4.5
Relative Emphasis on RPPs, Training, and
Socialization for Different Jobs

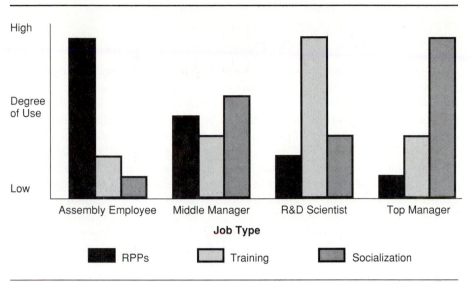

CENTRALIZATION

Centralization refers to the extent to which decision-making authority has been delegated to lower levels of an organization. It is best thought of as a continuum that ranges from centralized to decentralized decision making. A completely centralized organization is one where all decision-making authority rests in the hand of a top manager. A completely **decentralized** organization is one were every employee has a say in making decisions—an organizational democracy. Most organizations fall somewhere in between the two extremes. The degree to which an organization is decentralized is greater when the following conditions prevail:

1. More decisions are made lower down in an organization's hierarchy.

2. The importance of decisions made at lower levels of an organization's hierarchy increases. For example, the greater the sum of capital expenditures that a plant manager can make, the greater the decentralization in this area.

3. The number of functions affected by decisions made at lower hierarchical levels increases. Companies that permit only production decisions to be made at separate branch plants are more centralized, and those that permit personnel and financial decisions as well are more decentralized.

4. Less checking is required on the decision. Decentralization is greatest when no approvals from higher levels are required. Decision making is more centralized when superiors have to be informed of the decision, and still more centralized if superiors have to be consulted before the decision is made. The fewer people above that have to be consulted and the lower those people are in an organization's hierarchy, the greater the degree of decentralization.[27]

How and Why Decentralization Occurs

Most small organizations start out with centralized decision making where an owner/manager makes all the decisions. But as an organization grows, additional hierarchical levels usually are created to clarify roles and responsibilities. And, as additional hierarchical levels are added, the delegation of authority to lower levels is essential to maintain organizational flexibility.

Consider the case of Ed Conry, owner-manager of a small microcomputer store. When the store opened, decision making was highly centralized; Ed made all the decisions about the store's operations, products, vendors, employees, and so on. This is one of the virtues of small, owner-managed firms. Decisions can be made quickly and within the context of an overall organizational strategy because they are being made by a single person.

Ed's microcomputer store was successful. Sales increased, the number of employees grew, and new products and vendors were added. But as the store grew, Ed found it more difficult to make all the decisions about the store's operations. The difficulty was not because Ed lacked information about the decisions that had to be made. Information in Ed's store, like most, was more than abundant; it often was overwhelming. The difficulty was that there were too many decisions that had to be made, and individuals have cognitive limits in the amount of information they can process effectively.[28]

One day, after a regular customer switched his business to a competitor because of slow responses to his inquiries about new products, Ed came to the conclusion that he needed help managing the store. He appointed his best salesperson, Susan, to the position of sales manager. Her new responsibilities were to manage the store's day-to-day operations while Ed focused on strategic decisions, like what new products should be added to those the store already carried. Decentralization had begun.

This scenario is fairly common in small organizations. As they grow larger, decision-making authority needs to be delegated to employees at lower levels because an owner-manager's capacity to process and act on information is limited. As Table 4.3 shows, there are advantages to both centralization and decentralization. The key issue for managers is not whether to centralize or decentralize decision making, but to determine the balance (that is, the point between the two extremes) that best achieves effective coordination and control. Part of that balance will depend on the design of positions at lower organizational levels. The more horizontally and vertically specialized jobs are, the greater the need for centralized control, either through RPPs or by direct supervision. Conversely, as jobs become more complex, and less horizontally and vertically specialized, the more appropriate decentralization is.

Table 4.3
Advantages of Centralization and Decentralization

Centralization
1. A greater uniformity in decisions is possible.
2. Top-level managers are more aware of an organization's future plans and are more likely to make decisions in its best interests.
3. Fewer skilled (and highly paid) managers are required.
4. Less extensive planning and reporting procedures are required.

Decentralization
1. Decisions can be made more quickly.
2. Lower-level managerial problems can be dealt with on the spot.
3. Lower-level managers have an opportunity to develop their decision-making skills.
4. The motivation of lower-level managers is greater when they are entrusted to make decisions rather than always following orders issued at a higher level.
5. An organization's workload is spread so as to allow top-level managers more time for strategic planning.

Centralization and Reorganizations

Organizations wrestle with the issue of balancing centralization and decentralization on an ongoing basis. Changes in organization size, markets, and technology invariably affect the effectiveness of an organization's existing decision-making system. As a result, the issue of where decisions should be made in an organization is a common cause of restructuring. Many reorganizations, for example, during the past decade have focused on decentralizing decision-making authority to increase responsiveness to changing market conditions. The theory is that decentralization moves decision making closer to an organization's markets, which means that individuals lower in the organization's hierarchy—and who are in closer contact with customers—make more decisions. Not only are the decisions made by individuals that have the most information about a situation, but they are made more quickly, which is important in volatile markets.

During 1988 IBM announced a reorganization intended to reverse its earnings slump by reducing the time required to introduce new products tailored to its customers' needs. "Starting in the late 1970s," says the data processing director for an East Coast bank, "IBM got so bureaucratic that they lost sight of the customer. When customers delivered specifications for a system they wanted but IBM didn't have, IBM's sales people suggested there was something wrong with the request—not the products."[29]

A big part of the problem was IBM's cumbersome decision-making structure. Product-development decisions were handed down from a corporate management board composed of 18 senior executives at world headquarters in Armonk, New York, not by people in the field who were in direct customer contact. Consequently, product development often got "bogged down in reams of paperwork, endless management reviews and, often, battling among IBM divisions."[30] The result was that new products often reflected the needs of IBM's top managers, not those of its customers.

IBM reorganized its U.S. operations into seven autonomous business units: PCs, mainframes, minicomputers, communications, microchip manufacturing, programming, and software, with an eighth unit that handles marketing for all the others. Now the business units' general managers negotiate their business plans with top management and then go off and run their divisions, including product development. One of the first major product launches under the reorganized structure was the AS/400 minicomputer, which had been carefully designed to meet customer needs. In less than a year over 25,000 machines—worth $3 billion—were sold, making it the most successful product launch in IBM's history.[31]

Procter & Gamble (P&G) has found itself in a similar situation. Analysts suggest that P&G's historically highly centralized structure slowed its ability to introduce and market new products, and may have contributed to declining rates of growth and profitability during the mid 1980s. As one alumnus commented, "When the chairman has to approve ad copy on every brand, isn't it time to make changes?"[32] This particularly became a problem as P&G's mass markets began to fragment and hence required better targeting for specific consumer groups.

A reorganization of the marketing function at P&G moved authority downward so that decisions could be made more quickly and reflect consumer tastes that varied by market segment. And in some of its big divisions, the responsibilities of divisional advertising managers were divided and moved downward to several group product managers. One result was better tailoring of its advertising to specific market segments. For instance, P&G buys ad time on syndicated health-related TV shows for its low-saturated-fat Puritan oil. It also has six different ad campaigns for Crest toothpaste—including ads targeted for children, Hispanics, and blacks. P&G also began tailoring variations of its product for different market segments. Whereas it sold only one type of Tide detergent between 1947 and 1984, now there are four additional varieties, including Liquid Tide, and Tide with Bleach.[33]

RELATIONSHIPS AMONG SPECIALIZATION, FORMALIZATION, AND CENTRALIZATION

Mintzberg postulated a *congruence hypothesis* about the relationships among the components of organization design just reviewed—specialization, formalization, and centralization (Figure 4.6). He argues that effective structuring requires an internal consistency, or patterns of fit, among job

Figure 4.6
Relationships between Specialization,
Formalization, and Centralization

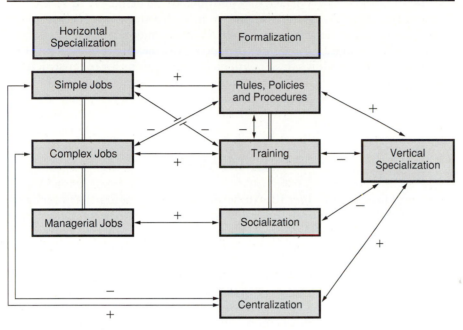

+ indicates positive relationship between design components
− indicates negative relationship between design components

specialization, formalization, and centralization.[34] For example, in two organizations of the same size, you would expect that the one with simpler jobs would have more horizontal and vertical job specialization with extensive RPPs for coordination and control. This organization also would be relatively centralized. In contrast, if jobs in the other organization horizontally enlarged and vertically enriched, you would expect a greater reliance on training for coordination and control, and a more decentralized decision-making system.

A number of other factors also affect the patterns of structuring in an organization. These include an organization's manner of grouping work units (Chapter 5), its technology (Chapter 6), and its strategy and environment (Chapters 7, 8, 9, and 10). As we proceed through the next six chapters, the importance of Mintzberg's congruence hypothesis will become increasingly clear.

The congruence hypothesis also is important because it directs attention to the fact that changing one aspect of an organization's design has implications for other parts of its structure. For example, if managers reduce the horizontal and vertical specialization of production jobs by moving to a team approach, extensive RPPs lose their usefulness as a mechanism of coordination and control. In fact, the continued use of extensive RPPs is likely to undermine the attempt to redesign jobs in such a situation. Such a change also requires some decentralization. In short, a major reason why many redesign efforts fail is that managers forget or are unaware that changing one aspect of an organization's design will have implications for other structural characteristics. We return to this theme in our discussion of the relationship between structure and technology in Chapter 6.

SUMMARY

Learning Objective 1: Identify three design components that managers can manipulate to assure effective organizational performance. Three design components that managers can manipulate to assure effective performance are job specialization, formalization, and centralization.

Learning Objective 2: Differentiate between horizontal and vertical job specialization. Horizontal job specialization refers to the scope of a job, or the extent to which employees perform a complete job. Vertical job specialization refers to the degree of control employees have over their jobs.

Learning Objective 3: Describe the problems associated with job specialization. Research indicates that a high level of job specialization is associated with reduced job satisfaction, worker alienation, decreased employee involvement, and lower levels of organizational commitment.

Learning Objective 4: Distinguish between job enlargement and job enrichment. Job enlargement involves extending the scope of a job so that the number of different activities an employee performs is increased. Job enrichment involves extending the depth of a job so that employee control over the job is increased.

Learning Objective 5: Identify five core job dimensions used to horizontally enlarge and vertically enrich jobs. The five core job dimensions are skill variety, task identity, task significance, autonomy, and performance feedback.

Learning Objective 6: Understand the role of rules, procedures, and policies as coordination and control mechanisms. Rules, procedures, and policies function as coordination and control mechanisms because they standardize employee behavior by informing them of expected job behaviors.

Learning Objective 7: Recognize the role of training as a coordination and control mechanism. Training acts as a mechanism of coordination and control in complex jobs by standardizing employees' skills. It informs them of the decisions and actions required under different circumstances, and provides them with the wherewithal to distinguish among different circumstances.

Learning Objective 8: Outline the importance of socialization to both individuals and organizations. Socialization is important to individuals because it informs them of an organization's behavioral norms. Socialization is important to organizations because it integrates individuals into their organizations by teaching them accepted standards of behavior.

Learning Objective 9: Appreciate how the use of job specialization, rules/policies/procedures, and socialization can vary by hierarchical level and function area within an organization. Horizontal and vertical specialization of jobs is usually found in units that have simple, repetitive tasks. As jobs become more complex, they will be less vertically specialized. More rules, procedures, and policies are likely to be used to achieve coordination and control when jobs are simple. The greater the complexity of a job, the more likely training will be used to achieve coordination and control. Socialization will be the primary mechanism of coordination and control at higher managerial levels, and when jobs are remote or sensitive.

Learning Objective 10: Explain centralization. Centralization of decision making refers to the extent to which decision-making authority is delegated within an organization. An organization is totally centralized if all decision-making authority rests in the hands of one individual. It would be totally decentralized if all members of the organization had an equal say in making decisions.

Learning Objective 11: Detail the advantages and disadvantages of decentralization. On the positive side, decentralization increases the speed and flexibility of decision making, and it motivates and trains managers to assume more responsible positions within an organization. On the negative side, decentralization can result in a loss of top-management control, in duplication of functions, and in a loss of decision-making expertise.

Discussion Questions

1. You have been called into a bank as a consultant to advise its management on problems of high turnover and low morale in the customer service department. This department is responsible for all activities within the bank lobby, including teller operations and the safety deposit vault. The jobs are horizontally specialized: some staff members work the reception area, others are window tellers, some work in the safety deposit vault area, and others are responsible for counting cash and processing checks. Because of the need for security, these jobs are highly regulated through the use of rules, policies, and procedures. What design options can you present to management to reduce turnover and improve morale? How would you justify these options?

2. The XYZ Widget Company has a production workforce of 100 employees. The market for widgets has mushroomed, and it needs to add 50 new production workers. The relationship between managers and production employees is strained because of misunderstandings about the dismissal of a group of workers for poor performance. There subsequently have been work slowdowns, some instances of sabotage, and increasing turnover. Managers are concerned that if they simply hire 50 new employees and introduce them into the existing situation, the new workers will be socialized to accept the current negative behaviors of the production employees. How can management deal with this problem?

3. As CEO of a *Fortune* 500 consumer products firm, you are concerned with the cosmetics division's declining market share. The corporate market research unit informs you that consumers feel the division's products are outdated. Similar reports are received with regularity from the division's sales representatives in the field. All new products are developed at a central R&D facility located at corporate headquarters. What can you do to revitalize this division?

4. You are a candidate to run a large corporation's training and development operation, and you have been asked to submit a statement of your beliefs about the role that training programs can play in making the corporation more competitive. How would you respond?

5. With the increasingly competitive economic environment, corporations around the globe have been busy eliminating layers of management, reducing administrative staff, and pushing decisions down to lower managerial levels. The result of this delayering is not just lower administrative costs but more autonomy for employees at almost every level. Reflecting this trend, Nucor Corp. CEO Ken Iverson says, "I'm a firm believer both in having the fewest number of managerial levels and in delegating authority to the lowest level possible."[35] Do you share Iverson's twin beliefs? Why or why not?

6. A typical General Motors assembly plant can produce more than 100 cars an hour. By comparison, it can take up to six months to build a Rolls-Royce, a car that may cost from $95,000 to $198,000. With this in mind, comment on the advantages and disadvantages of specialized jobs.

DESIGN AUDIT #4

Analyzing Job Specialization, Formalization, and Centralization in Your Organization

This design audit will help you understand the design components of job specialization, formalization, and centralization by having you apply the concepts to your organization.

Job Specialization and Formalization

1. Describe the major activities that are part of your job and the extent to which these activities are regulated by written rules, policies, and procedures (RPPs). (If you are not an employee of the organization, interview someone who is to obtain this information about his or her job.)

Position Title_____

Major Tasks	% RPPS
(a) _____	_____
(b) _____	_____
(c) _____	_____
(d) _____	_____
(e) _____	_____
(f) _____	_____
(g) _____	_____

Analysis: *If your description of tasks is fairly general or there are many (as opposed to just a few) specific activities, the less likely this job is horizontally specialized. The lower the proportion of activities governed by RPPs, the less likely this job is vertically specialized.*

2. Indicate the relative importance of RPPs, training, and socialization as coordination and control mechanisms for this job.

Mechanism	Very Important						Very Unimportant
(a) Written rules, policies, and procedures	7	6	5	4	3	2	1
(b) Training	7	6	5	4	3	2	1
(c) Socialization	7	6	5	4	3	2	1

(d) In the spaces below, give specific examples of these coordination and control mechanisms.

RPPS (examples of how job behavior is regulated through RPPS)

Training (examples of the types of training required for this job)

Socialization (examples of how you were socialized into this job, and how it regulates your behavior)

3. What changes could be made in this job to increase the core job characteristics of skill variety, task identity, task significance, autonomy, and feedback?

4. How would those changes affect the use of RPPs, training, and socialization of coordination and control mechanisms?

    Hint: *If this job is already high on one dimension, go on to the next dimension.*

5. Select five other jobs (or broad types of jobs) in this organization. As has been done in Figure 4.4, plot these jobs (and the one you described in Question 1) according to the extent that they are horizontally and vertically specialized.

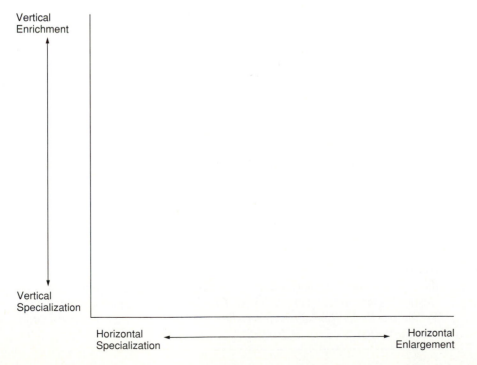

6. For each of these five jobs, how important are RPPs, training, and socialization as coordination and control mechanisms?

		Very Important						Very Unimportant
Job #1 _____	RPPs	7	6	5	4	3	2	1
	Training	7	6	5	4	3	2	1
	Socialization	7	6	5	4	3	2	1
Job #2 _____	RPPs	7	6	5	4	3	2	1
	Training	7	6	5	4	3	2	1
	Socialization	7	6	5	4	3	2	1
Job #3 _____	RPPs	7	6	5	4	3	2	1
	Training	7	6	5	4	3	2	1
	Socialization	7	6	5	4	3	2	1
Job #4 _____	RPPs	7	6	5	4	3	2	1
	Training	7	6	5	4	3	2	1
	Socialization	7	6	5	4	3	2	1
Job #5 _____	RPPs	7	6	5	4	3	2	1
	Training	7	6	5	4	3	2	1
	Socialization	7	6	5	4	3	2	1

Centralization

7. How many hierarchical levels are there between the organization's lowest hierarchical level and its top manager?

_____ Number of Levels

8. At what level are the following types of decisions made (i.e., what hierarchical level has the right of final approval)? [1 = top management]

Hint: You may find this part of the audit easier to do if you discuss where decisions are made with your superior.

Decisions		Comments ($$$ or other limits that apply)
Capital expenditure decisions	_____	
Hiring decisions	_____	
Marketing promotion decisions	_____	
Product change decisions	_____	
Equipment purchase decisions	_____	

Analysis: The higher the level at which decisions are made, the more centralized the organization. You may want to compare your responses with those of a classmate's for a different organization. This comparison should give you a better feel for how the location at which decisions are made can vary from organization to organization.

Notes

1. Richard H. Hall, *Organizations: Structures, Processes, and Outcomes*, 4th ed. (Englewood Cliffs, N.J.: Prentice-Hall, 1986), 98.

2. Lester A. Salamon, "The Goals of Reorganization: A Framework for Analysis," *Administration and Society* 12 (1981): 471–500.

3. William P. Sexton, ed., *Organization Theories.* (Columbus, Oh.: Merrill, 1970), 3.

4. Guy Benveniste, *Professionalizing the Bureaucracy* (San Francisco: Jossey-Bass, 1986), 27–44.

5. U. S. Department of Health, Education, and Welfare, *Work in America* (Cambridge, Mass.: MIT Press, 1973), xv.

6. Studs Terkel, *Working* (New York: Pantheon, 1972), xxix.

7. Interested readers can find historical overviews of quality of worklife programs and alternative job designs in Harry C. Katz, *Shifting Gears: Changing Labor Relations in the U.S. Automobile Industry* (Cambridge, Mass.: MIT Press, 1985), 73–104; Robert A. Rothman, *Working: Sociological Perspectives* (Englewood Cliffs, N.J.: Prentice-Hall, 1987), 231–252; Edward E. Lawler III, *High Involvement Management* (San Francisco: Jossey-Bass, 1980).

8. J. Richard Hackman and Greg R. Oldham, "Development of the Job Diagnostic Survey," *Journal of Applied Psychology* 60 (1975): 159–170; J. Richard Hackman and Greg R. Oldham, *Work Redesign* (Reading, Mass.: Addison-Wesley, 1980).

9. Gene L. Smith, "Improving Productivity in the Controller's Organization," *Management Accounting* (January 1986), 49–51.

10. Patricia Galagan, "Work Teams That Work," *Training and Development Journal* (November 1986), 33–35.

11. For example, see D. S. Pugh, D. J. Hickson, C. R. Hinings, and C. R. Turner, "Dimensions of Organizational Structure," *Administrative Science Quarterly* 13 (1968): 65–106.

12. Gerald Hage and Michael Aiken, "Relationship of Centralization to Other Structural Properties," *Administrative Science Quarterly* 12 (1967): 72–92; Stephen P. Robbins, *Organization Theory: The Structure and Design of Organizations* (Englewood Cliffs, N.J.: Prentice-Hall, 1983), 62–63; and Hall, *Organizations.*

13. Henry Mintzberg, *The Structuring of Organizations* (Englewood Cliffs, N.J.: Prentice-Hall, 1979), chapters 5 and 6. Our usage of terms differs from Mintzberg, who calls these three concepts behavior formalization, training, and indoctrination, respectively.

14. Robert K. Merton, *Social Theory and Social Structure* (Glencoe, Ill.: Free Press, 1957), 151–160.

15. See Hall, *Organizations*, 80–87, for a summary.

16. Peter M. Blau, "Decentralization in Bureaucracies," in Mayer M. Zald, ed. *Power in Organizations* (Nashville, Tenn.: Vanderbilt University Press, 1970); and John Child, "Strategies of Control and Organizational Behavior," *Administrative Science Quarterly* 18 (1973): 1–17.

17. Mintzberg, *The Structuring of Organizations*, 288–291.

18. Douglas McGregor, *The Human Side of Enterprise* (New York: McGraw-Hill, 1960).

19. Mintzberg, *The Structuring of Organizations*, 6.

20. Frank C. Spencer, "Deductive Reasoning in the Lifelong Continuing Education of a Cardiovascular Surgeon," *Archives of Surgery* (1976), 1182, quoted in Mintzberg, *The Structuring of Organizations*, 96.

21. John Van Maanen and Edgar H. Schein, "Toward a Theory of Organizational Socialization," *Research in Organizational Behavior* 1 (1979): 209–264.

22. Van Maanen and Schein, "Toward a Theory of Organizational Socialization," 210.

23. Mintzberg, *The Structuring of Organizations*, 98.

24. Anthony Jay, *Management and Machiavelli* (New York: Penguin, 1970), 70, quoted in Mintzberg, *The Structuring of Organizations*, 99.

25. Van Maanen and Schein, "Toward a Theory of Organizational Socialization," 222.

26. Richard H. Hall, "Professionalization and Bureaucratization," *American Sociological Review* 33 (1968): 92–104; Benveniste, *Professionalizing the Bureaucracy*, 10–14.

27. Adapted from Ernest Dale, *Planning and Developing the Company Organization Structure,* Research Report 20 (New York: American Management Association, 1952), 149–150.

28. Herbert A. Simon, *Administrative Behavior,* 3d ed. (New York: Free Press, 1976), 294.

29. "Big Changes at Big Blue," *Business Week,* February 15, 1988, 94.

30. David E. Sanger, "I.B.M. Forms 5 Autonomous Units," *New York Times,* January 29, 1988, Business Day Section, 30.

31. Joel Dreyfuss, "Reinventing IBM," *Fortune,* August 14, 1989, 30–39.

32. "Procter & Gamble Goes on a Health Kick," *Business Week,* June 29, 1987, 92.

33. "Stalking the New Consumer," *Business Week,* August 28, 1989, 54–62.

34. Mintzberg, *The Structuring of Organizations*, 219.

35. John Grossman, "Ken Iverson: Simply the Best," *American Way,* August 1, 1987, 24.

Unit Grouping and Integrating Mechanisms

Learning Objectives

Upon completing this chapter, you should be able to

1. Understand the concept of interdependence.
2. Explain the difference between functional and workflow interdependence.
3. Describe how unit grouping facilitates coordination.
4. Name the advantages and disadvantages of functional designs.
5. Name the major advantages and disadvantages of divisional designs.
6. Identify different ways of grouping market-based units.
7. Describe the role that integrating mechanisms play in organizations.
8. Name the advantages and disadvantages of matrix designs.
9. Explain why organizations employ a variety of design techniques.

KODAK GETS THE PICTURE

As the inventor of film photography, Kodak enjoyed a head start few companies could match. But the film giant eventually nodded off, leaving its market share relatively unprotected. In a celebrated marketing coup, Fuji Photo Film outbid Kodak to become the official film of the Los Angeles Olympic Games in 1984. The move gained Fuji immediate recognition that the company backed with a full advertising, promotion, and retail campaign.

Kodak got the picture. It began to unleash a series of product improvements, facilitated by a shift from a functionally designed structure to a divisional design of semiautonomous business units. It also reorganized its photographic products division into six distinct business units that focus on specific customer groups—professional photographers, for instance, and the motion picture industry. The divisional organization has helped spawn new ideas as well as improvements for existing products. The resulting films, most notably Ektar 25, 125, and 1,000, are demonstrably the best ever made, and should at least give Kodak some breathing space over Fuji and its other international rivals.

By giving its divisions the autonomy and resources they needed, Kodak was able to become more responsive to the individual areas of its environment. But as Chapter 5 explains, keeping independent units integrated enough to move an organization forward without inhibiting the units' progress is indeed a complex design task.

Source: Bill Saporito, "Companies That Compete Best," *Fortune*, May 22, 1989, 36.

THIS chapter examines how units are grouped within organizations to coordinate activities. After discussing the concept of interdependence, we examine the two primary designs used by organizations—functional and divisional—and the roles they play in coordinating functional and workflow interdependence. We then discuss integrating mechanisms that allow organizations to coordinate activities across unit boundaries. This leads to an examination of an intermediate design, the matrix, that attempts to provide the advantages of the functional and divisional designs without their drawbacks. The chapter closes with an examination of two common mixed designs—hybrid structures and incomplete divisionalization—that reflect the kinds of compromises that managers make in designing organizations.

UNIT GROUPING

The way that jobs are grouped into work units is an important determinant of how an organization's activities are coordinated. Unit grouping facilitates coordination because employees within a work unit (1) have a common supervisor, (2) share common resources, and (3) usually share the same evaluation and reward systems. Moreover, the typical physical proximity of employees within a work unit encourages mutual adjustment, meaning that they are more likely to communicate among themselves and informally coordinate their activities.[1]

In contrast, employees in different work units usually have different supervisors, evaluation and reward systems, and resource pools. Direct communication among different work units is thus more difficult than among employees within the same group. It helps for an organization to specify horizontal lines of communication among different work groups. Otherwise, formal communications must move up through a chain of command from one employee in one group to a common superior, and then back down to the other employee in the other group.[2] These factors, along with differences in the objectives of work units, can make coordination among units difficult.

Interdependence

Managers must make choices about which aspects of an organization's operations are most important to coordinate. As we show in this chapter, different methods of grouping units address different coordination needs. The key concept is **interdependence**, which is created whenever one person or unit does not entirely control all the tasks, information, or resources necessary for completing a project.[3]

Two primary types of interdependence are functional and workflow interdependence. **Functional interdependence** is related to job specialization, and it means that people who do similar jobs within an organization often depend on each other to complete a project. For example, individual specialists in a marketing department may depend on each other in preparing a marketing program. Copywriters draft text, graphic artists and photographers provide illustrations, layout artists prepare ads, and media buyers acquire space to run promotions. The efforts of all these specialists are required to perform the marketing function. A major advantage of grouping jobs by function is that "when like specialists are grouped together, they learn from each other and become more adept at their specialized work."[4] Thus, designing an organization to coordinate functional interdependencies increases operating efficiency.

Workflow interdependence refers to the interdependence of employees across functional areas in producing a good or service. The development, production, and sale of a good, for instance, need the expertise of employees in many different functional areas. R&D scientists develop a prototype, operations engineers translate the design into a production process, production employees make the intended good, and marketing staff arrange for promotion and distribution. When units or positions are grouped by workflow, mutual adjustment by employees across different functional areas is enhanced. Therefore, units grouped by workflow can respond more quickly to changing work conditions because communication is faster.

Both types of interdependence exist in most organizations. The choice of how to group units reflects decisions about which type of interdependence is most important to effective performance of that organization. Generally, a way that minimizes coordination costs is chosen.[5] The two most common ways are **functional** (grouping people by similarities in functional expertise) and **market-based** (grouping people by some aspect of the workflow). As we will show later, unit-grouping choices are not absolute—compromise in design is the rule rather than the exception. And as organization size, technology, and environments change, so will coordination requirements, which leads to redesign. But before we turn to a discussion of these grouping methods, and of their advantages and disadvantages, we will examine the uses and limits of organization charts in depicting unit grouping and organization structure.

Organization Charts

The most common method for depicting an organization's structure is an **organization chart**. The first such chart was constructed in 1854 when Daniel McCallum became general superintendent of the New York and Erie railroad, one of the world's largest railroads at the time, having nearly 500 miles of track. McCallum found that coordinating people and equipment became much more complicated as the railroad's size increased. The organization chart he developed showed who each person was supposed to report to. By 1910 organization charts had become a common feature on the landscape of American business.[6]

An organization chart is a graphic representation of an organization's positions or units and of their formal reporting relationships. The distance from the top to the bottom of a chart is generally viewed as a measure of the relative status of the different levels in an organization. Vertical connecting lines denote prescribed reporting and authority relationships between superiors and subordinates. Units or positions at the same horizontal level are equal in nominal authority.

The organization chart in Figure 5.1 has three hierarchical levels. The president has the most formal authority within the organization; unit heads 1 to 9 have the least. The horizontal lines indicate positions of equal nominal authority (i.e., vice presidents 1 to 3), and the vertical lines depict reporting relationships and formal communication channels. For example, unit heads 1 through 3 report to vice president 1, who in turn reports to the president.

The primary drawback of organization charts is that they present "static representations of what is in reality the dynamic process of organizational life."[7] Typically, "among the omitted details are most of the relationships among people who have no authority or reporting responsibility with respect to each other, but must coordinate their activities anyway [usually through informal communication channels]. Also omitted—by definition—are the informal norms which, in every organization concentrate more authority in certain positions than the [organization chart] anticipates; and all the personal preferences, alliances and coalitions, exchanges of favors, interferences by

Figure 5.1
Sample Organization Chart

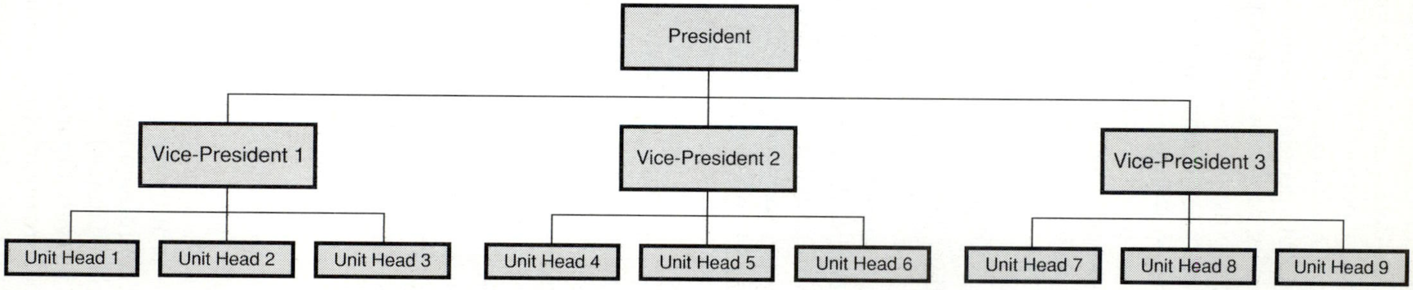

	President	

Vice-President 1	Vice-President 2	Vice-President 3

Unit Head 1 · Unit Head 2 · Unit Head 3

Unit Head 4 · Unit Head 5 · Unit Head 6

Unit Head 7 · Unit Head 8 · Unit Head 9

Figure 5.2
What an Organization Really Looks Like

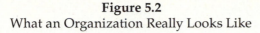
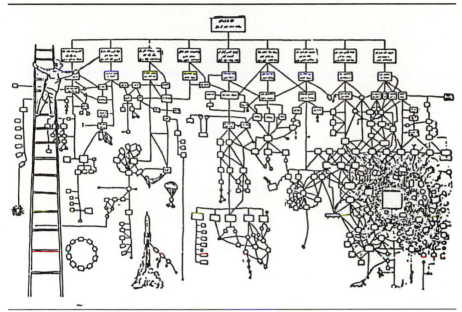

outsiders, and customary breaches of the rules that develop in any well-established organization."[8] What would an organization chart look like if it attempted to capture these dynamics? Figure 5.2 shows an unknown artist's attempt, found on a photocopier, to portray the realities of organizational life.

Although an organization chart falls short in depicting such dynamics accurately, it is a useful tool for understanding how an organization is structured. The labels in the boxes can tell us much about the way that units and positions are grouped. It thus provides a useful "shorthand" for depicting and studying organization structure and design. It also provides clues about the types of compromises that managers make in designing an organization, a major one being the use of different grouping principles at different organizational levels.

FUNCTIONAL DESIGNS

Development of Functional Designs: Games "R" Us, Ltd.

The easiest way to understand different structural configurations and the coordination needs they address is to examine how a small organization might change over time as it grows. Consider a hypothetical small toy

Figure 5.3
Games "R" Us—Original Structure and Three Years Later

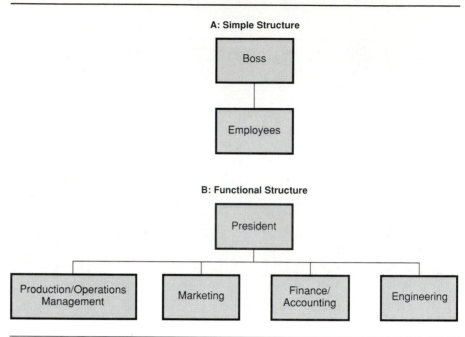

company, Games "R" Us, Ltd., whose founder and owner initially assembled a board game she had designed, with the help of her husband and children, in the basement of their home. As sales grew, she rented a warehouse and hired high school students to work part-time on Saturdays and weekends. Soon she had five full-time employees, then ten, then fifteen. At this point, the company's structure could be depicted as shown in Figure 5.3 (Panel A): the owner and several employees are grouped into a single work unit. All employees report directly to the owner, and she coordinates their activities through personal supervision. This type of structure, sometimes called a **simple structure** because tasks are not highly specialized, is quite flexible.[9] However, its ability to cope with complexity is constrained because all coordination depends on the owner, whose capacity is necessarily limited.

As Games "R" Us grows and its complexity increases, the owner will no longer be able to coordinate all its activities and effectively perform other necessary managerial tasks. Suppose that, informally, she asks one employee to help with sales (probably calling on small accounts), another to help schedule work hours, and another to order materials. They become her assistants. As these jobs become full-time for these employees, and other workers are hired to replace them as production workers, the company begins to develop a formal organization structure that is grouped along functional lines, as Figure 5.3 (Panel B) shows.

A functionally structured organization groups its activities into separate units or departments, each of which undertakes a distinctive function—marketing, production/operations, finance/accounting, engineering, and so on. Figure 5.4 presents a fully implemented functional structure for the toy company—now called Lots-of-Games, Inc.—after some ten years of successful growth. A deeper specialization of functional activities is clearly apparent.

Advantages and Disadvantages of Functional Designs

The principal strength of a functional structure is that as the number of employees performing the same function increases, functional unit grouping allows for an increasing refinement of specialized skills. For example, when all the engineers in an organization are grouped into a central engineering department, it is possible to distinguish among electrical, mechanical, industrial, and other engineering specialties. The combination of otherwise underutilized, scattered, and duplicated facilities and personnel into one functional unit allows for greater functional expertise, a gain in economies of scale, and decreasing overhead costs.

A functional design is particularly effective when an organization can coordinate its subunits' activities by means of various types of planning and budgeting mechanisms. Of course, the use of plans and budgets assumes that major operating contingencies are known, and that they lend themselves to the development of rules, policies, and procedures. Organizations where the same tasks are done over and over would be good candidates for a functional design. Those that mass produce commodity-type items, such as automobiles, refrigerators, or televisions to sell from on-hand stock, or that provide standardized services such as retail sales and food services often group jobs and positions by function. Focus on Design 5.1 shows a utility company management memo that captures the central role of planning in organizations with functionally grouped units—plans provide the basis of managerial control by specifying what actions should be taken to achieve an organization's goals.

Additional benefits of a functional design are that it

- Provides a simple communication and decision network.
- Facilitates the measurement of functional area outputs and results.
- Simplifies the training of functional specialists.
- Gives status to major functional areas.
- Preserves strategic control at top-management level.

The major shortcoming of a functional design is that the larger the number of work units, the more difficult it is to use plans and budgets to coordinate activities; hence cooperation among units may fail. This problem

Figure 5.4
Lots-of-Games, Inc.—Functional Unit Grouping Fully Implemented

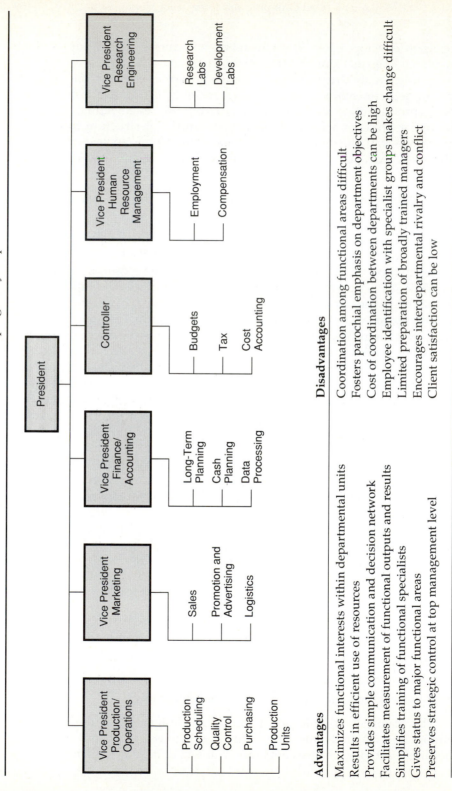

Advantages

Maximizes functional interests within departmental units
Results in efficient use of resources
Provides simple communication and decision network
Facilitates measurement of functional outputs and results
Simplifies training of functional specialists
Gives status to major functional areas
Preserves strategic control at top management level

Disadvantages

Coordination among functional areas difficult
Fosters parochial emphasis on department objectives
Cost of coordination between departments can be high
Employee identification with specialist groups makes change difficult
Limited preparation of broadly trained managers
Encourages interdepartmental rivalry and conflict
Client satisfaction can be low

FOCUS ON DESIGN 5.1

Planning and Coordination in the Functional Structure

**Without goals,
you cannot plan.**

**Without plans,
you cannot control.**

**Without control,
you cannot manage**

Either yourself or others.

fosters a parochial emphasis on work-unit objectives at the expense of broader organizational goals. For example, production/operations will want easily produced products, whereas research and engineering will want elegantly designed products, and marketing will want products that meet specific customer needs.

Other disadvantages of the functional design are that it often

- Requires higher coordination costs as an organization's size increases.
- Encourages employees to identify more with their work units than an organization as a whole, making change difficult.
- Fails to prepare broadly trained managers.
- Results in lower client satisfaction with service than other designs.
- Has a potential for information overload at the top of an organization.

DIVISIONAL DESIGNS

A functional design becomes unwieldy as an organization grows. Coordination becomes a problem, and then organizations often turn to *divisional* designs. Divisionalized structures group workflow interdependencies together, increasing an organization's ability to simultaneously manage operations in several markets. As a result, unit grouping in divisionalized structures can be referred to as *market-based grouping*. Three types are commonly used by organizations: by product, by location, and by customer. We will examine each.

Grouping Units by Product

With product grouping, each major product line is managed through a separate and semiautonomous division. Specialists of different types are grouped together to perform all the duties necessary to produce an individual good or service within each division. The result is a structure that provides both strategic responsiveness and efficient coordination of a larger number of specialized inputs. For example, 3M (which sells about 40,000 products) is organized into 40 autonomous product divisions, each doing its own research and development, production, and marketing.

Lots-of-Games Ten Years Later. If we returned to our toy company—now named MegaToy Corp.—after ten more years of growth, we might find that it has added other product lines such as dolls, soft goods, and mechanical toys. An organization chart for MegaToy Corp., reorganized along product lines, is shown in Figure 5.5. Each division (games, dolls, and mechanical toys) is a replica of an individual, often functionally structured, organization.

Figure 5.5
MegaToy Corp.—Product Grouping

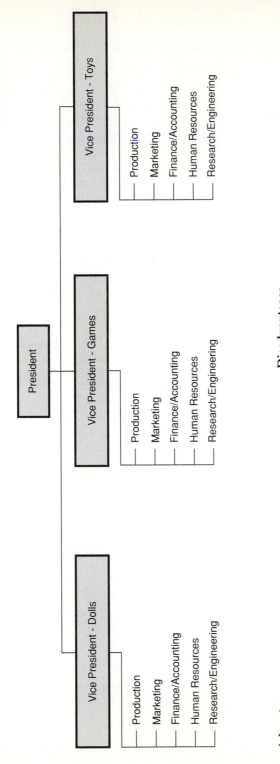

Advantages

Evaluates departments as autonomous profit centers
Accommodates growth
Facilitates coordination among functions for rapid response
Adds flexibility to an enterprise's structure
Focuses on client needs
Develops broadly trained managers

Disadvantages

Increases coordination problems among specialized product areas
Leads to decreased communication among functional specialists
Contributes to a duplication of services in each division

Advantages and Disadvantages of Divisional Designs

A major advantage of a divisional design over a functional design is it enables an organization to evaluate the use of cash and other resources. Departments in a functional structure can be assessed as either an expense center or a revenue center but not both. Inflows or outflows of cash can be linked to each unit, but a single unit usually does not contain both. In contrast, since units in a divisionalized structure are grouped to contain the workflow inter-dependencies for each product, they can be evaluated as profit centers, because they have identifiable cash flows of both revenues and expenses. This allows top managers to set profit targets for each division, which is not easily done for functional departments. And because workflow interdependencies are contained with a unit, there is usually no pressing need to closely coordinate activities across divisions. The result is more decentralization of decision-making authority to division managers than is common for department managers in functional structures. Division managers often are given considerable freedom in determining how to meet their divisions' performance goals, and this enables them to respond more quickly to changes in their markets.

Additional benefits of product-unit grouping, and divisional designs generally, are that they

- More easily accommodate growth. New divisions can be added on a self-contained basis having a similar relationship to headquarters as existing divisions.

- Have shorter lines of communication between functional experts within a division, increasing their ability to respond rapidly to changing market conditions.

- Provide a greater focus on customer needs, leading to more responsive customer service and increased customer satisfaction, because decisions are made closer to the market.

- Develop broadly trained managers, because division managers are responsible for all functional areas within their unit.

The major disadvantage associated with product-unit grouping, and divisional designs in general, is the relative lack of in-depth functional expertise they provide. Dividing functional experts among the divisions reduces the potential for developing specialized functional expertise. Other disadvantages of a divisional design are that it

- Decreases professional communication among functional specialists.
- Duplicates services, such as marketing research and accounting in each division, thus losing the advantage of economies of scale.

Grouping Units by Location

Also known as *territorial, geographic,* or *regional divisionalization,* grouping units by location is especially appropriate when an organization's operations are physically dispersed, or located in several regions with different legal, political, or cultural environments. Division boundaries are determined by these different environments or by distance. Its principal advantages are that it (1) reduces transportation costs by locating units near regional resources or markets, and (2) allows divisions operating in different regions to better sense and adapt to changes in local market needs. Consider McDonald's worldwide operations. Divisionalizing by location allows the firm to be responsive to local differences in consumer tastes. In Brazil, McDonald's serves a soft drink made from guarana, an Amazonian berry. In Malaysia, Singapore, and Thailand, it serves milkshakes flavored with durian, a foul-smelling (to non-Asian noses) southeast Asian fruit.[10]

Examples of organizations that are grouped by location to overcome coordination problems because of geographic dispersion include the Federal Reserve, Internal Revenue Service, and the U.S. Postal Service. Multinational organizations such as Massey-Ferguson, Singer, Ford, NEC, ITT, Matsushita, and Unilever, use geographic divisionalization to sense and adapt to the local needs of their diverse markets.

MegaToy Corp. Revisited. Our toy company has added a retail division to sell its products directly to customers. Managers of the retail sales division, understanding regional differences in toy tastes and the need to cater to them, have organized the division on a regional basis. Figure 5.6 shows the organization chart for this division. In this structure, regional managers are responsible for such functional areas as accounting, human resources management, and marketing within their divisions.

Grouping Units by Customer

Another common divisional design is organizing units by the specific customer segments that an organization serves. This grouping method often is selected when an organization's clients have very different needs. Commercial banks, for example, have different divisions for various types of customers—airlines, manufacturing companies, stock brokers, consumers, and so on. Grouping by customer (retail, government, and industrial) is shown in Figure 5.7.

While customer divisionalization has the advantage of tying performance to requirements of key market segments, it is not without disadvantages. Given the diverse nature of the customer groups served, establishment of uniform company-wide practices is difficult. As a consequence, pressure often develops for special treatment of various buyers, which may or may not be merited. An additional drawback emerges when customer-based

Figure 5.6
MegaToy Corp., Retail Sales Division—Grouping by Location

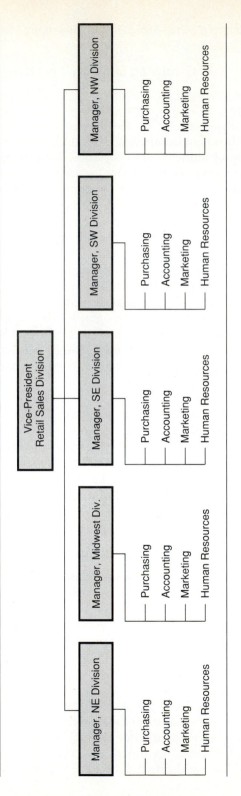

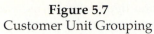

Figure 5.7
Customer Unit Grouping

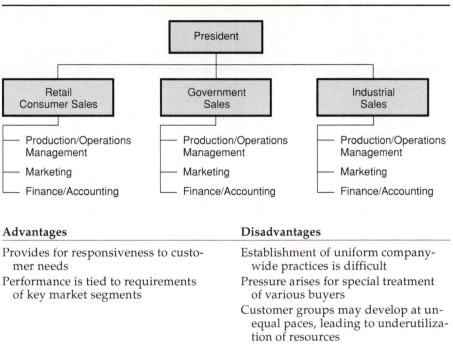

Advantages	Disadvantages
Provides for responsiveness to customer needs	Establishment of uniform company-wide practices is difficult
Performance is tied to requirements of key market segments	Pressure arises for special treatment of various buyers
	Customer groups may develop at unequal paces, leading to underutilization of resources

divisions develop at an unequal pace. During periods of recession, for example, banks may find the number of new construction loans to be processed too low to justify staffing a separate division. However, during economic expansion, that same market segment may grow at such a rapid rate that staff and facilities are strained to meet the demand.

COMPARING FUNCTIONAL AND DIVISIONAL DESIGNS

As might be expected, the two basic organization designs, functional and divisional, are related to the other structural components. Functional structures tend to have a higher degree of job specialization, a greater use of formal rules, regulations, and policies, and more centralized decision making than divisional structures. Moreover, as the preceding discussion shows, the advantages of functional designs parallel the disadvantages of divisional designs, and vice versa. A functional design is efficient because of economies of scale, and it leads to greater depth of expertise within the functional areas. But coordination among work units can become a problem as an organization grows. Also, the functional structure tends to be slow in responding to changes in its environment because of its reliance on plans, budgets, and vertical communication channels for coordination.

In contrast, divisional designs improve coordination among functional areas within a workflow (be it a workflow based on product, location, or customer). As a result, a divisional organization can respond more quickly to changing market conditions. But it also tends to be less efficient than its functional counterpart because of fewer economies of scale. Moreover, the smaller groupings of functional specialists within each division results in less depth of functional expertise. Clearly, managers make trade-offs in favoring one design over the other.

What kind of design seems to work best? Overall, functional structures tend to work best for small to medium-size organizations with one or a few goods or services, and for organizations that operate in relatively stable environments. Divisionalized structures appear to work best in medium-size to large organizations with several or many goods or services, and for organizations that operate in changing environments.[11]

INTEGRATING MECHANISMS[12]

Once managers have grouped units to take advantage of the efficiency and specialization of a functional design, or the responsiveness of a divisional design, they invariably encounter situations that prey on that design's weaknesses. Usually they are reluctant to completely redesign their organizations, particularly when the problem may be temporary or when the advantages of the existing structure are pronounced. So how do they deal with the problem challenging their organization design?

Most often, they use **integrating mechanisms** to increase horizontal communication and thus supply what their existing structural design lacks. Thus, an organization that emphasizes the coordination of functional interdependencies can use integrating mechanisms to manage important workflow interdependencies; and similarly, a divisionalized structure that emphasizes the coordination of workflow interdependencies can use integrating mechanisms to manage important functional interdependencies. Consider the following two scenarios:

Example 1. A small, functionally organized pharmaceutical company's R&D lab has developed a new compound that shows great promise in reducing the risk of coronary heart disease. Preliminary approvals have been acquired from the Food and Drug Administration, and industry analysts estimate a huge potential market. The company that is "first to market" will reap substantial short-run profits because of a lack of competition and, over the long run, the drug will remain profitable because of brand recognition and loyalty. Several of the company's competitors are working on similar drugs. The problem facing management is how to get the product to market quickly.

The effort will involve R&D scientists, process engineers, production staff, quality-control engineers, and the marketing and distribution units. The current functional structure works well in efficiently producing the company's existing inventory of drugs. But it is not designed for the rapid action and coordination across different functional areas needed to get the new drug to market. The use of vertical communication channels and the fact that each unit has other responsibilities are likely to further slow the process. What should top management do?

Example 2. A large, divisionally structured insurance company organized by product line has received notification through the *Federal Register* that the government is proposing regulations on underwriting practices across all lines of insurance. Underwriting specialists in the divisions estimate that the proposed regulations would, at best, lower company profits and likely create negative cash flows in some divisions, while not remedying the problems that they are supposed to correct. A 60-day period is allowed for interested parties to comment on the proposed regulations and recommend changes. The problem facing management is that its response must represent the concerns of all the divisions. None of the individual divisions have the depth of underwriting expertise to draft a response that would fit this requirement. What should top management do?

These types of problems are common. Organizations regularly encounter situations that require coordination across unit boundaries that cannot be readily accommodated by their existing design. The pharmaceutical company needs workflow coordination whereas its structure is adept at coordinating within functional areas. The opposite is true for the insurance company, in which the immediate need is for coordination within a functional area whereas the organization is designed to manage across functional areas.

Organizations frequently deal with these types of coordination problems by using the integrating mechanisms shown in Figure 5.8. The rectangle in the figure is divided to indicate the relative emphasis on coordinating functional or workflow interdependence. At the functional end, the primary emphasis is on coordinating functional interdependence; at the market-based end, it is on coordinating workflow interdependence. Note how using different types of integrating mechanisms shift an organization's emphasis in coordinating interdependence. For example, a liaison position (explained shortly) in a functional structure moves the coordination emphasis slightly away from functional interdependence toward workflow interdependence, but less so than would a *standing committee* (also explained shortly). Conversely, a liaison position in a divisionalized structure shifts the coordination emphasis away

Figure 5.8
Effects of Integrating Mechanisms on the Coordination of
Functional and Workflow Interdependence

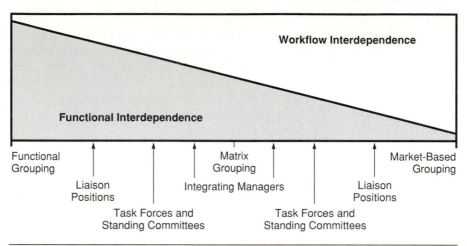

Source: Adapted from Jay Galbraith, *Designing Complex Organizations* (Reading, Mass.: Addison-Wesley, 1973), 114; Henry Mintzberg, *The Structuring of Organizations* (Englewood Cliffs, N.J.: Prentice-Hall, 1979), 176.

from workflow interdependence toward functional interdependence, but less than a standing committee would. The following sections describe these integrating mechanisms.

Liaison Positions

The simplest integrating mechanism is the **liaison position**. An individual in this position is designated to act as the common point of contact for two units that need on-going communication. For example, in the case of the pharmaceutical company, a process engineer might be designated by the engineering department to be the liaison with the production unit. He would be responsible for answering questions and assisting in implementing the new production process for the new drug—either while physically remaining in engineering or, more likely, being temporarily located in the production unit. A formal liaison increases horizontal communication between units and allows problems to be dealt with more quickly than through vertical communication channels.

Task Forces and Standing Committees

Task forces and **standing committees** bring together individuals representing units with a common problem or interest. Task forces are temporary, while standing committees are permanent (or at least of longer duration). In the case of the earlier mentioned insurance company, for instance, a task force of underwriters from all the product divisions could be assembled to discuss and draft a response to the proposed federal regulations. Its charge would be to develop a response accurately representing the views of all the divisions, and to make recommendations taking each division's concerns into account. Once a response was formulated, the task force would be disbanded. Because representatives from all the affected units would be included in the task force, differences in opinion and the potential impact of various recommendations could be explored quickly. Again, communication between units would be speeded up by creation of a horizontal communication channel.

Integrating Managers

Integrating managers, such as brand managers in consumer products firms, coordinate the efforts of the units involved in a particular project. Jay Galbraith notes that "managers who occupy [these positions] do not supervise any of the actual work. Instead they assist those who do, so that the work is coordinated in the best interests of the organization."[13] As a result, much of an integrating manager's job is negotiation between units, which requires that the manager understand each unit's goals and time frame and find a way to satisfy their differences. The following description of one brand manager's job illustrates the types of coordination problems integrating managers deal with.

> Ellen Fisher is a product manager responsible for the introduction of new soap products. She works through several functional departments, including market research, the development laboratory's production, and sales. In designing the new product, market research usually conducts a test of consumer reactions. In this case, the market research head, Hank Fellers, wants to run the standard field test on the new brand in two preselected cities. Ellen is opposed to this because it would delay the product introduction date of September 1; if that date can be met, sales has promised to obtain a major chain-store customer (using a house brand label) whose existing contract for this type of soap is about to expire.
>
> At the same time, manufacturing is resisting a commitment to fill this large order by the date sales established because, "new product introductions have to be carefully meshed in our schedule with other products in our schedule our facilities are producing . . . . "[14]

Integrating managers can have varying levels of formal authority. The first is the *power to approve*, meaning to accept or reject the plans formulated by units. The second level is the *power to propose*, meaning to suggest plans of action to the units, based on the manager's estimates or forecasts of activity and need. The third level is the *power to contract*, meaning to control the budget of a project and thus coordinate the activities of various units by contracting for their services. If an internal unit is unresponsive to project needs, an integrating manager often can contract for the needed services outside the organization. As the power of an integrating manager increases on all these levels, so does his or her ability to coordinate unit activities.[15]

In the case of the earlier mentioned pharmaceutical company, the most likely solution to the unit-coordination problem is using an integrating manager. Depending on how critical it is that the drug be produced quickly and well, the organization should give the integrating manager an appropriate amount of formal authority (and thus leverage in coordinating unit activities).

The final integrating device is a *matrix design,* which is also a technique for designing a whole organization.

MATRIX DESIGNS

Organizing activities by means of a matrix design entails an attempt to cross product unit grouping with functional unit grouping to obtain the best (and avoid the worst) consequences of each. In essence, the **matrix method** simultaneously coordinates both functional and workflow interdependence by overlaying functional and product (or project) lines of authority to form a grid or matrix. Many employees therefore belong to a functional or specialist group as well as a product or project group. They report to two or more superiors—a permanent boss in the functional unit and one or more temporary bosses (called *project managers*), who direct various projects.

This arrangement eliminates duplication of overhead costs, since basic activities such as engineering, purchasing, and human resource management are provided by an organization's customary functional units. Since employees report to project managers regarding project objectives and to their respective functional managers regarding technical-specialist objectives, the two kinds of managers have separate but complementary responsibilities. Functional managers are responsible for developing and deploying, in the form of skilled personnel, a technical resource. Project managers are responsible for project completion.

A typical matrix structure is shown in Figure 5.9. Universal Aerospace (a hypothetical company) is divided into functional departments (such as aerospace engineering, mechanical engineering, and electrical engineering), as well as into project groups based on unique product needs. As the figure shows, functional units with the expertise required by the project groups are incorporated into the matrix. Other units typically retain a more traditional place in an organization's structure. The diamond shape of the matrix indicates the equal authority of the project and functional managers. Consequently, an electrical engineer with expertise in navigation systems, for example, may report to several bosses over time. Suppose she is assigned to the Satellite Systems Project to design a navigation system. First she would report to the Satellite Systems' project manager. After completion of that

Figure 5.9

Universal Aerospace Company—Matrix Unit Grouping

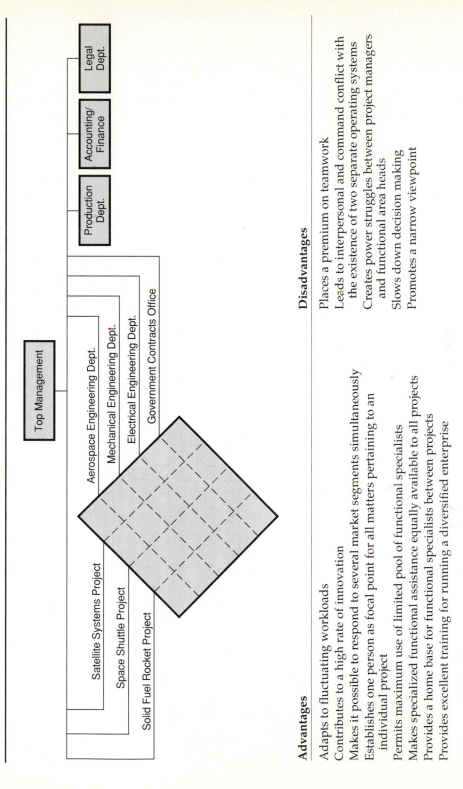

Advantages

Adapts to fluctuating workloads
Contributes to a high rate of innovation
Makes it possible to respond to several market segments simultaneously
Establishes one person as focal point for all matters pertaining to an individual project
Permits maximum use of limited pool of functional specialists
Makes specialized functional assistance equally available to all projects
Provides a home base for functional specialists between projects
Provides excellent training for running a diversified enterprise

Disadvantages

Places a premium on teamwork
Leads to interpersonal and command conflict with the existence of two separate operating systems
Creates power struggles between project managers and functional area heads
Slows down decision making
Promotes a narrow viewpoint

The diagram shows:

Top Management connecting to:
- Production Dept.
- Accounting/Finance Dept.
- Legal Dept.

And functional departments:
- Aerospace Engineering Dept.
- Mechanical Engineering Dept.
- Electrical Engineering Dept.
- Government Contracts Office

And projects:
- Satellite Systems Project
- Space Shuttle Project
- Solid Fuel Rocket Project

project, she might be reassigned to the Space Shuttle Project to test navigation system components and therefore report to the Space Shuttle project manager. All the while, as a member of the electrical engineering department's staff, she would continue reporting to the electrical engineering department manager.

Matrix as Integrating Mechanism

Matrix designs are commonly used as an integrating mechanism by large organizations with functional or divisional structures, often in the form of project teams. Instead of redesigning the whole organization as a matrix, a special matrix unit is established. Personnel with the different types of expertise necessary to complete a specific project are assigned to the matrix unit from other departments or divisions. The interdisciplinary nature of project teams can benefit a large organization by increasing the rate of new-product innovation.[16] If project teams are able to maintain autonomy while retaining access to the functional resources of the larger organization, they can operate with the flexibility of a small firm but all the benefits of a big firm's support. Moreover, it is common for project leaders to become "product champions," who act as entrepreneurs for their products and thus increase the chances of success. Focus on Design 5.2 describes how IBM used a matrix project team to develop the IBM PC.

Advantages and Disadvantages of Matrix Designs

The major benefits associated with a matrix design are that it

- Establishes one person (a project manager) as a focal point for all matters pertaining to an individual project.
- Makes possible the maximum use of a limited pool of functional specialists.
- Provides specialized functional assistance to all projects.
- Provides a home base for functional specialists as ongoing projects are completed.
- Produces well-trained managers for a diversified enterprise in which complex and conflicting interests must be balanced.

Although the matrix design offers many advantages, it is very prone to conflict because there are two separate lines of authority (project and functional). It is easy to understand how flare-ups can arise, particularly when a project manager needs the cooperation of a functional manager to obtain the resources needed to accomplish project objectives, or when the two types of managers make contradictory demands on an employee. Consider the conflict inherent in the fact that project managers are charged with completing specialized tasks within budget and time constraints, while functional

FOCUS ON DESIGN 5.2

How Do You Make an Elephant Dance?

After watching the personal computer market grow for five years, IBM decided to enter this entrepreneurial industry in August 1980. The problem, as former IBM chairman Frank T. Cary put it, was, "How do you make an elephant dance?" particularly in an industry where small, fast-moving companies are the rule, not the exception. The answer was the development of an "independent business unit" relatively unencumbered by the IBM bureaucracy in Armonk, New York. In a converted Boca Raton, Florida, warehouse with a leaky roof, few windows, and a malfunctioning air conditioner, manager Don Estridge's mandate was to get IBM into the personal computer business within a year. Estridge recruited people throughout the corporation to work in his small, integrated unit. "I had reporting to me," he explained, "R&D, the developers of activities for both programming and engineering, all of marketing, all advertising, all sales, manufacturing, and finance. So any decision we wanted to make was made at my level or below." Reviews and evaluations of the project were frequent but they were conducted at the highest levels of the corporation, which avoided tangling it up in the IBM bureaucracy.

This freedom allowed the unit to break with a number of IBM's traditional ways of doing business. Rather than relying on in-house expertise, the unit took the advice of outside software companies and chose a 16-bit microprocessor at a time when nearly all the personal computers on the market used 8-bit processors. Rather than treating the design as proprietary information, they published the PC specifications so that people outside the company could write software. Rather than manufacturing all the components, they bought extensively from outside vendors. And rather than using IBM's salesforce exclusively, they also recruited retail outlets to distribute the PC. Introduced in August 1981, the PC was an enormous success and quickly became the industry standard. The small group of 12 people that began working on the project in August 1980 grew to 10,000 by the end of 1984 with sales of about $5 billion. Indeed, the elephant danced.

Sources: "Here Come the Intrapreneurs," *Time*, February 4, 1985, 36–37; Robert Levering, Michael Katz, and Milton Moscowitz, *The Computer Entrepreneurs* (New York: New American Library, 1984), 20–27; "Personal Computers: And the Winner Is IBM," *Business Week*, October 3, 1983, 76–95.

managers must attempt to allocate their resources fairly across numerous projects. Moreover, experience indicates it is more efficient (and less stressful) for employees to report to only one superior.

Due to its complexities, matrix designs require effective teamwork, a lot of time for development, a different style of management, a willingness on the part of all concerned to learn new rules based on a new perspective, and a change in behaviors.[17] It is not an easy design to manage, and the costs of coordination are high. Focus on Design 5.3 shows how one firm dealt with the problems created by a matrix design.

Despite the potential for interpersonal conflict, matrix designs are valuable for their flexibility and responsiveness to organizing activities. They are particularly well suited to fluctuating workloads and have the advantage of allowing an organization to respond simultaneously to various market segments that may be critical for their success. As projects are completed, they are simply disbanded, and project members return to their respective functional units for reassignment.

When to Use Matrix Designs

Obviously, matrix designs should not be adopted indiscriminately. They should be considered only when functional and divisional designs are inadequate for the task at hand. These situations are most likely to occur when[18]

- Complex, short-run products are an organization's principal output.
- A complicated product design calls for both innovation and timely completion.
- Several kinds of sophisticated skills are needed for designing, building, and testing a product—skills that need constant updating and development.
- A rapidly changing marketplace calls for significant changes in products, perhaps even between the time they are conceived and the time they are delivered.

MIXED DESIGNS

As we noted earlier in this chapter, the design choices managers make often reflect compromises—as evidenced in the mixed structures that often result. Managers do not simply pull organization charts off the shelf and apply them. They design organizations to meet specific coordination needs. In this section, we'll examine how they mix and match different aspects of the designs discussed thus far, producing hybrid structures and incomplete divisionalization.

Hybrid Structures

An organization should use the unit-grouping strategies that best enable it to cope with a variety of contingencies—varying complexity in the work being done, different market conditions, changing technology—that may

---

FOCUS ON DESIGN 5.3

Managing a Matrix at Ebasco

Ebasco Services Incorporated, Enserch Corporation's energy-oriented engineering and consulting division, adopted a matrix design to manage large, complex construction projects. An internal survey showed that the matrix design was causing mounting tensions and rising levels of conflict at many of the projects' sites. To address the identified problems, the corporation's organization development (OD) staff designed and implemented a variety of training and troubleshooting programs.

The OD staff held more than 100 formal seminars on the matrix design for employees to reduce the misunderstandings that were identified in the survey. It also developed a dual performance-evaluation system to ensure that an employee who reported to two managers would be evaluated by both. This way an employee receiving conflicting orders would avoid being penalized by one manager for following the orders of the other.

A complex computerized career-tracking program was implemented to match employee skills with projected needs. The system is expected to give Ebasco early warning of potential skill shortages, and it assures employees that their strengths are on record, ready to be tapped as promotions become available. The OD staff also has conducted a number of team-building interventions in which a facilitator meets with project personnel who are in conflict in order to help identify and resolve the underlying causes of the conflict.

Follow-up surveys indicate that the problems have not been eradicated, but the level of tension and conflict at the project sites has been dramatically reduced.

Source: "How Ebasco Makes the Matrix Method Work," *Business Week,* June 15, 1981, 126.

---

differ across its levels and parts, particularly as it grows. In other words, different areas of operation may require different designs. Some parts of an organization's structure may be functionally organized, others market-based, and yet others a mix of the two. A **hybrid structure** is the result.

Let's take a final look at MegaToy Corp. Over time MegaToy has grown into a fully integrated designer, manufacturer, and distributor of entertainment products. Since our last visit some years ago, the company has entered the rapidly changing electronic games market, acquired a video rental chain, and developed its own nationwide toy store chain, MegaToys "R" Us.

Looking at MegaToy's current organization chart (Figure 5.10), we can see that its overall structure is divisionalized by product. Once we start looking at the divisions' structures (Figure 5.11), we see a variety of grouping principles being used. The board game division (Panel A) is functionally organized. Its major units are production, new-game development, sales, and

Figure 5.10
MegaToys, Inc.—Hybrid Structure

a variety of staff units such as human resources, accounting, purchasing, and so on. If we look at the next level in the structure, we find that the sales staff are grouped by customer: nationwide chains, independent toy stores, and MegaToys "R" Us. Each customer group has different needs, which customer-based unit grouping accommodates. In contrast, the production unit is functionally organized—printing, assembly, packing, and shipping—for maximum production efficiency.

In contrast, part of the electronics game division (Panel B) is organized as a matrix, which helps it develop and introduce new games consistent with rapidly changing consumer tastes and advancing technologies. MegaToys "R" Us (Panel C) is geographically divisionalized. Since consumers' toy-buying preferences differ by region, geographic divisionalization makes it easier for the stores in each region to carry the product mix that best fits their local markets. Individual store operations are fairly routine, and they are functionally organized into personnel, purchasing, sales, and accounting work units. In short, different design strategies are used in different parts of MegaToy's structure. The strategy used in each area reflects its particular coordination needs.

Incomplete Divisionalization

Another common mixed design is known as **incomplete divisionalization**. An organization is completely divisionalized when its staff functions (human resources, accounting, sales, purchasing, etc.) are included in its division's structures. It is incompletely divisionalized when some staff functions report directly to corporate headquarters. The greater the number of staff units reporting directly to corporate headquarters, the more incompletely divisionalized an organization is.

Figure 5.11
MegaToys, Inc.—Divisional Designs

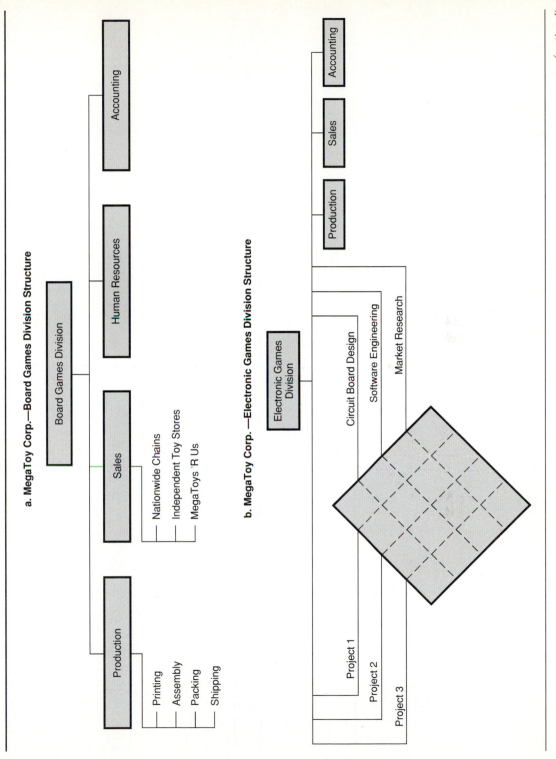

a. MegaToy Corp.—Board Games Division Structure

Board Games Division

- Production
  - Printing
  - Assembly
  - Packing
  - Shipping
- Sales
  - Nationwide Chains
  - Independent Toy Stores
  - MegaToys 'R Us
- Human Resources
- Accounting

b. MegaToy Corp. —Electronic Games Division Structure

Electronic Games Division

- Circuit Board Design
- Software Engineering
- Market Research
- Production
- Sales
- Accounting

Project 1
Project 2
Project 3

(continued)

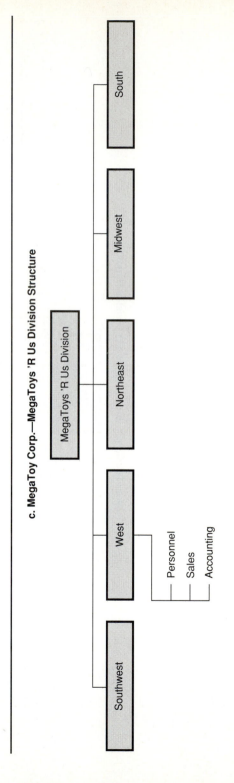

Figure 5.11 *(continued)*

c. MegaToy Corp.—MegaToys 'R Us Division Structure

a. Board Games Division Structure
b. Electronic Games Division Structure
c. MegaToys 'R Us Division Structure

When an organization's divisions produce similar goods or services and their operations are similar, incomplete divisionalization allows some economies of scale in staff functions despite divisionalized operations. This design is most common when geographic or customer unit grouping is used to form divisions. It is less common when product grouping is used, unless an organization's products are closely related.

Conglomerates are the best example of a completely divisionalized organization. These organizations have a number of divisions that typically produce a wide range of unrelated goods and services. ITT Corporation, for example, has a large number of product divisions, some manufacturing products like heat pumps, semiconductors, and aerospace controls, while others are divisionalized subsidiaries that provide a diversity of goods and services in different industries such as ITT Communication Services, Inc. (telecommunications), ITT Financial Corporation (consumer and commercial credit), ITT Life Insurance Corporation (life insurance), and ITT Rayonier Incorporated (wood products).

Conglomerates usually have a small headquarters staff composed primarily of financial and legal specialists who oversee the financial performance of the diversified businesses. Virtually all other functions are housed at the division level, and the design of each division reflects its particular coordination needs. Division managers in a completely divisionalized organization often operate as if they were running their own firm, although they adhere to the performance criteria and financial guidelines set by the organization's headquarters staff. Division managers usually have considerable freedom to determine how best to meet the division's objectives.

As the goods or services produced by an organization's divisions become more similar, incomplete divisionalization becomes more likely. Movie theater chains such as American Multi Cinema (AMC) usually divisionalize on the basis of location. AMC is divided into six regional divisions: five in the United States and one in Great Britain. These regional divisions are further subdivided into districts covering smaller territories. This type of divisionalization tends to be incomplete, with different staff functions reporting to different levels of the organization. The film-acquisition, accounting, marketing, and management-training functions are centralized at the headquarters level. Other functions—like payroll, computing, and security—are housed at the regional level. Still other functions are located at the district level, such as in-theater advertising and concessions. Most of the functions at the level of the individual theater or theater complex revolve around operations: projection, concessions, ushers, and cashiers.

In an incompletely divisionalized structure, many of the rules, policies, and procedures governing day-to-day operations are set by centralized staff units. At AMC, rules, policies, and procedures about financial performance, security, concession percentages, uniform requirements, required reporting documents, and so on, are issued by higher-level staff units. Thus, from the perspective of a division manager, the incompletely divisionalized organization tends to be more centralized than a completely divisionalized one.

Overall, managers should attempt to design structures that best enable their organization to achieve its goals while minimizing coordination costs. No single design works best. Each design needs to be tailored to the specific needs of each organization. Managers should select the aspects of the three basic designs—functional, divisional, and matrix—that best fit their needs. And, as we saw in the case of MegaToy, these needs will change over time, requiring periodic changes in design.

SUMMARY

Learning Objective 1: Understand the concept of interdependence. Interdependence is created whenever one person or unit does not entirely control all the tasks, information, or resources necessary for completing a project.

Learning Objective 2: Explain the difference between functional and workflow interdependence. Functional interdependence is related to job specialization, and it means that people who do similar jobs within an organization depend on each other to complete a project. Workflow interdependence refers to the interdependence of people across functional areas in producing a good or service.

Learning Objective 3: Describe how unit grouping facilitates coordination. Because individuals within a work unit share resources, a common supervisor, and evaluation and reward systems, they are likely to communicate among themselves and coordinate their own activities.

Learning Objective 4: Name the advantages and disadvantages of functional designs. Functional designs foster a greater depth of functional expertise, increase economies of scale, simplify communication and decision making, and enhance the training of functional specialists. Their disadvantages include high coordination costs among units, slow response to changing market conditions, lower levels of client satisfaction than that provided by other designs, and the potential for information overload at the top of an organization.

Learning Objective 5: Name the major advantages and disadvantages of divisional designs. The major advantages of divisional designs are that they facilitate workflow coordination, easily accommodate growth, lead to more responsive customer service, and develop broadly trained managers. The major disadvantages are difficulties in the coordination of functional specialities across divisions, decreased communication among functional specialists, less depth in functional expertise, and the duplication of services within an organization.

Learning Objective 6: Identify different ways of grouping market-based units. The three major ways of grouping market-based units are by product, location, or customer.

Learning Objective 7: Describe the role that integrating mechanisms play in organizations. Organizations use integrating mechanisms to retain the advantages of their existing structural design while enhancing communication across unit boundaries.

Learning Objective 8: Name the advantages and disadvantages of matrix designs. Matrix designs can contribute to a high rate of product innovation, maximize the use of a limited pool of functional specialists, and provide a home base for those specialists when projects are completed. But matrix designs are difficult to manage and work in because they are prone to high levels of stress and conflict.

Learning Objective 9: Explain why organizations employ a variety of design techniques. Managers try to design structures that will enable their organizations to achieve goals while minimizing coordination costs. No single design works best in every situation. Each organization's design needs to be tailored to its specific needs. Managers need to select the aspects of the three basic designs—functional, divisional, and matrix—that best fit their needs. Consequently, most organizations have mixed designs.

Discussion Questions

1. A large, functionally organized consumer products firm has expanded its product lines over the last five years to include cosmetics, detergents, and hair products. The firm produces house brands for department stores, grocery chains, drug stores, and discount outlets. As CEO, you are concerned with reports from the field sales offices that major customers are increasingly upset about lengthening delivery times and about inflexible sales and credit policies. You have to make a recommendation to the board of directors next week for a company reorganization. You need to outline the company's design options and the advantages and disadvantages of each option. What are you going to tell the board?

2. Your professor has informed the class that she is preparing a new book for this course, and that you and your classmates will write and evaluate test questions for each chapter as a group project. You have been elected by the class to manage the project. How will you organize the class members to best complete the assignment. What are the advantages and disadvantages of the design you have selected?

3. Why do organizations use hybrid designs? What are the advantages of using different design principles for different work units? What factors do you need to take into consideration when choosing a design for a work unit?

4. Your university implemented a new $4.2 million computerized, phone-in registration system this term. During the first day of add/drop, the system crashed, leaving 7,000 of 25,000 students without classes or with the wrong ones. About everything that could go wrong has. The students are outraged, the faculty is upset, and the administration is exceptionally embarrassed. As a member of the student governing body, you have been asked to make recommendations on how to go about untangling the mess so that all the parties are satisfied. What are you going to recommend and why?

5. You are a materials engineer working for a large, functionally organized semiconductor manufacturer. Its Japanese competitors are quickly eating away its market by introducing more powerful chips faster than your company can bring them to market. You are now working on a 10-billion bit chip, which your competitors also have under development. The first company to bring the chip to market will gain significant competitive advantages, but your organization's efforts have been slowed by technologically driven design changes that have ramifications for all the engineering departments working on the project. The material engineering department head has asked you for advice about how to break the logjam. What are you going to tell him? Explain the rationale for your answer and its implications for managing the development and production of this product.

6. You've been called in by Big Motors Corporation as a design consultant. BM's sales have been decreasing, and customers are complaining that its cars all look the same across divisions (e.g., Hudson, Studebaker, Arrow, Rambler, and DeLorean divisions). A few years ago BM began designing basic mechanical "platforms" (the guts of a car) to be shared across divisions by using integrating matrix units. The use of this integrating mechanism substantially cut design costs and considerably shortened the time it took to move a car from design to production. BM wants to retain these cost and time savings, but it also needs to design cars that appeal to its customers. What design options would you recommend to BM? What are their relative benefits and drawbacks?

DESIGN AUDIT #5

Analyzing Your Organization's Structure

This design audit will help you understand the concepts of unit-grouping and integrating mechanisms by applying the concepts to your own organization.

1. Draw an organization chart in the space below, identifying your organization's major units. How would you characterize the overall grouping technique used for the major units? Functional, divisional, matrix, or mixed?

    Hint: *If you work for a very large organization, sketch a broad organization chart for its major divisions and then focus on your division for the rest of the audit.*

2. Select one major unit with which you are familiar, and on a separate page draw an organization chart showing the subunits within it.

   a. To what extent do you find different types of unit grouping used?

   b. To what do you attribute these differences in unit grouping?

3. To what extent are integrating mechanisms used to increase horizontal communication between subunits (i.e., Question 2)? Sketch in these integrating linkages using dotted lines. Label the dotted lines to show the kind of integrating mechanisms being used. Are you aware of integrating mechanisms that are used between major units (i.e., Question 1)? Sketch these in as well.

4. Briefly describe three problems this organization has. For example, is it having problems attaining some of the goals you identified in Design Audit #2? Or, are there problems coordinating different units' activities (e.g., production bottlenecks, late product introductions, slow responses to changing market conditions, and so on)?

   a.   Problem 1:

   b.   Problem 2:

   c.   Problem 3:

5. Think about whether these problems indicate poor patterns of coordination and communication. What design options are available that might help resolve each problem?

   a. Design Alternatives for Problem 1:

   b. Design Alternatives for Problem 2:

   c. Design Alternatives for Problem 3:

Notes

1. Henry Mintzberg, *The Structuring of Organizations* (Englewood Cliffs, N.J.: Prentice-Hall, 1979), 106.

2. In reality, informal communication networks within an organization speed up communication by by-passing formal, hierarchical communication channels. The problem with informal communication is that unless employees are members of the appropriate network, they will be unable to coordinate with others except through formal hierarchical communication channels. This makes the use of informal communication for purposes of coordination a hit-or-miss proposition.

3. Jeffrey Pfeffer and Gerald R. Salancik, *The External Control of Organizations* (New York: Harper & Row, 1978), 40.

4. Mintzberg, *The Structuring of Organizations*, 1979, 122.

5. James D. Thompson, *Organizations in Action,* (New York: McGraw-Hill, 1967), 57.

6. Alfred D. Chandler, Jr., "Origins of the Organization Chart," *Harvard Business Review* 66, no. 2, (1988): 156–157.

7. Theodore Caplow, *How to Run an Organization: A Manual of Practical Sociology* (Hinsdale, Ill.: The Dryden Press, 1976), 18.

8. Herbert G. Hicks and Ray C. Gullett, *Organizations: Theory and Behavior* (New York: McGraw-Hill, 1975), 65.

9. Mintzberg, *The Structuring of Organizations*, 1979, 305–313.

10. "McWorld?" *Business Week,* October 13, 1986, 80–81.

11. Richard L. Daft, *Organization Theory and Design,* 2d ed. (St. Paul, Minn.: West, 1983), 232, 235.

12. This section draws heavily from Jay Galbraith, *Designing Complex Organizations* (Reading, Mass.: Addison-Wesley, 1973); and Mintzberg, *The Structuring of Organizations,* chapter 10.

13. Galbraith, *Designing Complex Organizations,* 93.

14. Leonard R. Sayles, "Matrix Organization: The Structure with a Future," *Organizational Dynamics* 5 (Autumn 1976): 11–12.

15. Galbraith, *Designing Complex Organizations,* 101–102.

16. Harvey F. Kolodony, "Matrix Organization Designs and New Product Success," *Research Management* 23 (September 1980): 29–33.

17. Stanley M. Davis and Paul R. Lawrence, *Matrix* (Reading, Mass.: Addison-Wesley, 1977), 129–144; Stanley M. Davis and Paul R. Lawrence, "Problems of Matrix Organization," *Harvard Business Review* 56, no. 3 (May–June 1978): 131–142.

18. Adapted from Sherman K. Grinnel and Howard P. Apple, "When Two Bosses Are Better Than One," *Machine Design,* January 9, 1975, 86.

CHAPTER 6

Technology and Organization Design

Learning Objectives

Upon completing this chapter, you should be able to

1. Give a general definition of technology.
2. Discuss Woodward's concept of technological complexity.
3. Discuss Thompson's concept of technological interdependence.
4. Discuss Perrow's concepts of the number and analyzability of exceptions as dimensions of technology.
5. Compare and contrast the results of the Woodward and Aston studies of the effects of technology on organization structure.
6. Describe the benefits of advanced information technologies for organizations.
7. Describe the benefits of computer-integrated manufacturing systems for organizations.
8. Explain how advanced information technologies and computer-integrated manufacturing affect organization design.

WAL-MART WINS WITH HIGH TECH

Leave the Wall Street eggheads behind and come to Bentonville, Arkansas, where some 100 of Wal-Mart's top managers—senior executives, divisional managers, regional managers—have flown back from visiting stores and are assembled for a weekly, no-holds-barred session with the sole agenda of moving merchandise.

For three hours, the managers pore over a printout that lists the inventory levels and rates of sale for key items that Wal-Mart stocks. Word on smaller stock decisions will reach all store managers by Monday, probably by phone. In more urgent cases, an executive can broadcast the message on TV from Bentonville to all stores over Wal-Mart's six-channel satellite system, which also gathers store data for its master computer, handles credit card approval in five seconds, and tracks Wal-Mart's complex distribution system. Technology is obviously quite alive and well in Bentonville, considering Wal-Mart's 46 percent average rate of return to investors and sales of about $25 billion. In fact, Wal-Mart is now poised to match and probably overtake rival Kmart in annual sales.

Nowhere is the technology of Wal-Mart more evident than in its merchandise distribution process. "Our distribution facilities are one of the keys to our success," says Wal-Mart's CEO. "If we do anything better than other folks, that's it." The distribution cycle at Wal-Mart has three basic steps. First, point-of-sale scanners track sales and monitor the supplies left on the shelf in the store. Second, stores beam stock orders via satellite to the mainframe at Bentonville. Finally, vendors schedule shipping to satisfy Wal-Mart's needs. The distribution centers themselves employ mechanized conveyor belts, bar coding, and computerized inventory to move needed products to stores as efficiently as possible.

According to one Wal-Mart manager, "A lot of companies use (technology). But no one runs it as hard as we do, and no one is as in touch with their business as we are." As Chapter 6 points out, matching the appropriate technology to an organization's structure can be a difficult endeavor. Clearly, Wal-Mart has implemented and managed technology to its competitive advantage.

Source: John Huey, "Wal-Mart: Will It Take Over the World?" *Fortune*, January 30, 1989, 52.

TECHNOLOGY is important to the study of organizations for several reasons. One obvious reason is that we live in a world pervaded by it. Technological developments are responsible for the "movement of people from farms to cities and from industrial to service operations. They have stimulated the evolution of the modern economic organization and affected political institutions."[1]

Technology also is a major spur to industrial productivity. Improved motivation techniques and incentives have not boosted production a fraction as much as technological innovations have. One need only review the evolution of technology from the first rudimentary hand tools to advanced information technologies and computer-integrated manufacturing systems to appreciate the truth of this statement. Technology also can be a prime determinant of job structure. As Litterer notes, "If technology and machines are changed, then jobs are changed."[2] Moreover, technology influences employee attitudes and behavior. While the assembly line immediately comes to mind, other examples of the effect of technology on the nature of work abound. Technology exerts influence on group composition, group size, patterns of social interaction, and individual control of personal activities.[3]

The study of these effects and organizations' responses to them provides the focus of this chapter. First, we review the early theory and research that has shaped thinking about the relationship between technology and organization structure over the last 30 years. Then we examine the effects of microelectronics-based technologies on organization structure. The chapter closes by integrating early and recent theory and research.

TECHNOLOGY DEFINED

There is little agreement as to the *exact* meaning of technology.[4] A general definition (based on the systems approach discussed in Chapter 1) with some measure of acceptance is that technology is the means by which an organization transforms inputs into outputs. More specifically, **technology** can be defined as the techniques or processes used to transform labor, knowledge, capital, and raw materials into finished goods or services. This general definition highlights a sometimes unappreciated fact: all organizations—regardless of whether they produce goods or services, or are profit or nonprofit—have technologies. An insurance company has its technology for converting capital, ideas, and labor into insurance services just as an oil company has its technology for converting crude oil and other resource inputs into petroleum products. And a welfare agency has a technology for serving clients just as an automotive company does for manufacturing automobiles.

The technology concept has been applied at three levels of organizational analysis: (1) the system or organization level, (2) the work-group level, and (3) the individual level. These levels are primarily a distinction between the overall, or core, technology of an organization, the basic characteristics of subunit workflow, and the nature of individual jobs. The first approach examines relationships such as the technology of industrial plants based on the complexity of their primary mode of production[5] or between technology and structural characteristics, such as type of ownership and number of employees.[6] The work-group level of analysis recognizes that different work units within the same organization may have different tasks and therefore different technologies.[7] The individual-level approach is typically concerned with the characteristics of tasks performed by individual employees and focuses on the design of jobs,[8] as discussed in Chapter 4. These differences reflect the diversity of orientations in the study of organizations. No one approach is right; each contributes something different to our understanding of the concept of technology and its relationship to structure.[9]

TECHNOLOGICAL TYPOLOGIES AND ORGANIZATION STRUCTURE

The effect of technology on organization structure has been a topic of debate since the 1950s. There is general agreement that the historical evolution from craft to more advanced technologies has increased the complexity of organizations. But "the extent to which technology *determines* structure has been disputed by organization theorists for some years."[10] Theory and research in this area can be separated roughly into two groups. One group, sometimes referred to as *technological determinists,* views technology as the primary determinant of an organization's structure. This group holds that different structures are required for different technologies, and that the former are strictly contingent on the latter. This notion is frequently referred to as the *technological imperative.* The second group views organizations as open systems, and recognizes that technology and structure are interdependent. It thus maintains that "technology can both influence the organization and be influenced by the organization."[11]

The conceptual schemes that have most influenced theory and research on technology and organization structure were developed during the 1950s and 1960s. We review the four streams of theory and research that have most influenced our understanding of the technology-structure relationship in the following sections: Woodward's technological complexity, the Aston group's workflow integration and production continuity, Thompson's technological interdependence, and Perrow's variability and analyzability.

Woodward: Technological Complexity

Begun in 1953 by the Human Relations Research Unit at the South Essex College of Technology in Great Britain, the research by Joan Woodward was the first major attempt to view organization structure from a technological perspective.[12] Her research gave rise to the aforementioned technological imperative—that organization structure is determined by technology.

Drawing on an empirical study of the structures of 100 British manufacturing firms, Woodward developed a scale of technology based on three related variables: (1) stages in the historical development of production processes,

Figure 6.1
Woodward's Classification of 100 British Manufacturing
Firms according to Their System of Production

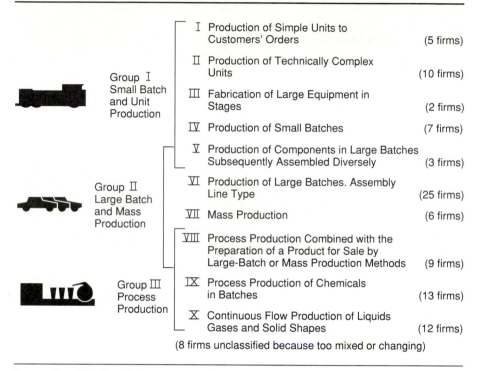

Group I Small Batch and Unit Production	I Production of Simple Units to Customers' Orders **(5 firms)**
	II Production of Technically Complex Units **(10 firms)**
	III Fabrication of Large Equipment in Stages **(2 firms)**
	IV Production of Small Batches **(7 firms)**
Group II Large Batch and Mass Production	V Production of Components in Large Batches Subsequently Assembled Diversely **(3 firms)**
	VI Production of Large Batches. Assembly Line Type **(25 firms)**
	VII Mass Production **(6 firms)**
Group III Process Production	VIII Process Production Combined with the Preparation of a Product for Sale by Large-Batch or Mass Production Methods **(9 firms)**
	IX Process Production of Chemicals in Batches **(13 firms)**
	X Continuous Flow Production of Liquids Gases and Solid Shapes **(12 firms)**

(8 firms unclassified because too mixed or changing)

Source: Joan Woodward, *Management and Technology* (London: Her Majesty's Stationery Office, 1958), p.11.

(2) the interrelationship between the equipment used for these processes, and (3) the extent to which the operations performed in the processes were repeated from one production cycle or sequence to the next. This scale resulted in a threefold classification of production technologies with numerous subgroups as shown in Figure 6.1. Woodward viewed these various subgroupings as increasing in order of chronological development (i.e., when they came into use) and in technological complexity (i.e., degree of predictability and control). **Technical complexity** ranges from the production of single units or small batches according to customer specifications (the oldest and simplest method of production), through an intermediate category involving large-batch and mass production, to continuous-flow process production (the most advanced at the time).

Later theorists, however, have raised questions about whether technical complexity increases from unit through mass to process production. Edward Harvey, for example, argues that this sequence can be viewed "as a move toward technical simplicity rather than complexity . . . . It is, after all, the frequent emergence of problems calling for innovation that characterize unit rather than process production."[13] In this sense, Woodward's technology scale is more accurately viewed as a set of categories, not a monotonic ordering.

Unit/Small-Batch Production. Organizations in the *unit/small-batch production* category are typically called *job-order shops*. Products are designed and manufactured on a "custom-made" basis. As a result, they are relatively heterogeneous, and the tasks performed on each unit or small batch vary. Examples of such output include custom-made accessories, specialty glass products, custom-tailored clothing, special-order printing, prototype electronic components, locomotives, satellites, and special-order machine tools.

Mass Production. High volumes of standardized goods are manufactured in **mass production** systems. The operations performed in this type of manufacturing are generally routine, repetitive, and predictable. In addition to the assembly-line manufacture of automobiles, television sets, and the like, other examples of mass production are bakeries, mechanized textile mills, and modern tobacco-processing plants.

Process/Continuous-Flow Production. Organizations using **process** or **continuous-flow** systems produce goods such as liquids, gases, and crystalline substances that are typically sold by weight or volume or, after further processing, are sold as a packaged product (e.g., acetylsalicylic acid packaged as aspirin tablets). Production is characteristically maintained at a set level, and lot sizes are large. Examples of process/continuous-flow products are petroleum products, gases, chemicals, and pharmaceuticals.

Woodward's Findings. From analyses and follow-up studies that spanned several years, Woodward's research group found that the structural characteristics of the most successful organizations using unit/small-batch and process technologies were quite similar. Specifically, for successful organizations Woodward found that

1. There was a tendency to use market-based unit grouping to coordinate workflow interdependence in unit/small-batch and process production organizations, while functional unit grouping was common in organizations using mass-production systems.

2. Relatively high degrees of horizontal and vertical job specialization were common in mass-production organizations, while more flexible, decentralized structures were characteristic of organizations with unit/small-batch and process/continuous-flow technologies.

3. Less differentiation of roles occurred in organizations with unit/small-batch and process/continuous-flow technologies, and it was difficult to distinguish between executive and advisory responsibility.

4. In organizations using unit/small-batch and process/continuous-flow production, managers' technical competence was important. In process production, however, it was based upon qualifications and knowledge, while in unit/small-batch production, it was based on long experience and know-how.[14]

Woodward's most important finding was that each organization's success was directly related to a proper match between technology and certain organizational characteristics. Within each technological classification—unit/small-batch, mass-production, process—there was a marked tendency for the most commercially successful firms to be appropriately structured for their technical systems. These findings suggested that while there seems to be no universal "best way" to design an organization, there did seem to be a particular structure most appropriate to each technical situation. Woodward interpreted these findings as showing that technology was the *dominant* factor affecting organization structure, which gave rise to the so-called technological imperative.

Aston Studies: Workflow Integration and Production Continuity

During the 1960s another group of English researchers, known as the Aston group, began an ambitious study of the relationship between organization structure and technology under the direction of Derek Pugh and David Hickson.[15] The Aston researchers are perhaps best known for their study of the structural and technological characteristics of 52 firms located in the Birmingham, England, area. They focused on two major facets of what they termed *operations technology,* meaning the equipping and sequencing of activities in a workflow. These facets were *workflow integration* and *production continuity*. Workflow integration was conceptualized as a general factor composed of the

1. Level of automation of workflow equipment.

2. Rigidity of workflow.

3. Degree of interdependence in the workflow.

4. Precision of criteria used in evaluating operations.

Production continuity was measured using Woodward's ten categories shown in Figure 6.1.

The Aston researchers began by comparing workflow integration with various measures of organization structure for the 31 manufacturing firms included in their sample to determine the extent to which operations technology and structure were related. Surprisingly, only 3 of 64 structural variables had even a weak relationship with this facet of technology, which contradicted Woodward's findings.

In an attempt to reconcile this result with Woodward's conclusions, the researchers conducted further analyses. They found that organization size moderated the relationship between technology and structure, which led them to conclude that Woodward's findings were valid only for smaller organizations where "everyone is closer to the 'shop floor,' and structural responses to the problems of size (for example) have not begun to show." This, the researchers believed, was in contrast to the situation in larger organizations where "managers and administrators are buffered from the technology itself by the specialized departments, standard procedures, and formalized paperwork that size brings with it." In other words, the researchers concluded that an organization's size, not its technology, was the primary determinant of organization structure.[16] The subsequent debate between advocates of technology versus size as the primary determinant of organization structure lasted through the 1970s.[17]

Thompson: Technological Interdependence

At the same time the Aston group was conducting its research, James Thompson offered an alternative view of technology based on the concept of **technological interdependence**.[18] Thompson's work focused on how organizations cope with uncertainties created by managers' cognitive limits and by events and influences that managers cannot control or predict.[19] He developed a classification of three technologies—mediating, long-linked, and intensive—based on organizational workflow patterns. The main differences among these three workflow patterns are "the amount of discretionary or problem-solving behavior required of the human operator in the production process,"[20] and the mechanisms used to coordinate different types of workflow interdependence. Generally, the greater the problem-solving behavior required by a workflow, the more expensive will be the coordinating mechanism required to satisfy coordination needs. These three technological types and their attendant coordinating mechanisms will be examined in turn.

Mediating Technology. As shown in Figure 6.2 (Panel A), a **mediating technology** entails the joining together of independent clients or customers. It is characterized as having **pooled interdependence**, where subunits within an organization may not directly interact but are interdependent nevertheless, because unless each performs adequately, the total organization—and the other subunits—are threatened. Examples of organizations using mediating technologies include commercial banks, real estate and commodity brokers, insurance claims units, post offices, gas and electric utilities, computer dating services, department stores, employment agencies, telephone companies, and even auction houses. To achieve coordination, mediating technology relies on categorization and standardization. For instance, banks categorize customers as either depositors or borrowers, who

Figure 6.2
Thompson's Technological Typology

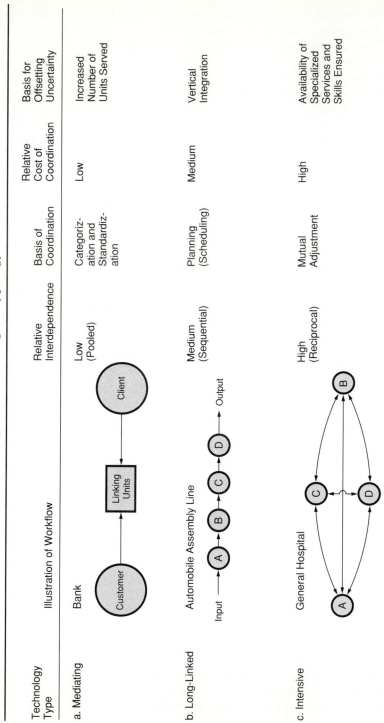

Technology Type	Illustration of Workflow	Relative Interdependence	Basis of Coordination	Relative Cost of Coordination	Basis for Offsetting Uncertainty
a. Mediating	Bank	Low (Pooled)	Categoriz-ation and Standardiz-ation	Low	Increased Number of Units Served
b. Long-Linked	Automobile Assembly Line	Medium (Sequential)	Planning (Scheduling)	Medium	Vertical Integration
c. Intensive	General Hospital	High (Reciprocal)	Mutual Adjustment	High	Availability of Specialized Services and Skills Ensured

Source: Based on James D. Thompson, *Organizations in Action* (New York: McGraw-Hill, 1967), pp. 15–18.

are then treated according to standardized procedures appropriate to that client category.

An organization with a mediating technology typically copes with uncertainty about future conditions by increasing the number of units served. For example, an insurance company reduces uncertainty by finding "enough poolers of risk to avoid the possibility of one loss destroying the coverage of the others."[21] Since mediating technology combines the outputs of different units by using predetermined categories and standard rules and procedures, it is usually the least costly of the three coordination mechanisms discussed by Thompson.

Long-Linked Technology. Typified by the mass-production assembly line, **long-linked technology** is characterized by the **sequential interdependence** of tasks or operations. The procedures necessary to complete a good or service are highly uniform and must be performed in a specified serial order. Task A must be performed first, then B, and then C before a good or service is produced. Consequently, a long-linked technology is rather inflexible in the face of changing product demands. Figure 6.2 (Panel B) diagrams such a system. The most obvious examples include cafeterias, relay teams, food and beverage processors, meat packing firms, and automated car washes.

An organization using a long-linked technology usually achieves coordination through planning and scheduling, which is more expensive than the categorization and standardization of a mediating technology. It typically uses vertical integration—broadening operations to include a larger number of processing stages—to accommodate possible future needs. Examples are the move backward of some automobile manufacturers into the production of parts and accessories to assure a stable source of supplies, and the move forward of aluminum companies into the marketing of finished goods to cultivate a demand for their product.

Intensive Technology. Exemplified by the use of a variety of different techniques and skills to produce a good or service, **intensive technology** is characterized by **reciprocal interdependence**. The selection, mix, and sequence of techniques and skills used to produce a good or service are largely determined by feedback from the object itself: the techniques applied at one stage of production are contingent on feedback from earlier production stages. Thus, the sequence of operations to be performed in producing a good or service cannot be predetermined.

> Intensive technology is most dramatically illustrated by the general hospital. At any moment an emergency admission may require some combination of dietary, x-ray, laboratory, and housekeeping or hotel services, together with the various medical specialties, pharmaceutical services, occupational therapies, social work services, and spiritual or religious services. Which of these,

and when, can be determined only from evidence about the state of mind of the patient.[22]

Other examples are military combat units, mental health centers, basketball squads, computer service firms, and certain research and development units. Their general structure is shown in Figure 6.2 (Panel C).

Because the workflow for producing a specific good or service cannot be predetermined, intensive technologies rely on mutual adjustment for coordination. That is, employees communicate among themselves to coordinate their activities. Organizations with intensive technologies attempt to reduce the workflow uncertainties by preparing for a wide variety of contingencies, which requires the availability of many specialized services and skills. A much publicized example is the tendency for hospitals to acquire sophisticated and specialized equipment such as magnetic resonance imaging units (MRI scanners). Intensive technology is typically the most expensive to coordinate. Coordination by mutual adjustment—frequent horizontal communication between units and among individuals—is required above and beyond the schedules, rules, and procedures generally associated with mediating or long-linked technologies.

Of the several technological typologies that have been developed, Thompson's is generally considered to be the richest conceptually. Although essentially a system-level model focusing on an organization's overall or core technology, it also is useful for categorizing subsystem units such as departments. Plus it has the advantage of being applicable to a wide variety of manufacturing and service organizations.

Perrow: Variability and Analyzability

At the same time Thompson's model was gaining attention, Charles Perrow proposed another technology framework.[23] Perrow's conceptual scheme went beyond those of Woodward and Thompson by including two dimensions:

1. The number of exceptional cases that occur during a technological process.

2. The extent to which these exceptions are *analyzable* (i.e., understandable and have routine solutions).

Using these dimensions, Perrow proposed the four categories of technology shown in Figure 6.3. He also discussed the effects of different technologies on organization structure, specifically their effects on coordination mechanisms, discretion, and the relative power of first-line supervisors and of the middle managers who supervise them. We examine these technologies and their relationship to structure in the following sections.

Figure 6.3
Perrow's Technological Typology

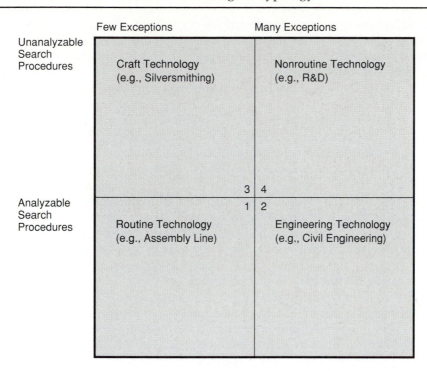

	Few Exceptions	Many Exceptions
Unanalyzable Search Procedures	Craft Technology (e.g., Silversmithing)	Nonroutine Technology (e.g., R&D)
Analyzable Search Procedures	Routine Technology (e.g., Assembly Line)	Engineering Technology (e.g., Civil Engineering)

Source: Adapted from Charles Perrow, "The Effect of Technological Change on the Structure of Business Firms," in *Industrial Relations: Contemporary Issues,* ed. Benjamin C. Roberts (London: Macmillan, 1968), p. 211. By permission of Macmillan. London & Basingstoke.

Routine Technology. Cell 1 portrays a *routine technology*. The extreme example is the mass-production assembly line where output is highly standardized. Few exceptions occur here, and they are readily analyzable when they do. As a result, policies, rules, and procedures can be established to resolve processing problems. To illustrate, there is little question about how a bumper should be attached to an automobile chassis moving down an assembly line. If an exception occurs, it is usually clear what the problem is and how to resolve it.

Since coordination in a routine technology is achieved through rules, policies, and procedures, both first-line supervisors and middle managers have little discretion (i.e., their jobs are vertically specialized). But middle managers have relatively more power because they write the rules, policies, and procedures that first-line supervisors must follow.

Nonroutine Technology. At the other extreme (Cell 4) are organizations with a *nonroutine technology*. Here numerous exceptions occur that are not readily analyzable. Solving problems requires the analytical skills acquired through professional training. Examples of this type of organization include research and development units, aerospace firms, noncustodial psychiatric clinics, certain kinds of advertising agencies, and manufacturers of exotic chemicals and nuclear fuels.

In contrast to organizations with routine technologies, coordination is achieved in those with nonroutine technologies through mutual adjustment at both the first-line supervisory and middle-management levels. Mutual adjustment is particularly necessary here because many workflow exceptions are encountered for which there are no ready solutions. As a result, both first-line supervisors and middle managers have a fair amount of discretion and relatively high levels of power. In fact, as Perrow points out, first-line supervisors usually work closely with middle management because "the latter cannot call the shots for the former on the basis of routine information sent upstairs."[24] With first-line supervision and middle management so closely involved, it often is difficult to distinguish between them.

Engineering Technology. Cell 2 portrays *engineering technologies,* characterized by a workflow with many analyzable exceptions. They are similar to routine technologies in that the variable tasks, including the exceptions, can be readily understood and analyzed. They differ from routine technologies (and are similar to nonroutine technologies) in the frequency with which exceptions occur. Civil engineering firms or manufacturers of customized heavy industrial machinery are typical of Cell 2. Every bridge or piece of machinery constructed presents problems different from those faced before, but standard decision procedures can be used to search for acceptable solutions.

Coordination at the middle-management level parallels that in a nonroutine technology because of the frequency of exceptions. Middle managers coordinate their activities through mutual adjustment, and they have a fair amount of discretion and power. But the situation of first-line supervisors parallels that in a routine technology, because exceptions are analyzable. Therefore activities can be coordinated through rules, policies, procedures, and plans, and the first-line supervisors have considerably less discretion and power than middle managers.

Craft Technology. In a *craft technology* (Cell 3), fewer exceptions occur than in nonroutine technology, but they need the artistic skills and knack of a craftperson to solve them; that is, they are not readily analyzable. Custom furniture, specialty ceramics and china, silversmithing, and other industries relying heavily on skilled artisans fall in this category. Coordination of first-level supervisors in a craft technology is through mutual adjustment, because the exceptions encountered are not readily analyzable. As a result, power and discretion shifts from middle management to first-line supervisors. Middle management is left in a relatively weak position.

An important aspect of Perrow's typology is that it is dynamic. For example, an organization could move from Cell 4 to Cell 3 by increasing production runs, clients served, programs administered, and so forth. This would allow more experience to be gained, reducing the number of perceived exceptions. Or if the amount of technical knowledge increases, increasing the speed and accuracy of problem solving, an organization could move from Cell 4 to Cell 2. If both experience and technical knowledge increase significantly, an organization could move from Cell 4 to Cell 1.

Another major implication of the multidimensional and dynamic nature of Perrow's technology is that it emphasizes the need to talk about *technologies* instead of a single technology in relation to the transformation processes within an organization. Modern organizations, especially those that are large and complex, typically have many specialized work units, and each can have a different technology. For instance, an organization may employ a nonroutine technology in its research and development department, but a relatively simple routine technology in its manufacturing department where products are mass produced. And, different work-unit technologies will require different types of unit structures.

WHAT THESE MODELS TELL US ABOUT TECHNOLOGY AND ORGANIZATION STRUCTURE

There are obvious similarities and differences among these technological frameworks. Viewing them together helps us gain a more complete understanding of the technology-structure relationship, because each framework tells us something different about it. Table 6.1 summarizes the overlap between these technological categories and their relationships with a number of different design components.

The work of Woodward and the Aston group, for example, provides information about the relationship among different types of technologies, organization size, and structure. It suggests that work units in organizations with **unit/small-batch** and process technologies tend toward market-based unit grouping, while those with mass-production technologies are more likely to be functionally organized. Consistent with these unit-grouping patterns, organizations with unit/small-batch and process technologies are less likely to employ extensive job specialization, widespread RPPs, and centralized decision making than organizations with mass-production technologies. They are more likely to use training and decentralized decision making for coordination and control. However, in larger organizations, these

Table 6.1

Comparison of the Woodward, Thompson, and Perrow Technological
Typologies and Their Relationships to Design Characteristics

| Technological Typologies | | | Job Specialization | |
Woodward	Thompson	Perrow	Horiz.	Vert.
Unit/small-batch	—	Craft	L–M	L–M
—	Mediating	Engineering	M–H	M–H
Mass production	Long-linked	Routine	H	H
—	Intensive	Nonroutine	L	L
Process/continuous-flow	—	—	L	M

L = Low
M = Medium
H = High

patterns might well be observed at the subunit level, though they do not apply to the whole organization.

Thompson's and Perrow's work help explain why these relationships exist. Thompson's technological interdependence indicates that increasing workflow interdependence increases uncertainty, which heightens the need for flexible coordination mechanisms. In Perrow's words, there is a growing need for flexible coordination as the number of exceptions increases, or as encountered exceptions become unanalyzable. Thus, coordination mechanisms that specify solutions in advance—rules, policies, and procedures—become less useful as an organization's work becomes more interdependent and uncertain.

For example, uncertainty is low in Woodward's mass-production technology because there are few exceptions and they are readily analyzable. Coordination needs can be predetermined; rules, policies, and procedures can be designed to fit these needs. In the opposite situation, Perrow's nonroutine technology and Thompson's intensive technology, the uncertainty created by an unpredictable workflow requires that coordination be ongoing and achieved through mutual adjustment. Rules, policies, and procedures are of limited value because coordination needs cannot be specified in advance. Also, mass-production jobs are likely to be highly specialized, both horizontally and vertically, while nonroutine/intensive jobs are relatively enlarged and enriched. And because of these differences in job design and coordination mechanisms, decision making in a mass-production organization is likely to be more centralized than in an organization with an intensive/nonroutine technology.

| Design Characteristics | | | |
| Formalization | | | |
RPPs	Training	Centralization	Unit Grouping
L	M	L–M	Market-based
M	M	M–H	Function/market-based
H	L	H	Function-based
L	H	L	Market-based
M	M	M	Market-based

Perrow's craft and engineering technologies (similar to Woodward's unit/small-batch production and Thompson's mediating technology) present intermediate cases. Operating uncertainty in a craft technology is created by unanalyzable exceptions, meaning that production employees have to coordinate among themselves to develop solutions to novel problems. With engineering technology, uncertainty is created by analyzable exceptions. Because these exceptions are readily understood, rules, policies, and procedures can be developed by middle managers to deal with them.

The difference in the effect these intermediate technologies have on organization structure is related to where uncertainties in a production process are handled. In craft technology, major uncertainties are dealt with at the production level, because they are unanalyzable, and employees thus require discretion to cope with them. In engineering technology, major uncertainties are analyzable, so are dealt with by rules, policies, and procedures formulated by middle managers. Thus, in a craft technology, the jobs of production employees tend to be more complex than those of middle managers, and vice versa in engineering technologies.

As a result, production jobs in a craft technology are likely to be less horizontally and vertically specialized than those in an engineering technology, because of the greater need for discretion. Craft organizations also are likely to be more decentralized than organizations with engineering technologies because major uncertainties are dealt with at lower organizational levels. Because these technologies are intermediate cases, the degree of job specialization and centralization is likely to be at a point between that observed in routine and nonroutine technologies.

Woodward's continuous-production/process technologies do not have a ready analog in Thompson's and Perrow's typologies. Workflow automation means that many of the rules, policies, and procedures governing routine activities are built into the hardware of a production system. Production employees no longer do the physical labor; they monitor and maintain equipment performing the actual work. Thus, the role of production employees becomes supervisory in that they supervise the operation of a production system and solve problems as they occur.

In this situation, jobs become less horizontally and vertically specialized because of their increased complexity, and training becomes more important as the reliance on rules, policies, and procedures decreases. Some decentralization is likely, enhancing production employees' ability to deal with problems quickly. And market-based unit grouping is more likely as work units are designed to contain the workflow interdependencies built into a production process.

THE MICROELECTRONICS REVOLUTION

A revolution in production technologies, based on the development of microelectronics, has occurred since the 1950s and 1960s, when the technology-structure models just reviewed were developed. Two facets of the microelectronics revolution are making new production technologies possible: *advanced information technologies* and *computer-integrated manufacturing*. These technologies are in their infancy, and their effects on organization structure are just beginning to be understood. The experiences of organizations, and the research done to date, indicate that a number of structural changes may be needed to realize their full potential.

Advanced Information Technologies (AIT)

Advanced information technologies (AIT), information management software using databases on distributed computer networks, have come about as the distinction between the computer and telecommunication industries blurred. As Michael Borrus and John Zyman explain,

> During the 1970s the communications industry moved away from the pure provision of communication pathways for analog voice transmission toward the provision of enhanced communications (voice, data, video, and facsimile) using computer technology. This change depended on the digitalization of information, be it voice or data. Simultaneously the computer industry moved away from stand-alone computers toward networks of geographically separate computers interconnected through communication pathways for data transmission.[25]

The merging of these industries is making the telephone system a distributed computer network and tying computers together into data networks. In turn, these changes are creating a new infrastructure that makes new production methods possible, much as the advent of railroads, highways, telegraph, and telephone systems made possible mass production technology early in the twentieth century.[26]

AIT provides a number of benefits. Its data networks streamline operations in four ways: (1) they increase efficiency by reducing the time spent and personnel involved in data collection and entry, (2) they decrease processing time by making a single source of information available throughout an organization, (3) they enhance coordination across an organization's subunits, and (4) they improve decision making and problem solving across geographically dispersed operations.

Increased Efficiency. AIT increases an organization's efficiency by automating information-processing tasks. Many colleges and universities, such as the University of Colorado, have automated their course registration systems. Under the old manual system, students were assigned a time period during which they could register on campus. The registration process required that students move from station to station—each school and college in the university having a different station—checking on course availability and signing up for those they needed. The process was time-consuming for both students and university staff. The new automated system allows students to check class availability and register for courses using a touch-tone phone anytime during the registration period. They also can change their class schedule any time during the registration period, as well as charge their tuition to a credit card. The automated system is considerably more efficient than the old system, requires fewer staff to operate, and is much more convenient for students.

Decreased Processing Time. By making a single source of information available throughout an organization, AIT decreases the amount of time required to respond to a customer's or client's needs. Godiva Chocolatier, Inc.—a subsidiary of Campbell's Soups and the leading maker of premium chocolates—equipped its field representatives with laptop computers in 1987. A field representative enters a customer's order on the laptop, which has the latest price information downloaded from a central factory computer. The central computer automatically calculates the total order, including any applicable discounts and special service needs. Orders are transmitted back to the central computer at the end of each day. Besides reducing field representatives' paperwork, the integrated information system provides complete and up-to-date information about changing demand for Godiva's products. This information allows Godiva to adjust its production mix to changes in the marketplace quickly.[27]

Enhanced Coordination. United Airlines uses an AIT at its Chicago terminal at O'Hare Airport to enhance coordination. Airports operate on a just-in-time basis, requiring the close coordination of passengers, equipment, customer-service agents, flight-crew management, station-operation control workers, ramp workers, flight-kitchen workers, fuelers, mechanics, and so on. United coordinates these people and their activities using an AIT featuring a main-frame-based Unimatic Flight Information System (UFIS) that feeds information to the Gate Assignment Display System, which in turn assigns aircraft to gates and then to the Flight Information Display System (FIDS) that displays information about United flights to passengers and employees on over 900 monitors. FIDS distributes information to the Baggage Information Display System and the Customer Information Display System. When a plane signals that it will arrive late, the information is fed into the UFIS, which distributes the information to the other systems. Gate assignments are modified to accommodate the late arrival, passengers are notified of the change, and the assignments of baggage handlers, customer-service representatives, mechanics, and so on, are adjusted. Considering that United's O'Hare terminal handles hundreds of departures and arrivals each day, coordination of all these people and activities would be almost impossible without an AIT.[28]

Improved Problem Solving and Decision Making. AIT can increase an organization's ability to coordinate decision making and problem solving when people and facilities are geographically dispersed. The decreased need for geographic proximity to coordinate activities gives organizations more options in siting offices and plants and locating personnel and provides an opportunity to reduce skill duplication. Victor Walling, strategic planner for information and computers with the Royal Dutch Shell Group, explains in Focus on Design 6.1 how AIT may affect coordination and problem solving over time and space in the future.

Computer-Integrated Manufacturing (CIM)

The data networks created by AIT are equally critical to the development of new production technologies in manufacturing. Internal computer networks link elements of the production system together, making **computer-integrated manufacturing (CIM)** possible, which can be loosely defined as an automated production system of people, machines, and tools linked electronically for the planning and control of the production process, which includes the acquisition of raw materials, parts, components, and the shipment and service of finished goods.[29] The basic components of a full-scale CIM are described in Table 6.2, and a graphic representation of a CIM is shown in Figure 6.4.[30]

CIM Benefits. CIM has a number of benefits related to product cost and quality. Computer-assisted design (CAD) and computer-assisted

---

FOCUS ON DESIGN 6.1

Advanced Information Systems and Coordination

Victor Walling, who does strategic planning for information and computers for the Royal Dutch Shell Group in the Netherlands, sketches a scenario: A small, out-of-the-way refinery with 300 or 400 employees, too small to have a world-class expert in corrosion on staff, develops a problem that only such an expert can solve. If the company doesn't find a solution in 24 hours, it will have to shut down the refinery—a costly move.

One solution is to fly in an expert, but that would probably use up most of the 24 hours.

Another is to use technology. "If we have a problem someplace and we can't move the problem, we need to bring in the expertise. The PC can help," Walling says.

"What we're working on is being able to put together a team to work in a task across time and space. We can load the problem into a computer conference, see who else around might have had a similar problem and what might have happened previously. We may ship out a problem to the experts, and several people in several different time zones may work on it within that 24-hour period. This way we can quickly get the best expertise in the world—no matter where the experts are."

Using computer conferencing and electronic mail to identify a problem and speed up its solution has a positive effect in more mundane areas as well. Walling says, "We can now reduce the number of meetings required when assigning a project. And management at higher levels can look in and review a project, eliminating the need for formal reports. This kind of computer communication represents a significant reduction in cost and an improvement in our ability to solve problems quickly."

Source: Excerpted from David DeJean, "The Electronic Workgroup," *PC Computing* 1, no. 3 (1988): 72, 74.

---

engineering (CAE) speed up product design and testing considerably, lowering the cost and aiding the process of modifying products to meet changing customer specifications. Computer-assisted process planning (CAPP) and materials-resource planning (MRP) help determine the most efficient manufacturing process for a product while ensuring that the required materials and labor are available. Better planning means less chance of having too many or too few materials and personnel on hand with the attendant cost or delay problems.

Automatic storage and retrieval systems (ASRS) and automated materials-handling systems (AMHS) reduce costs by ensuring that raw material and work-in-process are at the appropriate work stations when needed. They also reduce the size of the components and work-in-process inventories required to ensure a smooth production flow. Computer-assisted manufacturing

Table 6.2
Basic Components of a Computer-Integrated Manufacturing System

- *Computer-Assisted Design (CAD).* Software systems that do many of the routine tasks of product design, such as drafting, and that create instructions for the manufacture of the product to be used by an automated production system.
- *Computer-Assisted Engineering (CAE).* Software systems that allow engineers to test product designs without building prototypes.
- *Computer-Aided Process Planning (CAPP).* Software systems that aid in the transition between design and production by determining the optimal sequence of production operations, and the work stations and tools to be used in a production process.
- *Materials-Resource Planning (MRP).* Software systems that compile a master production schedule and that estimate material and human resource requirements.
- *Automatic Storage and Retrieval System (ASRS).* Consists of high-density storage racks for materials and work-in-process with vehicles that automatically load and unload them.
- *Automated Materials-Handling System (AMHS).* Systems that automatically transport raw materials or work-in-process to a work station where they are needed.
- *Computer-Aided Manufacturing (CAM).* Production system consisting of robotics, numerically controlled machines, computer-numerically controlled machines, and other devices that accept instructions from CAD/CAE systems.
- *Computer-Aided Testing (CAT).* Machine vision systems or other sensing mechanisms adjunct to a CAM system that detect deviations from standard and signal the machines to correct them.

(CAM) eliminates much of the direct labor involved in production and, coupled with computer-assisted testing (CAT) ensures that the goods are produced to specification. Because the operations are integrated through an AIT, the result is a flexible manufacturing system that produces high-quality goods, tailored to customer specifications, quickly, at a competitive price.

Dedicated versus Programmable Automation. The difference between CIM and the automation used by manufacturers since the 1950s lies in the distinction between dedicated automation and programmable automation. **Dedicated automation** uses automated machinery dedicated to a specific purpose. A dedicated machine can perform one or a few tasks. Production systems based on dedicated automation can be highly efficient, but they require product standardization, volume production, and marketing strategies to sell large numbers of the same products in mass markets.

This strategy worked well for many manufacturers during the 1950s and 1960s. But in the 1970s and 1980s, many mass markets began to break up because of shortening product life cycles and the growing consumer demand

Figure 6.4

General Design of a Computer-Integrated Manufacturing System

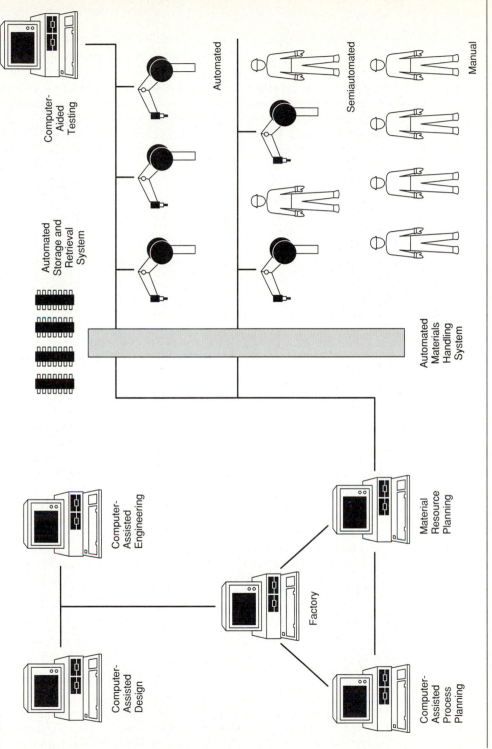

Source: Adapted from Richard L. Engwall, "Flexible Manufacturing System Pays Off for Both Westinghouse and the Air Force," *Industrial Engineering* 18 (November 1986), p. 49.

for more varied products.[31] This market instability creates a problem for mass-production organizations because dedicated automation is inflexible. For example, "a traditional, dedicated machine tool doesn't just cut metal, it cuts metal to make a specific part and no other. To alter its application is a slow and expensive process. In some cases, it simply is not possible to alter the application once a machine is in place."[32] If demand shifts away from a manufacturer's standardized product, it is left with an expensive plant that produces a good nobody wants. This is the situation U.S. automakers found themselves in during the period of 1974–1976, and again during 1980–1982. During both periods, demand shifted rapidly from large to small cars. Even though the automakers had excess production capacity, they could not produce small cars because their excess capacity was dedicated to the production of large cars.

Programmable automation, made possible by inexpensive microprocessors, provides a technological answer to this inflexibility problem. It differs from dedicated automation in that the machinery can be programmed to perform different tasks, which provides flexibility in the production process. Instead of changing the machines, you change the software. The advantages are obvious. They also were not lost on U.S. automakers. For example, GM's new Truck & Bus Group plants in Fort Wayne, Indiana, and Pontiac, Michigan, are designed as computer-integrated assembly systems using programmable automation. As Ernest O. Vahala, director of Manufacturing Engineering Operations at GM Truck and Bus Group, explains,

> When we went after a flexible assembly facility, we realized that we must have a flexible CIM system with it. When I say a flexible assembly system, I mean a flexible process where we can do a "soft" change (through reprogramming) rather than a "hard" change, when we get a product change or a model change.
>
> The savings that come in an on-going basis, as we get product engineering changes, that are "flex-soft" are in the magnitudes of 10 to 1 or even 100 to 1, depending on the kind of change. It becomes a software change in which the equipment reacts to the instructions, and we don't have to go through the design, debug, install, startup of different fixed automation. So that's the real driving motivation of CIM and of flexible manufacturing and flexible assembly.[33]

Economies of Scale versus Economies of Scope. CIM-associated reductions in product-modification costs are changing the economics of production. The cost per unit of an item produced using programmable automation lies in between that of unit/small-batch production and mass production. As Carol Parsons observes,

> The different economics of batch and mass production have traditionally been obvious. With very small batch or custom production, general purpose machines, usually hand operated by skilled workers, produce at most a few

items. Capital costs may be low but unit costs are high because set-up time can be considerable, individual machining is a demanding and time-consuming task, and all the costs must be spread over a very small number of units produced. Dedicated automation stands at the other extreme. Here initial fixed capital costs are quite high but total unit costs are typically very low because the automation of production increases speed and insures constant quality. Specialized equipment is set up once and from then on production proceeds in an almost continuous flow.[34]

Thus, programmable automation provides much of the flexibility of unit/small-batch production at unit costs approaching those of mass production. This creates **economies of scope** (the economies gained in the volume production of a set of goods) as opposed to **economies of scale** (the economies gained from volume production of a single good). Economies of scope are important because the economies of scale associated with mass production become unattainable in changing markets.[35] These economies of scope are possible because of the integration created by a system's software.

The flexibility provided by CIM enables organizations to respond quickly to changing consumer preferences and market conditions. Flexibility is becoming a prerequisite for success because of a rapidly changing business environment. Jack Ring, director of long-range planning at Honeywell, Inc., compares U.S. manufacturers in the year 2000 to Los Angeles freeway drivers—"All who are left will be very good." And, as Ring puts it, "The survivors in manufacturing are those who are now getting ready to live in CIM."[36] Focus on Design 6.2 explains how CIM has helped Allen-Bradley Co. become a flexible manufacturing organization that now relies on speed of response and economies of scope to compete.

MICROPROCESSOR TECHNOLOGIES AND ORGANIZATION DESIGN

There is growing consensus that organizations adopting AIT and CIM need to change their structures to gain the full benefits of these new technologies, which can change the nature of work done in organizations and impose new coordination requirements.[37] On one hand, CIM and AIT are similar to Woodward's unit/small-batch production (and Perrow's craft and engineering technologies) in that they provide organizations with the flexibility to produce customized goods and services, but more efficiently. On the other hand, they are similar to Woodward's continuous-production/process technologies in that the workflow becomes continuous, unlike unit/small-batch production. Moreover, the automation of a workflow's routine activities changes the nature of the remaining jobs. They become more similar to those

FOCUS ON DESIGN 6.2

Computer-Integrated Manufacturing at Allen-Bradley Co.

"CIM is the most effective tool manufacturers have in meeting the time-to-market challenge." That's how Tracy O'Rourke, president and CEO, Allen-Bradley Co. (A-B), views his $3½ million investment in a CIM (computer-integrated manufacturing) cell to produce surface-mount, printed circuit boards. Located in A-B's Twinsburg, Ohio, facility, the new implementation was inspired by the success of the company's 1982 CIM investment at its Milwaukee headquarters. The payback from that $15 million implementation gives the company the flexibility to produce over 600 variations in motor contractors and to control relays economically and efficiently in lot sizes of 1.

Mr. O'Rourke is convinced that "CIM is the marketing machine of the future. With it a company can respond rapidly to changes in the marketplace, producing products in a wider variety, at faster rates, and at lower costs." Says Don Davis, senior vice president of the Industrial Computer & Communication Group, "Time-to-market is one of the most critical factors in our business today. Rapidly changing technology shortens product life. Today, the average life of most of our products is about three years. If we're late in responding to market demand, we cut that product life even shorter—or miss the chance to compete entirely. We believe CIM helps everyone work as a team to produce better products faster."

How much faster? By automating the surface-mount assembly process and by integrating the information used in the operation, A-B managed to reduce assembly time from 15 days to less than 1. But the assembly savings on the plant floor are just one aspect of what A-B has achieved in the Twinsburg plant.

The process really begins with the perception of market need, according to Mr. Davis. To save time and eliminate waste from manufacturing, all the information required to build products had to be brought together on the plant floor—from four different divisional engineering departments. Three are in Highland Heights, Ohio, and one is in Ann Arbor, Michigan.

Originally the exchange of printed data took weeks. Extra manpower was needed to extract data from one system and regenerate the information. In effect, says Mr. Davis, people were using buckets to fill one data reservoir by dipping into another—and some data were being spilled in the process.

Careful control was required just to make sure that everyone was working with the same document versions and that no data had been lost or misinterpreted. With the new integration of information, Mr. Davis estimates that 50 man-hours of time and manpower per board design have been saved in test engineering alone. He says the time required to generate machine programs from engineering data has been reduced by two weeks or more. "Meanwhile, by controlling information better, we've improved control over production processes."

At this point, A-B can design, build, and test with common data. Next on the agenda is linking the surface-mount assembly with inventory and quality-information systems. Data, which have begun to flow as a trickle between business segments, will run more freely. Indirect labor will become more productive. "Not only will inventory and quality costs be lowered, but we will also be able to build our products better and faster than the competition," adds Mr. Davis.

Source: Excerpted from John Teresko, "Speeding the Product Development Cycle," *Industry Week*, July 18, 1988, 40–41.

of employees in Perrow's nonroutine technology and Thompson's intensive technology, where employees are required to solve problems and coordinate their own activities. Thus, AIT and CIM have a number of implications for how organizations design jobs, coordinate activities, people, and work units, make decisions, and solve problems.

Less Job Specialization

AIT and CIM technologies place different demands on employees than traditional production technologies. They decrease the number of routine, specialized jobs by building their activities—and the rules, policies, and procedures that govern them—into the hardware and software of a production system itself. Production workers in the new technologies supervise the operation of the hardware, maintain it, and solve problems that arise. These tasks call for a different set of skills than was required of production workers in the past: fundamental literacy, number and communication skills, the ability to learn and the ability to reason, to draw conclusions, to express ideas, and to exercise judgment.[38] As a result, workers need to be more educated than before, and flexible enough to learn new skills as their jobs change.

One indication of this change is provided by aerospace firms in southern California that have adopted AIT and CIM technologies. Northrop, McDonnell Douglas, Hughes Aircraft, TRW, General Dynamics, Lockheed, and Rockwell have formed a consortium with three local community colleges to ensure a supply of highly trained workers needed in AIT and CIM operating environments. The consortium developed programs offering degrees in manufacturing technology. "The courses provide training in as many as seven different areas, including manufacturing, materials processing, drafting, machinery, and computer-aided design. 'The purpose is to provide the most skilled and flexible employees for the aerospace industry,' says Susan Cotler, dean of industrial arts at El Camino College in Torrance, California. 'The key word is *flexible*.'"[39]

Organizations also are changing their reward systems to fit these new job requirements. At the General Electric plant in Bromont, Quebec, production employees are salaried, and their salaries are based on the number of skills learned.[40] Some organizations are beginning to reward employees on the basis of flexibility, not output; for what they can do instead of what they do.

Overall, changes in job design along the lines discussed in Chapter 4 are entirely consistent with the demands of the new technologies. Jobs tend to be horizontally enlarged because the new technologies increase job complexity. Jobs also tend to become vertically enriched because employees need more discretion to deal with the unexpected.

Reduced RPPs and Increased Training and Socialization

Because the rules, policies, and procedures that govern standardized jobs are built into the hardware and software of a production process, organizations that employ new technologies have less need for RPPs (rules, policies, and procedures) to coordinate and control employee behavior. Training and socialization play much greater roles, especially since most organizations need to change their cultures to use the new technologies effectively. And, as we discussed in Chapter 4, educational programs play a major role in socializing employees to a new organizational philosophy.

At the Centrilift-Hughes Division of Hughes Tool Company, for example, implementation of a materials-resource planning system required a substantial commitment to education and behavioral change. The system began by sending the six-man top-management team to special training sessions. Eventually, over 700 employees spent over 15,000 man-hours in in-house education. Everyone from the president to switchboard operators spent some time using video training tapes, and key personnel attended classes so they could teach others about the system. Besides providing people with information about how to operate the system, the extensive training was said to accomplish the following:

> [It] promotes a feeling of ownership and accountability that is crucial to the success of the implementation. If successful, that leads to behavioral change. People become convinced of the need to do their jobs differently because they recognize that the new way gives better and faster service, increases sales volume, and makes the company more competitive.[41]

Operational Decentralization and Strategic Centralization

AIT and CIM are likely to result in the decentralization of decision making in some areas and centralization in others. Operating decisions are likely to become more decentralized; strategic decision making may become more centralized. Decentralization in operating decisions is likely because these technologies eliminate the positions of middle managers and staff members whose sole role was to collect and process information, as well as those of employees who were in now automated production jobs. The removal of managerial layers leaves the technical and professional specialists who do an organization's work with more authority to make operational decisions. The result should be an increase in the speed with which such decisions are made.

Strategic decision making, on the other hand, may become more formally centralized. Because people can be linked electronically, AIT makes remoteness in time and location less of a factor in coordinating the involvement of people in decision making and problem solving. This is likely to have two effects: First, *formal* decision-making units (e.g., top-management teams) are likely to be smaller because these decision makers will have greater access to more information and expertise because of AIT. Second, more people will *informally* participate in decision making and problem solving because of the ease of linking them electronically. The overall result will be that experts within an organization will have less of a formal role in decision making but greater influence in an advising capacity because their expertise will be more easily accessed through AIT.[42]

More Market-Based Grouping and Greater Use of Integrating Mechanisms

CIM, in particular, appears to have a pronounced effect on unit grouping because of the high level of integration it provides. Brian Moore, general manager of Hewlett-Packard's Manufacturing Systems Group, says

> CIM is not a 'natural act' for a manufacturing organization, nor is integrating anything a 'natural act' for any organization. A business organization is designed in islands of [functional] authority, with activities conducted in discrete departments. In CIM, we wrap all these together in an integrated whole, so that everyone can be highly interdependent on one another.[43]

CIM integration amplifies workflow interdependence, which increases the need for market-based unit grouping to enhance coordination across functional areas. In the product-design phase, for example, computer-assisted design and engineering require that design engineers and production engineers work more closely together. One technique that accommodates increased workflow interdependence is the task-focused team, where specialists from all functional areas work together from the inception of research to a product's establishment in the market.[44] While this type of organizing device helps coordinate workflow interdependence for a product, the constantly changing mix of products makes it difficult to preprogram the overall pattern of an interaction among work units. As a result, the integrating mechanisms discussed in Chapter 5 are likely to play a large role in interunit coordination.

The overriding concern with coordinating workflow interdependence extends into the production area itself. Many organizations with traditional manufacturing systems group production units by function (i.e., by type of machine or by stage in the production process). A common technique for grouping in CIM organizations entails the placement of machinery and people into *manufacturing cells,* which means grouping by output rather than by function. William G. Rankin, general manager of Deere & Co. Technical Services, explains that at his company this means "rather than a lathe department or a milling department, we might have a department for production of a range of sizes of parts of rotation."[45]

This grouping method provides advantages both in product design and manufacture. In design, engineers can more easily avoid reinventing parts by checking to see if similar parts are already available. In production, the

Table 6.3
Comparison of the Characteristics of Mass Production and
Computer-Integrated Manufacturing (CIM) Organizations

Organizational Characteristics	Mass-Production Technology Organizations	CIM Organizations
Environment	Stable, little change, low complexity	Turbulent, dynamic change, complex
Strategy	Economies of scale, control environment, cost leadership	Economies of scope, adapt to environment, product quality, low cost, dependability, flexibility
Product life cycle	Long	Short
Products	Simple or complex, low differentiation	Complex, changing, high differentiation
Structure	Mechanistic	Organic
Span of control (First-level)	Wide	Narrow
Vertical levels	Many	Few
Tasks	Routine, repetitive	Responsive, craftlike
Specialization (Production)	High	Low
Integration	Low	High
Decision making	Centralized	Decentralized
Information flow	Vertical	Horizontal
Power base	Position	Knowledge
Behavior	Standardized	Adaptive
Management skills	Specific, detailed	Integrative
Rewards	Individual/production	Group/innovation
Control	Bureaucratic	Self-regulatory

Source: Patricia L. Nemetz and Louis W. Fry, "Flexible Manufacturing Organizations: Implications for Strategy Formulation and Organization Design," *Academy of Management Review* 13 (1988), 632.

proximity of all the functions required to produce a good or component reduces lead times and material-handling costs. Manufacturing-cell employees tend to be organized into *product teams* that share responsibility for the machines in their cell. Because manufacturing cells are organized by output, product teams typically perform all the operations needed to complete a "whole" product, and they often have discretion over a broad range of operating decisions.[46]

These changes in design are most apparent in contrasting the traditional, functionally organized mass-production organization with an organization that has adopted a CIM production technology. Table 6.3 summarizes the structural differences between these two types of organizations. Overall, these types of changes have the potential of simplifying management structures. Eliminating managerial levels and staff can increase an organization's rate of innovation and its speed of response to changing market conditions by empowering people at lower levels of an organization to take risks and make decisions.[47]

SUMMARY

Learning Objective 1: Give a general definition of technology. Technology can be defined as the techniques or processes used to transform labor, knowledge, capital, or raw materials into finished goods or services.

Learning Objective 2: Discuss Woodward's concept of technological complexity. According to Woodward, technological complexity reflects the degree of control and predictability in a production process. She derived three general categories of technology that she viewed as increasing in technological complexity: unit/small-batch, mass production, and process/continuous-flow production.

Learning Objective 3: Discuss Thompson's concept of technological interdependence. According to Thompson, technological interdependence is based on the pattern of an organization's workflows. He defined three different categories of technology—mediating, long-linked, and intensive—each having a different pattern of workflow interdependence—pooled, sequential, and reciprocal—that reflect the degree to which work units depend on each other to complete their objectives. As interdependence increases, the need for employee discretion in problem solving and associated coordination costs also increase.

Learning Objective 4: Discuss Perrow's concepts of the number and analyzability of exceptions as dimensions of technology. Perrow's concept of technology is based on two dimensions: the number of exceptions that occur in the technological process and the extent to which these exceptions are analyzable. The resulting typology (routine, engineering, craft, and nonroutine technologies) focuses attention on the likelihood that subunits within an organization may be designed differently because of differences in the nature of the work they perform.

Learning Objective 5: Compare and contrast the results of the Woodward and Aston studies of the effects of technology on organization structure. The results of Woodward's studies revealed that unit/small-batch and process/continuous-flow technologies were associated with similar organization structures (market-based grouping, relatively less job specialization, and relatively decentralized decision-making processes) that were different from that of mass-production technologies (functional unit grouping, relatively high degree of job specialization and centralization). She concluded that technology is the major determinant of organization structure.

In contrast, the Aston researchers found few relationships between technology and structural characteristics. They concluded instead that an organization's size intervenes in the relationship between technology and structure. Technology was viewed as likely to have an effect on structure in small organizations, but the effect would decrease as organizational size increased.

Learning Objective 6: Describe the benefits of advanced information technologies for organizations. The data networks created by AIT can streamline operations in four ways: (1) increase efficiency by reducing the time spent and personnel involved in data collection and entry, (2) decrease processing time by making a single source of information available throughout an organization, (3) enhance coordination across an organization's subunits, and (4) improve decision making and problem solving across geographically dispersed operations.

Learning Objective 7: Describe the benefits of computer-integrated manufacturing systems for organizations. Through electronic integration, computer-integrated manufacturing systems offer organizations a production technology that can produce high-quality goods, tailored to customer specifications, quickly, at a competitive price.

Learning Objective 8: Explain how advanced information technologies and computer-integrated manufacturing affect organization design. To gain the full benefits of AIT and CIM, it appears that organizations need to horizontally enlarge and vertically enrich jobs, shift their coordination and control emphasis from rules, policies, and procedures to training and socialization, delegate more authority to make operational decisions to lower levels, rely more heavily on market-based forms of unit grouping, and increase the use of integrating mechanisms to control interdependence.

Discussion Questions

1. A commercial bakery producing several lines of cookies and snack crackers has hired you as an organization design consultant. Management's problem is a high level of waste: errors in mixing remain undetected for long periods, and products are often under- or overbaked. The production unit is grouped into several functional departments—mixing, baking, packing, and shipping. Each type of baked good is produced on a separate line. Dough is mixed and formed in the mixing department and placed on a conveyor belt that travels through a continuous oven. As a conveyor belt exits an oven, it enters the packing department, where employees hand-pack the items. Completed packages then move to the shipping department. Communication between the departments is poor. What design options do you recommend to management and why?

2. You are a production supervisor in a company where top management has decided to introduce a computer-integrated manufacturing system. The system will replace a large number of horizontally specialized production jobs. To date, no changes in your functionally organized production department have been planned by top management, and production employees have resisted attempts to implement the new system. Your job depends on getting the new system up and running. What are the problems here, and what should you do to get the system implemented?

3. How would you classify the technologies of a McDonald's restaurant, your college, and a police department using Thompson's and Perrow's typologies? How are they different? What similarities do you detect? What implications do these different technologies have for the design of jobs in these organizations?

4. Explain why you agree or disagree with Jack Ring's statement that the survivors in manufacturing in the year 2000 will be those who are getting ready to enter the era of computer-integrated manufacturing? Under what circumstances do you think organizations using more traditional technologies will be able to compete in the future?

5. Libraries are among the many service organizations that have begun using advanced information technologies (AIT) in their operations. Computerized card catalogs, circulation operations, and reference services have become common. Do you think that AIT has had a major impact on the structure of these organizations? What effects might these changes have on the design of jobs, the efficiency of operations, and the accessibility of library services to the patrons? Explain your reasoning.

6. Search through a current issue of *Business Week, Fortune, Forbes,* or other business periodicals and see how many instances you can find of organizations adopting new information and manufacturing technologies. What benefits are these firms hoping to gain from these new technologies? What problems do they appear to be having in implementing them?

DESIGN AUDIT #6

Analyzing Your Organization's Technology

This design audit will help you gain an understanding of the relationship between technology and structure by applying the concepts in this chapter to your organization.

Hint: *If you are analyzing the structure of a large organization, you may want to complete the following steps for the division with which you are most familiar.*

Core Technology

1. What is the core or overall technology this organization uses to produce its primary good or service, using Woodward's, Thompson's, or Perrow's terminology. Which model fits your organization's technology best? Why does it fit? Draw a picture of how work flows through the organization's subunits in the space below.

Subunit Technologies

2. Using the organization charts you drew in Question 2 of Design Audit #5 as a guide, classify the technologies of the subunits you described earlier. Also provide a brief description of these subunits' major tasks.

   Hint: Use Thompson's technology classification (Figure 6.2) to classify these subunits' technologies, unless Woodward's or Perrow's classifications fit better.

a. Subunit #1 _____   Tech. Type _____

b. Subunit #2 _____   Tech. Type _____

c. Subunit #3 _____   Tech. Type _____

d. Subunit #4 _____   Tech. Type _____

e. Subunit #5 _____   Tech. Type _____

3. Outline the subunits' structural characteristics in the spaces below and indicate the extent to which each subunit's structure and technology fit together on the scales to the right. For example, if a unit uses a mass-production technology, is there evidence of functional grouping, high levels of job specialization, extensive RPPs, centralized decision making, etc? If there are inconsistencies between technology and structure, are there any identifiable problems that might be resolved by redesign?

Hint: Table 6.1 is a useful guide for examining structure-technology fit.

Subunit #1 characteristics   (Fit: Excellent   5   4   3   2   1   Poor)

Subunit #2 characteristics   (Fit: Excellent   5   4   3   2   1   Poor)

Subunit #3 characteristics   (Fit: Excellent   5   4   3   2   1   Poor)

Subunit #4 characteristics   (Fit: Excellent   5   4   3   2   1   Poor)

Subunit #5 characteristics   (Fit: Excellent   5   4   3   2   1   Poor)

Advanced Information Technologies and Computer-Integrated Manufacturing

4. **a.** To what extent are advanced information technologies (AIT) or computer-integrated manufacturing (CIM) used in your organization?

b. Do you see any potential uses for AIT or CIM in your organization? What are the potential benefits?

c. What changes in design would be required for successful implementation, or to improve the use of existing AIT and CIM applications?

Notes

1. Peter M. Blau, Cecilia M. Falbe, William McKinley, and Tracy Phelps, "Technology and Organization in Manufacturing," *Administrative Science Quarterly* 21 (1976): 20.

2. Joseph A. Litterer, *The Analysis of Organizations,* 2d ed., (New York: Wiley, 1973), 280.

3. Wickham Skinner, "The Impact of Changing Technology on the Working Environment," in *Work in America: The Decade Ahead,* ed. Clark Kerr and Jerome M. Rostow (New York: Van Nostrand Reinhold, 1979), 204–230.

4. Robert E. McGinn, "What Is Technology?" *Research in Philosophy and Technology* 1 (1978): 179–197.

5. Joan Woodward, *Management and Technology* (London: Her Majesty's Stationery Office, 1958), 12.

6. David J. Hickson, Derek S. Pugh, and Diane C. Phessey, "Operations Technology and Organization Structure: An Empirical Reappraisal," *Administrative Science Quarterly* 14 (1969): 378.

7. Andrew J. Grimes and Stuart M. Kline, "The Technological Imperative: The Relative Impact of Task Unit, Modal Technology, and Hierarchy on Structure," *Academy of Management Journal* 16 (1973): 583–597; Andrew Van de Ven and Andre Delbecq, "A Task Contingent Model of Work Unit Structure," *Administrative Science Quarterly* 19 (1974): 183–197.

8. Lawrence G. Hrebiniak, "Job Technology, Supervisor, and Work Group Structure," *Administrative Science Quarterly* 19 (1974): 395–410; Lawrence Mohr, "Organizational Technology and Organization Structure," *Administrative Science Quarterly* 16 (1971): 444–459.

9. The differences between approaches also leads to different types of results in studies of the relationships between technology and structure. For example, see Donald E. Comstock and W. Richard Scott, "Technology and the Structure of Subunits," *Administrative Science Quarterly* 22 (1977): 177–202; Denise M. Rousseau, "Measures of Technology as Predictors of Employee Attitude," *Journal of Applied Psychology* 63 (1978): 213–218; Denise M. Rousseau, "Assessment of Technology in Organizations: Closed versus Open Systems Approaches," *Academy of Management Review* 4 (1979): 531–542; Bernard Reimann, "Organization Structure and Technology in Manufacturing: Systems versus Work Flow Level Perspectives," *Academy of Management Journal* 23 (1980): 61–77.

10. John E. T. Eldridge and Alastair D. Crombie, *A Sociology of Organizations* (London: George Allen & Unwin, 1974), 107. [emphasis added]

11. Robert Albanese, *Managing Toward Accountability for Performance,* 3d ed. (Homewood, Ill.: Richard D. Irwin, 1981), 551.

12. Woodward, *Management and Technology*; Joan Woodward, *Industrial Organization: Theory and Practice* (London: Oxford University Press, 1965).

13. Edward Harvey, "Technology and the Structure of Organizations," *American Sociological Review* 33 (1968): 249.

14. Adapted from Joan Woodward, "Automation and Technical Changes—The Implications for the Management Process," in *Organizational Structure and Design,* ed.

Gene W. Dalton, Paul R. Lawrence, and Jay W. Lorsch (Homewood, Ill.: Richard D. Irwin, 1970), 300–301.

15. The original goal statement of this research program appeared in Derek S. Pugh, David J. Hickson, C. Robin Hinings, Keith M. MacDonald, Christopher Turner, and Tom Lupton, "A Conceptual Scheme for Organizational Analysis," *Administrative Science Quarterly* 8 (1963): 289–315.

16. David J. Hickson, Derek S. Pugh, and Diane Phessey, "Operations Technology and Organizational Structure: An Empirical Appraisal," *Administrative Science Quarterly* 14 (1969): 394–395.

17. Critical reviews of the Woodward and Aston studies over the past 25 years have pointed out a number of methodological weaknesses. Critics note that problems with the samples and methods in both studies, and the lack of sophisticated analyses in Woodward's study in particular, could limit the accuracy and generalizability of their findings. Despite these deficiencies, the Woodward and Aston studies are the only large-scale, programmatic research that has been undertaken on the relationship between technology and structure. Their results and the debates they generated have set the direction of theory and research on technology and structure since the mid-1960s.

For critiques of the Woodward studies, see Woodward, *Industrial Organization*, 10; Woodward, "Automation and Technical Change," 301, Terence K. Hopkins, "Review of Industrial Organization: Theory and Practice by Joan Woodward," *Administrative Science Quarterly* 11 (1966): 284–289; Louis F. Davis and James C. Taylor, "Technology, Organization, and Job Structure," in *Handbook of Work Organization and Society,* ed. Robert Dubin (Chicago: Rand-McNally, 1976), 380; Lex Donaldson, "Woodward Technology, Organizational Structure, and Performance—A Critique of the Universal Generalization," *Journal of Management Studies* 13 (1976): 255–273; Samuel Eilon, "Structural Determinism," *Omega* 5 (1977): 499–504.

For criticisms of the Aston studies, see C. Neville Osmond, "Organization—Is Technology the Key?" *Personnel Managment* 2, no. 5 (1970): 43–44; Howard E. Aldrich, "Technology and Organizational Structure: A Reexamination of the Findings of the Aston Group," *Administrative Science Quarterly* 17 (1972): 26–43; Edward A. Holdaway, John F. Newberry, David J. Hickson, and R. Peter Heron, "Dimensions of Organizations in Complex Societies: The Educational Sector," *Administrative Science Quarterly* 20 (1975): 47–58; William McKelvey, "Guidelines for the Empirical Classification of Organizations," *Administrative Science Quarterly* 20 (1975): 509–525; John L. Kmetz, "A Critique of the Aston Studies and Results with a New Measure of Technology," *Organization and Administrative Sciences* 8, no. 4 (1977–1978): 123–144; William H. Starbuck, "A Trip to View the Elephants and Rattlesnakes in the Garden of Aston," in *Perspectives on Organization Design,* ed. Andrew H. Van de Ven and William J. Joyce (New York: Wiley, 1981), 167–198; Richard S. Blackburn, "Dimensions of Structure: A Review and Reappraisal," *Academy of Management Review* 7 (1982): 59–66.

18. James D. Thompson, *Organizations in Action* (New York: McGraw-Hill, 1967) 15–18.

19. Thompson, *Organizations in Action,* 6.

20. Denise M. Rousseau, "Measures of Technology as Predictors of Employee Attitude," *Journal of Applied Psychology* 63 (1978): 214.

21. Thompson, *Organizations in Action,* 42.

22. Ibid., 17.

23. Charles Perrow, "A Framework for the Comparative Analysis of Organizations," *American Sociological Review* 32 (1967): 194–208; Charles Perrow, *Organizational Analysis: A Sociological View* (Monterey, Calif.: Wadsworth, 1970), 80–85.

24. Perrow, *Organizational Analysis: A Sociological View,* 81.

25. Michael Borrus and John Zysman, "The New Media, Telecommunications and Development: The Choices for the United States and Japan," BRIE Working Paper 7 (1984), quoted in Stephen S. Cohen and John Zysman, *Manufacturing Matters: The Myth of the Post-Industrial Economy* (New York: Basic Books, 1987), 182.

26. Cohen and Zysman, *Manufacturing Matters,* 178–185.

27. Jon Pepper, "Sweet Success in Sales Automation," *Working Woman,* April 1989, 59–62.

28. Paula Musich, "Airline Designs Software to Move Planes, People," *PC Week,* June 7, 1988, C11.

29. Johannes M. Pennings, "Technological Innovations in Manufacturing," in *New Technology as Organizational Innovation,* ed. Johannes M. Pennings and Arend Buitendam, (Cambridge, Mass.: Ballinger, 1987), 198.

30. The following definitions are drawn largely from James W. Dean, Jr., and Gerald I. Susman, "Strategic Responses to Global Competition: Advanced Technology, Organization Design, and Human Resource Practices," in *Strategy, Organization Design, and Human Resource Management,* ed. Charles C. Snow (Greenwich, Conn.: JAI Press, 1989), 305–309.

31. Arend Buitendam, "The Horizontal Perspective of Organization Design and New Technology," in *New Technology as Organizational Innovation,* ed. Johannes M. Pennings and Arend Buitendam (Cambridge, Mass.: Ballinger, 1987), 62–63.

32. Cohen and Zysman, *Manufacturing Matters,* 154.

33. Robert F. Huber, "Simulate, Integrate, Innovate," *Production* 99 (November 1987): 47.

34. Carol Parsons, "The Diffusion of New Manufacturing Technologies in U.S. Industry," Unpublished paper, BRIE, University of California, Berkeley, 1985, quoted in Cohen and Zysman, *Manufacturing Matters,* 154.

35. Cohen and Zysman, *Manufacturing Matters,* 156.

36. John Teresko, "CIM: Much More Than Adding Computers," *Industry Week,* February 9, 1987, 47.

37. For example, see John E. Ettlie, *Taking Charge of Manufacturing: How Companies Are Combining Technological and Organizational Innovation to Compete Successfully* (San Francisco: Jossey-Bass, 1988) and Richard E. Walton, *Up and Running: Integrating Information Technology and the Organization* (Boston: Harvard Business School Press, 1989).

38. Wayne F. Cascio and Raymond F. Zammuto, "Societal Trends and Staffing Policies," in *Human Resource Planning, Employment, and Placement,* ed. Wayne F. Cascio (Washington, D.C.: BNA/ASPA, 1989), 27.

39. "The Aerospace Labor Crunch," *Newsweek,* July 18, 1988, 45.

40. Teresko, "CIM: Much More Than Adding Computers," 52.

41. "Integrated Manufacturing II: Team Approach Pays Off," *Industry Week*, September 29, 1986, IM9.

42. George P. Huber, "The Nature and Design of Post-Industrial Organizations," *Management Science* 30 (1984): 934.

43. Teresko, "CIM: Much More Than Adding Computers," 49.

44. Peter F. Drucker, "The Coming of the New Organization," *Harvard Business Review* 88, no. 1 (1988): 47.

45. Huber, "Simulate, Integrate, Innovate," 44.

46. Dean, Jr., and Susman, "Strategic Responses to Global Competition," 322.

47. Robert H. Guest, "Management Imperatives for the Year 2000," *California Management Review* 28, no. 4 (1986): 66.

Organization Design in a Global Economy

Learning Objectives

Upon completing this chapter, you should be able to

1. Explain why managers develop new organization designs.

2. Describe how the shift from pre-industrial economies with local markets to industrial economies with national markets has changed organizational coordination needs.

3. Describe how the shift from industrial economies to post-industrial economies in a global market has further changed organizational coordination needs.

4. Identify the differences among international-trade, country-focused, and globally integrated designs.

5. Explain how unit grouping, technology, integrating mechanisms, and socialization facilitate coordination in a globally integrated design.

6. Discuss the reasons for organizations using interorganizational designs.

7. List a variety of interorganizational designs that organizations are now using.

HOW COKE BEAT PEPSI TO THE PUNCH

In the worst way, PepsiCo, Inc. wants to go global. "We are still basically an American company with offshore interests," PepsiCo Chairman D. Wayne Calloway recently told analysts. Pepsi's Frito-Lay division is by far the dominant U.S. company in snack foods, and Pepsi has more restaurants than any other company in the world (it owns the Pizza Hut, Kentucky Fried Chicken, and Taco Bell chains); in snack foods as well as restaurants, Pepsi is expanding aggressively overseas.

But soft drinks are a different story. In the still-growing U.S. soft drink market, Pepsi holds an estimated 32 percent of the market, versus 40 percent for rival Coca-Cola. But overseas Pepsi badly lags behind Coke. What's Pepsi's problem? The answer is simple: In a brilliant ploy by Coke patriarch Robert Woodruff during World War II, Coke has been the early bird in most major foreign markets. In the 1940s Woodruff declared that wherever American boys were fighting they'd be able to get a Coke. That artful bit of patriotism got Coke some useful waivers from wartime sugar rationing, and it made Coke the GI's drink of choice. By the time Pepsi tried to make its first major international push, in the 1950s, Coke had already established its brand name and a powerful distribution network tailored to the global marketplace.

Pepsi is working feverishly to make its foreign operations more profitable. The cola wars that have kept the U.S. market growing for both Coke and Pepsi have spilled overseas. Clearly, the "first in" advantage enjoyed by Coke in many foreign markets will be a formidable obstacle for Pepsi to overcome. And as you'll discover in this chapter, going global means implementing new design strategies as well.

Source: Subrata N. Chakravarty, "How Pepsi Broke into India," *Forbes,* November 27, 1989, 43.

ARE the functional, divisional, and matrix designs all managers have to work with in designing organizations? Do these designs and their variations meet the complete range of organizational coordination needs? The answer to both questions is no. New designs are developed when (1) available designs are unable to meet new coordination needs, and (2) social and technological conditions make new designs possible.[1] This chapter outlines two major economic transitions that have created new organizational coordination needs: the shift from pre-industrial economies with local markets to industrial economies of national markets, and the current transition from an industrial to a post-industrial economy with a global market. We show how new designs have been developed to meet these changing coordination needs. Then we look in detail at two current trends in organization design: (1) a shift from export-based and country-focused multinational designs to globally integrated operations and (2) the rapid proliferation of cooperative, interorganizational designs.

FROM A PRE-INDUSTRIAL TO AN INDUSTRIAL ECONOMY: THE SHIFT FROM LOCAL TO NATIONAL MARKETS

Pre-Industrial Organization Designs

The large organizations common in our everyday lives are creatures of the Industrial Age. Most organizations in pre-industrial Western societies consisted of small groups organized around a family unit. British historian Peter Laslett, for example, describes a common pre-industrial organization, the bakery, in seventeenth century London this way:

> In the year 1619 the bakers of London applied to the authorities for an increase in the price of bread. They sent in support of their claim a complete description of a bakery and an account of its weekly costs. There were thirteen or fourteen people in such an establishment: the baker and his wife, four paid employees who were called journeymen, two apprentices, two maid servants and the three or four children of the master baker himself . . . .
>
> The only word used at the time to describe such a group of people was "family." The man at the head of the group, the entrepreneur, the employer, or the manager, was then known as the master or head of the family. He was father to some of its members and in place of father to the rest. There was no sharp distinction between his domestic and his economic functions. His wife was both his partner and his subordinate, a partner because she ran the family, took charge of the food and managed the women-servants, a subordinate because she was woman and wife, mother and in place of mother to the rest.[2]

During this period of history, people were dispersed over large areas in small villages, in towns, and on farms. In the simple, undifferentiated design common to pre-industrial organizations, markets were limited to a local community and its surrounding area. Coordination needs were thus simple and could be dealt with by an owner's direct supervision.

Most small businesses today start out with and retain the undifferentiated, simple structure characteristic of pre-industrial organizations, with coordination being achieved by an owner/manager's direct supervision. But as an organization's size increases beyond a few handfuls of people, direct supervision becomes inadequate for coordination—as we saw in the cases of Lots of Toys, Ltd. (Chapter 5) and Ed Conry's microcomputer store (Chapter 4). Much of industrialization's effect on organization design has to do with changing coordination needs because of increasing organizational size and complexity.

Industrial Organization Designs

Functional Designs. Of the many changes brought about by industrialization, the effect that we are most interested in here is the shift from local markets to national markets. A number of technological and social factors contributed to this shift—the development of nation-wide rail, postal, and telegraph systems, and the growth of urban areas—all of which expanded market opportunities for many organizations. Nation-wide rail systems made possible the efficient movement of materials and finished goods over long distances. More efficient postal and telegraph systems increased the ability of organizations to coordinate activities over long distances. And the growing concentration of people in urban areas accelerated market growth.

Organizations taking advantage of these opportunities grew rapidly, and as their size increased, direct supervision became inadequate for coordination. Expanding railroads were among the first organizations to experience the need for new coordinating mechanisms. The problem railroad managers faced was how to coordinate the activities of numerous geographically dispersed employees. Their response was the *functional design*, where people and jobs were grouped by functional speciality, a clear chain of command was identified, and managers' jobs were differentiated from those of production employees.

As other organizations took advantage of the new market opportunities opened by the railroads, they encountered similar coordination problems. As business historian Alfred Chandler notes,

> By speedily enlarging the market for American manufacturing, mining, and marketing firms, the railroads permitted and, in fact, often required that these enterprises expand and subdivide their activities. Such subdivision or specialization, in turn, called for a concentration of effort on coordinating, appraising, and planning the work of the specialized units. Expanding markets also encouraged the use of more complex machinery in manufacturing establishments. This new and increasingly complicated machinery in turn spurred further increases in output and so provided another pressure for expansion and continued growth.[3]

Focus on Design 7.1 describes how the development of a national railway system made the creation of a national meatpacking industry possible. The situation described was typical of the birth of many nation-wide industries during this period.

But increasing size alone was not responsible for the new coordination needs, particularly in manufacturing organizations. In the 1870s most manufacturers were single-function organizations—they produced goods. Supplies were bought and finished goods sold through commissioned agents, wholesalers, and other middlemen. By 1900, however, many industries were dominated by a few large organizations that had incorporated these activities into their own operations by vertically *integrating forward* into retail distribution, and *backward* into the acquisition of raw materials. The multi-functional nature of these large organizations increased the complexity of management and created new coordination needs. The additional problem managers faced in these organizations was how to manage a diverse set of functional activities that earlier had been coordinated through market transactions. Building

FOCUS ON DESIGN 7.1

The Development of a National Meatpacking Industry

A New England wholesale butcher, [Gustavus] Swift moved to Chicago in the mid-1870s. Coming from Massachusetts, he was aware of the growing demand for fresh meat in the eastern cities. After the Civil War, Boston, New York, Philadelphia, and other urban areas were calling for much more meat than could be supplied locally. At the same time, great herds of cattle were gathering on the Western plains. Swift saw an opportunity to bring together the new supply and the new demand by exploiting the new technology of refrigeration. In 1878, shortly after his first experimental shipment of refrigerated meat, he formed a partnership with his younger brother, Edwin, to market fresh western meat in the eastern cities.

For the next decade, Swift struggled to put into effect his plans for building a nationwide distributing and marketing organization . . . . By the end of the decade, Swift's initial strategies had proved eminently successful. His fast-growing distributing organization constantly called for more and more supplies. Between 1888 and 1892, Swift, who had incorporated his enterprise in 1885, set up meatpacking establishments in Omaha and St. Louis, and, after the depression of the 1900s, three more in St. Joseph, St. Paul, and Fort Worth. At the same time, the company systematized the buying of cattle and other products at the stockyards. It expanded its marketing facilities abroad as well as in the United States. Before the end of the 1890s, Swift had created a huge vertically integrated industrial empire.

Other packers quickly followed his example . . . .

Source: Reprinted from Alfred D. Chandler, Jr., *Strategy and Structure: Chapters in the History of the American Industrial Enterprise* (Cambridge, Mass.: MIT Press, 1962), 25–26.

on the railroads' solution, they developed the fully elaborated functional design discussed in Chapter 5. By the end of the nineteenth century, the functional design had been adopted by large organizations in many industries.[4]

Divisional Designs. After 1900, Chandler notes that manufacturers begin pursuing two new expansion strategies.[5] One was the move to develop markets in other countries. By 1914, for example, a number of U.S. manufacturers—such as Parke Davis, Sherwin-Williams, Du Pont, Ford, General Electric, and Eastman Kodak—had significant production and marketing operations overseas.[6] Second, manufacturers began developing new products for a broader range of customers. Geographic expansion and product diversification placed enormous strains on the coordination capabilities of existing functional structures. As a result, a number of organizations, most notably General Motors, Du Pont, Sears, and Standard Oil (New Jersey), began experimenting with decentralized, "divisional" structures that better enabled them to coordinate the multiple workflow interdependencies that geographically dispersed and multi-product operations created. *Divisional designs*, "which hardly existed in 1920, had by 1960 become the accepted form of management for the most complex and diverse of American industrial enterprises."[7]

Matrix Designs. The next major design innovation came about in the late 1950s as organizations attempted to cope with increasingly complex techno-logical problems and rapid rates of technological change. The result was *matrix design*, developed in 1957 by TRW Inc. cofounder Simon Ramo when functional and divisional designs proved inadequate for managing complex technological developments in the aerospace industry, and in rapidly emerg-ing joint military-industrial ventures. Undertakings such as the Atlas, Titan, Thor, and Minuteman missile projects were so complex that it was impossible to make a single manager responsible for their execution. It became necessary not only to coordinate large numbers of people, materials, and facilities internally, but also to coordinate these activities with those of outside con-tractors. To complicate matters further, technological developments cut across traditional functional boundaries. What was needed was a structural design for blending the technical know-how of different disciplines. The available functional and market-based alternatives for grouping jobs and work units could not do this, so the matrix design was developed.

In short, managers have developed new designs to deal with new coordina-tion problems created by increased organizational complexity and size. The functional design met the problems of increased organization size and atten-dant multiple functional specialities. The divisional design met the problems of multi-market and multi-product operations. The matrix design met the problems of multi-function and multi-product/market organizations affected by rapidly changing technological conditions. But during the 1970s and 1980s, still more coordination needs appeared as economic, social, and tech-nological conditions continued to evolve, particularly as shaped by the globalization of markets and rapid advances in microprocessor technologies.

FROM AN INDUSTRIAL TO A POST-INDUSTRIAL ECONOMY: THE SHIFT FROM NATIONAL MARKETS TO A GLOBAL MARKET

Since the end of World War II, there has been gradual globalization of the world's economies. The United States emerged from World War II as the world's dominant economic power. The economies of Western Europe and

Japan had been devastated, and few other countries had industrialized. The rebuilding of the Western European economies and the gradual industrialization of Third World countries expanded existing markets and created new ones. U.S. firms took advantage of these new and expanding market opportunities (and helped create them) by becoming multinational organizations during the 1950s and 1960s. They dominated the international economic scene through the 1960s. But at least four major factors have changed the landscape of international trade since the 1960s: (1) the industrialization of many national economies, (2) the subsequent rise in many nations' standard of living, (3) the development of global telecommunication and transportation networks, and (4) the rapid pace of technological development.

Global Industrialization

As the economies of Western Europe and Japan were rebuilt, and as many lesser developed countries—such as South Korea, Taiwan, Brazil, Malaysia, and Mexico—began industrializing, U.S. firms faced new competitors. At first this competition was in the foreign markets where U.S. multinationals operated. Then the scope of competition became international as foreign firms also began exporting. Graham Astley and Richard Braham explain how the expanding global industrial base affected international trade in terms of the U.S. economy:

> Prior to 1960, foreign trade did not figure significantly in the U.S. economy. This situation had changed dramatically by 1980, when 70 percent of all the goods produced in the U.S. were actively competing with foreign-made goods. By 1980, America was importing 25 percent of its cars, 25 percent of its steel, 60 percent of its calculators, 27 percent of its metal-forming machine tools, 35 percent of its textile machinery, and 53 percent of its numerically-controlled machine tools. Twenty years earlier, imports had accounted for less then 10 percent of the U.S. market for each of these products.[8]

By the late 1980s, U.S. domination of the world's economy had ended. Table 7.1 presents a breakdown of the 1989 *Business Week* Global 1000, a ranking of the world's 1,000 largest firms based on market value. These firms had a combined market value of $6.4 trillion in 1989.[9] The data show that 384 North American firms accounted for 34.2 percent of the total, 376 Asian firms for 48.7 percent, and 240 European firms for 16.9 percent. The table also shows significant variation by industry. In 1989 large financial firms were fairly evenly divided among North America, Asia, and Europe. But over half the large energy companies and utilities were North American, as were almost half the large service firms. Asian firms, Japanese in particular, dominated the capital goods industries (electronic goods and components, construction and housing, data processing and reproduction, machinery, etc.). And almost 50 percent of the large materials companies (steel, chemicals, building materials and components, etc.) were located in Asian countries.

Table 7.1

1989 *Business Week* Global 1000 by Region, Country, and Industry Group

Industry Group	Energy	Materials	Capital Equipment	Consumer Goods	Services	Finance	Multi-Industry	Gold Mining	Total No. of Firms	% Total Market Value
North America	63	40	45	61	93	63	17	2	384	34.2
(% industry total)	60%	30%	30%	36%	47%	32%	45%	40%		
Canada	7	4	1	2	6	7	3	1	31	1.8
United States	56	36	44	59	87	56	14	1	353	32.4
Europe	18	32	27	43	39	65	16	0	240	16.9
(% industry total)	17%	24%	18%	25%	20%	33%	42%	0%		
Belgium	4	1	0	0	0	2	3	0	10	.5
Britain	4	11	9	19	24	19	7	0	93	7.1
Denmark	0	0	0	0	2	0	0	0	2	.1
Finland	0	1	0	0	0	3	1	0	5	.2
France	2	6	3	7	6	6	1	0	31	1.8
Italy	0	1	2	1	8	1	0	0	15	1.0
Netherlands	2	2	0	2	1	4	0	0	11	1.0
Norway	1	0	0	0	0	0	0	0	1	.1
Spain	3	1	0	0	1	6	0	0	11	.7
Sweden	0	4	5	4	0	4	2	0	19	.9
Switzerland	0	1	1	4	0	6	0	0	12	1.1
West Germany	2	4	7	6	3	7	1	0	30	2.4
Asia & Oceania	24	63	80	67	67	70	5	0	376	48.7
(% industry total)	23%	47%	52%	39%	33%	35%	13%	0%		
Australia	1	4	1	0	3	3	2	0	14	.9
Hong Kong	2	0	0	0	0	5	2	0	12	.6
Japan	21	58	79	67	60	60	0	0	345	47.0
Singapore/Malaysia	0	0	0	0	1	2	1	0	4	.2
New Zealand	0	1	0	0	0	0	0	0	1	.0
Africa	0	1	0	0	0	0	0	3	4	.2
(% industry total)	0%	1%	0%	0%	0%	0%	0%	60%		
South Africa	0	1	0	0	0	0	0	3	4	.2
Industry Group:										
Number firms	105	135	152	171	199	198	38	5		
Percent total	10%	13%	15%	17%	20%	20%	4%	.5%		

Source: Compiled from "The Business Week Global 1000," *Business Week*, July 17, 1989, pp. 145–176.

Figure 7.1
Motor Vehicles per 1,000 Population: 1960–1985

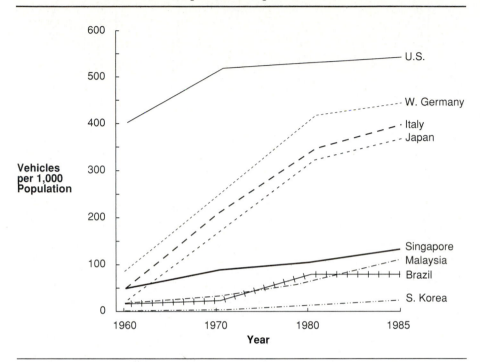

Source: United Nations, *World Statistics in Brief*, (New York: United Nations, 1977 and 1987).

A number of companies in newly industrialized countries are not included in the Global 1000 because their stock markets are closed to foreign investors and major corporations are often privately owned. But again there is evidence of significant industrial development having taken place. In South Korea, for example, twenty-one companies had over $1 billion in sales in 1988, in Taiwan five companies, in Brazil four companies; and in Mexico one company. These data simply emphasize the rapid expansion of the global industrial base that has taken place since World War II.[10]

Rising Living Standards

Industrialization has increased many countries' standard of living and provided people with more disposable income. Consider the demand for automobiles, which is the largest purchase most people make other than buying a home. Figure 7.1 shows changes in passenger vehicle ownership per 1,000 population in eight countries between 1960 and 1985. In the United States, the most car-intensive nation, the rate of vehicle ownership has steadily climbed from 403 cars per 1,000 population in 1960 to 547 cars in 1985. But the rate of increase has been considerably lower than demand growth in other countries. For example, the number of passenger vehicles per 1,000 population in Japan increased from 20 to 374 during the same period, in Italy 49 to 405, and in West Germany 91 to 450. And while the absolute numbers are smaller in the newly developing economies, the rate of growth over 25 years has been substantially higher than in the United States.

Growth in passenger vehicle demand is a strong indication that demand growth for other consumer goods and services has increased at even higher rates. Automobiles are expensive, often the most costly good that many individuals purchase. By the time people can afford automobiles, they usually have begun purchasing less expensive consumer goods. Focus on Design 7.2 provides an unusual example of how consumption grows as living standards rise.

In short, as living standards rise, markets expand and opportunities for organizations to sell their goods and services increase rapidly. Moreover, higher growth rates in other parts of the world indicate why U.S.–based organizations have become and are becoming global organizations: While the United States is the world's largest market, it is also relatively mature. Most of the major opportunities for growth lie outside the United States. And while the U.S. market is relatively mature, its size and the relative absence of trade barriers make it very attractive to foreign producers.

Global Transportation and Telecommunications

Industrialization and rising living standards alone do not account for the globalization of the world economy. A third factor is the increasing ease and decreasing cost of international transport and communication, which enable people to see the different lifestyles and range of goods and services available around the world. In 1950, for example, 676,000 U.S. citizens traveled to foreign countries, and 242,000 foreign nationals visited the United States. By 1985, 10 million Americans were traveling overseas, and over 8 million foreign visitors were received in the United States.[11] Moreover, global telecommunications expose people to much the same cultural, commercial, and news information worldwide. MTV, for example, is broadcast in Europe via satellite. The Cable News Network (CNN) is available in over 80 countries and is rapidly expanding. U.S. television programs are a fixture in most countries, and foreign programming has become common in the United States since the advent of cable television. Now people in all corners of the world "can see for themselves what the tastes and preferences are in other countries, the styles of clothing now in fashion, the sports, the lifestyles."[12]

Widespread international travel and global telecommunications are homogenizing consumer tastes. Or as Roberto C. Goizueta, chairman of the Coca-Cola Company, says, "People around the world are today connected to

---

FOCUS ON DESIGN 7.2

Consumption and the Rising Standard of Living in South Korea

Sales of consumer products less expensive than automobiles increase rapidly as an industrializing nation's standard of living rises. An unusual example is provided by the increased sales of Spam in South Korea, a country, which Figure 7.1 showed, with a rate of passenger vehicle ownership that is still far below that of many other industrial and industrializing countries. In the United States, Spam, manufactured by Hormel, is the stuff of children's lunch boxes and often the poor. In South Korea, it is a delicacy for which Koreans acquired a taste during the 1950s when it was a common item in American soldiers' C-rations. Now Spam is an upscale product, selling for over $3 per can. It also is considered a tasteful gift, appropriate for employees to give to their bosses and business associates.

The Spam boom began in 1987, when the South Korean government lifted its barriers against the import of canned pork products. The market grew rapidly with entry of European, Japanese, and U.S. producers, and a thriving black market emerged. Some Spam makes it into South Korea through Korean-American entrepreneurs who purchase it in bulk from U.S. supermarket warehouses and send it to Korea by the shipping container. More makes it to the market through U.S. Army PXs in Korea, which sell about 447,000 pounds a year to some 60,000 authorized personnel, most of which reappears on the black market.

Why do South Koreans buy Spam? As *The Wall Street Journal* noted, Koreans "now eat Spam not because they are poor, but because they are no longer poor . . . . [Its distributor has positioned Spam] as an upscale product, playing on America's trend-setting image. The luncheon meat is part of a boom in American products that includes Anne Klein fashions, Baskin-Robbins ice cream, and McDonald's hamburgers."

Source: Damon Darlin, "Something to Keep in Mind Next Time You Get a Fruitcake," *The Wall Street Journal*, September 20, 1989, A1, A10.

---

each other by brand name consumer products as much as by anything else. Tokyo, London, New York, and Los Angeles resemble each other today far more than they did 25 years ago because their residents' tastes in consumer products have converged."[13] This does not mean that all consumers in every part of the world desire exactly the same products. Rather, it means that consumers worldwide want the same diversity and quality in goods and services, and that many markets that used to exist only in industrialized countries are now globally distributed. Or as international marketing expert Ted Levitt notes, "The kinds of small market segments common in Switzerland now also appear in Sri Lanka and Swaziland."[14] Hence, consumer demand for many goods and services that was once limited to specific national markets is now global in scope.

Rapid Technological Change

A fourth major factor contributing to economic globalization has been the increasingly rapid pace of technological development. Product life cycles have grown shorter because of rapidly advancing technology. For example, Karlheinz Kaske, president and CEO of Seimens AG—the West German–based telecommunications manufacturer, notes that "in the past, 10 to 15 years went by before old products were replaced by new ones in our industry. Now it takes only four or five years."[15] In some developing industries the rate of new-product introductions based on technological advances is measured in months. In the semiconductor industry, for example, technological advances were doubling the power of chips every 18 months during the 1980s.[16]

Faster technological change and shorter product life cycles increase research and development costs. In the pharmaceutical industry, for instance, research and development costs have almost doubled every five years since 1970.[17] At the same time, production has become more capital-intensive. Between 1960 and 1980, for example, the labor content of manufacturing operations in the chemical, textile, steel, and many other traditional industries dropped from 25 percent to between 5 and 10 percent of total cost. In newer industries, such as semiconductors, direct labor content is below 5 percent.[18] Overall, these developments mean that the length of time during which an organization can recoup its development and production costs for a new product has decreased significantly. Operating profitably within a domestic market is no longer feasible for many. Profitability is becoming increasingly dependent on an organization's ability to produce and market goods and services in the global marketplace.

The changes leading to a global economy have increased organizational complexity. Organizations in global industries now have to coordinate multi-function, multi-product operations in rapidly changing technological environments *across national and cultural boundaries*. Existing designs have proven unable to coordinate these increasingly complex operations effectively. As a result, there have been two relatively new trends in organization design: (1) a shift from export-based operations with functional or product designs and from country-focused operations with geographically divisionalized designs to globally integrated operations, and (2) a rapid proliferation of inter-organizational designs. By interorganizational designs, we mean cooperative ventures among independent organizations. The following sections examine these design trends.

DESIGNS FOR GLOBAL ORGANIZATIONS

International-Trade and Country-Focused Designs

Organizations operating internationally during the 1960s and 1970s tended toward either the *international-trade* strategy or the *country-focused* strategy.[19] The international-trade strategy (Figure 7.2) is export-based with either a functional (Panel A) or divisional structure (Panel B), usually depending on the breadth of an organization's product lines. In both cases, an international division is usually responsible for marketing and sales outside a domestic market, while other divisions focus on domestic operations. Centralized control of critical operations—such as research and development, production, and finance—by managers at an organization's headquarters is typical, and these operations tend to be located within the organization's home country.

In contrast, the country-focused strategy is a federation of semiautonomous, geographically divisionalized operating units in different national markets (Figure 7.3). Critical operations are located in and under divisional control. Strategic and operational decisions are made by division managers based on the demands and opportunities in their local markets. Headquarter's managers primarily review financial performance and have a limited role in strategic and operational decision making.

Toyota's and General Motors' operations during the 1970s illustrate the differences between these design strategies. Toyota pursued an international-trade strategy. Strategic and operational decisions were made at corporate headquarters, and operations focused on the efficient production of standardized passenger vehicles and trucks in Japan for export to the world market. General Motors, on the other hand, pursued a country-focused strategy, operating a worldwide federation of semiautonomous divisions and subsidiaries. Products were tailored to each division's local market, and each division was responsible for its own research and development, production, and marketing.

The international-trade strategy is more efficient than the country-focused strategy. Product standardization and the lack of duplicated functions create global economies of scale. But the international-trade strategy does not readily lend itself to meeting varying consumer needs and preferences in different national markets, which is the strength of the country-focused strategy. Thus, the benefits and drawbacks of these two design strategies parallel those of the functional and divisional designs discussed in Chapter 5.

Globalization creates opportunities for organizations by expanding potential market size, meaning that less time is needed to recover initial development, production, and marketing costs. Consider, for example, an organization that annually sells 500,000 units of product in its domestic market. Over the past five years its product life cycles have decreased, pushing up research and development costs. And foreign competitors have entered its market as the industry becomes global in scope. The result is increasing competition and declining profitability. Suppose that the

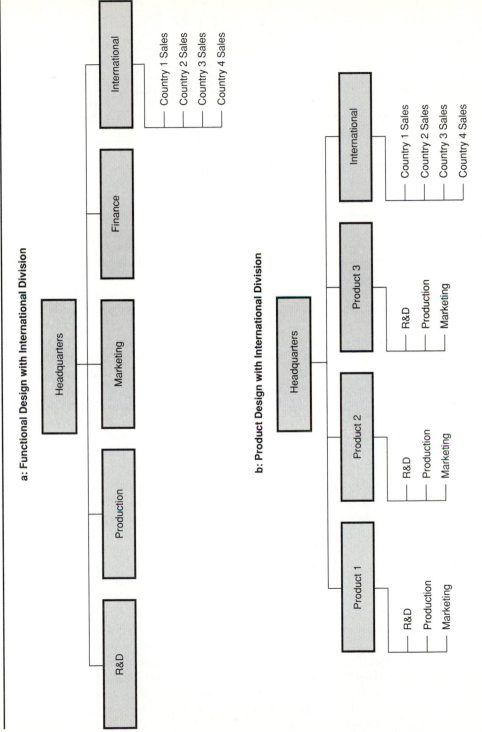

Figure 7.2
International-Trade Design Strategies

a: Functional Design with International Division

Headquarters

R&D

Production

Marketing

Finance

International
— Country 1 Sales
— Country 2 Sales
— Country 3 Sales
— Country 4 Sales

b: Product Design with International Division

Headquarters

Product 1
— R&D
— Production
— Marketing

Product 2
— R&D
— Production
— Marketing

Product 3
— R&D
— Production
— Marketing

International
— Country 1 Sales
— Country 2 Sales
— Country 3 Sales
— Country 4 Sales

Figure 7.3
Country-Focused Design Strategy

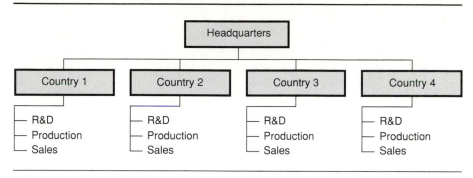

organization's market researchers discover that converging consumer preferences have created demand for an additional 500,000 units—with some modification—in other national markets. If the organization can sell its product in both its domestic and the emerging markets in other countries, it doubles its potential market size. Thus, penetrating the global market would help it recover development costs more quickly and increase profits.

An international-trade design could be used to export the product in this instance, but the organization might have difficulty adjusting to local market differences, and if so, its product will not sell well. If it pursues a country-focused design, it will be better able to sense local differences, but it will probably have difficulty coordinating production, logistics, and marketing across national borders and will therefore fail to gain the economies of scope needed to compete globally.

This is precisely the situation in which many organizations find themselves as their industries become global in scope. If they can develop designs enabling them to take advantage of global market opportunities, they are likely to compete successfully. But if not, they are likely to fall victim to the industry shakeouts that usually occur with globalization. Thus, taking advantage of global market opportunities requires that an organization's design successfully handle two different sets of coordination needs that pull in different directions: (1) the need for sensitivity to local market conditions, and the flexibility to adapt products, marketing, and distribution to them, and (2) the need to efficiently integrate operations across national borders within the context of a global strategy. The international-trade and country-focused design strategies each address one of these coordination needs but not the other. Consequently, there has been a move to an intermediate design—the globally integrated structure—which attempts a balance. Toyota, for example, is moving away from an international-trade design strategy, and General Motors from a country-focused strategy, toward global integration.[20]

Figure 7.4
Globally Integrated Design

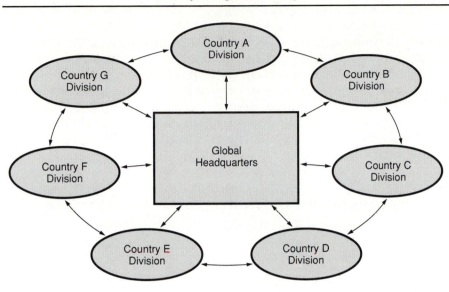

Globally Integrated Designs

The **globally integrated design** strategy creates an interdependent network of geographically dispersed divisions coordinated through a global headquarters (Figure 7.4). Interdependence is created by specialization among the divisions. One division, for example, may be responsible for research and development while others produce components, and yet others are responsible for final product assembly. Or each division may produce part of an organization's overall product line, which they then export to other divisions for distribution and sale. Some divisions will produce goods and services destined for their local, but not the global, market. And many divisions will have distribution and sales responsibilities for their local markets. The overall effect of this specialization is that individual divisions usually do not have the complete capabilities of a whole organization, making them dependent on other divisions for technology, products, resources, information, and export markets.[21]

Within a globally integrated design, top managers are responsible for (1) coordinating the development of strategic objectives and operating policies, (2) coordinating logistics between operating divisions, and (3) coordinating the flow of information among the divisions. Division managers are responsible for (1) adjusting an organization's global strategy to their divisions' markets and implementing it, and (2) acting as the organization's eyes and ears, communicating the demands and opportunities they see in their markets.[22]

These roles differ from those of top and middle managers in the international-trade and local-country models. For example, the responsibility for formulating a global strategy is shared by headquarters and divisional managers in the globally integrated design. Division managers identify the demands and opportunities on which strategic decisions are based, and headquarter's managers coordinate the give-and-take of the strategic development process. In contrast, top managers in an international-trade design formulate strategy, which middle managers implement. In a country-focused design, divisional (middle) managers formulate *and* implement strategies for their divisions' markets; top management is relatively uninvolved. Table 7.2 summarizes the major differences among these three designs.

Adjusting to Local Differences: The Coca-Cola Company

Sensitivity to local differences often makes the difference between success or failure in the global marketplace. Local differences can require adjustments to products, marketing, and distribution. Consider the case of the Coca-Cola Company, which owns the world's most recognized brand name. Coca-Cola is a global soft drink corporation distributing soft drinks in over 160 countries, with a 47 percent market share of the global soft drink market in 1988. Soft drink operations contributed 90 percent of the company's operating income, more than 79 percent of which came from operations outside the United States.[23]

Coca-Cola's strategic motto, "Think globally, but act locally," captures the essential dichotomy of pursuing a global strategy: planning for and coordinating operations globally but simultaneously adjusting that global strategy for local differences.[24] You might think there are few differences across national markets in the soft drink business. But as Coca-Cola's experience shows, there are many local preferences and cultural differences that have to be taken into account in making a global strategy work.

Products. Coca-Cola produces and markets the Coke, Fanta, and Sprite brands globally. Other products, Coke's Chief Marketing Officer Ira C. Herbert notes, "are tailored to a specific country or to a specific geography." Herbert explains, "For example, in Brazil, we make a product called Guarana Tai. In northern Latin America (El Salvador and Venezuela), we make another product called Fanta-Kolita, which is a cream soda type of drink. These products are not marketed globally."[25] Coke's Chairman Goizueta further notes that consumer taste in oranges varies across cultures, affecting the formulation of its Fanta orange drink. "In Germany, a tart orange taste is preferred, while in Italy, it is sweet. So to create a beverage that refreshes and appeals to people in every culture, we frequently use available local fruit to make our Fanta orange drink."[26]

Table 7.2
Comparison of International-Trade, Country-Focused, and
Globally Integrated Designs

	International-Trade Designs	Globally Integrated Designs	Country-Focused Designs
Strategic focus	Standardized goods and services for export	Global goods and services adjusted for local differences	Goods and services developed for specific local markets
Strategy responsibilities	Centralized at global headquarters	Shared among global headquarters and divisions	Decentralized to the divisions
Subunit relations	Hierarchical	Interdependent	Semiautonomous
Distribution of critical functions	Located in home-country	Dispersed throughout the divisional network	Located in each division
When appropriate	Consumers purchase good or service because of distinctive characteristics; few or no modifications required for sale in different national markets	Demand for good or service with some modifications exists in several national markets; variations in local needs, distribution systems, etc., require an insider's knowledge of the markets for success	Little or no overlap in demand across national markets
Example:	Toyota (1970s)→Toyota (1980s)	GM (1980s)←GM (1970s)	

Marketing. Language and cultural differences have a major impact on marketing. When Coke reentered China in 1979, it discovered that the literal representation of its name in Chinese characters was "bite the wax tadpole." A Chinese language expert developed an alternative ideograph that looked similar to Coca-Cola and meant "can happy, mouth happy." Attention to language and cultural differences has enabled Coke to avoid the kind of mistake one of its competitors made a few years ago when it launched an ad campaign in an Asian market based on a "Come Alive" theme. Translated, the advertising copy became, "[This product] makes your ancestors rise from the dead."

Coca-Cola avoids these marketing mistakes by following a *pattern-advertising* strategy that adjusts for local differences. Marketing Chief Herbert explains:

> Our pattern would follow a basic approach. Let's say we produce ten television commercials for Coca-Cola. Those commercials are targeted to a specific communication strategy and to a specific audience. The commercials are then sent out to our seventeen divisions around the world. The words and the lyrics

are translated into Spanish, German, Italian, etc. Basic adjustments are made to the copy. In some cases, even certain visual adjustments are made to ensure that what [happened to its competitor] doesn't happen.[27]

Coke's Goizueta describes the strategy in practice:

We are currently rolling out a global advertising campaign based on our very successful U.S. campaign, "You Can't Beat the Feeling." Our research showed us that the basic elements of that theme had wide universal appeal, but the message will be adapted and localized in many of the countries in which it will appear.

In the Caribbean, Africa, and the South Pacific, for example, the music will feature a distinctive reggae beat. In Japan our theme will translate as "I Feel Coke," in Italy, "Unique Sensation," and in Chile, "The Feeling of Life."[28]

Distribution. Local differences also affect distribution channels. Coke's distribution channels vary from country to country. Supermarkets are the primary outlet in West Germany, vending machines in Italy. In China, street vendors handle most sales, and in Indonesia the company uses small plastic coolers set outside stores for a significant part of its distribution. In Planta Vallarta, Mexico, where the city restricts truck traffic, Coke has developed a network of mini-warehouses from which motorized pushcarts deliver products to stores, restaurants, schools, and even individual residents.

Selecting a Global Organization Design

The extent to which an organization needs to adjust its operations will depend on the types of goods and services it produces. Fashion goods, such as Gucci bags, Chanel perfume, and Levi's jeans, may not need adjustment for local markets. Consumers worldwide buy these products because of their distinctive characteristics. Capital goods may need some tailoring for local markets, though. Boeing, for example, customizes jets sold to Third World countries to withstand rough operating conditions. Organizations producing consumer goods or services are likely to require the greatest adaptation to local market conditions. Some consumer goods can be sold worldwide with no modification, such as the Sony Walkman. Others, such as toothpaste and appliances, are likely to need some adjustment for local consumer needs and preferences. Services also may require extensive modification to fit local market conditions. International accounting firms, for example, have to modify the manner in which services are delivered as well as their content to fit local market conditions and government regulations and policies.

Overall, the less need for product modifications, the more likely an organization is to adopt an international-trade design strategy. As the need for local product modifications increases, the more appropriate a globally integrated design is. And if there is little or no overlap in the demand for goods or services across national markets, a country-focused design strategy is usually the best choice.

Integrating Global Operations

A globally integrated design obviously places a premium on efficient movement of information and materials through an organization's divisional network, much more so than international-trade or country-focused designs. Close coordination of specialized divisions is essential in making this design work. And this type of close coordination is made possible by the rapid development of microelectronic technologies, which have produced advanced information technologies and computer-integrated manufacturing (CIM) systems. Electronic mail, teleconferencing, fax machines, and global communications and data networks reduce the need for face-to-face contact to coordinate people's activities. Moreover, computer-integrated manufacturing provides organizations with the flexibility to customize products to meet local needs and preferences. In the following sections, we examine the roles that unit grouping, technology, integrating mechanisms, and socialization play in globally integrated designs.

Unit Grouping. Unit grouping in a globally integrated design often reflects specialization based on each division's distinctive competency. One division, for example, may have an edge over others in manufacturing costs because of lower prevailing wage rates in its local market, and may accordingly become a location for final product assembly. Others may have responsibilities related to emerging consumer or technological trends in their local markets. For instance, the product-development group in the United Kingdom division of Dutch-based Phillips N.V. was given responsibility for coordinating the development of the company's teletext TV product line because of the lead role that it played in sensing the opportunity in its local market.[29] At Nissan, product-development and production responsibilities are organized along a "lead country" model. Company engineers design vehicles to fit the needs and preferences of specific national markets. Then division managers are asked whether minor changes of any lead-country vehicle would make it suitable for their market. If the answer is yes, the vehicles are produced in the lead country and exported into the secondary markets. Nissan's CEO Yukata Kume notes that this type of unit specialization has a number of advantages:

> With this kind of thinking, we have been able to halve the number of basic models needed to cover the global markets and, at the same time, to cover 80% of our sales with cars designed for specific national markets. Not to miss the remaining 20%, however, we also provided each country manager with a range of additional model types that could be adapted to the needs of local segments. This approach allowed us to focus our resources on each of our largest core markets and, at the same time, provide a pool of supplemental designs that could be adapted to local preferences.[30]

In short, unit grouping in a globally integrated organization will reflect the specific competencies of its divisions. And this divisional specialization can increase the depth of an organization's functional expertise, provide it with flexibility to respond to changing market conditions, and, in addition, enable it to achieve global economies of scale.

Technology. Technology plays a major coordinating role in a globally integrated design. In fact, the kind of information exchange required in a globally integrated design would be practically impossible without global telecommunications. Consider the case of IBM, which has manufacturing, sales, and service operations in over 130 countries. Each country has its own import/export regulations, making the movement of goods and materials between divisions a very complex affair. Shipments are coordinated through IBM's Boulder, Colorado, office using its global telecommunications network. The network's database includes all the pertinent information about each country's import/export regulations, which is used to complete the various forms for transshipment across national borders. For example, suppose an employee at a facility in France signs on to the system and enters the information the system requests (in French) for a shipment to Japan. The system would print out the forms required to comply with French export regulations and Japanese import regulations in French and Japanese. The system also enables IBM to keep track of what goods and materials are in transit.

The Italian-based Benetton group, a manufacturer of fashion knitwear, uses a global telecommunications system to link its worldwide retail operations with its manufacturing facilities. Electronic point-of-sale systems in retail outlets feed information to Benetton's headquarters in northern Italy, which almost instantaneously provide them information about what styles, colors, and sizes are selling well. The information is transmitted to Benetton's manufacturing facilities, and the most marketable goods can be produced and delivered to retail outlets within a matter of days.[31]

Integrating Mechanisms. Integrating mechanisms also play an important role in coordinating globally integrated operations. Committees/task forces, integrating managers, and project/product teams (matrix units) appear to be the most commonly used.[32] Some mechanisms, like the integrating manager, can directly involve an organization's global headquarters in coordination. At AT&T, for example, senior corporate managers are assigned responsibilities for coordinating global marketing for a specific business line. Other integrating mechanisms provide more decentralized forms of coordination, where members of the divisional network coordinate their activities with major decisions subject to headquarter's approval. When Procter & Gamble (P&G) moved to develop a Europe-wide approach to product development and marketing, it created a number of special product teams with members drawn from its various European divisions. These teams developed product and marketing strategies for the European market, and the plans that had significant investment implications were automatically routed to corporate headquarters for approval.

Overall, integrating mechanisms serve two important needs in a globally integrated organization. First, they enhance its ability to respond to changing market conditions. The relatively ad hoc nature of many integrating mechanisms makes them well-suited for this task. As conditions change, organizations can create new integrating mechanisms that focus on specific coordination needs, and eliminate them when those needs are satisfied. Second, they aid globally integrated organizations in maintaining a balance between an integrated global strategy and specific local market conditions. By involving individuals from local divisions in collaboration with global headquarter's managers, they ensure that both the global and local interests of the organization are represented in the decision-making process.

Socialization. Socialization also plays an important coordination role in globally integrated organizations, particularly as the dispersion of its operations across nations and cultures increases. As we noted in Chapter 4, socialization is one of the few ways that organizations can coordinate the activities of employees in sensitive positions at remote locations. Such coordination is necessary because unless such employees have internalized their organization's norms, they may not make decisions in its best interest. Moreover, values and norms may differ across divisions. Collaboration therefore often requires subordination of divisional interests to those of the whole organization. Kenichi Ohmae, head of McKinsey & Company's office in Tokyo, makes the following observation:

> The more successful a company is at bringing both operational and strategic responsibility down to the regional or local level, the more likely that local or regional concerns, attitudes, affinities, and allegiances will shape the decisions of its far-flung managerial cadre. As the rulers of the old colonial empires learned from bitter experience, when you send officers to new territories across the ocean, you had better be sure that they have deeply internalized not only the official policies but also the values of the home government. Indeed, the more you try to coordinate and facilitate [instead of control] from the center, the more important the value system your people take with them becomes.[33]

Training plays an important role in the socialization process, and some globally integrated organizations run special training programs to communicate a sense of their global strategy and to firmly implant their norms in their managers. Some also rotate managers from divisions in other countries through their home-country operations on the theory that contact with employees there will help transmit the organization's norms. And some, like NEC and Eli Lilly, routinely rotate home-country employees through overseas divisions to help them gain a broader perspective on international operations.

Other tools that are used to socialize employees and expand their understanding of an organization's international operations include career-path planning, evaluation systems that are equitable across national borders, training for spouses of employees to be located overseas, and promotion systems that value international experience.

In short, the globally integrated design is a network of geographically dispersed, interdependent operations that implements a global strategy adjusted for specific local needs. Interdependence is created by divisional specialization, and it is usually managed using advanced information technologies and a wide array of integrating mechanisms. Socialization also plays an important coordination role by imparting to employees a sense of an organization's global mission and an understanding of its norms.

INTERORGANIZATIONAL DESIGNS

Economic globalization also has accelerated the use of **interorganizational designs**, which consist of two or more organizations that have chosen to cooperate by combining their strengths to overcome individual weaknesses. The concept of interorganizational design is not new,[34] but the virtual explosion in their use, particularly in high-technology industries such as computers, electronics, aerospace, and telecommunications, is. There has been a significant increase in interorganizational designs in mature industries such as automaking and steel as well.[35]

Organizations large and small can participate in interorganizational designs, both within domestic and global markets, and they can be of any structure. Organizations that participate range from those with globally integrated designs such as AT&T—which had over 20 interorganizational ventures in 1987—to a local physician's office with a simple structure that participates in an insurance company's preferred-provider network. As we'll show in the following sections, there are many different reasons that organizations use interorganizational designs, and there are many different forms these designs can take.

Uses of Interorganizational Designs

Interorganizational designs serve many purposes. Some organizations use them *to complement skills they have in-house.* Digital Equipment Corporation (DEC) has teamed with Apple Computer to develop communication and software to link Apple's personal computers with each other and with DEC's VAX minicomputers. Although they plan to market and distribute the resulting products independently, DEC and Apple expect that their combined, complementary expertise will help them develop better products more quickly than either could do alone. There are clear advantages for both partners in joining forces to do battle with their larger primary competitor, IBM, in the office network market.[36]

Other organizations cooperate *to gain economies of scale in research and development and in production.* Software manufacturers are teaming up to develop new relational database programs that can communicate with other software packages and be used on both minicomputers and personal computers. Apple Computer has teamed with Sybase, Ashton-Tate with Microsoft and Sybase, Informix with Innovative Software, and Relational Technology with Sun Microsystems. Each partnership expects that its combined resources and reputations will enable it to quickly develop and market these programs and have an opportunity to become the industry leader.[37]

Interorganizational designs also are a way *to share the risk* in a project that is beyond the financial and technological scope of a single organization. During the past decade, the three major firms in the commercial aircraft industry—Boeing, McDonnell Douglas, and Airbus Industries—have teamed up with other companies to produce new passenger aircraft. These cooperative ventures spread the capital requirements and risk inherent in developing and producing new aircraft.

Large organizations use interorganizational arrangements *to gain access to new technologies more quickly* than they can through in-house research and development. This movement away from in-house research and development reflects an awareness that smaller organizations are faster at, and more capable of, innovation and product development.[38] General Motors, for example, needed new technology to meet its goal of installing 10,000 robots by the end of the 1980s. It acquired that technology quickly by entering a joint venture with Japanese robotmaker Fanuc Ltd. to form GMF Robotics Corporation. GMF Robotics sells most of its output to GM, and it has become the world's largest industrial robot manufacturer.[39] Overall, there has been a significant increase in the use of external sources for research and development by large companies since 1980 through contract research, joint ventures, licensing, equity participation, and reciprocity agreements, and a corresponding decrease in internal research and development.[40]

Some organizations use interorganizational designs to *increase their ability to coordinate operations.* For example, a number of manufacturers are moving to just-in-time inventory systems, which require close coordination between a manufacturer and its suppliers. The Chrysler assembly plant in Belvidere, Illinois, began implementing a just-in-time inventory system in 1988. Its first partner, Johnson Control, manufactures seats. Johnson Control is tied into the plant's factory information system, which provides it with each day's production schedule. It manufactures and loads the seats onto semitrailers in the order they will be installed. The seats are automatically unloaded at the Chrysler plant onto a conveyer belt that delivers the seats to the assembly-line station where they are installed. The system reduces both organizations' costs by eliminating inventory and by minimizing the likelihood of damage in handling and storage.

Some organizations use interorganizational designs to *increase flexibility* by vertically disaggregating their operations. *Vertical disaggregation* means that critical functions such as product design, production, marketing, and distribution are performed by independent organizations within a cooperating network rather than by a single organization.[41] Typically, one participant—the broker—coordinates the efforts of the other members. Because each member of the network specializes in one or a few functional areas, the overall network displays the advantages of technical specialization associated with functional form. And because the individual members of the network are usually small companies, they remain in closer touch with their markets and are able to move more quickly than larger firms—a benefit typically associated with market-based designs.

Schwinn Bicycle Company is vertically disaggregated. Schwinn designs, markets, and distributes its bicycles, which are manufactured under contract by firms in Asia. The reason for getting out of manufacturing, top management explains, was that "the leverage of the business was no longer in manufacturing . . . when you are a manufacturing company, your mind set tends to be to sell what you make . . . . We're market driven now."[42]

Different Interorganizational Designs

Many different interorganizational designs are possible, depending on the closeness of the partners' relationship. Some involve equity positions of one partner in another, and others are nonequity forms of collaboration. Some of these designs involve whole organizations, while others involve only parts of organizations. In this respect, interorganizational designs are like a matrix design in that they are overlaid on existing organization structures. The closest interorganizational relationships are those that involve equity positions—such as minority equity investments and joint ventures. Some examples follow:

1. **Minority equity investments.** Chrysler Corporation has had a 15 percent equity position in Mitsubishi for over a decade. There are many benefits for Chrysler is this arrangement. Initially, it stabilized Chrysler's supply of small cars, which were produced by Mitsubishi and imported into the United States. Later, it provided Chrysler with access to new technologies, such as a joint venture with Mitsubishi known as the Diamond-Star Motor Corp. This jointly owned plant is an experiment in automation. Located just outside Normal, Illinois, the plant contains 470 robots, which is far more than most auto plants. The joint venture produces vehicles for both partners—the Plymouth Laser and the Mitsubishi Eclipse.[43] Similarly, Ford has a 25 percent equity position in Mazda Motor Corp., and General Motors holds 34.2 percent of Isuzu Motors Ltd. and 5.3 percent of Suzuki Motor Company.

2. **Joint ventures.** In 1984 General Motors and Toyota began a joint venture, NUMMI, to produce automobiles in a shuttered GM plant in Fremont,

California. The plant, managed by Toyota, originally produced Chevrolet Novas—and now Geo Prisms—based on the Toyota Corolla design. GM gained by studying Toyota's management and production techniques; Toyota gained by obtaining low-cost entry as a manufacturer into the U.S. market, and learning how to manage an ethnically diverse workforce.[44] Other examples in the auto industry include the Diamond Star joint venture just mentioned and a Ford-Mazda joint venture in Mexico.

Other interorganizational arrangements, such as marketing and distribution agreements, licensing arrangements, research grants and R&D (research and development) partnerships, value-adding partnerships, and dynamic networks, usually do not involve equity positions. These collaborative efforts provide partners with more flexibility because they can be more easily reconfigured without equity being at stake. Some examples follow:

1. Marketing and distribution agreements. American Telephone & Telegraph (AT&T) and Italy's Olivetti joined forces in 1984 through a marketing and distribution agreement. AT&T's capital and technology were combined with Olivetti's worldwide marketing expertise to compete against IBM and the Japanese in the world office-automation market. AT&T sold Olivetti UNIX-based personal computers in the United States, filling a gap in AT&T's product line. Olivetti sold AT&T UNIX-based minicomputers in Europe, and it helped AT&T market its office-automation products in Asia.[45]

2. Licensing arrangements. Ocean Pacific Sunwear Ltd. licenses the "Op" brand name to other companies that do much of the design and all of the manufacturing of "Op" products. Ocean Pacific's role is marketing and cultivating the mystique of the "Op" trademark. The arrangement helped Ocean Pacific's sales grow from $7 million to $270 million between 1976 and 1986, while limiting its downside risk in failed products, which the licensees absorb.[46]

3. Research grants and R&D partnerships. In 1982 Monsanto began moving out of the commodity chemical business into pharmaceuticals. Its strategy included a $52 million research fund for biological researchers at Washington University in St. Louis. In exchange for funding, Monsanto has first rights to commercialize subsequent patents.[47]

4. Consortia. Sematech, a consortium created in 1987 by the U.S. semiconductor industry, was formed to restore U.S. competitiveness in chip manufacturing. The consortium's goal is to develop the technologies needed to manufacture future generations of integrated circuits that would match the efficiency and quality of Japanese manufacturers by 1990. The consortium is partially funded by the Defense Department's Advanced Research Projects Agency, and project staff are on loan from the consortium's members.[48]

5. Value-adding partnerships. Value-adding partnerships are a form of a vertically disaggregated network that relies on cooperative agreements, often noncontract-based, to coordinate the partners. McKesson Corporation, distributor of drugs, health-care products, and other consumer goods, has transformed itself from a conventional wholesale distributor for independent drugstores into a value-adding partnership since the late 1970s. By fostering collaborative relationships and developing sophisticated information systems, McKesson has tied together its suppliers, retailers, third-party insurers, and consumers into a cooperating network. The effect: between 1976 and 1981 McKesson's sales increased from $900 million to over $4 billion, while it reduced the size of its warehousing operations and the number of employees they required.[49]

6. Dynamic networks. Dynamic networks are a form of a vertically disaggregated network that relies on market mechanisms such as contracts to coordinate partners' activities.[50] When IBM entered the personal computer market in 1981, its Entry Systems Division used the dynamic network concept to coordinate production. Rather than manufacture PC components in-house, it contracted with outside suppliers: Intel processors, an Epson printer, a TDK power supply, Tanden Shugart disk drives, IBM-designed keyboards for Keytronics and AMP, a motherboard from SCI Systems, and a monitor from Atlas. This arrangement allowed IBM to enter the desktop computer market more quickly than it could have otherwise, and at a relatively lower cost.[51]

Selecting an Interorganizational Design

While there has been very little research on the relative effectiveness of different interorganizational designs to date, there are a number of questions that managers should answer before deciding on a design. The first question managers need to ask is where their organization adds the most value in the design, production, distribution, and marketing of a good or service. In other words, what is its distinctive competence? Such an examination may reveal that an organization can better utilize its resources by entering into a partnership than by producing a good or service alone. Colby H. Chandler, CEO and chairman of Eastman Kodak, describes the rationale for taking a Japanese partner to manufacture its Supralife alkaline batteries.

> We could have done that in Rochester [New York], but alkaline technology has been around since the 1930s. So we decided that we could demonstrate more technology and market leadership by concentrating on our proprietary lithium battery. The alkaline batteries are important in terms of completing our product offering in this field, but Kodak's resources would not have been well spent if we had diverted some of them to reinventing existing technology.[52]

Similarly, Marriott Corp. recognized in the early 1980s that its distinctive competence was in the development and operation of hotels, but not in owning hotel properties. It subsequently sold most of its hotels to investors while retaining long-term contracts for their management.

A second question should concern the extent to which an organization needs to maintain legal control of assets and operations as opposed to being a minority partner. The prevailing management wisdom is that control increases the chance of success. But in many situations, striving for control can defeat a relationship's purpose. Consider why many organizations take on global partners—to gain access to expertise in new markets. Global partners are valuable because they have knowledge about consumer needs and preferences, distribution and marketing systems, and culture. Legal control, and the headquarter's mandates that often accompany it, can be self-defeating because they limit a partnership's ability to do what it is supposed to do—act like an "insider" in the local market. Thus, as Ohmae notes, "Good partnerships, like good marriages, don't work on the basis of ownership or control. It takes effort and commitment and enthusiasm from both sides if either is to realize the hoped-for benefits. You cannot own a successful partner any more than you can own a husband or wife."[53]

Finally, managers need to ask how flexible an interorganizational relationship should be. In rapidly developing industries, such as telecommunications, computers, semiconductors, and so on, it may be to an organization's advantage to enter into relatively flexible arrangements that do not involve equity positions of one partner in another. Nonequity arrangements are more flexible because organizations can more easily change partners as their industry develops and its technology progresses. Conversely, the more developed an industry's technology, the more likely it is that partners will opt for equity-based forms of collaboration. Such relationships are conducive to closer coordination between partners and more efficient operation, which is useful as an industry matures and becomes more competitive.[54]

The new designs that have emerged in response to the globalization of many industries, and their new coordination needs, reverse the trend of the functional and divisional designs that incorporated an increasing number of functions within a single organization. Management's primary concern at one time was reducing operational uncertainty by locking in sources of supply and distribution, and gaining greater control over internal operations. While these moves reduced uncertainty, they also reduced organizations' flexibility in responding to changing environmental conditions. With the development of globally integrated and interorganizational designs, managers are making the opposing trade-off: gaining flexibility to respond to complex and rapidly changing environments while giving up some of the stability associated with internal control of all operations.

SUMMARY

Learning Objective 1: Explain why managers develop new organization designs. Managers develop new designs when two conditions exist: (1) available designs are unable to meet new coordination needs, and (2) social and technological conditions make new designs possible.

Learning Objective 2: Describe how the shift from pre-industrial economies with local markets to industrial economies with national markets has changed organizational coordination needs. The development of nationwide rail, postal, and telegraph systems, and the growth of urban areas brought about the shift from pre-industrial to industrial economies. A major effect of these changes was to expand the market opportunities available to many organizations. Organizations grew in size and complexity as they took advantage of these opportunities. Increased size, the incorporation of multiple functions within an organization, and the move from one or few products/markets to many products/markets, increased the complexity of coordination. As a result, managers developed the functional and divisional designs. Later coordination problems caused by coordinating activities of multiple functions across multiple products/markets in rapidly changing technological environments led to the development of the matrix design.

Learning Objective 3: Describe how the shift from industrial economies to post-industrial economies in a global market has further changed organizational coordination needs. The industrialization of many national economies after World War II, rising standards of living, the development of global telecommunications and transportation systems, and the rapid pace of technological development have contributed to the globalization of many industries. Globalization has in turn increased the complexity of organizations operating in those industries. These organizations now have to coordinate multi-function, multi-product operations in rapidly changing technological environments *across national and cultural boundaries*. Existing designs have proven unable to coordinate these increasingly complex operations effectively.

Learning Objective 4: Identify the differences among international-trade, country-focused, and globally integrated designs. The international-trade design focuses on the production of standardized goods and services for export, typically using a functional or product-based design. Critical operations, such as research and development, production, and marketing, are located in an organization's home country under the control of a central headquarters. The country-focused design focuses on developing goods and services to meet local needs. Such organizations usually are geographically divisionalized and operate as a loose federation of semiautonomous divisions. Strategic and operational decisions are made in the divisions, and critical operations such as research and development, production, and marketing are housed at the divisional level. The globally integrated design focuses on a global strategy adjusted for local needs. It usually is structured as a network of geographically dispersed, interdependent divisions coordinated through a global headquarters. Interdependence is created through divisional specialization, where a particular division provides services to other divisions within the network as well as serving its own national market.

Learning Objective 5: Explain how unit grouping, technology, integrating mechanisms, and socialization facilitate coordination in a globally integrated design. Organizations with globally integrated designs make use of advanced information technologies, integrating mechanisms, and socialization to facilitate coordination. Advanced information technologies provide for the efficient movement of information across national boundaries and reduce the need for face-to-face contact to coordinate people's activities. Integrating mechanisms enable these organizations to adapt to rapidly changing conditions within the global market, and to balance their global strategy with the needs of local markets. Socialization provides managers with a shared vision of their organization's global strategy and helps ensure that the decisions they make will be in the organization's overall interest.

Learning Objective 6: Discuss the reasons for organizations using interorganizational designs. An interorganizational design consists of two or more organizations that have chosen to cooperate by combining their strengths to overcome their individual weaknesses. These designs can enable participating organizations to (1) complement the skills they have in-house, (2) gain economies of scale in research and development and in production, (3) share risk, (4) gain access to new technologies more quickly, (5) increase their ability to coordinate operations, and (6) increase flexibility.

Learning Objective 7: List a variety of interorganizational designs that organizations are now using. Organizations have created many different interorganizational designs. Two that involve equity positions are joint ventures and minority equity investments. Other interorganizational arrangements, such as marketing and distribution agreements, licensing arrangements, research grants and R&D partnerships, value-adding partnerships, and dynamic networks, are cooperative arrangements that do not involve equity.

Discussion Questions

1. Discuss the problems increasing organizational size and complexity have created for managers over time. What kinds of design solutions have been created to deal with these problems?

2. The shifts from a pre-industrial to an industrial economy, and then to a global economy, have changed organizations' coordination needs. Exactly how have these coordination needs changed, and what designs have managers developed to meet them? How have these designs addressed specific needs?

3. DigitMap, Inc., is the producer of an automated aeronautical mapping device that enables pilots to insert CDs into a reader and view routing maps instead of carrying conventional paper fold-out maps. DM feels that it can increase annual sales at least 35 percent annually by marketing its product internationally. Do you think this would be a good decision? Why or why not? What design options are open to DM? Which do you think might work best?

4. Compare and contrast the country-focused, globally integrated, and international-trade design strategies. What are their comparative strengths and weaknesses?

5. How have microelectronic-based technologies affected the abilities of managers to coordinate globe-spanning operations?

6. Search through a current issue of *Business Week* and find as many different examples of interorganizational designs as possible. What are the reasons stated in these articles for participating organizations to enter into these cooperative arrangements? How well do these arrangements appear to be working?

DESIGN AUDIT #7

Designing a Global Organization

This design audit will help you assess the extent to which your organization is engaged in and effectively designed for global operations. It will also help you examine any cooperative arrangements that your organization may be involved in with other organizations.

Global Operations

1. Briefly describe the extent to which the market for your organization's goods or services has become global in scope.

2. Does your organization currently produce, market, or distribute its goods or services outside its home country, or does it plan to do so in the future?

    _____ Yes

    _____ No

    If your organization doesn't currently produce, market, or distribute its goods or services outside its home country, or plan to do so in the future, skip to Question 7. If your organization is planning to engage in global operations in the future, answer the following questions based on how you think it should structure these operations in order to achieve its global objectives.

3. Outline the scope of and objectives for your organization's global operations in the space below.

4. Has your organization experienced any problems in achieving or moving toward these objectives? If yes, describe them in the space below.

5. How has your organization structured its global operations (i.e., international-trade, country-focused, globally integrated, or interorganizational design models)? Sketch an organization chart or diagram for your organization's global operations in the space below.

    Hint: Use solid lines to indicate global operations directly under the control of your organization (divisions, subsidiaries, etc.) and dotted lines to show the use of interorganizational designs (joint ventures, marketing and distribution agreements, etc.). In the case of interorganizational designs, indicate the nature of the relationship with the other participating organization(s).

6. Has this design worked well in helping your organization meet its global objectives? If it has not, describe the coordination and control problems you attribute to its current design. Also indicate what design changes might be made to alleviate these problems.

Interorganizational Designs

7. Many organizations use cooperative interorganizational arrangements regardless of whether their operations are domestic or global in scope. Is your organization currently involved in any interorganizational arrangements with other organizations?

    _____ Yes

    _____ No

    If you answered "no" to the above question, proceed to Design Audit #8.

8. Overall, how many different interorganizational relationships is your organization involved in?

    _____ Number of interorganizational relationships

9. In the spaces below, identify up to three interorganizational arrangements in which your organization is involved. Indicate whom the relationship is with, what its objective is, the type of interorganizational design being used, and the extent to which the relationship is meeting its objectives. Also describe any problems being encountered and whether you think a different interorganizational design would be more appropriate for this situation.

#1—With: _____

Type of I/O Design: _____

Objectives: Rating: *Very Successful* 5   4   3   2   1   *Very Unsuccessful*

Problems:

Recommendations:

#2—With: _____

Type of I/O Design: _____

Objectives: Rating: *Very Successful*   5   4   3   2   1   *Very Unsuccessful*

Problems:

Recommendations:

#3—With: _____

Type of I/O Design: _____

Objectives: Rating: *Very Successful*   5   4   3   2   1   *Very Unsuccessful*

Problems:

Recommendations:

_____

Notes

1. Arthur L. Stinchcombe, "Social Structure and Organizations," in James March, ed. *Handbook of Organizations* (Chicago: Rand McNally, 1965), 142–193.

2. Peter Laslett, *The World We Have Lost* (New York, Scribners, 1965), 1–2.

3. Alfred D. Chandler, Jr., *Strategy and Structure: Chapters in the History of the American Industrial Enterprise,* (Cambridge, Mass.: MIT Press, 1962), 23.

4. Ibid., 24–25.

5. Ibid., 42.

6. Alfred D. Chandler, *The Visible Hand: The Managerial Revolution in American Business* (Cambridge, Mass.: Belknap Press, 1977), 368.

7. Chandler, *Strategy and Structure,* 48–49.

8. W. Graham Astley and Richard A. Braham, "Organizational Designs for Post-Industrial Strategies," in Charles C. Snow, ed. *Strategy, Organization Design, and Human Resource Management* (Greenwich, Conn.: JAI Press, 1989), 240–241.

9. "Who's the Biggest of Them All?" *Business Week,* July 17, 1989, 139–178.

10. Ibid., 176.

11. Edmund T. Pratt, Jr., "Growing to Serve the Global Marketplace," in Jerome M. Rostow, ed. *The Global Marketplace* (New York: Facts on File, 1988), 130.

12. Kenichi Ohmae, "Managing in a Borderless World," *Harvard Business Review* 67 (May–June 1989): 153.

13. Roberto C. Goizueta, "Globalization: A Soft Drink Perspective," *Vital Speeches of the Day* 55 (1989): 351.

14. Ted Levitt, "The Pluralization of Consumption," *Harvard Business Review* 66, no. 3 (1988): 8.

15. Karlheinz Kaske, "Organizing for and Meeting the Global Challenge," in Jerome M. Rostow, ed. *The Global Marketplace* (New York: Facts on File, 1988), 85.

16. James E. Olson, "Toward a Global Information Age," in Rostow, *The Global Marketplace,* 96.

17. Richard Koenig and Joann S. Lubin, "Rx for Growth: Global Drug Industry Seems Headed for Big Consolidation Amid Rising Cost Pressures," *The Wall Street Journal,* April 13, 1989, A12.

18. Astley and Braham, "Organizational Designs for Post-Industrial Strategies," 251.

19. Michael E. Porter, "Competition in Global Industries: A Conceptual Framework," in Michael E. Porter, ed. *Competition in Global Industries* (Boston: Harvard Business School Press, 1986), 15–60.

20. Akihiro Okumura, "Toyota Transformation," Paper presented at the Academy of Management meeting, Washington, D.C., August 1989.

21. C. K. Prahalad and Yves L. Doz, *The Multinational Mission: Balancing Local Demands and Global Vision* (New York: Free Press, 1987), 161.

22. Christopher A. Bartlett, "Building and Managing the Transnational: The New Organizational Challenge," in Porter, *Competition in Global Industries,* 396–398.

23. Coca-Cola Company, *Annual Report*, 1989.

24. Roberto C. Goizueta, "Globalization: A Soft Drink Perspective," 361.

25. "How Coke Markets to the World: An Interview with Marketing Executive Ira C. Herbert," *Journal of Business Strategy* 9 (September–October 1988): 5.

26. Goizueta, "Globalization: A Soft Drink Perspective," 362.

27. "How Coke Markets to the World," 6.

28. Goizueta, "Globalization: A Soft Drink Perspective," 362.

29. Bartlett, "Building and Managing the Transnational," 384–385.

30. Ohmae, "Managing in a Borderless World," 155.

31. James E. Olson, "Toward a Global Information Age," in Rostow, *The Global Marketplace*, 101.

32. Prahalad and Doz, *The Multinational Mission*, 174–176.

33. Kenichi Ohmae, "Planting for a Global Harvest," *Harvard Business Review* 67, no. 4 (1989): 138.

34. The area of interorganizational relations has been of interest to organization theorists for some time. This section focuses on how interorganizational relationships have been used by organizations in recent years to cope with changing coordination needs. For reviews of the broader literature, see Howard Aldrich and David A. Whetten, "Organization-sets, Action-sets, and Networks: Making the Most of Simplicity," in Paul Nystrom and William H. Starbuck, eds. *Handbook of Organization Design*, vol. 1 (New York: Oxford University Press, 1981), 385–408; David A. Whetten, "Interorganizational Relations: A Review of the Field," *Journal of Higher Education* 52 (1981): 1–28; and Joseph Galaskiewicz, "Interorganizational Relations," *Annual Review of Sociology* 11 (1985): 281–304.

35. Deigan Morris and Michael Hergert, "Trends in International Collaborative Agreements," *Columbia Journal of World Business* 22, no. 2 (1987): 15–21.

36. "DEC's New Plan," *Business Week*, February 1, 1988, 83.

37. "It's Grab Your Partner Time for Software Makers," *Business Week*, February 8, 1988, 86–87.

38. Walter W. Powell, "Hybrid Organizational Arrangements: New Form or Transitional Development?" *California Management Review* 30 (Fall 1987): 72.

39. "GM and Fanuc: An Unlikely Pair—But a Winner," *Business Week,* July 21, 1986, 105.

40. Powell, "Hybrid Organizational Arrangements," 71–73.

41. Raymond E. Miles and Charles C. Snow, "Organizations: New Concepts for New Forms," *California Management Review* 28 (Fall 1986): 64.

42. "And Now, the Post-Industrial Corporation," *Business Week*, March 3, 1986, 66.

43. "Can Steel-Collar Workers Build Better Cars?" *Business Week*, September 12, 1988, 73.

44. Stephen E. Weiss, "Creating the GM-Toyota Joint Venture: A Case in Complex Negotiation," *Columbia Journal of World Business* 22, no. 2 (1987): 23–36.

45. "Olivetti and AT&T: An Odd Couple That's Flourishing," *Business Week*, March 4, 1985, 44–45.

46. "And Now, the Post-Industrial Corporation," 66, 71.

47. "Monsanto's College Alliance Is Getting High Marks," *Business Week,* May 12, 1986, 33–34.

48. "Bob Noyce Created Silicon Valley. Can He Save It?" *Business Week,* August 15, 1988, 76, 78.

49. Russell Johnston and Paul R. Lawrence, "Beyond Vertical Integration—The Rise of the Value-Adding Partnership," 95; "Foremost-McKesson: The Computer Moves Distribution to Center Stage," *Business Week,* December 7, 1981, 115–120.

50. Miles and Snow, "Organizations: New Concepts for New Forms," 62–73.

51. Astley and Braham, "Organizational Designs for Post-Industrial Strategies," in Snow, *Strategy, Organization Design, and Human Resource Management,* 256–257 and "And Now, the Post-Industrial Corporation," 66.

52. Colby H. Chandler, "Competition in the World Economy," in Rostow, *The Global Marketplace,* 172.

53. Kenichi Omhae, "The Global Logic of Strategic Alliances," *Harvard Business Review* 67, no. 2 (1989): 148.

54. Astley and Braham, "Organizational Designs for Post-Industrial Strategies," 260–262.

What Flexible Workers Can Do

By late 1987 the unemployment rate in Sarasota, Florida, had shriveled to 4%. That fact was of more than passing interest to executives of Lechmere Inc., a 27-store retail chain owned by Dayton Hudson. Lechmere was about to open an outlet in Sarasota and able workers were in short supply. Like other retailers, the company customarily hires hordes of entry-level part-timers, typically teenagers and housewives, plugging them into time slots as needed. That gives Lechmere the requisite flexibility in a business where store traffic ebbs and flows unpredictably across departments. But with unemployment low, there were no hordes to be had in Sarasota.

So Lechmere picked the new store to test a way of dealing with the shortages of labor it faces around the country. The company offers the Sarasota workers raises based on the number of jobs they learn to perform. Cashiers are encouraged to sell records and tapes. Sporting goods salesmen get tutoring in forklifts. That way Lechmere can quickly adjust to shifts in staffing needs simply by redeploying existing workers. The pay incentives, along with the prospect of a more varied and interesting workday, proved valuable lures in recruiting. The Sarasota store now has a work force that's 60% full-timers, vs. an average of 30% for the rest of the chain. What's more, says Paul Chaddock, senior vice president for personnel, the Sarasota store is substantially more productive than the others. Lechmere has extended the idea to several stores in the Carolinas and New Hampshire, and two others in Alabama will adopt it this year.

In Lechmere's case it was mainly a labor shortage that drove managers to try training workers in more than one skill. But a flexible work force is an

Source: "What Flexible Workers Can Do" by Norm Alster. Reprinted by permission from FORTUNE Magazine, February 13, 1989, pp. 62–66. © 1989 The Time Inc. Magazine Company. All rights reserved.

all-purpose Mr. Fixit for companies that want to increase speed, efficiency, quality, productivity, and job satisfaction—as many besides Lechmere have discovered. Recent examples:

• Unionized companies like General Motors and National Steel improved speed and efficiency by loosening up long-ossified job categories.

• Workers trained in several jobs helped Motorola solve critical quality problems with cellular telephones.

• USAA, a San Antonio insurance and financial services company with many military customers, made the most of a costly investment in office automation by consolidating departments and training salespeople to handle every step of processing a policy.

The cost of training can be substantial, and workers sometimes resist doing things differently. But in a quicksilver environment where technological change, global competition, and shrunken product cycles require a fast, fluid response, "multiskilling"—as academics insist on calling it—could be the human side of the answer. Says John Stepp, U.S. deputy undersecretary of labor: "Today's technology has telescoped product and process life cycles so much that skills are becoming obsolete at a breathtaking pace. Instead of paying for a job, employers are now paying for a variety of skills that workers acquire." Adds Robert Gilbreath, head of a group at Andersen Consulting that helps companies adapt to change: "Human beings are the corporation's most flexible form of capital. When change is the surest constant, it makes sense to develop a work force that can quickly adapt to unpredictable developments."

Manufacturers have led the way in multiskilling. In unionized industries, many companies reasoned that productivity would benefit by opening up rigid work classifications that restrict workers to precisely defined tasks. "The old system produced a lot of dead time," says Richard Coffee, vice president for human resources at National Steel. "You had a task that was 20% welding and 80% pipefitting, for example," he recalls. When either a welder or a pipefitter was unavailable, the work just sat there. "It was obviously a lot more efficient to have a pipefitter who could weld or a welder who could pipefit."

In 1985 and 1986, National posted net losses totaling $148 million. A landmark agreement with the United Steelworkers in 1986 allowed the company's major plant to consolidate 78 job classifications into 16 and generally broadened worker responsibilities and participation in operations and planning. These and other changes meant greater speed: National can now produce a ton of steel in 4.53 man-hours, vs. 5.5 in 1984. Quality has also been fine-tuned. The amount of steel that fails to meet customer specifications has been reduced 33% since the contract was signed. National earned $47.8 million in 1987 and $55 million through the first three quarters of 1988.

Many manufacturers have found that teams of cross-trained workers are vital to quality improvement. They can detect flaws in each other's work, apply problem-solving techniques more effectively, and fill in for each other as needed—critical in just-in-time systems that function without mountainous buffers of inventory and work-in-process. Says John F. Krafcik, consultant to MIT's International Motor Vehicle Program: "Around the world, there's a very strong correlation in durable-goods manufacturing between quality and productivity and the use of multi-skilling worker teams, and just-in-time." At General Motors' Detroit Gear & Axle plant, a team of 30 cross-trained workers building parts for rear-wheel-drive suspension systems cut warranty costs related to the suspensions by 400% in just two years.

In Motorola's case, too, groups of workers trained in several skills were the key to improving quality. The company won an antidumping suit in 1985 against Japanese manufacturers of cellular telephones. But cutthroat pricing was only half of Motorola's problem: even a member of the International Trade Commission remarked on "the relatively high failure rates reported by some purchasers." The company shifted responsibility for detecting defects from inspectors at the end of the assembly line to individual production workers. Then, because workers who understand the entire production process are the most adept at defect diagnosis, Motorola overhauled its compensation system to reward those who learn a variety of skills. The defect rate fell 77%, from 1,000 per million parts in 1985 to today's 233. Last year the company was one of three winners of a federal Malcolm Baldrige National Quality Award.

At the Arlington Heights, Illinois, cellular phone factory, Motorola abolished its system of half a dozen pay categories, each with its own maximum. Now all production workers are in the same category and each can qualify for the highest wage—27.5% more than some of the old caps. Adding a new skill means a pay increase, but a worker who has qualified does not get a raise until he has maintained zero-defect performance at his station for five consecutive days. All but three of the 400 workers have learned at least two skills. "Everybody's opportunity is enlarged," says Susan Hooker, director of planning, evaluation, and retraining. "The program has been so successful that the rest of the corporation has been learning from the example."

On one occasion, a worker saved the company from having to replace 20 printed circuitboards, which are the brains of a cellular phone. While machines add most of the electronic components to the board, some are oddly shaped and must be inserted by hand. A worker who was manually adding another part noticed that a capacitor, a device that stores an electrical charge, didn't look right. Workers checked an entire batch of 25,000 capacitors and found 19 others that were defective. Because the worker had previously run the machine that loads capacitors, she knew enough to spot the problem.

Alfred S. Warren, vice president of industrial relations at General Motors, says the increasing complexity of factory equipment has put a premium on workers who can do more than one thing. "We need a broader kind of tradesman, both skilled and unskilled, than we have in the past," he says. Adds Motorola's Hooker: "We used to hire people because they could manipulate parts, they could put things together with their hands . . . . Now we really need the whole worker. You have to have somebody to do simple programming, read, write commands, interpret information on terminals, and do preventive maintenance.

In service industries, multiskilling is an efficient response to office automation, which makes vast quantities of information available, say, to a customer-service representative who can then assume much broader responsibilities. At USAA new computer software allows a single operator equipped with telephone and terminal to combine what had been the work of several departments. In the old days, explains Bill Bowen, vice president for training and development, one person would take down insurance application information. Another would enter the data in a computer. A third would retrieve relevant data from files. A fourth would assess the applicant's risk. A fifth would actually write up the policy. Now a single service representative working one of USAA's 1,008 incoming WATS lines is trained to process the application from start to finish.

Apart from its salutary influence on efficiency and quality, multiskilling can make work more satisfying—and unlock hidden talent and energy within the organization. Says Bob Bowers, who was in charge of worker training at IBM's Tucson site before the company reeducated him as a software programmer: "I think people have to be flexible. For your own personal happiness, you need to be able to shift gears and change careers and explore new interests."

Kathleen Horan, hired to do customer service at Lechmere, studied on her own time to learn how to sell home health products, work the cash register, and fill in at the switchboard. She's now learning how to sell in the sporting goods, housewares, and photo departments. "I feel like I'm in charge of my own destiny," she says. Her co-worker Brad Davis has learned seven jobs, qualifying him for $2.50 an hour above base pay. "I love it," he says. "It's a chance to work with everybody."

For all its potential, the creation of a flexible work force is no walk through the parking lot. Land mines lurk all over. In the auto industry, while carmakers have had the cooperation of United Auto Workers leaders, they have met pockets of bitter resistance, especially from senior and skilled workers. Unions may insist on job guarantees in return for their cooperation. Even non-unionized workers often demand flexibility on management's part. Most frequently they want the brass to share more information, relax controls, and broaden employee participation in planning and operations. They also want incentives to learn new skills, so the cost of training plus incentive pay can be prohibitive.

At the same time, giving workers more skills and autonomy can confuse middle managers stripped of traditional responsibilities and thrust into roles that emphasize counseling and coaching over directing and enforcing. With workers doing their own sourcing, scheduling, and inspection, the middle-level managers who used to handle all that are often left in the lurch. One company that has been grappling with the issue is Eastman Kodak. Switching to flexible work teams at many plants has allowed the company to eliminate two or three layers of middle management, says Phil Leyendecker, director of human resource planning at the Kodak Park division. Those who remained had more people to supervise "but felt a little bit at a loss," Leyendecker says. With workers more autonomous, Kodak has tried to define a new role for foremen—now called team advisers—as well as department and division managers. Workers make up "core" teams. They are counseled and assisted, but not directed, by managers organized into "improving" teams.

In the end, the most powerful push toward flexible work forces may come as the whole U.S. begins to confront Lechmere's problem—a shortage of qualified labor. The decline of the nation's schools, the emergence of an uneducated underclass, and increasing dependence on immigrant workers mean that more people will need extensive remedial work in basic skills even before they can be trained to do several jobs. Motorola estimates that half its factory work force already requires such help—anything from a 32-hour math refresher to several years of English as a second language.

Even with qualified workers, businesses should be prepared for substantial investments in training and incentives. At USAA new service representatives require an initial 16 weeks of full-time training. And yet, laments Bowen, at that point they are only "minimally trained." National Steel calculates that it takes 320 hours of classroom instruction and costs about $21,000 to train an electronics technician, not counting the wages of a replacement worker while the technician is in class.

Corporations that can skim the cream of labor markets have an advantage in developing a flexible work force. USAA, one of the largest employers in San Antonio, has no trouble getting well-qualified workers, since it receives 22 applications for the average job opening. Without that luxury, other companies must confront the cold facts of more forbidding labor demographics. "We're probably going to have to pay a lot more in the early 1990s for labor," says Ana Hullinger, personnel manager for Lechmere in Sarasota.

To help attract workers in an increasingly competitive market, Marriott Corp. recently established a new corporate goal: recognition as the "preferred employer" in its industry and in any community where it does business. In workplaces plagued by lack of skills, flexible workers "get to be preferred workers," says Anthony Carnevale, chief economist at the American Society for Training and Development, a professional association of workplace trainers. Scarcity is certain to make all kinds of skills more valuable. Could one consequence be that the "social contract" between employers and employees—so recently tattered, dishonored, and pronounced dead—will come back to life?

THE BITTER SPLIT IN ORGANIZED LABOR

The dawn of the flexible work force has divided organized labor down the middle. The United Auto Workers leadership has generally supported flexibility, but at some plants opposition—particularly from skilled tradesmen and older workers—has been vociferous.

At Ford's Rouge Steel complex in Dearborn, Michigan, the battle has centered on the consolidation of skilled craft classifications. A 1987 membership vote on a contract that provided for flexible workers passed by just a whisker—1,333 to 1,326. Says Russ Leone, president of the tool-and-die unit of Local 600: "It's very hard to take a skilled tradesman who spent four years going through an apprenticeship and then try to tell him he's going to learn another trade in a few months." He adds that many workers fear that cross-training devalues their job skills, making them more vulnerable to layoffs.

Older workers have another bone to pick. The sharing of skills deprives them of their traditional right to an easier job as they approach retirement. With flexibility, says Pete Kelly, president of a UAW local in Warren, Michigan, "there are no easier jobs." Leone says Ford shelved its multiskilling plan after discovering how costly and time-consuming the training would be, but he expects the issue to resurface.

Merlin Christisen has been a blacksmith at General Motors for more than 30 years. When anyone suddenly needs a one-of-a-kind tool—a four-foot-long chisel, say—Christisen is the man of the hour. Last year GM consolidated job classifications at its Wentzville, Missouri,

assembly plant, and Christisen was made a millwright, a catchall category for repairmen and handymen.

Christisen protested, thus far to no avail. Like many other skilled tradesmen, he resents the change. "I've done this job for 30-plus years. I specialized in doing what I do and I took great pride in it. Some of these jobs that they want me to do as a millwright—they have no meaning. There's no skill involved in pouring concrete. There's no skill in putting up a fence around a parking lot."

Wentzville has also lumped welders with millwrights. Christisen feels that's a mistake: "There isn't any way you can take a man who doesn't have any expertise in welding and make a welder out of him in 30 days or six months. It takes years of training and a feeling for what needs to be done to become a good welder. It's not practical. It's unsafe."

Donald Ephlin, the UAW vice president who heads negotiations with GM, says much of the opposition comes from deep-rooted worker suspicion of management. Ephlin's response: "Some people look at this as helping the company and say, 'They never helped me. Why should I help them?' The other side of the coin is that we're not helping GM. We're improving the product so we can sell cars and provide job security." Some workers have bought the idea. Says Peter Downs, an assembly worker at Wentzville: "A large majority of the people here don't like the concept, but many are willing to accept it to keep the plant open."

Questions

1. Why are organizations enlarging and enriching jobs?

2. What benefits can organizations and their employees gain from jobs redesigned for greater flexibility? Provide examples from the case for each benefit you identify.

3. Given the significant benefits that organizations and their employees can gain from jobs redesigned for greater flexibility, why is there so much resistance to job redesign?

4. What changes in organization design appear to be necessary to effectively implement redesigned jobs?

Reinventing IBM

Say "IBM" to a Japanese executive and he's likely to nod knowingly and talk about *eye bee emu-san* in hushed, respectful tones. Many Japanese managers are openly scornful of the way U.S. corporations are run, but IBM remains cause for reverence, the rare American company that evokes admiration and even fear. Technologically powerful, selling in 130 countries, and wealthy enough to take on Japan Inc., the world's fifth-largest industrial corporation is emblematic of America's hopes for winning on the rugged fields of global competition.

It is also a symbol of America's lapse from greatness. "We took our eye off the ball," confesses John F. Akers, the 54-year-old chairman and CEO. IBM has yet to regain the double-digit growth rates that came as regularly as the sunrise just a few years ago. Revenues climbed 8% to $59.6 billion last year and nearly 8% in the first half of this year, a nice recovery from the 2.8% increase of 1986 but far from the 15% average of the early 1980s. The stock of this bluest of blue chips, once a favorite of institutions and individuals alike, has bounced around for years, trading recently around $115 a share, far beneath its precrash high of $175.

What ball did IBM lose sight of? Mainly the customer and his changing tastes. Companies are moving from big mainframe machines, IBM's bread and butter toward networks of smaller, ever more powerful desktop models. Concerned with protecting its basic business, IBM came late to personal computers, and the ones it built fell behind the competition in performance. The company surrendered such promising niches as laptops and technical workstations to newcomers. It let costs run away and failed to take full advantage of its acclaimed research prowess.

Critics wonder how a giant enterprise employing 387,000 people can keep pace in a market now teeming with small, nimble competitors. The

Source: "Reinventing IBM" by Joel Dreyfuss. Reprinted by permission from FORTUNE Magazine, August 14, 1989, pp. 31–35, 38, 39. © 1989 The Time Inc. Magazine Company. All rights reserved.

problem will be even more acute if, as many suspect, the industry evolves toward "open systems"—networks of computers from various manufacturers sharing a large body of software. With its high prices and proprietary software base, IBM looks ill-equipped to compete in such a world. Asks Sanjiv Hingorani, an analyst at Salomon Brothers: "What is going to make IBM grow 10% a year?"

The answer may not be long in coming. Akers has shattered tradition by publicly discussing IBM's shortcomings. And over the past three years he has set out to remedy them by reinventing the company. He has reorganized its bureaucratic management structure into one designed to address customers' needs and is transforming the IBM culture to the same end. So sweeping are the changes that Akers could stamp the most enduring mark on the company since Thomas Watson Jr. propelled it to world dominance. Says Bob Djurdjevic, whose Annex Research in Phoenix specializes in keeping IBM customers abreast of developments at Big Blue: "This is the most radical cultural change in IBM's history."

IBM is again flexing the technological muscle that made it the world's leader. The past few months have seen a razzle-dazzle burst of new products and good news about old ones. The AS/400 minicomputer is off to the best start ever for an IBM machine, slowing the gains Digital Equipment has been making at IBM's expense. Though the two-year-old PS/2 line of microcomputers has yet to achieve its goal of setting a new standard for desktop computers in the office, sales in the second quarter climbed 40% from last year. Even mainframe sales are up, especially in Europe, where companies are improving their information handling in preparation for 1992.

IBM researchers have won two Nobel Prizes in the past four years, for work on superconductivity and the scanning tunneling microscope. More to the point for customers, IBM is bringing its technical expertise—too often stuck behind the laboratory door in the past—to the marketplace more effectively. It is producing a four-megabit memory chip, the most complex of its kind to date, which puts it months ahead of the Japanese competition. Pointedly upstaging rival Compaq, it brought out a snap-in board for its top-end PS/2 model that incorporates Intel's latest 486 microprocessor. If anyone missed the message that IBM was back, it also unveiled the long-anticipated OfficeVision software that will finally let its disparate mainframes, minis, and micros communicate with ease.

The man behind these accomplishments is only the sixth CEO in IBM's 75-year history. Akers is a Bostonian who played hockey at Yale in the early 1950s and flew fighter planes in the peacetime Navy. Deliberate and unpretentious, he has spent his entire career at IBM, working his way up from sales trainee to the chairman's office. Akers was practically unknown to outsiders when the board handed him the top job and a bushel of troubles four years ago. His personal life remains low key in spite of his greatly enhanced total compensation, $2 million last year. He and his wife, Susan, live in a two-story, four-bedroom house in Westport, Connecticut, and have a summer home on

Nantucket. He drives a 1977 Mercedes. They have a son and two daughters, all in their 20s.

A golfing companion describes Akers as a fiery competitor on the links who—like many top managers—would be better at the game if he had more time. Akers can still recite the lineup of the 1949 Boston Red Sox team that lost the pennant to the hated Yankees. He often spends the early morning aboard an exercise bike at home, pondering his company. "After I've gone through that and showered and shaved," he says, "I'm pretty energetic and I've got my head clear."

Akers does not appear overwhelmed by the task of redirecting such a mammoth enterprise. "This is a pretty collegial place," he insists. "The chief executive always sets the course and the tone, but he gets an awful lot of help." One of IBM's outside directors says the board has not leaned on Akers during the company's tough times. "The pressure on John is self-inflicted," he says. "He's got a certain amount of pride." Sensitive about the impact of his position, Akers sets a style that lets people act freely. In meetings, he points out, "everybody watches the boss. What's his sense of urgency? What's his level of satisfaction? How aggressive is he?" He says he has always avoided taking advantage of a colleague in a business situation: "It's not my position to embarrass anyone."

It also takes humility to admit that you need to change in areas that have always been considered your strength. When IBM's near-monopoly eroded and new technologies began to explode in the early 1980s, the decision-making process that had served IBM well was suddenly cumbersome. Its corporate management board, with 18 senior executives, was handing down decisions from world headquarters in Armonk, New York, on everything from advertising campaigns to R&D allocations for specific products.

IBM was not thinking about the limitations of top-down management when the world began to get more competitive. Convinced that the biggest threat was Japan's awesome manufacturing prowess, the company spent $16.5 billion on new plants and focused on improving productivity and quality. Victims of their own achievements, IBM executives were extravagantly predicting that IBM would grow into a $100 billion company by 1990. (This year's likely revenues of $64 billion leave the old predictions far, far away.) The surest way to reach its goal, IBM concluded, was to play it safe in the marketplace. Akers acknowledges that the products the company introduced as a result were unexciting and middle-of-the-road. "We didn't want to tamper with success," he says. "We decided to be careful instead of aggressive."

When the boom in computer purchases fueled sales in the early 1980s, productivity goals and divisional politics became more important than the changing market. New products, like the PCjr, a personal computer for the home market, and the RT PC, a workstation, satisfied IBM's internal mandates but were embarrassingly weak competitors against rival products. Says Akers: "We were trying to solve some problems that were more IBM's than the customer's."

Reversing those priorities has been crucial to Akers's plan. Last year he reorganized the core company, IBM USA, into seven autonomous business units: PCs, mainframes, minicomputers, communications, microchip manufacturing, programming, and software, with an eighth unit that handles marketing for all the others. He left largely untouched the foreign operations, such as IBM Europe and IBM Japan. Though he got 6,500 employees to retire, he couldn't trim the company's size by firing. IBM has always hewed to a no-layoff tradition during even the toughest times. Instead he moved 20,000 from staff and laboratory jobs to the sales force, where they could boost revenues and increase contacts with customers.

Akers has preached endlessly that IBM must transform itself. "Our growth is really in our hands," he told an unusual meeting of 500 senior managers in January. "I believe the IBM company must become the world's champion in meeting the needs of our customers."

Underpinning Akers's cultural revolution is a systematic effort to push responsibility down the ranks. The decentralization has put the fate of the company squarely in the hands of the general managers of the autonomous business units, all large enough to be *Fortune* 500 companies on their own. Before, the management board kept close tabs on the performance of senior executives. Now general managers negotiate their business plans with Akers and the board each year and then go off to run their divisions. Frank Metz, the chief financial officer, told the January meeting of senior managers: "The corporate management board, to its delight, is spending two-thirds less time reviewing monthly measurements."

The leaders of this cultural revolution seem cut from the old mold, lifelong IBMers who toil in the still-requisite dark suit and white shirt. ("There's no rule about white shirts," insists an IBM manager, "but when I wear a striped shirt, my colleagues ask if I'm going to the beach.") But there's one important difference: Where sales used to be the route to the top, many of today's executives have strong technical backgrounds along with the characteristic IBM traits of competence, charm, and wariness. Among them: Jack Kuehler, 56, an engineer who championed memory chip technology and advanced microprocessors for workstations, whose elevation to president in May has been heralded as proof of IBM's new stress on technical strength.

Conversations with the new business heads reveal how much better IBM's management works these days. Ellen Hancock, 46, general manager of communication systems, which develops such products as modems and computer networks, has 10,000 employees reporting to her. The highest-ranking woman at IBM, she started as a programmer in 1966, became a manager of software programming for communications products, and was named a vice president in 1985.

Hancock, whose frequent hearty laughter belies her scholarly demeanor, says the reorganization has clarified lines of responsibility. "If there's something in telecommunications and we're not doing it, it's probably not being done," she says. "Before, you could assume somebody else in IBM was working on it, and perhaps that was true." Hancock says Akers is constantly prodding senior managers to be more daring and creative. She recently appointed two executives to pursue alliances with other companies in telecommunications to develop new products and services. Earlier, she notes, such moves would have required approval from the top. Says she: "It really has been fun."

Although they are autonomous, the general managers consult one another frequently. They say their dealings are remarkably free of red tape. "It's a one-level thing among us chickens," says George Conrades, 50, who heads U.S. marketing. One benefit is that the managers don't waste time politicking to curry the favor of superiors. Conflicts used to work their way up to the management board. Now, if the business heads can't resolve disputes, the final arbiter is one level up: Terry Lautenbach, 56, head of IBM USA. But Conrades says such adjudications are rare. "Peer group pressure," he says, "is greater than any fiat from on high."

Handing down responsibility is but one step in getting closer to customers. Long in the habit of telling buyers what it thought was good for them, IBM is having to teach its executives how to listen and become problem solvers. Akers forced the issue in the fall of 1986, when he invited several key customers to participate in the company's strategic planning conference. "I couldn't imagine former chairmen John Opel or Frank Cary doing that," says an IBM-watcher who knows the company well. The customers were unusually blunt. Akers, listening hard, firmly acknowledged the criticisms and vowed that IBM would take them seriously. Soon after that he declared that 1987 would be "the year of the customer" and launched a series of programs to bring users in during the design and introduction stages—a striking departure from IBM's notorious secrecy about new products.

The Glasnost paid off handsomely in the development of the AS/400 minicomputer, introduced last year as the overdue replacement for IBM's aging System 36 and System 38 machines. Digital Equipment's minis had been eating IBM's lunch for years because of their superior performance and the ability of different models to talk to each other. Engineers put together a prototype of the AS/400 in November 1985, and IBM decided to go ahead with the project in early 1986.

IBM created an advisory council of customers and shared its plans for the new computer. "It sounds easier than it was," says Stephen Schwartz, 54, the dour trouble-shooter who runs the Application Business Systems division, which manufactures minicomputers. "Developers become very protective of their thing." But the engineers eventually dropped their defenses. For example, potential buyers persuaded IBM to make it easier for them to transfer programs and data from the old machines to the new. Knowing that programming would be the key to selling the AS/400, the company also brought independent software companies into the planning in early 1987.

By the time IBM formally introduced the AS/400, potential buyers had tested 1,700 of the computers, and IBM made further changes in response to their criticisms. After tuning the system to foreign markets, IBM presented it around the world simultaneously and was ready with more than 1,000 software applications in 12 languages, including French, Japanese, and Chinese. IBM has called the AS/400 the most successful product launch in its history. In less than a year it sold more than 25,000 machines—worth an estimated $3 billion.

Outsiders are bringing a fresh understanding of the customer to IBM's Application Solutions division, the 30,000-strong software business unit headed by Ned Lautenbach, 45, brother of Terry Lautenbach. Ned Lautenbach's unit markets software and hardware to 17 major industries, from banking to automobiles, and is the fastest-growing part of IBM. Breaking with tradition, Lautenbach has recruited industry experts—from stock and bond traders to CPAs, from teachers to hospital administrators—to help develop and pitch products. "We've struggled to make sure we have all the right skills and abilities," he says.

Among IBM's sales and service forces, pleasing the customer has taken on almost mythic proportions. Conrades's instruction to his salespeople is simple and to the point: When the customer asks for something, "Just say yes." And autonomy makes saying yes easier. Ron Kilpatrick, an area manager, supervises 3,200 systems engineers and marketing representatives in Southern California, Arizona, and Hawaii from Los Angeles. Kilpatrick, who was a vice president in the division that handled dealers, jumped at the chance to go west and in effect run his own operation. He and a regional manager concluded recently that IBM wasn't paying enough attention to an important customer in Phoenix, so on the spot they created a new branch office. When fire in a Los Angeles high-rise knocked out the computer system of another major client, Kilpatrick was on the phone to the CEO immediately, offering to lend equipment and technicians. The system was back up and running before he thought to tell Armonk. In the past, he says, he would have had to call headquarters for approval first.

To make sure the troops keep their priorities straight, Akers has overturned the old commission system that rewarded salespeople for the number of units they rented or sold. Now IBM reps are measured on total revenue. They can concentrate on the customer's needs even if those don't maximize short-term revenue to IBM: smaller computers, software, networks, and, in the new spirit of entrepreneurship, even tying in other companies' products if that's what the customer must have.

The reps appear enthusiastic about the new approach. "My goal is to spend 80% of my time with customers," says Fred Liu, one of the thousands of IBMers redeployed to the field in the reorganization. An engineer who helped develop the AS/400, Liu now works with the information systems department of Farmers Group in Los Angeles, a large property and casualty insurer. He has spent many evenings helping his customer upgrade the software in its major system. "I'm part of Farmers' team," he says proudly. "I really felt the partnership when one of Farmers' employees came up to me, explained a decision the company was considering on a technical problem, and asked, 'Do you concur?' "

Bolstered with the redeployed technical and staff people, the sales force has more time for the smaller accounts IBM used to neglect. Computer usage surveys show that up to 70% of small businesses still don't have a computer, so future growth is clearly in this area. Roxanne Reynolds-Lair, information systems director of the Fashion Institute of Design and Merchandising in Los Angeles, recalls that when she called IBM's marketers a few years ago, "You left messages, and they wouldn't call you back." Now they not only call back, but when the institute moves to new quarters next year, IBM will design the computer center and install all the equipment. Says Reynolds-Lair: "They've entered the 1990s."

IBM's Service division is learning to embrace customers who mix and match brands. "We had built a tremendous skill base in solving problems," says David McDowell, 46, president of the 29,000-employee national service division. "Today we can help with everything." His troops will tackle whatever the customer asks: service other brands, tie them to IBM computers, or recover lost data after a disaster. This new ecumenism isn't a matter of charity. McDowell estimates that computer users spend $100 *billion* a year on maintenance and service, and he wants more of that.

In a change of no less import, IBM has abandoned its not-invented-here arrogance in favor of joint ventures with small outside firms that can help it develop new technologies or open new markets. Says Philippe Kahn, chairman of Borland International, a PC software developer: "They're more open to suggestions we make, and they're more open to interesting business relationships." IBM has invested in a dozen small software companies, licensed programming technology from Steven Jobs's Next Inc., and joined a consortium of investors in U.S. Memories, a company that aims to reduce the U.S. dependence on Japan for DRAMs, the most common variety of memory chip. When supercomputer whiz Steve Chen quit Cray Research, IBM quickly invested in his new company.

Foreign customers too are getting stroked as never before. IBM's best news recently has come from overseas, where revenues went up 15.5% to $34.4 billion in 1988, 58% of the total, and have kept rising in double digits for the first half of this year. Profits from abroad, always a large part of IBM's earnings, reached almost 75% of the total last year.

In Italy the company has formed alliances with European distributors and doubled its sales staff, spending 40% more "face" time with customers. IBM Japan has finally ended a 20-year slide from first to third place in its competition against NEC and Fujitsu, Japan's big computer makers. It has begun to match competitors by discounting and customizing products for the Japanese market. "We're no longer just offering what has been developed in other parts of the world," says Takeo Shiina, president of IBM Japan. For example, while U.S. customers still await a decent laptop, IBM Japan introduced one with full Japanese-language capability two years ago. Thanks to such efforts, *Nikkei Watcher on IBM*, a Japanese trade publication, expects IBM Japan to grow 13.5% next year, faster than its competitors.

Those technically oriented leaders eager to please customers are helping IBM get new technologies out of the laboratory faster. The company dismayed Japanese rivals recently with the announcement that it was producing the four-megabit chip in large volume. Patrick Toole, 52, the general manager of technology products, says the reorganization has helped. Now, like other heads of business units, he decides what products to make after negotiating with his customers: the other unit heads. Says Toole: "Much more of what I do now turns into successful products."

But technical prowess alone is not enough. IBM learned that when it introduced the Micro Channel, an internal connector for the PS/2 microcomputers that allowed data to be manipulated more quickly. Customers yawned. The company concedes now that it never sold the advantages of Micro Channel. "What's important to the customer is solving his problem, and the flow of technology is almost incidental," says Akers.

Unlike yesterday's computer specialists, today's executives use their machines as strategic tools. A shipping company, for example, can call up rates for all its competitors on a route and instantly offer a lower price to customers. Or it can look at prices and profit margins on a variety of goods and turn down a shipment with a low margin in favor of one with a higher payoff. Managers playing with such information have no patience for arcane commands, indecipherable screens, and rigid barriers between databases. They want to reach all their information easily without having to worry about where it is stored or what brand of computer it's on. The computer industry buzzword is "transparency."

Bewildered and frustrated by the proliferation of incompatible machines, buyers have spurred the movement toward "open systems," a universal standard that would allow software to run on many different brands of hardware. That clearly threatens IBM and other large computer makers such as Digital Equipment, which have traditionally clung to proprietary machines and programming. John Levinson of Goldman Sachs foresees what he calls an "industry standard chassis," a cheap, generic computer that would use Unix, an operating system popular in universities and engineering centers. Other analysts, looking further out, imagine networks that run just fine regardless of which operating systems the various machines linked to them use.

IBM's response is two-pronged: Beat 'em *and* join 'em. It wants to tighten its grip on its own broad base of customers who use its proprietary systems, while also offering its own version of Unix.

OfficeVision, a software bridge that straddles its three incompatible computer architectures, is IBM's bid to protect its home turf. OfficeVision allows PCs, minis, and mainframes to share programs and data, and presents an easy-to-use Macintosh-like screen to all users. It's a technological tour de force, a glimpse of what the billions in R&D money can deliver. It is also expensive at an estimated $8,000 per user. "It's not for people who are price-sensitive," says Richard Shaffer, publisher of *Technologic Computer Letter*, a trade publication. OfficeVision also makes customers more dependent on IBM, since it needs IBM's operating system and software.

The join 'em part, IBM's version of Unix, is called AIX. Last year IBM surprised many in the industry by hooking up with rival Digital and other companies in the Open Software Foundation, a group established to set a software standard for Unix-based computers, Joseph Guglielmi, 48, president of the Application Systems division, says IBM will develop links to let users pass data between AIX machines and its other computers. Akers says IBM is not at all ambivalent about proprietary vs. open systems. "We're spending more on Unix-based open systems than any other company in the world," he says. "That's a statement of commitment, and that's a statement of leadership. We're trying to do both very well." This fall IBM is expected to introduce a much more powerful family of workstations that should make it a serious competitor in the Unix market.

Still, IBM has good reason to sell OfficeVision as hard as possible: The system's heart is an IBM mainframe, doing less computing but serving as a central data library and switchboard for the desktop machines that are sprouting up all over.

IBM contends that Wall Street underestimates the future of the mainframe computer, which still delivers 70% to 75% of the company's profits. Domestic sales of mainframes have been modest, but the big machines are unmatched in handling huge quantities of data. And the trends in computing promise a need for more storage capacity, to accommodate image reproduction, voice recognition, corporate databases, and easier-to-use software. Brian Jeffery, managing director of International Technology Group, a consulting firm in Los Altos, California, expects the business to get a much-needed boost in 1991, when the company introduces its next-generation mainframe. The machine, code named Summit, may well incorporate such cutting-edge technologies as fiber-optic connectors and superfast gallium arsenide memory chips.

Though IBM makes more money than any other company in the world, it doesn't make enough. It has preserved its lush 70% gross profit margins on mainframes and proprietary software despite sharp competition from such makers of compatible machines as Amdahl and Hitachi. It also hopes to lift sales of high-margin software and small business systems fast enough to make up for slower sales of big systems.

Though IBM has closed plants, cut discretionary spending, and reduced capital expenditures, costs have risen faster than revenues during most of the reorganization. But the company may be getting somewhere. As recently as two years ago costs were climbing so fast that it needed annual revenue increases of more than 10% just to keep earnings steady. Frank Metz told security analysts in March that IBM could now maintain current earnings on 6% revenue increases. Analysts are taking heart. "They've been saying they're getting overhead down for quite a while," says John Jones, computer industry analyst at Montgomery Securities in San Francisco. "The results are finally surfacing."

One reason costs remain high is the no-layoff policy. Don Young, an analyst with the Sanford C. Bernstein investment firm, estimates that keeping those 20,000 redeployed people on the payroll is pulling profits down by 35%. But Akers's strategy in shifting those folks is to eventually make them a profit center.

Indeed, the new customer-friendly posture and the expanding role in software and service are the pillars of Akers's strategy for competing in a world IBM no longer dominates. Imagine squads of problem solvers living with customers and looking for opportunities to help out—at a price, of course. Focus just on the $100 billion a year that computer users pay various people and firms for maintenance and service. Today IBM captures about 9% of that. Each new percentage point of market share translates into $1 billion of revenue. And if the generic computer does eventually prevail, companies more than ever will need skilled, sympathetic service people to help them get the best performance and value from their systems. A vast army in dark suits and white shirts chanting "Just say yes" would be a force to reckon with— anywhere on the globe.

Questions

1. IBM was once the world's preeminent computer manufacturer but its market position eroded significantly during the 1980s. Why did IBM lose its preeminent position in the computer industry? How did its centralized decision-making style contribute to the decline?

2. Describe IBM's reorganization. How did it change the way decisions were made? What corresponding changes did IBM make to support decentralization and its renewed focus on the customer?

3. What evidence does the case provide that decentralization increased the speed of decision making and made it more responsive to customer needs?

P&G Rewrites the Marketing Rules

As annual meetings go, Procter & Gamble's promised to be pleasantly uneventful. Sales and profits were up; ditto the stock price and the outlook for the future. Even the animal-rights activists waving signs outside P&G's sleekly squat postmodern headquarters in Cincinnati seemed routine.

Which is why CEO John Smale's announcement a few minutes into the noon meeting that he was retiring at the end of the year to be replaced by vice chairman Edwin Artzt, 59, had the force of a grenade lobbed into the crowded auditorium. So impregnable is P&G that no word of Smale's plans had leaked beforehand. Indeed, a month earlier, the dark-haired, jowly 62-year-old had denied twice that he had any intention of stepping down.

P&G insiders took the appointment of Artzt as a sign that P&G was continuing with the most radical restructuring in its recent history. The man responsible for turning around Procter's international division, Artzt is known within the company for his aggressive style. Says he: "I feel most of the major things going on here have a lot of my blood and sweat already on them. I'm committed to the program, which is just about to blossom."

The transfer at the top shows that Smale, after overseeing two years of wrenching change, feels confident enough to let Artzt guide a new P&G through its completion. A *new* P&G? Yes. The peerless promoter that practically created modern marketing is re-creating it, profoundly altering the way consumer packaged goods are made and sold. Says Smale: "We've made watershed changes at P&G, the most significant changes since the Second World War. They will bear fruit well into the next decade."

Source: "P&G Rewrites the Marketing Rules" by Brian Dumaine. Reprinted by permission from FORTUNE Magazine, November 6, 1989, pp. 35–36, 38, 40, 42, 46, 48. © 1989 The Time Inc. Magazine Company. All rights reserved.

More balderdash from the big office? Hardly. Listen to consultant John Luther of Marketing Corp. of America, an adviser to scores of consumer products companies: "Procter is reinventing the packaged goods industry for the year 2000 and beyond." In the process, the company is providing American business with a case study of how a large and bureaucratic organization can change internally without totally destroying the culture that made it great. Says Smale: "We're not ancestor worshippers, but we do believe this company's culture is rooted very much in its past." Procter is taking the best of its past—a willingness to stay with long-term projects, job security, and a history of promotion from within—and grafting on to it a management style that calls for pushing authority down, speeding up decisions, and getting closer to the customer. Some examples:

- P&G now treats retailers—once considered tough, penny-pinching adversaries—as partners and assigns special teams to help big customers like Wal-Mart and Kroger improve inventory, distribution, and sales promotion.

- Into its famous brand management system, P&G has inserted a new level, called category manager. The supra-brand managers have the spending power and decision-making authority to respond to fast-changing markets.

- Another new position, the product supply manager, works with representatives from manufacturing, engineering, distribution, and purchasing to cut product development time. This middle-level manager has the authority to make decisions on the spot.

- To crack overseas markets, P&G is going native, spending heavily to learn what consumers from Oslo to Osaka want.

Make no mistake: These are sweeping changes. In the first two years of restructuring, Procter has reorganized marketing, sales, manufacturing, and distribution. Bonuses are now based on individual performance rather than corporate results, and head count in the U.S. is down by 2,000, to 43,600. Over one-third of the company's top 20 managers have been replaced since 1984.

Driving the reorganization is Smale's long-term strategy to be the market leader in each of P&G's 39 product categories. So far the company, which makes such household names as Crest, Ivory soap, Head & Shoulders, Pampers, Tide, NyQuil, Pepto-Bismol, and Folgers coffee, is first in 22 categories, up from 17 four years ago. In September the company announced the $1.3 billion purchase of Noxell, the manufacturer of Noxema skin cream and Cover Girl makeup, which will make P&G the largest mass-marketer of cosmetics in the U.S. Says Smale: "The money is made by those manufacturers that have major share." Hercules Segalas, head of the consumer products group at Paine Webber, estimates that bet-selling Crest, for instance, enjoys a 75% profit margin.

The reorganization has already produced some sprightly numbers. After a string of dismal years, earnings in fiscal 1989 (which ended in June) jumped 18% to $1.2 billion on sales of $21.4 billion. Unit volume growth, chugging along at 5% in 1985, is now rising at an average annual rate of 7%, a remarkable pace for a large company operating in mature markets.

Wall Street has not overlooked the new sparkle: Over the past year, P&G's stock has bubbled up 48% to a recent price of $120.75 a share. Says Morgan Stanley security analyst Brenda Lee Landry, who cites P&G's manageable debt, growing cash flow, and $1.6 billion in cash: "This large, stodgy company has been revitalized."

True enough. But change has its costs, and the long, drawn-out variety may be the most expensive kind. P&G's process of stretching its reorganization over years has proved demoralizing for some employees and even customers. Says a manager of a grocery chain, who anxiously awaits some sign of the new, improved P&G: "We hear a lot about the focus on Wal-Mart, and we want to know more about it."

Because Smale has been streamlining the company by attrition rather than layoffs, pockets of hardheaded, change-resistant bureaucrats remain. In some divisions and departments, the mix of old and new management levels makes for unnecessary confusion. Reporting lines in sales, for instance, are particularly unclear. An ex-P&Ger observes: "It's a nightmare right now." Though the company claims turnover is low, a headhunter who says he used to get five or ten calls a week from P&G people is now getting 30. "They're losing some of their best and brightest."

The company's rigid adherence to gradual promotion from within has prevented it from solving pressing problems in the food and beverage businesses. In the infamous soft-cookie wars of the early 1980s, Procter's Duncan Hines division got burned by Nabisco. Orange Crush soft drinks never came close to the Coke and Pepsi league and were finally sold last spring. P&G remains reluctant to hire outside food and beverage experts. Says a former high-level employee: "The biggest hang-up is that they don't let a lot of light in the window."

Though P&G plays down the turmoil, the selection of Artzt suggests that the company may be stepping up the pace of reorganization. Says an ex-P&G manager: "I think Ed will look at plans and timetables and force people to move them up. He will also reduce head count." For example, in the early 1980s, Artzt cut P&G's British work force 13%.

In guiding P&G's restructuring to its conclusion, Artzt has an advantage that managers in similar situations should envy: supportive shareholders. Thanks to a century-old profit-sharing plan and a brand-new employee stock ownership program, current and retired employees control 28% of the shares. Not only do workers have a stake in making the reorganization a success, but so much control in presumably friendly hands should discourage raiders.

Restructuring came to Cincinnati none too soon. In the mid-1980s, P&G's margins and earnings were eroding, and flagship products like Crest and Pampers were losing market share. The feeling among financial analysts and corporate customers was that P&G had become a corporate Kremlin: bureaucratic, risk averse, and arrogant. Says Leslie Dietzman, an executive vice president at Ames Department Stores and one of P&G's major customers: "It was do it P&G's way or hit the highway."

A manager at a large Midwestern supermarket chain, for instance, recalls how P&G once told him he would get his promotion money (funds the manufacturers give retailers to pay for special sales, coupons, and ad campaigns) only if he ran a two-column-inch newspaper ad on Tide. Recalls the retailer: "The P&G salesman would come into the store, measure the ad and say, 'Nope, it's only 1.9 inches, you won't get the money.' "

Many competitors like Colgate-Palmolive and Campbell Soup were already restructuring, and Smale realized that if he didn't do some heavy lifting, P&G would be left behind. Turning over such a huge boulder would be a hard job, but Smale, a 37-year veteran with an almost encyclopedic knowledge of the company, was the right man. In 1954, when he was the brand manager for what was then a little-known toothpaste called Crest, he asked the American Dental Association to endorse it. Six years later they did, giving Crest a leg up on the competition that it has never lost. A high-ranking manager who recently left the company describes Smale as "a tough, pragmatic man with a great command of the business. He can keep his hands on a lot of balls."

Though pleasant in social settings, Smale is considered aloof by colleagues. His lieutenant John Pepper, the company's president, is much warmer, and P&G security analysts, employees, and former employees tabbed him as the next CEO. When Artzt got the call, the speculation was that Pepper, at 51, needed more seasoning—an opinion that was reinforced when he was made the head of international, Artzt's old territory. Nonetheless, he remains the heir apparent. Known as a listener and consensus builder, Pepper invites managers on the spur of the moment for informal lunches. He represents a new generation at P&G hip to the latest in management thought who toss around buzzwords like "self-directed" and "empowerment." Not that he's exactly Silicon Valley: Employees still talk about the time he worked Christmas day.

In the summer of 1987, the company began organizing its 4,000-strong sales force to do something pretty obvious: focus more on the customer—in this case, supermarkets and department stores. Under the old system P&G had 11 national sales forces, each hawking a product line such as detergents or foods. Retailers were faced with numerous P&G salesmen pushing 11 different product lines with all sorts of different promotions. For years P&G got away with this awkward system. Says Paine Webber's Segalas: "Retailers hated P&G, but they needed it. It dominated the trade."

Then the balance of power shifted from big manufacturers like P&G to the retailers. What tipped the scales was consolidation among supermarket and drugstore chains and the widespread use of scanners at the checkout counter. As a result of industry mergers, 100 chains now account for some 80% of P&G's U.S. grocery sales, vs. 15% about 20 years ago. Electronic bar coding helped retailers gather their own sales data. P&G could no longer bully its way into the stores, waving figures a retailer couldn't dispute that showed Tide was outselling All and was therefore entitled to more shelf space.

Slowly P&G realized that it would have to start fussing over these power-punching retailers. Says Mike Milligan, one of P&G's top sales executives: "We're switching from a product to a customer approach." Now teams of people from finance, distribution, manufacturing, and other functions are assigned to cover the big retailers. Says an executive at a large supermarket chain: "We can call the shots now. If we want to run a Duncan Hines ad, P&G has given its local sales managers the autonomy to say, 'We'll give you $20,000 for it.' "

A team of a dozen or so attends solely to the needs of Wal-Mart. Working with the crew from P&G, the discount giant has set up a just-in-time ordering and delivery system for Pampers and Luvs disposable diapers. When the diapers run low in a store, a computer sends an order by satellite to a P&G factory, which in turn automatically ships more diapers directly to the outlet. As a result, Wal-Mart can maintain smaller inventories and cut the number of times it runs out of Pampers. Says Smale: "This is what people refer to as a win-win situation. Our costs go lower and their costs go lower. Our objectives and the objectives of our customers are going to be much more aligned."

Here's another example of working with—rather than against—the retailers. P&G through a joint venture has installed a state-of-the-art checkout system called Visions in a Dahl's supermarket in Des Moines, Iowa. A Dahl's customer gets an electronic card that he inserts in a black box hooked to the register to call up his account. Let's say the customer buys Downy on sale. When the clerk scans the bottle of fabric softener, a color monitor at the counter shows a video of a woman holding Downy and purring, "You've saved 50 cents on Downy." That amount is deducted from the tab. Visions also automatically tallies points for certain products—50 for Downy. When the customer accrues enough points, he or she gets a prize, perhaps a watch (4,745 points) or a VCR (22,035). Not only is Visions attracting customers to Dahl's stores, but it is also giving both Dahl's and P&G valuable market data about consumer spending.

Once Smale tackled sales, he turned to the heart of P&G, the vaunted brand management system. The company doesn't know for sure how many brand managers it has—one inside source stopped counting at 92. Some shepherd $700-million or $800-million-a-year businesses. Only one of every three new hires makes it to brand manager, a process that usually takes four years. Those who do earn between $60,000 and $77,000. They are responsible for every aspect of their brands—marketing, advertising, sales, and development.

The rub: To get a major decision, brand managers often had to go through three or four layers of management. With up to 14 brand managers in each division, getting the attention of the division chief wasn't easy. One manager recalls waiting a year for an OK on a simple package design change. Another difficulty: Brand managers were so focused on a single product that they lost sight of the marketplace, even of what their colleagues were doing. Says one who left P&G: "The brand managers were butting heads. There was a lot of cannibalization. You'd issue coupons at the same time for P&G's liquid and powdered detergents."

That's why Smale, in late 1987, created the category management system, a move which promises to revolutionize consumer marketing much as brand management did nearly 60 years ago. He broke the company into 39 product categories and named 26 category managers (some have more than one category). Brand managers report to the category manager, who is like a small businessman. He has total profit-and-loss responsibility for an entire product line—all laundry detergents, for example, which would include such competing brands as Tide, Cheer, and Ivory Flakes.

The idea is to have someone who thinks in terms of product groups and who will make sure the brand managers aren't sabotaging each other. Now the brand managers can go directly to the category manager, who has the authority to make quick decisions and to back them up with as much as $1 million per project. Says Smale: "The creation of these category profit centers was really a continuation of the basic philosophy that small is good, that you bring focus to a specific business when you create a stand-alone operation."

Last year's severe drought in the Midwest put the new system to the test. The price of soybeans, a crucial ingredient in Puritan and Crisco oils, started to shoot up. What to do? Buy now or wait? Under the old system, says category manager Neil DeFeo, "We'd write a lengthy memo with exhibits and send it to senior management for agreement." Instead, DeFeo gave an OK on the spot to the purchasing agent to buy more soybeans and avoided a pounding on escalating prices.

Critics of the category management system say that P&G is moving in the right direction but not far enough or fast enough. For the most part the company has not eliminated any of the division vice presidents or other executives whose authority is being usurped by the category managers. Observes one ex-P&Ger: "You've got these vice presidents, all with their corporate jets, who make a lot of money and have been there forever. It's not easy to get rid of them."

When he launches a new product or repositions an old one, the category manager forms a small team made up of the brand manager plus people from sales, finance, and manufacturing. Key to P&G's success here is another new position called the product supply manager, who reports to the category manager but has broad responsibility over every aspect of manufacturing, engineering, purchasing, and distribution. Says Smale: "I have the growing conviction that the product supply concept is perhaps the single most important thing that can influence our profit performance over the next several years." He estimates that the creation of product supply managers will slash costs by $1 billion over the next two years.

At the old P&G a brand manager would come up with a new concept for a product or package. The idea, usually traveling in memo form, would be tossed over the transom to engineering, then to manufacturing, and then maybe to distribution. Progress was slow and awkward.

The product supply manager has changed all that. This spring, for example, the category manager for dishwashing detergent wanted a new cap for liquid Cascade. Though the cap in use was childproof, it was also somewhat adultproof. The team got together, and the product supply manager, as its leader, was able to get everyone to work out all the cost, design, and manufacturing problems. The cap went into production without any glitches after only nine months, nearly twice as fast as under the old system.

To instill a sense of what P&G calls "total quality," the company spreads tales like this one as well as other corporate heroics. In a war story making the rounds this fall, the company's Hatboro, Pennsylvania, plant was gearing up to launch a new children's NyQuil cough syrup in time for the winter cold season.

Just days before the line was to start rolling, the factory received from a supplier three million NyQuil boxes printed upside down. If the faulty boxes were run through the machine that inserted the bottles, the tops of the bottles would end up at the bottom of the boxes, and the packages would be unstable on the store shelves. Without enough time to bring in engineers or have new parts designed, two mechanics, George Rowan and Ed Scott, worked around the clock for three days, missing the plant's annual picnic. The pair came up with a system of springs and brushes that turned the boxes around and kept them open so NyQuil bottles could be inserted properly. Amen.

And how about this for getting *really* close to the customer? At the Duncan Hines angel food cake factory in Jackson, Tennessee, the line workers are given letters from customers who have problems with the product. One factory hand called up a customer whose angel food cake didn't rise, and helped figure out why by asking such questions as "How long did you beat the mix?" and "At what temperature did you bake it?" Says Smale: "What we've said to the workers is, this is the only place we make angel food cake, and you're responsible for it, and if you want to talk to the consumer, we'd like you to talk to the consumer."

The quality quest explains the $652 million P&G allocated to R&D in fiscal 1988. As a percent of sales, that amount represents half again as much as such competitors as Unilever and Colgate-Palmolive spend developing packaged goods. Even so, P&G has had few megahits since it launched disposable diapers in the 1960s. But olestra, the fake fat now undergoing Food and Drug Administration testing, may be that long-awaited home run.

Olestra is sugar and vegetable oil chemically combined so that its molecule is too large for the stomach to digest; so it never enters the bloodstream, where it can clog arteries and veins. The body simply excretes it. Olestra rolls over the tongue much like fat but without the calories or cholesterol. It can be used to replace the silky consistency fat gives ice cream or to fry fat-free French fries, potato chips, and donuts. At Procter's R&D labs, this *Fortune* writer dined on steak with wine sauce, sauteed zucchini, and apple tart, all cooked in vegetable oil cut with olestra. The meal tasted just as good as food cooked in regular vegetable oil. Potato chips fried in olestra, however, flunked a blind taste test; they lacked the delightfully greasy aftertaste of the real thing.

The FDA is expected to rule on olestra's safety within the next two years. If approved for sale, olestra will likely be used initially as an additive in Crisco and Puritan vegetable oils. Nutritionists are concerned that if P&G marketed a 100% olestra product, some Americans would scarf down ice cream and French fries until scurvy got them. Estimates of how much money olestra will make for P&G range wildly. Some financial analysts believe the fake fat will add $1 billion to sales over the first few years; others a few hundred million. Even Smale can't guess, but he firmly believes that olestra heralds a change in the American diet.

Want to know how P&G's restructuring will play out? Take a look at the international division. During his nine-year tenure as its head, Artzt helped P&G expand rapidly overseas. In 1986 the international business—P&G peddles its products in 140 foreign countries—represented 29% of sales; now it is 40%. Nearly 35% of earnings in fiscal 1989 came from offshore, up from 23% three years ago. In fiscal 1989 international's profits shot up 37% from the year earlier.

Feeding the growth spurt is P&G's entry into new business categories overseas, such as feminine protection products. Always is now marketed in the Far East, where it's called Whisper and is the biggest selling sanitary napkin in Japan. The acquisition of Richardson-Vicks, the maker of NyQuil cough syrup and Oil of Olay skin creams, has provided P&G with strong international distribution channels in Australia, New Zealand, Singapore, and Hong Kong. But perhaps the most important element in P&G's overseas success is its new willingness to go native, and nothing illustrates this better than the company's experience in Japan.

Smale predicts that—after 16 years of struggle—sales in Japan will top $1 billion in 1990. In the next three years Japan should replace West Germany as P&G's biggest foreign market. The key to cracking Japan: realizing that the company would have to fine-tune its "world products"—defined by P&G as the best you can buy anywhere—to the Japanese market.

Not such a revelation, you say. Well, remember that P&G once truly believed its marketing prowess could ignore cultural differences. That attitude is changing. Says Artzt: "We need to develop the ability to deliver globally what we do well regionally. We have to adapt to overseas markets." For example, a Camay soap commercial showed a Japanese husband in the room while his wife was bathing, an invasion of privacy the Japanese found distasteful. After P&G switched to a more abstract commercial, sales improved.

In the early 1980s, P&G was getting soaked in the Japanese diaper market. After years of painstaking market research, the company finally realized that Japanese parents are very concerned with keeping their babies clean, and changed their kids' diapers far more often than Americans do. In response, P&G devised Ultra Pampers, a more absorbent diaper that keeps the tyke drier and makes frequent changing a less messy task. P&G also discovered that in land-starved Japan, shelf and closet space is almost as precious to housewives as their kids. It made the diapers thinner so the same number fit in a much smaller box. The popularity of the new diapers spread like a baby's rash, and today Ultra Pampers is the market leader.

P&G sells a total of 20 products in Japan, including Colac, the leading laxative. To keep the momentum going, in September the company announced a new $215 million R&D center to be built in Osaka Bay in the early 1990s.

The company has also made some inroads into the Japanese distribution system, whose arcane network of mom and pop wholesalers has frustrated many American firms. Procter's executives in Japan try to establish an unofficial partnership with the Japanese distributors the same way that the Japanese companies do, by showing a keen personal interest in their lives, inside and outside work. Not only do top executives help the distributors run their businesses, but they also hold elaborate lunches for them and, in some cases, even attend their weddings and funerals.

What's truly amazing about P&G's historic restructuring is that it is a response to the consumer market, not the stock market. No raider has the company in his cross hairs—at least not yet. So P&G can rewrite the rules of marketing in its own deliberate way, continuing to pour money into R&D and toughing out a turnaround for businesses like Citrus Hill orange juice despite years of losses. After all, taking the long view paid off for Folgers coffee, which took 25 years to become the best-selling java in the U.S. A new management structure, a fresh global approach, an enduring corporate culture, and a commitment to the long term: Sounds like P&G is just about ready for the year 2000.

Questions

1. Procter & Gamble (P&G)—perhaps the most successful U.S. consumer-products firm in U.S. history—began a massive, long-term organization restructuring during the late 1980s. Why?

2. Characterize the design of P&G's sales operations prior to restructuring. What were its drawbacks? How did P&G change its sales operations in terms of unit grouping? What were the benefits of this reorganization?

3. Characterize the design of P&G's product management system prior to restructuring. What were its drawbacks? How did P&G restructure its brand-management system? What were the benefits of this reorganization?

CASE 6

Deere's "Factory of the Future"

The Wilson Learning Corporation of Eden Prairie, Minnesota, publishes a colorful and appealing poster in which organizational performance is graphically represented as a bicycle, the front wheel of which is "people," and the back wheel "technology." In the Wilson poster, none of the bicycles have front wheels, symbolizing the undeniable fact that American managers over the last three decades foolishly ignored the human factor in their businesses. In overreaction to this managerial error, many consultants are now selling bicycles with no rear wheels (search as one might, the word "technology" is hard to find in any of the five management bestsellers of the 1980s). The problem is that bicycles without rear wheels have no mechanism for forward propulsion—they lack the productive drive of technology. This is no better than a bicycle that lacks the steering power of the human mind. Wilson's point is that all bicycles must stand and move on two wheels. It is a message that has been absorbed at the Vanguard—these companies are as balanced on two wheels as any in America.

Like the concepts "innovation," "productivity," and "pay for performance," "technology" is also hard to define. Let us call it "the systematic application of scientific knowledge to practical tasks" (with the understanding that "scientific" includes all organized and replicable knowledge, both quantitative and qualitative). The reason why most recent books on management pay scant attention to technology is because management professors know nothing about it (for example, of the 140 professors of business at the USC business school where I work, only four have any background in technology, and only one—not me—can lay claim to being an expert). And

Source: "Deere's Factory of the Future" excerpted from VANGUARD MANAGEMENT by James O'Toole, pp. 187–198, copyright © 1985 by James O'Toole. Used by permission of Doubleday, a division of Bantam, Doubleday, Dell Publishing Group, Inc.

technology frightens the hell out of most managers (who were educated, after all, by that very same technologically illiterate mob just mentioned).

The state of most managers' knowledge of technology is frozen at about the level of Eli Whitney's great idea that, if parts could all be standardized, they would be interchangeable. This led to the introduction of efficient mass production of manufactured goods (as opposed to the slow and expensive process of making things one by one). Beyond that, all most managers know about manufacturing technology is that it is complicated, it creates a constant demand for costly reinvestment, and that it often involves unionized workers. To learn more, managers know they would have to visit a hot, noisy, and grimy factory where they would not only get their Brooks Brothers suits soiled, they would get grunted at (at best) by people who are supposed to be *their* employees. Is it any surprise that so many managers come to the conclusion to shut the factory down and acquire a burger chain?

At Deere, they had a different idea. Until 1970, Deere & Company's "mass produced" tractors were built mostly by hand in an odd collection of grimy, sixty-year-old brick factories spread over half a square mile near the center of a sleepy Iowa town (improbably named Waterloo). The factory, like many manufacturing operations, had grown a little like my Uncle Fred's house— add a bathroom here, a bedroom there. At the beginning, an entire tractor was made in one building but, as tractors became more complicated (and bigger), additional steps in the manufacturing process—and the introduction of new, complex tools—necessitated adding a new wing, building a new plant, and all manner and sorts of other "amendments" to the original facility. By the late 1960s, building a tractor had become a miracle of orchestration, a cacophonous symphony involving thousands of workers, engaged in hundreds of different tasks, making thousands of parts in a score of different buildings.

A miracle, yes, but to Deere it seemed like a far too complex and inefficient process. A tractor is built up from its basic parts—gears, drive shafts, axles, and the like. In the old Deere Waterloo works, for example, a slug of uncut steel would be sent to a man on the second floor of Building A operating a hobbing machine, and he would start the process of turning that piece of metal into a gear. When he was finished with it, another man would transport the hobbed piece of metal to a worker on the fifth floor of Building B, who operated a drilling machine. When she was finished with the proto gear, it would be transported to the first floor of Building C for grinding, then back to Building A for cleaning, and then shipped to the assembly building where it was stored in a "crib" (a giant parts supply room). An assembly worker in need of a gear was at the mercy of a materials handler who lined up at the crib, waiting his turn to give the inventory manager an order, which, when filled, he would take back to the assembly worker.

If one mapped the path of a part as it moved around the old Waterloo plant, the path resembled that of an errant Ping-Pong ball bouncing from here to there as men and women dragged it back and forth in various stages of preparation. Then, when the part was put into a transmission or a hydraulic system, workers would drag that assembled component to where it would be bolted into a tractor chassis. If one had walked by the old Waterloo plant, one would have seen tractors in various stages of completion being schlepped from one building to another until, finally, they would come to a hot and stinking building where they would all be painted a glorious gleaming green (the shade of fresh alfalfa). The tractors would then be finished and, as any Iowa farmer would tell you, they were the best damn tractors in the world. The production process may not have been textbook neat but, by God, it worked!

In the early 1970s, business was going swimmingly for Deere & Company. The CEO, William Hewitt, was in the process of turning Deere, traditionally a domestic producer of farm equipment, into an international manufacturer as well. Hewitt was also enlarging Deere's product line from farm machinery into construction machinery—smack into the bailiwick long-dominated by the big, yellow monsters of Caterpillar Tractors. Around about that time, engineers in the grand, new Eero Saarinen-designed Deere headquarters in Moline, Illinois, had a daring idea: Deere could build the factory of the future, an automated factory with wondrous machines, with efficiencies beyond anything yet realized. And not just new machines here or there, but an entirely new *system*, starting with the design of the tractor right on down to fueling her up! The old Waterloo works had reached its capacity and had become unmanageable—what with a foundry, an engine works, a transmission plant, and what-have-you all at one location. It was obvious that the company would have to do something to both expand production and to break it down into more manageable units. But who would have expected such a bold plan from the country slickers in Moline? When others were retreating from manufacturing—conceding markets to foreigners and diversifying into "cleaner" white-collar businesses—Deere decided to remain the best at what they did so well. Hewitt was not an engineer, but he instinctively understood the importance of engineering and the significance of the grand scheme being laid before him. He asked: How much would this cost? Oh, it will drive our total capital expenditures to some two hundred million a year for, say, ten years. That will take every penny we've got, it will depress earnings, it will drive us perilously close to the edge . . . It's risky, Hewitt said, but we've got to do it.

In 1974, Deere bought a corn farm, a big one, on the outskirts of Waterloo. That's where they would build their factory of the future, in the midst of working farms, to symbolize the company's tie to the soil. The factory opened in 1981. Forget about assembly lines, forget even about robots, forget everything you've ever seen in factories or heard about them. This one is different. Not just that it is clean, quiet, and well lighted. Not just that it is architecturally pleasing sitting out there, across the field from several classic red barns with silos and all. Not just that the bloody place is twenty-four times the size of a football field (and several stories high, to boot). Not just that there are few people to be seen on the factory floor. No, what strikes you most is the *lines*. The factory looks like one of those Piet Mondrian paintings, all color and geometry. Geometry, especially. The interior of the factory is dominated by vertical lines running from the floor to the ceiling, and horizontal lines connecting them all in an eye-catching grid. Thin pipes, beams, pillars, girders, rails . . . the only thing like it was one of those German factories designed by Walter Gropius in the early part of the century, one in which the skeleton of the building—stark, naked lines—was exposed on the outside. But this is the *inside* of a factory, not the exterior. (The outside is clean and smooth and white.)

The inside of the new Deere Waterloo Tractor Works is dominated by the geometric pattern of a 68-foot high-rise stack of some ten thousand storage bins—wire cages that look like shopping carts. All the parts used in assembling a tractor are stored in these bins. Like a giant Rubik's Cube, this structure is puzzling. How do they get parts out of a bin that's up there on the top and over there in the middle? And where is the crib manager and the queue of workers waiting to get their parts?

The answer, one discovers, is that a computer finds the part, directs an automated hoist to retrieve the bin that it is in, delivers it to a waiting "robocarrier" (a computer-controlled cart), and this carrier transports the part to the worker who had requested it by simply punching a number on a terminal at his workstation. (The robocarriers strike terror in the visitor's heart. Seemingly hundreds of them are gliding about at all times, unmanned, going their own ways at the breakneck speed of 135 feet per second, each carrying up to a 4,000-pound payload. One would, indeed, break your neck if it hit you. But you are shown that a robocarrier is a smart little devil. Stand in its way, and it stops dead in its path.)

Gone, then, are people dragging parts around. Gone are people going up and down elevators to get parts out of the storage crib. Gone are workers standing around in queues waiting for parts. At this plant, computers "talk" to each other and coordinate the delivery of parts—and they arrive just in time for assembly. There are miles of guide-wire paths that the robocarriers run along, miles of conveyors and monorail tracks—all those lines! The system saves the workers time and labor. And it saves the company money: Deere now needs to have only about 50 percent of the inventory required by their competitors.

Another source of increased productivity is reduced set-up time. The plant is unlike the typical assembly operation in which identical products are produced by men and machines engaged, over and again, in the same repetitive tasks. Instead, nearly every tractor built at Waterloo is different, *customized*. Farmers are finicky folk. One wants a 15-gear transmission, another will pay less and get fewer. One wants a closed cab, another wants fresh air. The Waterloo Tractor Works can turn out some five thousand different tractor configurations, customizing each without the time and cost of retooling, without so much as stopping production to remind a worker that the next tractor needs a stereo tape deck.

This system is called "flexible manufacturing" and it is to the historical development of manufacturing processes what computer-assisted instruction (a la PLATO) is to the historical development of teaching. When Eli Whitney invented the "American Method" of assembly based on standardized parts and standardized products, could he ever have guessed that one day manufacturing would evolve to the point where his *mass* production would also be *customized* production? Eli, you've met your Waterloo!

Please, it is not the case that Deere's engineers invented all of the methods utilized in their marvelous system. Rather, Deere has had the audacity to bring together various state-of-the-art technologies developed elsewhere and to combine them in innovative ways that increase their productivity through synergistic coordination. Here are some of the techniques Deere is using:

Computer-Assisted Design and Engineering Deere spends more than 4 percent of their annual sales on research and development—about 50 percent more than the average for the entire machinery industry. The lion's share of Deere's R&D is spent at their spanking new Product Engineering Center (also near Waterloo) where 125 people with advanced professional and technical degrees lead an even larger team of technicians and assistants in designing, developing, and testing engines, transmissions, hydraulic systems, and electronic components. In cold rooms, hot rooms, sound rooms, wind tunnels, and other chambers of horror, Deere engineers and scientists will take a tractor and freeze it, broil it, blow on it, bump it, shake it, pound it, and twist it, all to the end of producing the highest quality product possible. The lab is also the "conscience" of the firm on safety and environmental issues, paying close attention to such factors as operator safety, noise levels, pollution emissions, and so forth.

While the lab sits in the middle of a cornfield, it has the air of a sophisticated university campus (indeed, some 40 employees are pursuing master's degrees in engineering while on the job). The lab is among the nation's leaders in the industrial application of computer-assisted design and computer-assisted engineering. Deere engineers now do their drawings on computer screens. The computer then generates design specifications which it feeds to machine tools, instructing the tools what to make and how to make it. The computer is also used to search through Deere's inventory of some 250,000 parts, looking for an existing part that can be used in a prototype product, saving the expense of designing and making a new part.

Group Technology Better utilization of parts is a key to almost all of the increases in productivity that Deere has realized in the last decade. "Group technology" is an approach to improving productivity based on identifying the underlying commonality found among "families" of parts. Deere has developed a system for scientifically clustering parts based on their shapes and functions. By rationalizing parts in this way, the company has been able to: achieve greater standardization across product lines (they can now use tractor parts in construction vehicles, for example); reduce the total number of parts in their inventory; get greater economies of scale in production (making more each of a smaller variety of parts); and avoid reinventing a part when an existing one would work just fine.

Group technology also leads to reduced costs by minimizing materials handling and by allowing common tools to make an entire family of parts. For example, prior to the introduction of group technology, only 7 percent of the parts used in one Deere manufacturing department were made completely within the confines of that department. In the past, a part from this department would be sent to the first floor milling department, moved to the fifth floor for drilling, sent half a mile away for grinding, then back to the original department for cleaning and shipping. Now, using group technology, 72 percent of the parts used in this department are made from beginning to end within its walls. The savings—as measured by schlepping, storing, inventory, lost parts, and quality—are enormous.

Focused Factories When Deere opened its new assembly facility out in the cornfield, this permitted them to reorganize the cluster of old factories in downtown Waterloo. Deere then redesigned them and turned them into the component works of the future. Deere engineers rationalized operations, creating "factories within a factory," each responsible for the complete production of a single component (for example, transmissions, hydraulics, gears). In this way, workers came to feel they were part of a small company (the largest having 3,000 employees), instead of working in a single big, impersonal factory with 14,000 workers.

Within each small factory, operations were further broken down into "cells." Here is how a cell is different from a traditional manufacturing department: In the production of gears in traditional plants, for example, a slug of metal was moved around from machine to machine, from a worker turning a lathe, to another working a hob, to another on a shaper, to another on a shaver, and, finally, to one operating a mill. This process would employ five workers on five different machines (and at least one other worker to transport the part between them). By grouping the production of gears into a single "cell," three operators now run their own little cluster of two lathes, three hobs, three shapers, a shaver, and a milling machine. And, by bringing the machines into close proximity, it is now possible to move gears automatically from one machine to the other, thus eliminating the need for transportation. All of this sounds simple, but it cost $15 million for Deere to improve the efficiency of just the production of three sizes of gears—that is, only three parts of the thousands that go into the making of a tractor. That's why the entire Deere transformation cost $2 billion.

Flexible Machinery Because numerically controlled machines permit rapid retooling, they have become increasingly popular in American industry. But Deere goes one step further by linking dozens of numerically controlled machines together through a common computer. The computer not only constantly reprograms each machine to do different tasks, it rationalizes the overall systemic efficiency of all the machines by directing parts and work to each machine at the proper pace and in the optimal amount. This system eliminates both machine idle time and long queues of parts.

Robotics It is curious that one of the nation's most advanced manufacturing operations utilizes the services of only a very few of those machines most commonly associated with futuristic production. Robots are unloved by Deere engineers for two reasons: Robots weld, but Deere's high-quality tractors are bolted together; robots work on high-volume assembly lines, but the manufacturing of tractors is a low-volume business. But robots also do dirty, unsafe work—like spray painting—and it is in such jobs that Deere employs a few of these mechanical workers, saving the lungs of dozens of *real* workers.

Deere has been able to introduce the factory of the future without having workers pay the price of the transition. Through careful planning, there have been no layoffs as the result of automation. (Thousands of Deere workers *were* laid off as the result of the severe 1980–84 depression in the farm industry, but not as a result of technology. Indeed, because of low demand for tractors, the Waterloo plant never, in its first three years, operated at more than 50 percent of capacity.) The jobs of many workers have also been upgraded. For example, workers who once drove forklifts have been retrained and they now operate complex machines. In addition to finding their tasks more interesting, workers also appreciate the cleaner, quieter, lighter work environment and the much improved amenities (cafeterias, dressing areas) off the shop floor.

Significantly, one problem Deere has with this marvelous system is that it complicates pay for performance. Historically, almost all of Deere's workers have been on an incentive system that rewards output. Now, in many cases, machines do all the labor—which is fine with the workers—but the machines are *also* responsible for work quality and quantity—which isn't so fine. In the factory of the future, automation makes it difficult to measure and reward the contributions to productivity of individual workers. To put some incentives back into the system, Deere is now experimenting with group rewards a la Motorola and with profit sharing and other alternatives to traditional piecework. Why do they care about employee incentives if machines make the tractors? Because, while the machines may do all the *labor*, they do not do all the *work*. There is still plenty of brainwork left. This is work that, if it isn't done well, is costly to repair. For instance, a bored worker who neglects to monitor the maintenance schedule of machines can cost the company tens of thousands of dollars in downtime. It is no wonder that Vanguard managers often say that the two key variables in corporate performance are technology and human motivation!

One other problem that Deere may or may not have with their factory of the future is with the colossal size and scale of the undertaking. Deere went ahead and built the giant Waterloo facility in the midst of a trend toward small manufacturing plants. In the 1960s and 1970s, Pratt & Whitney and General Electric both built giant plants in which to assemble jet engines—and both quickly learned that they could not make these mammoth facilities anywhere near as productive as their much smaller plants. As a result, both companies—and hundreds of others that soon followed—adopted a "small is beautiful" manufacturing philosophy to avoid the diseconomies of scale that result from workers feeling like ants in a giant colony. Deere, instead, gambled that they could create the sense of smallness that motivates workers by stressing teamwork and their factory-within-a-factory concept. They reasoned that, if demand picked up and if there was a major shakeout in the industry (which, in fact, occurred when International Harvester went out of the tractor business in early 1985), they could capture the economies of scale of fully integrated production. In addition, through sound management, Deere has made the Tractor Works break even while operating at only 40 percent of capacity. Nonetheless, the risk is great. Not only did Deere lock themselves into high overhead, they locked themselves into the relatively small expensive end of the tractor market (one couldn't build small, cheap tractors profitably in Waterloo). In this regard, Deere has a possible failing in common with the two giant leaders of the Old Guard—IBM and GM—both of which are addicted to manufacturing megalomania, which is the most likely cause of any future failures they may experience.

This future vulnerability not withstanding, what is the bottom line at Deere? Does all of this effort have a payoff? Between 1971 and 1981, Deere's sales went from $1.5 billion to $5.4 billion. (During that period Deere's earnings were higher than the average for *high-tech* companies!) Beginning in 1980, Deere weathered the worst farm depression in fifty years without experiencing a losing year, while their chief competitors International Harvester and Massey-Ferguson were driven to the brink of bankruptcy. Deere boosted both capacity and efficiency during the farm depression of 1980–84, even though they were already the low-cost producer in the industry. They emerged from the depression poised to move from a 40 percent share to 60 percent of the domestic market for farm equipment.

Deere proves that it is possible to be innovative, productive, and dynamic in a sleepy, mature, cyclical, and highly competitive heavy manufacturing business. If Deere can do it, why not U.S. Steel or Chrysler? Why did Deere find the way to become fully competitive in world markets (the Japanese don't dare take them on in anything but the small tractors that Deere has no interest in producing) while International Harvester, Massey-Ferguson, and, in fact, almost all of the largest North American manufacturers did not?

There is nothing magic or exotic about what Deere accomplished. Automated materials handling, automated inventory management, group technology, customization, focused factories, flexible machinery, and computer-assisted design, engineering, and manufacturing—none of these ideas was invented by Deere. Yet Deere invested in them—even in bad years—while others did not. Why? The answer, according to James F. Lardner, Deere's vice president of manufacturing development, is none other than differing *managerial assumptions:*

> If our foreign competition can recognize the advantages of these technologies and has been willing to accept the risks involved in adopting them, why haven't American companies done the same? Our present concepts of organizational structures, manufacturing management qualifications, and financial-analysis-and-control systems used to evaluate investment—all of these stand in our way.

For example, traditional financial analysis causes managers to miss out on new technologies because "hurdle rates," "discounted cash flow," and other cost-accounting measures are ad hoc. That is, they may be appropriate for analyzing the value of single machines, but they are not useful in evaluating an entire *system* in which, when a critical mass is reached, unheard-of economies may be realized. Applying traditional analysis, there is no financial justification for replacing a conventional $175,000 numerically controlled machine with a $350,000 computer-controlled machine. Only if one can see the whole of production as a *system* with long-term benefits will one be able to see the justification for the greater investment. Hence, the desire for short-term profit maximization will cause managers to skimp on the investments that will insure long-term profitability.

Most American managers simply don't understand production technology, don't understand the long-term opportunities presented, for example, by a system that allows for the cheap manufacture of small batches of goods. It is no wonder, then, that in the United States 34 percent of all machine tools are twenty years old or more (as opposed to 24 percent in England, and 18 percent in Japan). It took American managers some twenty years to be able to understand the advantages of numerically controlled tools; now these same technological illiterates are resisting the move to flexible manufacturing and, worse, they are having their predilections reinforced by the currently ascendant school of consultants who tell them the future is in marketing *not* in manufacturing. As Deere's William Hewitt recognized, the future is, in fact, to those who think *systemically:*

> We have no special advantage that cannot accrue to any other company. The primary way we can maintain and advance our position is through better planning, design, engineering, fabricating, distributing, selling, and servicing—through better work on the part of John Deere people and groups.

That's what productivity and innovation are all about in the end: a balanced system of people and machines—bicycles with two fully inflated wheels.

Questions

1. Why did Deere & Co. decide to invest $2 billion in a computer-integrated manufacturing system? Do you think it was a wise decision? Why or why not?

2. Compare and contrast job design, formalization, and unit grouping at the old and new Deere & Co. plants.

3. What elements of computer-integrated manufacturing did Deere & Co. integrate into its new plant? What benefits did Deere & Co. gain from the new system?

Your Rivals Can Be Your Allies

American Companies once rode into alien country as fearlessly as the Lone Ranger without Tonto. Nowadays they enlist a partner who knows his way around the local gullies. In their quest for new markets and technology, U.S. corporations have formed over 2,000 alliances in the Eighties with European companies alone. Some joint-venturers assert that if you don't go abroad in these days of global markets, you will sooner or later get slaughtered at home.

Alliance fever has turned even bitter rivals into bedfellows. Texas Instruments, which in 1986 sued Hitachi of Japan for patent infringement, is now teamed up with its old enemy to develop the next generation of memory chips. Says Larry Woodson, manager of strategic marketing for the American company's semiconductor group: "No single company can cover all the bases, all the technologies." That's no news to Corning Glass Works, an old hand at international partnerships. Corning wrings over half its profits from 23 joint ventures, two-thirds of them with foreign companies.

Corporate alliances take many forms, from straightforward marketing agreements to joint ownership of world-scale operations. The arrangements must pass antitrust muster, of course, and companies teamed up in one country may go on battling everywhere else in the world. Lowering the costs and risks of high-tech product development is only one of the hoped-for gains. More and more U.S. companies need global markets to get maximum economies of scale in manufacturing, and foreign alliances offer a cheaper and faster way to achieve the needed volume than building plants or making acquisitions. By joining up with a foreign rival, the American partner also gains a lookout post for tracking other rivals preparing to invade its turf.

Source: "Your Rivals Can Be Your Allies" by Louis Kraar. Reprinted by permission from FORTUNE Magazine, March 27, 1989, pp. 66–68, 72, 76. © 1989 The Time Inc. Magazine Company.

Alliances may be the only recourse for companies seeking to fill the whole spectrum of market niches. Mighty Ford Motor, though a longtime multinational with plants on several continents, has found itself forced to join such erstwhile enemies as Nissan and Volkswagen. The new relationships, says Philip E. Benton Jr., president of Ford's automotive group, are prompted by "insatiable consumer appetite for more variety than any one company can handle."

Old-line companies with new international goals are eagerly boarding the alliance bandwagon. In the past few years General Electric has formed eight major tie-ups in such fields as fluorescent lamps and factory automation; its partners include companies in Europe, Japan, and South Korea. Meanwhile, fledgling outfits are quickly learning the game. Nynex, one of the seven Baby Bells, has formed about a dozen relationships with counterparts in Asia and Europe. Its latest venture with British Telecom, called Phonepoint, has just won a license to operate a unique service in Britain in which subscribers will use pocket-size cordless phones to make calls on the run.

Many alliances are aimed not at winning markets abroad but defending them at home. With no orders coming in for nuclear power plants, Bechtel Group has teamed up with West Germany's Siemens to service existing American nukes. Inland Steel and Nippon Steel are jointly building what they describe as "the world's most advanced continuous cold steel mill" at New Carlisle, Indiana. Under the arrangement Inland gets Nippon Steel's technology and an injection of low-cost capital to help it supply a better product to its American customers. Nippon, which is entitled to part of the mill's output, is able to leap over import quotas and supply Japanese auto plants in the U.S.

Tie-ups carry the risk of disappointment, or worse. Working with foreign partners is a new experience for most U.S. executives, who must master the subtle art of sharing power and information without giving away too much. They talk about alliances in terms ordinarily used to describe marriages, such as compatibility and trust. As in the case with modern marriages, the divorce rate is high. Companies that rush into too many alliances at once, as AT&T did a few years ago in Europe, can stumble badly. Kathryn R. Harrigan, a professor of strategic management at Columbia University who studied U.S. corporate tie-ups at home and abroad during a ten-year period ended in 1985, found that 57% did not work out well. Nevertheless, she views the arrangements as a growing business necessity: "Within a decade most companies will be members of teams that compete against each other."

Nothing shatters a corporate alliance faster than a partner's jealous rage. Big players like Ford, which practice a kind of polygamy, strive to avoid any sign of favoritism. Ford has just teamed up to build a new minivan in the U.S. with Nissan, but has managed not to anger Mazda, in which it has long held a 25% stake.

The relationship with Mazda, formed two decades ago when Ford felt the need for a Japanese connection after it had been caught napping by that country's auto blitz, is more fruitful than ever. Among other things, the two companies make components and design cars for each other. Mazda created the Mercury Tracer, which Ford assembles in Mexico, and the Ford Probe, which Mazda builds in Flat Rock, Michigan. Reversing roles, Ford will supply Mazda with a sporty compact utility vehicle to sell in North America in the next few years.

That partnership also gives Ford extra thrust in fast-growing Asian markets, where the U.S. automaker's line includes its own versions of Mazdas. Moreover, Mazda brought Ford into South Korea, which Benton describes as "an opportunity of unknown dimensions." Already the South Koreans are among the lowest-cost producers of small cars, including the Ford Festiva sold in this country. That model comes from Kia Motors, a Korean automaker long associated with Mazda and now 10% owned by Ford. In the future Kia may be able to develop new products that Ford's own engineers are too busy to handle, and provide a way into the elusive China market. Insisting that Ford's far-reaching relationship with Mazda is unique, Benton says: "To us they are a member of the family. The others are close friends."

Ford's friendships can be quite intimate. The Ford-Nissan minivan, a front-wheel-drive affair that complements a current Ford offering with rear-wheel drive, will be assembled at a Ford truck plant in Avon Lake, Ohio, starting in late 1991. Ford is investing over $1 billion to tap what it regards as a relatively limited market. It gets the vehicle faster by using Nissan's design and at a lower cost by sharing the plant's projected annual output of 130,000 units. The companies are splitting production costs, and Nissan has no equity in the venture.

The U.S. State Department could learn from the artful ways in which Ford has striven to keep both Japanese associates happy. Mazda got first crack at joining the minivan project and spurned it, but Ford made certain that its old Japanese ally was not surprised by the new relationship with Nissan. Says Benton: "I'm not saying that Mazda was enormously enthusiastic about it, because you never quite know how something like that is going to evolve over time." The new relationship is already blossoming. Nissan and Ford are supplying each other with light utility trucks and sharing a passenger car in Australia. They are considering joint production of a four-wheel-drive vehicle for Europe.

Ford has a friend in Latin America too. Hit by rough economic conditions, Ford and Volkswagen merged their operations in Brazil and Argentina about two years ago to create Autlatina. Nowadays the Ford plant in Argentina also assembles Volkswagens, and the two companies are designing common engines for their cars in Brazil. The jointly owned company, which claims to be the largest nongovernmental manufacturer in South America, turned profitable last year but discloses no figures. Benton stresses that Ford went into the arrangement purely to survive: "I'm looking for a competitive advantage. I'm not out there to make Volkswagen stronger."

To break into the Soviet Union, Ford has joined another association unlikely to offend other partners. The six-company American Trade Consortium, which also includes Archer-Daniels-Midland, RJR Nabisco, Johnson & Johnson, Eastman Kodak, and Chevron, is negotiating with Moscow over the ground rules for investors and hopes to nail down an agreement this spring. The Russians need hard currency to support joint ventures. The U.S. consortium's proposed solution: Chevron, which plans to develop and export Soviet oil, would generate foreign exchange for the other American partners. Ford is discussing with Minavtoprom, the Soviet automotive ministry, a joint venture that would initially import European-made Ford Scorpios and later build them at a plant in Gorky.

In the curious workings of global business, some alliances have their birth on the battlefield. After Texas Instruments sued Hitachi, contempt bred familiarity, which ripened into romance. The legal battle came amid U.S. complaints that Japanese manufacturers dumped memory chips several years back, forcing most American companies to quit making them. Pat Weber, president of TI's semiconductor group, says that when the company saw no hope of making any money, "we decided to raise the ante on using our intellectual property." In 1986, TI filed suits against eight Japanese companies, including Hitachi, and demanded stiff royalties. Negotiated settlements have brought TI payments totaling $315 million so far.

But a funny thing happened on the way to court. "Hitachi had to lay its cards on the table to negotiate royalty payments," says Weber. The haggling gave the companies not only "a damned good understanding of each other's technology," Weber adds, "but a good respect for each other's capability."

In late December, TI stunned the semiconductor industry by announcing a cooperative arrangement with Hitachi to develop a 16-megabit dynamic RAM chip. Jerry R. Junkins, 51, TI's chairman and CEO, makes no bones that licensing know-how to a rival "comes back to haunt you in the form of a very, very strong competitor." This venture, however, is a leap into the future. Explains Wally Rhines, executive vice president of TI's semiconductor group: "We both needed a partner to minimize our risks." Since Hitachi and TI have taken different approaches, teaming up represents a gigantic hedge. Even before the chip is fully developed, TI has to start pouring money into production facilities, raising its stakes as high as $1 billion. "If something goes wrong with either company's design," says Rhines, "we both have a fallback position."

Cooperating with competitors is such a new concept at TI that its executives gingerly refer to alliances as "business arrangements." A co-inventor of the integrated circuit, the company long banked on its proprietary know-how to capture markets. "We were a pretty closed society," says Weber. "Prior to 1987 I wouldn't even be talking to you." Customers brought the semiconductor recluse out of its shell by demanding faster development of a wide variety of chips. Rather than trying to invent everything itself, TI now has arrangements with other partners—small U.S. companies and Acer, an innovative

Taiwan computer maker—for swapping and buying chip designs. Says Weber: "We've become more realistic about what it takes to be successful in the complexities of global markets."

Lest misunderstandings arise, Hitachi has endorsed TI's formal list of "ingredients for successful alliances," which resembles the recipe successfully followed by other American corporations. For starters, both players must agree on a common need and admit their weaknesses, but they must also believe, as one TI executive puts it, "that we're both going to win." Secondly, "trust and openness" between the competitors are essential. And each company has to make a top-to-bottom commitment of executives.

For all its new acceptance of interdependence, TI is zealously guarding its technological jewels. The agreement with Hitachi catalogues precisely the intellectual property that belongs to each company. Whatever they develop together will be jointly owned, but won't be shared with outsiders unless the allies agree. Once the new chip is perfected, each company is free to manufacture it independently. Still, Weber admits, "We don't know if it's going to work."

TI is not the only high-tech warrior to make a common cause with the enemy. Motorola, a militant critic of Japanese semiconductor tactics a few years ago, is doing what then seemed unthinkable: sharing chip designs and manufacturing facilities with Toshiba. In essence, Motorola is exchanging technology for help in gaining greater access to the Japanese market. James A. Norling, executive vice president and general manager of Motorola's semiconductor products sector, says that one way to solve trade tensions with Japan is for companies to "partner up." That technique has enabled Motorola to return to the memory chip business that it quit in 1985. At that time, Norling says, "we were pushed out by Japanese dumping." Motorola will get memory chip designs from Toshiba and half ownership of a new $300 million semiconductor plant in Japan.

Like a wary bride, Motorola has placed incentives in a prenuptial agreement to ensure cooperation from its Japanese competitor turned ally. Toshiba craves access to Motorola's knowledge of microprocessors, the logic chips that form the core of personal computers. The danger for Motorola is not getting enough in return. Consequently it is handing over its microprocessor technology in stages—in direct proportion to Toshiba's delivery on its pledge to help the U.S. company crack the Japanese market for chips.

Corning Glass Works, the veteran alliance builder, sees no need for a guarded approach. Corning gets a lot of its market penetration abroad through partnerships, and Chairman James Houghton, 52, describes his company's collaboration as "a form of leverage." Corning's optical fiber, for instance, spreads through Europe and Australia via six joint ventures. Says Roger Ackerman, Corning's group president of specialty materials: "You need allies to invade a market."

Though widely hailed as one of America's most innovative companies, Corning also gets vital infusions of technology from its foreign tie-ups. In

Corning's business of making medical diagnostic equipment and supplies, the need for fresh know-how was downright desperate when Switzerland's Ciba-Geigy showed up four years ago. At first Ciba wanted to acquire Corning's medical business, but Chairman Houghton flew to Switzerland and sold the idea of teaming up. "What we had was years of old technology in blood analyzers packaged in fancy boxes," says E. Martin Gibson, group president of Corning's laboratory sciences. By forming the joint venture, he adds, "we harvested cash and stayed in the business with Ciba's science."

Ciba Corning Diagnostics, based in Medfield, Massachusetts, is only now moving into the black. For all Corning's gentle ways, the joint venture initially suffered from a culture clash. The American managers were great at spinning entrepreneurial ideas orally, but had to learn writing them in a formal, documented manner for the Swiss parent.

Foreign collaboration has put new life in another Corning product, which was past its prime at home. The company's profits on its estimated $250-million-a-year business of making glass bulbs for TV picture tubes have withered along with TV set production by U.S. companies. Last October, Corning folded the operation into a venture with Japan's Asahi Glass. The Japanese partner had soaked up Corning know-how through earlier licenses and improved upon it, but shipping TV glass across the Pacific is prohibitively expensive.

The joint venture gives Asahi immediate access to Corning's plants in the U.S. and Mexico. For Corning, the alliance opens the door to Japanese customers in the U.S. and provides superior technology for large TV screens. Explains John Loose, Corning's international vice president and CEO of the new joint venture, called Corning Asahi Video Products: "A lot of Japanese tubemakers have moved to the U.S., and Asahi has good relationships with them that we want to take advantage of."

Corning has also forged strong links with South Korea. Samsung-Corning, another TV glass venture, is staffed entirely by Koreans from Samsung Group, one of the conglomerates that dominate the country's industry. The joint venture got injections of Corning technology in the Seventies, but now has a life of its own. Samsung-Corning is diversifying into integrated circuit packages and into processing such materials as soft ferrite for videotape recorders. Having TV glass partners in both Korea and Japan gives Corning valuable research leverage. "The technical synergy is remarkable," says Loose, "and we're the focal point of the relationship."

As the Ciba and Samsung partnerships show, Corning does not insist on top billing in its name. The company, which likes to think of itself as a long-term stockholder in its multiple ventures, usually prefers fifty-fifty ownership but often lets its ally run the show. Says Ackerman: "There's no need for dominance if it's a successful, growing enterprise." Corning insists, however, that its joint ventures have strong management teams that can operate without constant intervention from the corporate parents. Though most problems can be worked out "behind bedroom doors," says a Corning executive, a few ventures have flopped. Several years ago an Indonesian businessman who signed on to make dinnerware with Corning introduced his own competing products simultaneously—grounds for instant annulment.

Overeagerness is one of the worst failings of companies in pursuit of foreign partners, as AT&T has painfully learned. Foreign markets are vital to the telephone giant, which lost its captive U.S. customers when the old Bell System was broken up five years ago. Having long restricted itself to the U.S., AT&T needed to go global fast. "After looking at acquisitions, the alliance approach seemed the fastest way into international business," says Blaine Davis, corporate vice president for strategic and market planning. Like a nervous debutante, AT&T has filled its dance card with 28 alliances, most of them with highly suitable foreign partners. But it has stepped on a lot of feet, including its own.

In 1983, AT&T linked up with Philips, the Dutch electronics leader, to sell switching equipment to government-owned telecommunications companies in Europe. Almost simultaneously AT&T formed a separate alliance with Italy's Olivetti in the hope of becoming an international force in computers and office automation. "Philips and Olivetti would handle the marketing, and we would handle the technology," says Davis. The theory sounds reasonable, but AT&T wound up with a hangover and little market penetration.

From the very start the American company found itself at the hub of conflicts. Philips, which hoped to develop ties with AT&T in office automation, apparently resented the Olivetti connection. Moreover, neither of the European companies wanted to inject capital and research effort into the alliances as rapidly as AT&T expected. "Europeans are comfortable with long-term results," Davis says delicately. "Americans want results up front." Jack Grubman, a security analyst at Paine Webber, is blunter: "AT&T was arrogant about swaggering into Europe."

The link with Olivetti seemed in earnest because AT&T bought 25% of its Italian partner for $260 million. But the two companies have found little to do together. They first tried sharing production of computers, with Olivetti providing the smaller models and the American company the larger ones, but sales proved disappointing. Robert Kavner, president of AT&T's Data Systems Group, says the arrangement "became too difficult to manage." The allies subsequently dropped the agreement to fill each other's product lines and are still thrashing out how to cooperate. Plainly the alliance is not strategically important for either company anymore.

The Philips connection, begun as a fifty-fifty joint venture, has also been troubled. The Dutch company wanted to stay in the telephone central-switching business without investing heavily to modernize its products. Adapting AT&T's switches to Europe turned out to be a longer and more costly exercise than expected, resulting in four money-losing years. In the end Philips flinched, cutting its equity to 40% and turning over operating control of the venture to the U.S. company early last year.

AT&T is wiser now. "We took it for granted that technology would sell our products," says John Heck, president of the switching venture, based in

Hilversum, the Netherlands. "We're just starting to recognize that we must create a European identity." AT&T's uneasy alliances have at least provided valuable contacts and coaching. Last month, with Olivetti's help, AT&T prevailed over three European competitors to become the leading contender to partner with Italtel, Italy's state-owned telecom equipment company. This promises access to a market worth an estimated $28 billion over the next four years.

Ma Bell might have done well to emulate one of its offspring. "We approach alliances cautiously," says Susan Simon, director of strategy assurance for Nynex's international subsidiary. Nynex has found, Simon says, that "a bit of courtship," such as exchanging people and ideas with foreign companies, paves the way for successful alliances. Gary Hamel, a lecturer at the London Business School and an authority on alliances, offers two other tips. A tense relationship may mean that members of the alliance have conflicting goals and should split. And alliances are a way of gaining strength from rivals. "Westerners tend to approach alliances as teachers," says Hamel, "while the Japanese act like students and get more out of them." So there's another lesson we can learn from Japan.

Questions

1. Identify the different reasons that organizations use strategic alliances and give an example of each.

2. Corning Glass Works is involved in a large number of alliances with different partners. Identify the benefits that Corning hopes to gain from each alliance. How similar or dissimilar is each of these alliances?

3. What kind of management orientation is needed to make a strategic alliance work? Why did AT&T's early alliances run into trouble?

P A R T I I I

Strategy, Structure, and Environmental Change

Organizations and Their Environments

Learning Objectives

Upon completing this chapter you should be able to

1. Distinguish between an organization's general environment and its task environment.
2. Explain the concept of an organizational domain and its relationship to an organization's task environment.
3. Differentiate among contingency theory, strategic choice, and population ecology.
4. Describe the general implications of contingency theory for the relationship between organization design and environmental conditions.
5. Describe the general implications of strategic choice theory for the relationship among organization structure, strategy, and environment.
6. Describe the general implications of the population ecology approach for the relationship between organizational forms and environmental change.

DOING BUSINESS IN AGING AMERICA

Once upon a simpler time not so long ago, "workforce" meant white men in ties or blue collars. Male Caucasians in their prime were in such plentiful supply that few employers had to reach beyond them except for the least-wanted jobs. But the boss is losing that confident glow. The decline in birth rates after 1960 slashed the numbers of young people available to fill jobs, and today's employers are looking to the nonmale, the nonwhite, and the nonyoung to fill the gaps. But not only are the years of picky hiring over; in ways both subtle and obvious, this change in demographics is rapidly transforming everything from the types of goods and services offered to organizational policies and procedures.

For instance, with more than half of all mothers working, and three-quarters of working women in their childbearing years, companies are being forced to make it easier for workers to balance work and family needs. As a result, some are offering company-sponsored child care or making job-sharing available in order to recruit such women. Others, like AT&T, are hiring retirees instead, particularly in sales, where they can be effective in winning over other consumers their age.

Additionally, many organizations are altering their product offerings to meet the needs of an older clientele. On the cruise ship Crown Odyssey, *for example, passengers take water aerobics classes, order broiled fish with lemon, and attend seminars on stress reduction. Sounds like a shipful of health-conscious yuppies, right? Wrong. Royal Cruise Line, the operator of the* Crown Odyssey, *is simply trying to please its 55-and-older customers, who comprise the majority. Almost all marketers will have to reject their conventional wisdom of targeting 18-to-49 year-olds and find new ways to appeal to the active aging consumers who will soon make up the bulk of U.S. buying power.*

In sum, because of the dramatic change in U.S. population demographics, companies are being forced to change their strategies, goods, and services, and redesign structures that had been successful in the past. Chapter 8 examines three perspectives on how the changing business environment affects organizations' strategies and structures.

Sources: Elizabeth Ehrlich, with Susan B. Garland, "For American Business, a New World of Workers," *Business Week*, September 19, 1988; Walecia Konrad and Gail DeGeorge, "U.S. Companies Go for the Gray," *Business Week*, April 3, 1989, 64; and bureau reports.

IN the preceding chapters, we alluded to the central role that the relationship between organizations and their environments plays in organization design. In Chapter 1 we noted that organizations are open systems interacting with their environments. In Chapter 2 we showed that organizations often formulate goals with external stakeholders in mind. In Chapter 3 we explained how both an organization's ability to acquire scarce resources from its environment and its stakeholders' judgments can be used as measures of organizational effectiveness. Finally, Chapters 4 through 7 detailed how decisions about the mechanisms of coordination and control, delegation of authority, unit grouping, and technology are affected by an organization's environment. Clearly, an organization's environment is important.

In the next three chapters, we examine the concept of an organization's environment, and the implications of different environmental conditions for organization design. We begin by discussing the meaning of the term *environment*. Then we look at three approaches to understanding organization-environment relations. Each approach raises different questions about environmental effects on an organization's structure and design. Many theorists and researchers view the three approaches as competing perspectives.[1] In Chapters 9 and 10, we present a different line of reasoning and show how the approaches complement each other by presenting an integrative model that draws from all three.

ENVIRONMENTS AND DOMAINS

The concept of an organization's environment and its relationship to structure and design has been a central theme in the study of organizations since the late 1950s. Not surprisingly, the term *environment* has been used in many different ways. Indeed, William Starbuck, in a review of organization-environment relations, noted at least twenty different uses of the term.[2] Part of the reason for so many different definitions lies in the fact that each organization has both a *general* and *task* environment.

General and Task Environments

The **general environment** is the sum of factors outside an organization's boundaries that influence, or may influence, its structure, goals, and effectiveness. To make this broad concept more manageable, most researchers distinguish among different sectors of the general environment. Table 8.1 lists and describes some of these major sectors: cultural, technological, educational, political, legal, natural resource, demographic, sociological, and economic. For example, the cultural component includes the values, ideologies, beliefs, and norms that are a society's underpinnings and thus determine, to a large extent, the nature of social relations common to all organizations within a society. In other words, the general environment is a shared environment.

An organization's **task environment** consists of those aspects of the general environment relevant to the organization's goal setting and goal attainment.[3] It can be defined specifically in terms of its customers, suppliers, employees, competitors, and government regulatory agencies. Hence, the difference between the general environment and the task

Table 8.1
General Environment Sectors

Cultural. Including the historical background, ideologies, values, and norms of the society. Views on authority relationships, leadership patterns, interpersonal relationships, rationalism, science, and technology define the nature of social institutions.

Technological. The level of scientific and technological advancement in society, including the physical base (plant, equipment, facilities), the knowledge base of technology, and the degree to which the scientific and technological community is able to develop new knowledge and apply it.

Educational. The general literacy level of the population, the degree of sophistication and specialization in the educational system, and the proportion of the people with a high level of professional and/or specialized training.

Political. The general political climate of society, the degree of concentration of political power, the nature of political organization (degrees of decentralization, diversity of functions, etc.), and the political party system.

Legal. Constitutional considerations, nature of legal system, jurisdictions of various governmental units. Specific laws concerning formation, taxation, and control of organizations.

Natural Resources. The nature, quantity, and availability of natural resources, including climatic and other conditions.

Demographic. The nature of human resources available to the society; their number, distribution, age, and sex. Concentration of urbanization of population is a characteristic of industrialized societies.

Sociological. Class structure and mobility, the definition of social roles, and the nature of the social organization and development of social institutions.

Economic. General economic framework, including the type of economic organization—private versus public ownership, the centralization or decentralization of economic planning, the banking system, and fiscal policies. The level of the investment in physical resources and consumption characteristics.

Source: Fremont E. Kast and James E. Rosenzweig, *Organization and Management: A Systems and Contingency Approach,* 3rd ed. (New York: McGraw-Hill, 1979), p. 131. Reprinted by permission.

environment is the difference between the broad social context within which all organizations exist and those general environmental aspects relevant to a specific organization's functioning. The general environment is thus one step removed from the direct experience of an organization; the task environment is the subset of the general environment that is of more immediate concern.

While conceptually distinct, an organization's general and task environments are not independent. Changes occurring in the former affect the latter. Consider, for instance, the effects of the 1950s and early 1960s "baby boom" and the subsequent "baby bust" of the late 1960s and 1970s on almost any organization's task environment. As baby boomers grow older, the median age of the population increases, and the number of younger people in American society decreases. The composition of the U.S. labor force reflects these changes. Projections indicate that the number of people in the entry-level labor pool (ages 16 to 24) reached a peak in 1980 that probably won't be matched until the late twenty-first century. Organizations such as fast food restaurants and grocery stores that depend on a steady flow into the labor force have had to develop new ways of attracting and retaining employees as a result.[4] Other organizations have had to change their product offerings, since changes in the population's age structure affects the demand for different goods and services. Focus on Design 8.1 describes how many organizations are carefully assessing future changes they may have to make in their goods and services to accommodate changing product demands.

Organizational Domain

An organization's task environment reflects its domain of operation.[5] Simply stated, an **organizational domain** is defined by the goods and services an organization produces, and by the customers or clients it serves. Different organizations have different domains and, therefore, different task environments—even within the same industry. Consider, for instance, two universities. They are alike in that they both offer postsecondary educational services. But they may differ significantly in the services they provide, their clients, and the markets they serve. Suppose one offers a traditional liberal arts and science program for undergraduates between ages 18 and 21 on a residential campus in a rural setting. The other specializes in graduate professional programs for working individuals over age 25 in an urban location. Both are universities, but their domains of operation and therefore their task environments are dissimilar.

In short, the general environment provides the broad context within which all organizations in a society operate. Task environment refers to the specific parts of the general environment relevant to a particular organization's functioning, and this is determined by its domain of operation. These relationships are shown in Figure 8.1. The different approaches to organization-environment relations that we examine in the following sections focus on different aspects of this general environment-task environment-organizational domain configuration.

Three Approaches to Organization-Environment Relations

Since the 1950s a primary theme in the organization sciences has been that successful performance is the outcome of a proper "fit," or alignment, between an organization (its management processes, structure, and strategy) and its environment.[6] Regardless of the underlying perspective, most theory and research on organization-environment relations is based on this proposition. Consequently, research focuses on how organizations adapt to changing

---

FOCUS ON DESIGN 8.1

Quality International's Response to an Aging Population

The management of Quality International, the world's third largest lodging chain, made a commitment to move into the rapidly growing senior travel market in 1986. Their decision was prompted by the fact that consumers over age 50 today control over 50 percent of the nation's disposable income, adding up to over $132 billion in uncommitted moneys. Moreover, a study on the over-50 traveler by the U.S. Travel Data Center showed that they account for 30 percent of all travel, 30 percent of all passenger air travel, 72 percent of all recreational vehicle trips, 34 percent of package tours, and 32 percent of all hotel-room nights booked. Quality's own market research also showed that the over-50 traveler accounted for more frequent trips, trips covering greater distances, and longer stays than those of younger travelers. It found that the over-50 traveler was more likely to patronize hotel restaurants, more apt to consume name brand liquors, and generally spent 30 percent more per visit than younger travelers.

Quality International also surveyed older guests in its hotels, conducted focus groups, and did extensive phone surveys to determine what hotel services the over-50 traveler wanted. Based on its findings, Quality made a major shift in strategy to capture more of the over-50 travelers' business. Among the changes it made were

- Its "Prime Time" program that provided year-round discounts for over-50 travelers in all its hotels.
- Converting a minimum 15 percent of its rooms at every location into non-smoking accommodations.
- Addressing small details that over-50 travelers indicated were important, such as adding special in-room amenities, bellmen to help carry luggage, and guest service personnel to answer questions about shopping, restaurants, special services, and local attractions
- Marketing its program through senior clubs and organizations such as the American Association of Retired Persons.
- Producing advertising and special publications directed toward the over-50 traveler.
- Developed joint programs with United Airlines—the "Silver Wings Club"—and Dollar Rent-A-Car that focused on the over-50 traveler.

The result: Quality's senior business began to rise rapidly, and it finds itself in an excellent position to benefit from the aging of the U.S. population.

Source: Adapted from Bill Todd, "Marketing to Older People: Quality International's Prime Time Travel Program," *Generations* (Summer 1989): 58–60.

---

environments (to produce a better "fit"). As we'll show in this chapter, there is a wide difference of opinion on how this occurs.[7]

Contingency theory, the first approach we discuss in this chapter, was developed during the late 1950s and 1960s as an outgrowth of the application

Figure 8.1

Relationships between the General Environment, Task
Environment, and an Organization's Domain

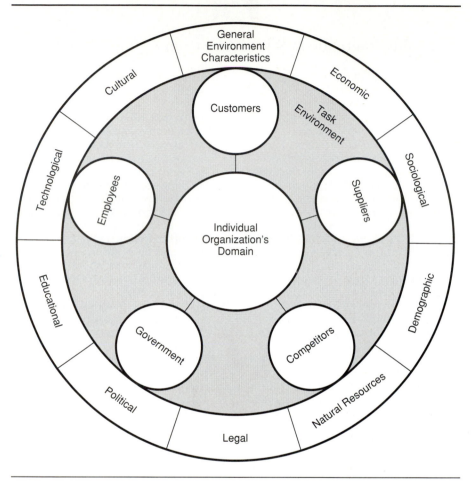

Source: Adapted from Fremont E. Kast, "Scanning the Future Environment: Social Indicators," *California Management Review* 23, 1(1980), p. 24. © by the Regents of the University of California. Used by permission of the Regents.

of systems theory (Chapter 1) to the social sciences. Contingency theorists
examined whether some organization designs fit different environmental
conditions better than others and concluded that managers should choose
the design that best fits prevailing environmental conditions.

During the 1970s two other approaches to organization-environment
relations were developed. **Strategic choice** theory emerged as a response to
what many organization theorists saw as the overly deterministic thrust of
the contingency approach (i.e., the environment *determines* appropriate

organizational form). Strategic choice theorists argued that managers create and select environments by making decisions about their organization's domain of operation; that is, they actively change their organization's environment. **Population ecology** differs from contingency and strategic choice in two ways. First, it focuses on aggregates of organizations, such as industries, instead of individual organizations. Second, it asks different kinds of questions about organization design. Population ecologists ask why there are so many kinds of organizations in society, suggesting that adaptation occurs through the rise and fall of different organizational forms.

Because these three approaches focus on different aspects of the organization-environment relationship, they generate different insights into its nature. We use these insights in Chapters 9 and 10 to construct an integrated model of organization-environment relations that ties together the concepts of environment, strategy, and structure.

THE CONTINGENCY APPROACH

Organic and Mechanistic Designs

A study conducted in the late 1950s by Tom Burns and George Stalker was the first major attempt to identify the types of organization structures and managerial practices appropriate for different environmental conditions.[8] The particular environmental conditions examined involved the changing scientific technology and product markets of 20 English and Scottish manufacturing firms' task environments. "Two divergent systems of management practice" were identified: organic and mechanistic. As shown in Table 8.2, in **organic systems**, structure is flexible, tasks are loosely defined, and communication resembles consultation rather than order-giving. Organic systems are especially appropriate for changing environments in which novel problems continually arise:

> Organic systems are adapted to unstable conditions, when problems and requirements for action arise which cannot be broken down and distributed among specialist roles within a clearly designed hierarchy. Individuals have to perform their special tasks in the light of their knowledge of the tasks of the firm as a whole. Jobs lose much of their formal definition in terms of methods, duties, and powers, which have to be redefined continually by interaction with others participating in a task. Interaction runs laterally as much as vertically. Communication between people of different ranks tends to resemble lateral consultation rather than vertical command. Omniscience can no longer be imputed to the head of the firm.[9]

In contrast, organizations with **mechanistic systems** are characterized by distinct functional specialties, precisely defined tasks and responsibilities, and a well-defined chain of command. Mechanistic systems, containing

Table 8.2
Comparison of Mechanistic and Organic
Systems of Management Practice

Mechanistic	Organic
1. Tasks are highly fractionated and specialized; little regard paid to clarifying relationship between tasks and organization objectives.	1. Tasks are more interdependent; emphasis on relevance of tasks and organizational objectives.
2. Tasks tend to remain rigidly defined unless altered formally by top management.	2. Tasks are continually adjusted and redefined through interaction of organizational members.
3. Specific role definition (rights, obligations, and technical methods prescribed for each member).	3. Generalized role definition (members accept general responsibility for task accomplishment beyond individual role definition).
4. Hierarchic structure of control, authority, and communication. Sanctions derive from employment contract between employee and organization.	4. Network structure of control, authority, and communication. Sanctions derive more from community of interest than from contractual relationship.
5. Information relevant to situation and operations of the organization formally assumed to rest with chief executive.	5. Leader not assumed to be omniscient; knowledge centers identified where located throughout organization.
6. Communication is primarily vertical between superior and subordinate.	6. Communication is both vertical and horizontal, depending upon where information resides.
7. Communications primarily take form of instructions and decisions issued by superiors. Information and requests for decisions supplied by inferiors.	7. Communications primarily take form of information and advice.
8. Insistence on loyalty to organization and obedience to superiors.	8. Commitment to organization's tasks and goals more highly valued than loyalty or obedience.
9. Importance and prestige attached to identification with organization and its members.	9. Importance and prestige attached to affiliations and expertise in external environment.

Source: Richard M. Steers, *Organizational Effectiveness: A Behavioral View* (Santa Monica, Calif.: Goodyear, 1977), p. 90. Adapted from Tom Burns and George M. Stalker, *The Management of Innovation* (London: Tavistock, 1961), pp. 119–122.

many bureaucratic elements, are particularly appropriate for stable environments:

> In mechanistic systems the problems and tasks facing the concern as a whole are broken down into specialisms. Each individual pursues his task as something distinct from the real tasks of the concern as a whole, as if it were the subject of a subcontract. "Somebody at the top" is responsible for seeing to its relevance. The technical methods, duties, and power attached to each functional role are precisely defined. Interaction within management tends to be vertical, i.e., between superior and subordinate. Operations and working behavior are governed by instructions and decisions issued by supervisors. This command hierarchy is maintained by the implicit assumption that all knowledge about the situation of the firm and its tasks is, or should be, available only to the head of the firm. Management, often visualized as the complex hierarchy familiar in organization charts, operates a simple control system, with information flowing up through a succession of filters, and decisions and instructions flowing downwards through a succession of amplifiers.[10]

Organic and mechanistic systems are ideal types defining two ends of a continuum. Burns and Stalker suggest that few, if any, management systems are purely mechanistic or purely organic; most combine characteristics of both. In addition, no part of their research indicates that one system is superior to the other. Rather, the nature of an organization's environment determines which system is appropriate.[11]

Differentiation and Integration

Building on the findings of Burns and Stalker and others, Paul Lawrence and Jay Lorsch, during the 1960s, studied ten U.S. firms with various levels of economic effectiveness in three different industry environments: six in the plastics industry, two in the consumer foods industry, and two in the container industry.[12] The plastics industry was chosen because, at the time, it operated in a dynamic environment characterized by high rates of technological and scientific innovation and by rapidly changing customer needs and preferences. The container industry, on the other hand, had a stable environment, where customer needs were predictable and technical requirements were constant. Finally, the consumer foods industry environment was of intermediate stability, characterized by a moderate rate of change—slower than the plastics industry, but faster than the container industry.

Lawrence and Lorsch argued that as an organization's task environment becomes more complex and uncertain, it tends to segment itself into subunits, each concentrating on a particular part of its task environment. This segmentation into distinct subunits is known as **differentiation**. They also noted that structural differentiation leads to differences in subunit goals and structure, time perspectives, and interpersonal orientations, reflecting the task and the environmental uncertainties with which each unit copes. Thus efficiency may

FOCUS ON DESIGN 8.2

The Effects of Differentiation as Seen from inside an Organization

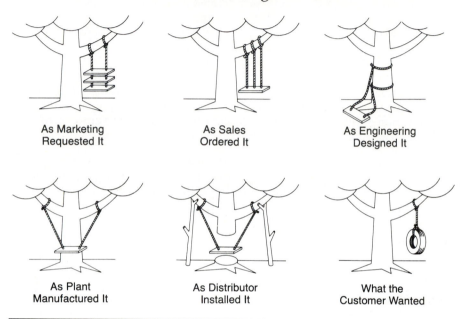

| As Marketing Requested It | As Sales Ordered It | As Engineering Designed It |
| As Plant Manufactured It | As Distributor Installed It | What the Customer Wanted |

Source: A corporate bulletin board.

be the primary goal for a production unit, while a sales unit is more likely to focus on satisfying specific customer needs. Correspondingly, subunit time perspectives are likely to be different. A sales unit usually has a short time frame because of the need to rapidly respond to customer needs. In contrast, a production unit tends to have a longer time perspective because planning and long production runs are necessary for maximum production efficiency.

In effect, differentiated units *see* the world in different ways, as the drawing in Focus on Design 8.2 indicates. The greater the differentiation among units, the greater the chance that their goals, time perspectives, and interpersonal orientations will conflict. Lawrence and Lorsch hypothesized that it would be more difficult to integrate functional subunits' efforts as differentiation increased. **Integration** is defined as "the process of achieving unity of effort among various subsystems in the accomplishment of the organization's task."[13]

Table 8.3
Comparison of Integrating Mechanisms in
Three High-Performing Organizations

Degree of Differentiation	High	Medium	Low
Major Integrative Devices	1. Paper system	1. Paper system	1. Paper system
	2. Managerial hierarchy	2. Managerial hierarchy	2. Managerial hierarchy
	3. Direct managerial contact	3. Direct managerial contact	3. Direct managerial contact
	4. Permanent cross-functional teams at three levels of management	4. Temporary cross-functional teams	
	5. Integrative department	5. Individual integrators	

Source: Adapted from Paul R. Lawrence and Jay W. Lorsch, *Organization and Environment* (Homewood, Ill.: Richard D. Irwin, 1969), 138.

The production, sales, and research and development units in these ten organizations were more differentiated in organizations operating in highly diverse and uncertain environments. Organizations operating in the plastics industry, for example, were more highly differentiated than those in the consumer foods industry, which were more highly differentiated than organizations in the container industry. In other words, the more complex and dynamic the environment is, the greater the differentiation of subunit goals and structure, time orientation, and interpersonal orientation.

Perhaps most important, Lawrence and Lorsch also found that the more economically effective organizations in each industry, with one exception, exhibited a higher degree of integration. Effectiveness was judged using economic criteria such as change in profits over the preceding five years, change in sales volume over the preceding five years, and the number of new products introduced in the preceding five years as a percentage of total current sales. Thus, not only was a higher degree of differentiation needed to deal with diverse and uncertain environmental demands, but a matching degree of integration was needed to achieve effective performance.

When comparing the most effective firms across industries, Lawrence and Lorsch also discovered differences in how they achieved integration (see Table 8.3). In the dynamic and uncertain environment of the plastics industry, the more effective (and most differentiated) organization largely relied on a formal integrating department to coordinate subunit activities. In the moderately stable consumer foods industry, the more effective (and relatively less differentiated) firm principally utilized individual integrators. And in the more stable and more certain container industry, the better-performing (and least differentiated) organization mainly employed direct managerial supervision through a formal chain of command.

In Chapter 5, we noted that organizations attempt to balance coordination needs with the costs of satisfying them. Lawrence and Lorsch's findings indicate that the greater an organization's coordination needs (caused by differentiation), the more elaborate (and expensive) the mechanisms required to satisfy them. But their findings also suggest that economically effective organizations select the least costly coordination mechanisms that satisfy their particular needs. In short, integrating mechanisms should be more elaborate when an organization's units are highly differentiated and integration is hence more difficult. Conversely, when an organization's subunits are not highly differentiated, less elaborate coordination mechanisms appear to work quite well.

Consistent with Burns and Stalker's findings, Lawrence and Lorsch's study implies that there is no universal best way to design an organization. The specific design of an organization and its subunits must "fit" its environment. Successful organizations are those able to diagnose and meet environmental requirements for differentiation and integration. Thus, appropriate patterns of structure vary, and they are contingent on the relationship between an organization and its environment.

Environmental Complexity and Stability

Later work by Robert Duncan helped synthesize these observations about environmental uncertainty and organization design.[14] He identified two primary environmental dimensions, simple-complex and static-dynamic. The *simple-complex dimension* refers to the degree to which an organization deals with a few or many environmental sectors. An organization has a simple environment when only a few sectors are relevant to it. As an example, dry cleaners, barber shops, and corner drugstores have few relevant environmental sectors. In contrast, an organization faces a complex environment when it must deal with a diversity of environmental sectors. Hospitals, universities, auto companies, and aerospace companies have complex environments, with many environmental sectors relevant to their operations. Generally, the larger an organization is, the more complex its environment.

The *static-dynamic dimension* refers to the degree to which the sectors of an organization's environment are changing. The basic issue here is one of stability: "When an organization faces a regular set of demands from the same environment, such as producing the same product or service for the same or very similar clients, the organization faces stable conditions."[15] For example, the commodity chemical, glass container, and utility industries exist in relatively stable environments. Dynamic environments are characterized by high rates of change, often occurring at the same time in different environmental sectors. For instance, the electronics, aerospace, pharmaceutical, and computer industries exist in relatively dynamic environments that change rapidly.

Duncan used these two dimensions to construct a four-cell model of environmental conditions, shown in Figure 8.2. Each cell is associated with a different level of environmental uncertainty, occurring because of (1) a lack of information about the environmental sectors associated with particular decision-making situations; (2) an inability to accurately assess how the environment may affect an organization's success or failure; and (3) a lack of knowledge about the costs associated with an incorrect decision. The model suggests that an organization operating in a static-simple environment (Cell 1) experiences the least amount of perceived environmental uncertainty in decision making, while an organization in a dynamic-complex environment (Cell 4) experiences the most. Duncan's research indicates that the static-dynamic dimension makes a more significant contribution to perceived environmental uncertainty than the simple-complex dimension. He concluded as follows:

> [D]ecision units with dynamic environments always experience significantly more uncertainty in decision making regardless of whether their environment is simple or complex. The difference in perceived uncertainty between decision units with simple and complex environments is not significant, unless the decision unit's environment is also dynamic.[16]

Implications for Organization Design

The contingency approach has been a fertile research area for 30 years. Many of its findings can be synthesized using Duncan's model to show prospective fits between environmental conditions and structure. Table 8.4 presents an overview of the types of structural characteristics that appear to fit in different environmental conditions, drawing on the material presented in Chapters 4 and 5.

In simple-static environments, functionally designed organizations (such as Lawrence and Lorsch's container firms) tend to rely on rules, policies, and procedures to achieve coordination and control. In complex-static environments, organizations face moderately low perceived environmental uncertainty and tend to have divisional designs, rely on training for coordination, and have moderately decentralized decision-making systems. Universities and hospitals during the 1970s are examples of organizations in this type of environment.

Organizations with simple-dynamic environments, such as small entrepreneurial firms in the software industry, tend to have simple, functionally designed structures that are moderately centralized and that rely on direct

Figure 8.2
Characteristics of Various Environmental States

		Simple	Complex
Static		1 *Low perceived uncertainty*	2 *Moderately low perceived uncertainty*
		Small number of factors and components in the environment	Large number of factors and components in the environment
		Factors and components are somewhat similar to one another	Factors and components are not similar to one another
		Factors and components remain basically the same and are not changing	Factors and components remain basically the same
		Example: Soft drink industry	*Example: Food products*
Dynamic		3 *Moderately high perceived uncertainty*	4 *High perceived uncertainty*
		Small number of factors and components in the environment	Large number of factors and components in the environment
		Factors and components are somewhat similar to one another	Factors and components are not similar to one another
		Factors and components of the environment are in continual process of change	Factors and components of the environment are in a continual process of change
		Example: Fast food industry	*Example: Commercial airline industry*

Note: *Simple-complex* refers to the degree to which a decision unit (an individual or organization) must deal with few or many elements that are similar or dissimilar to one another. *Static-dynamic* refers to the degree to which elements of a decision unit's surrounding environment remain the same or are marked by change. *Perceived uncertainty* is seen as resulting from an interaction of the simple-complex and static-dynamic components and as comprised of: (1) a lack of information concerning environmental factors; (2) an inability to accurately assess environmental probabilities; and (3) lack of knowledge regarding the costs associated with an incorrect decision.

Source: Reprinted by permission of the publisher from Robert B. Duncan, "What Is the Right Organization Structure? Decision Tree Analysis Provides the Answer," *Organizational Dynamics* 7 (Winter 1979), p. 63. © by AMACOM, a division of American Management Associations. All rights reserved.

Table 8.4
Environmental Uncertainty and Organization Design

	Environment			
	Simple-Static	Complex-Static	Simple-Dynamic	Complex-Dynamic
	(Cell 1)	(Cell 2)	(Cell 3)	(Cell 4)
	Perceived Uncertainty			
	Low	Low-moderate	Moderate-high	High
	Design Characteristics			
Unit Grouping	Functional (Bureaucracy)	Market-Based (Divisional)	Functional (Simple)	Market-Based (Matrix)
Centralization	High	Medium	High	Low
Job Specialization (Horizontal) (Vertical)	High High	Medium Low	Low High	Low Low
Coordination	Rules, policies, procedures	Training	Direct supervision	Training, socialization, mutual adjustment

supervision to accomplish coordination and control. Finally, organizations in complex-dynamic environments, such as aerospace, engineering consulting, and large computer companies, tend toward relatively decentralized divisional or matrix structures and rely on training, socialization, and mutual adjustment to achieve coordination and control.

It also should be emphasized that an organization's subunits can face different environmental conditions, and these differences will be reflected in their design. For example, the research and development unit of an organization may have a complex-dynamic environment, which requires an organic design such as a matrix. In the same organization, a sales unit serving a heterogeneous customer-base with stable needs might face a complex-stable environment. This type of environment would result in moderately decentralized work units grouped by customer. In contrast, if its production unit's technology is relatively stable and the rate of product innovation is relatively slow (a simple-stable environment), the production unit would likely employ a centralized functional design that relies on rules, regulations, and procedures for coordination and control.

The challenge for managers in organizations with highly differentiated structures is, as Lawrence and Lorsch point out, a problem of integration.

This means that organizations that can effectively use the types of integrating mechanisms discussed on Chapter 5 are more likely to achieve effective coordination. Thus, the contingency approach implies that managers have a relatively restricted range of designs from which to select, based on conditions in their organization's environment. Consequently, selecting a design that "fits" environmental conditions, and developing mechanisms to integrate the efforts of differentiated units, should result in effective performance.

STRATEGIC CHOICE

During the 1970s a number of organization theorists began to express reservations about the central theme of contingency theory. John Child, who coined the term "strategic choice," argued that contingency theory was in error "because it fails to give due attention to the agency of choice by whoever have the power to direct the organization."[17] Child noted that managers take steps to define and manipulate their organizations' domains, thereby choosing to ignore or restrain the effects of the environment that might require modification of existing structural arrangements.[18] In the following passage, Child foresaw the direction that much theory and research on organization-environment relations would take over the ensuing 20 years.

> [T]he analysis of organization and environment must recognize the exercise of choice by organizational decision-makers. They may well have some power to 'enact' their organization's environment . . . . Thus to an important extent, their decisions as to where the organization's operations shall be located, the clientele it shall serve, or the types of employees it shall recruit determine the limits to its environment—that is, to the environment significant for the functions which the organization performs . . . . In view of these essentially strategic and political factors, environmental conditions cannot be regarded as a direct source of variation in organizational structure, as open systems [contingency] theorists often imply.[19]

Subsequent theory and research using a strategic choice approach has substantially increased our understanding of how organizations perceive and manage their environments.

Enacted Environment

Over 60 years ago sociologist William I. Thomas made the observation that "if men define situations as real, they are real in their consequences."[20] A few organization theorists, notably Karl Weick and William Starbuck, began making the same argument about the relationship between organizations and their environments—that managers respond to what they perceive.[21] Given human perceptual limits and the concept of bounded rationality discussed in Chapter 2, managers' perceptions of their organizations' environments may or may not reflect *objective reality*—the world as an omniscient observer might see it. But regardless of whether managers' perceptions of the environment are accurate, they are the basis for managerial action.

In describing how managers perceive their organizations' environments, Weick argued that particular attention should be paid to how and why individual managers focus their attention on specific aspects of an environment to the exclusions of others, and how they acquire and process information necessary for learning about "what is really out there" and "what they have to do to deal with it." In this regard, Weick used the phrase **enacted environment** to refer to the parts of the general and task environment that an organization's managers perceive. Weick states that "the human actor does not *re*act to an environment, he *en*acts it. It is this enacted environment and nothing else that is worked upon by the process of organizing."[22] Those environmental factors not perceived are not considered in an organization's deliberations and actions. Consequently, Starbuck notes, "The same environment one organization perceives as unpredictable, complex, and evanescent, another organization might see as static and easily understood."[23] The implication is that managers in different organizations facing the same "objective" environmental conditions may design those organizations differently because they "see" different environments.

The importance of enactment processes for understanding the effectiveness of different organization designs depends on the pressures placed on an organization by its environment. If an organization is in a very competitive environment, then perception is unimportant. A concern with perceptions of organizational reality is only meaningful to the degree that an organization is immune to, or at least partially insulated from, environmental effects. If its managers don't perceive the environment accurately, their organization will soon go out of existence. In contrast, if an organization's environment does not closely constrain its activities, its managers' environmental perceptions will be important in understanding their organization's structure, strategy, and process.[24]

Accordingly, the relationship between effective design and environmental conditions is likely to approximate that suggested by contingency theorists when the environment severely constrains an organization's performance. But when an organization has more latitude, enactment processes can be an important source of innovation and learning. As Weick noted, "Whatever people do during enactment, whether it be operating without goals, misplacing personnel, operating a technology that no one understands, improvising instead of forecasting, dwelling on opportunities, inventing solutions rather than borrowing them, cultivating impermanence, arguing, or doubting, if those 'strange' actions promote rapid adaptation to shifting conditions, they're likely to persist . . . ."[25] In other words, enactment processes in the absence of severe environmental constraints can be an important source of learning, a topic we examine in Chapter 13.

Resource Dependence

Following from the premise that managers enact their organizations' environments, Jeffrey Pfeffer and Gerald Salancik proposed a **resource-dependence model** of organization-environment relations.[26] They argue that most organizations are unable to internally generate all the resources necessary for their operations and, as a result, must enter into transactions with (and depend on) other organizations to obtain them. Relying on others in the environment creates uncertainty for an organization's managers. But as Pfeffer and Salancik note:

> The fact that organizations are dependent for survival and success on their environments does not, in itself, make their existence problematic. If stable supplies were assured from the sources of needed resources, there would be no problem. If the resources needed by the organization were continually available, even if outside their control, there would be no problem. Problems arise not merely because organizations are dependent on their environment, but because this environment is not dependable. Environments can change, new organizations enter and exit, and the supply of resources becomes more or less scarce. When environments change, organizations face the prospect of either not surviving or of changing their activities in response to these environmental factors.[27]

Thus, the perceptual inaccuracies inherent in the enactment process, coupled with environmental change, creates uncertainty for managers. The resource-dependence model suggests that managers reduce this uncertainty through their transactions with other organizations. They do this in a number of ways. For example, they alter patterns of environmental dependence through mergers, diversification, and vertical integration. Each type of linkage incorporates potential sources of uncertainty within an organization's boundaries and control. Mergers between competing organizations reduce uncertainty by decreasing the competition the merged organizations face. Diversification attempts to stabilize an organization's dependence on the environment by reducing the uncertainty associated with economic cycles and with the growth and decline of individual industry markets. Vertical integration reduces uncertainty by assuring supplies of raw materials and markets for finished goods and services.

Organizations also reduce uncertainty by coordinating their activities with other organizations through arrangements such as joint ventures, interlocking directorates, trade associations, coalitions, and cartels. As discussed in Chapter 7, interorganizational cooperation enables organizations to exchange information, pool resources, and reduce risk. Organizations also use political action to decrease environmental uncertainty. They promote government regulation that reduces uncertainty by increasing barriers to entry, mandate price supports, limit foreign competition, and so on. They use the legal system, as well, to change their environment, as when MCI's antitrust suit eventually led to the breakup of AT&T. Or political action can be directed at the larger public to enhance an organization's legitimacy, such as corporate "public service" advertising unrelated to an organization's primary domain of operation. Overall, the resource-dependence model directs attention to the plasticity of the environment and the many ways organizations shape it through deliberate managerial actions.

Strategy and Structure

Other strategic choice researchers have examined how organizations enact and modify their environments through the selection of and changes in strategy, and how those strategic choices are related to organization design. Raymond Miles and Charles Snow were among the first to examine whether "an organization's form of enactment—its selection of and development of a particular domain within the larger environment—produces predictable patterns in organizational structure and process."[28] Consistency between strategy and structure, they argue, is necessary for effective performance. Based on a series of studies in the textbook publishing, hospital, electronics, and food processing industries, Miles and Snow identified three types of consistent and stable strategy-structure configurations, which they labeled defender, prospector, and analyzer.

The **defender** has a relatively narrow, stable domain of operation that encompasses a limited range of goods and services.

> [It] attempts to locate and maintain a secure niche in a relatively stable product or service area. The [defender] tends to offer a more limited range of products and services than its competitors, and it tries to protect its domain by offering higher quality, superior service, lower prices, and so forth. Often this type of organization is not at the forefront of developments in the industry—it tends to ignore industry changes that have no direct influence on current areas of operation and concentrates instead on doing the best job possible in a limited area.[29]

A functional structure emphasizing efficiency is consistent with the defender's strategy (see Table 8.5). As we discussed in Chapter 5, this also implies that the defender is relatively slow to perceive and react to threats and opportunities in its environment. Typical of the functional structure, positions at a defender's lower levels are usually horizontally and vertically specialized, and decision making tends to be centralized. Planning and rules, policies, and procedures are the primary mechanisms for coordination and control. Often, defenders vertically integrate their operations to reduce their dependence on the environment for resources.

In contrast to the defender, the **prospector** pursues a strategy of quick movement within a broad domain of operation.

> [The prospector] typically operates within a broad product-market domain that undergoes periodic redefinition. The organization values being "first in" in new product and market areas even if not all these efforts prove to be highly

Table 8.5
Domain Strategies

Strategy	Defender	Analyzer	Prospector
Strategic Emphases:			
Efficiency	High	Medium	Low
Speed of response	Low	Medium	High
Breadth of domain	Narrow	Broad	Broad
Strategic predisposition	Domain Defense	Domain Offense	Domain Creation
Design Characteristics:			
Unit grouping	Functional	Market-Based	Market-Based
Centralization	High	Medium	Low
Use of integrating mechanisms	Low	Medium	High
Job specialization	High	High in estimated areas of operation; low in emerging areas of operation	Low

Sources: Raymond E. Miles and Charles C. Snow, *Organizational Strategy, Structure, and Process* (New York: McGraw-Hill, 1978), 31–80; Robert H. Miles, *Coffin Nails and Corporate Strategy* (Englewood Cliffs, N.J.: Prentice-Hall, 1982), 237–241.

profitable. The organization responds rapidly to early signals concerning areas of opportunity, and these responses often lead to a new round of competitive actions. However, this type of organization may not maintain market strength in all of the areas it enters.[30]

The structure consistent with the prospector's strategy is a decentralized, divisionalized design that facilitates quick responses to product and market opportunities. Training and socialization are common coordinating mechanisms in this situation, and the need for quick action results in the extensive use of integrating mechanisms such as project and product teams. Formalized rules, policies and procedures often are most noticeable by their relative absence.

The third strategy-structure configuration, the **analyzer**, pursues an intermediate strategy, which combines aspects of the defender and prospector strategies.

[The analyzer] attempts to maintain a stable, limited line of products or services, while at the same time moving out quickly to follow a carefully selected set of the more promising new developments in the industry. The organization is seldom "first in" with new products or services. However, by carefully monitoring the actions of major competitors in areas compatible with its stable product-market base, the organization can frequently be "second in" with a more cost-efficient product or service.[31]

Miles and Snow characterize analyzers as having a parallel structure. Sub-units operating in the stable parts of the analyzer's domain will have a functional design like that of a defender. But those operating in the changing parts of the analyzer's domain will have market-based, divisionalized designs similar to a prospector's. Thus, an analyzer can be viewed as an intermediate strategy-structure configuration.

A fourth strategic type, the *reactor*, is an organization with an inconsistent strategy-structure configuration, such as an organization attempting to pursue a prospector strategy with a defender structure.[32] Subsequent research in the plastics, semiconductor, automotive, and air transportation industries showed that defenders, prospectors, and analyzers financially outperformed reactors in competitive industries, but not in regulated industries.[33] Another study comparing the relative performance of defenders, prospectors, and analyzers found that the best-performing strategic type depended on whether industry environments were mature or growing, innovative or noninnovative.[34]

Robert Miles extended this line of argument in a study of the strategies employed by the six major tobacco companies between 1950 and 1975,[35] the period during which the health risks of tobacco were discovered and publicized and the rate of increase in cigarette smoking declined. Miles was interested in examining how organizations adapted to a threatening environment by modifying their domains of operation, activities that we will refer to as **domain tactics**. He identified three primary domain tactics: domain defense, domain offense, and domain creation. As Table 8.6 shows, **domain defense** is undertaken to protect the legitimacy of an organization's domain through both the creation and control of information and through political action. For example, Ford Motor Company and the United Autoworkers jointly used domain defense to stem the flow of Japanese imports into the U.S. market during the early 1980s by bringing an action before the International Trade Commission and, later, pushing for Congressional import restrictions.

Domain offense focuses on increasing the economic performance of an organization by expanding its domain of operation into adjacent product or market areas. For example, Gerber Foods used domain offense to move into new, related areas of operation when a declining birth rate shrunk its market during the 1960s. Its acquisition of rubber pants and baby wash cloth manufacturers, and the development of a child care division, built on its existing expertise and reputation for baby care products.

Domain creation focuses on the development of new opportunities for an organization outside of its traditional domain through diversification. An organization can pursue domain creation in a number of ways, most notably through research and development or by acquisition. The tobacco manufacturers, for example, created new domains of operation beginning in the 1960s by acquiring consumer products companies in order to reduce their dependence on tobacco products for long-term growth and revenues. RJR's acquisition of Nabisco in 1988 is just one in a long history of such acquisitions.

Table 8.6
Domain Tactics in the Tobacco Industry

Adaptive Modes	Goals	Strategies
Domain Defense	Preservation of legitimacy and autonomy of traditional domain **(Legitimacy)**	Creation and control of vital information; lobbying and coopting institutional gatekeepers
Domain Offense	Enhancement of economic performance in traditional domain **(Efficiency)**	Product innovation; market segmentation
Domain Creation	Creation of new performance oppor- tunities; minimization of risk exposure **(Growth and security)**	Diversification; overseas expansion

Source: Robert H. Miles, *Coffin Nails and Corporate Strategy* (Englewood Cliffs, N.J.: Prentice-Hall, 1982), 51.

Miles showed that organizations tend to have a *strategic predisposition,* which he defines as "the extent to which an organization exhibits a consistent pattern over time in the choices it makes about the formulation and implementation of its strategies."[36] Within the context of Miles and Snow's typology, he found that the strategic predisposition of the Big Six tobacco companies was evident in their diversification strategies. Defenders attempted domain defense first, then either domain offense or creation if domain defense was not effective. Analyzers tended to use domain-offense tactics, while prospectors engaged in domain creation. Ongoing strategic actions thus tended to be consistent with their overall strategy-structure configuration.

Implications for Design

The general thrust of the strategic choice approach can be summarized as follows: Managers actively enact their organization's environment, and the enacted environment is likely to be less complex than the "objective environment," which consists of all the factors that may affect an organization's operations. Differences in enactment by organizations in the same overall environment mean that they may perceive different environmental opportunities and threats, choose different strategic options, and as a result design themselves differently.

Referent Domain	Primary Target	Relations among Traditional Competitors
Traditional product/market	Agents in the institutional environment surrounding the traditional product/market	Cooperative
Traditional product/market	Rivals for the traditional product/market	Competitive
New product/markets	Rivals for the new product/markets	Independent

By making choices as to what goods and services they produce, and what markets and customers they choose to serve, organizations define their task environments. They also manipulate these environments over time through a variety of actions and strategies such as mergers, acquisitions, joint ventures, political action. These actions further shape an organization's environment. In turn, the type of strategy that an organization pursues has implications for its design. As Miles and Snow suggest, some strategies are better served by some structural designs than by others. The strategy-structure configuration also appears to have an impact on the strategic disposition of an organization. That is, once a strategic direction is set through the choices of managers, it affects the subsequent selection of strategic actions.

Notice that the strategic choice approach does not contradict the findings from contingency theory about the relationship between environmental conditions and the organization designs that result in effective performance. Instead, the difference lies in the way each approach sees the environment-strategy-structure alignment coming about. Contingency theorists indicate that organizations reactively adapt to changing environmental conditions, that is, the environment drives organization design. Strategic choice advocates, on the other hand, argue that managers create and shape the environments to which their organizations adapt, and structural design follows from these choices. But both approaches indicate that structure needs to be aligned to environmental conditions, regardless of whether the environment is imposed or enacted.

POPULATION ECOLOGY[37]

In the late 1970s a more environmentally based approach to the study of organization-environment relations, known as population ecology, was proposed by Michael Hannan and John Freeman.[38] Population ecologists are interested in the processes that generate organizational diversity, and in how the diversity of organizational forms within industries and societies changes in response to long-term environmental pressures. Drawing heavily from the biological ecology literature, Hannan and Freeman suggest that organizational adaptation should be examined by looking at changes in organizational populations instead of studying individual organizations. **Organizational populations** consist of organizations with similar forms, with **organizational form** being defined by organizations' goals, technologies, structures, and markets.[39] Hannan and Freeman state that adaptation to changing environmental conditions takes place primarily through the creation of populations with new forms that replace existing populations. The reason, they propose, is that there are strong inertial forces in existing organizations that make it difficult for them to change.

> Some of the factors that generate structural inertia are internal to organizations: these include sunk costs in plant, equipment, and personnel, the dynamics of political coalitions, and the tendency for precedents to become normative standards. Others are external. There are legal and other barriers to entry and exit from realms of activity. Exchange relations with other organizations constitute an investment that is not written off lightly. Finally, attempting radical structural change often threatens legitimacy; the loss of institutional support may be devastating.[40]

Because existing organizations change slowly, new organizations taking advantage of emerging environmental opportunities have an opportunity to gain a foothold in an industry.

> One of the most important kinds of threats to the success of extant organizations is the creation of new organizations designed specifically to take advantage of some new set of opportunities. When the costs of building a new organization are low and the expected time from initiation to full production is short, this kind of threat is intense (unless there are legal barriers to the entry of new organizations). If the existing organizations cannot change their strategies and structures more quickly than entrepreneurs can begin new organizations, new competitors will have a chance to establish footholds. Other things being equal, the faster the speed with which new organizations can be built, the greater is the (relative) inertia of a set of existing structures.[41]

The result, Hannan and Freeman suggest, is that adaptation to environmental change occurs through the failure and replacement of existing organizations by new ones better suited to altered environmental conditions. Focus on Design 8.3 shows some of the major opportunities that existing organizations have bypassed, giving rise to new organizations

FOCUS ON DESIGN 8.3

Inertia and Some Less Than Great Moments in Innovation

"This 'telephone' has too many short-comings to be seriously considered as a means of communication. The device is of no value to us."
> Western Union internal memo, 1876

"A cookie store is a bad idea. Besides, market research reports say that America likes crispy cookies, not soft chewy cookies like you make."
> Response to Debbi Fields' idea of starting Mrs. Fields' Cookies

"We don't like their sound, and guitar music is on the way out."
> Decca Recording, rejecting the Beatles, 1962

So we went to Atari and said, 'Hey, we've got this amazing thing, even built with some of your parts, and what do you think about funding us? Or we'll give it to you. We just want to do it. Pay our salary, we'll come to work for you.' And they said, 'No.' So then we went to Hewlett-Packard, and they said, 'Hey, we don't need you. You haven't got through college yet.' "
> Apple Computer Inc. founder Steve Jobs on attempts to get Atari and H-P interested in his and Steve Wozniak's personal computer

"The concept is interesting and well-formed, but in order to earn better than a 'C,' the idea must be feasible."
> A Yale University management professor in response to Fred Smith's paper proposing reliable overnight delivery service. Smith went on to found Federal Express Corp.

Source: James C. Collins, "Wet Blankets Through History," Stanford University Graduate School of Business, 1989. Used with permission.

and industries. Population ecologists study these processes by examining how environments change and the subsequent creation, growth, and demise of organizational populations.

Ecological Niches and Organizational Domains

Fundamental to the ecological approach is concept of a **population niche**, the ecologist's version of the organizational environment, defined as a resource space within which a population of organizations can survive.[42] Population niches are defined in relation to the organizations inhabiting them: "niches define forms and forms define niches."[43] By choosing strategies and structures based on market opportunities and resource availability, organizations define their niche. An *industry* consists of multiple niches, each occupied by a population with a distinct organizational form. The extent to which competition exists among these populations depends on the degree to which their niches overlap.

Generalist and Specialist Strategies

Population ecologists use the distinction between generalist and specialist strategies as one dimension for distinguishing among organizational forms.[44] Organizations offering a broad range of goods or services, or serving a broad range of customers or markets, are known as **generalists**. Organizations providing a narrower range of goods or services, or serving more limited markets or customer groups are known as **specialists**. For example, IBM is a computer industry generalist because it offers a broad range of products, from personal computers to supercomputers. Cray Computers, on the other hand, is a specialist manufacturing only supercomputers. Generally, specialists outcompete generalists in the narrow area in which their niches overlap because they are more efficient. But while the generalist is less efficient, the breadth of its domain buffers it from some effects of environmental change. While demand is decreasing for some of the generalist's goods or services, it usually is increasing for others. Moreover, the diversity of goods, services, and markets defining a generalist's domain allows it to reallocate resources internally to accommodate changing environmental conditions, an option not open to a specialist.[45]

Glenn Carroll suggests that the extent to which specialists will be found in an industry depends on the degree of industry concentration and the extent to which the domain of the industry's generalists overlap.[46] He notes

> [T]he success of generalism creates the conditions for the success of specialism. By attempting to serve large market shares through universalistic appeal to all potential customers, generalists avoid making extended particularistic appeals to special groups of customers (the more special the appeals made, the less is the general appeal). The net result of these dynamics is that markets highly concentrated by one or several generalists leave open many small, specialized pockets of consumers. These pockets are where specialists pop up and thrive.[47]

In other words, the more that one or a few generalists dominate the market's center, the more opportunities there will be for specialist organizations to serve small pockets of demand at its periphery.

Resource-Exploitation Strategies and Population Density

A second strategic dimension population ecologists use to distinguish among organizational forms is based on the manner in which organizations exploit resources within a population niche.[48] Some organizations innovate quickly to take advantage of new resource opportunities, and they gain a competitive advantage by being first-to-market. The benefits of being first-to-market include setting industry standards and high profits. Organizations pursuing

Figure 8.3
Logistic Model of Industry Growth

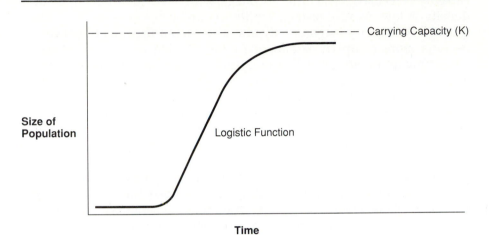

Verhulst-Pearl logistic equation: $\dfrac{dN}{dT} = rN\left(\dfrac{K-N}{K}\right)$

Where
K is a niche's carrying capacity,
r   is a population's reproductive rate, and
N is the number of organisms in a population.

a first-to-market strategy are known as *r-strategists*. Apple Computer, which pioneered the personal computer industry, is a *r*-strategist. Other organizations follow *r*-strategists into a market once it is established and compete on the basis of their efficient use of resources. These organizations are known as *K-strategists*. IBM, which usually follows the leader after new market opportunities have been established, is a *K*-strategist.

The *r* and *K* labels are derived from the Verhulst-Pearl logistic equation that ecologists use to model population growth. *K* refers to a niche's **carrying capacity**, defined as the maximum number of organizations a niche can support at equilibrium; *r* refers to the rate of population growth. The extent to which a population has fully exploited a niche's available resources is called **population density**.[49] The greater the extent that a niche's resources are being used by a population, the higher the population's density is.

Population ecologists use logistic equations to study changes in population growth and density. As Figure 8.3 shows, the logistic equation generates an S-shaped curve, indicating that a niche will attract occupants at an initially slow but exponentially increasing rate. As population density increases, entry into a niche becomes less attractive and the rate of population growth slows. Eventually population growth stops when the niche's carrying capacity is reached. Generally, *r*-strategists are favored when population density is low because of their ability to exploit resource opportunities quickly. As density increases, dynamics between organizational forms become more competitive and favor the efficiencies of *K*-strategists. Over time, populations of *K*-strategists replace populations of *r*-strategists within an industry.

Cross-classification of the generalism/specialism and *r*/*K* dimensions yields a typology of strategic types: *r*-specialists, *K*-specialists, *r*-generalists, and *K*-generalists.[50] The *r*-specialists operate within a narrow domain, and compete by moving quickly to take advantage of emerging market opportunities. *K*-specialists also have a narrow domain of operation, but they compete on the basis of efficient operations, whereas *r*-generalists operate in a broader domain of activities, competing on the basis of their ability to move quickly to take advantage of new opportunities. *K*-generalists also operate in a broad domain, but they compete through efficient operations.

In the computer industry, for example, Cray Computer is an *r*-specialist competing in a narrow domain (supercomputers) by continually advancing technology through research and development. Hewlett-Packard is an *r*-generalist that competes through the development of innovative products in many segments of the computing (personal computers, work stations, minicomputers) and scientific equipment industries. Compaq Computer is a *K*-specialist, competing in a relatively narrow domain (personal computers) on the basis of price and quality. IBM is a *K*-generalist that operates in a broad domain (personal to supercomputers) on the basis of price and service.

According to the logic of the population ecology model, *r*-specialists and *r*-generalists will be the most common organizational forms early in an industry's development. Once *r*-strategists establish the viability of an industry, there will be an increasing number of entrants, and many of these later entrants will be *K*-specialists and *K*-generalists. As more organizations enter the industry, increasing population density and competition will favor the greater efficiency of *K*-strategists. Unless *r*-strategists can find or develop new areas of operation, they are likely to be replaced by *K*-strategists as an industry matures.

Implications for Design

The primary message from population ecology for managers is that once they make choices about strategy and structure, success or failure is largely determined by ensuing environmental conditions. For example, the population ecology approach suggests that an entrepreneurial start-up organization—an *r*-strategist—will succeed as long as there are not many competing organizations. But as later entrants—often pursuing a *K*-strategy—are attracted into the industry, a less efficient entrepreneurial firm will find it difficult to remain competitive.

Strategic choice theorists would argue that the entrepreneurial start-up organization has a number of options open to it. It could remain a small, specialized organization that rapidly creates and exploits new opportunities through research and development, enabling it to avoid head-on competition with K-strategists. Or it could change its strategy as it grows, develop a functional structure and become an efficient producer—much like Games 'R Us as discussed in Chapter 5. Or it might be acquired by a generalist looking for quick entry into that part of an industry.

Population ecologists, on the other hand, argue that the first two scenarios are unlikely. First, new organizations have a significantly higher failure rates than organizations that have survived their first few years, making a successful transition to an efficient functional form problematic.[51] Second, if new opportunities develop within an industry, it is easier for entrepreneurial individuals to take advantage of them by forming new organizations than it is to change an existing organization's direction. The third option, population ecologists would argue, is simply a form of organizational death.

It is important to understand that these differences in perspective are more a matter of beliefs about how the environment-strategy-structure alignment comes about than about the nature of this alignment. Contingency theorists, strategic choice advocates, and population ecologists largely agree about the patterns of organizational design that fit different environmental conditions. We present a model of environmental change and organizational adaptation that draws from all three approaches in the next two chapters. It shows how these approaches complement each other and, by viewing the approaches together, it provides a richer understanding of the relationship between structure, strategy, and environment.

SUMMARY

Learning Objective 1: Distinguish between an organization's general environment and its task environment. The general environment refers to the sum of factors outside an organization's boundaries that influence, or may influence, its structure, goals, and effectiveness. An organization's task environment consists of the aspects of the general environment that are directly relevant to its goal setting and goal attainment. The task environment can be defined specifically in terms of an organization's customers, suppliers, employees, competitors, and government regulatory agencies. Thus, the difference between the general environment and an organization's task environment is the difference between the broad social context within which all organizations exist and those aspects of the general environment relevant to a specific organization's functioning.

Learning Objective 2: Explain the concept of an organizational domain and its relationship to an organization's task environment. An organizational domain is defined by the goods and services an organization produces, and by the customers or clients it serves. Different organizations, even within the same industry, have different domains and therefore different task environments.

Learning Objective 3: Differentiate among contingency theory, strategic choice, and population ecology. Each of these approaches differs in its underlying view of how the alignment between environments, strategies, and structures come about. Contingency theorists envision managers operating in a reactive mode, responding to changes in their organization's environment. The primary managerial problem is one of ensuring a proper "fit" between an organization's design and environmental conditions. Strategic choice theorists see managers playing a more proactive role, actively selecting and shaping their organizations' environments and then designing their organizations to fit those environments. Population ecologists, on the other hand, argue that the inertia inherent in organizational strategies and structures makes it difficult for managers to accurately perceive or respond to environmental change. As a result, the alignment of strategy and structure with environmental conditions occurs through the creation of new organizational forms that "fit" prevailing environmental conditions and the demise of those that do not.

Learning Objective 4: Describe the general implications of contingency theory for the relationship between organizational design and environmental conditions. Contingency theorists point out that effective organizations have designs that fit the demands of their environments, and their research indicates that mechanistic designs fit stable environments and organic designs fit changing environments. The greater the complexity and instability of an organization's environment, the more likely it is to create specialized units that deal with each environmental sector. However, the greater the degree to which an organization has differentiated units, the more elaborate and costly are the coordinating mechanisms needed for effective integration.

Learning Objective 5: Describe the general implications of strategic choice theory for the relationship among organization structure, strategy, and environment. Strategic choice advocates see managers in a less reactive mode than contingency theorists. They believe that managers select their organizations' environments when they develop strategies and choose domains of operation, and that they continually reshape their environments by changing strategies and domains of operation—and by making transactions with other organizations and taking political action. However, strategic choice advocates agree with contingency theorists that managers must design organizations and create management processes consistent with the strategies they select.

Learning Objective 6: Describe the general implications of the population ecology approach for the relationship between organizational forms and environmental change. Population ecologists argue that inertial forces make organizational change a slow, problematic process, preventing significant adaptation to changing environmental conditions. As a result, they indicate that adaptation to changing environmental conditions occurs through the creation of new organizational forms that replace older organizational forms. Population ecologists study the dynamics of adaptation in industries and societies by examining how different environmental conditions create selection pressures that favor some organizational forms and not others.

Discussion Questions

1. You are the owner/manager of a small electrical components manufacturer in a rapidly growing market. Over the past five years, there have been a number of small, innovative manufacturers producing similar components using different formats. Six months ago a major electronics firm entered the market, and its product has rapidly set an industry standard. As that firm has brought more production capacity on line, prices have begun to fall, and demand for your version of the component is decreasing. What advice would a contingency theorist, a strategic choice advocate, and a population ecologist give you?

2. What are the likely differences in the task environments of a small, independent grocery store and a large grocery chain operating in the same area?

3. When Ted Turner began the Cable News Network (CNN) in 1980, the major broadcasters made little of it. After all, who would be interested in an around-the-clock news network. But by 1989 Turner's SuperStation TBS, CNN, and Turner Network Television (TNT) were among the six highest rated basic cable stations. And including his Headline News channel, they accounted for 31 percent of all basic-cable viewing in the first quarter of 1989.[52] Turner operates in the same environment as ABC, CBS, and NBC. Why has he done so well?

4. The videotape rental market grew rapidly during the 1980s. How would you classify the strategies of organizations renting videotapes in your area? Which are r-specialists, r-generalists, K-specialists, and K-generalists? Explain the reasons for your classifications.

5. You are the manager of a large high-tech company that manufactures circuit boards for alarm systems. The company has, as the inventor of the product, been very successful during its first three years of operation. However, sales steadily declined during the first two quarters of this year. Several factors appear to have contributed to this situation: two suppliers have had great difficulty shipping needed components; two new manufacturers have entered the market, one with an innovative product design that it is marketing in Europe as well as the United States; and overall economic growth is beginning to slow. How might you interpret this situation from the perspective of contingency theory? From the strategic choice perspective? From the population ecology perspective?

6. Identify changes occurring in the general environment of your college or university (e.g., changing population demographics, changing student interests for fields of study, rapid technological change, and so on) that might affect its operations in ten years. What opportunities and threats do these changes pose for its future?

DESIGN AUDIT #8

Mapping Your Organization's Environment

This design audit will help you "map" your organization's environment by specifying important environmental sectors, how they are changing, and how well designed your organization is in meeting those environmental changes.

Organizational Domain

1. Describe your organization's domain by specifying the types of goods and services it produces, customers served, and specific market segments.

   Hint: Under "goods and services" identify the broad lines of goods and services your organization produces. If your organization is fairly specialized, you may have only one or two entries. Under "customers" identify the broad groups of customers your organization serves. These groups might differ by product line, or they might vary according to some consumer characteristic, such as age, income level, industry, or so on. Under "market segment" identify the distinctive market niches that your organization operates in, which will reflect your responses in the first two columns. For example, a housing developer might be in a segment described as "custom-homes in the high-priced end of the Orange County housing market."

Goods and Services	Customers	Market Segments
_____	_____	_____
_____	_____	_____
_____	_____	_____
_____	_____	_____
_____	_____	_____
_____	_____	_____
_____	_____	_____

General and Task Environment

2. Keeping in mind the domain you have specified in Question 1, identify trends in the different sectors of the general environment that may affect your organization's operations over the next five years. (In effect, by identifying trends and changes relevant to your organization, you are specifying factors that are changing your organization's task environment.)

Hint: Each general environmental sector is defined in Table 8.1. Think about each in terms of trends or events that may affect your organization. For example, in the political domain, the increasing emphasis on improving air quality is likely to affect the oil and gas industry as regulations require cleaner fuels for automobiles. In the technological domain, rapid advances in the semiconductor industry are likely to affect organizations that use semiconductors as a component in their goods. In the demographic domain, the aging of the population will have an impact on organizations with goods and services targeted at or differentially used by different age groups. In the economic domain, the entry of new competitors, industry-wide consolidation, or industry globalization can have an impact on your organization's competitive position. You may find industry-specific publications helpful in identifying trends, as well as managers in your organization.

Think about each environmental sector carefully. Some of the changes that end up being important in your analysis may not be obvious at first. If you find that an environmental sector is not relevant to your organization after giving it some thought, write "not applicable" in that section and move on to the next one. Finally, you are likely to find that changes in one environmental sector are related to changes in others. Don't worry too much about which section you put the information in. The important point is identifying those trends and events that may affect your organization's future.

Environmental Sector	Changes and Trends
Cultural	(Ex: Decreasing emphasis on the "Protestant work ethic," greater ethnic diversity)
Technological	(Ex: Accelerating rate of technological change, increased applications of computers)
Educational	(Ex: Shortages of trained personnel, increasingly educated consumers)

Political   (Ex: Decreased funding for national defense, in-
                                         creased pressures for regulation/deregulation)

Legal   (Ex: Increased liability for inappropriate managerial
                                         behavior, increasing government reporting
                                         requirements)

Natural Resources   (Ex: Increasing prices for a critical raw material,
                                         shortages of raw materials)

Demographic   (Ex: Aging of the population, increased proportion
                                         of minorities)

Sociological   (Ex: Increasing number of two-income families,
                                         changing social attitudes about business)

Economic   (Ex: Increased industry competition, rising/falling
                                         interest rates, globalization)

Criticality of Environmental Changes
for Your Organization

3. Based on your analysis in Question 2, indicate the relative importance of each environmental sector to the future success of your organization in the first column, where 5 = very important and 1 = not important at all. In the second column, indicate the extent to which these general environmental trends create uncertainty about the future for your organization, where 5 = creates very high uncertainty about the future, and 1 = creates little uncertainty. Multiply these two scores for each environmental sector, and write the product in the "Product Score" column. These scores provide you with a rough indication of the relative criticality of each environmental sector to your organization's future.

Environmental Sector	Importance	Uncertainty	Product Score
Cultural	5 4 3 2 1	5 4 3 2 1	_____
Technological	5 4 3 2 1	5 4 3 2 1	_____
Educational	5 4 3 2 1	5 4 3 2 1	_____
Political	5 4 3 2 1	5 4 3 2 1	_____
Legal	5 4 3 2 1	5 4 3 2 1	_____
Natural Resources	5 4 3 2 1	5 4 3 2 1	_____
Demographic	5 4 3 2 1	5 4 3 2 1	_____
Sociological	5 4 3 2 1	5 4 3 2 1	_____
Economic	5 4 3 2 1	5 4 3 2 1	_____

Design Implications

4. Examine these environmental trends and their relative criticality for your organization's future. Taken together, what are the three most pressing issues your organization is likely to face over the next ten years. Write these issues in the spaces provided below with a brief explanation. Then, looking back at the design audits for Chapters 4 through 7, assess how well your organization's design is prepared to cope with them. Outline *two* design options that would better position your organization to deal with each issue.

    For example, if you have identified changing consumer preferences for goods or services as a critical issue (because of demographic, cultural, or technological trends), how well does your organization's existing design allow it to cope with it. Is the organization's decision-making system adequate to perceive and react to these changes (implications for the extent to which decision making is centralized), or is the design conducive to engineering, producing, and selling new or modified goods or services to existing customers or new customers (implications for unit grouping and/or integrating mechanisms)? What design options might improve your organization's ability to deal with these environmental changes? Use separate sheets of paper if needed.

Issue #1: _____
Design Alternatives:

Issue #2: _____
Design Alternatives:

Issue #3: _____
Design Alternatives:

Notes

1. W. Graham Astley and Andrew H. Van de Ven, "Central Perspectives and Debates in Organization Theory," *Administrative Science Quarterly* 28 (1983): 245–273.

2. William H. Starbuck, "Organizations and Their Environments," in *Handbook of Industrial and Organizational Psychology,* ed. Marvin D. Dunnette (Chicago: Rand McNally, 1976), 1069–1123.

3. William R. Dill, "Environment as an Influence on Managerial Autonomy," *Administrative Science Quarterly* 2 (1958): 410; William R. Dill, "The Impact of Environment on Organizational Development," in *Concepts and Issues in Administrative Behavior,* ed. Sidney Mailick and Edward H. Van Ness (Englewood Cliffs, N. J.: Prentice-Hall, 1962), 29–48.

4. Wayne F. Cascio and Raymond F. Zammuto, "Societal Trends and Staffing Policies," in *Human Resource Planning, Employment, and Placement,* ed. Wayne F. Cascio (Washington, D.C.: American Society of Personnel Administrators and the Bureau of National Affairs, 1989), 19–27.

5. Sol Levine and Paul E. White, "Exchange as a Conceptual Framework for the Study of Interorganizational Relationships," *Administrative Science Quarterly* 5 (1961): 395–420; James D. Thompson, *Organizations in Action* (New York: McGraw-Hill, 1967), 26.

6. Andrew H. Van de Ven and Robert Drazin, "The Concept of Fit in Contingency Theory," *Research in Organizational Behavior* 7 (1985): 333–365; Raymond E. Miles and Charles C. Snow, "Fit, Failure, and the Hall of Fame," in *Strategy and Organization: A West Coast Perspective,* ed. Glenn Carroll and David Vogel (Boston: Pitman, 1984), 1–19; N. Venkatraman, "The Concept of Fit in Strategy Research: Toward Verbal and Statistical Correspondence," *Academy of Management Review* 14 (1989): 423–444.

7. For extensive reviews about the development of theory and research on organization-environment relations, see W. Richard Scott, *Organizations: Rational, Natural, and Open Systems,* 2d ed. (Englewood Cliffs, N.J.: Prentice-Hall, 1987); Howard E. Aldrich and Peter V. Marsden, "Environments and Organizations," in *Handbook of Sociology,* ed. Neil J. Smelser (Beverly Hills, Calif.: Sage, 1988), 361–392.

8. Tom Burns and George M. Stalker, *The Management of Innovation* (London: Tavistock, 1961).

9. Ibid., 5–6.

10. Ibid., 5.

11. Ibid., 125.

12. Paul R. Lawrence and Jay W. Lorsch, *Organization and Environment: Managing Differentiation and Integration* (Homewood, Ill.: Richard D. Iwrin, 1969); Paul R. Lawrence and Jay W. Lorsch, "Differentiation and Integration in Complex Organizations," *Administrative Science Quarterly* 12 (1967): 1–47. See also Paul R. Lawrence, "The Harvard Organization and Environment Research Program," in *Perspectives on Organization Design and Behavior,* ed. Andrew H. Van de Ven and William F. Joyce (New York: John Wiley & Sons, 1981), 311–337.

13. Lawrence and Lorsch, "Differentiation and Integration," 3–4.

14. Robert B. Duncan, "Characteristics of Organizational Environments and Perceived Environmental Uncertainty," *Administrative Science Quarterly* 17 (1972):

313–327; Robert B. Duncan, "Multiple Decision Making Structures in Adapting to Environmental Uncertainty: The Impact of Organizational Effectiveness," *Human Relations* 26 (1973): 273–291; Robert B. Duncan, "Modifications in Decision Structure in Adapting to the Environment: Some Implications for Organizational Learning," *Decision Sciences* 5 (1974): 705–725.

15. Joseph A. Litterer, *The Analysis of Organizations*, 2d ed. (New York: Wiley, 1973), 335–336.

16. Duncan, "Characteristics of Organizational Environments," 325.

17. John Child, "Organizational Structure, Environment, and Performance: The Role of Strategic Choice," *Sociology* 6 (1972): 3.

18. Ibid., 9.

19. Ibid., 10.

20. W. I. Thomas, *The Child in America* (New York: Alfred A. Knopf, 1928), 572.

21. Karl E. Weick, *The Social Psychology of Organizing* (Reading, Mass.: Addison-Wesley, 1969); Karl E. Weick, "Enactment Processes in Organizations," in *New Directions in Organizational Behavior*, ed. Barry M. Staw and Gerald R. Salancik (Chicago: St. Clair Press, 1977), 267–300; Starbuck, "Organizations and Their Environments," 1069–1123.

22. Weick, *The Social Psychology of Organizing*, 64.

23. Starbuck, "Organizations and Their Environments," 1080.

24. Howard E. Aldrich and Jeffrey Pfeffer, "Environments of Organizations," *Annual Review of Sociology* 2 (1976): 89.

25. Weick, *The Social Psychology of Organizing*, 185.

26. Jeffrey Pfeffer and Gerald R. Salancik, *The External Control of Organizations: A Resource Dependence Perspective* (New York: Harper & Row, 1978).

27. Ibid., 3.

28. Raymond E. Miles and Charles C. Snow, *Organizational Strategy, Structure, and Process* (New York: McGraw-Hill, 1978), 9.

29. Charles C. Snow and Lawrence G. Hrebiniak, "Strategy, Distinctive Competence, and Organizational Performance," *Administrative Science Quarterly* 25 (1980): 336.

30. Ibid., 336.

31. Ibid., 336.

32. Miles and Snow, *Organizational Strategy, Structure, and Process*, 14, 93.

33. Ibid., 331.

34. Donald C. Hambrick, "Some Tests of the Effectiveness and Functional Attributes of Miles and Snow's Strategic Types," *Academy of Management Journal* 26 (1983): 5–26.

35. Robert H. Miles, *Coffin Nails and Corporate Strategies* (Englewood Cliffs, N. J.: Prentice-Hall, 1982).

36. Ibid., 238.

37. Population ecology is one of several models that applies evolutionary or ecological logic to the study of organizations. Others focus on different levels of

analysis, ranging from that of the individual organization to organizational communities. For an overview of these models, see Glenn R. Carroll, "Organizational Ecology," *Annual Review of Sociology* 10 (1984): 71–93.

38. Michael T. Hannan and John Freeman, "The Population Ecology of Organizations," *American Journal of Sociology* 82 (1977): 929–963.

39. Michael T. Hannan and John Freeman, "Structural Inertia and Organizational Change," *American Sociological Review* 49 (1984): 155–156.

40. Ibid., 149.

41. Ibid., 152.

42. Michael T. Hannan and John Freeman, "Where Do Organizational Forms Come From?" *Sociological Forum* 1 (1986): 57.

43. Ibid., 57.

44. Howard E. Aldrich, *Organizations and Environments* (Englewood Cliffs, N.J.: Prentice-Hall, 1979), 113–115; John Freeman and Michael T. Hannan, "Niche Width and the Dynamics of Organizational Populations," *American Journal of Sociology* 88 (1983): 1116–1145.

45. Raymond F. Zammuto, "Three Propositions on Organizational Growth and Decline," in *Proceedings of the Academy of Management,* ed. Kae H. Chung (1983): 271–275.

46. Glenn R. Carroll, "Concentration and Specialization: Dynamics of Niche Width in Populations of Organizations," *American Journal of Sociology* 90 (1984): 1262–1283.

47. Glenn R. Carroll, "The Specialist Strategy," in *Strategy and Organization: A West Coast Perspective,* ed. Glenn R. Carroll and David Vogel (Boston: Pitman, 1984), 123.

48. Jack W. Brittain and John H. Freeman, "Organizational Proliferation and Density Dependent Selection," in *The Organization Life Cycle,* ed. John R. Kimberly and Robert H. Miles (San Francisco: Jossey-Bass, 1980), 311–313.

49. Michael T. Hannan and John Freeman, "Density Dependence in the Growth of Organizational Populations," in *Ecological Models of Organizations,* ed. Glenn R. Carroll (Cambridge, Mass.: Ballinger, 1988), 7–32.

50. Jack W. Brittain and John H. Freeman, "Organizational Proliferation and Density Dependent Selection," 321–326; Jack W. Brittain and Douglas R. Wholey, "Competition and Coexistence in Organizational Communities: Population Dynamics in Electronics Components Manufacturing," in *Ecological Models of Organization,* ed. Glenn R. Carroll (Cambridge, Mass.: Ballinger), 195–222.

51. Jitendra Singh, Robert J. House, and David J. Tucker, "Organizational Legitimacy and the Liability of Newness," *Administrative Science Quarterly* 31 (1986): 171–193; John Freeman, Glenn R. Carroll, and Michael T. Hannan, "The Liability of Newness: Age Dependence in Organizational Death Rates," *American Journal of Sociology* 48 (1983): 692–710.

52. "Captain Comeback," *Business Week,* July 17, 1989, 99.

Environmental Change and Strategic Adaptation

Learning Objectives

Upon completing this chapter you should be able to

1. Define the concept of an industry niche.

2. Distinguish between niche size and niche shape.

3. Distinguish between continuous and discontinuous environmental change.

4. Identify different types of changes in niche conditions that are conducive to industry growth and industry decline.

5. Identify different types of changes in niche conditions that affect the success and failure of different domain strategies.

6. Explain why the concept of environmental change is so complex.

It was a field day for Germany Inc. when electronics giant Siemens swooped down to snap up ailing Nixdorf Computer, keeping the computer maker safely out of non-German hands. The acquisition sets the stage for a new round of bloodletting in the congested European computer industry, where U.S. giants are setting a fast pace. But the Siemens purchase gives it a hardy position in minicomputers, and greatly improves its chances for being one of the few industry survivors.

The Nixdorf takeover fits the aggressive expansion strategy at Siemens; it has recently bought into or signed cooperation deals with at least five other major mid-range computer manufacturers. Nixdorf's huge customer base of 50,000 installed mid-size computer systems, coupled with Siemens's quick move to use its own chips in Nixdorf computers, gives Siemens the critical mass it needs to be a major player in the minicomputer market.

As Chapter 9 explains, competition becomes more fierce as an industry matures, and smaller firms can be pushed out of business. It's not surprising, then, that other European computer makers, caught in the wake of the Nixdorf deal, are now actively looking for partners.

Source: Igor Reichlin and Thane Peterson, "Why Siemens Wrote Such a Big Check," *Business Week*, January 22, 1990, 42.

IN the last chapter we reviewed three major approaches to organization-environment relations: contingency theory, strategic choice, and population ecology. Each presents a different explanation of how organizational adaptation occurs. During the late 1970s and early 1980s, many organization theorists viewed these as competing perspectives.[1] In recent years, however, there has been a shift toward viewing them as complementary.[2] Because each approach addresses a different aspect of organization-environment relations, they are not inherently mutually exclusive. Strategic choice theorists, for instance, are interested in how individuals' *perceptions* of the environment affect the selection of strategy and structure. Contingency theorists, on the other hand, focus on *structures* that effectively cope with the demands of different environmental conditions. Population ecologists examine how different resource-exploitation *strategies* affect the relative success of organizational populations as environmental conditions change.

Our view is that each perspective provides unique insights into the process of environmental change and organizational adaptation. Together the three perspectives should provide a better understanding of the subject. This chapter and Chapter 10 present an integrative model of organization-environment relations that draws from all three approaches.

Table 9.1

Comparison of Domain Strategies from the Strategic Choice
and Population Ecology Perspectives

	Breadth of Domain	
	Narrow	*Wide*
Basis of Competition		
Efficiency	SC: Defender	SC: Analyzer
	PE: *K*-Specialist	PE: *K*-Generalist
First-to-market	SC: Entrepreneur	SC: Prospector
	PE: *r*-Specialist	PE: *r*-Generalist

SC = Strategic Choice
PE = Population Ecology

Source: Adapted from Raymond F. Zammuto, "Organizational Adaptation: Some Implications of Population Ecology for Strategic Choice, " *Journal of Management Studies* 25 (1988): 110.

CORRESPONDENCE BETWEEN STRATEGIC CHOICE AND POPULATION ECOLOGY VIEWS OF STRATEGY[3]

In linking the three main approaches to organization-environment relations, we begin with the concept of strategy. This concept plays a particularly important role in strategic choice theory and population ecology. Strategic choice theorists see strategy as arising from the perception and interpretation of environmental information; population ecologists see it as being a primary determinant of whether an organizational form will be favored by changing environmental conditions. Despite the different perspectives, which afford very little overlap, similar classifications of strategy have been developed by strategic choice theorists and population ecologists.

Recall the discussion in Chapter 8 of Miles and Snow's strategy classification (defenders, analyzers, and prospectors) and that of population ecologists Brittain and Freeman (*r*-specialists, *r*-generalists, *K*-specialists, and *K*-generalists). Both classifications are based on the relative breadth of organizational domains (broad versus narrow) and the manner in which organizations compete within those domains (efficiency versus innovation).[4] With the addition of one domain strategy to Miles and Snow's work—the entrepreneur—there is a close correspondence between the classifications.[5] Briefly, the entrepreneur is typically a small organization (often a start-up) that has a narrow domain of operation and competes by innovating and moving quickly to take advantage of new opportunities. The correspondence between these views of strategy is shown in Table 9.1.

This correspondence provides a way to link the insights of contingency theory, strategic choice, and population ecology. Throughout the rest of this chapter, we present a model of environments and environmental change based, with modification, on the population ecology approach. We also discuss how different conditions of environmental change affect organizational success. Different environmental conditions favor different domain strategies. In Chapter 10, we use the strategic choice approach and contingency theory to see why and how organizations modify their domain strategies in response to changing environmental conditions, why variations in strategic responses to environmental change are observed within industries, and to consider the implications of changing domain strategies for organization structure. Overall, these two chapters address the complicated phenomenon of environmental change and organizational adaptation.

INDUSTRY NICHES AND ENVIRONMENTAL CHANGE

We use a number of concepts from population ecology in our model of environments and environmental change, but we deviate from its precepts in one important way. Population ecologists believe that adaptation occurs through the failure and replacement of existing organizational forms by new forms. We argue that adaptation also occurs through the transformation of existing forms. In other words, organizations change their goals, strategies, and structures as their environments change. And as organizations change their forms, they enter and exit different populations. This means that population boundaries are permeable and their rise and fall is a less compelling mechanism of organizational adaptation. Increased importance is therefore assumed by changes in the distribution of organizational forms within an industry, which brings us to focus attention on births and deaths, *and* transformations of existing organizations.[6]

We use the term *industry niche*, instead of *population niche*, to signify this difference in orientation. An **industry niche** is bounded by resource opportunities and constraints that form a resource space within which member organizations can operate and survive. Many different factors define a resource space, such as consumer demand, technological development, government policy, and so on. And, as a resource *space*, a niche can be described in terms of its shape and size.

Niche Shape

Niche shape refers to the *range or types* of activities that a niche's resources will support. A variety of factors shape niches, such as consumer preferences, technological development, and government regulations and policies, by determining what is possible and what is not. Consider the following examples:

- *Technological development.* Personal computers were not commercially feasible until the development of semiconductors.

- *Government regulation.* Government regulation of the airlines prohibited them from experimenting with new route and fare structures until the industry was deregulated in 1978.

- *Consumer preferences.* During the 1950s and 1960s, Americans had an affinity for large cars, buying virtually anything the American automakers could produce. But when the 1973 Arab oil embargo increased gas prices and uncertainty about future oil supplies, consumer preferences rapidly shifted to smaller cars, and sales of large cars dropped precipitously.

In short, niche shape defines the boundaries of what organizations can do.

The limits on what organizations can do are often short-term constraints to which they must adjust. But over the long-term, these constraints are often quite manipulable. For example, organizations overcome current technological barriers through research and development; their political activities change current government regulatory policies; advertising and consumer education build demand. Organizations use such activities to shape industry niches over the long term.

Niche Size

Population ecologists use the term *carrying capacity* to denote the number of organizations a niche will support at equilibrium. We use an analogous concept—**niche size**—to refer to the *level or amount* of performance a niche will support.[7] A niche's size is determined by several factors. Consumer demand is one of the most important, particularly since it defines the upper limit of a niche's size. But other factors, such as the availability of raw materials, economic conditions, and the like, will affect niche size, too. For example, the health care industry's niche size is constrained by the availability of financial resources, not consumer demand, which far outpaces the funds available to finance health care services. While many different factors can define a niche's size, the most limiting factor at a given point in time is usually the most important in understanding industry behavior. Thus, the difference between niche shape and niche size is that niche shape defines *what* organizations can do while niche size defines *how much* can be done.

Changes in Niche Shape and Size

An industry niche's shape and size change over time as the factors defining them change. We use the drawings in Figure 9.1 to represent some of the types of changes that can occur in niche shape and size. Panel a is a hypothetical

Figure 9.1
Examples of Changes in Niche Shape and Size

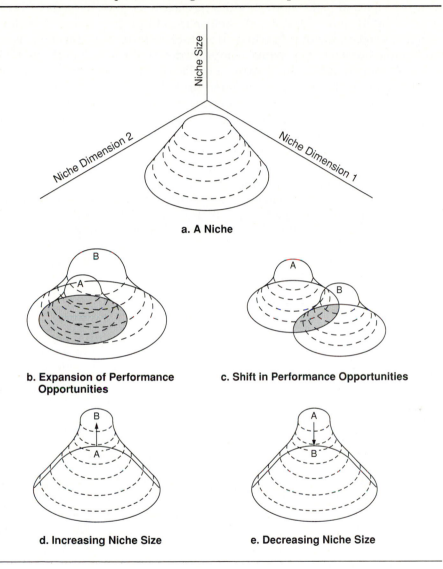

a. A Niche

b. Expansion of Performance
Opportunities

c. Shift in Performance Opportunities

d. Increasing Niche Size

e. Decreasing Niche Size

niche, where the horizontal axes represent two dimensions or factors defining niche shape, and the vertical axis represents niche size.[8]

A niche's shape changes as the social constraints, consumer preferences, technologies, and other factors defining it evolve. A simple way of thinking about changes in niche shape is that a niche's location in the potential resource space (defined by the axes in Figure 9.1, Panel a) changes. As a niche's shape changes, the range of goods and services organizations can produce also changes.[9] Technological advances, for example, can expand a niche's shape and make more activities possible over time. In Panel b, this is represented by the expansion of the bell-shaped figure from A to B. Developments in semiconductor technology (from 8-bit to 16-bit to 32-bit chips) have made rapid advances in personal computer design possible. But technological developments also can eliminate or replace existing opportunities (Panel c). For example, the personal computer virtually eliminated the market for home video game systems in the early 1980s. Thus, changes in technology, government regulation, political and economic climate, demographic change, consumer preferences, and the like, continually redefine what is possible for organizations to do.

Many of these factors can affect niche size as well. Growing consumer acceptance of a recently introduced product, for instance, can expand a niche's size by increasing demand. Demographic change also can expand or shrink a niche's size. As the U.S. population ages, the niche of the nursing home industry is expanding (Panel d), and the niche of the popular music industry shrinking (Panel e). Economic conditions also affect niche size. Many industry niches expand when good economic conditions prevail, and they shrink as economic downturns occur.

Continuity of Change

Some changes in niche size and shape are continuous; others are not. **Continuous changes** occur gradually so that conditions within a niche are not noticeably different over relatively short periods of time. Such changes are often linked to long-term trends, such as changing population demographics. The aging of the U.S. population is a slow process that spans decades, and its effect on the size and shape of industry niches becomes apparent over years, not days.

At the other extreme are **discontinuous changes,** which can significantly change conditions in a niche from one day to the next. Many discontinuities are caused by events such as the October 19, 1987, stock market crash, which discontinuously shrunk the securities industry niche. Government actions are a major source of discontinuities. New regulations can eliminate goods, services, or organizational practices overnight. They also can create opportunities, the way the passage of air and water quality legislation in the 1960s and 1970s created the pollution control industry. Focus on Design 9.1 shows how changing government regulations discontinuously opened, enlarged, modified, and then closed the niche of one small industry in less than ten years. Some environmental discontinuities result from long-term trends: gradually rising interest rates usually have little effect on consumer demand for home mortgages until they reach a critical or threshold point, after which demand drops rapidly.

FOCUS ON DESIGN 9.1

Environmental Discontinuities: Government Regulation and Casino Nights in Colorado

The history of "casino nights" in Colorado provides a clear example of how government actions can discontinuously open, expand, modify, and close an industry niche. In 1979 the Colorado legislature opened a new niche by passing legislation that permitted charitable organizations to sponsor seven gambling events (subsequently known as "casino nights") in licensed liquor establishments for fund-raising purposes. In 1981 the state expanded this niche by amending the original legislation to allow all nonprofit organizations to host casino nights. This change made the casino-night fund-raising activity available to thousands more organizations, up from the original few hundred. Growth of an industry began slowly, then increased at an accelerating rate. Thirty casino-night operations were active in 1981, 92 in 1982, and 500 by August 1983, with an estimated gross revenues of $25 million for the first eight months of the year.

Stories began to surface in the Denver newspapers during the spring of 1983 suggesting the possibility of criminal elements infiltrating casino-night operations. Concern grew in the Colorado legislature, and it authorized the

State Liquor Enforcement Agency of the Department of Revenue to police casino nights. As his first action, the Revenue Department's director requested an opinion from the state attorney general on the constitutionality of casino nights. The attorney general responded in August 1983 that they violated the Colorado Constitution's prohibition of games of chance. Casino-night operations were closed down a few days later.

The attorney general's opinion had a loophole; poker is not a game of chance and hence is not prohibited by the state constitution. The first "poker night" was hosted in October, and by December 27 permits for other poker nights had been issued. During the first few months of 1984 the number of permits issued grew rapidly: 100 in January, 255 in February, and 431 in March. As the number of poker nights increased, specialized "poker palaces" sprang up, some advertising poker 12 hours a day, 7 days a week. The legislature, concerned about the rapid proliferation of poker nights and the potential for abuse closed the niche altogether by banning them as of July 1, 1984.

Sources: T. Coakley, "Poker Becomes Ace in Hole for State Non-Profit Groups," *Denver Post*, March 25, 1984, 1-A, 4-A; L. Kilzer and N. Weaver, "Casino Nights Ruled Illegal," *Denver Post*, August 6, 1983, 1-A, 4-A; C. Parameter, "Greed Deals Charity Poker Games a Busted Flush," *Denver Post*, April 15, 1984, 1-E, 6-E; S. Sherman, "Casino Nights Bill Approved by Panel," *Denver Post*, May 6, 1983; S. Sherman, "Gaming Curbs Left to Agency," *Denver Post*, May 18, 1983.

Finally, one should keep in mind that change ranges on a continuum from continuous to discontinuous. So the continuity of environmental change is a matter of degree. Some changes are more continuous or discontinuous than others. To simplify our discussion, however, we have classified all change as either continuous or discontinuous.

Changes in niche size and shape, and in the continuity of these changes, influence the level of competition within an industry and the success and failure of different domain strategies. Many of the effects are density-dependent, meaning that they depend on the extent to which an industry niche is filled. (This subject will be discussed next.) Others are related to whether organizations in an industry niche pursue generalist or specialist strategies and the distribution of domain strategies within a niche, which we examine in Chapter 10.

DENSITY-DEPENDENT EFFECTS OF ENVIRONMENTAL CHANGE

Recall that population ecologists use the term *density* to refer to the extent to which organizations fill a niche. Low density means that the organizations inhabiting a niche have not satisfied available demand, a situation characteristic of the early stages of industry development. High density means that member organizations have filled available demand, a characteristic of mature industries. Briefly, population ecologists argue that when niche conditions are stable, *r*-strategists (entrepreneurs and prospectors) will be the most successful in the early stages of an industry's development because low density favors their ability to quickly exploit resource opportunities (area a in Figure 9.2). As density increases, a greater diversity of strategic types will be observed as *K*-strategists (defenders and analyzers) enter the industry (area b in Figure 9.2). Then, as an industry approaches maturity and density increases, analyzers and defenders will drive out entrepreneurs and prospectors as efficiency becomes the primary mode of competition (area c in Figure 9.2).

The density-dependent effects of environmental change are variations on this basic theme. Changes in niche size and shape affect the density of organizations within a niche. Some changes increase relative density, whereas others decrease it. Increasing density favors defenders and analyzers; decreasing density favors entrepreneurs and prospectors. In the following sections we elaborate on how changes in niche size and shape, and the continuity of change, affect density and the subsequent success of different domain strategies within an industry.

Changes in Niche Size

Increasing niche size (a move from NS to NS' in Figure 9.3), effectively reduces density. In mature industries, increasing niche size may create opportunities for the reentry of entrepreneurs and prospectors. If change is

Figure 9.2
Density Dependence and Prevalence of Different Domain Strategies

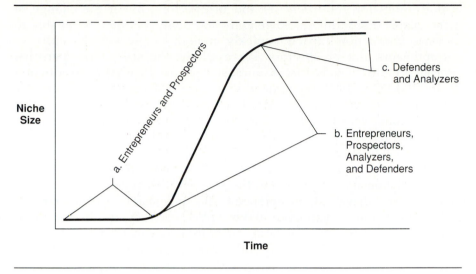

Figure 9.3
Effects of Changing Niche Size on Industry Density

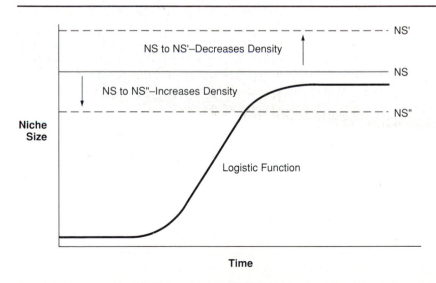

continuous, existing defenders and analyzers often can increase their production capacity at the rate of demand growth, providing few, if any, opportunities for entrepreneurs and prospectors. But if the change in niche size is discontinuous, defenders and analyzers may be unable to increase production capacity quickly enough to prevent the entry of entrepreneurs and prospectors. For example, the size of the personal computer industry niche discontinuously increased with the introduction of the IBM PC in 1982. As demand exceeded IBM's production capacity over the next two years, hundreds of new, primarily entrepreneurial organizations were formed to produce IBM-compatible equipment. In developing industries, increasing niche size simply increases the period of industry development.

Conversely, when niche size decreases (a move from NS to NS" in Figure 9.3), density increases, and the greater efficiency of defenders and analyzers will drive out entrepreneurs and prospectors. At the extreme, defenders should prevail over analyzers because they are the most efficient strategic type. The declining birthrate between 1965 and 1975 decreased the size of the baby food market, leading to intense price competition in the baby food industry. Gerber Foods, the industry's defender and most efficient producer, gained market share and profits at the expense of the industry's analyzers.[10]

Similar dynamics are sometimes found in rapidly growing industries when total supply exceeds demand (i.e., the total production of an industry's firms collectively overshoots maximum niche size). This happens when a large number of entrepreneurial firms attempt to emulate the success of earlier entrants by rushing into an industry.[11] A subsequent shake-out typically results in the demise of many prospectors and entrepreneurs. This dynamic occurred in the personal computer industry during the mid 1980s when the rate of demand growth slowed, and many of the hundreds of newly formed IBM-compatible personal computer manufacturers failed. Similar situations have also occurred in the software, hard disk, and 5¼-inch floppy disk segments of the computer industry during mid to late 1980s.

Changes in Niche Shape

Changes in niche shape also affect the relative density of organizations within an industry niche. When the performance opportunities within a niche multiply, the emerging area of the niche will have a relatively low density, favoring entrepreneurs and prospectors. This situation is often created by the development of new products, services, technologies, or the extension of existing goods and services to new markets. For example, the application of a developed technology to a new market segment modified the shape of the optical character reader industry's niche. Originally, firms in this industry produced expensive, customized equipment to sort checks, credit card receipts, and mail. The development of small, hand-held wands for use with retail point-of-sale terminals opened up significant new opportunities for firms in the industry.[12] This new product expanded the overall configuration of the industry niche (Figure 9.1, Panel b) because it did not replace existing products. All four domain strategies can succeed in this situation because the relatively high density of the established portion of a niche favors the efficiencies of defenders and analyzers, while the relatively low density in the emerging portions of a niche favor the quick movement of entrepreneurs and prospectors.

When a change in niche shape causes a shift in demand from existing goods or services to new ones, competition within the established portion of the niche will increase. As the established area shrinks (the shaded area in Figure 9.1, Panel c), defenders and analyzers will outcompete entrepreneurs and prospectors because of their more efficient use of resources. Prospectors and entrepreneurs in the established niche area can survive, however, by making a transition to an emerging area of a niche, which has a relatively low density that favors their ability to move quickly.

Competition will increase, and the rates of failure and exit will rise, as performance opportunities are eliminated by the shifting niche shape, the speed of which depends on the rate at which new goods or services replace old ones. The more quickly a change takes place, the more quickly increases in competition, failure, and exit will be observed. An example is provided by the shift from mechanical to electronic watches in the early 1970s. Looking for new uses for their products, U.S. semiconductor manufacturers introduced inexpensive, electronic digital watches that rapidly replaced demand for mechanical watches. The effect on the Swiss watchmaking industry's niche—a major source of high-priced mechanical watches—was dramatic. Sales of Swiss-made mechanical watches fell by half over two years, competition among mechanical watchmakers quickly increased, and large numbers of firms failed. Many that survived did so by acquiring the capacity to manufacture electronic watches.[13]

ENVIRONMENTAL CHANGE AND INDUSTRY DYNAMICS

The type of change occurring in niche configuration (size or shape) and the continuity or discontinuity of those changes are featured in the eight-celled model of environmental conditions shown in Figures 9.4 and 9.5. Four cells reflect environmental conditions conducive to industry growth, and another four focus on industry decline. The density-dependent dynamics described earlier are used to explain how environmental change affects competition and the relative success and failure of the four domain strategies.

Figure 9.4
Niche Conditions Favoring Industry Growth

| | **Continuity of Change** | |
	Continuous	Discontinuous
Change in Niche Size	**Expansion** Competition: No Increase Success: Defenders, analyzers Failure: Randomly distributed, related to problems managing organizational growth	**Eruption** Competition: Decreases Success: All types Failure: Randomly distributed, related to problems managing organizational growth
Change in Niche Shape	**Evolution** Competition: Increases in established areas, little competition in emerging areas Success: Defenders and analyzers in established areas, entrepreneurs and prospectors in emerging areas Failure: Randomly distributed, related to problems managing organizational growth	**Creation** Competition: None Success: Entrepreneurs and prospectors that are able to establish the legitimacy of the market Failure: Randomly distributed, related to problems of establishing legitimacy and managing growth

(Row group label at left: "Type of Change in Niche Configuration")

Niche Conditions Favoring Industry Growth

Expansion. Continuous increases in niche size are termed **niche expansion.** Often, niche expansion is related to long-term trends such as the aging of a population, changes in the composition of a workforce, and so on. If the rate of increase in niche size is slow, niche expansion is unlikely to have much effect on density because the industry's organizations will attempt to expand production at the same rate. Generally, defenders and analyzers will be at an advantage in this situation. If expansion occurs in a developing industry, or if existing organizations in a mature industry cannot increase capacity at the same pace as the growth in niche size, new organizations will enter. All four domain strategies can do well in this situation because it decreases density and reduces competition. Any failures are likely to stem from internal management problems associated with organizational growth (a topic examined in detail in Chapter 11) rather than from environmental pressures.

One example of niche expansion has been the increasing demand for child care services.[14] A number of factors have contributed to the expansion of the child care industry's niche, the foremost being the increasing numbers of women in the labor force since the 1960s. In 1970 about one-quarter of

Figure 9.5
Niche Conditions Favoring Industry Decline

| | **Continuity of Change** | |
	Continuous	Discontinuous
Change in Niche Size	**Erosion** Competition: Slow increase Success: Defenders, Analyzers Failure: Slow increase in the failure of entrepreneurs and prospectors	**Contraction** Competition: Rapid increase Success: Defenders Failure: Rapid increase in the failure of entrepreneurs and prospectors, likely exit of analyzers
Change in Niche Shape	**Dissolution** Competition: Slow to moderate increase in shrinking area, low level in expanding area Success: Defenders, analyzers in in shrinking areas; analyzers, prospectors, and entrepreneurs in expanding area Failure: Slow to moderate increase in failures of entrepreneurs in shrinking area; internal, growth related in expanding area	**Collapse** Competition: Intense among all organizations in shrinking area, rising between organizations in shrinking and expanding areas Success: Defenders in shrinking area; analyzers, prospectors and entrepreneurs in expanding area Failure: Rapid increase in failures of all domain strategies in shrinking area; internal, growth related in expanding area

Type of Change in Niche Configuration

mothers with children under the age of one were in the workforce. By 1987 the proportion had doubled. And there will be 10 million working women with small children by 1990, double the number of 1980.

Historically, the child care needs of working parents with small children have been met by "mom-and-pop" operations—small, child care operations with four or fewer facilities. As demand grew in the late 1960s, for-profit corporation chains began entering the child care industry, opening centers at multiple locations. The four largest chains (Kindercare, La Petite Academy, Daybridge/Children's World, and Gerber) have grown quickly, from a total of 237 centers in 1974 to 2,285 centers in 1987. Smaller chains (with 5 to 99 centers) are expected to exhibit the highest rate of growth through the 1990s. But even with this rapid growth of large and medium-sized national chains, 90 percent of all for-profit child care centers were operated by organizations with four or fewer centers in 1988.

Expansion in this industry's niche is likely to accelerate over the next decade as corporations add child care benefits to their compensation plans. Such benefits range from providing discounts at specific child care centers to sponsoring on-site child care, often managed by a corporate child care chain. Between 1982 and 1987 the number of employers offering some form of child care assistance increased eight-fold, from 400 to over 3,000, and industry analysts expect this rate of growth to continue into the next decade.

Eruption. A discontinuous increase in industry niche size is termed **niche eruption**. It is often the result of rapidly growing consumer acceptance after a new product's or technology's introduction. The discontinuous increase in demand reduces industry density and usually leads to a spurt of entrants into the industry niche as organizations attempt to exploit a lucrative market. All four domain strategies are likely to be successful because of the relative lack of competition. Failures within an industry will be randomly distributed, related more to internal management problems associated with rapid growth than to environmental selection pressures.

An example of eruption is the current market for facsimile (fax) machines that transmit documents over phone lines.[15] Prior to 1980, fax machines were expensive ($3,000 to $4,000), bulky, and produced relatively poor quality copies. In 1980, however, a fax using advanced digital technology was introduced and gradually established a market, with worldwide sales of 56,000 units in 1981. The eruption in demand occurred when two Japanese office equipment firms—Sharp and Canon—introduced small, low-cost machines, then priced between $2,000 and $3,000. By 1987 worldwide sales hit 423,000 units, and they are projected to reach 2.3 million units annually by 1992. New entrants have been streaming into the industry, with more than 20 firms entering the fax market in 1987 alone. The fax industry also provides a good example of how changes in one industry niche can lead to changes in other industry niches. Focus on Design 9.2 describes how the erupting fax market expanded the niches of other industries and caused decline in yet others.

Evolution. A continuous change in an industry's niche shape is termed **niche evolution**. It is often due to technological advances that expand the range of performance in which member organizations can engage. As a niche evolves, competition increases among organizations within the established parts of the industry niche as that part of the market matures. But there will be relatively little competition in the evolving part of the niche where the new technology is introduced. Defenders and analyzers will dominate the maturing niche areas because of their production efficiencies. Prospectors and entrepreneurs, the organizations most likely to pioneer new technologies, will do well in the emerging niche area, where speed of movement is critical for success. As a result, all four domain strategies can succeed in an evolving niche because there are conditions within different parts of the niche that favor each. Failures within the industry niche tend to be isolated. Entrepreneurs and prospectors that do not make the transition from the established to the emerging area of the niche are likely to fail because of the greater efficiencies of the defenders and analyzers. But failures in the evolving part of the industry niche are more likely to stem from internal management problems than environmental pressures.

FOCUS ON DESIGN 9.2

How Changes in One Industry's Niche Can Affect Others

Changes in one industry niche are often associated with changes in others. For example, the eruption in the fax market created a decline in certain other industry niches. Western Union reported a 50 percent decrease in its U.S. telex traffic between 1984 and 1987, largely due to fax and electronic mail. Overnight letter services, such as Federal Express, also expect to experience some erosion in demand because fax is cheaper and quicker than overnight mail.

The telecommunications industry niche, however, experienced growth rather than decline as a result of the eruption of the fax industry niche. MCI Communications, estimating that the fax transmission market will grow from $3 billion in 1988 to $9 billion in 1991, announced in 1988 that it would offer its business customers a special fiber optic transmission network to ensure better transmission quality and lower prices. And Nippon Telephone and Telegraph estimates that half its long distance traffic between Japan and the United States by 1988 was fax transmissions.

Such effects can clearly be seen in the industry examples throughout this chapter—evolution in the electronics industry leading to the creation of the personal computer industry and, later, growth in the personal computer industry resulting in the collapse of the home video game industry. The point to remember is that changes in the size or shape of one industry's niche often lead to changes in the size or shape of other industry niches.

Niche evolution characterizes the changes in the electronics industry niche as it moved from vacuum tubes to transistors, then to integrated circuits.[16] The first transistor was developed in 1947 at Bell Laboratories. The device did not have immediate commercial value, being considerably more expensive than vacuum tubes. Western Electric developed a production technology that considerably lowered unit costs in 1950–1951 and licensed it to other manufacturers. By 1954 there were 18 firms manufacturing transistors. Transistor technology advanced through the 1950s, increasing potential uses and expanding the market. Then, in 1960, Texas Instruments and Fairchild Semiconductor developed a production process for multi-layer integrated circuits that contained all the functions performed by multiple transistors on a single silicon chip. This development further changed the electronics industry niche's shape and led to rapid growth in the size and number of organizations producing semiconductors.

In 1971 Intel began selling microprocessors, which represented a further evolution of industry technology. The new technology's introduction further

Figure 9.6
Value of Shipments of Electronic Components,
1939–1978 (in Billions of Dollars)

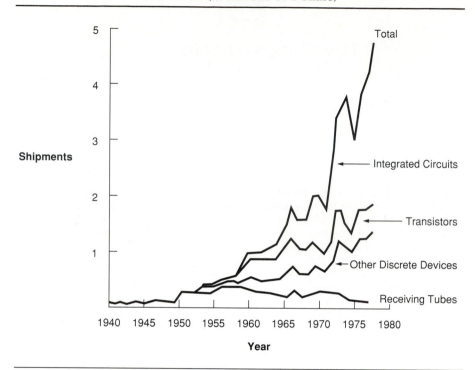

Source: Jack W. Brittain and John H. Freeman, "Organizational Proliferation and Density
Dependence," in *The Organizational Life Cycle*, ed. John R. Kimberly and Robert H. Miles (San
Francisco: Jossey-Bass, 1980), 300.

expanded potential applications and was followed by more new firms entering the industry. Subsequent developments have resulted in an almost
continuous stream of more powerful microprocessors with a greater range of
uses. The electronics industry niche has therefore continued to grow in size
and to expand in shape. As Figure 9.6 shows, each of the new technologies
had an additive effect on overall industry demand between 1940 and 1980.

Creation. The discontinuous emergence of a new industry niche is termed
niche creation. It often results from the development of a new technology,
good, or service that is qualitatively different from those preceding it, or that
arose in response to developments in other industry niches. In the first
instance, the legitimacy of the new niche must be established. Many innovations that could result in niche creation fail because the organizations introducing them are unable to establish a market. For example, consumer

electronic firms tried to introduce quadraphonic stereo players (four-channel sound) in the 1970s. After floundering for a few years, they withdrew the product because they were unable to establish a market. In contrast, some of these same firms were able to establish a market during the early 1980s for compact discs players, which are now making turntables obsolete.

In the second type of niche creation, developments in other industry niches create demand for a good or service that is not being produced. When this occurs, there will be a rush of entrants into the market because legitimacy is relatively easy to establish. In either case, once the legitimacy of the market is established, industry conditions are likely to move to niche expansion or niche eruption.

An example of the latter type of niche creation is the rapid development of a systems integration industry.[17] Systems integration involves developing software that coherently links a client organization's diverse computer systems together. The industry resulted from rapid growth in the computer hardware and software industries. As companies added more computers, they discovered that systems from different vendors couldn't communicate, creating operating problems and inefficiencies. Early on, large firms handled the development of systems integration software in-house. But developing systems integration software became more complex as the number of vendors increased. Moreover, as it became more common for smaller organizations to use systems from multiple vendors, it also became less costly to contract for systems software development than to do it in-house. The result was a growing need for organizations specializing in writing systems integration software.

The term *systems integration* was coined by IBM in 1985, when it signed a $300 million contract with United Airlines to develop software that would integrate its disparate reservations computers into a coherent system. By 1988 systems integration had become a $1.4 billion industry with over 20 competitors, among them IBM, Control Data, Unisys, Electronic Data Systems, AT&T, Boeing, and Arthur Andersen, who had already developed the capacity in-house and were in a position to market the service to other organizations. Analysts project annual growth of 26 percent through the early 1990s, which will lure other organizations into the industry.

Niche Conditions Favoring Industry Decline

Erosion. A continuous decrease in industry niche size is termed **niche erosion**. Under conditions of erosion, competition will increase as demand drops, with the most efficient producers—usually defenders—outcompeting other competitors on the basis of price,[18] and the least efficient producers will fail. Over the long term, defenders are likely to push analyzers out of mature industries, and existing entrepreneurs and prospectors will either fail or exit. Successful organizations find ways to become low-cost producers, or to expand their markets.

U.S. firearms manufacturers experienced erosion during the early 1980s.[19] Demand for U.S.-manufactured firearms peaked in 1981 and turned down because of a soft economy, a saturated market, and a strong dollar cutting into import sales. Between 1981 and 1984 the dollar value of guns sold in the United States dropped 35 percent. A price war followed the onset of the slump, with the most efficient producers gaining market share. Several manufacturers filed for bankruptcy or were liquidated as competitive pressures increased: U.S. Repeating Arms Co. (manufacturer of Winchester), Harrington and Richardson, Inc., and R.G. Industries.

Contraction. An environmental discontinuity that reduces the size of an industry niche is termed **niche contraction**. At the extreme, contraction means that demand for an industry's goods or services significantly decreases from one day to the next. There is a rapid increase in competition when an industry niche collapses, with the most efficient producers—defenders and analyzers—surviving and the less efficient—entrepreneurs and prospectors—failing or exiting the industry niche.

The oil industry niche contracted in 1985 as the average U.S. wellhead price dropped from about $25 per barrel to about $13 per barrel. A massive industrywide shakeout followed over the next two years. Hundreds of small, independent firms (entrepreneurs and prospectors) failed, with their assets being sold for as little as $.10 on the $1.00. And a wave of consolidations occurred among the larger industry firms, the defenders and analyzers. For example, Gulf Oil was purchased by Chevron, Superior by Mobil, Marathon Oil and Texas Oil and Gas by USX, and Getty by Texaco.

Dissolution. A continuous shift in niche shape that results in the gradual replacement of one set of performance opportunities by another is termed **niche dissolution**. Dissolution results in a gradual rise in competition in areas where performance opportunities are decreasing. Generally, dissolution favors the efficiencies of analyzers and defenders as competition increases in established performance areas, and prospectors and entrepreneurs move quickly to exploit new opportunities in emerging areas. There is likely to be a slow to moderate increase of failures among entrepreneurs and prospectors that do not move into the evolving portion of an industry niche, and then among analyzers and defenders as old performance opportunities continue to disappear.

The niche of the savings and loan industry has undergone dissolution from the late 1970s to the present.[20] The industry was created to finance home loans by pooling local investor deposits and making the funds available for home mortgages. After World War II, rapid shifts in the U.S. population caused an imbalance in local markets, and the mortgage banking industry arose. Mortgage banks originate mortgages for resale to investors and lenders in other regions where capital exceeds the demand for credit. The continued development of a national secondary mortgage market, the creation of new home financing vehicles, and the deregulation of financial markets acceler-ated the dissolution of the savings and loan niche in the late 1970s and 1980s. These changes fostered the development of a national market where mort-gage loans are pooled into securities and traded like government bonds. Also, the entry of new organizations into the home mortgage market was facili-tated. The result was increasing proportions of home mortgages being fi-nanced by insurance companies, pension funds, and other financial institutions, as well as by organizations such as Ford, Sears, Owens-Illinois, and General Motors. Between 1978 and 1988 the value of home mortgages in the savings and loan industry's portfolio decreased from 46 percent to 28 percent, and the industry's share of the home mortgage business dropped from 48 percent to 39 percent.

Until the mid 1980s, savings and loan failures were relatively rare be-cause of the Federal Savings and Loan Insurance Corporation (FSLIC), which insures deposits and props up failing savings and loans. But the number of savings and loans that have been liquidated or sold through the FSLIC has increased steadily through the 1980s. By 1988 nearly 1,000 of the approxi-mately 3,000 U.S. savings and loan associations were losing money, and half of those were insolvent. Furthermore, the federal government estimated that over $150 billion will be required to pay off depositors covered by FSLIC insurance. Potentially, the industry could collapse.

Collapse. A discontinuous shift in niche shape that changes the types of performance in which member organizations can engage is termed **niche collapse**. Often niche collapse is related to technological change, where one good or service replaces an existing good or service very quickly. When a niche collapses, competition will increase sharply among organizations oc-cupying the collapsing segment of the niche. Failures and exits are wide-spread, with the least efficient members of the industry, usually entrepreneurs and prospectors, failing or exiting quickly. If the collapse is severe, analyzers and defenders will follow them out.

The home video game industry experienced niche collapse at the end of 1982.[21] Through 1982, industry sales had grown rapidly to $3 billion, with 29 organizations in the industry. But then declining prices in the personal computer industry erased the cost difference between personal computers and home video game systems. This meant that people could buy a personal computer for games *and* other uses for about the same price as a home video game unit. The result was disastrous for the video game manufacturers, and just before Christmas 1982, video game sales evaporated. Stephen J. Ross—chairman and CEO of Atari's parent, Warner Communications—re-called, "We shipped $98 million (in game cartridges) the week before Thanks-giving . . . . And then a week and a half later—nothing." Retailers canceled Christmas orders, "as if someone had brought down an invisible shield."[22] The video game companies collectively lost over $1 billion in 1983, more than they had made in all the good years. Atari alone lost over $500 million.

Price competition was fierce during 1983. A few popular video cartridges sold at full price in 1983, but for every one that did, five were discounted 70 percent to 80 percent. Some sold for as little as $.99. Firms large and small began failing or exiting the industry niche, and within a year and a half most of the industry's firms had moved out: Warner Communications divested Atari (which then suspended its electronic games operations), Mattel and Milton Bradley closed their electronics divisions, and a number of others simply went bankrupt, such as Games by Apollo and Data Age. By mid 1984 the home video game industry was at a standstill, its market having been absorbed by the personal computer industry.

COMPLEX CHANGE AND INDUSTRY NICHES

Simultaneous Changes in Niche Size and Shape

So far we've painted a reasonably simple picture of how industry niches change over time. The picture becomes more complicated when you realize that changes in niche size and shape can occur simultaneously. For example, during the 1980s the size and shape of the college and university niche underwent both types of changes as the number of 18 to 21 year olds decreased (erosion), and student interests in fields of study continued to move toward the professions and applied sciences (dissolution). We'll show in the next chapter that the complex nature of environmental change is one reason why managers perceive it in varying ways and thus select different strategic responses.

It is also important to understand that industries have environmental histories. Most industries more than a few years old have passed through a variety of environmental conditions. New industries usually follow the pattern described by the logistic model (Figure 9.2), beginning with a period of niche creation (area a). After an industry establishes its legitimacy, its niche goes through an expansion or eruption phase (area b), which is then followed by a period of maturity and an industry shake-out (niche erosion or contraction), often triggered by an environmental event such as an economic downturn. As a niche moves through different conditions, there are shifts in the observed mix of domain strategies. Entrepreneurs and prospectors dominate during niche creation; they are joined by analyzers and defenders during the niche expansion or eruption phase, who then force many entrepreneurs and prospectors out when demand growth slows or declines.

Once an industry moves through these early, somewhat predictable, developmental stages, the types of niche changes that occur tend to be unpredictable and complex. We show in the following chapter that an industry's history of niche changes can have a major impact on its member organizations' ability to adapt to subsequent environmental changes. The mix of domain strategies present at the onset of new environmental conditions has much to do with the subsequent success or failure of an industry's organizations, and that mix is largely determined by earlier niche conditions.

For example, defenders do well when the size of an industry's niche contracts, because they focus on efficient operations. Entrepreneurs and prospectors, on the other hand, are more likely to fail under contraction, because their innovation focus makes them relatively inefficient. If an industry niche enters a period of expansion after a prolonged contraction, surviving defenders and analyzers will likely prosper because they already are efficiently doing what is in demand. But if dissolution follows contraction, surviving defenders may have a hard time adapting. Their efficiency-driven strategy makes it difficult for them to innovate and track changes in niche shape. Prospectors and entrepreneurs, on the other hand, are relatively adept at tracking changes in niche shape, but likely will have been eliminated during the previous period of contraction. In short, domain strategies that enhance an organization's ability to survive one set of niche conditions may work against it at a later time if there are substantive changes in those conditions.

The Evolution of the Auto Industry Niche[23]

The changes that occurred in the size and shape of the auto industry's niche over time provides a clear illustration of the complexity of environmental change. (Figure 9.7 graphically presents these changes.) The auto industry traces its beginnings to the 1890s with the development of the "self-propelled carriage." Niche creation best describes the conditions that existed during the industry's first 10 years, where growing numbers of small entrepreneurial organizations attempted to establish the niche's legitimacy (Figure 9.2, area a). As consumers began accepting and buying "horseless carriages," "run-abouts," and "buggies," the niche erupted. In 1900, 58 manufacturers produced 4,192 automotive vehicles. By 1910, about 250 manufacturers were producing more than 180,000 vehicles.

As often happens during niche eruption (Figure 9.2, area b), analyzers and defenders entered the industry, changing the nature of competition from innovation to efficiency. One of the first analyzers was General Motors, which William C. Durant founded between 1908 and 1910 by acquiring about 25 small automotive manufacturers. One of Durant's motives in forming GM was to build an auto company whose broad product line had something to offer to all the segments of the automotive market. The collection of small companies that eventually resulted in Chrysler Corporation—another analyzer—began during this period as well.

Ford Motor Company—the industry's preeminent defender—also was founded during this period. Ford's strategy, in contrast to GM, was to produce an inexpensive car available to the masses—the Model T. In 1913 Ford introduced the assembly-line method, which expanded its production capacity and lowered vehicle prices. Ford produced 78,611 Model T cars in

Figure 9.7

Changes in the Auto Industry Niche's Size and Shape Over Time

	1890s	1900s	1910s	1920s	1930s	1940s	1950s	1960s	1970s	1980s	1990s
Niche Size		Eruption		Expansion					Cont.	Cont.	Exp.
Niche Shape	Creation	Evolution						Dis.	Coll.	Coll.	Dis.
									Exp.	Exp.	
									Dis.		

Coll. = Collapse
Cont. = Contraction
Dis. = Dissolution
Exp. = Expansion

1912, the last year it solely used traditional production methods. Introduction of the assembly-line method rapidly increased production to 260,720 Model T cars in 1914, and more efficient production enabled Ford to lower the Model T's price from $850 when it was introduced in 1908 to $350 in 1916. Falling prices and the establishment of national dealer networks by GM, Ford, and a few other automakers fueled demand growth. By 1920 over 1.9 million vehicles were being sold annually.

Demand growth slowed during the 1920s as the automotive market matured, ending the period of niche eruption (Figure 9.2, area c). A recession in 1920–1921 (niche contraction) led to an industry shakeout, resulting in the failure of many of the industry's entrepreneurs and prospectors. The emergence of a used car industry further reduced market opportunities for these organizations. By the end of the 1920s, there were fewer than 25 manufacturers, with the 7 largest producers accounting for 90 percent of industry sales.

From the 1930s to the 1970s, niche expansion and niche evolution best characterize the auto industry environment. There were minor perturbations in niche size—an occasional recession leading to short-lived contractions in demand—but long-term demand growth was the rule rather than the exception. Evolution in the niche's shape was caused largely by the automakers own actions as they introduced technological innovations, such as the automatic transmission, power steering, and power brakes. As the dynamics of competition gradually played out during this period, most of the remaining small producers were acquired or went out of business, and the Big Three automakers (GM, Ford, and Chrysler—all of whom pursued an analyzer strategy after World War II) shared about 90 percent of industry sales.

Beginning in the mid 1960s, the shape of the auto industry niche began undergoing a period of dissolution because of government regulation. The industry had been virtually unregulated during the first six decades of its existence, a situation that changed with the rise of social activism in the United States during the 1960s. The first federal safety and environmental regulations were enacted in 1966. By 1973, 44 federal safety standards applied to one or more classifications of automotive vehicles. And by 1975, emission standards called for 90 percent reductions over unregulated levels of hydrocarbon, carbon monoxide, and nitrous oxide emissions. Both sets of regulations placed constraints on automotive design. On the whole, niche conditions remained fairly stable from the 1930s through the 1960s with a gradual expansion of demand in the U.S. market, and a gradual evolution of niche shape caused by technological innovation and, after 1966, by government regulation.

The benign niche conditions of the 1950s and 1960s changed for the worse in October 1973 with the onset of the OPEC oil embargo. Rapidly rising gasoline prices, consumer fears about its continued availability, and the onset of a recession contributed to both a contraction of auto industry's niche size and a discontinuous shift in niche shape. Demand fell from a peak of 11.35 million vehicles in 1973 to 8.7 million vehicles in 1974. Consumers began buying small cars, shunning the large vehicles that were the mainstay of the Big Three's production.

Most of the small cars sold were imports. Imports had been around for many years but the Big Three never took them seriously. Now they gained market share rapidly. The Big Three tried to shift production to smaller vehicles, but their plants were tooled to produce large cars and they had few vehicle designs that appealed to consumers. The government also added new regulations in 1974 mandating substantial improvements in fuel economy. Then, as the economy pulled out of the recession and gas prices stabilized in 1976, the shape of the industry niche again shifted as consumers flocked back to large cars, leaving the Big Three with huge inventories of small vehicles.

Through the late 1970s, the automakers faced a cross-cutting set of demands. Government regulation required automakers to build safe, low-emission, high-mileage automobiles, which the automakers saw as a contradiction in terms. They had met earlier safety and emissions standards by increasing vehicle weight and detuning engines, which reduced fuel economy. The fuel economy regulations meant that this strategy for meeting government regulations was no longer viable. The result: U.S. automakers had to rethink and reengineer automotive transportation, and this required huge investments in research and development, engineering, and facility retooling. At the same time, the import's market share continued increasing—from 11.2 percent in 1969 to 22.6 percent in 1979—exerting severe competitive pressures on the U.S. manufacturers, which reduced their ability to finance the needed product changes. Moreover, the industry began undergoing rapid globalization as consumer preferences worldwide converged. The shape of this industry niche was rapidly moving away from what it had been in the past. And while its size increased during the late 1970s, it remained below its high of 1973.

Disaster struck again in 1979. Ayatolla Khomeni's Iranian revolution early in the year pushed gas prices up, and the seizure of hostages at the U.S. embassy in Tehran that November increased uncertainty about the future supply of oil. Coupled with the onset of a worldwide recession, auto sales rapidly contracted. To make matters worse, those consumers still in the market were buying small imports. By April 1980, imports accounted for over 40 percent of U.S. sales. By mid-year, almost a quarter-million U.S. auto employees had been laid off, and domestic vehicle sales were at their lowest point in 20 years. The Big Three collectively lost over $4 billion during 1980. Chrysler's $1.7 billion loss was the largest in U.S. history, and it was kept afloat only by federal loan guarantees. Ford posted a $1.5 billion loss, the largest in its history. GM reported a $763 million loss, its first in 59 years.

As the worldwide recession ended, demand increased, and the slimmed down Big Three earned record profits. Then Japanese manufacturers, operating under "voluntary" import restrictions, changed their tactics. To get the most out of limited sales, they began importing higher-priced, higher-margin luxury compacts into the U.S. market, a market segment they had not entered before. They also began locating plants in North America (ten were in operation by 1989). By the late 1980s competition in the U.S. market had intensified. The Big Three struggled to reengineer their products, retool their plants, and redesign themselves into global manufacturers.

As the industry entered the 1990s, buying preferences had begun to stabilize, with consumers worldwide demanding high-quality, fuel-efficient automobiles. On the other hand, automotive design and materials technologies were evolving rapidly as global manufacturers attempted to meet these preferences. Production technologies also were undergoing significant changes as the automakers attempted to lower costs and build better quality vehicles. In short, the 1990s promises to be a decade of intense global competition in a niche characterized by rapidly evolving technology. Where the Big Three had controlled their environment during the 1950s and 1960s, they now have to respond to rapidly evolving conditions in the global marketplace over which they have little control.

SUMMARY

Learning Objective 1: Define the concept of an industry niche. An industry niche is bounded by resource opportunities and constraints that form a resource space within which member organizations can operate and survive. Many different factors define a resource space, such as consumer demand, technological development, and government policy.

Learning Objective 2: Distinguish between niche size and niche shape. Niche shape refers to the *range or types* of activities that a niche's resources will support. A variety of factors shape niches, such as consumer preferences, technological development, and government regulations and policies, by determining what is possible and what is not. Niche size refers to the *level or amount* of performance a niche will support. A niche's size is determined by several factors, including consumer demand, availability of raw materials, and economic conditions. The difference between niche shape and niche size is that niche shape defines *what* organizations can do while niche size defines *how much* can be done.

Learning Objective 3: Distinguish between continuous and discontinuous environmental change. Continuous changes occur gradually so that industry niche conditions are not noticeably different over relatively short periods of time. They are often linked to long-term trends, such as changing population demographics. At the other extreme are environmental discontinuities that can significantly change niche conditions from one day to the next. Many discontinuities are caused by events and government regulation. Continuous and discontinuous change are really the polar ends of a continuum. Most environmental changes fall somewhere in between.

Learning Objective 4: Identify different types of changes in niche conditions that are conducive to industry growth and industry decline. Four niche conditions described in this chapter are conducive to industry growth: expansion, eruption, evolution, and creation. Four other identified niche conditions are conducive to industry decline: erosion, contraction, dissolution, and collapse.

Learning Objective 5: Identify different types of changes in niche conditions that affect the success and failure of different domain strategies. Changes in niche conditions affect the density (the extent to which the industry niche is filled) of organizations within the industry niche. Low density favors quick movement to exploit resource opportunities; high density favors efficient use of available resources. Thus, changes that decrease density favor the success of entrepreneurs and prospectors, who pursue domain strategies based on innovation and quick movement to exploit new opportunities. Changes that increase density favor defenders and analyzers, whose domain strategies focus on the efficient use of resources.

Learning Objective 6: Explain why the concept of environmental change is so complex. Environmental change can be very unpredictable. Industries can experience simultaneous changes in both niche shape and size, which can impose different, and sometimes conflicting, requirements for survival. Moreover, industries can experience a wide variety of environmental conditions over time, favoring different types of domain strategies.

Discussion Questions

1. Using a current issue of a business periodical such as *Business Week, Fortune,* or *Forbes,* find examples of the types of changes in industry niche size and shape depicted in Figure 9.1.

2. What types of factors define the niche size and shape of the aerospace industry, the consumer electronics industry, and hospital industry? To what extent are these factors similar or dissimilar across industry niches?

3. You are the vice president of a ten-year-old entrepreneurial company that designs and manufactures video games. The company was profitable until the last two years, when its sales dropped after a number of small competitors were acquired by large toy manufacturing companies. How would you explain to the president why your firm is in trouble and what strategic options are open.

4. Explain the difference between continuous and discontinuous changes in the shape or size of an industry niche. Under what circumstances can a continuous change have a discontinuous effect on an industry niche?

5. The development of the personal computer industry niche has had an impact on the niches of other industries. How do you think it has affected the niches of the mainframe computer, automobile, and the health-care industries?

6. Increasing concern about overflowing landfills, toxic waste, the greenhouse effect, deterioration of the ozone layer, and so forth, is likely to result in a resurgence of environmentalism during the 1990s. What impact do you think the environmental movement will have on the niche size and shape of the coal, automobile, and fast food industries over the next ten years?

DESIGN AUDIT #9

Analyzing Your Organization's Industry Environment

This design audit will help you gain a better understanding of your organization's industry environment. You will examine the structure of your organization's industry niche, changes occurring in the industry niche, and your organization's position with respect to those of its competitors.

Changes in the Industry Niche

1. In the space below, briefly describe major changes that have taken place in your industry's niche over the past 20 years (less if the industry hasn't been around 20 years). Then draw a time line like the one in Figure 9.7, identifying changes that have occurred in the niche's size and shape over time. Use separate sheets of paper as needed.

2. Write the three major environmental issues you identified in Question 4 of Design Audit #8 in the appropriate spaces below. Then identify the current and potential effects of these changing environmental conditions on the size and/or shape of the industry niche.

Issue #1: _____

Current and potential effects on the industry niche's size and/or shape:

Issue #2: _____

Current and potential effects on the industry niche's size and/or shape:

Issue #3: _____

Current and potential effects on the industry niche's size and/or shape:

Effects of Change on Industry's Organizations

3. List your organization and its major competitors in the spaces below. Using the descriptions on the following page, identify which best describes each listed organization by placing the corresponding letter in the first column (STR).

   In the three columns under (DMD), indicate whether these changes are likely to increase (I), decrease (D), or have no effect (0) on the demand for each organization's goods or services. You can use one column for each issue if the issues you've identified have different effects on demand, or use one column if all three issues have the same effect.

   Tables 9.4 and 9.5 indicate how different niche changes affect organizational domain strategies. In the third column (FIT), assess how well these organizations' current strategies position them to deal with the niche changes you have identified, using the following codes: (F) = projected environmental changes favor this strategy, (0) = unclear whether this organization has a strategic advantage or disadvantage given projected environmental changes, or (P) = strategy is likely to cause problems given the projected changes. For example, assume that the industry niche is undergoing dissolution. One of the organizations is a defender in the shrinking part of the industry niche and does not have a reputation for innovativeness. Demand for its products is declining and you don't think that it can redevelop its product line to move with the changes in demand. In this instance you would record a P in the FIT column.

Organization Name	STR	DMD			FIT
		(#1	#2	#3)	
1. _____ (Your organization)	____	____	____	____	____
2. _____	____	____	____	____	____
3. _____	____	____	____	____	____
4. _____	____	____	____	____	____
5. _____	____	____	____	____	____
6. _____	____	____	____	____	____
7. _____	____	____	____	____	____
8. _____	____	____	____	____	____
9. _____	____	____	____	____	____

Domain Strategy Profiles

Defender (D) This organization attempts to locate and maintain a secure niche in a relatively stable product area. The organization tends to offer a more limited range of products than its competitors, and it tries to protect its domain by offering higher quality, superior service, lower prices, and so forth. Often this type of organization is not at the forefront of developments in the industry—it tends to ignore industry changes that have no direct influence on current areas of operation and concentrates instead on doing the best job possible in a limited area.

Prospector (P) This organization typically operates within a broad product-market domain that undergoes periodic redefinition. The organization values being "first in" in new product and market areas even if not all these efforts prove to be highly profitable. The organization responds rapidly to early signals concerning areas of opportunities, and these responses often lead to a new round of competitive actions. However, this type of organization may not maintain market strength in all of the areas it enters.

Analyzer (A) This organization attempts to maintain a stable, limited line of products, while at the same time moving out to quickly follow a carefully selected set of the more promising new developments in the industry. The organization is seldom "first in" with new products or services. However, by carefully monitoring the actions of major competitors in areas compatible with its stable product-market base, it can frequently be "second-in" with a more cost-efficient product or service.

Entrepreneur (E) This organization offers a limited range of products, often only a single line. It typically is owner-managed, and it reflects the interests, abilities, and limitations of the owner-manager. The organization moves quickly to take advantage of new opportunities within its limited domain of operation, and it is constrained only by owner-manager's adeptness and energy.

Prognosis

4. If the projected environmental changes occur, what is your prognosis for your organization over the next five years if it continues to pursue its current strategy?

Notes

1. Howard E. Aldrich and Jeffrey Pfeffer, "Environments of Organizations," *Annual Review of Sociology* 2 (1976): 79–105; W. Graham Astley and Charles J. Fombrun, "Collective Strategy: The Social Ecology of Organization Theory," *Academy of Management Review* 8 (1983): 576–587; W. Graham Astley and Andrew H. Van de Ven, "Central Perspectives and Debates in Organization Theory," *Administrative Science Quarterly* 28 (1983): 245–273; Lawrence J. Bourgeois, "Strategic Management and Determinism," *Academy of Management Review* 9 (1984): 586–596; Michael T. Hannan and John Freeman, "The Population Ecology of Organizations," *American Journal of Sociology* 82 (1977): 929–964; Raymond E. Miles and Charles C. Snow, *Organizational Strategy, Structure, and Process* (New York: McGraw-Hill, 1978); Jeffrey Pfeffer and Gerald R. Salancik, *The External Control of Organizations* (New York: Harper & Row, 1978).

2. Arthur G. Bedeian, "An Interactionist Perspective on Organizational Adaptation," *Leadership and Organizational Development Journal* 8(3) (1987): 31–32; Lawrence G. Hrebiniak and William F. Joyce, "Organizational Adaptation: Strategic Choice and Environmental Determinism," *Administrative Science Quarterly* 30 (1985): 336–349; Masoud Yasai-Ardekani, "Structural Adaptations to Environments," *Academy of Management Review* 11 (1986): 9–21; Anna Grandori, *Perspectives on Organization Theory* (Cambridge, Mass.: Ballinger, 1987); Raymond F. Zammuto, "Organizational Adaptation: Some Implications of Organizational Ecology for Strategic Choice," *Journal of Management Studies* 25 (1988): 105–120.

3. The model of environmental change and organizational adaptation presented in this chapter and the next draws heavily from Raymond F. Zammuto and Kim S. Cameron, "Environmental Decline and Organizational Response," *Research in Organizational Behavior* 5 (1985): 223–262; and Zammuto, "Organizational Adaptation."

Readers should note that the model is focused at the level of individual organizations within single or related industries. As an organization's goods and services become less similar, portfolio models from the strategic management field may provide a better overall model of organization-environment relations. But even in this situation, the model presented here is applicable to individual strategic business units.

4. Michael Porter's concept of generic strategies [*Competitive Strategy* (New York: Free Press, 1980)] and its derivatives also could be examined in this context. Miles and Snow's work was selected over that of Porter because it is more clearly linked to the strategic choice perspective (see Miles and Snow, *Organizational Strategy, Structure, and Process,* Chapter 1, for a description of the model's lineage). Porter's work is based on industrial economics.

While Porter's model is rooted in a different tradition, it also has a number of similarities with the ecological classification system of Brittain and Freeman. For example, Porter's focused and differentiated strategies represent two aspects of specialism, and his low-cost strategy is clearly analogous to the *K*-strategy from the ecological model.

5. Miles and Snow discussed the entreprenuer in *Organizational Strategy, Structure, and Process,* (pp. 118–119) but did not include it in their classification of strategic types. The addition of the entrepreneurial strategy, however, logically completes their typology and does no violence to the underlying concepts of their model.

6. Bioecologists do not have this problem because an organism's form is genetically determined and fixed; once a duck, always a duck. Thus, population

membership is genetically fixed. Organizations, on the other hand, can change form over time. If form is defined as goals, technologies, structures, strategies, and markets, then organizations can change form by modifying their goals, technologies, structures, strategies, and markets. Numerous examples in Chapters 2 through 7 make it clear that they do, even with the difficulties described by the population ecologists and in Chapter 12.

Some might argue that biological organisms also change form as they grow. But biological organisms follow a genetically predetermined developmental sequence. Organizations change form, but not in a predetermined developmental sequence (a topic discussed in more detail in Chapter 11). Consider the case of a small start-up firm. If it is successful during its first few years, a variety of different developmental paths are possible:

1.   Remaining a small entrepreneurial organization by choosing not to grow larger.

2.   Developing into a functionally organized defender by emphasizing efficient operations, and perhaps later transforming itself into an analyzer, either through the development of new products or through acquisition.

3.   Becoming a prospector by retaining its strategic orientation of moving quickly to enter emerging product-market areas.

While we disagree with population ecologists over these points and have doubts about the utility of the population concept as currently formulated, our observations about the relationships between different organizational forms and environmental change are the same as theirs. In other words, their observations about the dynamics of change and the effects of environmental selection on different organizational forms (such as the effects of density dependence on r- and K-strategists) are not bound to the concept of populations. Thus, the emphasis in this chapter is on change and adaptation in organizational forms instead of the rise and fall of organizational populations.

7. Consistent with the bioecology literature, population ecologists define a niche's *carrying capacity* as the number of organizations a niche will support at equilibrium. We use the term *niche size* to refer to the amount of goods and services that can be produced and sold. As such, it is as an analog to carrying capacity. The reason for this change in definition is that the size of organizations within a population can vary considerably. More often than not, the distribution of organizations by size is skewed, with many more small organizations than large ones. Studies of organizational size often use a logarithmic transformation to control for skewedness. This is unlike biological populations, where organism size is normally distributed around a population mean, and each organism can be considered a "unit" in terms of resource usage. Hence, a count of organization does not have ratio properties as does a count of organisms.

As a result, the number of organizations is not a good measure of carrying capacity because models, such as the Verhulst-Pearl logistic equation, require ratio-level data. On the other hand, counts or estimates of goods and services do have the properties of a ratio scale. Therefore, the change in definition makes explicit the fact that population properties, such as population size and the bases of competition, can be inferred only indirectly when using tools derived from bioecology.

8. We use the bell-shaped representation of a niche in a fairly loose, heuristic manner. Actual graphic representations of an industry niche would be more complex

with all sorts of bumps and curves that reflect variations in niche size according to the dimensions used to define niche shape. As such, we are simply trying to convey the *idea* of changes in niche shape and size through these diagrams. The bell-shaped form used to represent a niche in Figure 9.1 is borrowed from bioecology, where the peak represents optimal resource conditions for a population. Movement away from the optimal results in a smaller carrying capacity.

9. In the most general sense, changes in niche shape mean both the location of the feasible performance area (the industry niche) within the potential resource space, and changes in the actual shape of the feasible performance area itself. Keep in mind that we use the bell-shaped volume only as a heuristic, and actual plots of an industry's niche would be odd-shaped volumes.

10. Zammuto and Cameron, "Environmental Decline and Organizational Response," 239–240; Kathryn Rudie Harrigan, *Strategies for Declining Businesses* (Lexington Mass.: Lexington Books, 1980), 139–184.

11. Jacques Delacroix and Glenn R. Carroll, "Organizational Foundings: An Ecological Study of the Newspaper Industries of Argentina and Ireland," *Administrative Science Quarterly* 28 (1983): 274–291.

12. Michael E. Porter, *Competitive Strategy: Techniques for Analyzing Industries and Competitors* (New York: Free Press, 1980), 169.

13. Zammuto and Cameron, "Environmental Decline and Organizational Response," 243.

14. "Labor Letter," *The Wall Street Journal,* December 4, 1986, 1; Gretchen Morgenson, "Where Big Profits Will Be Made Next," *Money,* November 1985, 142; Joani Nelson-Horchler, "Benefit of the Future," *Industry Week,* April 20, 1987, 18–19; Roger Neugebauer, "How's Business? Status Report #4 on For Profit Child Care," *Exchange,* January 1988, 29–34; John P. Fernandez, *Child Care and Corporate Productivity* (Lexington, Mass.: Lexington Books,1986), 19–21.

15. "It's a Fax, Fax, Fax, Fax, World," *Business Week,* March 21, 1988, 136; "Fax Sweeps the World with Corporate Memos," *Denver Post,* April 24, 1988, 1G; "Fax Fever," *Boulder Daily Camera,* November 8, 1988, 10D–11D.

16. Information for this example was adapted from Jack W. Brittain and John H. Freeman, "Organizational Proliferation and Density Dependence Selection," in *The Organizational Life Cycle,* ed. John R. Kimberly and Robert H. Miles (San Francisco: Jossey-Bass, 1980), 291–341.

17. "A Market Is Born Out of Computer Confusion," *Business Week,* April 25, 1988, 124–125.

18. This assumes that other things—such as age and quality of equipment, financial strength, and so on—are equal.

19. Johnnie L. Roberts, "Gun Makers Forced to Be More Aggressive in Face of Falling Sales, Shrinking Market," *The Wall Street Journal,* June 27, 1983, 27; "USRAC: Shooting Beyond the Gun That Won the West," *Business Week,* February 27, 1984, 65, 69; "U.S. Gunmakers: The Casualties Pile Up," *Business Week,* May 19, 1986, 76, 78.

20. "The S&L Mess—And How To Fix It," *Business Week,* October 31, 1988, 130–136; Robert Ebisch, "Poor Housing Market Hurts Mortgage Lenders," *Boulder Daily Camera,* September 13, 1988, D1, D10-11; "It's the Morning After for Mortgage Bankers," *Business Week,* August 8, 1988, 66

21. James E. Braham, "Computers Haunt Videogame Makers," *Industry Week,* May 16, 1983, 53–54; Laura Landro, "How Headlines of 1982 Lead to 1983's Doldrums for Warner and Atari," *The Wall Street Journal,* July 25, 1983, 1; Laura Landro, "Video-Game Firms Face Tough Christmas as Industry Approaches a Major Shakeout," *The Wall Street Journal,* September 23, 1983, 33; "A Holiday Massacre in Video Games," *Fortune,* December 26, 1983, 100; Stephen J. Sansweet, "Mattel Will Concentrate on Making Toys After Decision to Leave Two Other Lines," *The Wall Street Journal,* February 6, 1984, 18; Dennis Kneale, "Atari's Jack Tramiel Begins Big Effort to Cut Costs 3 Days After Acquiring Firm," *The Wall Street Journal,* July 6, 1984, 6; William M. Bulkeley, "Earnings for Three Toy Makers Reflect Appeal of Tradition, Slide of Electronics," *The Wall Street Journal,* July 20, 1984, 29

22. Landro, "How Headlines of 1982 Lead to 1983's Doldrums," 1.

23. Material for this example was drawn from Paul R. Lawrence and Davis Dyer, *Renewing American Industry* (New York: Free Press, 1983), 17–33; Raymond F. Zammuto, *Assessing Organizational Effectiveness: Systems Change, Adaptation, and Strategy* (Albany, N.Y.: SUNY Press, 1982), 107–145.

Organizational Adaptation and Design

Learning Objectives

Upon completing this chapter you should be able to

1. Describe the organization designs that are consistent with the entrepreneur, prospector, analyzer, and defender domain strategies.

2. Identify the domain tactics that fit the different conditions of niche change.

3. Explain how different individual and organizational factors influence managers' perceptions and interpretations of environmental change.

4. Describe the effects that a change in an organization's structure, strategy, or environment can have on one another.

NEW USES FOR "PIGS"

Williams Cos. has always been interested in getting from here to there. It started out building sidewalks, then pipelines. Then a bunch of "pigs" with rope on their tails marched through 1,000 miles of unused Williams pipe, and now the pipes are transmitting messages from here to there.

Pipeline "pigs" are plastic balls just a bit smaller than a pipe's diameter. They are pushed along, squeezing out remnants of crude oil, gasoline, or liquid fertilizer— whatever it was that last oozed through the pipe. The pigs that Williams turned loose pulled behind them sheaths of fiber optic cable. Thus, pipes that once moved crude oil at three miles an hour now carry dots of information at the speed of light, and help Williams use its existing resources to lessen the damages of an oil industry downturn.

Suddenly Williams is in the high-tech telecommunications business, competing with AT&T, MCI, and US Sprint, and facing a test that confronts many companies trying to break out of hard-hat industries: It must make the transition from tangibles to intangibles, from delivering products to selling services. Williams markets its cable-in-the-pipeline trick heavily because a broken fiber optic line, carrying far more data than a regular phone line does, is a big disaster. The industry giants nevertheless have been chipping away at Williams, and as industry capacity increases, prices are falling.

The creativity used by Williams is one way of adapting to industry changes. Chapter 10 discusses other ways as well and outlines how industry evolution occurs, including how organizations creatively responded to industry changes.

Source: Caleb Solomon, "How Williams Cos. Turned Oil Pipelines to Conduits of Data," *The Wall Street Journal*, July 11, 1989, 1.

THE last chapter approached the topic of environmental change by focusing on industries. It described how industry niches change over time, and how different niche conditions affect the relative success or failure of different organizational strategies. This chapter examines the implications of environmental change from the perspective of individual organizations. First, we look at the relationship between strategy and structure, and discuss the organization designs that "fit" the entrepreneur, prospector, defender, and analyzer domain strategies. We also examine how organizations both create and respond to environmental change by modifying their domains of operation. Then we consider the resulting implications for an organization's design. Next, we address the issue of why organizations within the same industry choose different strategies for responding to changes in an industry niche. To answer this question, we look at how individual and organizational factors affect managers' perceptions and interpretations of environmental change. The chapter closes with a discussion of how the integrative model of organization–environment relations presented in this and the last chapter differs from the strategic choice, population ecology, and contingency theories.

STRATEGY AND STRUCTURE

As we noted in Chapter 7, research findings indicate that certain organization designs appear better suited for some strategies and environmental conditions than others. These findings also indicate that organizations with a good "fit" between strategy and structure perform better. Table 10.1 displays the strategy-structure "fits" for the entrepreneur, prospector, defender, and analyzer domain strategies.

Entrepreneurs

Entrepreneurs take advantage of environmental opportunities by moving quickly within a limited domain of operation. They tend to be small organizations, often start-ups, and have simple, undifferentiated to functionally based designs. Their relatively small size allows for coordination and control through the direct supervision of an owner/manager. As a result, they tend to be highly centralized, use few integrating mechanisms, and have a low degree of horizontal specialization.

Such designs enable an entrepreneurial organization to move quickly. The owner/manager can perceive and act on opportunities without delay. For this reason, entrepreneurs are often a source of environmental change, creating conditions to which other organizations must respond. Often they perceive opportunities not evident to others. Pursuing such opportunities often opens new niches (*niche creation*), as in the case of Apple Computer and the personal computer industry niche, or results in the evolution, dissolution, or collapse of an existing niche (*niche evolution,* as in the case of Cray Computer and the supercomputer). At the same time, entrepreneurs are vulnerable to decreasing niche size because defenders and analyzers operate more efficiently. And, because of their narrow domain of operation, entrepreneurs are vulnerable to changes in niche shape if they do not accurately perceive changes occurring.

Prospectors

Prospectors move quickly to create and exploit opportunities over a broad domain of operation. They use decentralized market-based designs, integrating mechanisms, and low job specialization to support this strategy. Divisionalization enables market-based units to focus their attention on specific markets. The containment of workflow interdependencies within divisions allows prospectors to create new divisions to explore new and

Table 10.1
The "Fit" between Strategy and Structure

	Domain Strategy			
	Entrepreneur	Prospector	Defender	Analyzer
Strategic Emphases				
Efficiency	Moderate	Low	High	Moderate
Speed of Resp.	High	High	Low	Moderate
Breadth of Domain	Narrow	Wide	Narrow	Wide
Strategic Predisposition	Domain Creation	Domain Creation	Domain Defense	Domain Offense
Most Vulnerable to Changes in	Niche Size and Shape	Niche Size	Niche Shape	Niche Shape
Design Characteristics				
Unit Grouping	Undifferentiated to Functional	Market-Based	Functional	Market-Based
Centralization	High	Low	High	Medium
Uses of Integrating Mechanisms	Low	High	Low	Medium
Job Specialization	Low	Low	High	High in established Areas Low in New Areas
Organization Size	Small	Medium to Large	Medium	Medium to Large

discontinue old opportunities with relative ease. As a result, prospectors have relatively fluid structures that are constantly being reorganized.

Like entrepreneurs, prospectors are creators of environmental change. Research and development that results in new goods or services, or the application of existing goods and services to new markets or customers, affect niche shape by redefining what is possible. But prospectors are vulnerable to decreasing niche size because of their relative inefficiency, and they often must abandon domains as more efficient analyzers and defenders enter an industry and increase competition.

Analyzers

Analyzers operate in a broad domain within or across industry niches and rely on a moderate to high degree of efficiency to compete. They have moderately decentralized market-based structures. Job specialization tends to be high in units operating in established product/market areas, and moderate to low in units operating in emerging areas. Analyzers play *follow-the-leader,* entering industry niches and market segments after they have been established by entrepreneurs and prospectors. As the market for a new division stabilizes, analyzers focus on increasing operational efficiency. Thus, there is movement toward a functional structure within divisions as markets mature.

Analyzers create order within an industry, taking the innovations pioneered by entrepreneurs and prospectors and increasing their marketability and ease of production.[1] Their greater efficiencies change an industry's basis of competition by lowering prices and setting industry standards, often leading to an expansion or eruption of niche size (the entry of IBM into the personal computer industry was an example). Over time, an analyzer's greater operating efficiency often forces out less efficient entrepreneurs and prospectors. Conversely, an analyzer's functionally designed divisions are vulnerable to changes in niche shape because of their emphasis on efficiency. Entrepreneurs and prospectors often attempt to counter the entry of analyzers by innovating and thus changing the shape of an industry's niche.

Defenders

Defenders operate in a narrow domain, and their operations are characterized by a high degree of efficiency. They usually are small to medium-size organizations employing a functional structure. Decision-making authority tends to be centralized and jobs specialized. Rules, policies, and procedures are the major forms of coordination and control. The appearance of defenders often is a sign of approaching industry maturity. They drive out entrepreneurs and prospectors by further lowering costs, facilitating mass consumption of a good or service.[2] Because of their narrow domain and slow movement, they are vulnerable to changes in niche shape. But they do well when niche size decreases because of their efficient operations.

ORGANIZATIONAL RESPONSES TO CHANGES IN INDUSTRY NICHES

While the foregoing descriptions characterize the fit between structure and strategy, they do not address the issue of how organizations contend with changing environmental conditions. This is done by modifying their domains of operation. In Chapter 8 (Table 8.6), we briefly reviewed three tactics for modifying organizational domains: domain defense, domain offense, and domain creation. Table 10.2 shows an expanded classification of domain tactics, which extends these general concepts to a broader range of environmental conditions. Two tactics have been added—domain continuity and domain abandonment—and the domain-offense and domain-creation tactics

Table 10.2
An Expanded Typology of Domain Tactics

Domain Continuity	Maintaining an existing organizational domain while focusing on operational issues within it.
Domain Defense	Building and preserving the legitimacy of an organizational domain.
Domain Offense	Expansion into new products/markets/customers adjacent to those in a current organizational domain.
Domain Consolidation	Consolidation of an existing domain to an organization's areas of core expertise.
Domain Creation	Development of new performance opportunities through the creation of new operational domains, usually through research and development or by acquisition.
Domain Substitution	Substitution of one operational domain for another through research and development, acquisition, or other interorganizational arrangements.
Domain Abandonment	Exiting an industry niche, usually through divestiture or by closing a division's operations.

have been refined. Figure 10.1 shows the domain tactics and operational emphases that are commonly used to respond to different changes in niche size and shape (although these are not the only tactics used). In the following sections, we explain each of these responses.

Domain Continuity

Domain continuity refers to maintaining an organization's current domain. This is often the most appropriate domain tactic when niche size is increasing and niche shape is stable. The primary concerns of organizations in this situation are operational—how to increase production capacity and reap the benefits of increasing demand. When an increase in niche size is continuous (niche expansion), the operational emphasis is typically one of controlled growth. For example, during the 1950s and 1960s the primary issue for organizations in the electric utility industry was planned growth in generating capacity as electric consumption rose at an annual rate of 7 percent.

When an increase in niche size is discontinuous (niche eruption), the emphasis shifts to rapidly expanding production capacity, often through innovations in production processes. In the cellular phone industry, for example, the number of customers increased from a few hundred thousand in 1984 when cellular was first offered to over 3 million by the end of 1989. The rapid increase in demand severely strained cellular phone systems'

Figure 10.1
Strategic and Operational Responses to Niche Change

a. Changes Conducive to Growth

Expansion
  OpEm: Controlled growth
 	
  DomTac: Continuity
	Eruption
	  OpEm: Rapid expansion of capacity
	
	  DomTac: Continuity

Evolution
  OpEm: Diversification
 	
  DomTac: Creation
	Creation
	  OpEm: Legitimacy
	
	  DomTac: Defense

b. Changes Conducive to Decline

Erosion
  OpEm: Fine-tuning operations
 	
  DomTac: Offense
	Contraction
	  OpEm: Retrenchment of operations
	
	  DomTac: Defense & Consolidation

Dissolution
  OpEm: Creation of new performance
      opportunities
  DomTac: Defense & Creation
	Collapse
	  OpEm: Survival
	
	  DomTac: Substitution

OpEm = Operational Emphasis
DomTac = Domain Tactics

---

capacity. The solution for existing companies was to convert from analog technology to digital technology. Indeed, the use of digital technology is expected to triple capacity, increase the quality of communications, and lower the per call cost.[3]

Domain Defense

Domain defense refers to actions undertaken to build or protect the legitimacy of an organization's domain. Common domain-defense tactics often involve political or legal actions, public image advertising, and coalition building. During the 1980s, for example, automotive, steel, textiles, and semiconductor manufacturers attempted to stop or slow foreign competitors' penetration of the U.S. market through domain defense. They filed complaints with the International Trade Commission, lobbied for protectionist legislation, and ran ad campaigns to "Buy American." The primary function of domain defense is to buy time for organizations to realign themselves to a changing environment.

Textile manufacturers, for example, used domain defense to gain time to modernize their plant and equipment. During the 1970s they had been slow to adopt the more efficient shuttleless looms their foreign competitors used, and the import share of the U.S. textile market doubled from 15 percent to over 30 percent between 1973 and 1983. To match their more efficient foreign competitors' prices, U.S. manufacturers had to update their production technologies. The textile manufacturers used domain defense to curtail imports while they replaced their old looms with new shuttleless looms that were three to four times more efficient. The tactic paid off, and many U.S. textile manufacturers regained a competitive position by the mid 1980s.[4]

While domain defense can buy time, it can backfire as well. When the U.S. passenger car market contracted in the early 1980s, and Japanese imports gained a larger share of the shrinking market, Ford and the United Auto Workers jointly filed a complaint with the International Trade Commission and lobbied Congress for import restrictions. No formal restraints were forthcoming, but the Japanese producers "voluntarily" agreed to import restrictions of 1.7 million cars annually. But then the Japanese manufacturers altered their strategy. They changed the mix of cars imported into the United States, sending more profitable luxury vehicles, and they began moving production operations to the United States. These actions significantly increased competition, which obviously was not the intent of U.S. industry's domain-defense efforts.[5] In short, domain defense tactics buy time for organizations to realign themselves to a changing industry niche by slowing the effects of changing niche size and shape on their operations. But they also can have unintended consequences, and they are rarely effective unless used in conjunction with another domain tactic.

Domain Offense

Domain offense enhances an organization's performance through expansion into product or market customer areas adjacent to its existing domain of operation. This way an organization is able to more thoroughly exploit resource and demand opportunities even though they may be becoming scarcer. This tactic is commonly used as a response to niche erosion, and organizations usually fine-tune their operations to increase efficiency at the same time.

Consider Champion Spark Plug Co. What was once a $900 million annual domestic market for replacement spark plugs in the 1970s shrank to $600 million by 1988 as the automotive companies started using smaller, more fuel-efficient engines. Champion fine-tuned its operations: management was cut back, factories revamped, and less profitable assets divested. And capitalizing on the Champion name, it entered other segments of the auto replacement parts market with 21 new products, including air filters, ignition cables, and fuel additives.[6] Similarly, Educational Testing Service (ETS), best known for the Scholastic Aptitude Test (SAT), saw its market shrink in the late 1970s as the number of 18-to-21 year-olds declined. During the early 1980s, ETS used its testing and measurement expertise to expand into other markets, such as certification tests for travel agents, energy auditors, construction-code inspectors, and electricians.[7]

Domain Consolidation

In **domain consolidation**, which is the reverse of domain offense, an organization consolidates its operations by eliminating areas peripheral to its central expertise. This tactic is employed when an organization experiences niche contraction. The primary operational emphasis is increasing efficiency through retrenchment, that is, divesting, or closing an organization's least efficient operations. In this way, consolidation enhances an organization's cash flow and increases its chances of survival when industry competition increases substantially.

The year 1987 was a bad one for the securities industry. A spike in interest rates early in the year lead to substantial losses for many securities firms prior to the October stock market crash. For the quarter ending September 30, 1987, no fewer than 107 of the 392 member firms of the New York Stock Exchange were operating at a loss. Then came the October 19th crash, which pushed down trading volume and rapidly increased competition for the remaining business. Within weeks, many small, specialist securities firms failed or were acquired. Others survived by massive consolidations in operations. L. F. Rothschild & Co., which lost $44 million in the crash (more than a quarter of its net worth), laid off over half its employees, lowered administrative costs, cut salaries, and pulled out of the firm's less profitable areas of operations. Salomon Brothers Inc. announced that it was pulling out of the commercial paper market days before the crash because of competition from more efficient commercial banks. PaineWebber closed its commercial paper operations a month later for the same reason. Overall, securities firms laid off about 45,000 employees in the year following the stock market crash. In the New York City area alone, an estimated 28,000 of 156,000 securities jobs disappeared. Virtually all the surviving companies consolidated operations, withdrawing into areas where they were more efficient and competitive.[8]

Domain Creation

Domain creation refers to the development of new areas of operation that supplement an organization's current domain. This tactic is commonly used by organizations in industries experiencing changes in niche shape. In the case of niche evolution, entrepreneurs and prospectors are likely to engage in domain creation through research and development, which is a primary cause of these two environmental conditions. Analyzers are more likely to follow entrepreneurs and prospectors into the evolving area of a niche through acquisition. For example, the accidental discovery of aspartame by a G. D. Searle researcher is an example of domain evolution in the artificial sweetener market caused by a prospector's research and development. Monsanto, an analyzer that manufactured another artificial sweetener, saccharin, engaged in domain creation by acquiring G. D. Searle. Now the Nutrasweet Division of Monsanto engages in domain creation through research on new uses for aspartame.

When environmental change results in niche dissolution, domain creation enables organizations to track changes in niche shape by adding to its domain while cutting back declining operations. For example, when student preferences for college and university programs shifted from the arts and sciences to the professions and applied sciences, the majority of specialized liberal arts colleges responded by developing high-demand professional programs. The number of schools offering business programs, for example, doubled during the 1970s.[9] The overall effect on many liberal arts and sciences colleges was a shift from a specialist to a generalist strategy.

Domain Substitution

Domain substitution focuses on replacing an organization's existing domain with a new one, usually when an industry niche collapses. If an organization is forewarned of a collapse, it may try to substitute one domain for another in a way that builds on existing expertise. Rolm Corporation, for example, began corporate life in the 1960s as a manufacturer of heavy-duty computers sold primarily to the military. In 1971 co-founder Kenneth Oshman projected that the $15 million military-specification computer market was saturated. Moreover, the navy had announced plans to use only one standard computer design, with specifications identical to those for a computer manufactured by Sperry Univac. Believing that Rolm's market was about to collapse, Oshman searched for a new domain of operation that built on Rolm's existing competencies. He moved the company into the telephone switching business, believing that Rolm's expertise in computers would allow it to design and manufacture digital switching equipment more sophisticated than that produced by AT&T and other industry competitors. The risk paid off. Rolm grew at an annual compound rate of 57 percent to sales of $660 million and a 16.7 percent market share by 1984, when it was acquired by IBM for $1.9 billion. And, as it turned out, Oshman was wrong about the military-specifications computer market. The navy loosened its design requirements in 1976, and the market grew to $220 million annually by 1984.[10]

More often, domain-substitution tactics are called into play after an industry's niche collapses, leaving little time to develop a new domain internally. Swiss manufacturers, for example, historically dominated the high-priced end of the global mechanical watch market. But in the early 1970s, the growing popularity of digital watches and the rising value of the Swiss franc caused an industry-wide collapse. Between 1973 and 1975, worldwide sales of digital watches grew from 200,000 units to over 2.5 million units. The effect on the Swiss watch industry was dramatic. The number of Swiss watchmakers dropped from about 1,300 in the mid 1960s to under 900 by the mid 1970s. Because of the rapid onset of the collapse, many surviving Swiss manufacturers used the technique of domain substitution, replacing much of their mechanical watchmaking capacity with an electronic watchmaking capacity. Ebauches, the world's largest manufacturer of watch movements, contracted with Texas Instruments and Hughes Aircraft to supply needed components. Bulova, a U.S.–owned Swiss manufacturer, entered into a joint venture with semiconductor manufacturer Integrated Display Systems (itself a joint venture between General Electric and Solid State Scientific) to gain needed components. Another large Swiss manufacturer, S.S.I.H., entered the electronic watch market through a series of joint ventures, acquisitions, and supply contracts.[11]

Domain Abandonment

Domain abandonment occurs when an organization exits an industry niche, and it is a valuable tactic for analyzers and prospectors that have operations across many areas in a segmented industry niche or across different industry niches. Generalist organizations will abandon an industry niche if their managers believe they can earn a higher rate of return by moving into another domain. For example, when the home video game industry collapsed in 1983, three of the largest producers quickly exited the industry niche. Mattel and Milton Bradley closed down their electronic toy divisions; Warner Communications divested Atari.

When domain abandonment occurs through divestiture, a divested division is often transformed into a specialist organization. In some cases, a divested division can become profitable, even in a declining industry niche. During the early 1980s, the size of the glass container industry market shrank because of a recession and increasing competition with plastic container manufacturers. Most of the glass container operations were owned by large divisionalized firms that spun them off into free-standing organizations. These specialized glass container firms made money because they could operate at lower volumes with fewer overhead expenses.[12] Similarly, Beatrice Corporation—a major conglomerate that once had over 300 divisions—sold off poorly performing operations in the mid 1980s after a leveraged buyout. Many of the operations, such as Playtex, Revlon, and Danskin, became profitable because of reduced overhead and a better ability to focus on their specific markets.[13]

The Strategy-Structure Linkage

Theoretically, all these domain tactics are available to entrepreneurs, prospectors, defenders, and analyzers. But their strategic dispositions differ, meaning that certain types of organizations are more likely to respond to environmental change with particular domain tactics rather than others. For example, prospectors are predisposed to domain creation, and their initial response to changing environmental conditions is likely to be further domain creation.[14] In contrast, a defender's strategic predisposition is toward domain defense and domain offense—preserving its current domain and often expanding it at the margin. In effect, an organization's strategy-structure alignment (Table 10.1) has a major impact on how it will initially respond to changing environmental conditions because the alignment reflects what it does well.

If changing environmental conditions—such as niche dissolution and niche collapse—favor a domain-creation response, prospectors are likely to do well because they are strategically predisposed to acting in a way that addresses that type of environmental change. Their multidivisional structures and propensity to innovate help them adapt to changes in niche shape. Defenders, on the other hand, are at a considerable disadvantage when changing niche conditions favor domain creation, because their structure and strategic predisposition emphasize efficiency, not innovation. In other words, their structure makes domain creation difficult to implement. Conversely, defenders are better positioned to deal successfully with environmental changes that favor domain offense or consolidation—such as niche erosion and contraction. These conditions fit the defender's strategic predisposition and emphasis on efficient operations. But decreasing niche size creates problems for prospectors, because they are not structured to effectively implement efficiency-oriented domain tactics.

Organizations are not locked into their strategic dispositions, though. Defenders can engage in domain creation, and prospectors can pursue domain consolidation or offense. To change their basic strategic orientation, however, they must modify their structures to support such a change. And as we've seen in earlier chapters, changing an organization's underlying structure is a large task, often requiring the redesign of jobs, coordination and control mechanisms, decision making, and unit grouping.

Looking at Table 10.1 from a slightly different perspective can give you a sense of the relative difficulty of these transitions. For example, look at the table with an eye toward the design changes required to make a prospector into a defender, and vice versa. Their structural configurations are quite different, and the structural changes required to support the switch from one strategy to the other are significant. In contrast, moving from an entrepreneurial domain strategy to that of a prospector or defender is not quite so hard because there is not much of an existing structure to be dismantled and reassembled.

In summary, an organization's strategic orientation and corresponding structure constrain the domain tactics it is likely to use in response to changing environmental conditions. Organizations may pursue domain tactics other than those to which they are strategically predisposed, but such tactical shifts require corresponding changes in their structure. And some transitions are more difficult than others.

PERCEIVING AND INTERPRETING ENVIRONMENTAL CHANGE

An organization's strategy, strategic predisposition, and structure also filter its managers' environmental perceptions, affecting their ability to detect changes in its industry niche. As noted in Chapter 8, strategic-choice theorists claim that strategy and structure are determined by managers' perceptions and interpretations of their organization's environment. In other words, what managers "see" affects the strategies they select, the structures they choose, and how they modify them in response to changing environmental conditions. It follows that if managers do not perceive changes in an industry niche's size or shape, they will behave as if those changes are not occurring. For example, managers in the baby food industry did not perceive that a declining birth rate in the mid 1960s was eroding their industry niche. It was not until a few years after the downturn began that they noticed the decline and responded.[15] If managers do perceive changes in their industry niche, they may have widely varying interpretations of what is occurring, as we will discuss next.

Organizational Factors Affecting Perception

A number of organizational factors affect managers' perceptions. For example, an organization's culture can filter out environmental information that is inconsistent with its values and beliefs. This is often the case with successful entrepreneurs, who sometimes refuse to acknowledge their vulnerability to growing competition as a market matures. An organization's structure also affects perception. For instance, decision makers in decentralized organizations tend to perceive more information about environmental conditions than managers in centralized organizations, because there are more decision makers, and they are closer to their markets. As a result, centralized organizations may miss changes in customer preferences that their decentralized counterparts take advantage of.

One fairly simple organizational factor having a major influence on managers' environmental perceptions that has received little attention is an organization's location within an industry niche. *Where* an organization is located within an industry niche affects what managers perceive for two reasons. First, an organization's location in a niche may cause it to experience environmental changes differently than the industry as a whole. Second, because managers view changes from their organization's niche location, they may see different conditions.

Where You "Sit" Affects What You "See." Think about being part of an audience watching a play in a large theater. Where you sit influences what you see. If you are seated to the theater's far left, the action you see is going to be somewhat different than someone seated at center stage or to far right. Your friend, who was seated far right, comments after the performance that "the facial expressions of so-and-so playing Juliet really added to the scene's romantic quality." You, on the other hand, were unimpressed. But then you couldn't see the details of that particular scene because it took place on the side of the stage away from you. Though at the same performance, you each may end up with a different perception of it.

Perceiving Changes in Niche Shape. Much the same is true on a larger scale for organizations. Individual organizations choose their locations in an industry niche when they select a domain of operation. Organizations that produce similar goods or services, or serve similar customers, have similar locations in their industry niche. As a result, they are more likely to perceive similar environmental conditions than managers in organizations that produce different goods or services, or serve different customer groups. But even then, their relevant environments may differ.

Figure 10.2 shows two different "seating arrangements" for organizations in an industry niche. The two large circles in each panel represent the base of an industry niche at Time$_1$ and Time$_2$, as you would see looking down on the horizontal surface of Figure 9.1, Panel D. The smaller circles represent individual organizations. A circle's width indicates the extent that an organization pursues a generalist or specialist strategy. The smaller the circle, the more specialized an organization's strategy is.

The overlapping circles in Panel A indicate that these three organizations produce similar goods or services. If the shape of this industry niche changes from Time$_1$ to Time$_2$, managers in these organizations are likely to perceive the environmental changes similarly, because the changes have similar effects on their organizations. For example, when consumer preferences shifted from home video games to personal computers in 1982, all the manufacturers perceived and experienced the change in niche shape in much the same way because they were located in the part of the industry niche that was collapsing. This type of "seating arrangement" is common in industries that produce commodity-like goods and services.

In contrast, Panel B shows an industry with a highly segmented market. The central area of the industry's niche is dominated by a generalist organization (Organization B), and small pockets of demand at the niche's periphery are served by specialist organizations (Organizations A and C). If the niche shape changes continuously from Time$_1$ to Time$_2$, each organization will

Figure 10.2
Two Different Industry Structures

a. Overlapping Domains: Commodity-like Market

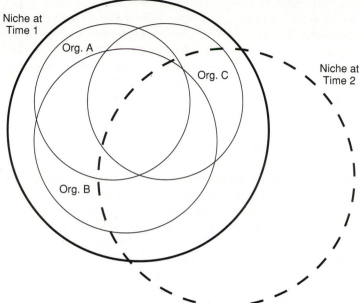

b. Non-overlapping Domains: Highly Segmented Market

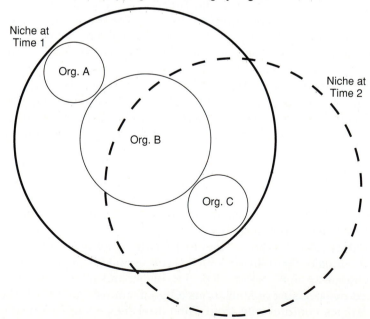

experience the change differently, and their managers will perceive the change in different ways.

Organization A experiences niche dissolution as the change in niche shape closes off performance opportunities. Organization B, on the other hand, finds that the change has reduced demand for some of its goods and services while increasing it for others. Organization C experiences niche expansion because the shift in niche shape favors its domain. Managers in each organization are likely to perceive the change in niche shape differently because it affects their organizations differently. Consequently, the extent to which organizations' domains overlap affects the similarity of their managers' environmental perceptions.

For example, there was a continuous change in student preferences for fields of study during the 1970s and 1980s from arts and science programs to professional and applied science programs. Specialist liberal arts and sciences colleges experienced niche dissolution as student preferences moved away from the programs they offered. For generalist comprehensive universities, declining demand for some programs was offset by increasing demand for others. Specialized professional schools, on the other hand, experienced niche expansion, with a continuous increase in demand for the services they offered.

Perceiving Changes in Niche Size. Changes in niche size can differentially affect organizations within an industry niche as well. When member organizations produce a commodity-like good or service, changes in niche size are likely to affect them similarly. But when an industry's markets are segmented and different organizations serve different segments, changes in niche size may have differing effects. For example, higher education enrollment markets are highly segmented. Relatively few colleges and universities compete for students in the national enrollment market, since most draw students from small, local areas. As a result, while the size of the 18-to-21-year-old population declined nationwide, it affected some local enrollment markets more than others. Schools drawing students from the Northeast were more severely affected by decreasing niche size than schools in the Southwest, where the decrease in traditional college age students was less severe.

Individual Factors Affecting Perception

A number of individual factors also influence managers' perceptions and interpretations of environmental events and trends—namely, managers' personalities, past experiences, ego involvement, and personal goals. Or, to use the flip-side of an old adage, "I see what I believe."[16]

Differences in perception mean that some managers see opportunities that others miss. Whether these perceptions are accurate is often irrelevant. Remember Kenneth Oshman's (of Rolm Corporation) perceptions of the military computer market discussed earlier in this chapter. His mistaken beliefs about the future of the military computer market led to the development of digital switching systems that revolutionized the telecommunication industry's niche shape. Sometimes, however, an inaccurate perception can harm an organization, such as when managers miss shifts in niche shape away from an organization's domain or decreases in niche size, ultimately leading to the organization's decline and failure (see Chapter 12).

One clearly documented example of how managers' perceptions and interpretations of the environment affect strategy is provided by the case of Montgomery Ward and Sears after World War II.[17] In 1946 Ward and Sears were close competitors, Ward with 632 stores and Sears with 610. When the war ended, the U.S. economy entered a long period of economic expansion, and Sears accordingly began expanding its chain of retail outlets, particularly in the rapidly growing suburbs of major urban areas. Ward, on the other hand, opened no new stores and began closing marginal outlets in its existing chain. By 1955 Sears had 718 retail stores, Ward had 568. These differences in strategy were reflected in financial performance: Sears' net income was $35.8 million in 1946 and $117.9 million in 1954. Ward's was $22.9 million in 1946 and $41.2 million in 1954.

What prompted Ward's no-growth decision as the economy rapidly expanded? The answer lies in Ward's Chairman Sewell Avery's beliefs about what would happen to the economy after World War II:

> He [Sewell Avery] had an adamant belief that a depression was imminent after the cessation of hostilities in World War II. His basis for this belief was the depression that did occur after World War I. Avery foresaw that the nation would have difficulties trying to readjust to a peacetime economy, as industries halted production of war materials and reverted to peacetime production, and as millions of returning servicemen tried to find employment. He predicted that "economic conditions are terrorizing beyond what we have known before." And he noted, "We (Ward) are starting nothing of any size, we are being cautious."[18]

Ward's no-growth policy continued until 1957—ten years after the expansion began—when Avery retired at age 83. Between 1957 and 1965, 182 new stores opened, and these new stores accounted for 72 percent of Ward's 1965 sales and 73 percent of its pretax operating profits.

In summary, a number of factors influence how managers perceive, interpret, and respond to changes in their industry's niche. As explained earlier, an organization's location within a niche determines the particular environmental conditions that it experiences. The greater the degree to which organizations' domains overlap, the more likely it is that their managers will perceive similar environmental conditions. Thus, organizations with overlapping domains are more likely to pursue similar strategies than organizations located in different parts of an industry niche. But while organizations with overlapping domains may experience similar environmental conditions, their managers' perceptions and interpretations may nevertheless differ due to past experiences, personal goals, personalities, and their organizations' cultures and structures. The end result is that organizations pursue many different strategies in response to changing industry niche conditions, some because of the differential effects of environmental change, others because of differences in managers' perceptions and interpretations of the change.

CHANGING ENVIRONMENTS, STRATEGIES, AND STRUCTURES

The relationships described in the preceding sections can be summarized by saying that strategy affects both an organization's structure and environment, and an organization's structure and environment affect its strategy (Figure 10.3). In effect, this describes an open system (Chapter 1) where there are feedback loops (the arrows in the figure) between one of the system's components and the other (structure, strategy, and environment). This may seem to be a complex way to portray these relationships, but the relationships themselves are complex.

An Example: Digital Widget

Consider the case of Jim Hernandez, an engineer who develops the digital widget. Jim is unable to convince his employer, U.S. Widget—a major mechanical widget producer, that the digital widget is the product of the future. Frustrated, Jim organizes his own small entrepreneurial firm, Digital Widget. He and a half-dozen employees began assembling their first product, the DW-1, in Jim's garage.

The primary problem facing Digital at this point is establishing the legitimacy of the digital widget market. Jim spends much of the organization's first year legitimating the digital widget by promoting the DW-1 at trade shows and making calls on prospective clients. Progress is slow, but after a year of living hand-to-mouth, Digital Widget gets a break: a major manufacturer agrees to test the DW-1 as a component in one of its products. The manufacturer finds that the DW-1 is more reliable than the mechanical widget it replaces and is easier to install, reducing its production and warranty costs. Suddenly Digital Widget is swamped in orders. By year-end, it has become a 500-employee firm, renting space in a renovated factory complex.

The rapid growth in demand for digital widgets results in the collapse of the mechanical widget market, forcing U.S. Widget into a major retrenchment. From Digital Widget's standpoint, life couldn't be better, since demand

Figure 10.3
The Interrelated Nature of Changes in Structure,
Strategy, and Environment

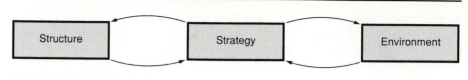

exceeds its capacity to supply digital widgets. Other entrepreneurial organizations enter the market with "clones" and slightly different widget designs that expand the range of widget applications. These new entrants do not concern Jim Hernandez; there is more than enough demand for everybody. Digital Widget's primary problem is adding capacity quickly. But the organization runs into problems as it adds capacity. Some orders are delivered late, and quality problems crop up because of bottlenecks in production and poor communication between production and sales. Being an astute entrepreneur, Jim realizes (with a bit of urging from his bankers) that he can no longer cope with all the demands for his time, and that the simple structure that worked well when Digital Widget was small is now causing problems. Jim hires a staff of MBA-trained managers to redesign Digital Widget's operations and to set up managerial controls. These new managers structure the organization along functional lines with a more formal management hierarchy and reporting systems. Product quality and delivery times improve, and Digital Widget's operations become more efficient, allowing it to become more price-competitive.

One unintended effect of the reorganization, though, is a shift from an entrepreneurial to a defender strategy. Part of this is reflected in the subtle reorientation of Digital's R&D unit, whose focus shifts from basic widget research in the hope of inventing radically new widget designs to refining existing products based on current widget technology. R&D delivers, bringing out designs for a series of improved products—DW-2 through DW-7— based on the original DW-1 design. The shift in strategy works well for Digital Widget, and the new products enable it to expand its customer base. It rapidly grows over the next three years at an annual rate of 76 percent. The move to a functional structure and a defender strategy turns out to be a good one, particularly since the eruption of digital widget demand has attracted a number of other firms into the industry, including the industry's biggest competitor, International Business Widgets (IBW), who buys in by acquiring some small entrepreneurs that are having problems managing rapid growth. Competition heightens as industry capacity catches up with demand. But Digital Widget's market position is enviable: it is the low-cost producer, and the DW-brand is synonymous with digital widgets.

One day, Jim wakes up to discover that the market has crashed because of an industry-wide strike in the biggest digital widget end-user market. Demand for digital widgets drops by one-half overnight. In the next few weeks, prices plummet, and a number of the industry's late entrepreneurial entrants file for bankruptcy, pushed out of the market by more efficient firms. Digital Widget cuts back its operations to enhance cash flow, and it pulls out of market segments where other firms, such as IBW, have become the low-cost producer. This consolidation allows the company to focus on DW models that have the largest market share in their product class and that can be produced very efficiently.

Within a year, only a few major players remain in the industry, demand has leveled out, and prices slowly rise. Digital Widget has weathered the crisis. Then one afternoon, a young engineer comes into Jim Hernandez's office excited about some ideas she has on the design of an opto-electronic widget . . .

Digital Widget Analysis

Although hypothetical, the outline of Digital Widget's story is not unusual, and it captures the interrelated nature of how an organization's strategy, structure, and environment change over time. Figure 10.4 diagrams the history of the digital widget niche and Digital Widget's strategy and structure, and points to some of the choices that Jim Hernandez now faces. In the following analysis, we parenthetically note the direction of the changes in environment, strategy, and structure.

Jim Hernandez's invention and the founding of Digital Widget lead to the creation of the digital widget industry niche (strategy → environment), which is a common example of managerial action influencing an organization's environment. Appropriate to this entrepreneurial strategy was the simple, undifferentiated structure that characterized Digital Widget's first couple of years (structure ← strategy). Once Digital Widget established the industry's legitimacy, niche eruption occurred, leading to a change in tactics—from domain creation and defense to domain continuity with an emphasis on expanding production capacity (strategy ← environment). Digital Widget's subsequent rapid growth created operational problems that it resolved by developing a more formal functional structure (structure ← strategy). The development of a functional structure then results in a shift away from an entrepreneurial to a defender strategy (structure → strategy) that emphasizes domain offense and efficient operations.

As the rate of demand growth slows, and analyzers such as IBW enter the digital widget market, the industry's competitive dynamics change, shifting away from product innovation toward product price and quality. Fortunately for Digital Widget, the defender strategy it assumed to manage rapid growth has positioned it to be an efficient competitor. Then the industry-wide strike in the major end-user market results in niche contraction, forcing Digital Widget to pursue domain consolidation (strategy ← environment).

Figure 10.4
Industry Niche and Digital Widget Chronology

Time →

	Creation / Expansion	Eruption / Evolution	Contraction	Evolution, Dissolution, or Collapse
Niche Conditions Niche Size Niche Shape				
Domain Strategy	Entrepreneur	Defender		Defender or Analyzer?
Domain Tactics	Domain Creation & Domain Defense	Domain Offense	Domain Consolidation	Domain Defense or Domain Creation?
Structure	Simple	Functional		Functional or Divisional?
Primary Operating Issue	Devel. product & est. legitimacy	Expand capacity	Retrench operations	Defend or Innovate?

We left Digital Widget with some potentially significant changes in the offing. Will Jim Hernandez develop the opto-electronic widget technology? It would require a shift in strategy—from a defender to being something more like an analyzer. If successfully developed, the opto-electronic widget would change the shape of the industry niche (strategy → environment). Niche dissolution or collapse would occur if the new technology replaced the old one, depending on the rate of replacement. Or niche evolution would result if the new technology added to the range of products widget manufacturers could produce and sell.

The change in strategy, from domain offense to domain creation, also would require a change in Digital Widget's structure (structure ← strategy). If Jim Hernandez wants to minimize the organization's investment and downside risk, he might set up a matrix unit and recruit people with the necessary expertise from the various functional areas to staff the project. If the project failed, the unit could be disbanded without much disruption to the organization. If product development was successful, the organization's overall design could be changed from a functional structure to a product-based divisional structure. If Jim Hernandez is an optimistic risk-taker, he might create a separate product division to handle development, production, and marketing of the new product at the outset. Either alternative would likely result in quicker development than if the project were handled within the confines of a functional structure.

Alternatively, Jim Hernandez may forget about the frustrations of being a young engineer with a revolutionary idea and not develop the opto-electronic widget. The success of his own invention earlier may predispose him against the potential of the new widget. And then, much as he did, the young engineer might set up her own small company to develop the new technology. If successful, her actions would change the environment, to which Digital Widget would in turn have to react. The same type of scenario with which Jim Hernandez's story began might ensue, with the collapse of Hernandez's digital widget industry niche due to a discontinuous shift in widget technology caused by the introduction of the opto-electronic widget. In any event, successful development of the new technology would create a set of environmental conditions to which Digital Widget would have to respond (strategy ← environment), with its attendant implications for the organization's structure (structure ← strategy). Will Jim Hernandez's experience as a young engineer with a revolutionary idea cause him to act again as a creator of environmental change? Or will he continue on Digital Widget's current course? Only the future will tell. After all, changes in the widget industry have never been easy to predict.

The essential point of Chapters 9 and 10 is that environmental change and organizational adaptation are complex processes. Contingency theorists, strategic choice proponents, and population ecologists each present us with a partial understanding of these processes. Contingency theorists help us understand the linkage between environmental conditions and structure, strategic choice theorists enlighten us about the relationships between managerial action and the environment and about the fit between structure and strategy, and population ecologists explain the relative success of different strategies under varying environmental conditions. But none of these approaches alone provides a complete picture. The model presented in Chapters 9 and 10 helps us understand that environmental change and organizational adaptation present managers with many challenges. Effectively meeting these challenges requires that managers remember that strategies, structures, and environments affect each other.

SUMMARY

Learning Objective 1: Describe the organization designs that are consistent with the entrepreneur, prospector, analyzer, and defender domain strategies. Simple, undifferentiated designs that provide owner/managers with a high degree of control appear to be consistent with the entrepreneur's strategy. Prospectors, on the other hand, tend to employ divisionalized structures that are relatively decentralized. The analyzer generally employs a divisionalized structure with a moderate degree of decentralization. Divisional structures within an analyzer reflect prevailing market conditions. The more mature a division's market is, the more the division will move toward a functional design. Defenders tend to be functionally structured and centralized.

Learning Objective 2: Identify the domain tactics that fit the different conditions of niche change. Domain continuity, which refers to continued operation in the same domain over time, is most appropriate for organizations in expanding or erupting niches. Domain defense refers to efforts to build or maintain the legitimacy of an industry niche. It is often used when niche creation occurs to establish the legitimacy of a new niche, and to protect existing niches when niche contraction or erosion occurs. Domain creation refers to actions taken to expand an organization's domain by increasing the types of performance that it engages in. This tactic is commonly used by organizations that face niche evolution or dissolution. Domain offense expands an organization's domain of operation by moving it into product, market, or customer areas adjacent to its existing domain of operation. It often is employed when an organization experiences niche erosion. Domain substitution refers to replacing one domain of operation with another. It is employed when an organization experiences niche collapse.

Learning Objective 3: Explain how different individual and organizational factors influence managers' perceptions and interpretations of environmental change. Both organizational factors (e.g., an organization's structure, culture, position within an industry niche) and individual factors (e.g., personality, ego involvement, past experiences, personal goals) can affect managers' perceptions of environmental change by coloring their interpretations. In some instances, differences in perception and interpretation may benefit an organization, such as when a manager "sees" an opportunity that others don't. In others, it may work to an organization's disadvantage, such as when a manager fails to perceive or correctly interpret information about environmental changes that could adversely affect an organization. The differences in perception arising from individual and organizational factors is a primary reason why organizations pursue different domain strategies and tactics even though they are experiencing similar environmental conditions.

Learning Objective 4: Describe the effects that a change in an organization's structure, strategy, or environment can have on one another. Organizations that survive past their first few years experience a variety of niche conditions over time. These changing niche conditions differentially affect the entrepreneurial, prospector, defender, and analyzer domain strategies, favoring the success of some and the failure of others. As a result, organizations often find it necessary to either adapt their domain strategy to fit changing niche conditions, or to change the niche conditions to fit their strategies. Moreover, different organization designs are necessary to effectively implement the different organizational strategies. Thus, a change in strategy usually requires a change in design. The primary implication is that organizational adaptation is a continual process. Environments change and organizations adapt, either by creating environmental change or by responding to it through their strategic actions. Regardless of whether an organization creates or responds to changing environmental conditions, managers' primary task is to constantly manage the alignment between an organization's strategy, structure, and environment over time.

Discussion Questions

1. In the Digital Widget scenario, we noted that Jim Hernandez left U.S. Widget because his boss wouldn't consider developing his new digital widget design. Write a scenario for U.S. Widget after Jim Hernandez left to found Digital Widget. Describe the environmental changes U.S. Widget might have experienced and its strategic response to these changes.

2. You work for a small firm that writes automation software for radio stations and bundles it with hardware from a major computer manufacturer. This has been a very profitable enterprise for the past ten years, and the firm has needed to spend little on research and development because there are no real competitors. Unfortunately, sales of new systems in the United States are beginning to decline because the market is getting saturated. The firm has to change its strategy if it is to continue growing. What options might this firm pursue? How would you classify these options in terms of domain tactics?

3. Examine a current issue of *Business Week, Fortune,* or *Forbes* and find examples of organizations using the different domain tactics listed in Table 10.2. Do you think the domain tactics these organizations have chosen are appropriate given the articles' descriptions of what they are trying to accomplish? Why or why not?

4. You are a senior manager in an old-line, vertically integrated steel company. Increased competition from foreign manufacturers, and from domestic mini-mills that reprocess scrap, have undercut your operations. Prices for many of your products are no longer competitive, and many product lines have become unprofitable. What domain tactics are options for your organization? What are the advantages and drawbacks of each option?

5. Two common ways of implementing domain creation are through research and development and acquisition. What are the advantages and disadvantages of these different approaches to domain creation? What conditions do you think are more appropriate for each?

DESIGN AUDIT #10

Responding to Changing Environmental Conditions

This design audit will help you analyze your organization's position within its industry niche relative to its competitors, examine the specific effects of environmental change on it, determine the range of strategic options open to it, and explore the design options needed to implement the identified domain tactics.

Competitive Structure

1. Think about the domain of your organization relative to that of its competitors. What are the most important dimensions on which these organizations compete? These dimensions can reflect inputs such as scarce resources and personnel (e.g., nonprofit organizations often compete for funding) or outputs such as customer demand. How segmented is the industry on these dimensions? For example, how segmented is the industry in terms of geographic regions served, types of goods or services produced, types of customer served, price or quality, etc. By definition, competitors' domains will overlap your organization's domain on at least one dimension. But there may be other factors that differentiate their domains from your organization's. In the space below list the competitors you identified in Question 3, Design Audit #9. Label the columns to the right to reflect the major dimensions (e.g., product, customer,

geographical, price, etc.) on which your organization competes with them. You will be identifying where these organizations' domains overlap and where they differ. (An example is presented on the following page.)

Organization	Dimension 1 ( )	Dimension 2 ( )	Dimension 3 ( )	Dimension 4 ( )
_____	_____	_____	_____	_____
_____	_____	_____	_____	_____
_____	_____	_____	_____	_____
_____	_____	_____	_____	_____
_____	_____	_____	_____	_____
_____	_____	_____	_____	_____
_____	_____	_____	_____	_____
_____	_____	_____	_____	_____
_____	_____	_____	_____	_____

Example: There are many different types of colleges and universities. Some compete for student enrollments, others do not. Consider the following public university: University A specializes in graduate professional programs, such as business, education, and law, and has undergraduate programs in business and in the arts and sciences. Its educational services are targeted primarily at nontraditional students in their late 20s and 30s who live within 50 miles of the school.

It has a number of competitors. University B is a public university in A's service area with similar undergraduate programs and graduate professional programs. But the majority of its students are between ages 18 and 25, so competition between them is limited. College C also is a public institution located in A's service area, enrolls students between ages 18 and 40, but offers only undergraduate programs. It competes head-on with A in the areas where they have similar undergraduate programs. University D is a private school in A's service area that offers a number of competing graduate professional programs. University D also offers undergraduate programs, but its tuition is three times that of A so the two do not compete in this area. College E is a private for-profit school that offers graduate and undergraduate programs in business that are directed at 25- to 40-year-old students. While its tuition is slightly higher than A's, many potential students see it as an alternative to A, so these two schools compete head-on in this area. The form for Question 1 would be filled out as follows:

Organization	Dimension 1 (Programs)	Dimension 2 (Students)	Dimension 3 (Price)	Dimension 4 (Service Area)
Univ. A	Grad prof & ungrad bus, A&S	late 20s-30s	low	same
Univ. B	Grad prof & ungrad bus, A&S	18-25	low	same
College C	Ungrad bus, A&S	18-40	low	same
Univ. D	Grad prof & ungrad	18-30	high	same
College E	Grad & ungrad bus	25-40	medium	same

2. Look at the industry niche changes you identified in Question 2, Design Audit #9, with an eye toward their specific effects on your organization. In the space below, note whether these changes will have the same effect on your organization as they do on the industry as a whole, or whether they create different niche conditions for your organization?

Example: Relevant environmental changes in the college and university niche are the aging of the population and the shift in students' interests away from the arts and sciences to the professions and applied sciences. While the overall college and university niche is undergoing niche dissolution, University A is in a good position to capitalize on the changes since it is located in that part of the niche that is growing—it is experiencing niche expansion.

Identify the type of niche change that your organization is experiencing. If it is different from that of the industry niche as a whole, explain why.

Strategic and Tactical Domain Responses

3.   Describe any strategic and tactical responses your organization is undertaking or plans on in response to the changes described in the last section.

Example: University A's overall response has been domain continuity within the framework of its analyzer domain strategy. Most actions have been operational in nature: it is downsizing programs in areas with declining demand, expanding programs in areas of increasing demand, and shifting resources among existing areas of operation.

4. If you think your organization's response (or lack of response) will not effectively reposition it within its changing industry niche, what changes in domain strategy and tactics do you recommend. Note why you think these changes would better position the organization than what it is currently doing, or planning to do. Keep in mind your competitors' domains and what they might do in response to the environmental changes. (Refer to your response to Question 4 in Design Audit #8. Which of the options you've identified would best position your organization to meet these changes in its industry niche?)

Implications for Organization Design

5. What changes in design does your organization need to effectively implement the domain strategy and tactics identified in Question 3, or Question 4—if you think it should respond differently than it is responding? (See Table 10.1.)

Notes

1. Raymond E. Miles and Charles C. Snow, "Organizations: New Concepts for New Forms," *California Management Review* 28 (1986, Spring): 66.

2. Ibid., 66.

3. Robert H. Miles, *Coffin Nails and Corporate Strategie*s (Englewood Cliffs, N.J.: Prentice-Hall, 1982). This book refers to domain defense, domain offense, and domain creation as "domain strategies." We have chosen the term "domain tactics" to distinguish these actions from the larger defender, entrepreneur, analyzer, and prospector domain strategies.

4. Calvin Sims, "Meeting Mobile Phone Demand," *New York Times,* July 19, 1989, C1; Julie A. Lopez, "Phone Fixation: Once High Tech Toys, Celluar Telephones are Becoming Staples," *The Wall Street Journal,* August 11, 1989, A1, A9.

5. Scott Kilman and Linda Williams, "While Textile Manufacturers Bemoan Imports, They Are Modernizing, Too," *The Wall Street Journal,* September 19, 1984, 1, 19.

6. "Will the Auto Glut Choke Detroit?" *Business Week,* March 7, 1988, 54–61.

7. "Champion Is Starting to Show a Little Spark," *Business Week,* March 21, 1988, 87.

8. Virginia Inman, "Educational Testing Service Adopts Tactics from Business World as Old Markets Shrink," *The Wall Street Journal,* November 30, 1982, 31.

9. "The Big Chill on Wall Street," *Business Week,* December 7, 1987, 54–57; "Wall Street Faces a Long Morning After," *Business Week,* January 11, 1988, 126–127; "The Splintering of Wall Street," *Business Week,* March 21, 1988, 128–134; "Can Young Blood Revive L.F. Rothschild?" *Business Week,* July 18, 1988, 74.

10. Raymond F. Zammuto, "Are the Liberal Arts an Endangered Species?" *Journal of Higher Education* 55 (1984): 184–211.

11. Myron Magnet, "How Top Managers Make a Company's Toughest Decision," *Fortune,* March 18, 1985, 52–57; Peggy Berkowitz, "Rivalry is Fierce in Growing Market for Telephone Switching Systems," *The Wall Street Journal,* February 10, 1984, 17. (Rolm was sold to Seimens AG—the West German telecommunications manufacturer—by IBM in 1989.)

12. "Time for a Change," *Barron's,* October 15, 1973, 11+; "Digital Watches: Bringing Watchmaking Back to the U.S.," *Business Week,* October 27, 1975, 79–92; Norris Willatt, "The Swiss Watch Lesson," *Management Today,* December 1980, 50–53, 124; Walter Galling and Robert Ball, "How Omega and Tissot Got Ticking Again," *Fortune,* January 14, 1980, 68–70; Michele Ingrassia, "Watchful Gumby Enters a Digital Quagmire," *Denver Post,* December 19, 1985, 15C.

13. "How Glass Container Manufacturers Are Breaking Their Fall," *Business Week,* December 23, 1983, 38.

14. "How Sweet It Is to Be Out from Beatrice's Thumb," *Business Week,* May 9, 1988, 98–99.

15. Robert H. Miles, *Coffin Nails and Corporate Strategies,* 237–247.

16. Raymond F. Zammuto and Kim S. Cameron, "Environmental Decline and Organizational Response," *Research in Organizational Behavior* 7 (1985): 249–250.

17. A serious discussion of factors affecting individual perception and subsequent behavior is well beyond the scope of this book. For our purpose, we simply note that individual differences result in varied interpretations of and beliefs about the external world that affect subsequent decisions and actions. For a recent review of the topic, see Charles I. Stubbart, "Managerial Cognition: A Missing Link in Strategic Management Research," *Journal of Management Studies* 26 (1989): 325–347.

18. Robert F. Hartley, *Management Mistakes,* 2d ed. (New York: Wiley, 1986), 120–121.

Where the Next Fortunes Will Be Made

Where will the next great fortunes be created? The question, like what song the sirens sang, is difficult, but not beyond intelligent conjecture. History shows that each successive age has been characterized by a distinctive mode of wealth creation. Since the Industrial Revolution, the prevailing pattern has been that of the entrepreneur catching a major social, economic, or technological wave at just the right moment and riding it to enormous riches.

Over the next few decades big money will be made by prescient individuals who seize on one of four overarching trends:

- Information as the new transformative resource, replacing energy.
- The aging of the population of the developed world.
- The emergence of tightly integrated regional economies, embracing several nations.
- The exploitation of new technologies.

In the static economies of precapitalist days, attaining great wealth was a Hobbesian affair, the result of winning a zero-sum game. Behind most great fortunes there really was a great crime, often the appropriation of somebody else's assets—as in a war—or perhaps peculation. In first-century B.C. Rome, for example, conventional ways of achieving riches included extortion and the bribery of public officials. The triumvir Crassus, from whose name we get the modern word "crass," operated the first fire brigade in the imperial city. If a citizen whose house was aflame didn't pay an obscene price, Crassus

Source: "Where the Next Fortunes Will Be Made" by Brett Duval Fromson. Reprinted by permission from FORTUNE Magazine, December 5, 1988, pp. 185–186, 188, 192, 196. © 1988 The Time Inc. Magazine Company. All rights reserved.

would tell his men to let the blaze burn. The next day the enterprising Roman would try to buy whatever remained, at fire-sale prices.

Wealth creation as we know it today emerged in 18th-century England, with the first Industrial Revolution. Gradually royal monopolies on just about every branch of commerce were swept away, under pressure from men and machines who could produce better products more efficiently. The eminent business historian Alfred Chandler, a professor at the Harvard business school, calls these modern entrepreneurs first movers: Even if they didn't invent a new technology—the steam engine, say, or the power loom—they had the vision to organize and dominate emerging industries in those initial states with the highest growth and profitability.

The people who amassed great fortunes in the past few years were still first movers. In the U.S. they found fertile soil in finance, computers, real estate, and retailing. Again, the critical factor was not necessarily invention, but some degree of foresight and the ability to adapt quickly to evolving conditions. Messrs. Kohlberg, Kravis, and Roberts did not invent the leveraged buyout, nor Michael Milken the junk bond. But these financiers did see potential uses for the devices that others didn't, and they made the new forms of financing ubiquitous. Software whiz Bill Gates built a $1.4 billion fortune not just by creating another operating system for personal computers, but by seeing to it that his system became the standard in an industry about to take off. Urban landlords such as New York's Harry Helmsley and Donald Trump weren't scared off by predictions that the center city was finished, and made pots of money when Manhattan came roaring back. In retailing Sam Walton amassed some $7.4 billion from the realization that theretofore ignored small-town shoppers had become affluent enough to buy brand-name goods in volume at discount prices.

Where should the first movers of today be looking? Into the morning, not the dawn, of the information age, for starters. Daniel Bell, professor of sociology at Harvard University, says, "Codification of theoretical knowledge is replacing capital and energy as the primary transforming resource." He cites electricity, oil, and nuclear power as examples of "transforming resources" in industrial society. According to Bell's research, industries where knowledge represents the largest input to production—as opposed to labor—already dominate the U.S. economy. Think investment banking and software development, vs. old-line manufacturing.

So far, excitement about making money with information has mostly fastened on two businesses, electronic databases and communications. Yes, the airline with the best reservation system can outgun competitors with its ability to manage scheduling, load factors, and a frequent-flier program. And yes, the telecommunications company with breakthrough technology in, say, digital data transmission stands to make a tidy sum in electronic mail or on-line database services. But this still leaves a lot of room for the individual entrepreneur in more mundane, less capital-intensive areas of information management.

Like the business of getting some of this new information into people's heads. By almost every estimate, workers from the lowliest to the loftiest will need progressively higher levels of education and more frequent retraining to keep them up to date. Fortunately, new technologies, particularly computer and video technologies, are available to help. It all adds up to opportunity for any entrepreneur who can boost productivity in both teaching and learning. Paul Strassmann, a consultant and former vice president of Xerox, predicts that by the turn of the century, 25% of the gross national product of the U.S. will be spent on education and professional training, compared with 10% today.

Steven P. Jobs, late of Apple Computer, apparently is eyeing this same trend. With the workstation from his new company, Next, he has taken dead aim at the university market. The experts predict, though, that there may be even more money to be made in job training. In the future workers may need to be intellectually retooled every year, or even more frequently. If you're turning out monoclonal antibodies, you're going to have to find some way to get your production people the latest scientific information about genetic engineering, including the papers presented at the conference in Tokyo last week.

This imperative extends even to the science—art?—of management. William Sahlman, an associate professor at the Harvard business school, sees glowing prospects for the entrepreneur who can help executives keep abreast of their craft, and not just through boring sessions in the classroom. No, imagine the hard-driving honcho at the end of the day, on his exercise bicycle or in the hot tub, after popping an instructional tape into his videocassette recorder. Later he can measure his progress with a diagnostic program on his home computer or participate in discussion on a computer network or videophone. Predicts Sahlman: "The entrepreneur who can help put that instructional package together will add value and, by the way, make himself rich."

In the new world of information, holding on to your intellectual property will be essential to reaping its benefits. A political stump speech, a computer software program, or a new financial formula—each will have monetary value. New laws, both national and international, are probably needed to protect such intangibles. Donald Elliott, professor at Yale law school, foresees the equivalent of a General Agreement on Tariffs and Trade for information, to prevent one nation's wealth from being unfairly appropriated by pirates abroad.

The aging of the population in the developed world will present opportunities galore. By the year 2020 elderly Americans will number about 60 million, representing about 20% of the population. Already more interested in fitness than prior generations, baby-boomers are likely to look to medicine and technology for all sorts of magic to stave off or minimize the effects of aging. The current mania for health clubs is just the beginning. Tom Mandel, senior management consultant of SRI International in Menlo Park, California, says, "People's demand for health care will be insatiable."

Entrepreneurs who can provide inexpensive diagnostics and medicine to meet this growing appetite should be well rewarded by a society progressively more worried about the cost. Biotechnologists will deliver many new wonders. Expect disease-specific pharmaceuticals targeted ever more precisely at particular illnesses, such as multiple sclerosis or diabetes. And don't leave engineers out of the ranks of the potentially wealthy. Designers of the next generations of prostheses, artificial organs, and aids for the visually and hearing impaired can anticipate a voracious market. So, too, manufacturers of medical equipment. Mandel looks for the day when the aerobically fit oldster will drop by the club, jog a bit, go for a swim, and then get a full body scan by a fourth-generation magnetic resonance imaging system that will deliver— ta-dah—a complete physical report. Time to replace those hip joints again?

This and other trends will influence a chameleonlike business that is as old as history and yet forever new. By nature a limited resource, real estate waxes and wanes in value depending on how preferences shift in response to large forces at play in society. As baby-boomers get older, for example, some will want to live closer to where they work. Why? Because commuters will face ever more crowded highways and because smoke-belching, earsplitting factories will become relics of our industrial past. Landlords who own commercial properties in predominantly residential areas and, conversely, residences in commercial areas should stand to benefit. Over the long term, the best play may be in owning real estate in up-and-coming university towns. These communities should benefit as a generation of college-educated retirees seek stimulating settings for their golden years and as entrepreneurs settle nearer centers of intelligence. Watch out, Williamstown, Massachusetts.

Would-be creators of wealth should be monitoring another trend of global significance: the emergence of regional—as opposed to national— economies. The political opposition that the U.S.-Canada free-trade pact faces is but a cough in a hurricane blowing in the opposite direction. Neighboring countries are banding together as never before to compete more effectively. The Europeans have embarked on an ambitious plan for economic integration post-1992. The Japanese have launched their own attempt at hegemony in the Pacific, negotiating country by country with their neighbors South Korea, Taiwan, Hong Kong, and Singapore to achieve new ground rules on trade and competition. The U.S. has lowered barriers between itself and Mexico. Evidence already points inexorably to the ultimate rise of three great regional blocs—the Western Pacific, the Americas, and Europe.

The Pacific region has all the necessary ingredients for 3.5%-plus per year real economic growth: Japanese capital, world-class technology, and an increasingly skilled work force. Even a poor Asian nation such as Indonesia may prove fertile ground for someone interested in creating wealth. Indonesia? Yes, there is more to it than Bali's beaches and the oil fields outside Jakarta.

Robert Hormats, vice chairman of international operations at Goldman Sachs investment bank, explains: "The country has been remarkably stable since Suharto took over after the bloody coup d'etat in 1965. There is a big population, a big market, a reasonably educated middle class, a lot of oil." He looks for Indonesia to take over a share of the manufacturing now done by Korea and other more developed East Asian countries. In the process, those who anticipate change will get rich. This should come as no surprise. Throughout history, most of the great fortunes have been made in newly industrializing countries.

Within Europe the Mediterranean countries, especially Spain, seem promising sites for wealth creation. Spaniards have shown themselves surprisingly entrepreneurial and internationally minded after the stultifying years of General Franco. As one of the EEC's newest members, Spain also has a chance to expand into a host of new markets.

William Johnston, a vice president of the Hudson Institute in Alexandria, Virginia, looks for Eastern and Western Europe to become more integrated and for the Easterners to benefit thereby. "Historically," he says, "Eastern Europeans are economically successful peoples who have been politically repressed." Any thawing of the cold war should hasten their chances to recover some of that success.

Regionalization and the economic development of emerging nations will hasten the return of megaprojects, those high-risk feats of complex engineering and construction, after a hiatus of a few years. An increase in trade within regions would perforce require new energy, transportation, and distribution links. Someone will have to build new factories and roads in Indonesia if it becomes an exporter of manufactured goods. Someone will have to integrate and rebuild the energy grids of the U.S., Canada, and Mexico if the Western Hemisphere is to become a more efficient competitor in world markets. Someone will have to develop the high-tech industrial parks that are sure to go up in Spain. While the overall responsibility for such projects may fall to governments, plenty of money will be made by carrying out their plans.

New technologies just lifting off will offer entrepreneurs a shot at out-of-this-world fortunes. Take space, for example. Three young businessmen are already using today's most advanced technology to make booster rockets and satellite-tracking systems for space missions. David Thompson, 34, Scott Webster, 36, and Bruce Ferguson, 34, pilot Orbital Sciences Corp. of Fairfax, Virginia. The private company's first product was a rocket that NASA astronauts will use to launch satellites into orbit from the space shuttle. Their latest, an air-launched booster called Pegasus, is being developed for the Defense Advanced Research Projects Agency (Darpa) and commercial customers. It holds out the prospect of launching satellites from highflying airplanes. Six-year-old Orbital Sciences, already profitable, projects 1988 revenues in excess of $60 million.

For a truly spectacular look ahead, consider the entrepreneurial possibilities inherent in molecular-scale machines capable of extracting gold from seawater or diamonds from egg yolks. This is nanotechnology, the 21st century's answer to alchemy. Theoretician K. Eric Drexler, a visiting scholar at Stanford University, is the leading champion of the new technology, which could build objects atom by atom. ("Nano" means "dwarf" in Greek.)

Drexler's idea is to create not just new molecules, but whole, visible structures composed of these molecules. The tiny machines—akin to miniaturized robot arms—would be provided with raw material from which they could build anything, including copies of themselves to hasten the production process. Every hour entire factories no larger than a grain of sand might produce billions of new assemblers. He cites enzymes that function as jigs and machine tools to shape large molecules as examples of nanomachines that exist in nature.

Properly instructed by computer software—the big challenge is figuring out just how—nano-assemblers in short order could turn out just about anything that can be designed at a fraction of the current cost and of a structural integrity far superior to anything on the market today. In Drexler's vision these machines could swim in a vat of chemicals and fuel, and in a few days manufacture a roomful of computers or rocket engines. Or they might roam through your body destroying cancer cells. Manufacturing and engineering as we know them would become obsolete.

Far-fetched? Perhaps, but then 20 years ago, who envisioned the possibility of designing and testing a new machine at a desktop engineering workstation? Extrapolating from recent developments in molecular biology and biochemistry, Drexler has been drawing blueprints for nanotechnology for over a decade. Marvin Minsky, a professor of computer science at Massachusetts Institute of Technology, writes in the forward to Drexler's book *Engines of Creation* that Drexler "has built on the soundest areas of present-day technical knowledge." Drexler predicts: "Nanotechnology is probable within 30 years. It will make developing a room-temperature superconductor look trivial by comparison." The likeliest people to profit from nanotechnology? Software designers who will write the programs to tell the nanomachines what to produce.

Replacing the world's manufacturing with a new technology. Building superprojects to link nations together. Moving beyond the Industrial Revolution into the Age of Information. They sound like tall orders. Too much for the individual entrepreneur? Work that only governments or giant corporations can do? Don't be too sure. Says Harvard's Sahlman: "As long as the entrepreneur relentlessly pursues new opportunities without regard to the resources he currently controls, he will always have the best shot at creating the most wealth." A recent study of 6,000 Harvard business school MBAs shows that 15 years or more after graduation, 25% of those who ran their own businesses were worth over $2.5 million, while only 12% of those employed by someone else were as affluent.

Increasingly, though, the entrepreneur will have to combine his wit and willingness to work with a good bit of managerial sophistication. The main reason? Increased competition. The proliferation of new companies in the past 15 years signals an abundance of rivals in just about every industry for years to come. To survive, the biggest companies will have to get smart and keep getting smarter. Foreign corporations will continue to invade others' home markets. Concludes Sahlman: "Superior management will be at a huge premium in the next 50 years."

The growing importance of managerial skill is good news for senior executives who should be able to command chunks of equity in any company that covets their talents. A forerunner of the emerging entrepreneur-manager may be James Tappan, a former group vice president at General Foods. He recently received a 10% equity stake in a new $100 million partnership established to buy and run existing consumer products companies. This in return for managing whatever operations are acquired. While not as great as the fortune of a John D. Rockefeller, $10 million, and the prospect of more to come, should keep the wolf from the door, at least until the 21st century.

Questions

1. What are the potential implications of the aging population and rapidly advancing technologies for a hospital and an automobile manufacturer?

2. How would you expect the trend toward an information-based economy to affect job design in the future?

3. If you view these changes through the lenses of the contingency, strategic choice, and population ecology approaches to organization–environment relations, what would each say are the implications of these changes for organizations in the future?

C A S E   9

Insurers under Siege

Obscure. Abstruse. Boring.

For years that was the image most people had of the insurance industry, a remote monolith shrouded by a cloud of mystery. Everybody bought insurance, but few buyers gave much thought to those who produced it. The insurance business, as a result, operated free from public scrutiny. Exempt from federal regulation, including most anti-trust laws, and subject only to feckless state regulation, the industry was a "private government," as Wyoming Senator Joseph C. O'Mahoney put it in 1945. As a legal cartel, it reaped bountiful profits and came to control enormous assets, now more than $1.8 trillion. Its premium income is 9% of the GNP. Few industries have ever enjoyed such unchecked political and economic power.

Now, the once-tranquil world of insurance is in turmoil. Instead of the most ignored industry in America, it has become perhaps the most reviled. Consumers, corporate executives, and lawmakers are lambasting insurers for everything from profiteering to an unseemly attitude of arrogance and insensitivity. "We're being besieged. It's a holocaust that's going on," complains Robert E. Vagely, president of the American Insurance Assn., the most prominent commercial-insurance trade group. Adds Chief Executive John J. Byrne of Fireman's Fund Insurance Co.: "We're at the bottom of everyone's list. Our name is mud."

'Long Decline.' A muddy image is only the most obvious sign of a far-reaching deterioration in the industry's well-being. Everywhere they look today, insurance executives see their power eroding, their markets contracting, and their profits evaporating. "They're in a state of panic," says J. Robert Hunter, president of the National Insurance Consumer Organization and the

Source: "Insurers under Siege" by Chris Welles and Christopher Farrell. Reprinted from August 21, 1989 issue of *Business Week*, pp. 72–78, by special permission, copyright © 1989 by McGraw-Hill, Inc.

industry's best-known critic. Consumers and other insurance buyers are benefiting from these developments, which are producing better insurance services at more competitive prices. The insurance industry, however, may end up losing its status as the chief provider of these services. It is threatened, says consultant Orin S. Kramer, "by a period of long-term decline"—a reversal of fortunes that would be among the most dramatic for a major industry in American business history.

Insurers are suffering from many forces beyond their control, notably surging liability damages that have beset property/casualty companies and high interest rates that have squeezed life insurers. Yet, says Washington attorney T. Lawrence Jones, Vagley's predecessor at the AIA, "they've created a lot of their own problems."

Insurance executives have long been known for their obstinate resistance to change and new ideas—a not surprising shortcoming for individuals used to the stability of cartel life and whose business is predicting the future by extrapolating from the past. "They're the nicest, most honorable people in business," says Jones. "But they're not the most imaginative or creative."

They are, though, working on strategies to clean up their image and befriend their antagonists. "The industry's instinct is to say no, do nothing," says Vagley. "We're trying to develop affirmative responses." But the outlook is not propitious, for the industry faces many noxious changes:

• Its customers are rebelling. The revolt by California consumers against soaring automobile-insurance rates last year culminated in voter approval of Proposition 103, whose sweeping reforms include a 20% rollback in auto and other insurance rates. The fever is spreading. As many as 10 similar voter initiatives are possible in 1990, and 300 insurance-reform bills have been introduced in dozens of state legislatures. Corporations are bypassing insurers in favor of do-it-yourself approaches, which are siphoning off a third of the property/casualty industry's premiums. "We have largely ignored and mistreated our customers," concedes Leslie Cheek III, head of Crum & Forster Insurance Cos.' Washington office.

• The industry's political clout is crumbling. State legislators and insurance commissioners, once comfortably in the industry's pocket, are now more independent, even adversarial. In Washington, the industry has suffered some embarrassing legislative defeats. "They're losing control of their destiny," says Bruce A. Bunner, a partner at accounting firm KPMG Peat Marwick and former California insurance commissioner.

• Some insurance markets face possible government takeover. The auto and health markets have become so dysfunctional, with millions of people unable to get affordable coverage, that these markets may be increasingly assumed by state and federal insurance mechanisms. Insurance consultant Barbara J. Lautzenheiser sees "a real tendency toward socialization of all insurance."

• The cartel is dying. Competition has become vicious. "Soft" markets, when insurers often lose money underpricing each other, are more protracted, while "hard" markets, when companies can raise prices and rebuild balance sheets, are briefer. Critics are seeking to abolish insurers' antitrust immunity, which could make competition even worse.

• Insurers' financial health is deteriorating. "There will almost certainly be a major shakeout, major insolvencies, and financial dislocations," says Robert H. Moore, senior vice-president of Alexander & Alexander Services Inc., a large insurance broker. Morgan Stanley & Co. analyst Norman L. Rosenthal foresees "a fundamental downsizing of the property/casualty industry." Life insurers also face shrinkage. While they have mostly escaped serious image-tarnishing, their profits are also under severe, perhaps irreversible, pressure.

The proximate cause of the property/casualty industry's traumas was the widely publicized liability-coverage crisis of 1984-86. After a six-year price war, insurers hiked some premiums several-fold. They refused to write or renew other coverage, which closed down facilities from jails to day-care centers. They blamed excessive liability litigation. But mainly, they had simply panicked, in typical herd-like fashion, when their profits sunk to new lows. Their actions set off a fierce public backlash—"retribution beyond the industry's wildest imaginings," according to Cheek.

Jolting Blow. Yet the roots of the industry's traumas extend back much further, to attitudes engendered by the insurance cartel, organized during the 1800s by fire insurers, forerunners of today's property/casualty companies. The temptation to slash prices has always been intense in insurance markets because insurance is sold primarily on price. To protect profits, insurers erected mechanisms to fix prices, standardize products, and share information.

In 1944, the cartel suffered a jolt—the Supreme Court held the industry subject to federal antitrust laws. But the industry flexed its political muscle and won passage in 1945 of the McCarran-Ferguson Act, which exempted it from anti-trust laws so long as it was regulated by the states. McCarran left intact the cartel's price-fixing mechanism, a group of industry-controlled rating bureaus, most of which were consolidated in 1971 into the Insurance Services Office. The ISO issued "advisory" rates that were high enough to protect even the most inefficient concerns from insolvency.

The cartel began unraveling in the 1950s. Auto and homeowners insurance came to be dominated by large "direct writers" such as State Farm Mutual Automobile Insurance Co., with in-house sales forces. They underpriced other insurers that sold policies through vast networks of high-commission independent agents. The agency writers were forced to discount ISO rates.

Commercial insurers followed ISO until the 1970s, when supply and demand became badly imbalanced. On the supply side, the cartel, like all cartels, had chronic excess capacity and excess cartel membership. Returns on equity of around 25% a year started enticing billions of dollars of new underwriting capacity, especially from the booming London market, where insurers lay off some of their risk with reinsurers.

Demand growth, meanwhile, was already slowing. Increasingly sophisticated corporate risk managers began insuring themselves. Companies, industry groups, even municipalities and nonprofits set up alternative facilities such as their own "captive" insurers. According to the Tillinghast division of Towers, Perrin, Forster & Crosby, a consulting firm, the alternative market now has a 35% market share, depriving insurers of $50 billion in annual premiums. By 1995, Tillinghast projects, the alternative share could reach 50%.

Insurers could not have forestalled the alternative market. But they are to blame for its rapid growth. In hard markets, they acted as if buyers had nowhere else to go, jacking up prices and walking away from lines that seemed unattractive. "Their heavy-handedness really turned off a lot of their clients," says Richard C. Heydinger, risk manager for Hallmark Cards Inc. Now, hundreds of major companies and large portions of industries such as pharmaceuticals and chemicals are self-insured. After the industry all but abandoned the medical-malpractice market in the 1970s, doctors and hospitals set up their own insurance vehicles. Insurers have made little headway trying to regain market share. ISO President Fred R. Marcon concedes that most of the business lost is "gone forever."

Insurers for years ignored the alternative market, refusing, for instance, to deal with captives. Insurance brokers, though, created a lucrative business by helping to set up and manage captives. Insurers' belated efforts to offer services to captives have not been very successful. "They could have been the leaders," says Charles L. Ruoff, head of strategic planning at Fred S. James & Co., a large insurance broker. "But by the time they got interested, the ship had left the dock."

The business that insurers are losing to alternative markets tends to be their best business. The reason is a pernicious process known as "adverse selection." Companies with low insurance risks tend to insure themselves, while risk-prone companies tend to buy insurance. And the risks that self-insurers retain tend to be their most predictable, such as workers' compensation. They go outside mainly for high-risk coverage, such as the catastrophic loss of an off-shore oil rig. "The insurance industry is being left with a much worse book of business," says consultant Barbara D. Stewart. A few venturesome insurers, notably American International Group Inc., developed the skills to handle new, tough risks, on which they make big profits. Most companies, though, chase the shrinking supply of routine low-risk business, exacerbating overcapacity and competition.

The alternative market and growing overcapacity have made insurance cycles hazardous. Hard and soft markets each used to last about three years. But the soft market that began in the late 1970s was the longest (six years) and deepest in history. And despite the sharp price hikes, the latest hard market was about the shortest (18 months). Aggravating the severity of recent cycles has been a big shift in the industry's business mix. Once it wrote mainly property coverage, where claims are made soon after an accident. Now it mainly sells liability coverage, where damages are less predictable and often do not surface until years after a policy is written. And while property loss costs have been dropping, liability costs keep rising. Still, with claims costs so far off and uncertain, many insurers feel less inhibited in cutting prices, often recklessly.

Life insurers for years avoided the competitive havoc of their property/casualty brethren. They had something of a cartel of their own. Everyone followed the pricing lead of the large Eastern mutual companies. They grew fat on the wondrous creation known as whole life, with its huge spread between the niggardly yield to policyholders and the lush return on insurers' investments.

Double-digit interest rates in the early 1980s wrecked the business. Customers bought cheap term insurance and defected to high-yield investments offered by banks and mutual funds. Insurers were forced to counter with market-rate products such as universal life. Their spreads are now so wafer-thin that some big players such as Cigna Corp. and Travelers Corp. are sharply reducing their life business.

Coalition for Change. The already badly tattered property/casualty cartel, meanwhile, faces further damage. Last year, 19 states filed suits alleging that 32 insurance defendants conspired, starting in 1983, to restrict the availability of commercial-liability coverage, mainly by altering the terms of the industry's most widely used policy. The suits say the defendants used acts of "boycott, coercion" and "intimidation," which are excluded from the McCarran-Ferguson Act's antitrust immunity. The alleged aim was to end the price war by limiting supply. According to the states, this was "an important contributing factor" to the liability crisis.

A federal judge recently said he intends to dismiss the litigation on the grounds that the defendants' actions were immune from prosecution under McCarran. Such a ruling, which will be appealed by the states, would likely intensify the already broad political assault being mounted against McCarran. Congress is considering several bills that, while allowing some joint activities, would sharply modify the act. To industry critics, McCarran symbolizes the industry's privileged status.

Consumerists, many of whom consider insurance reform their top priority, have put together a formidable coalition that includes groups representing women, minorities, labor, senior citizens, and small business. They have even enlisted the influential American Bar Assn., many of whose members resent being blamed by insurers for causing the liability crisis.

Once, such a coalition would have been no match for the insurance lobby. But now, says a Capitol Hill staffer, the insurers "don't have anybody on their side." State insurance commissioners and legislators are distancing themselves from the mud-splattered industry. Insurance brokers, once close to insurance executives, are now loyal to corporate risk managers.

Waning Power. Insurers' most powerful allies have been the 150,000 independent insurance agents who, says a lobbyist, are "the industry's shock
troops." Aided by fat PAC budgets, they have intimate political connections
at the state and federal level. Officially the agents back McCarran. However,
says Dennis Jay, a spokesman for the National Association of Professional
Insurance Agents, "we're no longer following with blind faith what the big
carriers want."

Signs of the industry's waning political power are abundant. In what the
AIA's Vagley calls "a major defeat," the industry failed to derail the 1986
Liability Risk Retention Act, which made it much easier for businesses to
self-insure. Vagley has been quietly exploring a compromise on McCarran.
"A number of our members feel its benefits are outweighed by the political
mischief it creates," he says. The ISO, meanwhile, recently announced that
next year it will stop issuing advisory rates and instead estimate future losses
and related costs. Insurers will then have to factor in their own projections of
profits and overhead. While critics claim that ISO figures will still facilitate
price-fixing, the move is likely to heighten rate competition.

Some of the industry's most important markets face an even more serious
threat: government takeover. The reason is a big shift in society's view of
certain kinds of insurance. Affordable auto and health insurance is now seen
less as a voluntary option than as a necessity, even an entitlement. Insurers,
though, don't want to sell affordable insurance to everyone. They deliberately discriminate. They charge people thought to be good risks relatively
low rates. Bad risks, who are often poor, are charged high premiums, regardless of whether they can afford it, and they may be denied coverage altogether. The result: millions of Americans with little if any insurance.

James M. Stone, former Massachusetts insurance commissioner who
now runs a small auto insurer, says the insurance industry "should have
taken the initiative" and worked with the government to develop a mix of
public and private mechanisms "to make sure its products were available and
affordable to all." Instead, the industry ignored the problem. It paid little heed
to loss prevention and simply passed costs to customers. Now, the auto and
health markets are in such disarray that demands are growing for government insurance covering everyone.

In auto insurance, which produces 42% of the property/casualty
industry's volume, the impetus for socialized insurance stems from relentlessly rising claims costs and public pressure on state regulators to keep
premiums low. Plagued by losses, some insurers are leaving the auto business. Others are turning down more bad risks. In large urban states with the
highest costs and premiums, notably New Jersey and Massachusetts, drivers
who can't afford or get insurance are relegated to "residual" markets of last
resort subsidized by insurers and states. New Jersey's state-run residual
market has half the state's autos and a $3 billion deficit.

Auto insurers are now pushing such measures as broader no-fault laws
and cheap no-frills policies. But some observers feel these solutions do not

go far enough. "If this situation continues," says Crum & Forster's Cheek, "I don't see any alternative to a government takeover." As states have to foot more of the bill for the bad risks, observers feel, some will want to insure all motorists. With monopoly power, they could control costs and subsidize poor risks with premiums from good ones. States that don't socialize will still likely continue to subject insurers to low-return, utility-type regulation.

The outlook for health insurance is also grim. Their market is already a patchwork of public and private systems. In theory, it makes sense: private insurers, mainly life companies, who get a third of their premiums from health, serve the good risks who can afford to pay. Through medicare and medicaid, the government subsidizes coverage for the old and poor. Non-profit Blue Cross/Blue Shield helps the government by selling coverage to all comers.

Minimum Standards. But this arrangement is breaking down. Government programs have become more restrictive and cover a declining portion of the needy. And the loss-plagued Blues are targeting better risks. This is raising the number of people without coverage, now 37 million. Many hospitals treat the uninsured but then inflate bills for clients who are able to pay, mainly employers. To arrest skyrocketing costs, which have resisted years of contain-ment programs, 60% of all large employers self-insure. Most insurers serving the rest have been operating in the red. They've been unable to raise rates fast enough to keep up with cost inflation. They're losing market share to "man-aged care" facilities such as health maintenance organizations. And they're losing big money on their own HMOs.

Things could get even worse. Ohio and several other states are consider-ing state-run health plans. In part to avoid picking up the tab for the uninsured, many large employers such as Chrysler Corp. and American Airlines Inc. now support a federal plan. National health insurance has always been a political long shot, but corporate backing could change that. A federal system would not necessarily threaten insurers. Their role, for instance, would be preserved under a bill sponsored by Senator Edward M. Kennedy (D-Mass.) that would impose minimum standards on employers and guarantee similar coverage to others through medicaid.

But critics, including many physicians, claim the best, maybe only, way to control costs and make sure everyone is covered is to make the government the sole payer. They cite as a model Canada's tax-financed national health system, which is far less expensive than that of the U.S. Insurers claim its quality is inferior. Still, only 3% of Canadians favor a switch to a U.S.-style system, while 61% of Americans would prefer the Canadian system, accord-ing to Louis Harris and Gallup polls.

Thin Margins. Socialized health insurance would usurp insurers' under-writing business, except for excess coverage not provided by the government.

Insurers could serve as administrators, much as they do today for corporate self-insurers. But they would face heavy competition from the Blues and noninsurance administrators. And they would lose the income from premium investment. Says David F. D'Alessandro, head of group health for John Hancock Mutual Life Insurance Co.: "Processing margins are very thin. It's not a very good business."

Over the next few years, companies with thin margins may consider themselves lucky, for they will at least be alive. That may not be the case for dozens, even hundreds, of their compatriots.

On the surface, the property/casualty business looks fit. The 1984-86 price hikes, coupled with investment gains from the booming stock and bond markets, boosted the industry's surplus, or net worth, to $117 billion. From a $3.0 billion loss in 1985, net income jumped to $12.8 billion in 1988.

But appearances are deceiving. The quality of the policies that the industry is writing is deteriorating. Price-cutting is rampant. To compensate, insurers are skimping on reserves for future claims. As a result, says Shearson Lehman Hutton Inc. insurance analyst Udayan D. Ghose, current earnings are "grossly exaggerated." Earnings, further, do not reflect the danger that insurers will never be able to collect on claims against some fly-by-night reinsurers who popped up during the last price war. That hit, says Oppenheimer & Co. analyst Myron M. Picoult, could be $16 billion.

Losses from insurer insolvencies are already escalating. The eventual tab for recent liquidations could be as much as $20 billion, much of which will have to be picked up by state guaranty funds underwritten by solvent insurers. Former Colorado Insurance Commissioner John Kezer has called the problem "huge, growing, and . . . unchecked." A probe of three failed casualty companies by Representative John D. Dingell (D-Mich.) and his oversight and investigations subcommittee revealed, he says, "a deadly mix of incompetence, greed, self-dealing, and fraudulent activity." These practices, coupled with weak regulation, his staff said, "are disturbingly similar" to those that produced the S&L crisis.

Life insurers are not in much better shape. Many have been subsidizing losses on new universal-life products with profits from old whole-life policies. Some are precariously leveraged, and the quality of some of their investments is dubious. "There are many companies in deep, fundamental trouble," says Robert McDonald, chief executive officer of LifeUSA, a Minneapolis life company. "People would be scared if they knew what was happening."

An Earthquake? A wave of insurance collapses could have a domino effect. It could overwhelm often weak and understaffed state regulators, drag down healthy companies, and ultimately bring on federal regulation. Many analysts think a hair-curling shakeout is inevitable, and would even be salutary, to wring out overcapacity and other inefficiencies still burdening the dying cartel. The industry would end up smaller but with a chance to rebuild its health.

But looming down the road may be some big hits for property/casualty insurers that could make overcapacity seem like a fender-bender claim. If court rulings turn decisively against them, they could get stuck with much of the $175 billion cost of cleaning up Superfund toxic-waste sites. A worst-case Los Angeles earthquake could sock insurers with a $60 billion bill. Says Tillinghast Vice-President H. Felix Kloman: "You're talking about a sequence of events that could topple the whole industry."

There isn't much insurers can do to prevent the quake but pray. There is a lot they can do to arrest their slow slide into a permanent eclipse. It would require a heavy dose of enterprise, imagination, and hustle—in short, a cultural revolution. But if insurers are to regain anything close to their former power and glory, they have no other choice.

AIG THRIVES ON BUSINESS OTHER COMPANIES WON'T TOUCH

Shanghai's teeming port drew many a dreamer and adventurer at the century's turn. One enterprising American, 27-year-old Cornelius Vander Starr, founded an insurance company in a two-room office in 1919. Only in 1926, by which time he had offices throughout the Far East, did Starr open a New York branch. That's a circuitous origin for what evolved into American International Group Inc., the largest shareholder-owned commercial insurance company in America. But then again, AIG is unlike any other U.S. insurer.

'Genius.' While most ignore overseas markets, AIG operates in more than 130 countries. As many American rivals posted anemic returns, AIG earned an average return-on-equity of 18% this past decade by cannily exploiting less popular markets and keeping a tight check on costs. While its rivals mostly sell commodity products, AIG excels in exotic niche markets—all for a pretty penny.

The company's success clearly bears the stamp of Maurice R. "Hank" Greenberg, its tough, combative chairman, president, and CEO. A trim, fit New Yorker of legendary discipline, he took the helm from Starr in 1968, when AIG's net income was $17.2 million. Its stock market value the following year, after going public, was some $285 million. In 1988, AIG earned $1.2 billion, and the company's market value is now $15.5 billion. Says New

York State Insurance Superintendent James P. Corcoran: "The guy's a genius."

As with Michael R. Milken on junk bonds, when the 63-year-old Greenberg talks insurance, people listen—if uncomfortably. Charming and wryly humorous, Greenberg can turn acerbic when holding forth on common industry practices, such as lax underwriting standards. Indeed, says an insurance broker, he's "widely loathed" by his peers, regarded as a brilliant loner who refuses to join major industry trade groups or schmooze with competitors. Greenberg, often trotting the globe, runs an entrepreneurial, high-stress workplace. For executives who can hack it, the reward is a slice of management's 31% stake in AIG, with Greenberg alone owning or controlling stock worth $670 million. Says T. Lawrence Jones, former head of the American Insurance Assn.: Greenberg is the only man to make an absolute fortune in insurance over the last 20 years."

He did it by taking risks others shun. Although AIG sells a broad range of insurance products, "we look for markets without a lot of competition," says Thomas R. Tizzio, vice-chairman of AIG's North American property/casualty business.

Only Game in Town. Among its specialty products are liability insurance for directors and officers, coverage it's flogging in Europe as deal mania sweeps the Continent, and for professionals, mostly lawyers and accountants. AIG's trademark is seizing opportunities, says Jones, recalling that during the difficult market of the late 1970s, AIG's directors and officers policy was the only one the trade group could buy. Currently, the company is among a handful selling tailor-made pollution liability policies.

For its multinational clients, AIG often underwrites worldwide coverage. Unlike other U.S. insurers, it has eagerly provided services and backup coverage to the offshore "captive" insurers since the movement's early days. And AIG is comfortable creating markets. For instance, it plowed new ground starting in 1979 by entering joint ventures with East Bloc nations.

In a classic Greenberg move to take advantage of others' ineptitude, AIG is about to expand its minor presence in a troubled Main Street business—auto insurance. It aims to tap the latest marketing and servicing techniques to hold down expenses while reducing claims costs through other innovations—including possibly its own repair shops. "We expect to be a major underwriter of the business in the future," says Greenberg.

Financially, however, AIG is conservative. It tries to earn a buck the old-fashioned way in insurance—through underwriting profits. Its executives are almost cult-like in their insistence that premiums be high enough to reflect a policy's risk. "Expecting investment income to bail you out is a dangerous game," says Vice-Chairman Edward E. Matthews. AIG can also compete hard without lowballing rates since it's a tightwad company. It is a low-cost producer with an expense ratio of about 20%; most competitors have a ratio of around 30%.

Global Roots. The company's global network comes directly out of its foreign origins. AIG shifted headquarters from Shanghai to New York only in 1939. In sharp contrast to its U.S. competition, some 31% of its property/casualty

operating profits and 93% of its life insurance operating income were generated overseas in 1988. About 65% of all pretax earnings came from foreign markets during the past 11 years. "We understand doing business globally," says Greenberg. "We feel comfortable in any part of the world."

AIG's foreign operations are a source of stable profits, with income from many less competitive markets, especially in fast-growing Southeast Asia, offsetting the earnings drag from vicious pricing cycles in the U.S. In Japan, AIG is a strong niche player, ranking third in personal accident insurance, for one, and is about to expand there through a new company closely tied to Japan Travel Bureau Inc. In anticipation of Europe 1992, AIG recently restructured its Continental operations by replacing 13 different national companies with a new one, Paris-based UNAT. AIG is expanding into financial services and is already a factor in such markets as international interest-rate swaps and overseas merchant banking.

One-Man Show. Although it's still able to turn a profit selling life policies in Beirut, some of AIG's foreign adventures do go sour. After years of struggle, AIG finally broke into the South Korean life market, but business is moribund with half its agents out on strike. And while it's still insuring foreign interests in China despite the Great Leap Backward, hopes for expanding into the domestic market of AIG's historic homeland have dimmed for now. Back in the U.S., even AIG's earnings machine will sputter if price-cutting in the commercial market continues. Wall Street is edgy, too, about the lack of an obvious corporate heir to the dominating Greenberg.

Still, Greenberg is confident that AIG is set to make the most of the upheaval he sees racking the property/casualty business these next few years. After all, in China, AIG's birthplace, the word crisis is made up of the characters for danger and opportunity.

Questions

1.   Trace the development of the insurance industry niche and the major changes it has experienced over time.

2.   How have these changes affected the size and shape of the insurance industry niche?

3.   To what extent did/does the insurance industry control its environment? How has this relationship changed over time?

4.   Using the model presented in Chapter 10, explain what types of insurance firms and what types of strategies are likely to do well during the 1990s.

Hard Road ahead for Auto Insurers

The biggest puzzle about auto insurance—apart from why it costs the earth—is why so many property and casualty companies sell so much of it for so little gain. Detested by consumers as price-gouging fat cats and dismissed by investors as dogs, auto insurers are confronting a fast-approaching tidal wave of regulation, soaring costs, and fierce competition. By most measures, the $69 billion business—bigger in total revenues than the airline industry—has been only marginally profitable for a decade.

The future looks dismal. A massive consumer revolt, sparked by surging premiums, is winning powerful supporters in state-houses and Congress. Consumer activists hope to clone all or part of California's Proposition 103, now under review by the state supreme court, in 14 other states. Along with provisions that permit banks to sell their own competing auto policies and that require the state to give consumers price and service information, Proposition 103 calls for a 20% rollback from November 1987 rates, another 20% discount for the more than 80% of policyholders that the law defines as good drivers, and a rigid system of regulating rate increases.

The rate rollback will have far-reaching effects on the auto insurance industry if it is upheld, but they are not likely to be felt for quite a while. Insurers will appeal an unfavorable decision to the U.S. Supreme Court, a process that could take years. Travelers Corp. already has attempted to pull out of the California auto insurance market but has been prevented from leaving by regulators. And Geico Corp., which has stopped signing up new customers in the state, has made it clear that it will decamp if it sees no prospects for profits. Says Chairman William Snyder: "We will not, I repeat, not knowingly write policies at a loss for long."

Even as angry consumers threaten to jam a lid on premiums, the industry is feeling a profit pinch that promises to turn into a permanent squeeze. Survival in this treacherous environment demands that insurers do two things: First, face up to their appalling customer relations and join with consumer advocates in offering car owners a better deal. Second, realize that only large, low-cost specialists and superskilled niche players can succeed in the business. "There will be fewer insurance companies down the road," predicts Eugene Meyung, president of Geico, one of a handful of highly profitable auto insurers.

As anyone who gets behind the wheel knows, insuring that wheel is expensive. Most states require drivers to carry minimum coverage, costing anywhere from $200 to $1,000 per car, and the average premium per car, about $500 last year, roughly doubled during the Eighties. This rise outpaced gains in take-home pay by a factor of more than two.

To the injury of high prices, insurers often add the insult of high-handed treatment when policyholders report a claim. But there are signs that some companies are going out of their way to treat their customers fairly. State Farm, for example, no longer automatically boosts premiums for a longtime policyholder who reports an accident—even if he caused it. Says CEO Edward Rust Jr.: "We value our long-term customers who have had good records." Both Geico and 20th Century Insurance have increased the number of drive-in centers at which customers can get on-the-spot payments.

But the legacy of soaring premiums and poor customer relations is coming back to haunt the industry. The present system of auto coverage—which encourages, if not forces accident victims to turn to the courts for recompense even for minor injuries—is breaking down, especially in high-cost urban areas. Awards are rising because jurors don't hesitate to soak insurers, and fraud is rampant on small claims that companies don't bother to investigate closely. Except in states such as New York and Michigan that have true no-fault laws—which trade off faster, more generous compensation from the policyholder's company for the victim's right to sue—there are few effective mechanisms for limiting litigation or fraud.

Auto insurers need to take the lead in revamping coverage to include no-fault provisions, but they are moving too slowly. Says Peter Walker, a director at McKinsey & Co.: "The industry got burned in the Seventies when watered-down no-fault laws failed to deliver the expected savings." Under a strict no-fault system, insurers could sell policies that require them to pay the medical expenses, repair bills, and lost earnings of their own customers regardless of who caused the accident. But they could be sued for pain and suffering only in cases of serious, permanent injury or death.

Consumers benefit from no-fault because with it rates would rise much more slowly than they do now. In New York, for example, premiums have increased at just two-thirds of the California pace since 1982. Moreover, to gain consumer support for no-fault, companies will likely have to cut rates perhaps as much as 10% initially. Insurers would gain because, as claims came under control, they would be able to earn a reasonable return without charging ruinous rates.

Unfortunately, no-fault would do little to hold down premiums for auto collision and theft insurance. That is why the industry also must persuade government to adopt stricter safety standards for cars, step up highway enforcement, and crack down on body shop rip-offs. But insurers have to do more than crank up the lobbying machine, says Kemper Property & Casualty President Gerald Maatman, and there are signs that they are getting the message. Fireman's Fund and Travelers, for instance, have recently announced a plan to give discounts to policyholders who participate in a program to combat auto theft that tags cars so that police can easily recognize them if they are stolen.

In addition to repairing their image with consumers, auto insurers must also deal with the changing dynamics of their industry. Powerful forces have been driving profitability down. Claims are spiraling. Payouts for bodily injury, the largest component of claims, have risen faster than premiums for most of the 1980s, and the price of car repairs is rising too. But the threat of more regulation and growing price competition are restraining companies from bringing their rates in line with the jump in claim costs.

Judged purely on operating results, private passenger auto insurance is, on average, not profitable at all. Based on the operating numbers the industry reports to regulators, returns on revenues have been averaging −1% and returns on net worth an estimated −2% during the 1980s. On a more liberal measure that includes investment income from shareholders' equity or, in the case of mutual companies, policyholders' net worth, the industry's after-tax return on net worth has been running around 10% over the decade. That figure falls short of the average 12.6% return of the Standard & Poor's 500 over the same period. Admits industry critic Robert Hunter, head of the National Insurance Consumer Organization: "Profit is not where you are going to cut rates."

Some insurers are in better shape to survive in the bleak, high-cost, low-profit world ahead. They are the specialists in auto and other personal insurance that market directly to consumers either through their own exclusive agents or by telephone or mail. Direct writers' expenses average just 20% of premiums, vs. 30% for agency writers, the multiline companies that sell through independent agents. Independent agents represent two or more insurers and cream off some 15% of premiums in commissions, putting agency companies' total selling costs at 20% or more. Direct writers' selling costs, on the other hand, range from 12% of premiums to less than 2%.

Because their costs of doing business are lower, direct writers can undersell the agency companies 10% or more and grab market share. Indeed, they now control 63% of the auto insurance market, vs. 52% in the early 1970s. Direct writers benefit from a virtuous cycle. Initially these companies used their lower rates and underwriting abilities to assess risk to siphon off the best drivers from the agency concerns. The best drivers, in turn, are cheaper to service, produce smaller losses, and tend to have high renewal rates.

As pressures on rates intensify, direct writers are working even harder to extend their competitive edge. The most successful is State Farm Mutual Automobile Insurance Co., as it is formally known. Located in Bloomington, Illinois, it derives two-thirds of its revenues from personal auto premiums. State Farm insures nearly one-fifth of all U.S. cars, almost twice as many as Sears Roebuck's Allstate Insurance Co., the No. 2 company. Says one reverent competitor: "State Farm is the McDonald's—no, the IBM—of this business: best prices, best service."

The heart of this operation is a remarkable force of 17,000 agents who sell only State Farm's products, mostly auto, homeowners, and life policies. These "good neighbors" are considered among the finest salespeople in the business. They work on lower commissions than independent agents—10% vs. 15%—but benefit from State Farm's excellent sales management programs and support services.

As the regulatory climate gets stormier, State Farm's top priority will be protecting its agents. If it pulled out of states like California, where hurricanes threaten, its agents would have to stop selling profitable homeowners and life policies as well as the unprofitable auto insurance. So when the warnings reach gale force, the company will just stop hiring agents in the state and pursuing new auto business aggressively. It will continue to service existing policyholders, however. "Our commitment is to keep our promises," says Edward Rust, whose father was chief executive before him.

Geico, a shareholder-owned company in Washington, D.C., that markets mainly by telephone and mail, has very few agents, and 90% of its business comes from selling auto insurance. As a result it can enter sunny states and exit chilly ones more easily than an insurer like State Farm can. Geico got its start during the Depression peddling policies to federal workers and nearly went belly up in the mid-Seventies when it expanded feverishly by insuring too many bad drivers. Today it practically mints money. Geico has been averaging an annual 31% return on equity for the past decade.

The company's discipline and prowess as an underwriter are widely admired. It insures middle-aged, middle-class drivers with clean accident records and insists on pricing policies to secure an average underwriting profit of 4% even if it has to sacrifice revenue growth. That means Geico is one of the few that makes money from selling auto insurance before counting its investment income.

Geico wants to increase policies in force at a rate of 5% to 6% a year if it can do so profitably. In pursuit of this goal, it is trying to refine its underwriting still more by investing in a new database that tracks policyholders' past claim records with other insurers. This information helps the insurer boost growth by culling the good risks from among the applicants it now rejects and enables Geico to reduce the number of liars and frauds that slip through its screening.

Some multiline agency writers, such as Travelers, have responded to the more aggressive competition from direct writers by trimming their personal auto insurance divisions. But Aetna Life & Casualty, a diversified financial services giant in Hartford and the No. 5 personal auto insurer, is making an all-out effort to turn its unprofitable auto insurance business around.

Aetna is trying to make its agents more productive. By selling auto insurance only through those agents who already handle a high volume of the company's other policies, the division has been able to justify a $156 million investment in computer systems. Now most agents have a direct computer link to Aetna's underwriting and claims handling departments, speeding up transactions between the agency and the company.

A select few agency players prosper by slipping into niches where the State Farms of the world can't—or won't—follow. Progressive Corp. of Cleveland sells through over 41,000 independent agents, claims it has higher service costs per policyholder than anyone else in the business, and concentrates on customers that other companies reject. Believe it or not, Progressive is also one of the most profitable companies in auto insurance.

The alchemists at Progressive turn dross to gold by carefully screening drivers who can't get anyone to insure them. Progressive uses remarkably detailed data on drivers in highly sophisticated ways to separate the guy with too many speeding tickets from the woman who built her car from a kit, so it can price its policies accordingly. Joyce Culbert, an insurance analyst at S. G. Warburg & Co., a merchant bank, describes the method as "take the best of the worst risks, charge the average of the worst risks, and make a ton." "Ton" is something of an understatement for a firm with an average annual return on equity of more than 23% for the past ten years. Like Geico, Progressive also makes an underwriting profit: an average 2.9% a year over the past decade.

The niche for 20th Century is Los Angeles County, and it is mining 24% returns on equity, but from the other extreme of the market. Founded in 1958 by a curmudgeonly independent agent named Louis Foster—he believes that one day the K marts of the world will drive the full-price emporiums out of business—the company boasts rock-bottom prices and one of the lowest ratios of expenses to premiums, less than 0.09:1, in the business.

What's the secret? "We don't insure Porsches," Foster growls. The company also doesn't insure drivers under age 25, speeders, and job hoppers—refusing even to mail applications to half the people who ask for them. Its marketing expenses are microscopic because it does not need to advertise. More than 90% of its customers renew their policies, and the company gets new names by word of mouth. Occasionally 20th Century exerts itself and mails a note to policyholders asking them to mention the company to a few other pillars of the community. One of Foster's earliest breaks came when a client mailed him a list of his entire church membership.

With no fat to trim and no place to run, 20th Century is especially vulnerable to Proposition 103's rate rollback. But California regulators would be likely to grant whatever requests for rate relief are allowed under 103 to this popular home-grown company.

The winners in the auto insurance race are going to be the low-cost producers, especially those who work effectively to get drivers a better deal. If the result of California's consumer revolt is that prices are held below the cost of providing the product, the consequences will be totally predictable. Losses will mount, insurers will issue fewer policies, and the state itself will be saddled with the responsibility of insuring the growing number of motorists—typically those who live in the highest-cost, urban areas—who will be turned away by private companies.

For a while, the state can force company shareholders, drivers in rural areas, and buyers of other types of property and casualty insurance to subsidize this pool. But eventually a mass exodus of companies becomes inevitable, leaving behind a wrecked insurance market. This is precisely what has already happened in New Jersey and Massachusetts, where regulators held rates below costs for years. Their residents now pay the highest premiums in the land.

Questions

1. How would you describe environmental conditions within the auto insurance market?

2. What are the domain strategies of State Farm, Geico, Travelers, Aetna, Progressive Corp., and 20th Century? Describe each organization's domain of operations.

3. To what extent is each of these companies vulnerable to change in the auto insurance industry's niche size and niche shape?

A 19th-Century Firm Shifts, Reinvents Itself and Survives 100 Years

Gainesville, Ga.—In a long box in a narrow closet in a low building by a road, there is an old photograph, in sepia, of a man feeding turkey quills into the rollers of a machine. The man is making featherbone.

Featherbone was a popular sewing notion around the turn of the century. It was made of finely split turkey quills bound to form a cord, and it was used to stiffen and shape corsets and collars and bustles and gowns. It was patented in 1883 by Edward K. Warren, a Three Oaks, Mich., merchant, whose Warren Featherbone Co. grew into the world's mightiest featherbone producer. "I have always Warren's Featherbone used in my costumes," actress Sarah Bernhardt wrote in 1901, "for I believe it to be the best dress boning material in existence."

Featherbone fell victim to changing fashions and the development of plastics. But Warren Featherbone Co. still exists as a thriving small business, headquartered here. It makes baby clothes now, and it is controlled and run by descendants of Mr. Warren. In its own quiet way, the company is a reminder that, even in this restive financial era, there is a core to U.S. business that has value and tradition, and that endures.

A Survivor. "We've asked ourselves how it is we could be over 100 years old when so many other companies, particularly in the apparel industry, haven't survived," says 44-year-old Charles E. "Gus" Whalen Jr., a great-grandson of

Source: "A 19th-Century Firm Shifts, Reinvents Itself and Survives 100 Years" by Eric Morgenthaler. *The Wall Street Journal*, May 9, 1989, pp. A1, A10. Reprinted by permission of The Wall Street Journal, © Dow Jones & Company, Inc. 1989. All Rights Reserved Worldwide.

the founder, who now heads the company. "Probably the No. 1 thing that has kept us alive is our ability to adapt."

For Warren Featherbone, adapting has meant virtually reinventing itself twice and weathering some very hard years. Instead of small-town Michigan, the company now is based here in small-town Georgia. It expects to post $20 million in sales this fiscal year and employs some 535 people, not many more than in 1915 but more than double the number of 1975.

The evolution of Warren Featherbone Co. is, in many ways, a grass-roots look at more than a century of American business, from the days when accounts were posted by grandly flowing hand to the days when they whirled through grandly flowing computers.

Offering Stability. But what makes Warren Featherbone especially notable is that it is a rather ordinary company, not at all unlike thousands of small and medium-sized businesses in the U.S. It is unflashy, low-keyed and conservatively run—a world apart from today's yellow-tied investment banker and avaricious corporate raider. Over the years, it has done some big things right and some big things wrong, but it has survived, creating hundreds of jobs along the way. It is representative of that huge mass of often-overlooked businesses that give breadth and stability to the U.S. economy.

> Three Oaks, Mich.—1989: "This was his office," says Larry G. Bubb, chairman of the Bank of Three Oaks, as he walks a visitor into the high-ceilinged, corner room from which E.K. Warren once ruled his company town. It's Mr. Bubb's office now, for his bank a few years ago bought the old Warren office building and restored it beautifully.
>
> You know, there was a bicycle shop in here. The electricity didn't work. There was no heat. It was just a big white elephant, really.
>
> Time was when things were different.

A phone call to the company office was once front-page news. At 22 minutes, it was "probably the longest conversation that will ever be carried on in this place by long distance," the Three Oaks Press reported, somewhat breathlessly, in its edition of Jan. 14, 1898. The call linked Warren Featherbone's officers in Three Oaks with its New York office.

Modern times! McKinley was in the White House, Victoria was on the throne and Warren Featherbone Co. was developing big-league telephone habits. Which seemed altogether proper, for it was turning into a big-league business.

Aside from the factory in Three Oaks—a little country town across Lake Michigan from Chicago—it had or was opening offices in New York, Boston, San Francisco, Chicago, London, Paris, Hamburg and Sydney and Melbourne, Australia. Its factory records for March 25, 1899—by all appearances, an ordinary day—show shipments to 57 customers in 23 states. It advertised in the Ladies Home Journal and Good Housekeeping. Its products were listed in the Sears Roebuck catalog. It was starting its own little consumer publication, the Featherbone Magazinette. The Spring 1901 issue would include such articles as "What Waists Will Be." And in its offices, it kept a long blue volume with a burgundy-colored binding. "Record of Quills—Out-Going and In-Coming Shipments," its label read.

As a young merchant in Three Oaks around 1883, or so the story goes, E.K. Warren saw the need for a new elastic boning material, for giving form to the often spectacularly formed ladies clothing of the time. Whalebone, the leading product, was becoming scarce and expensive. One day, while visiting a feather-duster factory, Mr. Warren noticed that certain supple quills on turkey's wings were being discarded as unsuitable for dusters, because they had plumage on only one side.

Two thoughts—"an elastic material wanted" and "an elastic material wasted"—ran through his mind, one company history noted, until "they finally met and the idea of making a bone out of the quill substance was conceived. The next day the word 'Featherbone' was coined."

Not everyone believes that. Some people in Three Oaks say the invention actually originated with a clerk in Mr. Warren's store, a woman named Retta Hollet. Whatever the truth, it was Mr. Warren who knew what to do with the idea. In June 1883, at age 36, he organized Warren Featherbone Co. with capital stock of $100,000. On Oct. 16, he and an associate received a patent for a "corset stiffener" that he called featherbone.

Locals scoffed at first, but by December the factory was running at full tilt with a crew of nine. Within a decade or two, thanks largely to Mr. Warren's business, the population of Three Oaks doubled to around 1,500, and featherbone was prospering.

The Profits Roll In. Meaningful financial records aren't available, but Mr. Warren was making so much money that in 1904 he chartered an ocean-liner and—at his own expense, it appears—took some 600 U.S. delegates to a meeting in Jerusalem of the International Sunday School Association.

Meanwhile, the company was diversifying into other notions and fashion items, such as ribbons and braids and bustles. The minutes of a department-heads meeting on Aug. 17, 1914, preserved in archives at Western Michigan University in Kalamazoo, make no mention of the war that was breaking out in Europe. But they do say that the factory made 7,326 dozen girdles the previous week—a record for a five-day period—and that there were 452 people on the payroll. At a managers meeting the following April 12, the minutes report, one man "was fined 50 cents for using the word 'can't' during the course of the meeting."

The company's operations by then sprawled through a cluster of buildings in the heart of Three Oaks, next to the railroad tracks. The main factory was a block or two long and two stories high. There was a box-making shop, a print shop, a greenhouse and a power plant. The company also had a liquor license, for Mr. Warren, a minister's son, felt so strongly about the evils of drink that he had the company buy up all the saloon licenses in Three Oaks so no one could sell alcohol. Mr. Warren and his family also owned the bank, the department store and, for a while, the newspaper.

The Company Town. "The success of the whole town was dependent on Warren Featherbone Co.," says Edward Drier, a kinetic 69-year-old butcher whose shop is just up Elm Street from the old corporate offices. Mr. Drier pulls out of an old cabinet the shop ledger for 1913—the year his father bought the business—and opens it randomly to Thursday, Nov. 6. It shows the shop waited on 150 people and took in $46.47. "So you see, there was a lot of street traffic from the Featherbone factory," he says.

The pay was low, but Warren Featherbone literally kept Three Oaks in business during the Depression. It hired only locals, and it would hire any local who needed a job. "Maybe we worked just a couple of days a week," says Maybell Dellinger, who started there in 1931, at age 18. "But they never laid us off."

The Depression doesn't seem to have seriously dented the company. But changes were taking place in the competitive environment that threatened to destroy it altogether.

"Featherbone was very profitable, but plastics were coming into being," says Mr. Whalen of those years. The company saw the trend and signed on. It began working with B.F. Goodrich Co., based in Akron, Ohio, to develop uses for the new material and came up with the idea of plastic baby pants—to go over diapers and replace the heavier, hotter, rubber baby pants that then were in use. In 1938, it introduced what it says were the world's first plastic baby pants. Soon, it expanded into a whole line of plastic apparel, from bibs to raincoats to aprons.

Missing the Boom. The transition was interrupted by World War II. The company directed much of its output to the war effort, even making machine-gun belts on equipment that formerly wove belts for Venetian blinds. Workers remember those as exhausting years. "I was putting in so many darn hours that I had to complain about it," says Alvin Keefer, age 82, who started in 1929 and stayed for nearly a quarter century, most of it as a dyer.

The war work may have masked serious problems at Warren Featherbone. By the late 1940s, as the U.S. was taking off on an era of unparalleled growth, the company, its conventional business waning, was struggling simply to keep afloat. It had an old and increasingly outdated plant. It had a shrinking, aging work force. Its relations with its union, the Amalgamated Clothing Workers, were deteriorating.

For Three Oaks, there were even worse developments. In 1956, following a generational change in management, Warren Featherbone announced that the company and its $500,000-a-year payroll would migrate south, to Georgia, abandoning Three Oaks and its work force. The move came as a shock to employees, who had come to view Warren Featherbone as a paternal mainstay in their lives. It also symbolized the most dramatic transformation in Warren Featherbone's history.

In 1950 the company had discontinued its notions business, the foundation of Warren Featherbone, and three years later expanded its clothing operations by buying Alexis Inc., an Atlanta-based maker of infants wear. For its new headquarters, Warren Featherbone chose Gainesville, Ga., a country town about 50 miles northeast of Atlanta. Gainesville had an abundant labor supply, low costs, low taxes—and no unions. It was near textile mills, it was eager for industry, and it offered financing, through industrial-development bonds, for Warren Featherbone's new plant.

> Gainesville, Ga.—1989: Irene Saxon is standing near a machine that cuts plastic for baby pants, trying to explain the ties that bind the Warren Featherbone workforce. She turns to Perry Smith, a man in red suspenders who works nearby.
>
> Perry is my husband's cousin, Mrs. Saxon explains. And this lady—she points to Montrella Dunagan, who is sitting at a work table—is my first cousin. And her daughter works here, in the office. Everybody is kin around here.
>
> So don't say anything about anyone.

In people terms, it wasn't all that hard for Warren Featherbone to make the switch from Michigan to Georgia. It traded a town with a historic cannon in the park for one with a Confederate soldier statue in the square; but both were sleepy, close-knit little communities, and the corporate culture transferred easily.

The business adjustment, however, was much rockier. The company was in the red, and sales were shrinking. It knew what it was getting out of—sewing notions—but it was less sure what it was getting into. Its main product, plastic baby pants, was under growing competitive attack. Its baby-clothes business (based in Atlanta and separate from its baby-pants business) wasn't taking off as hoped, and it was soon moved to Gainesville, resulting in more expense and turmoil.

"We were finding our way," says Doris Whalen, a family manager and Gus Whalen's stepmother. "If you make a product that has been popular for 40 years, getting into a new product takes a little while."

Working in the Red. The company was now thrashing about. It tried to diversify into diaper bags and cosmetic purses with the acquisition of a small manufacturer. The effort quickly flopped. It tried to expand its line of infant-wear clothes into toddler-wear. That, too, failed. It introduced a discount line. It fiddled with different "looks" for its baby clothes. Nothing worked.

Sales were spiraling down and the company kept losing money. In fiscal 1957, the year of the move, sales were just under $4 million. They fell steadily for most of the next decade, to a low of $1,999,000 in fiscal 1966.

But the company kept reworking its product and redefining its niche. By the early 1970s, it had decided to focus on its plastic baby-pants business and expand into medium-priced, nicely styled baby clothes for department stores and specialty shops. It revamped and substantially beefed up its sales and marketing staff—a key move, in Gus Whalen's view. Gradually, things began turning up.

Sales have risen almost every year since fiscal 1965, the last year the company showed a loss. Warren Featherbone doesn't release earnings results, but Mr. Whalen says it now regularly out-performs the industry. It has managed that growth despite a second product crisis that easily could have been as daunting as the demise of featherbone.

As late as 1975, plastic pants accounted for the bulk of Warren Featherbone's sales. But the era of disposable diapers, which arrived in the mid-1960s, spelled trouble for that business, which relied on the use of cloth diapers.

Co-Opting Adversity. But the company successfully offset the decline with growth in its other, baby-clothes lines. It also responded with a tactic reminiscent of its response to the onset of plastics: Instead of fighting the change, it co-opted it. It brainstormed something called "diaper dress-ups"—fancy coverings worn over disposable diapers. They now account for about 7% of Warren Featherbone sales.

"So you say, what is 7%?" Mr. Whalen asks. "Well, it is 7% that we didn't have before. And theoretically, the more Procter & Gamble spends on advertising Pampers, the bigger our market becomes."

In another era, the company did quite well abroad, but all that ended when Warren Featherbone slipped into decline. In recent years, however, the company has begun stepping overseas again, and now it is targeting Europe. It recently entered a venture with a Scottish clothes company to produce and distribute its baby wear in Europe, in anticipation of the creation of a unified market there in three years. "We think 1992 will be a good opportunity for us," Mr. Whalen says.

The company still stumbles now and then. It oversold last year's spring line, for instance, and fell behind on delivery schedules. The cost of making that up to customers, including liberal credit and return conditions, contributed to a steep decline in earnings for fiscal 1988, even though sales rose. Mr. Whalen says those problems are over and that both sales and earnings should set records this year.

All in the Family. At a publicly traded company, such an earnings lapse could send the stock into a tailspin. Mr. Whalen doesn't have such pressures. A Whalen family trust controls almost all the outstanding shares. The family also is heavily involved in running the company. In addition to Gus (the president) and Doris (the executive vice president), there is Gus's stepbrother, Jeffrey Whalen (director of merchandising), and half-brother, William Whalen (who heads the Chicago office).

The company now turns out about 7 million pieces of infants wear a year, mostly under its Alexis label. It has 4,500 commercial customers, from Saks to Sears. Its most popular line of bibs, with decorations which squeak, has annual sales of over $1 million. It is using computers in everything from purchasing to production. Yet it remains a decidedly homespun place. Employees already are working on this year's Christmas quilt, a scale model of which hangs on the cafeteria wall.

In its own way, Three Oaks has also adapted since it was abandoned by Warren Featherbone. Many of the laid-off workers found new jobs in other towns within commuting distance. Today, Three Oaks still has about 1,600 people, and the old featherbone factory complex is still the biggest thing in town—physically, at least. It is a hulking industrial ghost. It is so big, in a town so small, that no one knows quite what to do with it. "It was just a shame when Warren Featherbone folded up," Maybell Dellinger says. "Just a big shame."

As for featherbone itself, the company still made it as late as 1962. The machinery had been brought down to Georgia from Michigan—the only notions line that wasn't discontinued with the move—but after a while, even sentiment couldn't justify its continued production. Among the last customers was the Douglas Aircraft Co., which used it somewhere in planes—no one remembers where. The featherbone workers were given other jobs in the plant. The featherbone machinery was junked. The word featherbone still is listed in the dictionary.

Questions

1. Construct a time line for Warren Featherbone Company that is similar to the one in Figure 10.4, and show how its industry niche, domain strategy, and domain tactics changed over time. Provide examples of each change.

2. To what extent did Warren Featherbone's strategy shape its environment? To what extent did changes in the environment force changes in Warren Featherbone's strategy? Provide examples to support your answer.

PART IV

Organizational Processes

CHAPTER 11

Managing Growth and Development

Learning Objectives

Upon completing this chapter, you should be able to

1. Name various motives for organizational growth.
2. Explain the general nature of the Greiner organizational growth model.
3. Describe Greiner's five phases of organizational growth.
4. Recount several managerial implications of the various phases of organizational growth.

PHOENIX'S RISE AND FALL

Phoenix Technologies Ltd. was once living proof that little guys can beat big guys. The company sells a crucial piece of software that makes PC clones work just like IBM PCs. But now, after laying off 25 percent of its employees, Phoenix faces a fall from its rapid-growth heyday.

Phoenix wrote long-term contracts with nearly every small clone-maker, taking in $10 every time a clone was sold. It enjoyed a near monopoly, with 80 percent gross margins. Then its CEO hired extra staff to develop software that would let computer makers build workstation clones based on the SPARC chip from Sun Workstations Inc. But demand never materialized, and the project created a $1 million loss. And PC demand began to slow, hurting smaller clone-makers the most.

A resumption of growth for Phoenix depends on new products, but a Boston partnerhsip has bought 7.8 percent of Phoenix's shares and says it may attempt a tender offer for the company. Chapter 11 explains the management of growth and development in organizations and why, like Phoenix, so many organizations experience problems after achieving rapid growth.

Source: Keith Hammonds, "Phoenix Keeps Getting Its Feathers Ruffled," *Business Week,* January 22, 1990, 70.

L IKE human beings, organizations have life histories. That is, they are conceived, born, and nurtured in the hope that they will develop and mature. Also, as will be discussed in Chapter 12, organizations can die. Indeed, as Orzack and Oldham observe, "Some organizations die . . . shortly after conception, others prematurely, some during infancy, some after a lengthy period of growth and survival."[1] In theory, however, organizations can be immortal. Corporations such as The Hudson Bay Company (founded in 1670) have existed for centuries, as have many universities, churches, and nations. In this sense, there is no "developed" organization. Development is a continuous process, so organizations that successfully adapt to their surrounding environment are continually developing. (See Focus on Design 11.1.) This growth and development is the subject of the present chapter, the first of two chapters on managing growth and decline processes.

WHY PURSUE GROWTH?

There are numerous motives for organizational growth. Perhaps the most obvious is that growth brings economic security to an organization. Smaller organizations have a greater probability of failure since they are subject to

FOCUS ON DESIGN 11.1

The U.S.'s Oldest Companies

In theory, organizations can be immortal, long outliving their founders. The British Royal Mint celebrated its 1,100th anniversary in 1986. The oldest company in Sweden, Stora Kopparberg, is first mentioned in historical records in the year 1288. The Lowenbrau brewery in Munich was founded in 1383. In Italy, the Banco de Napoli first opened its doors for business in 1539. The Saint Gobain glass company was established in France by a charter of King Louis XIV in 1665.

In the United States, thousands of businesses flourished before the American Revolution. At the time of the bicentennial in 1976, only 20 were veterans of pre-Revolutionary War days, existing as independent companies or recognizable divisions of other companies. They were as follows:

Founded	Company
1702	J. E. Rhoads & Sons, Inc., (Wilmington, DE), a manufacturer of industrial belting, and the nation's oldest company.
1717	Presbyterian Minister's Fund (Philadelphia), an insurance company.
1728	Franklin Printing Co. (Primos, PA), Ben Franklin's printing firm.
1740	James E. Pepper & Co. (Lexington, KY), a distiller, and the oldest company west of the Allegheny Mountains.
1742	Taylor-Wharton Co. (Easton, PA), steel fabrications.
1743	Skillman Express, Storage & Furniture Exchange (Princeton, NJ), a furniture warehousing company.
1752	Caswell-Massey Co., Ltd. (New York), chemists and perfumers.
1752	Philadelphia Contributorship for the Insurance of Houses from Loss of Fire (Philadelphia), the nation's oldest fire insurance company.
1754	Devoe & Reynolds Co., Inc. (New York), a paint manufacturer.
1760	P. Lorillard & Co. (New York), a manufacturer of tobacco products.
1760	American Lawn Equipment Corp. (Lyndhurst, NJ), a lawn mower sales company.
1761	Kirk & Nice (Philadelphia), undertakers.
1764	The Hartford Courant (Hartford, CT), a daily newspaper.

(continued)

FOCUS ON DESIGN 11.1 *(continued)*

Founded	Company
1766	New Haven Journal-Courier (New Haven, CT), a daily newspaper.
1767	Dexter Corp. (Windsor Locks, CT), an industrial paper manufacturer.
1770	Demuth Tobacco Shop (Lancaster, PA), tobacconists.
1771	Philadelphia Inquirer (Philadelphia). a daily newspaper.
1773	Baltimore New American (Baltimore), a daily newspaper.
1774	O. Ames Co. (Parkersburg, W VA), a farm tool manufacturer.
1775	Bowne & Co. (New York), a financial printing firm.

Sources: "America's Oldest Companies," *Nation's Business* 64, no. 7 (1976): 36–37; "Members Forum," *National Geographic* 76, no. 6 (1987): 684

elimination due to relatively minor environmental fluctuations. In contrast, larger organizations are not only more likely to have the resources to withstand even major environmental disruptions, but also the critical mass needed to compete with foreign enterprises that are often gigantic and subsidized or even state-owned. IBM, master of the great growth industry of the age, towers over its competitors. Despite industry downturns and mounting worldwide competition , IBM's size allows it to invest billions of dollars in new research and products. Similarly, Exxon, the world's largest oil company, was able to lose billions of dollars on synfuels, and General Motors, the nation's largest manufacturing firm, was able to lose its position in the small-car market in the 1970s but yet survive. Such mismanagement would have quickly destroyed smaller competitors. As O'Toole emphatically observes, this suggests a possible "law": "If an organization is going to be mismanaged, the chances of survival are improved if [it is] the biggest company in [its] industry!"[2] In this sense, growth is an effect, not a cause, of an organization's success. (See Focus on Design 11.2.)

Prestige, power, perks, and pay are also obvious motives for organizational growth. According to a *Business Week* survey of "hot" growth companies, managers who run these exceptional organizations are "proud" and "ornery." They like money, but that's not all that motivates them. They want to make a mark.[3] R. E. "Ted" Turner, owner of the Turner Broadcasting System, declares he's no longer interested in money. "I'm not concerned with myself," he says. "I'm trying to get bigger so I'll have more influence. It's almost like a religious fervor."[4]

FOCUS ON DESIGN 11.2

Strength in Size: The Nation's Goliaths

One motive for organizational growth is economic security. Smaller organizations have a greater probability of failure since they are subject to elimination due to relatively minor environmental fluctuations. In contrast, larger organizations are more likely to have the resources to withstand even major environmental disruptions. *Fortune* magazine annually ranks both the 500 largest U.S. industrial corporations and 500 largest diversified service companies by sales. The 1989 rankings were as follows:

Industrial Corporations

Rank	Company	Sales ($ mil)	Profits ($ mil)
1.	General Motors (Detroit)	121,085.4	4,856.3
2.	Ford Motor (Dearborn, MI)	92,445.6	5,300.2
3.	Exxon (New York)	79,557.0	5,260.0
4.	International Business Machines (Armonk, NY)	59,681.0	5,806.0
5.	General Electric (Fairfield, CT)	49,414.0	3,386.0
6.	Mobil (New York)	48,198.0	2,087.0
7.	Chrysler (Highland Park, MI)	35,472.7	1,050.2
8.	Texaco (White Plains, NY)	33,544.0	1,304.0
9.	E. I. du Pont de Nemours (Wilmington, DE)	32,514.0	2,190.0
10.	Philip Morris (New York)	25,860.0	2,337.0

(continued)

Such a fervor was perhaps no more evident than in the management style of former International Telephone and Telegraph Corporation (ITT) chairman, Harold Geneen. During his 25-year tenure, ITT became one of the world's largest conglomerates. His preoccupation with growth is told best in his own words:

> I never let up. I talked about growth, how we were going to achieve it, and I talked about more growth. In the beginning at ITT, I spent night after night talking with our management teams . . . discussing how we intended to do it. As the years went on, every time we acquired a new . . . company's management, we would talk about our goal of at least 10 percent annual growth. It did

FOCUS ON DESIGN 11.2 *(continued)*

Service Companies

Rank	Company	Sales ($ mil)	Profits ($ mil)
1.	American Tel. & Tel. (New York)	35,210.0	(1,669.0)
2.	Fleming Cos. (Oklahoma City)	10,467.0	65.4
3.	Super Valu Stores (Eden Prairie, MN)	9,371.1	111.8
4.	McKesson (San Francisco)	7,297.7	95.0
5.	American Financial (Cincinnati)	6,901.7	102.4
6.	United Telecommunications (Westwood, KS)	6,493.0	508.9
7.	MCI Communications (Washington)	5,137.0	346.0
8.	Fluor (Irvine, CA)	5,132.5	56.4
9.	Ryder System (Miami)	5,029.6	197.2
10.	Halliburton (Dallas)	4,838.7	93.6

Sources: "The *Fortune* 500 Largest Industrial Corporations," *Fortune,* April 24, 1989, 354–373; "The *Fortune* 500 Largest Corporations," *Fortune,* June 5, 1989, 358–385.

not make any difference if times were good or bad . . . . When they were bad, we had to work harder.[5]

Obviously, there are many other motives for organizational growth. These might include adventure and risk, greater profit, and even monopolistic dominance. Many of these motives, however, are interrelated, and their relative importance will depend on the individual situation. It should also be noted that although motives are necessary, alone they are insufficient to produce growth. Organizations must overcome both internal and external pressures to succeed.[6] In this respect, as we have seen with the Penn Central, once our nation's largest railroad, and W. T. Grant, once one of the world's largest retailers, growth can be too extreme, exceeding an organization's ability to assimilate, control, and provide necessary resources. On balance, it is clear that either extreme—reckless headlong growth or maintaining the status quo—is dangerous.

The growth of an organization is thus more than a chance occurrence. It involves thought, worry, and effort. More specifically, it depends on a host of managerial decisions combined with appropriate execution of the actions that follow from them. Finally, as the preceding illustrations involving Ted Turner and Harold Geneen attest, these decisions, in turn, are related to the goals pursued by an organization's key participants.

THE GREINER FIVE-PHASE GROWTH MODEL

Organization theorists have developed some two dozen models for delineating phases of organizational growth. While each is somewhat different in the number of phases identified and the issues addressed, all presuppose a sequence of phases through which organizations—corporations, universities, hospitals, or museums—pass as they grow over time. A similar sequencing of phases can also be observed in divisions, departments, and project teams within organizations.

Of the many different models, perhaps the most useful was proposed by Larry E. Greiner in a now classic article titled, "Evolution and Revolution as Organizations Grow."[7] Based on an analysis of case histories, the Greiner model is essentially a theory of organizational adjustment that identifies both internal and external forces for stability and change, and that recognizes the relative impact of top management leadership on organization behavior over time. It presents organizations as moving through five phases of growth as they make the transition from small to large (in sales and employees) and from young to mature. These phases are shown in Figure 11.1.

Each phase is distinguished by an *evolution* from the prior phase and then by a *revolution,* or crisis, which precipitates movement into the next phase. Thus, each phase is comprised of a relatively calm and prolonged period of growth (evolution) that ends with a period of substantial turmoil or crisis (revolution). Management's critical task during each revolutionary period is to identify and implement appropriate new practices to enter another period of evolutionary growth. With time, these new practices will likewise become inadequate, prompting another period of evolution. Thus, each evolutionary period is seen as "breeding" its own revolution.

Other key dimensions of Greiner's model include:

1. *Age.* An organization's age is considered the most essential dimension in the model, since each succeeding crisis is believed to be a function of past decisions.

2. *Size.* Since succeeding crises are thought to vary as an organization's workforce and sales increase, size is also believed to be an important dimension.

3. *Growth rate.* The speed with which periods of evolution are punctuated by revolution is believed to be closely related to the growth rate of an organization's environment. While it is impossible to predict the amount of time (months or years) that will elapse between times of revolutionary transition, Greiner contends that the *slope* of the diagonal line in Figure 11.1 depends on whether an organization is in a high- or low-growth industry. Evolutionary periods will be relatively shorter and revolutionary periods will come more quickly in high-growth or expanding industries than in low-growth or mature industries.

Figure 11.1
Greiner's Five Phases of Organizational Growth

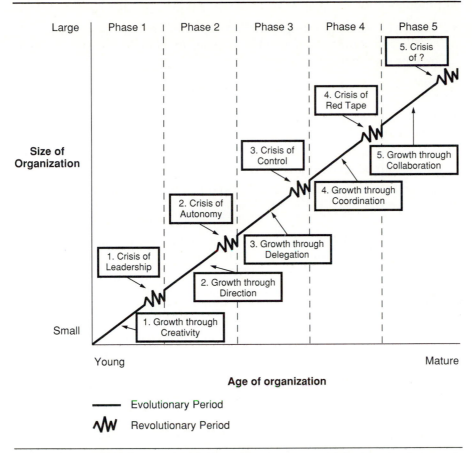

Five Phases of Growth

As envisioned by Greiner, an organization's life can thus be seen as a five-phase evolutionary process punctuated by periods of revolutionary change. During revolutionary periods, practices that were previously satisfactory are found to be inadequate. This results in substantial turmoil or crisis as management identifies and implements new practices that will serve the organization through a new evolutionary period. Hence, *each phase* is both an effect of the previous phase and a cause for the next phase. The five phases comprising Greiner's growth model (Figure 11.1) can be described as follows:

Phase 1: Creativity ... At an organization's birth, emphasis is on creating both a product and a market. The characteristics of this phase of creative evolution include

- Being technically or entrepreneurially oriented, an organization's founders disdain management activities; a majority of their time is devoted to making and selling a new product.
- Structure is rudimentary; facilities "make-do"; communication among participants is frequent and informal.
- The organization is comprised of a small group of dedicated people; esprit de corps is high.
- Salaries are modest; long hours of work are motivated by the promise of ownership benefits.
- Control comes from immediate marketplace feedback; management acts as customers react.

... and the Leadership Crisis. As an organization grows, however, it encounters a crisis of leadership. The individualistic activities essential for a new undertaking quickly become ineffective. A steady increase in employees makes it more and more difficult to manage by relying on informal communication. The organization's founders find themselves saddled with unwanted managerial responsibilities requiring skills they most likely do not possess. The need at this point is to locate and install a capable professional manager, someone more temperamentally suited to the new managerial responsibilities—but who must also be acceptable to the founders. The founders may not recognize this need, or may be unwilling to step aside, and as a consequence some organizations fail to survive this crisis.

Example. Entrepreneur-founders bring creativity to new markets and opportunities. Experience shows, however, that the skills needed to found an organization—ambition, self-confidence, even obsessiveness—are radically different than those needed to ensure its continued growth. As has been observed, "Most high-tech companies don't make that transition mainly because they can't overcome conflicts between the geniuses who come up with the ideas and the 'doers'—the business people who actually run the company."[8] Indeed, it has almost become a "rite of passage" for many high-tech start-ups to fail as they try to grow into industry leaders. Says one authority, "The oldest story in the Silicon Valley is the entrepreneurial founder finding he no longer belongs at the company that bears his name."[9] Seemingly, growing organizations wait for no one, not even their founders. What is typically required are professional managers who can see beyond the brilliance of the founder's original vision.

Apple Computer offers a classic example of this phenomenon. The Apple II personal computer, which in 1977 launched a whole new industry, was born in co-founder Steven P. Jobs's garage. Described as brilliant, Jobs had an uncanny ability to mesmerize employees and to inspire them to achieving more than they thought possible. He, however, was also known as a brash and obsessive perfectionist. It took seven scant years for a palace revolt to strip Jobs of all day-to-day company responsibilities. In 1985 John Sculley, recruited from Pepsi (USA), was named company president. Having racked up 100 percent annual growth year after year, Apple attempted to go toe-to-toe in the big-business market with IBM. It made the move, however, without altering its "designer jeans and T-shirts culture." Apple's loose-as-a-goose can-do practices were not in stride with a big-business mentality. Following a series of conflicts over Sculley's attempts to impose a more businesslike atmosphere at Apple, Jobs quit "in a huff" to begin a new company called Next Inc. With $90 million in Apple stock, his goal was to produce a "fourth wave" microcomputer even glitzier and easier to use than the Macintosh, his last project at Apple.

This example is counterbalanced by the high-tech stars, such as Microsoft's Bill Gates and Compaq Computer's Rod Canion, who have remained successful in running the businesses they founded. It is rare, however, to be both an entrepreneur and a good manager.

Phase 2: Direction . . .   Those organizations that survive Phase 1 by installing a professional manager typically enter an era of growth through direction. This is a time of sustained growth under competent and directive management characterized by the following:

- An organization is likely reorganized along functional departments; job assignments become more specialized.

- Accounting systems are introduced.

- Work standards, incentives, and budgets are installed.

- Communication becomes more formal; a management hierarchy is created.

- Direction is provided by top management, leaving lower-level managers little opportunity for autonomous decision making.

. . . and the Autonomy Crisis.   While these new directive techniques result in more efficient growth, they eventually become inappropriate as an organization becomes larger and more diverse. Lower-level managers, often possessing more knowledge than executives at the top, find themselves burdened with an overly centralized and impersonal hierarchy. They are torn between following management directives and taking initiative. Ultimately, this begets a crisis of autonomy as they demand greater decision-making latitude, something they may not be ready for given their inexperience as decision makers. Numerous organizations flounder during this revolutionary period, with top managers adhering to centralized practices while disenchanted lower-level employees quit.

Examples. Growing organizations almost inevitably face a challenge that threatens their continued survival: transforming themselves from exuberant start-ups into mid-size high-growth ventures that need direction and structure to stay efficient. While unfettered enthusiasm was likely crucial to their early success, it must now be channeled in an organized way. Yet, the increased direction and structure that is necessary might crush the unique attributes responsible for an organization's success. Clifford and Cavanaugh describe well the risk a Phase 2 organization faces:

> Opportunities for breakdowns and malfunction multiply. Layers of organization can add drastically to response time. Functional specialization can lead to major problems for coordination and control: Is manufacturing really providing what sales is selling at the time it was promised? Systems may fail to monitor costs that get out of line. Leaders may lose their in-depth understanding of business dynamics or even their fundamental zeal . . . . People throughout the company may lose motivation and morale, adopting a nine-to-five mentality.[10]

To avoid the downside of this risk, the top management of Phase 2 organizations must ultimately push authority down to lower-level managers. For some founders this is particularly difficult. Notes one observer, delegating authority "can be like getting a babysitter for the first time. You don't trust anybody."[11] For retailers like Toys "R" Us, Businessland, and Price Club, the transition from Phase 2 to Phase 3 has occurred smoothly, since they treat each of their stores as a business unto itself. Says Toys "R" Us founder Charles Lazarus, "No matter how big we get, the key unit in this company is the store. We want our store managers to take the business home in their stomach. We want them to think that their store is the only store in the world. We reward them with bonuses and stock options, and we've made a lot of millionaires."[12] (See Focus on Design 11.3.)

Phase 3: Delegation . . . For organizations that survive Phase 2 by balancing the need for direction against employee desires for autonomy, a new era of growth typically emerges. Successful delegation of authority and the introduction of a geographically decentralized organization structure give rise to a phase of evolution characterized by the following:

- Managers of plant facilities and market territories acquire greater responsibility and authority.
- Profit centers and bonuses are introduced to stimulate motivation.
- Top management uses periodic field reports to "manage by exception."
- New acquisitions are added to other decentralized units.
- Communication from top managers is infrequent.

. . . and the Control Crisis. Phase 3 is useful in stimulating expansion through increased motivation at lower management levels. With more authority and incentive, decentralized unit managers invade larger markets and

FOCUS ON DESIGN 11.3

How Hot Is Hot?: The Top 100 Growth Companies

Each May *Business Week* magazine releases its annual ranking of "The Top 100 Growth Companies" in the United States. To qualify, a company must have sales less than $150 million, a current market value greater than $1 million, a current stock price greater than $1, and be actively traded. Banks, insurers, real estate firms, and utilities are excluded.

To determine the listing, over 7,700 publicly traded corporations are ranked three ways—according to three-year return on invested capital, three-year sales growth, and three-year earnings growth. A company's composite rank is the sum of 0.5 times its rank in return on total capital plus 0.25 times each growth rank.

The top ten growth companies for 1989 were as follows:

Rank	Company	Three-Year Averages		Return on Capital
		Increase (%)		
		Sales	Profits	
1.	T^2 Medical (Roswell, GA) In-home intravenous therapy	213.3	368.2	64.8
2.	Software Toolworks (Chatsworth, CA) PC software	148.3	244.3	39.7
3.	Critical Industries (Houston) Asbestos removal equipment	104.6	261.9	43.3
4.	American Power Conversion (Peace Dale, RI) Computer power systems	167.7	422.6	33.9
5.	Adobe Systems (Mountain View, CA) Graphic software	160.9	237.6	35.4
6.	Aldus (Seattle) Desktop publishing software	230.9	222.7	34.4
7.	Catalina Lighting (Miami) Lighting fixtures	99.1	164.6	45.3
8.	Silk Greenhouse (Tampa) Silk flowers, plants, trees	151.6	144.1	35.0
9.	Home Office Reference Laboratory (Lenexa, KS) Blood and urine testing	98.1	156.3	37.1
10.	Rainbow Technologies (Irvine, CA) Software protection systems	122.1	203.9	31.4

Source: "The Best Small Companies," *Business Week,* May 22, 1989, 101–108.

develop new products. A crisis develops, however, as top management fears it may be losing control over a highly decentralized field operation. Being autonomous, unit managers prefer running their own shows and resent having to coordinate their activities with other units. Freedom breeds a narrow attitude. The Phase 3 revolution begins when top management moves to regain control by returning to a centralized structure. This usually fails, however, because field operations are too vast. Those organizations that grow into Phase 4 find a solution in the use of various coordinating techniques.

Examples. If an organization survives, it will eventually develop other acceptable products and start to mature rapidly. During Phase 3 an organization must be responsive to increasing market demands. It must concentrate on increasing its market share so that it can become an accepted industry member. This will require a broader (geographically decentralized) operational base, so responsibility and authority must be likewise dispersed. While unit managers must possess a certain flexibility and freedom of action, top-management direction is still required for organization-wide control. Herein lies the crux of the problem for growing Phase 3 organizations.

Example. Consider the example of Lotus Development Corporation. Founded in 1981, Lotus's once freewheeling management style has been replaced with tight controls in an effort to increase company-wide coordination. This change reflects Lotus's increasing struggle to cope with its own remarkable growth. Thanks mainly to 1-2-3, its first product, in less than four years it grew from zero to $283 million in sales and from 90 to 1,300 employees. Where Lotus was once characterized by a casual atmosphere complete with Hawaiian shirts and impromptu hallway meetings, it became evident that increased control and coordination were necessary. Commenting on Lotus's transformation from an eccentric start-up to a mature industry leader, founder Mitchell D. Kapor remarked: "People here pine for the good old days, but we're growing up, and we have to grow up organizationally."[13] Controls at Lotus for achieving increased coordination include planning groups and official policies on matters ranging from hiring to press queries.

Phase 4: Coordination . . . This phase of growth is marked by the introduction of various techniques for achieving increased coordination. Typical techniques might include strategic planning groups and official policies, as occurred at Lotus, as well as special councils, committee meetings, interdepartmental task forces, and labor-management project teams. Their common purpose is to achieve a more efficient allocation of resources by subjecting individual decisions to a wider audience. It is believed that such scrutiny will prompt managers to look beyond the needs of their own units. The characteristics of this phase of evolution include the following:

- Decentralized units are combined to form product divisions.
- A formal planning process is established.
- Numerous headquarters staff are hired to monitor company-wide control and review programs for line managers.
- Capital expenditures are carefully evaluated and allocated to competing units.
- Product groups are treated as investment centers where return on investment is used to measure efficiency in generating profits.
- Technical functions, such as data processing, are centralized at headquarters, while many daily operating decisions remain decentralized.
- Stock options and organization-wide profit sharing are instituted to foster identity with the organization as a whole.

. . . and the Red-Tape Crisis. Eventually a lack of trust develops between headquarters and product groups in the field. As a consequence, line-staff conflicts emerge. Line managers increasingly resent the paperwork and programs originated by staff unfamiliar with local conditions. Staff, in turn, complain about what they consider uncooperative and uninformed line managers. Soon both groups condemn the paper blizzard that has developed. Procedures take priority over problem solving, and creativity is dampened. The organization has grown too large and complex to be managed through formal controls. The Phase 4 revolution has begun.

Example. As an organization moves into Phase 4, it permanently leaves behind its small and less structured early days. Informality is replaced with formality as the inevitable need for increased control results in a creeping bureaucracy. Complexity has increased—more customers, more employees, more locations, more products—and informal control/coordination techniques no longer suffice. Red tape appears as project outlines become detailed plans, impromptu meetings become scheduled meetings with agendas and minutes, and verbal instructions evolve into job descriptions.

Reebok International, whose sales jumped from $13 million in 1983 to $1.4 billion in 1987, is a ready example of an organization that has entered Phase 4. It dealt with its problems of coordination by organizing its eight different lines into five separate product divisions. At the time, a majority of its 2,200 employees had less than two years' experience and needed better supervision. This prompted an emphasis on paperwork and procedures that almost led to disaster when Reebok entered the sportswear business. Sales jumped almost immediately to $39 million. Reflects Reebok president C. Joseph LaBonte:

> The brand was so hot that anything we put on the racks just blew out of there. But we didn't know what we were doing. The product quality was not high. The good news was that our distribution was so bad that we didn't ruin

ourselves. Most of the clothes never reached the shelves in time for the holiday sales. We eventually destroyed the rest.[14]

Few organizations are so fortunate as Reebok to actually benefit from excessive red tape that results in poor coordination between distribution and sales. In any case, Reebok now has in place an effective infrastructure to assure adequate coordination.

Phase 5: Collaboration . . . The final phase of growth stresses strong interpersonal collaboration to overcome the red-tape crisis. Whereas Phase 4 emphasizes formal controls, Phase 5 emphasizes greater spontaneity in managerial action, teamwork, and the skillful resolution of interpersonal differences. Social controls and self-discipline replace formal controls. This change is especially troublesome for those managers who created previous control systems. The characteristics of this phase of evolution include the following:

- Team action is emphasized to solve problems quickly.
- Key managers confer frequently to review major issues.
- Educational programs are offered for training managers in behavioral skills to enhance teamwork and conflict resolution.
- Experiments in new practices are encouraged at all hierarchical levels.

. . . and the ? Crisis. The nature of the revolution in response to this evolutionary period is yet to be determined. Numerous organizations throughout the world are now in Phase 5, so the answer is critical. No doubt this yet to be named crisis will require new structures and practices. Only the future will tell.

Example. Almost every large organization in the world was once young and small. Companies such as General Electric, Xerox, or Johnson & Johnson were once fledgling undertakings. While these companies are unquestionably among the world's best managed, perhaps no other company exemplifies a Phase 5 organization better than IBM. Originating as the Computing-Tabulating-Recorder Co., a maker of time clocks, butcher scales, and tabulators, IBM today is a vast, decentralized democracy run by committee. Marked by its collegiality, an eight-member management committee meets twice weekly to make key decisions. A 17-member corporate management board meets throughout each year to plot broad strategy. The members of these committees are noted for their close-knit teamwork and skillful conflict resolution. As one observer has remarked:

> All of them know how to argue issues and escalate disputes to include higher management levels without "breaking glass," or offending colleagues along the way. They excel in the company's politely combative "contention management" system, which spells out the procedures by which corporate-staff members must challenge the decisions they question.[15]

Whether this fundamental philosophy will foster the kind of visionary, long-haul leadership necessary for IBM to move through Phase 5 awaits to be seen.

Managerial Implications

As the foregoing discussion suggests, managers can learn much by analyzing the various phases of organizational growth. Because organizations are dynamic systems, they constantly undergo changes as they grow and develop. Many of the crises they face are never fully resolved—they are ongoing dilemmas. In this sense, optimal organization is not a constant, but rather a set of parameters that depends on an organization's past history, the stability of its environment, and the nature of its current strategies. Several important managerial implications exist:

1. By knowing an organization's developmental phase and future plans, managers can make more informed decisions and prepare themselves and their organizations for future challenges. While every organization is unique in many ways, all face similar problems. An understanding of the patterns and forces of organizational growth will not only aid managers in diagnosing current problems, but enable them to predict and thus control what happens as an organization develops.

2. Organizations are subject to developmental transitions that can jeopardize performance, if not survival. To minimize this risk, they must use managerial practices appropriate to their phase of development. With each new phase of growth, old ways of managing are likely to become inappropriate. Thus, organizations must not only be willing to change, but must be capable of doing so. Obviously, an understanding of the practices likely to be successful at different developmental phases can aid greatly in effectively managing the transitions between phases. As cases in point, consider the actions of Cypress Semiconductor. In an effort to fight the seemingly inevitable bureaucratic inertia and resulting innovative sluggishness that overtake Phase 4 organizations, Cypress is trying what might be termed "small-company management." Rather than developing a new product line within its existing structure, Cypress creates a separate start-up company under the Cypress aegis. This "organization of tomorrow" differs from a traditional divisionalized company in several notable ways. Each start-up is headed by a president who can alter product design, construct factories, issue stock, raise funds, increase wages, and hire and fire. Cypress maintains a majority interest in each start-up, with the remaining stock owned by employees as an incentive. As a result, Cypress has reached annual sales of over $200 million in six years.

3. Organizations exist in uncertain environments and must reactively and practically adapt to their surroundings in order to grow and develop. Consequently, the appropriateness of goals, priorities, and even criteria of effectiveness (see Chapter 3) will vary over an organization's life span. System resource model criteria (for example, effectiveness in acquiring inputs) would seem to be the most important in early growth phases when uncertainty, complexity, and turbulence are typically high. On the other hand, goal model criteria (for example, effectiveness in producing outputs) would seem to be the most important in later stages when an organization is mature and its procedures are formalized. Moreover, it is likely that the importance of effectiveness criteria will vary in different growth phases as different constituencies become more or less dominant. In early phases, for example, resource providers are typically more important than regulators, while the opposite is true in later phases. This suggests that in order to be judged successful, organizations should satisfy the primary criteria of effectiveness held by their dominant constituencies.[16]

4. Leading an organization through its developmental phases requires an extraordinary range of talents as well as motivations. Managers must adjust their roles and behavior as the needs of their organizations and positions evolve, as well as be prepared to encounter great personal stress. Yet people capable of presiding over an organization from entrepreneurial kick-start to industry powerhouse are seemingly rare. All too often leadership skills that are necessary to be effective during one phase of growth are of limited value in a subsequent phase. So it is important for top managers to try to prepare themselves for transitions between phases in order to avert the necessity of frequent top-management succession. The truth of this observation is well illustrated by the growth of Xerox Corp. from a small, entrepreneurial concern to an impersonal, multibillion-dollar corporation.[17] Under the guidance of entrepreneur Joseph C. Wilson, Xerox introduced the 914 copier, one of the most successful products in business history. During Wilson's reign as chief executive from 1961 to 1968, Xerox boasted an entrepreneurial culture marked by informality, innovation, and bold risk taking. Camaraderie was strong and motivation high. As Xerox entered a phase of sustained growth in 1968, C. Peter McColough became CEO. McColough, a professional manager with an MBA from Harvard, oversaw a major change in Xerox's culture. Bureaucratic controls were installed to ostensibly monitor Xerox's growth, but soon Xerox became stodgy and formal with layers of watchdog managers. New-product development was delayed with a resulting loss of market share and increase in costs. Xerox's rejuvenation began in 1982 when David T. Kearns, a former IBMer, was named CEO. To reestablish Xerox's competitive edge, Kearns trimmed the number of employees, stressed quality, and greatly decentralized authority. Xerox soon moved outside its core business and by 1986 was earning almost half of its profits from financial services. It is unlikely that the range of talents and motivations demonstrated by Wilson "the Entrepreneur," McColough "the Bureaucrat," and Kearns "the Rejuvenator" could be found in one individual.

5. Despite its appearance, the Greiner model is not meant to suggest that all organizations move in a linear progression, proceeding sequentially from Phase 1 to Phase 5 or that these transitions automatically occur. In reality, the length of time that organizations remain in each phase will vary, and the dividing lines between phases typically will be blurred, with considerable overlap. Moreover, resistance to change (see Chapter 14) may well impede movement from one phase to another. In addition, the impression that all units in an organization proceed simultaneously, in lockstep fashion, through the various developmental phases should be avoided. Indeed, organizations with different divisions and departments can be in several phases at once.

6. Because of unusual environmental events, loss of key participants, or a substantial decrease in resources, an organization may revert to an earlier phase of development. In this respect, managerial actions can be used to purposely speed up, slow down, or turn back an organization's growth and development. NCR Corporation is a prime example of an organization that has been reborn through managerial actions. After revamping its outmoded products with the latest technology, the former cash register goliath has become a cutting-edge computer company with a soaring growth rate. Thus, decay and decline are not inevitable given sound management.

7. For whatever reason, the life span of many organizations is short. Many die before passing through all five phases of development. Consequently, as will be discussed in Chapter 12, decay and decline are the most important concerns of many organizations.

8. The Greiner model is principally applicable to organizations that have the express intent of growing over time. Whether it is also relevant for purposefully small organizations is questionable,[18] and the vast majority of small organizations remain small.

SUMMARY

The sole purpose of this chapter has been to familiarize the reader with the patterns and forces of organizational growth.

Learning Objective 1: Name various motives for organizational growth. There are numerous motives for organizational growth, including (1) security, (2) prestige and power, (3) adventure and risk, (4) increased compensation, (5) greater profit, and (6) monopolistic dominance.

Learning Objective 2: Explain the general nature of the Greiner organizational growth model. The Greiner model presents organizations as moving through five phases of growth as they make the transition from small to large (in sales and employees) and from young to mature. These phases are shown in Figure 11.1. Each phase is distinguished by an *evolution* from the prior phase and then by a *revolution,* or crisis, that precipitates movement into the next phase. Management's critical task during each revolutionary period is to identify and implement appropriate new practices to enter another period of evolutionary growth.

Learning Objective 3: Describe Greiner's five phases of organizational growth.

1. Representing the birth of an organization, the emphasis of the *creativity phase* of growth is on creating both a product and a market. This phase ends in a crisis of leadership.

2. The *direction phase* of organizational growth is a time of sustained growth under competent and directive management. This phase ends in a crisis of autonomy.

3. The *delegation phase* of organizational growth is an era of growth evolving from the successful introduction of a geographically decentralized organization structure. This phase ends in a crisis of control.

4. The *coordination phase* of organizational growth is marked by the introduction of various techniques for achieving increased coordination. This phase ends in a crisis of red tape.

5. The *collaboration phase* of organizational growth emphasizes greater spontaneity in management action, teamwork, and the skillful resolution of interpersonal differences. The crisis ending this phase has yet to be determined.

Learning Objective 4: Recount several managerial implications of the various phases of organizational growth.
Managerial implications suggested by the various phases of organizational growth include the following: (1) by knowing an organization's development phase and future plans, managers can make more informed decisions and prepare themselves and their organizations for later challenges; (2) organizations are subject to developmental transitions that can jeopardize their performance, if not survival; (3) organizations exist in uncertain environments and must reactively and proactively adapt to their surroundings in order to grow and develop; (4) leading an organization through its developmental phases requires an extraordinary range of talents, as well as motivations; (5) not all organizations grow in a smooth and linear fashion; (6) due to various reasons, organizations may revert or recycle to an earlier phase of development; (7) the life span of many organizations is short; and (8) the growth and developmental patterns of organizations with the express intent of growth over time may be different from those of purposefully small organizations.

Discussion Questions

1. Security is one motive for organizational growth. Bigger organizations seldom find their backs to the wall. Indeed, as a result of government intervention on the grounds of national security (for example, Lockheed Aircraft) or unacceptable social costs (for example, Chrysler), larger business organizations have long enjoyed "womb to tomb" protection. Moreover, the Federal Bankruptcy Act is structured in such a way as to assure continuity of larger business enterprises—albeit under new management. Commenting on the nature of this continuity, Cole has described the high stakes of business survival particularly well.

> If . . . railroads may be kept running despite financial embarrassment in the treasurer's office, if manufacturing establishments can persist in the employment of personnel and the production of goods despite the need of red ink in the controller's reports, the business world is spared the repercussions which a break in the preexisting skein of business relationships would otherwise have caused, the extent of the disturbance varying, of course, with the size of the enterprise that had gotten itself into difficulties. The series of repercussions which a sudden closing of the doors of General Motors or General Electric would touch off is almost inconceivable; but the damage to the whole country would surely be tremendous.[19]

Given this reasoning, it has been argued, even as such companies as those described become atrophied and inefficient, they become "too big to fail." Does bigness carry any downside risk? Explain.

2. British economist Jack Downie has remarked, "Growth involves thought, effort and worry, and there is ample evidence that willingness to undertake these is by no means an immutable, instinctive characteristic of humans."[20] Reflecting on the observation that "empire-builders are made, not born," comment on the growth motives of such top managers as R. E. "Ted" Turner, (president and chairman, Turner Broadcasting System) and Lee A. Iacocca (chairman, Chrysler Motors).

3. The chapter acknowledges that there are various motives for organizational growth. In addition to the motives it identifies, it also could be argued that a growth-oriented organization is better able to attract qualified employees, more likely to be viewed by customers as reliable and eager to please, and more likely to be given preferential treatment by suppliers and creditors who hope to retain its business as it expands. Comment on this argument, being sure to identify other motives for organizational growth.

4. Do you agree with the following opinion?

> The words "big" and "small" are *relational* terms. A "big" dog is simply a dog larger than most dogs; a "small" house is simply a house smaller than most houses. Hence, when someone asserts that a corporation is "too big," the question, "Big in relation to what?" must be asked. Simply, the claim that a corporation is "too big" in the sense that the corporation is big in relation to a solitary

individual, is little more than an expression of the sort of disquiet some people experience when observing the vastness of the Grand Canyon. The claim, as noted, is understandable. Nonetheless, it is irrational.[21]

In explaining your position, reflect on the following facts: (1) The U. S. state department has over 16,500 employees overseas; IBM has over 163,000; (2) IBM's revenue of more than $50 billion is larger than the gross domestic product of Greece, Iceland, Ireland, Luxembourg, New Zealand, Portugal, or Turkey; and (3) IBM's worldwide tax provision exceeds $5 billion annually. It would take over 1 million Americans, paying average taxes to equal those revenues.

5. In answering the question, "How large should a company be?" noted management authority Peter F. Drucker has given the following response:

> Let's say you need to enter a hospital. If it's fewer than 180 beds, don't go there. If it's more than 500 beds, don't go there. The smaller hospital really cannot do everything well. Neither can the big one. If you have a bypass, don't go to a hospital that does fewer than 500 a year. They don't have to learn on you.
>
> The real growth and innovation in this country has been in medium-size companies that employ between 200 and 4,000 workers. If you are in a small company, you are running all out. You have neither the time nor the energy to devote to anything but yesterday's crisis.
>
> A medium-size company has the resources to devote to new products and markets, and it's still small enough to be flexible and move fast. And these companies now have what they once lacked—they've learned how to manage.[22]

Comment on the logic underlying Drucker's response.

6. Noted organization theorists Peter M. Blau and W. Richard Scott have observed that "large and complex . . . organizations do not spring into existence full-blown but develop out of simpler ones."[23] Given your knowledge of the growth and development of organizations, do you agree? If so, why? If not, why not?

7. In a lead story devoted to the need of growing organizations for new leadership, *USA Today* issued the following warning: "To all 'T-shirt tycoons': Grow up and join the mainstream, or move aside. Growing corporations wait for no one, not even brilliant and headstrong visionaries."[24] Comment on this warning in light of the turmoil or crises ultimately faced by a growing Phase 1 organization.

8. Looking at a map of the United States studded with red pushpins for each Toys "R" Us store, founder Charles Lazarus commented, "Growth creates problems, yes, but it also eliminates them. The only thing I know how to manage is growth. We're in the growth business. What we sell is toys."[25] Discuss the problems a growing organization is likely to encounter as it moves from Phase 2 to Phase 3 and then from Phase 3 to Phase 4 of Greiner's organizational growth model.

DESIGN AUDIT #11

Managing Organizational Growth

This design audit will help you assess the effects of growth on your organization's structure and determine whether its design fits its current coordination and control needs. You will diagnose the extent to which growth has caused coordination and control problems for your organization, and explore potential design options to correct these problems.

1. How many employees has your organization added in the past 24 months?

    _____ Number of new employees

    _____ Percent increase over 24 months

    Note: If the number of employees has grown by less than 15 percent over the past 24 months, you may want to skim through this design audit and go to Design Audit #12.

2. How would you classify your organization's current life-cycle stage?

    _____ Creativity stage

    _____ Direction stage

    _____ Delegation stage

    _____ Coordination stage

    _____ Collaboration stage

3. Is there evidence that your organization has outgrown its current structure and entered one of the crises described in Chapter 11? If so, indicate which crisis your organization is experiencing, and, on a separate sheet of paper, briefly describe the nature of the crisis. If your organization is not experiencing one of the crises described in Chapter 11, skim through the rest of this design audit and go to Design Audit #12.

    _____ Crisis of leadership

    _____ Crisis of autonomy

    _____ Crisis of control

    _____ Crisis of red tape

    Description of crisis

4.   Look again at Design Audits #4 through #7 and think about whether any of the problems identified and design alternatives suggested would alleviate the crisis identified in Question 3. Indicate in the space below what design changes are needed to help your organization resolve its current life cycle crisis.

Notes

1. Louis H. Orzack and Jack Oldham, "Toward a Theory of New Organizations," in *The New Social Sciences,* ed. Baidya N. Varma (Westport, Conn.: Greenwood Press, 1976), 197. This entire paragraph draws on this source.

2. James O'Toole, *Vanguard Management: Redesigning the Corporate Future* (Garden City, N.Y.: Doubleday, 1985), 39.

3. Judith H. Dobrzynski, John P. Tarpey, and Rebecca Aikman, "Small Is Beautiful: A New Survey of Hot Growth Companies," *Business Week,* May 27, 1985, 88–90.

4. Stratford P. Sherman, "Ted Turner: Back from the Brink," *Fortune*, July 7, 1986, 26.

5. Harold Geneen, *Managing* (Garden City, N.Y.: Doubleday, 1984), 131.

6. Barry D. Baysinger, Roger E. Meiners, and Carl P. Zeithaml, *Barriers to Corporate Growth* (Lexington, Mass.: Lexington Books, 1981), 4.

7. Larry E. Greiner, "Evolution and Revolution as Organizations Grow," *Harvard Business Review* 50, no. 4 (1972): 37–46.

8. William Dowdy quoted in Brenton R. Schlender, "Apple Tries to Achieve Stability but Remain Creative," *The Wall Street Journal,* July 16, 1987, 1.

9. Michael S. Malone quoted in Kathy Rebello and John Hillkirk, "Apple's Story 'Oldest in Silicon Valley,'" *USA Today,* June 5, 1985, 1B.

10. Donald K. Clifford, Jr. and Richard E. Cavanaugh, *The Winning Performance: How America's High-Growth Midsize Companies Succeed* (New York: Bantam Books, 1985), 168.

11. William C. Dunkelberg quoted in Carrie Dolan, "Entrepreneurs Often Fail as Managers," *The Wall Street Journal,* May 15, 1989, B1.

12. Charles Lazarus quoted in Stuart Gannes, "America's Fastest-Growing Companies," *Fortune,* May 23, 1988, 32–33.

13. Mitchell D. Kapor quoted in Barbara Buell, "Coming of Age at Lotus: Software's Child Prodigy Grows Up," *Business Week,* February 25, 1985, 100.

14. C. Joseph LaBonte quoted in Gannes, "America's Fastest-Growing Companies," 32.

15. Randall Smith, "IBM, Once a Dictatorship, Is Now a Vast, Decentralized Democracy," *The Wall Street Journal*, April 7, 1986, 20.

16. Kim S. Cameron and David A. Whetten, "Perceptions of Organizational Effectiveness Across Organizational Life Cycles," *Administrative Science Quarterly* 26 (1981): 525–544. See also Cameron, "The Enigma of Organizational Effectiveness," in *New Directions for Program Evaluation: Measuring Effectiveness,* ed. Dan Baugher (San Francisco: Jossey-Bass, 1981), 1–13; Robert E. Quinn and Kim S. Cameron, "Organizational Life Cycles and Shifting Criteria of Effectiveness: Some Preliminary Evidence," *Management Science,* (1983): 33–51.

17. John A. Byrne, "Culture Shock at Xerox," *Business Week,* June 22, 1987, 108.

18. Bernard Barry, "Human and Organizational Problems Affecting Growth in Smaller Enterprises," *Management International Review* 20, no. 1 (1980): 39–49; Estelle James, "How Nonprofits Grow: A Model," *Journal of Policy Analysis and Management* 2 (1983): 350–366.

19. Arthur H. Cole, "A Note on Continuity of Enterprises," *Business History Review* 35 (1961): 82.

20. Jack Downie, *The Competitive Process* (London: Duckworth, 1958), 63.

21. John K. Williams, "A Bad Time for Giants," *The Freeman* 36 (1986): 12.

22. John A. Byrne, "Advice from the Dr. Spock of Business," *Business Week,* September 28, 1987, 61.

23. Peter M. Blau and W. Richard Scott, *Formal Organizations: A Comparative Approach* (San Francisco: Chandler, 1962), 224.

24. Rebello and Hillkirk, "Apple's Story," 1B.

25. Gannes, "America's Fastest-Growing Companies," 36.

Managing Decline and Turnarounds

Learning Objectives

Upon completing this chapter, you should be able to

1. Explain the statement that "success breeds failure."
2. Outline the organizational and interpersonal dynamics that are common in declining organizations.
3. Discuss the basic steps required to turn around a declining organization.
4. Identify five basic workforce redeployment and reduction strategies.
5. Explain the importance of maintaining workforce morale in a declining organization.

INTERCO SLIMS DOWN, BUT IS IT ENOUGH?

Is there life after death for Interco? Since the consumer products company's recapitalization a few years ago, things have gone dreadfully wrong. The deal saved Interco Inc., which owns several retail units including Florsheim Shoes and Broyhill Furniture, from a hostile raid. Unfortunately, Interco was left leveraged to the eyeballs. To make matters worse, the sale of choice assets didn't fetch the cash expected, and support from angry bondholders and jittery lenders is tenuous at best.

Cleaning up this sad mess has fallen to Richard B. Loynd, Interco's new CEO. According to Loynd, the freedom that Interco's operating units have traditionally enjoyed is a thing of the past. He has placed the entire organization on a strict budget; gone is the company jet, along with a third of the headquarters staff. Projects have been shelved, and Loynd is subleasing half of Interco's corporate suite to a law firm.

So far, Interco has shaved about $75 million in costs, but analysts doubt that will be enough. Cash flow problems, as you'll see in Chapter 12, are only one of the several indicators that can signal an organization's decline. And, as the situation at Interco suggests, it may be necessary to empower a leader or management team to make the drastic cost-cutting measures needed in order to turn around an organization in decline.

Source: Brian Bremner, "Interco: Another Day Older and $1.4 Billion In Debt," *Business Week*, January 22, 1990, 58.

IN the last several chapters we examined how both environmental change and organizational growth can create situations that lead to organizational decline and failure. After having read these chapters, you might ask why managers don't see potential problems in advance and correct them. This chapter attempts to answer that question. We also look at the structural and interpersonal dynamics that are common during decline and failure, and how managers turn around declining organizations.

Managing decline and failure are important topics that have been ignored to a large extent by the academic and business communities. David Whetten suggests that part of the reason lies in the pervasive success ethic in American society:

> The dark side of this philosophy . . . is its implication that failure reflects personal incompetence. This logical trap is also reflected in the tendency to treat organization growth as evidence of youth and vitality; decline then becomes equated with old age and senility. So powerful is the association between growth and success and between decline and failure in our society that Scott[1] has proposed that the chief issue in the management of declining organizations is not whether managers are capable of saving them but whether they are willing to make the attempt.[2]

The effect, *The Wall Street Journal* says, is "a corporate and academic complex that has long had a nearly paranoid aversion to admitting to, discussing, or teaching about failure."[3]

But ignoring the management of failing organizations denies reality because decline and failure are common in the world of organizations. As Figure 12.1 shows, during the 1980s the rate of business failures was higher than at any time since the Great Depression. High rates of inflation during the late 1970s, followed by a recession, major intrusions in U.S. markets by foreign competitors, deregulation, accelerating technological change, and rapidly changing consumer preferences all contributed to the increased incidence of decline and failure.

Decline and failure are not limited to the private sector, either, since their effects spill over into the public sector. As the fortunes of the business community have waned, so have those of government and nonprofit organizations. Declining tax receipts and cuts in federal, state, and local funding have shrunk government operations. Charitable and nonprofit organizations also have suffered as government grants and contracts and private contributions have decreased. In short, managing declining organizations has become an important aspect of the everyday lives of both private- and public-sector managers.

WHY ORGANIZATIONS GET INTO TROUBLE

If, as we have outlined in the preceding chapters, there are identifiable environmental conditions and internal organizational dynamics that can lead to decline, why not simply take steps to prevent it? There are two parts to the answer to this question. One is related to an organization's past successes; the other to the imperfections of human perception. Both affect managers' abilities to perceive and interpret information that would forewarn of an impending downturn.

Success Breeds Failure

Three things typically happen when an organization is successful. First, it amasses slack resources. This has both good and bad effects. As noted in Chapter 2, an organization uses slack resources as side payments to satisfy divergent stakeholder interests. Employees want higher pay, shareholders want increasing dividends, banks want timely payments, and so on. An expanding pool of slack resources allows an organization to satisfy these stakeholder demands. But at the same time, accumulated slack resources can make it less sensitive to its environment because they buffer it from the initial effects of internal problems and environmental change. Consequently, managers in a successful organization perceive the world around them less accurately.[4]

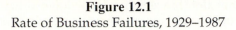

Figure 12.1
Rate of Business Failures, 1929–1987

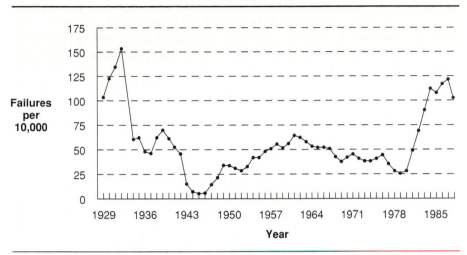

Source: Dun & Bradstreet Corporation. *Business Failure Record*, 1987.

Second, increased slack resources allow an organization greater freedom to act more autonomously than it could otherwise—to choose among alternative courses of action, to take risks, and to experiment. One common manifestation of this new freedom is diversification into new lines of business, particularly by firms in cyclical or mature industries. Buoyed by their past successes, managers then often become less cautious about the types of businesses into which they enter. Diversification into unrelated businesses is often unaccompanied by the expertise to manage them.

William C. Verity, Secretary of Commerce during the last year of the Reagan administration, had previously served as the chairman of Armco Inc., a diversified steelmaker, between 1971 and 1982. To reduce the impact of the steel industry's cyclical downturns, Verity diversified Armco's operations into oil rigs, petroleum exploration, building products, insurance, and strategic metals and materials. But diversification created a problem, because Armco's top management was dominated by managers brought up in the traditional steel business. These managers clung to power, which resulted in major decisions being made by people who did not understand the diversified operations. The result: Armco lost $1.9 billion between 1982 and 1986, mainly in newly acquired divisions. Armco was forced to dismantle in order to stave off bankruptcy. Its insurance division alone lost $520 million, primarily because of high-risk ventures such as insuring Colonel Muammer Quadaffi's Libyan navy.[5]

A third and related problem caused by past success is that an organization's managers often begin to believe that their management style and methods cannot fail. Since what they have done in the past was successful, they tend to rely too much on past experience as a guide to future action. Successful policies and procedures become set practices, patterns of communication and coordination become rigid, and managers become complacent.[6] As long as an organization's original competitive situation persists, those practices and patterns will maintain its success. But if the situation changes, the organization may find itself perched on the brink of a crisis. Focus on Design 12.1 describes how the Howard Johnson restaurant chain lost its position as the premier roadside restaurant business in exactly this way.

Overall, accumulated slack resources and growing operational rigidities make it difficult for managers to perceive environmental changes as they occur. Thus, previously successful organizations falter as they lose their ability to adapt. A graphic illustration is provided by the fortunes of some of the 43 firms that Peters and Waterman identified in *In Search of Excellence* as being paragons of successful management. Two years after publication of the book, a *Business Week* report indicated that 14 of the 43 companies were stumbling badly—and 12 were having problems because of fundamental changes in their markets to which they had not responded.[7]

The Limits of Perception

Another reason managers sometimes fail to detect potential problems is that human perception is shaped by individual factors, such as values, beliefs, and past experiences.[8] For example, unless managers believe that something can happen, they are unlikely to recognize it when it does.

Such was the case with auto industry executives during the 1973–1974 Arab oil embargo. General Motors executives had studied the possibility of an energy shortage and its potential effect on sales months prior to the onset of the oil embargo. Because they believed such a problem might occur, they responded quickly by downsizing their vehicles. Ford and Chrysler executives could not believe that the oil embargo signaled a fundamental change in the auto industry environment, and they took no action. As a result, GM gained two years on its domestic competitors in realigning its products to an environment where supplies of gasoline were expensive and uncertain.[9] The difference in the way that these executives perceived and responded points out the value of strategic as well as contingency planning. It lies not so much in having developed plans of action, but in developing a perceptual readiness that allows managers to "see" the unexpected.[10]

An individual's past experience is a major factor in perception. For example, a manager who has not experienced an industry decline is less likely to interpret correctly information about fundamental environmental changes than one who has encountered a similar situation. Until experience teaches otherwise, people tend to believe that what has worked in the past will work in the future. Past experience also may influence the interpretation of perceived

FOCUS ON DESIGN 12.1

How Success Killed HoJo's Orange Roofs

Howard Johnson founded the restaurant chain bearing his name in 1925 by combining a patent medicine store and newspaper agency in suburban Quincy, Massachusetts, next to a commuter train station. He added a soda fountain with store-made ice cream, which was an instant hit. Within a few years, Howard Johnson was franchising family-oriented restaurants. The chain expanded and prospered until World War II, when it was forced to close many of its outlets because of food and gasoline rationing. Its near collapse left Howard Johnson leary of long-term debt. If a growing and prosperous business could be pushed to the brink of failure, he reasoned, the world was a too dangerous place for those in debt.

With the expansion of the highway system during the 1950s and 1960s, HoJo's orange roofs became a roadside fixture. Its cash flow was sufficient to launch hundreds of new restaurants along with a chain of franchised, family-oriented motor lodges. By 1965 its revenues exceeded the combined sales of McDonald's, Burger King, and Kentucky Fried Chicken. The elder Howard Johnson stepped down and passed control to his son, Howard Johnson, Jr.

By the early 1970s, HoJo's had amassed a cash reserve of almost $90 million, but the environment in which it had been so successful began to change. Rapidly expanding inexpensive, franchised fast food chains increased competition in the family segment of the market, while higher-priced theme and ethnic restaurants challenged it at the market's higher end. At the same time, franchise operators began expanding the HoJo's motor lodges to compete with the increasing number of roadside hotel and motel chains. These expanded facilities brought in a new clientele—businesspeople, whose tastes differed from that of the average family traveller, significantly complicating the restaurants' operations as they tried to serve both customers. HoJo's might have acquired a fast food chain to reposition itself, but that would have meant going into debt. Remembering his father's experience, the younger Howard Johnson refused.

Instead, HoJo's response was to run its operation with more of an accountant's eye than that of an entrepreneur. It was preoccupied with controlling expenses instead of monitoring changing consumer tastes. Said the younger Howard Johnson, "We ran a very tight operation. We kept our expenses low. We wanted to have earnings improvement. We were on top of the numbers daily." The chain relied on comment cards left on its tables to gauge consumer tastes, compared to the sophisticated market-testing operations of competitors such as Marriott and Denny's. This system meant that Howard Johnson's received market information from only those people who still patronized its restaurants. The result: the menu, decor, and presentation that had made the firm successful during the 1950s and 1960s changed very little as the market rapidly evolved. By 1984 Howard Johnson was running a negative cash flow. In 1985 Marriott acquired the company, sold the motor lodges and some of the restaurants, and converted the rest into Big Boy restaurant franchises.

Source: Adapted from John Merwin, "The Sad Case of the Dwindling Orange Roofs," *Forbes,* December 30, 1985, 75–79; "Howard Johnson: Is It Too Late to Fix Up Its Faded 1950s Image?" *Business Week,* October 22, 1984, 90.

change as threatening instead of presenting an opportunity. So might several other factors, such as personality, personal goals, and attitudes toward change. In summary, many organizations experience a downturn simply because their managers "didn't see it coming."

ORGANIZATIONAL AND INTERPERSONAL DYNAMICS

The best way to understand what happens in a declining organization is to examine a hypothetical but typical pattern of the organizational and interpersonal dynamics involved. Figure 12.2 traces out the general dynamics.

Organizational Dynamics

The initial reaction by managers in many successful organizations to a downturn is "weathering the storm," which literally means doing as little as possible and waiting for the situation to pass. Minor actions that address the symptoms of a downturn by increasing cash flow are the norm—deferring maintenance, reducing spending on new-product development, decreasing capital spending to modernize plant and equipment, halting new hiring, reducing R&D funding, cutting advertising budgets, and so on. Little attention is paid to diagnosing the causes of declining profitability or decreasing cash flow. This response creates a problem if a downturn is not temporary: managers have squandered valuable time and resources that could have been used to turn around an organization's operations. And if the response of "curing" the symptoms is initially successful, the motivation to understand environmental changes is reduced, usually resulting in a major crisis a short time later.[11]

If the cause of a downturn doesn't resolve itself, the types of actions taken to fine-tune operations will no longer work: profitability and/or market share drop further, and cash flow worsens. At this point, managers can no longer ignore the situation, and a number of things start to happen. Decision making becomes more centralized, and the authority for making previously delegated operating decisions is consolidated at higher levels.[12] Senior managers often find themselves making decisions about hiring secretaries, authorizing the purchase of pens and pencils, and the like, in an effort to gain tighter control over cash flow. The information (and attendant paperwork) needed to make these decisions now must be communicated upward from lower hierarchical levels. The sheer quantity of information previously handled by several lower-level managers creates information overload at higher management levels. It also can lead to information distortion as more information passes through more hands.[13]

Figure 12.2
The Downward Cycle of Decline

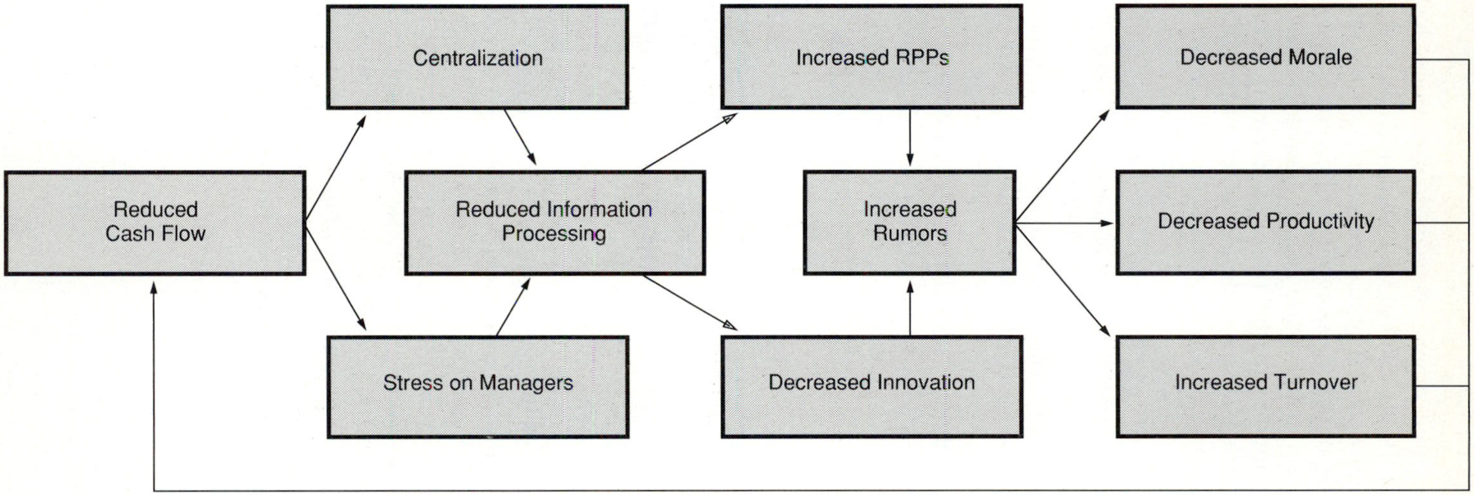

At the same time, managers begin to experience high levels of stress as they realize that the survival of their organization is threatened. This stress in turn decreases their ability to accurately perceive and interpret information. Individuals under stress typically become: (1) less able to deal with complex issues for which there are no standard operating procedures, (2) increasingly reliant on personal preferences and decision-making styles that have worked in the past, regardless of whether they are appropriate for the current situation, and (3) less able to estimate the consequences of alternative courses of action.[14] Thus, the potential for poor decisions increases—and errors are more costly during a period of decline than in a period of growth.[15] Strategic miscalculations that may be painful during a period of growth can be fatal during a period of decline when little organizational slack exists.

Chrysler's introduction of the K-car in 1980 provides a clear example. Because the extensive publicity that the K-car received during the federal loan guarantee hearings ensured that thousands of curious potential customers would visit dealer showrooms, executives decided to load the cars with options in order to increase cash flow from their sales. As expected, dealer traffic was heavy when the cars were introduced, but their price, which was as high as that of many larger models, kept sales down until Chrysler initiated a rebate program. The effect of the miscalculation on cash flow was almost fatal. Chrysler was in the process of posting its second consecutive year of losses and would have gone under without the federal loan guarantee obtained a few months earlier. If the company had been in better financial condition, a botched vehicle introduction would have been painful, but not nearly fatal.[16]

Because decision-making authority has been centralized, organizations begin to increasingly rely on rules, policies, and procedures to coordinate and control activities at lower hierarchical levels.[17] Unit objectives and criteria for evaluating them become more explicit and resource allocation is centralized to higher managerial levels.[18] These actions increase top management's control of an organization's operations. But they also decrease an organization's flexibility, reducing its capacity to innovate.[19]

The capacity to innovate also can be dampened by two other factors: (1) a heightened fear of failure and its associated costs, which in turn reduces managers' willingness to experiment, and (2) scant slack resources, diminishing the likelihood that innovative responses can be developed or implemented.[20] An inability to innovate can be fatal if an organization is experiencing decline because of changes in the shape of its industry niche. Innovations in product offerings and customers served will be required to reposition the organization within its evolving environment.

Interpersonal Dynamics

Decreasing resources also have a major impact on the interpersonal dynamics within an organization. Resource allocation tends to become a zero sum game where one party gains only at the expense of another, because there are fewer resources available to satisfy the divergent needs of different units and stakeholders. Conflict becomes more intense in the organization,[21] and resource allocation tends to conform to the relative power of the participants.[22]

Increased centralization causes other problems. If top management has not kept employees informed (they usually do not in this situation), rumors abound as employees try to make sense of the situation.[23] As uncertainty increases, morale drops, and commitment to the organization declines. Productivity then decreases, forcing managers to further cut operations.

When the climate within an organization worsens, the most mobile—and usually the best—employees look for jobs elsewhere.[24] Their departure further decreases productivity, necessitating further cuts. At this point, an organization will enter a downward spiral, where cuts are followed by further decreases in productivity, requiring more cuts. And that organization will go under unless management can break out of the downward spiral.[25]

Usually, the situation is forced at some point by one of an organization's stakeholders as they become aware of its troubles. Banks may refuse to extend loan payments, suppliers may demand cash payment for materials and components, the board may confront management, or a hostile takeover attempt may occur. Managers can no longer keep an organization's condition under wraps, and a crisis of confidence in top management and in the organization's chances of survival occurs. Stakeholders typically try to withdraw from or minimize their contact with the organization at this point.[26] Shareholders sell their stock, banks call loans due, customers abandon the organization for more stable sources of supply, and so on.

In the next stage, top management is replaced by the organization's board of directors.[27] The most common reason for replacing top management is that a new management team is not wedded to the policies of the past, which, more often than not, have led to the organization's decline. Because a new management team enters an organization with a fresh perspective, it can redefine problems and develop new strategies. Whether a new management team can turn around a declining organization depends on a number of factors, including

1. The extent to which an organization's resources have been depleted.
2. The extent to which stakeholders, including employees, have been alienated.
3. The extent to which the new management team understands an organization's underlying problems, can develop a strategy to correct them, and can implement that strategy.

Implementation is particularly affected by the first two factors.

MANAGING A TURNAROUND

Four basic steps are involved in managing a turnaround:

1. Diagnosing the nature of underlying problems and developing a long-range strategy for countering them.
2. Deciding what to cut from current operations.
3. Developing the support of key stakeholders, including nonmanagerial employees, for a turnaround strategy.
4. Rebuilding workforce morale and redesigning the current organization.

Diagnosing the Problem and Developing a Long-Term Strategy

The first step in turning around a declining organization is diagnosing underlying problems. Diagnosis seems simple in hindsight, but on a real-time basis it can be difficult for a number of reasons. As we noted earlier, the stress created by a threat to an organization's survival can diminish the quality of decisions, as can factors affecting individual perception.

Cash Flow Symptoms of Decline. Diagnosing a decline situation requires that managers carefully evaluate information about internal organizational operations and about how an organization's environment is changing. A good place to start is by examining decline symptoms as reflected in an organization's cash flow. This means that attention has to be shifted from income statements that reflect historical performance to the cash flow of current operations. Richard Sloma, author of *The Turnaround Manager's Handbook,* identifies four stages in the development of a cash flow crisis.[28] From least to most severe they are

• *Quality of profit:* The decreasing value of the ratio of operating pretax sales to net sales is an early indicator that an organization may be losing its competitive edge.

• *Quantity of profit:* A detectable erosion in an organization's current profit compared to recent periods is caused by increasing fixed and variable expenses, indicating further slippage in an organization's position relative to its competitors.

• *Cash shortfall:* Increasing unit costs and decreasing revenues are depleting an organization's resources and will lead to a cash flow crisis in the near term if not resolved.

• *Cash crunch:* Bankruptcy is imminent because an organization can no longer meet short-term obligations such as debt service, accounts payable, and payroll.

Sloma's stages and their corresponding symptoms are shown in Table 12.1.

Table 12.1
Stages Leading to a Cash Flow Crisis

Quality of Profit
  Inconsistent valuation of inventory input/output
  Increasing warranty expense
  Decreasing plant utilization
  Decreasing product-line profitability
  Decreasing unit sales
  Decreasing customer profitability

Quantity of Profit
  Increasing people-related fixed and variable expenses
  Increasing plant-related fixed and variable expenses
  Increasing sales/marketing expense
  Increasing finance/administration expense
  Increasing engineering expense

Cash Shortfall
  Excessive debt/equity ratio
  Flat, falling sales
  Eroding gross margin
  Increasing unit labor cost
  Increasing unit material cost

Cash Crunch
  Inability to pay the following:
    Debt service
    Taxes
    Contractual obligations
    Accounts payable
    Salaries, wages, commissions
    Fringe benefits, pensions, etc.
    Purchase commitments

Source: Adapted from Richard S. Sloma, *The Turnaround Manager's Handbook* (New York: Free Press, 1985), 39–68.

It should be obvious that the earlier managers recognize that a problem exists, the more resources they will have to work with in reversing a decline. Unfortunately, because of the complacency often created by past successes, many managers do not recognize the need for action until their organization experiences a cash shortfall or cash crunch (the last two of Sloma's stages), resulting in too little being done too late.

Identifying the Causes of Decline. Identifying symptoms of decline through cash flow analysis provides managers with information and the impetus to ask what the underlying causes are. Is the decline attributable to internal factors, such as poor financial controls, faulty product quality, or increasing unit costs? Or is it related to changes in an organization's environment, such as increased competition, changing consumer preferences, changing technology, or economic conditions? Often the causes are a combination of internal and external factors.

Diagnosis requires participation of the people with the greatest knowledge about an organization's operations and environment. In large organizations, and in those with a professionalized workforce, much of the expertise for accurate diagnosis is located at lower hierarchical levels. If decision making is centralized in response to a cash flow crisis, it is less likely that an organization's top managers will have ready access to information about the causes of its problems and, hence, to the solutions. As a result, a decided effort must be made to include people with relevant knowledge in the diagnosis process, particularly when crisis conditions prevail.

Once causes have been identified, a response strategy can be formulated. As noted in Chapter 10, several domain tactics can be used by organizations, each addressing a particular type of environmental change. For example, if an organization is facing erosion of demand, fine-tuning operations to increase efficiency and employing domain offense to move the organization into adjacent customer or product markets is a viable retrenchment plan. If a decline in operations is related primarily to the types of internal life cycle transitions discussed in Chapter 11, managers need to redesign an organization's structure and processes to meet existing needs for coordination and control. For example, many small entrepreneurial organizations encounter crises as they grow larger because they do not have adequate controls in place or because owner/managers have failed to decentralize decision-making authority as their capacity for control is exceeded. Finally, a response strategy has to be realistic about available financial and human resources. Grandiose strategies that an organization has little hope of implementing are sure to fail. And the more severe an organization's cash flow problems, the less time and fewer resources will be available to implement a turnaround strategy.

Targeting Cuts

Implementing an organization's turnaround strategy usually begins by cutting back current operations. Such cutbacks serve two purposes: (1) they scale down or eliminate areas of operation that are no longer in demand, and (2) they make available resources that can be used to reposition an organization in its environment. How cuts are made has much to do with whether a turnaround strategy will work. Many of the internal problems encountered by a declining organization are caused not by decline itself, but by how its managers respond. In other words, the dynamics described earlier are, to a large degree, preventable. Focus on Design 12.2 shows how AT&T created a lot of its own problems the first time it made major cuts, and what it learned from that experience.

FOCUS ON DESIGN 12.2

Creating Your Own Problems—AT&T
Learns the Hard Way

AT&T, an organization that eliminated 66,000 positions between 1984 and 1988, learned that rumors are very costly when it began laying off employees. When AT&T first began its layoffs, word leaked out through Wall Street analysts to the newspapers that it was planning massive cuts, which was the first information that many employees received that they might lose their jobs. Work rapidly ground to a halt as employees speculated about what was coming next. Little information was provided to employees after the layoffs began, fueling further rumors. One former manager notes, "No one in top management stepped forward and said the rumors weren't true. Nobody told us anything official at all, in fact. So the grapevine went berserk." It took many months to get people back to work and to improve survivors' morale.

AT&T learned from this debacle. It hoped to alleviate survivors' fears and to keep morale and productivity from plummeting when it planned to lay off 24,000 Information Systems Division employees in 1985. The layoff was managed much differently. The announcement was made by Chairman Robert T. Allen in a closed-circuit address, who explained how the cuts would make AT&T more competitive. AT&T also flooded employees with literature explaining the situation; provided a toll-free number for questions; sent Mr. Allen on a company-wide tour to meet with employees; ran ads in newspapers seeking jobs for laid-off employees; offered generous severance plans; and provided outplacement services that included counseling, coaching on interview skills, and resume preparation. Although AT&T has had more layoffs, none has had the devastating impact that the first one had on employee morale and productivity. Subsequent layoffs were handled more skillfully.

Sources: Anne B. Fisher, "The Downside of Downsizing," *Fortune,* May 23, 1988, 46; Larry Reibstein, "Survivors of Layoffs to Receive Help to Lift Morale and Reinstill Trust," *The Wall Street Journal,* December 8, 1985, 31.

Deciding on Cuts. The presence of a turnaround strategy is essential for making decisions about how much to cut and where. Otherwise, many private- and public-sector organizations are likely to respond to the onset of a cash flow crisis by ordering across-the-board cuts: "All units will reduce their expenditures by 7 percent." Across-the-board cuts are attractive because they provide an illusion that all units will share the pain equally,[29] and they avoid the difficulty of making painful choices among units and people.[30] Unfortunately, such cuts are subject to the "efficiency paradox."[31] Efficient units have fewer slack resources than less efficient units with which to absorb cuts.

As a result, across-the-board cuts can have three serious, unintended consequences. First, they provide managers with a disincentive to operate efficiently because inefficiencies can be used to absorb the effects of cuts—a self-defeating behavior for an organization during a turnaround. Thus, across-the-board cuts punish efficient units and reward inefficient units. Second, because efficient units have fewer slack resources than inefficient units, their productivity will decrease disproportionately more than that of less efficient units.[32] Third, because of the inequitable effects of across-the-board cuts on efficient units, top management ends up sending the wrong message to its most productive employees—that it does not know what it is doing, which can begin or speed up an exodus of the people an organization most needs to turn it around.

Selective cuts made without a well-thought-out turnaround strategy can damage an organization's chances of survival as well. For example, when the video game market collapsed, and demand shifted to home computers, Atari selectively cut back its operations. But misunderstanding the changes taking place in the industry environment, Atari's managers made cuts and layoffs in its home computer division and not video game operations, further reducing its ability to adapt to changing consumer demand.[33]

In short, effectively targeting cuts requires that managers have an overall guiding strategy. Cuts made on the basis of perceived "equity" usually turn out to be inequitable, jeopardizing an organization's future. Selective cuts made without an eye toward an overall strategy may eliminate people and operations that are essential to an organization's future success.

Managing Workforce Redeployment and Reductions. Redeploying employees and reducing workforce size are two of the major tools that organizations can use to realign themselves to changing market conditions. The purpose of reconfiguring an organization's workforce is to assure that it has the people and skills required to implement its turnaround strategy. In some cases this means an organization needs fewer employees, such as when its industry niche contracts and demand for an organization's goods or services quickly decreases. In other cases, this means an organization needs different skills than its employees currently possess, such as when there is a major technological shift within an industry.

As Figure 12.3 shows, a variety of strategies and tactics can be used to redeploy personnel and reduce workforce size. Some protect employee welfare better than others, and some provide more short-term cost savings to an organization.[34] Redeployment strategies typically provide fewer short-run cost savings but greater long-term benefits, particularly in terms of employee morale and productivity. For example, natural attrition is usually a slow method of reducing workforce size, and an organization typically accrues cost savings slowly from this process. But then remaining employees usually experience few disruptions in their existing employment

Figure 12.3
Strategies and Tactics for Workforce Redeployment and Reduction

Strategy	Sample Tactics
Redeployment Strategies	
Natural Attrition	Selective hiring freeze Selective transfer-in freeze Total hiring freeze Total transfer-in freeze

Induced Redeployment	Transfer-out incentive
	Early retirement incentive
	Severance pay incentive
	Curtailing of advancement
	  opportunities
	Compensation freeze
	  or reduction
	Optional part-time or
	  short-week schedules,
	  work sharing, or
	  leave-without-pay

Involuntary Redeployment	Involuntary transfer-out
	  within plant
	Involuntary transfer-out
	  within firm
	Demotion/downgrading
	Involuntary part-time or
	  short-week schedules,
	  work sharing, or
	  leave-without-pay

Layoff Strategies	

Layoff with Outplacement Assistance	Layoff with:
	  Retraining
	  Job search counseling
	  Severance pay
	  Continuation of benefits
	  (medical, life)
	  Advance notice of layoff

Layoff without Outplacement Assistance	With recall rights Without recall rights

Increasing Protection of Employee Well-Being

Increasing Short-Term Cost savings for Organization

Source: Leonard Greenhalgh, Anne T. Lawrence, and Robert I. Sutton, "Determinants of Work Force Reduction Strategies in Declining Organizations," *Academy of Management Review* 13 (1988): 243.

relationship with an organization, so morale and productivity do not suffer. Layoffs, on the other hand, provide an organization with quick short-term cost savings, but often at the expense of longer-term costs since they are very disruptive and thus harm the morale and productivity of remaining employees.

Redeployment versus Reduction. Many factors influence whether an organization chooses redeployment or reduction strategies. A major determinant is the speed with which a decline occurs. If a decline is caused by a rapid drop in demand (contraction or collapse), an organization may need to lay off employees to bring costs in line quickly. Examples provided earlier include the actions of brokerage firms after the October 1987 stock market crash, and of the auto companies following the contraction of demand in the early 1980s. If environmental conditions change relatively slowly (by erosion or dissolution), redeployment strategies with extensive employee retraining are more beneficial.

For example, technology in the printing industry has changed extensively over the past decade with computerization. These technological advances have changed how printed materials are produced and have reduced the amount of labor needed in the production process. Kansas City–based Hallmark Cards has coped with changes through its philosophy of continually retraining its workforce. Camera operators who once made color separations photographically have been retrained to make them with computer scanners, which requires a different set of skills. The company has also retrained factory workers whose jobs have been eliminated to perform clerical jobs. Overall, its redeployment efforts have enabled it to adapt to changes in its industry, improve productivity, and eliminate 1,300 positions out of more than 20,000 without resorting to layoffs.[35]

Another major determinant is an organization's cash flow. If cash flow has reached the cash-shortage or cash-crunch stage, an organization is more likely to use layoffs, because of an immediate need to conserve cash. If it is experiencing decreasing quality or quantity of profits, and the need for cash is not pressing, redeployment strategies are more likely to be beneficial.

Characteristics of an organization and its workforce also influence whether an organization chooses to redeploy employees or reduce workforce size. Public-sector and unionized organizations, for example, are more likely to redeploy employees than to lay them off, as are organizations with highly skilled workforces.[36]

Effects of Workforce Reductions on Survivors. Managers have become increasingly aware that the manner in which layoffs are handled has a major impact on an organization's future. Long-term survival is the ultimate objective of a turnaround strategy, and its success depends on the employees who remain after a layoff.[37] Mass layoffs can be extremely demoralizing, and the treatment of laid-off employees is a major determinant of how quickly survivors bounce back.[38] *Fortune* reporter, Anne Fisher observes

> Above all, say managers who have been through the downsizing mill, the people being let go must be treated with respect, kindness, even solicitude. That sounds idealistic, but in practice it is less a matter of human decency than of hard-nosed pragmatism, because the employees who remain will be watching closely to see how the laid-off are treated. Notes a Midwestern manufacturing

company manager who has had to lay off a number of people: "If you're nasty to the people who are leaving, morale takes a terrible dive because those who stay conclude that they're working for a bunch of sadistic idiots."[39]

Surviving employees appear to react better to layoffs if an organization has offered some sort of meaningful outplacement assistance, which they interpret as a sign that an organization cares about its employees and which can relieve some of their anxieties about "what if I'm next."[40] Outplacement services, such as career counseling, resume writing, the provision of office space and services, and so on, may be expensive in the short run, but costs are quickly recovered in four ways: (1) direct savings from workforce reductions, (2) lower unemployment insurance premiums as laid-off employees are placed in new jobs, (3) a less negative impact of the layoffs on survivors, and (4) the continued goodwill of stakeholders and the larger community.

The treatment of laid-off workers also has legal implications. Between 1980 and 1987, for example, the number of age-discrimination suits filed against employers more than doubled to 27,000 per year. Many of these suits focused on how organizations chose employees to be laid off.[41] And it appears that outplacement services reduce the likelihood that laid-off employees will sue their former employers.[42]

Managing Information

Developing stakeholder support for an organization's turnaround strategy requires skillful management of information. The instinctive reaction of most managers in a declining organization is to keep the situation under wraps. But almost everything about an organization's condition and its turnaround strategy eventually becomes known to people inside and outside the organization. Being secretive creates rumors, which usually portray a situation as worse than it really is. It also alienates stakeholders, undermining management's credibility and resulting in a loss of trust. Thus, the real issue for management is one of timing—"who should know what when"—not whether to be forthcoming.

Developing External Support. External stakeholders, such as creditors, shareholders, and customers, should be kept reasonably informed of an organization's situation and made aware of the corrective actions being undertaken. When important stakeholders discover that information has been withheld or distorted, they will not trust top management to be truthful in the future. A loss of trust leads to a loss of support: shareholders sell their stock, bankers call loans due, and suppliers refuse to deliver materials on credit—all of which worsen an organization's predicament.

Thus, the challenge facing top management is to be reasonably open about the organization's problems while convincing stakeholders that the survival of the organization is in everyone's best interest. This requires that managers have a turnaround strategy that stakeholders can support. For example, rather than have a bank call loans due and precipitate a cash crunch when it independently finds out that an organization is having financial difficulties, top management may want to approach the bank, explain the organization's situation and proposed turnaround strategy—and explain how that strategy ensures that the bank will be fully repaid as opposed to recovering only a portion of its investment through a bankruptcy proceeding—and then negotiate a new schedule of payments.[43] Overall, top management has to convince important external stakeholders that it understands the situation and has a viable strategy for reversing it. If top management is no longer perceived as credible or trustworthy by external stakeholders, the chances of convincing them that a turnaround is in progress are small, and so is the likelihood of survival.

Developing Internal Support. Managing information within an organization is equally important. If employees are not kept informed about the organization's condition and how it will reverse a decline, they will, as suggested earlier, create their own information in the form of rumors. In the absence of other information, rumors help reduce anxiety by giving meaning to a situation.[44] Keeping employees informed saves the time they will otherwise spend trying to make sense out of a decline situation and thus reducing productivity when the organization can least afford it. For example, during 1987 Bell & Howell was subject to a three-way takeover attempt, and rumors pervaded the organization about impending layoffs. Sales representatives spent half their time on the phone with co-workers at Bell & Howell's Chicago headquarters trying to find out what was happening, and everybody else was too distracted and dispirited to work much. Bell & Howell executives estimate that the resulting drop in productivity dragged the company's second-half profits down as much as 11 percent, or $2.1 million.[45]

Symbolic Information. An important form of information often overlooked by managers is the symbolic content of their actions. Actions speak louder than words, particularly in turnarounds. Or, stated differently, stakeholders and employees watch what managers do, not just what they say. If verbal pronouncements are inconsistent with actions, the meaning inherent in the actions usually takes precedence.

For example, when Lee Iacocca became chairman of Chrysler Corporation, he announced that his salary would be $1.00 per year until the company turned a profit. Chrysler was in the process of negotiating wage and benefit rollbacks with the United Auto Workers, and Iacocca's message was, "We are all in this together." Similarly, the fact that the chief executive of the Tithwal Mills, an Indian textile company going through a downturn, left standing instructions that his office air conditioner be shut off during power cuts so that one or two extra looms could be operated was apparently a significant factor in the cooperation he got from his staff.[46]

Compare the message content of these actions with some that are more common:

- Demanding wage and benefit cuts from lower-level employees while top managers receive bonuses.
- Closing the company-subsidized employee cafeteria as an economy measure while leaving the executive dining room open.
- Laying off production employees but not managerial employees.

The symbolic content of such actions can further decrease employee morale when an organization can least afford it. Atari's experience during the early 1980s is instructive.

> The focus on layoffs of lower-level employees, especially in the early phase of decline, . . . hurt the company because it sent a symbolic message to lower-level people. The message: Management (especially top management) would not share equally in what James Morgan (Atari's last president) described as "painful and bloody" work force reductions. Morale was seriously damaged by the apparent inequities.[47]

Even small things—burnt out light bulbs in a hallway, litter in a parking lot, or a lack of paper towels in a restroom—can be interpreted as evidence of a worsening situation and further decrease morale. Conversely, small symbolic actions—a company party, an extra day off, or simple acknowledgment of the stress and pain that people are feeling—can improve morale.

Rebuilding Morale and Redesigning the Organization

One of the most difficult tasks for a manager during a turnaround is rebuilding the morale of survivors after a workforce reduction. Open and honest communication during the reduction helps, but there is still a necessity to rebuild workforce confidence, trust, and support. As Steven Appelbaum and his colleagues note,

> Management must be visible, honest, and supportive during this highly unstable period. Communication will facilitate the reassurance process. Above all, management must be open and honest in answering employees' questions, including those about the possibility of future terminations . . . . The company's management must now direct their energy toward planning for the future, communicating their new goals to the employees, and infusing the company with confidence.[48]

Part of this rebuilding process involves redesigning the organization. It is usually a mistake to think that what an organization has done in the past can still be done with fewer people. Often this results in overloading the remaining employees. For example, after one layer of management had been eliminated in GE's Medical Systems Group, one manager commented,

Quite honestly, I feel overworked. I work hard, and sometimes I don't enjoy it anymore. Before the de-layering last October, I had a total of 10 people who would report to me, and four of them were managers who had people reporting to them. After that, I wound up with 20 people . . . . The other day, one of my managers, a happy-go-lucky guy, walked up to me, put out his hand, and said: 'Hi! Remember me? I work for you.' And that's part of the problem—you don't see as much of your people. That makes me feel bad as a manager. I need to let my people know that I'm there and that I care about them. Somehow I'm going to have to off-load some of my work.[49]

One way to minimize these problems is by enlarging and enriching jobs to give employees more latitude in performing their tasks. As an organization gets smaller, it usually requires a less complex structure, with fewer hierarchical levels and less need for rules, policies, and procedures.[50] Thus, redesigning an organization can help bring its structure in line with new operating realities. It also can increase morale by getting people back to work in productive, challenging jobs. For example, managers at Du Pont—which laid off more than 35,000 employees between 1982 and 1987—reacted well to the increased responsibilities because of the company's adoption of a new team concept that called for each department to set its own goals. But there are two requirements to make job design effective in this situation: training and decentralization.

Redesigned jobs require that employees learn new behaviors. Formal retraining is helpful. Ford and Apple Computer successfully used retraining programs in the 1980s after massive layoffs to help employees cope with added responsibilities. In addition to helping the employees accomplish their new tasks, training also can play an important role in resocializing them to new organizational realities. Often there is a need to change an organization's culture after a turnaround, such as moving people from a bureaucratic orientation to a more innovative or entrepreneurial one.

Training also helps an organization communicate its new expectations for employees. It is best to be realistic about what can be accomplished during the first stages of a turnaround. Morale is likely to be shaky, and having achievable near-term goals can bolster it. Therefore, it is smart policy to avoid overly ambitious goals in the first months following a reorganization resulting from a major workforce reduction.

Enlarged and enriched jobs also require a move toward decentralization. Many organizations accordingly downsize their workforces to eliminate bureaucratic barriers that slow their ability to respond to changing market conditions. Generally, organizations will not become more flexible unless decision-making authority is delegated to lower hierarchical levels. Cutting management levels and then not delegating authority downward defeats the purpose of a turnaround.

While managing a declining organization back to health is probably not as much "fun" as managing a rapidly growing enterprise, it has become an everyday part of managerial life. Virtually every manager can count on having to reverse a declining situation at some point during his or her career. With a good strategy, an ability to communicate, a sensitivity to employee needs, and a little luck, managers can meet the challenge.

SUMMARY

Learning Objective 1: Explain the statement that "success breeds failure." The slack resources that a successful organization accumulates allow it to act more autonomously than it did in the past, which often results in diversification into areas in which it has no expertise. Success also lulls managers into a sense of complacency as they begin to believe that they can do no wrong. The result is that they become less accurate in perceiving and responding to changes in their organization's environment.

Learning Objective 2: Outline the organizational and interpersonal dynamics that are common in declining organizations. Organizations centralize decision making as top management attempts to gain greater control over operations and cash flow. Centralization reduces the number of communication channels carrying information, resulting in information overload and distortion. Combined with the effects of stress on perception and decision making, this increases the likelihood that poor decisions will be made at the very time when they are most costly. Centralization also increases an organization's reliance on standardized rules, policies, and procedures (RPPs) to guide action at lower organizational levels, which increases structural rigidity and decreases its capacity to innovate. Morale decreases, conflict becomes more intense, productivity drops, and the most mobile—and usually best—employees begin to abandon the organization.

Learning Objective 3: Discuss the basic steps required to turn around a declining organization. To turn around a declining organization, managers need to (1) diagnose the nature of the problem and develop a turnaround strategy to counter it, (2) decide what to cut from current operations, (3) develop the support of key stakeholders, including employees, for the turnaround strategy, and (4) rebuild the morale of workforce survivors and redesign the organization.

Learning Objective 4: Identify five basic workforce redeployment and reduction strategies. Five major workforce reduction strategies are natural attrition, induced redeployment, involuntary redeployment, layoffs with outplacement assistance, and layoffs without outplacement assistance.

Learning Objective 5: Explain the importance of maintaining workforce morale in a declining organization. The ultimate purpose of a turnaround is to ensure an organization's long-term survival. Thus, the success of a turnaround strategy relies largely on the ability of the surviving work-force to implement it. If management alienates the survivors, chances of success are slim.

Discussion Questions

1. You are the human resource manager at Slinger Sewing Machine, Inc. The CEO has called you into her office and told you that the company needs to reduce its workforce size because of slipping sales. She wants your advice on how to conduct a workforce reduction. What are the company's options? What are the benefits and drawbacks of those options? What factors are going to influence the option you recommend to the CEO?

2. You are the CEO of a small, high-tech manufacturing firm whose major competitor has just introduced a new product that makes yours obsolete. Sales are plummeting, and you have cash reserves sufficient to last for only six months. What do you do?

3. Your company is in a real cash crunch. Today two vendors suspended the company's credit and are demanding cash on delivery (COD). If you don't receive the shipments, you will have to close down production, but you don't have enough cash on hand to meet the COD requirement. Top management is developing a plan to decrease workforce size and to increase the efficiency of manufacturing operations. You believe the planned actions are sufficient to turn around the company, but only if the company keeps operating. What can you do to get out of this bind?

4. Club Blub, an exclusive vacation destination for the pleasantly plump, is a seven-year-old resort operation that has been expanding its operations rapidly. It now operates 27 resorts worldwide. These resorts have been amazingly successful with the thirty-something set, as vacationers can be virtu-ally guaranteed that there will be someone on the beach whose thighs and buttocks are lumpier than their own. While sales are booming, Club Blub's profitability has been sinking fast. What do you suspect its problem might be?

5. You have been called in as a consultant to a large sales company that has just laid off 25 percent of its employees because of falling revenues. Layoffs eliminated two layers of middle management and a significant number of redundant sales personnel. Management believed that by reducing the num-ber of hierarchical levels, they would speed up decision making and increase productivity. The result has been the opposite: almost no decisions are being made, and productivity is decreasing. What are the possible causes of these problems? What options are available to reverse them?

6. You are the CEO of a municipal hospital in financial trouble. Decreasing reimbursement rates from government sources and private insurers have pushed your hospital to the financial wall. At the same time, employees are quitting in droves because your pay scale is below that of other hospitals in the area. Cash flow is decreasing, and you are concerned about the hospital's ability to meet its financial obligations in coming months. As was discussed in Chapters 2 and 3, different organizational stakeholders have different interests in how an organization performs. You have to put together a turnaround plan that addresses the concerns of a number of different stakeholders, including patients, physicians, other employees, creditors, suppliers, and the city council. What do you expect the concerns of these groups would be? What kind of plan would you put together to address these concerns? How would you communicate this plan to the different stakeholder groups?

DESIGN AUDIT #12

Assessing the Need for Turnaround Management

This design audit will help you assess the need for a current or potential turnaround, and to explore some of the options open to your organization.

1. Reexamine the industry analysis you completed in Design Audits #9 and #10. To what extent has your organization's position within its industry improved or deteriorated in the last three years? On a separate sheet of paper, describe your projection for your organization's position three years from now if it continues its current course of action?

    Note: If your organization is in "good shape," you may want to skim through the rest of this design audit and advance to Chapter 13.

2. Has your organization's cash flow improved, remained the same, or deteriorated over the past three years? What's your projection for cash flow if the organization continues its current course of action over the next three years? Use additional sheets of paper as needed.

    Note: Obtaining cash flow information can be difficult. Most organizations guard this information closely. Others simply haven't generated it. Often the best you can do is get a sense of how an organization's cash flow has changed over time. Table 12.1 provides some useful hints for determining whether an organization's cash flow is worsening. Also keep in mind that a worsening market position may not be related to a deteriorating cash flow. If an organization is consolidating operations and pulling out of areas in which it is least efficient, loss of market share may be accompanied by improved cash flow. On the other hand, an organization may be improving its market position, but its cash flow may be deteriorating if operations are becoming less efficient or if margins are declining.

3.   If your organization's market position is poor or deteriorating, what domain tactics or operational emphases would help it reposition itself?

Hint: See Table 10.2 and Figure 10.1 (Chapter 10). They outline available domain tactics and operational emphases, and indicate the different types of environmental conditions under which they are appropriate.

4.   In concrete terms, how would these domain tactics and operational emphases change your organization's operations? Will some operational areas increase in importance? Will others become less important? Use additional sheets of paper as needed.

5. Think about the human resource implications of your answer to Question 4. How would the changes you propose affect your organization's staffing requirements? Would there be less need for some types of personnel? Increased need for others?

    Note: *If you are recommending domain creation or offense tactics, for example, will efforts to create a new domain of operation require different types of skills than your organization now possesses? If you are suggesting that your organization "downsize," what types of skills would become less important?*

6. How should your organization make this transition in its labor force?
    Given its cash flow situation, what options are open to it? What are the
    benefits and drawbacks of those options?

    *Hint: Figure 12.3 lists some of the options that are available for workforce
    redeployment and reduction.*

7. Would these options change if your organization waited one year to
    implement them. If so, in what way?

8. What other actions are available to your organization (e.g., sell underutilized assets, spin off poorly performing operations, contract for services rather than provide them in-house)?

9. Does top management perceive that there is a problem that needs to be addressed? Does this management team have the ability to communicate a vision of what your organization should be doing? Do relevant stakeholders (i.e., employees, shareholders, customers, creditors) have enough confidence in the top management team that they would be willing to "buy in" to a turnaround strategy? What might this strategy look like? What stakeholder concerns would have to be addressed?

Notes

1. William G. Scott, "The Management of Decline," *Conference Board Record* 8, no. 6 (1976): 56–59.

2. David A. Whetten, "Sources, Responses, and Effects of Organizational Decline," in *The Organizational Life Cycle,* ed. John R. Kimberly and Robert H. Miles (San Francisco: Jossey-Bass, 1980), 343.

3. "The Neglected Side of Business," *The Wall Street Journal,* December 15, 1986, 29.

4. William H. Starbuck, Avent Greve, and Bo L. T. Hedberg, "Responding to Crisis," *Journal of Business Administration* 9, no. 2 (1978): 114–115.

5. "Smeltdown at Armco: Behind the Steelmaker's Long Slide," *Business Week,* February 1, 1988, 48–50.

6. Bo T. L. Hedberg, Paul C. Nystrom, and William H. Starbuck, "Camping on Seesaws: Prescriptions for a Self-Designing Organization," *Administrative Science Quarterly* 21 (1976): 49.

7. "Who's Excellent Now?" *Business Week,* November 5, 1984, 76–86.

8. Jeffrey D. Ford, "The Effects of Causal Attributions on Decision-Makers' Responses to Performance Downturns," *Academy of Management Review* 10 (1985): 770–787; Beth M. Haenke, Steven A. Harrison, Karen L. Lollar, David L. Sutter, and Gregory L. Trouth, "Perception and the Formation of Response Strategies," in *Understanding Turnaround Management: A Manager's Guide,* ed. Raymond F. Zammuto (Denver: University of Colorado Graduate School of Business Administration, 1988), 4/1.

9. Raymond F. Zammuto, *Assessing Organizational Effectiveness: Systems Change, Adaptation, and Strategy* (Albany: SUNY Press, 1982), Chapter 5.

10. Raymond F. Zammuto, "Managing Decline: Lessons from the U.S. Auto Industry," *Administration and Society* 17 (1985): 71–95.

11. Hedberg, Nystrom, and Starbuck, "Camping on Seesaws," 50–51.

12. That centralization occurs with the recognition of a downturn is a common research finding. For example, see Douglas T. Hall and Roger Mansfield, "Organizational and Individual Responses to External Stress," *Administrative Science Quarterly* 16 (1971): 533–546; Pradip N. Khandwalla, "Crisis Responses of Competing versus Noncompeting Organizations," in *Studies on Crisis Management,* ed. Carolyne F. Smart and William T. Stanbury (Toronto: Butterworth, 1978), 151–178; Jeffrey D. Ford, "The Ocurrence of Structural Hysteresis in Declining Organizations," *Academy of Management Review* 5 (1980): 589–598.

13. Charles F. Hermann, "Some Consequences of Crisis Which Limit the Viability of Organizations," *Administrative Science Quarterly* 8 (1963): 61–82.

14. Ole R. Holsti, "Limitations of Cognitive Abilities in the Face of Crisis," *Journal of Business Administration* 9, no. 2 (1978): 39–55; Carolyne F. Smart and Ilan Vertinsky, "Designs for Crisis Decision Units," *Administrative Science Quarterly* 22 (1977): 640–657.

15. Kenneth E. Boulding, "The Management of Decline," *Change* 64 (June 8–9, 1975): 64; William G. Scott, "The Management of Decline," 56–59; Charles H. Levine, "Organizational Decline and Cutback Management," *Public Administration Review* 38 (1978): 316–325.

16. Zammuto, "Managing Decline: Lessons from the U.S. Auto Industry," 81–82.

17. Smart and Vertinsky, "Designs for Crisis Decision Units"; Khandwalla, "Crisis Responses of Competing versus Noncompeting Organizations"; Barry Bozeman and E. Allen Slusher, "Scarcity and Environmental Stress in Public Organizations: A Conjectural Essay," *Administration & Society* 11 (1979): 335–355.

18. Dan E. Schendel and G. R. Patton, "Corporate Stagnation and Turnaround," *Journal of Economics and Business* 28 (1976): 236–241; Irene Rubin, "Universities in Stress: Decision Making Under Conditions of Reduced Resources," *Social Science Quarterly* 58 (1977): 242–254.

19. David A. Whetten, "Organizational Responses to Scarcity: Exploring the Obstacles to Innovative Approaches in Education," *Educational Administration Quarterly* 17 (1981, Summer): 80–97.

20. Bozeman and Slusher, "Scarcity and Environmental Stress in Public Organizations: A Conjectural Essay"; Smart and Vertinsky, "Designs for Crisis Decision Units"; Warren E. Walker and Jan M. Chaiken, "The Effects of Fiscal Contraction in the Public Sector," *Policy Sciences* 15 (1982): 141–165.

21. Laurence Iannacone, "The Management of Decline: Implications of Our Knowledge in the Politics of Education," *Education and Urban Society* 11 (1979): 418–430; Richard M. Cyert, "The Management of Universities of Constant or Decreasing Size," *Public Administration Review* 38 (1978): 344–349; David A. Whetten, "Organizational Decline: A Neglected Topic in Organizational Science," *Academy of Management Review* 5 (1980): 577–588.

22. Jeffrey Pfeffer and Gerald R. Salanacik, "Organizational Decision Making as a Political Process," *Administrative Science Quarterly* 19 (1974): 135–151; Gerald R. Salancik and Jeffrey Pfeffer, "The Bases and Use of Power in Organizational Decision Making," *Administrative Science Quarterly* 19 (1974): 453–473.

23. Larry Hirschhorn, "Managing Rumors," in *Cutting Back: Retrenchment and Redevelopment in Human and Community Services,* ed. Larry Hirschhorn (San Francisco: Jossey-Bass, 1983), 49–57.

24. Charles H. Levine, "More on Cutback Management: Hard Questions for Hard Times," *Public Administration Review* 38 (1979): 179–183; Lena Kolarska and Howard Aldrich, "Exit, Voice, and Silence: Consumers' and Managers' Responses to Organizational Decline," *Organization Studies* 1 (1980): 41–58;

25. Bozeman and Slusher, "Scarcity and Environmental Stress in Public Organizations: A Conjectural Essay," 343; Cyert, "The Management of Universities of Constant or Decreasing Size," 344–349.

26. Robert I. Sutton and Anita L. Callahan, "The Stigma of Bankruptcy: Spoiled Organizational Image and Its Management," *Academy of Management Journal* 30 (1987): 405–436.

27. The replacement of top management for cause, or as scapegoats, is very common in declining organizations. For example, see Schendel and Patton, "Corporate Stagnation and Turnaround"; Dan E. Schendel, G. R. Patton, and James Riggs, "Corporate Turnaournd Strategies: A Study of Profit Decline and Recovery," *Journal of General Management* 3 (1976): 3–11; William H. Starbuck, Avent Greve, and Bo L. T. Hedberg, "Responding to Crisis," 111–137; Charles H. Hofer, "Turnaround Strategies," *Journal of Business Strategy* (Spring 1980): 19–31.

28. Richard S. Sloma, *The Turnaround Manager's Handbook* (New York: Free Press, 1985), 20–21.

29. Levine, "Organizational Decline and Cutback Management," 316–325; Whetten, "Organizational Responses to Scarcity," 88.

30. Todd D. Jick and Victor V. Murray, "The Management of Hard Times: Budget Cutbacks in Public Sector Organizations," *Organization Studies* 3 (1982): 141–169.

31. Levine, "More on Cutback Management," 179–183.

32. Robert D. Behn, "Leadership for Cutback Management: The Use of Corporate Strategy," *Public Administration Review* 40 (1980): 613–620.

33. Robert I. Sutton, Kathleen M. Eisenhardt, and James V. Jucker, "Managing Organizational Decline: Lessons from Atari," *Organizational Dynamics* (Spring 1986): 28.

34. Leonard Greenhalgh, Anne T. Lawrence, and Robert I. Sutton, "Determinants of Work Force Reduction Strategies in Declining Organizations," *Academy of Management Review* 13 (1988): 242.

35. Bill Saporito, "Cutting Costs without Cutting People," *Fortune*, May 25, 1987, 27.

36. Ibid., 246–250; Robert G. Sheets and Yuan Ting, "Determinants of Employee-Termination Benefits in Organizations," *Administrative Science Quarterly* 33 (1988): 607–624.

37. Cynthia Hardy, *Strategies for Retrenchment and Turnaround: The Politics of Survival* (New York: DeGruyter, forthcoming); Cynthia Hardy, "Investing in Retrenchment: Avoiding the Hidden Costs," *California Management Review* 29, no. 4 (1987): 111–125.

38. Joel Brockner, Steven Grover, Thomas Reed, Rocki DeWitt, and Michael O'Malley, "Survivors' Reactions to Layoffs: We Get by with a Little Help from Our Friends," *Administrative Science Quarterly* 32 (1987): 526–541.

39. Anne B. Fisher, "The Downside of Downsizing," *Fortune*, May 23, 1988, 48.

40. Larry Reibstein, "Survivors of Layoffs Receive Help to Lift Morale and Reinstill Trust," *The Wall Street Journal*, December 5, 1985, 31.

41. Sydney P. Freedberg, "Forced Exits? Companies Confront Wave of Age Discrimination Suits," *The Wall Street Journal*, October 13, 1987, 39

42. Stanley E. Garner and Morgan M. Wheaton, "Implementing a Reduction in Force," in *Understanding Turnaround Management: A Manager's Guide*, ed. Raymond F. Zammuto (Denver: University of Colorado Graduate School of Business, 1988).

43. There are dangers here of which readers should be aware. If a stakeholder cannot be persuaded that a turnaround strategy is workable, this may precipitate the crisis that management is trying to prevent.

44. Hirschhorn, "Managing Rumors," 50.

45. Fisher, "The Downside of Downsizing," 42.

46. Pradip N. Khandwalla, "Turnaround Management of Mismanaged Complex Organizations," *Journal of Organization and Management* 13, no. 4 (1983–84): 34.

47. Sutton, Eisenhardt, and Jucker, "Managing Organizational Decline: Lessons from Atari," 20–21.

48. Steven H. Appelbaum, Roger Simpson, and Barbara T. Shapiro, "The Tough Test of Downsizing," *Organizational Dynamics* 16(2), 1987: 78.

49. "Caught in the Middle: Six Managers Speak Out on Corporate Life," *Business Week,* September 12, 1988, 83–84.

50. Robert I. Sutton and Thomas D'Aunno, "Decreasing Organization Size: Untangling the Effects of Money and People," *Academy of Management Review,* 14 (1989): 203–204.

Managing Decision Making and Learning

Learning Objectives

Upon completing this chapter, you should be able to

1. Specify the three conditions under which managers make decisions.
2. Explain the concepts of bounded rationality and satisficing.
3. Discuss incremental decision making.
4. Describe the so-called garbage-can model of decision making.
5. Define what is meant by organizational learning.
6. Explain how individual and organizational learning relate.
7. Discuss the importance of organizational memory.
8. Identify the different ways organizations learn.
9. Define what is meant by deutero-learning.
10. Describe how self-designing organizations operate.

GE FIGHTS ITS BUREAUCRACY

Speed is crucial to competitive advantage. "Making the right decision late is the same as making the wrong decision" is the belief driving the current fight at GE to end information overload and unleash individual decision-making power.

In the 1980s GE went from a chronic state of cash shortage to immense financial strength. But the bureaucracy also flourished, with the addition of more complex financial reporting to the military-type command-and-control systems already in place. The bureaucracy, in an attempt to eliminate as much uncertainty as possible, routinely overwhelmed top executives with useless information, and enslaved middle managers with the need to gather it. Mastery of the facts became impossible. Only its illusion had to suffice in the decision-making process.

Now, after a major restructuring, GE is staking its future on reducing that bureaucracy. As Chapter 13 explains, the conditions under which most decisions are made can vary. And as GE discovered, those conditions, especially when combined with an inadequate decision-support structure, can lengthen the time needed to make good-quality decisions.

Source: Stratford Sherman, "Inside the Mind of Jack Welch," *Fortune,* March 27, 1989, 38.

HUNDREDS of decisions are made daily at all levels in a busy organization. For example, should raw materials be ordered from one source or another? Is now a good time to enter into a joint-venture agreement, or is it better to wait? Should new equipment be purchased now or later to improve productivity? Regardless of its goals, an organization's long-term survival is based on its decision-making performance.

Proficiency in decision making calls for diagnostic skills and keen judgment. The development of both qualities is closely related to an organization's ability to learn. It is this link between organizational learning and decision-making performance that is the focus of this chapter. The quality of an organization's decisions over time is a function of how it has learned to identify and respond to new situations and to take a proactive stance relative to its surrounding environment. A high learning capability, then, is basic to an organization's continued success.[1]

Thus, in this chapter we begin by defining the term *decision making* and identifying the various conditions under which organizations make decisions. Next, after questioning the fundamental assumptions of classical economic analysis, the alternate concepts of bounded rationality, incrementalism, and the so-called garbage-can model of organizational decision making are introduced. It is likely that evidence of all three decision modes can be found in every organization. Following this, we will comment on how individual and organizational learning relate and introduce the notion of organizational memory. Finally, different forms of organizational learning are described, along with various means for creating and sustaining an organization's capacity for learning.

THE NATURE OF DECISION MAKING

Decision making may be defined as the act of choosing between two or more alternatives. As such, it involves identifying alternatives and selecting the one judged best. This identification and selection can occur under conditions that vary dramatically. In a free-enterprise system, managers make decisions under conditions of certainty, risk, and uncertainty (Figure 13.1). Each condition will be discussed in turn.

Certainty

A decision is made under conditions of **certainty** when the available alternatives and the benefits (or costs) associated with each are known. In such situations, there is perfect knowledge about available alternatives and their consequences. No element of chance intervenes between an alternative and its outcome. Exact outcomes are known in advance with complete (100 percent) certainty. Alternative 1 will lead to Outcome A, Alternative 2 will lead to Outcome B, and so on. Under such conditions, a manager simply identifies the consequences of available alternatives and selects the outcome with the greatest benefit.

As one would expect, organizations rarely make decisions under these conditions, since rarely is the future known with perfect reliability. Indeed, it is difficult to think of examples of any but the most trivial managerial decisions that are made under such conditions. One illustration often cited as a decision made under at least near certainty is the purchase of U.S. savings bonds. Barring the fall of the federal government, $1,000 invested in a savings bond for one year at 10 percent will yield $100 in interest. It should still be realized, however, that despite the unlikeliness of the government defaulting on its obligations, the possibility exists. This observation reinforces the point that very few decisions are made under conditions of certainty.

Risk

A decision is made under conditions of **risk** when the available alternatives, the likelihood of their occurrence, and the potential benefits (or costs) associated with each are known. Decisions under conditions of risk are perhaps the most common. Alternatives are clearly known, but their outcomes are in doubt. As an illustration, a gambler who bets on number 6 for a single roll of a fair die has a one-sixth probability of winning, in that there is only one

Figure 13.1
Decision-Making Conditions

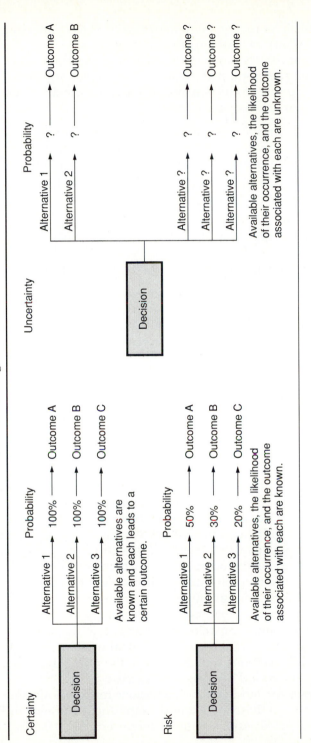

chance in six of rolling a 6. While the alternatives are clear, the outcome is doubtful. Thus, a condition of risk exists.

In business, "gambling" is not a popular word, but "risk taking" is. Continued successful performance requires that organizations take risks in introducing new products, in borrowing capital, in diversifying, and so forth. Examples of risk taking abound:

• Security Pacific, once known as "Security Pathetic" for its reluctance to risk capital, now underwrites Eurodollar debt securities, makes consumer loans in Spain, and lends to companies in Macao and Kuala Lumpur.

• In 1985 Sears, Roebuck challenged MasterCard and Visa by launching a new credit card, the Discover card. It expected an after-tax first-year loss (risk) in 1986 of $115 million.

• Chrysler Corp. spent $1.5 billion in 1987 to acquire American Motors Corp. While industry analysts and labor leaders applauded, some observers wonder if Chrysler has taken on too great a risk, especially if the auto market softens.

Making bold decisions such as these is a way of life at many organizations. PepsiCo is proud that its emphasis on risk taking is what sets its managers apart from those of many other companies. As one analyst has observed, "[PepsiCo] simply doesn't allow them to not take risks."[2]

Risk, of course, has its downside. Nevertheless, aggressive organizations realize that growth requires risk taking. Consider the remark made by RCA CEO Thornton Bradshaw after taking a $580 million write-off on a failed attempt to enter the VCR market: "No one's to blame. This is a risk company, and we're going to take more risks in the future."[3]

Uncertainty

A decision is made under conditions of **uncertainty** when the available alternatives, the likelihood of their occurrence, and their potential outcomes are unknown. Decisions under conditions of uncertainty are unquestionably the most difficult. In such situations, there is no knowledge on which to base even an estimate of the likelihood of various outcomes. Decisions under uncertainty generally occur in cases where no historical data are available from which to infer probabilities or in instances that are so novel and complex it is impossible to make comparative judgments.

Decisions under conditions of uncertainty are often those that make or break careers and companies. As described in the business press, these are the decisions that "challenge conventional wisdom—sometimes even laugh at it."[4] Such decisions are likely to be the only kind that can catapult an organization toward dramatic new success.

Perhaps the most common occasions for decisions under conditions of uncertainty are those involving the introduction of new technology. Examples of "gutsy" decisions made under uncertainty include

• The Texas Instruments (TI) decision to bet $50 million annually on the development of artificial intelligence (AI) technology. High-tech enthusiasts forecast a $4.2 billion AI market by 1990. However, the possibility remains that in its race to market, TI could lose out to rivals.

• The Compaq Computer decision to launch a personal computer with the advanced "386" 32-bit microprocessor chip—ahead of IBM. By launching a "clone" before IBM, Compaq faces the possibility that IBM could alter the architecture of its machine and render the "clone" only partially compatible, thus wrecking Compaq's strategy.

• The Federal Express decision to begin its ZapMail venture, a network of facsimile machines capable of shooting instant mail—words or graphics—across the country. A first-of-a-kind venture, its likelihood of success was unknown at the time it was launched. After some $400 million in losses, ZapMail was discontinued in 1986.

RATIONALITY OF DECISIONS

Bounded Rationality

Ideally, organizational decisions should be completely **rational**, that is, fully objective and logical. In practice, however, rationality is seldom achieved. As the preceding discussion suggests, organizations must often make decisions based on incomplete knowledge. It should come as no surprise, then, to find that the results of those decisions may range from wild success to total disaster.

Traditional economic analysis nevertheless assumes that organizational decisions are made under conditions of certainty. For the most part, it portrays decision makers as "supersmart" people able to instantly formulate and solve problems of great complexity. In doing so, it assumes that they possess the following characteristics (see Figure 13.2):

1. Perfect knowledge of available alternatives.

2. Perfect knowledge of the consequences of available alternatives.

3. The ability to objectively evaluate the consequences of available alternatives.

4. A well-ordered and stable set of preferences.

These assumptions flow from two basic traditional economic principles: (1) organizations seek to maximize expected benefits (or minimize costs) and (2) decision makers are completely rational.

The validity of these principles was first questioned by Nobel laureate Herbert A. Simon, who drew a distinction between the theoretical **economic man**—a completely rational decision maker who would always seek to

Figure 13.2
Assumptions of Rationality

1. Perfect knowledge of available alternatives

2. Perfect knowledge of the consequences of available alternatives

3. The necessary ability to objectively evaluate the consequences of available alternatives

4. A well-ordered and stable set of preferences

maximize benefits—and the real-life **administrative man**, who is not completely rational.[5] Initially focusing on the process by which decision makers identify and evaluate alternatives, Herbert A. Simon advanced the view that organizational decisions, far from being completely rational, are bounded by the limited mental capacity and emotions of the individuals involved, as well as by environmental factors over which they may have no control. This situation he described as one of **bounded rationality**. It not only reflects the limited capability of the human mind and emotions to grasp the full complexity of organizational decisions, but also the uncertainty of future events with which organizations must cope. Given that organizations exist in highly complex environments in which many possible alternatives and their consequences may remain unknown, all intended rational behavior is inherently bounded.

As this suggests, **optimum decisions** (meaning "best possible" decisions) are almost never made—except perhaps by chance. Even if it were possible to acquire perfect knowledge of all alternatives and their consequences, it is doubtful, given the limitations of human beings as processors of information, that an adequate evaluation could be made. In response to this dilemma, Simon believes that decision makers typically reduce the complexity they confront by constructing a simplified model of the real situation that encompasses only the information they feel equipped to handle. Thus, only a limited number of alternatives and a limited range of consequences are considered.

Simon further believes that once decision makers have identified a limited set of alternatives, they typically deviate from the demands of rationality by selecting the first alternative deemed "satisfactory" or "good enough," rather than searching for the optimum choice. That is, rather than examine all possible alternatives and attempt to rank them according to a well-ordered and stable set of preferences, they settle for the first one that satisfies some predetermined **aspiration level**—a subjectively defined goal for organizational performance that is a product of past organizational goals, past organizational performances, and past performances of comparable organizations. As a shorthand label for this process, Simon uses the Scottish word **satisficing** (satisfying). Examples of satisficing criteria include "share of market" versus "total market," "adequate profit" versus "maximum profit," and "fair price" versus "best price." Thus, satisficing is evident in a business firm whose managers are willing to hold to a decision alternative that results in a 25 percent return on investment even if they are aware that there *may* be other alternatives that *might* raise profits still higher.

An example of satisficing on a more personal level occurs when a person seeks a job. To make a completely rational decision, that is, to select the best alternative, an individual would have to investigate all the available jobs in the world. Thus, instead of searching for the "optimum" employment opportunity, the individual will settle for the first job judged "good enough."

For practical purposes (for example, purchasing a car or selecting a source of raw materials), it is important that satisficing not be seen as irrational. Given the limitations of human information processing, the cost of searching for alternatives, and the uncertainty of future events, satisficing is actually quite sensible, suggesting two important implications.[6]

1. Although there is only one optimum solution to most problems, there are likely several equally good satisficing solutions. For example, two decision makers may evaluate alternatives in a different order. If they each stop when they find an alternative that is "good enough," they could easily find themselves disagreeing about what should be done. This will likely mean that a final decision will have to be made on some other basis than the logic of the problem itself. Such factors as seniority, persuasiveness, and politics then come into play—something that would not happen if decisions were made on purely rational grounds.

2. Optimizing and satisficing are fundamentally complementary.[7] To a decision maker, performance that meets or exceeds a level of aspiration is success, and performance that falls short is failure. If a decision maker's level of aspiration tends to rise after success (or drop after failure), this resetting will often edge in on an optimum solution. Thus, decision makers do not necessarily have to be permanently satisfied with the first acceptable alternative that pops into their minds. For example:

> Suppose you are in charge of a small manufacturing plant, and have to make a decision as to how much the plant will produce. If you set production targets too low, the plant will have idle capacity, sales will be lost, and profitability will suffer. On the other hand, if you try to produce too much, machine maintenance may be neglected, people will work too hard (and perhaps get sick or injured), and so on. Finding the optimal balance is clearly a very tricky decision.

As a satisficer, however, suppose you set a target at 105 percent of last month's production. If you achieve this level without too much strain for a few months, you may reset your aim to 110 percent. Perhaps this level shows a number of danger signals, and cannot be reached without stress. You reset your aim down a little, perhaps to 108 percent, and find that this works satisfactorily on a regular basis. You have found an acceptable balance between overproduction and underproduction—without ever having to solve the highly complex problem of finding the analytic optimum.[8]

On balance, Simon's work rejects the basic traditional economic principles mentioned earlier. Whereas economists have typically focused on how decision makers *should* behave, the focus of Simon's work has been on how they *do* behave. He posits that organizations do not merely seek to maximize expected benefits, and decision makers are not completely rational. The Simon concept of bounded rationality replaces the idea of the so-called economic man with the more realistic administrative man.

Incrementalism

Developed originally to describe policy formulation in government and bureaucratic organizations, a second theory of decision making, called **incrementalism**, has been advanced by Charles E. Lindblom.[9] Building on Simon's notion of bounded rationality, Lindblom likewise contends that organizational decision making is simplified by limited search and satisficing behavior. He claims that rather than consider all options, decision makers tend to limit their search to a few alternatives that differ only slightly (that is, incrementally) from the status quo. Further, for each alternative considered, only a few (rather than all) of its main expected effects are evaluated. Decisions are then continually adjusted as they unfold. Problems are not "solved" all at once, but repeatedly attacked.

Policy formulation is thus best viewed as reflecting the impact of countless decisions that have been made, *one at a time,* over a period of years. At any given point, decision makers can learn from the results of earlier choices and reconsider alternatives in the light of experience. Hence, decision making is remedial, moving *away* from trouble at hand rather than consciously *toward* known goals. In sum, decision makers simply bumble along, or in Lindblom's term, "muddle through," without ever attempting to survey all possible alternatives for achieving superior performance.

Incremental decision making deals with risk and uncertainty by assuming that small decisions will not produce big effects (in particular, will not produce big negative effects) that cannot be reversed by further incremental adjustments. In this way, it "protects" an organization from negative consequences that cannot be anticipated in advance.

Kroger Co. offers an example of successful incremental decision making. It discovered that it could minimize its operating costs by holding at least a 20 to 25 percent market share in each geographic region where it did business since warehousing, transportation, and advertising costs could then be spread among several stores. As a result, it closed over 1,200 supermarkets in areas where it believed it could not obtain an acceptable market share. The profitability of the remaining stores is being increased gradually by enlarging them in size and also by adding other types of services to them: cheese shops, delis, flower shops, health food shops, beauty salons. Each of these services is tried in a limited market before being expanded. Future expansions will depend on the results.[10]

Assessment

As the Kroger example suggests, a principal advantage of incremental decision making is that it allows an organization to maximize security in making changes. Incrementalism has several serious weaknesses, though, as well. Two are particularly noteworthy in an organization theory context.

1. Incrementalism is best suited for organizations in stable environments where routine is the best policy. With turbulent organizational environments of the kind described in Chapters 8 through 10, the conditions essential to incremental decision making are the exception rather than the rule. Indeed, incrementalism is a poor method for decision making unless three unlikely conditions exist:[11]

- The results of present policies are reasonably satisfactory, so that small changes are sufficient to yield improvement in performance. By contrast, when present policy results are unsatisfactory, radical departures in policy may be preferable despite the accompanying risk. This would seem to describe the segregation problem during the 1960s in the United States.

- There is continuity in the nature of problems. Note, however, that when no past policies exist with respect to a policy issue, incremental decision making is in fact impossible. Many of the problems encountered during the New Deal, for instance, were so novel that most policies were a radical departure from the past, making invalid the option of incremental decision making.

- There is continuity in the knowledge available for dealing with problems. Unless ignored, however, changes in knowledge often lead to radical new policies since they offer decision makers new means for dealing with problems. Modern innovations in medical knowledge, for example, have recently prompted drastic new policies with regard to smoking in both public and private places.

2. A long series of incremental adjustments may result in a major policy reorientation, without consideration of the associated consequences. Incremental changes can be so gradual and drawn out that decision makers are slow to recognize a major policy change. For instance:

[T]he involvement of the United States in the Vietnam War gradually increased during a long series of small escalations, without careful consideration that these escalations were bringing about a shift in foreign policy from providing material assistance to conducting a major land war in Asia. Before they fully realized what had happened, policymakers became committed to a foreign policy that would result in domestic political unrest, dislocation of the economy, and erosion of the nation's image and credibility.[12]

Garbage-Can Model

An even broader attack on the concept of rationality in decision making has been mounted by James G. March and Johan P. Olsen.[13] A basic insight of their so-called **garbage-can model** (see Focus on Design 13.1) is that organizational decisions are not exclusively exercises in purpose and control. They contend that traditional theories underestimate the confusion surrounding most decisions. Observations of actual organizations do indeed suggest that in a typical decision-making situation many things are happening at once: "Technologies are changing and poorly understood; alliances, preferences, and perceptions are changing; problems, solutions, opportunities, ideas, people, and outcomes are mixed together in a way that makes their interpretation uncertain and their connections unclear."[14] Such decision-making situations are referred to as **organized anarchies**.

March and Olsen suggest that decisions in organized anarchies occur as a consequence of the interdependent, but partially fortuitous, confluence of four "streams" over time:

1. *A stream of choice opportunities.* Occasions when an organization is expected to make a decision—for example, weekly staff meetings, a customer that needs a new product, budget hearings.

2. *A stream of participants.* Persons who have access to choice opportunities.

3. *A stream of problems.* The concerns of people inside and outside an organization—for example, formal organizational requirements such as recruiting, exceptional events such as declining sales or the initiation of a new product line, or personal concerns such as one's own career advancement.

4. *A stream of solutions.* Answers actively seeking questions—from the efficiency expert, the systems analyst, the market consultant.

In this view, choice opportunities act as garbage cans in which are mixed problems, solutions, and participants. The major point is that managers work amid a great deal of disorder. Preferences are rarely well-ordered or stable, and criteria for judging the relevance of information are typically vague. Consequently, decision processes rarely unfold in a logical and orderly manner. Choices are sometimes made before problems are understood, solutions sometimes discover problems, and only rarely are problems resolved when choices are made.

Examples of such situations abound.[15] A few follow:

FOCUS ON DESIGN 13.1

A Garbage-Can Decision

The garbage-can model of decision making has been studied in the context of large universities. Universities usually consist of many units. There are dozens of different colleges and academic departments. The administrative structure also consists of many units to manage academic affairs as well as those concerned with finance, student services, registration, physical plant, to name just a few. Many committees and councils also exist. Participants are numerous and varied.

In one university, a final decision was eventually made to discontinue the Music Department and its programs. Students in the program were allowed to complete their studies, but no new ones were accepted. Faculty were urged to resign or seek administrative posts. On the surface, this decision to close the Music Department appeared orderly and rational. Enrollment was dropping, and costs were skyrocketing. The university was under legislative pressure to trim such operations to meet new funding levels for higher education in the state. It seemed reasonable that the Music Department be the first to be cut.

A closer examination revealed that the decision was much more complex. It resulted from the fluid interaction of many people and problems in the university over a four-year period. Different events and forces came into play that produced dozens of small decisions. Some favored the Music Department, but most eventually worked against it. For example, in the early stages of budget pressure, the Music Department was put on probation by a national accrediting association. Soon afterward, a new academic vice-president called for a review of all programs on campus. In the midst of this,

the chair of the Music Department retired and a search began for a replacement. The energy and time of the Music faculty was eaten up preparing reports for the vice-president's review, and searching for a new chair. As a result, little time was left for improving themselves to get off their probationary status.

During the vice-president's review, the search committee for a new chair was disbanded. It hadn't received good applications, and this provided the vice-president an excuse to discontinue the search rather than extend it. Throughout the process, other departments were competing for funds. Yet some faculty outside music joined with alumni and local citizens to support the music program. Student groups also got involved. Despite this support, the administration dragged its feet on replacing a key faculty member who took a job elsewhere.

Two years after its original visit, the accrediting association returned for a reevaluation. It recommended withdrawing accreditation because of lack of administrative backing for the Music Department. They cited failure to hire a chair and replace faculty. They also noted that other recommendations they had made two years earlier were not implemented. Soon after the loss of accreditation, the university decided to close the Music Department.

The garbage-can model is quite evident in this example. One interesting aspect is that loss of accreditation was used as a major reason to end the music program. It was the university itself that had made it difficult if not impossible to meet accreditation requirements. It did so by forcing a review, and failing to replace the chair and faculty.

Source: Henry L. Tosi, John R. Rizzo, and Stephen J. Carroll, *Managing Organizational Behavior* (Marshfield, Mass.: Pitman, 1986), 431.

- Sales representatives try to interest potential buyers in new equipment for which there was previously no recognized need.

- Confronted with surplus funds to spend before the end of the fiscal year (or else lose them), a manager begins to look for projects to fund.

- Eager to buy the latest generation of computers, a programmer becomes alert for opportunities to suggest buying this equipment.

- A corporate director learns that a former classmate is displeased with his current position. The director proposes that her board hire the classmate as a general vice president, a position that had not previously existed.

- As a result of government funds being made available for demonstration projects in developing social services for the elderly who suffer from speech difficulties, novel interests are likely to be stimulated—gerontologists expressing a sudden interest in speech pathology and speech therapists developing an immediate interest in the elderly.

Assessment. The value of the garbage-can model lies in its highlighting of the way chance and timing often determine organizational decisions. Decisions may be made because a problem arises, but they may also be made for other reasons. Despite its realism, the garbage-can model has two shortcomings:

1. It can produce only reactive rather than proactive solutions, which in the long run may cause important problems to be neglected and certain solutions to be overworked.[16] In this regard, the idea that organizations work toward goals is perhaps not given enough attention in the garbage-can model.

2. The question remains whether value of the garbage-can model has been overstated. While there is no doubt that decision making occurs in this manner sometimes, precisely when and how often it does is unclear. While ends and means do not always perfectly match, individual intention and organizational action are not usually as disjointed as the garbage-can model suggests. As at least one critic has observed, there is generally a greater consistency of actions, as well as a stronger cause-effect connection between actions and outcomes than implied by this model.[17] While it may describe a portion of almost any organization's activities, it does not describe all.

ORGANIZATIONAL LEARNING

Throughout Chapters 8 through 10, the continual interaction between organizations and their surrounding environments was explored from several perspectives. In line with prevailing contingency theory, it was argued that the degree to which an organization thrives depends largely upon how well it adapts, or "fits," into its surrounding environment. Building on this logic, it follows that as environmental demands change, relevant structural and behavioral attitudes must also change to maintain tightness of fit. In other words, in order for an organization to prosper, it must be able to respond appropriately to the changing demands of its environment. If it cannot, its performance will eventually deteriorate. The ultimate consequence of this deterioration was the focus of Chapter 12, "Managing Decline and Turnarounds."

For an organization to resist deterioration and, indeed, to grow and develop (Chapter 11), it must learn to cope with environmental changes. Given the complexity of many of these changes, and the sometimes rapid succession of changes, a high capacity for learning is a crucial organizational requirement. As generally defined, **organizational learning** is the process by which an organization develops knowledge about the relationship of its actions to environmental outcomes. In the 1980s and 1990s, learning to create new goods and new services, as well as new methods of producing both more efficiently, has become the most urgent concern of organizations everywhere. A high learning capability is basic to an organization's continued survival.

HOW INDIVIDUAL AND ORGANIZATIONAL LEARNING RELATE

Just as in the case of organizational goals (Chapter 2), the concept of organizational learning raises the issue of reification and whether organizations can in fact learn except in a purely metaphorical sense. Despite the fact that organizations do exhibit adaptive behavior over time, it still seems naive to assume that they learn in the same manner as human beings. However, as social systems, organizations are manifestations of their human participants and therefore subject to the same processes.

Argyris states that organizational learning is produced through the actions of individuals acting as "agents" for an organization.[18] This idea, however, does not contradict the tenet that organizational learning is an organizational process rather than an individual process. "Although individuals are the agents through whom the learning takes place, the process of learning is influenced by a much broader set of social, political, and structural variables. It involves sharing of knowledge, beliefs, or assumptions among individuals."[19]

ORGANIZATIONAL MEMORY

While all organizational learning begins with individual learning, it would be erroneous to assume that the total learning of an organization is equivalent to the sum of its individual participants' learning. While organizations have no other brains than those of their present participants, they do have memories extending beyond that. Hedberg states the matter well: "Members come and go, and leadership changes, but organizations' members preserve certain behaviors, mental maps, norms, and values over time."[20] Thus, job descriptions, computerized algorithms, employee handbooks, planning systems, and standard operating procedures define a stock of sanctioned behaviors that apply throughout an organization and are frequently inherited by new generations of employees.

Socialization patterns are perpetuated by organizational customs and symbols, and the traditions and norms that they reinforce. Legends, rituals, and myths function as long-term organizational memory banks from which environmental definitions (mental maps) are derived. Culture, values, and ways of thinking (ideology), are sustained by ceremonial acts, stories, and languages. All of these phenomena influence the learning of organizational participants and serve to transmit an organization's heritage to succeeding generations of employees. With each new round of officeholders, another layer of learning is added to an organization's memory. Thus, long after original learners have departed, their knowledge remains.

Accordingly, as described by Covington, memory contributes to two organizational attributes: (1) a learning capability that informs and conditions decisions with knowledge of the past and (2) an independent and self-sustaining identity—a continuing characteristic sense of mission.[21] In this respect, organizational memory serves as a source of continuity in the behavior of organizations by answering such questions as "Where are we?" and "How did we come to be where we are?" and, perhaps most important, "Now that we are here, where might (could or should) we be going?"[22]

HOW ORGANIZATIONS LEARN

All organizations learn. Some learn more quickly than others, but in any instance, learning is a continuous process that takes place over time. In addition to learning from day-to-day direct experience, organizations learn from (1) imitation, (2) innovation, (3) errors, and (4) superstition.

Imitative Learning

Imitation, or simply copying others, is a form of organizational learning so widespread among organizations that it has been compared to the spread of measles among a population of children.[23] IBM got into computers as an imitator, Holiday Inns into motels as an imitator, RCA into television as an imitator, and Texas Instruments into transistors as an imitator. Private brands are totally imitative, as are most toys and "new" packaged foods.[24]

Imitation allows borrowing organizations to start further along the "learning curve" and possibly thus outperform their competition. *Reverse engineering,* one technique for imitative learning, has been routinely used for years to duplicate and improve the successful products of competitors. A form of "me-too technology," reverse engineering involves examining in detail a competitor's products as they appear in the marketplace and then copying the features deemed desirable—or improving on them. Marriott Corp., for example, sends employees to all of its competitors' hotels. It then simulates the rooms and tests them on customers. Similarly, researchers at Eastman Kodak methodically analyze Fuji film to uncover its "magic." Xerox goes so far as to maintain a completely equipped lab for ripping apart each new Canon and Minolta copier just to see how it ticks. Other well-known cases of imitative learning based on reverse engineering include the rapid copying of Sony's Walkman and, until recently, Nissan's standard practice of duplicating Toyota's technical and design specifications. Imitation is clearly one way for an organization to neutralize an advantage enjoyed by a competitor. In fact, it has been suggested that the inability of many *Fortune* 500 companies to maintain or replicate past successes may be due to competitors imitating their successful techniques.[25]

Although less publicized, spying is a second technique used for imitative learning. GTE, General Electric, General Motors, IBM, and AT&T all have "competitive intelligence" departments doing everything they can to "learn" from their competition this way. Reviewing public filings of every description, touring plants, hiring a rival's best employees, cultivating telephone relationships with trade associations, regulatory agencies, suppliers, and customers, and even information trading are all popular methods in this endeavor. Kellogg Co. was forced to end an 80-year tradition of cereal-plant tours after two spies from a European competitor toured its Battle Creek, Michigan, plant and stole invaluable manufacturing secrets.

Innovative Learning

A second form of organizational learning, opposite to imitation, is innovation. As noted in Chapter 2, in their analysis of America's best-run companies, Thomas J. Peters and Robert H. Waterman, Jr., found that excellent companies possess an almost radical preoccupation with innovation.[26] As examples, AT&T's Bell Labs (with its seven Nobel laureates and 20,000 patents) and General Electric (which files more patents every year than any other U.S. company) are both known for their prolific innovations.

The distinguishing feature of an organization with a capacity for innovative learning is a willingness to experiment. At Digital Equipment, the axiom is "do it, fix it, try it." Controlled experiments abound in such organizations. As Tom Peters explains, "The attitude of management is to 'get some data, do it, then adjust it' rather than wait for a perfect overall plan."[27]

This attitude reflects an appreciation for the fact that "a firm can only remain adaptive to its environment by seeking out new data, looking honestly at it, and continually assessing what actions—if any—should be taken. To this extent, an experimenting organization is a learning organization."[28]

Kohler Co., a major maker of plumbing fixtures, offers an unusual example. Each summer it invites small groups of ceramists to spend a few months designing experimental products—brightly decorated sinks and toilets that may someday be for sale. The guest ceramists have proven to be mind-stretchers for Kohler's employees, who see themselves as "artists."

Another example of an experimenting organization is Control Data Corporation, known as one of the most visionary corporations in America. This computer and financial-services giant grows vegetables hydroponically on rooftops, imports products such as Yugoslavian wine, draws up urban-renewal plans, and provides health care on Indian reservations. Over the last 25 years it has spent almost $1 billion on Plato, a computer-education project that has yet to make a penny. In response to its critics, CDC says these experiments are placing it in a position to enjoy prosperity for years to come.

General Motors (GM) has taken a somewhat different tack. It has hired a "corporate thinker" whose sole job is to ponder the future and then design cars that will fit into that vision. He thinks about politics, economics, and social trends. He has no deadlines or day-to-day responsibilities. The only proviso is that his thoughts be ultimately useful to GM's future.

Learning from Errors

Organizations also learn through their errors. Indeed, it has been argued that "the learning organization is, by definition, an erring organization."[29] In considering errors, "two things are worth noting: (1) even the most successful organizations make mistakes, but can and do survive as long as they maintain a good batting average; and (2) making mistakes can be an effective teaching tool."[30] As August A. Busch, III, Anheuser-Busch CEO puts it, "You learn from your mistakes, not your successes."[31]

Certainly, what Ford Motor Co. learned about market research from the Edsel debacle of the 1950s was put to good use in introducing the phenomenally successful Mustang in the early 1960s. Former Johnson & Johnson CEO James E. Burke sums up this lesson well in what might be termed a "growth through failure" philosophy. "Any successful growth company is riddled with failures, and there's just not any other way to do it," he says. "We love to win, but we also have to lose in order to grow."[32]

Some amazing opportunities have been produced by errors. One day in 1879, for example, a Procter & Gamble (P&G) workman broke for lunch, forgetting to turn off his soap-mixing machine. When he returned, the soap contained tiny air bubbles and floated. P&G saw the opportunity in this new product and put it on the market. The public loved it and clamored for more of the "soap that floats."

Similar stories abound. Post-it Notes were developed by two 3M product researchers from an unsuccessful glue. Another 3M researcher investigating industrial compounds spilled some liquid on her tennis shoe while working. After several days, she noticed that the shoe repelled water and dirt. The result was the highly successful Scotch-Guard fabric protector. A Raytheon engineer was working with some experimental radar equipment one day when he noticed that the candy bar in his shirt pocket had melted. Fascinated, he brought in some popcorn, and cooked that too. The result was eventually the first microwave oven. Finally, consider the G. D. Searle chemist who accidentally spilled some experimental fluid one morning and hurriedly cleaned it up. Later in the day he licked his finger to turn a book page and was shocked by a sweet taste. The result was Nutrasweet. In each of these examples, learning took place as errors became recognized opportunities.

Superstitious Learning

Finally, organizational learning can be superstitious. As suggested earlier, most decision situations are accompanied by varying degrees of uncertainty. Decision makers act to elicit a hoped for response from an organization's environment. Whether the responses that occur are due to their actions or completely independent of them is often difficult, if not impossible, to determine. Notwithstanding, subsequent actions are usually modified according to those responses. Despite the fact that the real situation may be substantially different from what is believed, this superstition-based "learning" continues as more and more implications are drawn from the supposed relationship between environmental events and immediately preceding organizational actions.

The marketing efforts of most major corporations probably qualify as superstitious learning. While advertising and other marketing efforts doubtlessly have an impact on consumer expenditures, the full extent of that impact remains unknown. It is simply too difficult to measure. While an increase in advertising expenditures may be accompanied by an increase in product sales, whether the former prompted the latter is often an open question. Sales increases could easily be a consequence of other unidentified environmental factors. Therefore, the decision to increase advertising expenditures due to sales increases that accompanied an earlier advertising increase could be viewed as reflecting a form of superstition rather than a proven means for eliciting a desired environmental response. Indeed, it could be easily argued that the marketplace is actually indifferent to much advertising, and that advertising expenditures are based as much on superstition as on fact.

Other organizational actions that have been labeled superstitious behavior include long-range planning, forecasting, new-product market research, capital budgeting, and employee-assessment centers. Each may be viewed as an example of an anxiety-relieving superstitious behavior rather than as a legitimate predictive device.[33]

Whatever the truth, it would seem that organizations interpret and try to make sense of their experiences. They try to find meaning in environmental happenings and provide explanations for how they come to believe what they believe. The process by which their beliefs are established (that is, through direct experience, imitation, innovation, error, or superstition) clearly affects what they learn and the subsequent logic of their ensuing actions.

LEARNING TO LEARN

Deutero-Learning

A major implication of the preceding discussion is that a primary managerial task involves creating an organizational capacity for change and new learning. Bateson has coined the term **deutero-learning** to refer to the notion that organizations must be able to learn to learn.[34] "This type of learning is not merely the rote accumulation of data and facts; rather, it is the ability to remain open to new ways of seeing, to question appearance, to reflect on and reframe situations, and to find previously ignored patterns and meaning."[35] The Philip Morris Co. offers a classic example of deutero-learning. Moving into the beer industry, Philip Morris considered the same facts available to its competitors, but did so in a way that questioned conventional industry wisdom. The introduction of Lite Beer through the company's Miller Brewing unit flew in the face of the dogma that a diet beer could not be successfully marketed.

This example highlights the fact that "unlearning," or the discarding of old knowledge is essential for an organization's continued success. As knowledge is accumulated, much of it becomes obsolete as environmental conditions change. Perhaps no other organization has had to unlearn on such a massive scale as AT&T. Since that fateful day—"one-one-eight-four" as AT&Ters call it—when "Ma Bell" was forced to go from the calm life of a regulated monopoly to the frantic pace of a competitor in a heated marketplace, the necessity of unlearning has been felt from telephone operators to the highest managerial levels. To illustrate:

> A management style based on referring decisions to higher levels has been discarded in favor of rewards for decision making and risk taking at lower levels. A century-long commitment to the highest production standards made it necessary to produce everything in-house so that tight control could be exercised.

> AT&T has now discarded this single-minded attention to quality in order to pay at least as much attention to design, price, and value considerations. To do so, for the first time, it has entered into joint ventures with such firms as United Technologies, N. V. Philips, and Olivetti, from whom it hopes to learn a great deal about these other matters. The "Ma Bell" culture based on lifetime careers, exclusive promotion from within, stability of organizational structures, and pride in service and technical excellence has been replaced. Increased recruiting of outsiders, changing organizational structures, and a high value on innovation are redirecting career paths and shaping new behavior patterns that in time will determine a new corporate culture. The old culture is being unlearned slowly and will eventually be forgotten by all but the "oldtimers."[36]

Just how successful AT&T will be in continuing to unlearn its past will determine nothing less than its future survival.

Self-Designing Organizations

Creating a learning organization requires a sustained effort in which the capacity for self-regulation is widespread. Wildavsky writes of an ideal "self-evaluating organization" that would "continuously monitor its own activities so as to determine whether it was meeting its goals or even whether these goals should continue to prevail."[37] Similarly, White writes of the "dialectical organization," "a type of organization which is structured so as to attempt constantly to discover and respond to its own inconsistencies, internal contradictions, and irrationalities."[38] Both ideas are basically identical to the more well-developed concept of "self-designing organizations" introduced by Hedberg, Nystrom, and Starbuck.[39]

Self-designing organizations—"organizations that continually appraise and revise their behaviors and that invent their futures as well as survive them"—are structured to maintain maximum long-term viability.[40] The main requirement for self-design is an unwavering commitment to organizational learning. As described by Weick, self-designing organizations value improvisation more than forecasts, they dwell on opportunities rather than constraints, they invent solutions rather than borrowing them, they devise new actions rather than defending past ones, they cultivate impermanence rather than permanence, they value argument more highly than agreement, they use diverse measures rather than relying on accounting systems as their sole means to assess performance, they encourage doubt rather than discouraging it, they continuously experiment rather than searching for final solutions, and they seek rather than discourage contradictions.[41]

As should be clear, self-designing organizations are purposefully dynamic, incorporating a certain amount of inconsistency and much heterogeneity. The image of the self-designing organization developed here is perhaps best described as a "tinkering organization" dedicated to continual learning.

SUMMARY

This chapter is divided into two principal sections. The first focuses on decision making, a key activity in all organizations. The second deals with organizational learning. The quality of an organization's decisions over time is a function of how well it has learned to identify and respond to new situations and to take a proactive stance relative to its surrounding environment.

Learning Objective 1: Specify the three conditions under which managers make decisions. In a free-enterprise system, managers make decisions under conditions of certainty, risk, and uncertainty.

Learning Objective 2: Explain the concepts of bounded rationality and satisficing. Bounded rationality refers to the view that managerial decisions, far from being completely rational, are bounded by the limited mental capacity and emotions of the individuals involved, as well as by environmental factors over which they may have no control. Satisficing refers to the decision process in which, rather than examining all possible alternatives and attempting to rank them according to a well-ordered and stable set of preferences, managers settle for the first alternative that is judged "good enough."

Learning Objective 3: Discuss incremental decision making. Incrementalism is the theory that organizational decision making is simplified by limited search and satisficing behavior. In addition, it holds that, rather than considering all options, decision makers usually limit their search to a few alternatives that differ only slightly (that is, incrementally) from the status quo. Further, for each alternative considered, only a few (rather than all) of its main expected effects are evaluated. Decisions are continually adjusted as they unfold. Problems are not "solved" all at once, but repeatedly attacked.

Learning Objective 4: Describe the so-called garbage-can model of decision making. The garbage-can model argues that rather than being exercises in purpose and control, decisions occur as a consequence of the interdependent, but partially fortuitous, confluence of four "streams" that occur over time: (1) a stream of choice opportunities, (2) a stream of participants, (3) a stream of problems, and (4) a stream of solutions.

Learning Objective 5: Define what is meant by organizational learning. Generally defined, organizational learning is the process by which an organization develops knowledge about the relationship of its actions to environmental outcomes.

Learning Objective 6: Explain how individual and organizational learning relate. Organizational learning is produced through the actions of individuals acting as "agents" for an organization. This is not to say that organizational learning is not an organizational process rather than an individual process. As an organizational process it is influenced by a much broader set of social, political, and structural variables than an individual process would be, and it influences the sharing of knowledge, beliefs, or assumptions among individuals.

Learning Objective 7: Discuss the importance of organizational memory. Organizational memory is important because it contributes to (1) a learning capability that informs and conditions decisions with knowledge of the past and (2) an independent and self-sustaining identity—a continuing characteristic sense of mission.

Learning Objective 8: Identify the different ways organizations learn. In addition to learning from day-to-day direct experience, organizations learn from (1) imitation, (2) innovation, (3) errors, and (4) superstition.

Learning Objective 9: Define what is meant by deutero-learning. Deutero-learning refers to an organization's capacity to learn how to learn.

Learning Objective 10: Describe how self-designing organizations operate. Self-designing organizations are structured to maintain maximum long-term viability. They continually appraise and revise their behaviors and invent their futures. The main requirement for self-design is an unwavering commitment to organizational learning.

Discussion Questions

1. You have just returned from an open lecture given by the College of Business's Executive-in-Residence, a CEO for a major oil company. During her address, she quoted author John McDonald: "The business executive is by profession a decision maker. Uncertainty is his opponent. Overcoming it is his mission."[42] Explain what McDonald means.

2. Imagine that you have one item to complete on your final exam for this course, and it must be completed within five minutes: "Give an example of a decision made under each of three conditions: certainty, risk, and uncertainty." How would you respond?

3. Assume you are on a dinner date. You and a companion have just completed a delicious meal at one of San Francisco's finest restaurants. The conversation has turned to conditions in the world today. Your companion insists that if he (she) were "King [Queen] for a Day," he'd (she'd) make nothing but rational decisions. What would your response be to this assertion?

4. You are representing your school in this year's College Bowl. The category for the next question is "Decision Making." As the moderator is halfway through reading the question, you sound your buzzer, indicating that you know the answer. For 15 points and the national championship, "Distinguish between 'economic man' and 'administrative man.'"

5. Imagine that the guest speaker in your class today is the distinguished economist and Nobel laureate Milton Friedman. Recognizing as you do that the traditional economic assumption of extreme rationality in decision making is false, you wonder why economists persist in ignoring reality. Your curiosity gets the best of you, and you ask Professor Friedman for an explanation. What justification does he offer?

6. According to political scientist Lloyd S. Etheredge, many U.S. government agencies follow the "gray head" theory of memory. That is, they "deliberately make efforts to keep people whose memories of top-level issues extend back 20 years or more."[43] Of what advantage is a well-developed organizational memory?

7. In his book, *Thriving on Chaos: Handbook for a Management Revolution,* Tom Peters advises managers to facilitate innovative learning in their organizations by supporting *failure.* He comments: "If you haven't yet cheered at least one interesting failure today, applauded an act of defiance, and removed one tiny hurdle from a champion's path, you are not foursquare behind fast innovation."[44] Explain the importance of experimentation to organizational learning.

8. What is your reaction to the following reasoning?

> Quaker Oats Chairman William Smithburg tells his managers: "I want you to take risks. There isn't one senior manager in this company who hasn't been associated with a product that failed, or some project that failed. That includes me. It's like learning to ski. If you're not falling down, you're not learning."[45]

9. In an essay appearing in the *Harvard Business Review,* its former editor, Theodore Levitt, offered the following observation:

> Nothing characterizes the successful organization so much as its willingness to abandon what has been long successful. Of course, not all that is new is better. Good things have good reasons for enduring. It may be good to be skeptical of fashionable new prescriptions for achieving organizational vitality and competitive virtuosity, but it's bad to be resistant to the kind of healthy self-examination that might prescribe new medicine.[46]

Explain the importance of learning to unlearn, or to use Levitt's phrase, "healthy self-examination," for an organization's continued success.

10. Eric Hoffer, the deceased sage of San Francisco's Embarcadero, summed up the spirit of organizational learning in this way: "In a time of drastic change, it is the learners who inherit the future. The learn*ed* find themselves equipped to live only in a world that no longer exists."[47] Reflecting on this statement, explain how an organization can learn to slough off yesterday in order to build its tomorrow.

DESIGN AUDIT #13

Assessing Your Organization's Capacity for Decision Making and Learning

This design audit will help you assess your organization's current decision making and learning mechanisms. It also helps you think about whether these mechanisms are appropriate for the future, given environmental changes that may occur over the next few years.

1. Indicate the extent to which strategic and operational decisions in your organization are made under conditions of certainty, risk, or uncertainty by dividing 100 points among the conditions in the spaces below. How do you see these decision-making conditions changing in the next five years, given the types of environmental and industry changes you identified in earlier design audits?

    Hint: Strategic decisions are future-oriented and related to the goals of an organization. Operational decisions are present-oriented and related to the day-to-day operations of an organization.

	Strategic Decisions		Operational Decisions	
	Now	In 5 Years	Now	In 5 Years
Certainty	_____	_____	_____	_____
Risk	_____	_____	_____	_____
Uncertainty	_____	_____	_____	_____
	100	100	100	100

Provide an example of strategic and operational decisions in your organization made under each condition.

Certainty

Risk

Uncertainty

2. To what extent does your organization's structure support decision making under each of these conditions? If you've projected changing decision making conditions over the next five years, are there changes in design that might improve decision making under these new conditions?

Hint: Generally, the more uncertain the decision-making context, the greater the need for flexibility and information in the decision-making process. Functional designs with extensive RPPs, reporting procedures, and vertical communication channels tend to be somewhat inflexible but work reasonably well when decision-making conditions are relatively certain. As the decision-making context becomes more uncertain, more flexible structures that increase horizontal communication and information flows tend to work better. For example, many functionally designed organizations move toward divisional designs as uncertainty increases. Other organizations make greater use of integrating mechanisms that increase the amount and flow of information in the decision-making process.

3. To what extent does your organization rely on imitative, innovative, error-based, and superstitious learning processes in coping with changing environmental conditions? Divide 100 points among each of the processes in the spaces below. Also provide a short example of the operation of these learning processes in your organization.

    Given the environmental and industry changes you've identified in earlier design audits, to what extent do you think your organization needs to change the way it learns? Identify the relative learning emphases you think your organization will need in order to cope with changing environmental conditions five years from now.

Learning Processes	Now	In 5 Years	Example
Imitative	_____	_____	
Innovative	_____	_____	
Error-based	_____	_____	
Superstitious	_____	_____	
	100	100	

4. If you've indicated that you think the organization needs to change the way it learns in the future, explain below why you think changes need to occur. What are the likely benefits to the organization? Would these changes affect the way decisions are made?

Notes

1. Richard Norman, "Developing Capabilities for Organizational Learning," in *Organizational Strategy and Change,* ed. Johannes M. Pennings and Associates (San Francisco: Jossey-Bass, 1985), 221.

2. Gary Stibel, quoted in "PepsiCo's Fast Track," *Business Month* 129 (June 1987): 50.

3. Quoted in Robert Heller, *The Naked Manager* (New York: Dutton, 1985), 168.

4. Charles R. Day, Jr., "The Year's Gutsiest Decisions," *Industry Week*, February 23, 1987, 26.

5. Herbert A. Simon, *Administrative Behavior: A Study of Decision-Making Processes in Administrative Organization,* 3d ed (New York: Free Press, 1976).

6. The following discussion draws on Terry Connolly, *Scientists, Engineers, and Organizations* (Monterey, Calif.: Brooks–Cole, 1983), 22–24.

7. William H. Starbuck, "Level of Aspiration," *Psychological Review* 70 (1963): 51–60; William H. Starbuck, "The Aspiration Mechanism," *General Systems Journal* 9 (1964): 191–203.

8. Connolly, *Scientists, Engineers, and Organizations,* 23–24.

9. Charles E. Lindblom, "The Science of 'Muddling Through,'" *Public Administration Review* 19 (1959): 79–88; David Braybrooke and Charles E. Lindblom, *A Strategy of Decision: Policy Evaluation as a Social Process* (New York: Free Press, 1963); Charles E. Lindblom, "Still Muddling, Not Yet Through," *Public Administration Review* 39 (1979): 517–526.

10. This example is paraphrased from Edwin A. Locke and Gary P. Latham, *Goal Setting for Individuals, Groups, and Organizations* (Chicago: Science Research Associates, 1984), 26.

11. Yehezkel Dror, "Muddling Through—'Science' or Inertia?" *Public Administration Review* 24 (September 1964): 154.

12. Kenneth N. Wexley and Gary A. Yukl, *Organizational Behavior and Personnel Psychology,* rev. ed. (Homewood, Ill.: Richard D. Irwin, 1984), 111.

13. Michael D. Cohen, James G. March, and Johan P. Olsen, "A Garbage Can Model of Organizational Choice," *Administrative Science Quarterly* 17 (1972): 1–25; James G. March and Johan P. Olsen, *Ambiguity and Choice in Organization* (Bergen, Norway: Universitetsforlaget, 1976), v; James G. March and Johan P. Olsen, "Garbage Can Models of Decision Making in Organizations," in *Ambiguity and Command: Organizational Perspectives on Military Decision Making,* ed. James G. March and Roger Weissinger-Baylon (Marshfield, Mass.: Pitman, 1986), 11–35.

14. James G. March, "Theories of Choice and Making Decisions," *Society* 20 (1982): 36.

15. The following examples have been paraphrased from Albert A. Einsiedel, Jr., "Decision-Making and Problem Solving Skills: The Rational Versus the Garbage Can Model of Decision-Making," *Project Management Quarterly* 14, no. 4 (1983): 52–57; C. Edward Weber, "Strategic Thinking—Dealing with Uncertainty," *Long-Range Planning* 7, no. 5 (1984): 60–70; Wexley and Yukl, *Organizational Behavior,* 118.

16. Einsiedel, "Decision-Making," 55–56.

17. Andrew M. Pettigrew, "Examining Change in the Long-Term Context of Culture and Politics," in *Organizational Strategy and Change,* ed. Pennings and Associates, 278.

18. Chris Argyris, "Developing with Threat and Defensiveness," in *Organizational Strategy and Change,* ed. Pennings and Associates, 421.

19. Paul Shrivastava, "A Typology of Organizational Learning Systems," *Journal of Management Studies* 20 (1983): 16–17.

20. Bo L. T. Hedberg, "How Organizations Learn and Unlearn," in *Handbook of Organizational Design,* vol. 1, ed. Paul C. Nystrom and William H. Starbuck (New York: Oxford University Press, 1981), 6.

21. Cary R. Covington, "Development of Organizational Memory in Presidential Agencies," *Administration & Society* 17 (1985): 173–174.

22. Omar A. El Sawy, Glenn M. Gomes, and Manolete V. Gonzalez, "Preserving Institutional Memory: The Management of History as an Organizational Resource," in *Proceedings of the Annual Meeting of the Academy of Management,* ed. John A. Pearce II and Richard B. Robinson, Jr. (Columbia, S.C.: 1986), 118.

23. James G. March and Guje Sevo'n, "Gossip, Information, and Decision Making," *Advances in Information Processing Organizations* 1 (1982): 99. See also Barbara Levitt and James G. March, "Organizational Learning," *Annual Review of Sociology* 14 (1988): 319–340.

24. Theodore Levitt, "Innovative Imitation," *Harvard Business Review* 44, no. 5 (1966): 63–70.

25. John M. Dutton and Richard D. Freedman, "External Environment and Internal Strategies: Calculating, Experimenting, and Imitating in Organizations," *Advances in Strategic Management* 3 (1985): 41.

26. Thomas J. Peters and Robert H. Waterman, Jr., *In Search of Excellence: Lessons from America's Best-Run Companies* (New York: Harper & Row, 1982), 12.

27. Thomas J. Peters, "Putting Excellence into Management," *Business Week,* July 21, 1980, 196.

28. Alan J. Zakon, "Strategy and Style: Ten Rules for the CEO," in *Annual Perspective 1985* (Boston: Boston Consulting Group, 1983), 7. See also L. Jay Bourgeois III and Kathleen M. Eisenhardt, "Strategic Decision Processes in High Velocity Environments: Four Cases in the Microcomputer Industry," *Management Science* 34 (1988): 816–835.

29. David Dery, "Erring and Learning: An Organizational Analysis," *Accounting, Organizations and Society* 7 (1982): 217.

30. Robert F. Hartley, *Management Mistakes,* 2d ed. (New York: Wiley, 1986), 275.

31. Michael O'Neal, "How Do You Follow an Act Like Bud?" *Business Week,* May 2, 1988, 12.

32. H. John Steinbreder, "Taking Chances at J & J," *Fortune,* June 6, 1988, 60.

33. Martin L. Gimpl and Stephen R. Dakin, "Management and Magic," *California Management Review* 27, no. 1 (1984): 125–136.

34. Gregory Bateson, *Steps Toward an Ecology of Mind* (New York: Chandler, 1972), 166–176. See also Donald A. Schon, "Deutero-Learning in Organizations: Learning for Increased Effectiveness," *Organizational Dynamics* 4, no 1 (1975): 2–16.

35. Gloria Barczak, Charles Smith, and David Wilemon, "Managing Large-Scale Organizational Change," *Organizational Dynamics* 16, no. 2 (1987): 33.

36. Paraphrased from Warren Bennis and Burt Nanus, *Leaders: The Strategies for Taking Charge* (New York: Harper & Row, 1985), 202–203.

37. Aaron Wildavsky, "The Self-Evaluating Organization," *Public Administration Review* 32 (1972): 509.

38. Orion White, Jr., "Psychic Energy and Organizational Change," *Sage Professional Paper in Administrative and Policy Studies* 1, no 03–007 (1973): 30.

39. Bo L. T. Hedberg, Paul C. Nystrom, and William H. Starbuck, "Camping on Seesaws: Prescriptions for a Self-Designing Organization," *Administrative Science Quarterly* 21 (1976): 41–65.

40. Bo L. T. Hedberg, Paul C. Nystrom, and William H. Starbuck, "Designing Organizations to Match Tomorrow," *North-Holland/TIMS Studies in the Management Sciences* 5 (1977): 171.

41. Paraphrased from Karl E. Weick, "Organization Design: Organizations as Self-Designing Systems," *Organizational Dynamics* 2, no. 6 (1977): 37.

42. Quoted in *Macmillan Book of Business and Economic Quotations,* ed. Michael Jackman (New York: Macmillan, 1984), 127.

43. Lloyd S. Etheredge, "Government Learning: An Overview," in *Handbook of Political Behavior,* vol. 2, ed. Samuel L. Long (New York: Plenum, 1981), 122.

44. Thomas J. Peters, *Thriving on Chaos: Handbook for a Management Revolution* (New York: Knopf, 1987), 258.

45. Warren Bennis and Burt Nanus, "Organizational Learning: Management of the Collective Self," *New Management* 3, no. 1 (1985): 6.

46. Theodore Levitt, "The Innovating Organization," *Harvard Business Review* 66, no. 1 (1988): 7.

47. Eric Hoffer quoted in James O'Toole, *Vanguard Management: Redesigning the Corporate Future* (Garden City, N.J.: Doubleday, 1985), 54.

CHAPTER 14

Managing Change and Innovation

Learning Objectives

Upon completing this chapter, you should be able to

1. Identify the key factors upon which successful change hinges.
2. Explain why people resist change.
3. Discuss tactics for overcoming resistance to change.
4. List the four major methods an organization may use to introduce change.
5. List several reasons why careful evaluations of change efforts are relatively rare.

MOTOROLA TAKES OFF THE GLOVES

Motorola CEO George Fisher is insisting on battling Japan Inc. in as many markets as he can—including Japan itself. And the wins for Motorola are beginning to stack up, especially with two new products, both marvels of miniaturization, that helped it knock the wind out of Japanese telecommunications rivals. First came the MicroTac cellular phone, a Star Trekky unit that slips into a coat pocket and flips open for use. Motorola followed that act with the first wristwatch pager—an ultra-small product resembling the wrist-radio familiar to Dick Tracy fans. These two innovations represent a dramatic change for this once staid company whose virtual lock on the U.S. market for pagers and cellular phones was shattered in the early and mid-1980s.

When Motorola embarked on its daring plan to out-Japan Japan Inc., it changed both its philosophy and design. It embraced such Japanese tactics as driving relentlessly for market share, sharply upgrading quality, and constantly honing manufacturing processes to pare costs. To foster more team spirit, Motorola tore down the traditional walls that had isolated various departments, such as design, manufacturing, and marketing. Now, people from each discipline get involved in new projects early on, so products are designed from the outset to be cost-effective and to provide features that customers want. Additionally, Motorola continues to pour billions into research and development, training, and capital improvements. The MicroTac would never have happened if Motorola had not been prepared to make a long-term investment, pumping in $100 million over ten years before it saw any return. The pocket-slim phone has just 400 parts, and is assembled by robots and workers in only two hours, down from the forty hours required to build cellular phones just four years earlier.

Motorola's massive changes have not come easily. Organizations in its position have to battle many forms of resistance to change. As you'll see in this chapter, any organization that wishes to change itself needs to understand why people resist change and how to overcome that resistance.

Source: Lois Therrien, "The Rival Japan Respects," *Business Week*, November 13, 1989, 108; bureau reports.

As previous chapters have suggested, the most unchanging aspect of organizational life is change itself. To survive and grow in contemporary society, an organization must be highly adaptive. It must be able to monitor and anticipate change, assess its goals in the light of change, and alter its capabilities accordingly. Over the last decade, the economy has gone from deep recession to rapid expansion, the government has imposed new regulations on some industries and vastly deregulated others, and rapid technological developments have continued to outpace many organizations' abilities to absorb them. Each of these developments—and many others we haven't mentioned—has forced managers to accept change, even destructive change, as part and parcel of the everyday organizing process.

Change is a universal aspect of all organizations in many senses. Over time, as organizations grow, their members come and go, their environments change, their product lines and customer sets evolve. As a consequence, every organization must confront the challenge of continually reorganizing itself (even redesigning its basic structure if necessary).

While change can threaten the survival of an organization, it also frequently offers an unprecedented opportunity for growth. Indeed, some organizations seek out rapidly changing markets for this very reason. This explains Northern Telecom's move into Japan in advance of the privatization of Nippon Telegraph and Telephone (NTT). The changing market there presented Northern Telecom with the opportunity to land a seven-year $250 million contract to supply NTT with digital switching machines.

The purpose of this chapter is to explore the manifold nature of organizational change. After first considering change as a paradox, we will examine a model of successful organizational change. We will then consider some of the reasons people resist change and will suggest several ways for overcoming this resistance. Next, we will identify four different methods of introducing change. Finally, we will comment on the importance of systematically evaluating the extent to which an implemented change achieves its purposes.

CHANGE AS A PARADOX

Organizational change is a process, not an event. It results from both internal and external pressures. New employees are hired while older employees retire, established products are discontinued and new products introduced, old markets expire and new ones are exploited. Paradoxically, an organization's success depends on its ability to maintain stability while managing change. Change without order and order without change are equally crippling.

Since change is a perennial issue for every organization, an organization's ability to manage change better than its competitors may well be its only sustainable competitive advantage. There is therefore a clear need to recognize the requisites for change and know how to introduce it effectively.

CHANGE AND INNOVATION

The terms *change* and *innovation* are frequently treated as synonyms. In reality, though, organizational **innovation**, which involves the implementation of new ideas, is a principal process by which change occurs. Clearly, both involve organizational learning (see Chapter 13). Perhaps for this reason nothing so characterizes a successful organization as its ability to challenge old assumptions and old practices. It has been repeatedly observed that "the history of long-surviving and thriving enterprises is a history of innovation."[1] Organizations on the move are receptive to self-examination and make innovation and change their open ally.

SUCCESSFUL CHANGE

There have been many attempts to develop a model of successful change. The model most general in its application was developed by Larry E. Greiner.[2] Building upon evidence collected in a survey of the change literature, Greiner sought to identify conditions that distinguished successful from unsuccessful change. He found two key factors:

1. Successful change was accompanied by a redistribution of power within an organization so that traditional decision-making practices moved toward greater use of *shared power*.

2. Such a power redistribution occurred through a *developmental change process*. Successful changes did not take place in one dramatic step, but involved a series of momentum-building phases.

In analyzing this evidence further, Greiner was able to identify six phases common to successful change, each involving a *stimulus* to, as well as a *reaction* from, the power structure (typically, top management) within an organization. These phases can be completed at different rates, depending on the situation, and they overlap in actual practice. A general overview of the six phases is presented in Figure 14.1. Let's examine each.

Phase 1: Pressure and Arousal

The process of successful change begins as a result of *pressure* on top management. Such pressure may arise either externally from environmental factors such as lower sales, or internally from events such as interdepartmental disagreements. In successful changes, the result is the same—*arousal* to take action.

Phase 2: Intervention and Reorientation

Arousal in itself does not automatically ensure proper response. It is quite likely that top managers will be tempted to see problems as temporary or to blame them on "that lousy union" or "that meddling government," rather than concede that their performance could be improved. As a consequence, successful change typically involves *intervention* by an outsider (called a *change agent*). It is important that this individual be known to have an ability

Figure 14.1
Dynamics of Successful Change

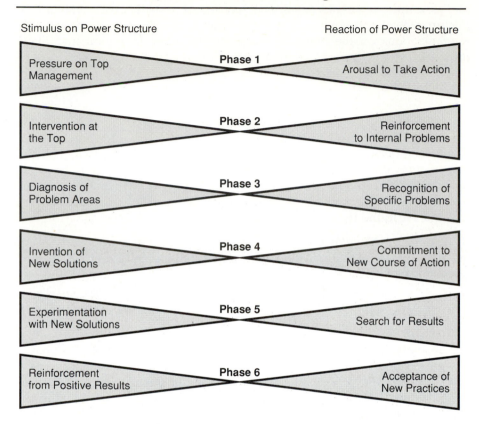

Sources: Larry E. Greiner, "Patterns of Organization Change," *Harvard Business Review* 45 (May–June 1967): 119–130; Larry E. Greiner and Louis B. Barnes, "Organization Change and Development," in *Organizational Change and Development*, ed. Gene W. Dalton, Paul R. Lawrence, and Larry E. Greiner (Homewood, Ill.: Irwin, 1970), 1–12.

to introduce improvements, and that he or she enter an enterprise at the top, or as a consultant who reports directly to the highest level of management. This places the newcomer in an ideal position to encourage top managers to reevaluate past practices as possible causes of current internal problems. Such reevaluation should lead to appropriate *reorientation*.

Phase 3: Diagnosis and Recognition

The third phase of successful change is characterized by a *shared approach to power*, as the newcomer, with top-management support and active personal involvement, engages organization members at several lower levels in collaborative, fact-finding, problem-solving discussions in order to *diagnose and recognize* current and potential problem areas, as well as to reduce any anticipated opposition. This phase is significant because it provides subordinates with evidence that (1) top management is willing to consider change, (2) problems are being recognized and acknowledged, and (3) ideas of lower-level employees are valued. In short, this phase serves to reflect top management's sincerity and interest.

Phase 4: Invention and Commitment

Once current and potential problem areas are identified and diagnosed, attention switches to the *invention* of solutions capable of generating a sustained *commitment* to new courses of action. As in the previous phase, the newcomer plays an active role, involving all organization levels in developing ideas and methods for solving problems and taking action. Solutions are based on shared power, emphasizing participation in the invention of group solutions to the problems recognized in Phase 3. Such collaboration has been shown to be particularly effective in developing high-quality solutions and, as previously suggested, sustained commitment to action. Employees are much more likely to endorse their own solutions than those directed from above.

Phase 5: Experimentation and Search (Testing)

Once new solutions to problems are developed, *experimentation* and *testing* follow. In this phase, Phase 4 solutions are tested for credibility on a small scale before they are introduced on an organization-wide basis. In addition, the method previously used to generate solutions (interaction and shared power) is carefully evaluated. Further, rather than implementing major changes at the top, numerous small changes are introduced at all levels on an experimental basis. In turn, reinforcement from positive results marks the beginning of Phase 6.

Phase 6: Reinforcement and Acceptance

The last phase of successful change is an outgrowth of the acceptance and internalization of change previously experienced. As a change is found to be successful, and as participant support grows, it is introduced on a much larger scale, ultimately being absorbed into all parts of an organization. Accordingly, Phase 6 involves *reinforcement* from positive results, leading in due course to an *acceptance* of new practices. Greiner suggests that, aside from change itself, the most significant outcome of this phase is a greater acceptance at all hierarchical levels of the use of shared power as an approach for introducing change.

An Evaluation of Greiner's Six Phases

In evaluating Greiner's six phases, it should be realized that all models are inevitably oversimplifications of reality. Because of the complex variables involved, no model is capable of explaining fully the change process or its results. Moreover, given the contingent nature of change, it is impossible to formulate a standard recipe for all situations. Nevertheless, an appreciation of the six phases common to successful change is useful in three ways:

1. It is helpful in understanding what typically contributes to successful change. By understanding the major challenges of each phase of successful change, managers can better anticipate roadblocks to change.

2. By understanding Greiner's six-phase sequence, managers can design their activities so that the challenges of each phase can be openly addressed and resolved. This should help an organization operate more smoothly and productively.

3. The six-phase sequence makes the point that effectiveness in introducing a change depends as much on how the change is implemented as on what it is.

RESISTANCE TO CHANGE

Although change is universal and inevitable, it is rarely received without protest. Resistance to change is a natural human reaction. Reasons are varied and often difficult to determine. Whether soundly based or not, however, resistance should always be considered an important signal for further inquiry.

Managers are often unfamiliar with even the most basic reasons for resistance and are therefore unprepared to deal with it. The following is an abbreviated discussion of four of the most common reasons (Figure 14.2).[3] Space does not permit a detailed discussion.

Parochial Self-Interest

Virtually all organizations can be expected to behave in ways that will maximize those goals that they personally consider most important. Consequently, to the extent that all proposals for change represent a threat to the status quo, individuals (and groups) are likely to resist if they believe they stand to lose something of value. In such circumstances, the individuals involved will usually focus on their own self-interest, and only incidentally on an organization's overall good. A sample listing of personal goals that, when threatened, will almost inevitably provoke resistance would include[4]

1.   *Power.* Authority and control over organization resources.

Figure 14.2
Four Reasons for Resistance to Change

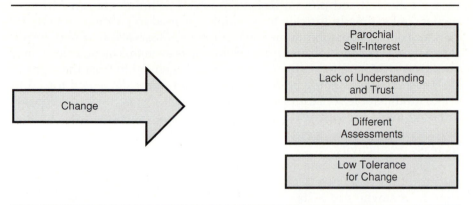

2. *Money.* Increases in income or income substitutes.

3. *Prestige.* Respect and approval from those responsible for funding, determining promotions, hiring and firing.

4. *Convenience.* Avoidance of conditions that will require additional personal efforts.

5. *Job security.* Protection against loss of position.

6. *Professional competence.* Respect from peers for knowledge, technical proficiency, or professionally ethical behavior.

At Digital Equipment Corp. (DEC), a highly successful job-enrichment program clearly threatened the self-interests of many managers. The program, which relies on "bossless" 18-member teams to assemble printed circuit boards, has resulted in dramatic productivity gains and an enviable standard of quality. Team members divide the work among themselves and produce the circuit boards from start to finish. Each member knows how to do each of the 20 jobs involved in assembling a board. Employees set their own hours, arrange their own schedules, and check their own work. There are no time clocks or quality-control managers. Every employee has a key to the front door. But not everyone likes these changes. In fact, many people don't want to work in a place where everyone is equal in authority and there is no opportunity to become a supervisor.

Lack of Understanding and Trust

People also tend to resist when they do not understand the intended purpose of a planned change. Such a predicament is most likely to occur when there is a lack of trust between the parties involved in initiating and those involved in adopting a proposed modification. Distrust and suspicion often produce widespread rumors and distorted information. This makes effective communication difficult and poses a real problem in instituting change. The new owners of Reading Industries, for example, resorted to putting out periodic "rumor-control" memorandums when employees' fears about a plant closing threatened to become too disruptive. Sometimes even this tactic failed, since employees had seen too many changes in management to trust the word of the latest owners. Having been buffeted by constant change and forced to make innumerable concessions to each group of owners, they had become angry, cynical, and distrustful. Their unhappiness expressed itself in high absenteeism, endless complaints, and a resistance to changes intended to increase productivity.

It is important to note that people do not resist change per se, only the uncertainties that change can bring. Such resistance is easier to prevent than to remove once it has developed. Therefore, it is important to tell employees in advance why a change is being made and how it will affect them.

Different Assessments

Resistance to change frequently occurs when organization members or other stakeholders differ in their evaluation of a change's likely costs and benefits. Such evaluations obviously depend on what these individuals think a proposed change will mean for themselves and also for their organization. Take the example of hospitals. Hospital managers, finding themselves caught in the squeeze between legislation that imposes a ceiling on Medicare reimbursements and the increased reluctance of private insurers to foot the tab for staggering medical costs, have begun to seek ways of trimming expenses. But physicians worry that patients' welfare will be jeopardized as hospitals push to become more cost-effective. As a former American Medical Association president remarked of the cost-control programs, "It's treating the patient as if he were a number—the 62-year-old cardiac in 4B who's been here for 18 days when the average stay should be 13 days."[5] The challenge in such cases is to bring these differing assessments into line, so that each party understands the concerns and constraints motivating the other.

Differing assessments of the effectiveness of proposed changes often occur when information concerning a change is inadequate. For example, various stakeholders may possess different degrees of information about the change in question and consequently arrive at different analyses.

We should point out, however, that opposition to change is not always bad. Change initiators are not infallible. Constructive opposition mounted by knowledgeable organization members may save an enterprise from the unproductive or even disastrous consequences of an ill-conceived change.

Low Tolerance for Change

Finally, people may resist change because of personal concerns about their ability to be effective after the change. The unknown consequences of change may present a psychological threat to the self-esteem of many individuals. While research confirms that personal anxieties are to be expected in the face of change, there are individuals who let their anxieties go beyond the norm and will oppose a new plan or idea even when they recognize its soundness. These are people with an excessively low tolerance for change. They may be afraid they will be unable to develop the skills and behavior demanded by a new position or by the unfamiliar circumstances associated with a reorganization. Can I do it? How will I do it? Do I have the ability to learn a new way? These and other concerns may produce active resistance to change while never being stated out loud.

For example, a person who receives a significantly more important job as a result of an organizational change will probably be very happy. But it is just as possible for that person also to feel uneasy and to resist giving up certain aspects of his or her current situation. A new and very different job will require new and different behavior, new and different relationships, and the loss of some satisfactory activities and relationships. If the changes are significant, and the individual's tolerance for change is low, the person might begin to actively resist the change for reasons not consciously understood.

Questions to Ask When Contemplating Change

As we suggested, these are just a few of the reasons that change might be resisted. No doubt, there are innumerable others. They will vary in importance from situation to situation. Realizing this, managers might do well to ask themselves the following questions when contemplating a change.

1. What are the consequences of implementing or not implementing the proposed change?
2. Has the process for change and its effect on individuals been clearly explained?
3. How much resistance will the proposed change generate?
4. In what form will resistance show itself?
5. What is the level of trust between the parties involved?
6. Do all parties involved have the information necessary to understand the reasons for the proposed change and benefits that will result?
7. Have real incentives been provided for accepting the proposed change?

OVERCOMING RESISTANCE TO CHANGE

Several effective tactics for dealing with resistance to change have been identified.[6] Six of these tactics are shown in Figure 14.3 and will be discussed. Choice of a tactic will, of course, depend on the combination of factors present in each individual situation. (See Focus on Design 14.1 for guidelines relevant to this discussion.)

Education and Communication

Change initiators often possess information about a situation that is not readily available to other organization members. By sharing this knowledge, they may be able to counter opposition to proposed changes. This tactic of education and communication assumes that organization members share common objectives and that resistance can therefore be overcome by training people to recognize the existence of problem areas and, hence, the necessity for change. Furthermore, it assumes that resistance is based largely on misinformation or poor communication. If these assumptions are true, resistance can be overcome by securing relevant facts, eliminating misunderstandings due to incorrect or incomplete information, and resolving different viewpoints through discussion.

Depending on the nature of the change, this tactic may involve mass media educational campaigns, one-on-one discussions, memos, group presentation, and reports. To be successful, such education and communication programs must always be unquestionably and firmly grounded in mutual trust and credibility.

Participation

Perhaps the most effective way to reduce anticipated opposition and to engender commitment to a proposed change is to involve potential resisters in its planning and implementation. As Mary Kay Ash, founder of Mary Kay Cosmetics, advises, "People will support that which they help to create."[7] When Allstate Insurance undertook a reorganization, it enlisted the help of employee "growth teams" representing all departments and employees. Acting on their suggestions, Allstate relocated many of its 40,000 employees, stripping away an entire managerial level. Allstate attributes the success of its reorganization to this employee participation.

As a tactic for overcoming resistance to change, participation involves open communication among all parties involved. It is assumed that all parties are rational, possess the required expertise to contribute meaningfully, and are willing to act in good faith. When these assumptions are true, it is generally accepted that participation shortens the implementation process and aids its success, although it necessarily lengthens the actual change process.

Figure 14.3
How to Deal with Resistance to Change

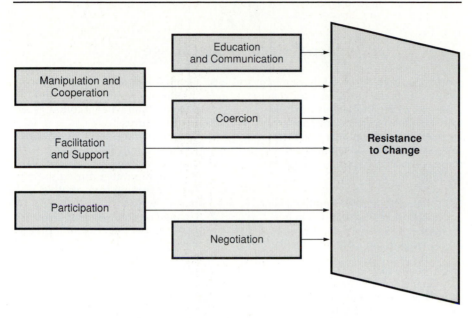

Sources: John P. Kotter, Leonard A. Schlesinger, and Vijay Sathe, *Organization,* 2nd ed. (Homewood, Ill.: Irwin, 1986): 354–359; John P. Kotter and Leonard A. Schlesinger, "Choosing Strategies for Change," *Harvard Business Review* 57 (March–April 1979): 106–114.

Facilitation and Support

Another tactic that has proven helpful in decreasing resistance to change, especially when such resistance develops as a result of fear, involves the use of facilitative and supportive skills. The origins of supportive methods such as employee counseling and therapy programs may be traced to the earliest stirrings of the human relations movement. Perhaps the most succinct expression of the philosophy that underlies this approach is that by a noted psychologist: "Resistance will be prevented to the degree that the changer helps the changees to develop their own understanding of the need for change, and an explicit awareness of how they feel about it, and what can be done about those feelings."[8]

Although written some 30 years ago, this declaration is just as applicable now as it was then. It provides a nutshell description of the basic framework of the facilitative approach, underscoring its behavioral origin. However, note the major drawbacks of this approach: It can be time-consuming, expensive, and still fail.

FOCUS ON DESIGN 14.1

Ten Guidelines for Change

It often has been observed that human nature resists change. Like most generalities, however, this is only partially true. People welcome some changes. To be effective, a manager must make proposed changes desirable to all those concerned. Experience suggests the following guidelines.

1. Change is more acceptable when it is understood than when it is not.
2. Change is more acceptable when it doesn't threaten security than when it does.
3. Change is more acceptable when those affected have helped to create it than when it has been externally imposed.
4. Change is more acceptable when it results from an application of previously established impersonal principles than when it is dictated by personal order.
5. Change is more acceptable when it follows a series of successful changes than when it follows a series of failures.
6. Change is more acceptable when it is inaugurated after a prior change has been assimilated than if it is inaugurated during the confusion resulting from another major change.
7. Change is more acceptable if it has been planned than if it is haphazard.
8. Change is more acceptable to people new on a job than to veterans.
9. Change is more acceptable to people who share in its benefits than to those who do not.
10. Change is more acceptable if people have been trained to plan for improvement.

Source: Adapted from Ralph M. Basse, "Company Planning Must Be Planned!" *Dun's Review and Modern Industry* 69 (April 1957), 62–63. Reprinted with the permission of *Dun's Review*, April 1957, © 1957, Dun & Bradstreet Publications Corporation.

Negotiation

Another tactic for dealing with resistance to change involves conferring and bargaining—negotiating—to reach an agreement. Since bargaining implies reciprocity, this tactic suggests that a change initiator is willing to tailor a change to meet the needs and interests of active or potential resisters. Negotiated agreements are particularly appropriate in situations where some individual or group will clearly lose an advantage in a change and has considerable power to resist. However, while negotiation with those affected may succeed temporarily in quelling resistance, it often begins a process of continuing give and take. Once it becomes known that an initiator of change is willing to modify a stance to avoid resistance, the invitation is open for continual bargaining and even blackmail.

Manipulation and Cooptation

In the present context, manipulation involves the use of covert attempts to sidestep potential resistance to change. Manipulation goes beyond persuasion. It is actually a devious tactic for convincing opposing individuals or groups that a proposed change should be adopted by giving them incomplete or slanted knowledge, appealing to their particular interests. Dishonest emotional appeals and deliberate misrepresentation of facts may be involved.

Cooptation, a form of manipulation, has long been a popular method to avert opposition and gain support. It involves absorbing key resisters or various influential people into an enterprise's decision-making structure, but unlike participation, cooptation seeks only an individual's or group's endorsement, not advice. Candidates for corporate directorships are thus often selected not only for their ability, but also for their potential influence in an enterprise's larger environment.

To illustrate, organizations can use their board of directors as vehicles for coopting important stakeholders such as banks, representatives of labor, or environmental groups. Or organizations can absorb influential stakeholders into their decision-making structure by affording them special privileges. Some observers would suggest that this took place when the National Aeronautics and Space Administration (NASA) selected Senator Jake Garn, the Utah Republican, to be the first congressional observer to fly in space. Senator Garn is also chairman of the Senate subcommittee overseeing the NASA budget.

Coercion

Use of coercion assumes that the principal opposing parties are operating from relatively fixed positions. When efforts at consensus are abandoned, at least temporarily, there may be an effort to compel acceptance of a change by means of orders accompanied by virulent arguments, as well as threatened firings, transfers, and loss of promotion possibilities. For obvious reasons, coercion is used sparingly.

In this respect, as former General Motors' Chairman Roger B. Smith observed in connection with the reorganization of GM's North American car operations: "You can't push people to do what we're trying to do. And you can't drag them. If they don't want to do something—and if they aren't dedicated to doing it—the human being . . . has a marvelous capacity for screwing things up. And he feels justified in doing it too. He just says, 'I don't believe in it. I'm not going to do it.'"[9]

METHODS OF INTRODUCING CHANGE

As we saw in our opening discussion of organizations, initial changes of one type often create a need for further changes of another type. The four major methods of introducing change in an organization are task change, structural change, people change, and technological change (see Figure 14.4). Table 14.1 gives examples of each.

1. *Task change* involves the redesign of jobs using the methods described in Chapter 4. Principal among these are job enrichment and job enlargement. Because of their ease of implementation, task changes are among the most frequently used methods for introducing change.

2. *Structural change* involves modifying any of the basic components of structure discussed in Chapter 5. Included would be changes in departmentalization, authority, delegation, spans of control, and hierarchical levels.

3. *Technological change* involves modifying means whereby an organization transforms inputs into outputs, as described in Chapter 6. Examples would include introducing new equipment, new computer-support systems, new tools, or new forms of automation such as robots.

4. *People change* involves modifying the way employees think and act. Above all, the process of change is essentially a process of altering the relationships of employees with one another and with their jobs. Among the many "people" approaches for introducing change are survey feedback, process consultation, team building, intergroup interventions, and sensitivity training. These approaches are standard topics covered in a typical organizational behavior course.

An important point illustrated by Figure 14.4 is the interrelated nature of the four methods for introducing change. Indeed, change cannot be introduced using one method without causing implications for the others. For example, changes in technology are almost inevitably accompanied by task changes. In turn, changes in task and technology usually produce changes in structure. Likewise, changes in task, technology, and structure typically require changes in people. This point is well underscored by H. Ross Perot, a former GM director, in commenting on the problems GM has encountered in its high-tech drive to build "factories of the future": "GM cannot become a world-class and cost-competitive company simply by throwing technology and money at its problems."[10] Perot warns that fundamental changes in people, their jobs, and GM's tradition-bound structure will be required.

Practical people have long recognized the extreme difficulties involved in changing complex systems, for it is difficult to foresee all the consequences. Some of these consequences may be intended, but others are not. Consider the hospital that installed a computerized scheduling system for its nurses in an effort to give them greater working-hour flexibility and thus reduce turnover. An unanticipated result of the new scheduling system was that nurses' awareness of their marketability increased, leading some to seek jobs elsewhere. While the system was still judged a success, it clearly illustrates how a change in one area (technology) can have an unintended consequence in another (people). Identifying potential unintended consequences is essential

Figure 14.4
Methods for Introducing Change

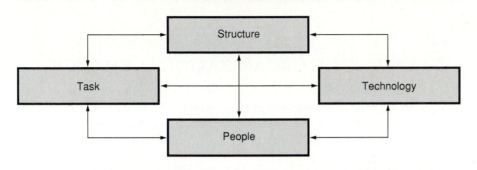

Source: Harold J. Leavitt, "Applied Organization Change in Industry: Structural, Technical, and Human Approaches," *New Perspectives in Organizational Research,* ed. William W. Cooper, Harold J. Leavitt, and Maynard W. Shelly II (New York: Wiley, 1964), 56.

Table 14.1
Examples of Methods for Introducing Change

Method	Examples
1. Task	Job enrichment, job enlargement
2. Structure	Modify bases of departmentalization, authority delegation, spans of control, hierarchical levels
3. Technology	New equipment, new computer-support systems, new tools, new forms of automation
4. People	Survey feedback, process consultation, team building, intergroup interventions, sensitivity training

for successful organization performance. In this sense, the incredible complexity of change may be a cliche, but it is a fact.

Figure 14.4 is thus useful in three ways:

1. It is helpful for interpreting the relationships among an organization's subsystems. In this respect, the systemic interdependence of task, people, technology, and structure clearly implies that the case for implementing changes with multiple foci is strong. It is not only necessary to understand the basic cause-and-effect relationships governing the performance of subsystems, but also the effect on system performance of the complex chains of interrelationships between subsystems.

2. Following from number 1 above, Figure 14.4 can be used as a guide for diagnosing organizational problems and choosing points of intervention for initiating change.

3. Figure 14.4 is useful for analyzing solutions to organizational problems in terms of their meaning for task, structure, technology, and people, as well as the interrelationships among these variables.

EVALUATING ORGANIZATIONAL CHANGE

Before concluding our discussion, it is appropriate to comment, if only briefly, on the importance of evaluating change efforts. As Brager and Holloway recognize, "Determining the extent to which . . . [an] implemented change achieves its purposes, or has the potential for achieving them is a central evaluation issue."[11] If properly undertaken, systematic evaluation of change can provide feedback on the success or failure of a change strategy.

Although the importance of such a determination can hardly be questioned, available evidence suggests that careful evaluation of organizational change efforts are relatively rare. Several reasons have been offered for this seeming incongruity.[12]

1. Criteria for success are typically multiple and generally vague.

2. Successes and failures are equally likely to be highlighted.

3. Evaluation of change can be expensive and time-consuming, especially if viewed from a short- rather than long-run perspective.

4. Simply specifying, let alone explaining, the results that have been produced is not an easy task.

5. Few organizations possess the expertise required to undertake adequate evaluation.

6. Some organizations avoid evaluation, fearing that it will be used for negative (or political) purposes.

Despite the recognized importance of evaluating organizational change—or lack of it—efforts at evaluation are scarce. Yet, the development of a more complete understanding and, in turn, a more general acceptance of organizational change is directly dependent upon the ability not only to generate valid and reliable information about the outcomes of change efforts but to establish clear criteria against which the resulting effects can be evaluated. Both needs are among the most pressing in the analysis of organizational change. See Focus on Design 14.2 for further discussion of this problem.

SUMMARY

Change is a universal aspect of all enterprises. This chapter has identified conditions for successfully introducing change, discussed why people resist change, suggested tactics for overcoming resistance to change, described

FOCUS ON DESIGN 14.2

Evaluation: Where Art Thou?

Many reasons have been offered for the rarity of careful studies evaluating organizational change efforts. One common reason mentioned is the fear that such evaluations will be used for negative purposes—that is, to withhold rewards.

Supposedly, people are rewarded for doing what their job requires and not rewarded when they do something else. Real life isn't always so simple and straightforward, though. Organizations often create forces that lead to unwanted consequences by rewarding behaviors that are not desired and by discouraging behaviors that are desired. And this phenomenon seems to be an obstacle to careful evaluations of implemented changes.

The individuals (whether in personnel, human resource planning, or wherever) who normally would be responsible for conducting such evaluations are the same ones often charged with introducing the change effort in the first place. Having convinced top management to spend the money, they usually are quite animated afterwards in collecting rigorous vignettes and anecdotes about how successful the program was. The last thing many desire is a formal, systematic, and revealing evaluation. Although members of top management may actually *hope* for such systematic evaluation, their reward systems continue to *reward* ignorance in this area. And if the personnel department abdicates its responsibility, who is to step into the breach? The change agent himself? Hardly! He is likely to be too busy collecting anecdotal "evidence" of his own, for use with his next client.

Source: Adapted from Steven Kerr, "The Folly of Rewarding A, While Hoping for B," *Academy of Management Journal* 18 (1975): 769–783.

different methods an organization may use to introduce change, and stressed the importance of evaluating change efforts.

Learning Objective 1: Identify the key factors upon which successful change hinges. Successful change almost invariably hinges on two key factors: (1) a redistribution of power within an enterprise so that traditional decision-making practices move toward greater use of shared power and (2) the occurrence of such a power redistribution through a developmental change process.

Learning Objective 2: Explain why people resist change. People resist change for many reasons. The four most common are (1) parochial self-interest, (2) lack of understanding and trust, (3) different assessments, and (4) low tolerance for change.

Learning Objective 3: Discuss tactics for overcoming resistance to change. The chapter discussed six methods for overcoming resistance to change: (1) education and communication, (2) participation, (3) facilitation and support, (4) negotiation, (5) manipulation and cooptation, and (6) coercion.

Learning Objective 4: List the four major methods an organization may use to introduce change. Four major methods for introducing change are (1) task change, (2) structural change, (3) technological change, and (4) people change.

Learning Objective 5: List several reasons why careful evaluations of change efforts are relatively rare. Careful evaluations of organizational change efforts are relatively rare because (1) criteria for success are typically multiple and generally vague, (2) successes and failures are equally likely to be highlighted, (3) evaluation of change can be expensive and time-consuming, especially if viewed from a short- rather than long-run perspective, (4) simply specifying, let alone explaining, the results that have been produced is not an easy task, (5) few organizations possess the expertise required to undertake adequate evaluation, and (6) some organizations avoid evaluation, fearing that it will be used for negative (or political) purposes.

Discussion Questions

1. After reading the following opinion, explain how organizational survival in today's competitive environment is shark-ism.

> "Consider the shark," says Irwin Federman, founder of Monolithic Memories, a major Silicon Valley semiconductor company. "The shark has been around for 15,000 years. And do you know why? It's because the shark adapts, constantly moves, never sleeps. It's the ultimately flexible animal, with no bones, only cartilage. And the shark keeps renewing its weapons, discarding its old teeth, new teeth continually moving forward. It is ever-vigilant, the shark, always on the prowl, able to adjust to changing circumstances like a rise in the water temperature or an ice age. Whatever happens, the shark survives."[13]

2. A noted organization theorist has stated that the same properties enabling organizations to survive and keep on course under changing conditions also make them resistant to change in general. Given your reading of Chapter 14, explain this statement.

3. You are the well-known author of a best-selling book titled *Successful Change*. Moments ago you completed a telephone conversation with a representative of a large corporation pleading for advice on successfully implementing a company-wide reorganization. What advice did you offer?

4. As a seasoned manager with some 40 years of service, you've experienced both the good and the bad. Reflecting on your career, you've repeatedly observed that the old saying, "Human nature resists change," is only partially true. People do welcome some changes. What advice would you offer new managers for introducing changes that are welcome?

5. You are commander of the U.S. Pacific Fleet. You've just received an order to further integrate female personnel in all aspects of sea duty. You anticipate varying degrees of resistance on the part of both male and female personnel, as well as their spouses. What tactics would you use to deal with this resistance to change?

6. Being a successful manager, you realize that change cannot be introduced without potential unintended side effects. Your department is in the process of changing to a computerized production system. What task, structural, and people difficulties might you anticipate?

7. Thomas J. Peters, author of the best-selling book, *Thriving on Chaos,* reasons that "if the word 'excellence' is to be applicable in the future, it requires wholesale redefinition." In this respect, he suggests that "Excellent firms don't believe in excellence—only in constant improvement and constant change."[14] Comment on Peters's suggestions, being sure to relate your remarks to Chapter 14 and the following quote: "Learning is the process that underlies and gives birth to change. Change is the child of learning."[15]

8. Modern management has been described as a baseball game in which both the ball and the bases are in motion. "As soon as the ball is hit, the defending players can pick up the base bags and move them to anywhere in fair territory. The offensive players never know in advance where they must run to be safe."[16] This metaphor highlights the terrific pace of change in today's world—not only in the way things are organized within an enterprise, but in its supporting environment. Recognizing that change is the status quo, further develop this metaphor.

DESIGN AUDIT #14

Organizational Change and Implementing Your Redesign Plan

This design audit helps you integrate the analyses done in earlier design audits into a redesign plan. Approach this design audit as if you were preparing a presentation for your organization's top managers.

1. Review the design audits you've completed to this point and, on separate sheets, compile an inventory of the problems/issues you've identified and the redesign options you've proposed. Examine this inventory of problems/issues and design options for common themes. To what extent have you suggested similar design options for the various problems/issues?

For example, in Design Audit #4, you might have identified some problems that could be addressed by enlarging and enriching jobs, reducing reliance on RPPs, and decentralizing decision-making authority. In Design Audit #5, the use of integrating mechanisms and the redesign of some units were suggested as potential solutions to coordination problems arising because of poor inter-unit communications. In Design Audit #6, it was suggested that implementing an advanced information technology would reduce communication and coordination problems and speed the organization's responses to changing consumer needs. Later, in Design Audits #8 through #10 you might have suggested that a more flexible design would help the organization cope with the environmental changes you see lurking in the future. All these problems/issues and suggested design changes have a common theme—increasing organizational responsiveness and flexibility—and the suggested changes in design all move toward this end. In short, to what extent are the design changes you've proposed interrelated?

2.   After examining your inventory, think about how you would present these problems/issues and recommendations to your organization's top managers. Within this context, write a summary statement on separate sheets of paper of the major problems/issues facing your organization over the next few years and outline your recommendations on how to best redesign the organization to meet these challenges. What are the costs or the problems/issues you've identified? What are the benefits of the redesign you are proposing? Also consider the following issues:

   a.   What resources would have to be committed to make your redesign plan work?

   b.   How long will it take to implement the redesign? Can it be done in stages?

   c.   How will the success of the redesign be evaluated? Can you suggest any specific criteria that might be monitored? How long will it be before the organization should expect to see any benefits of the new design?

3. Now you need to consider implementing these changes. Identify major barriers to implementing the design changes. Who is likely to resist these changes and why? (Figure 14.2 provides a summary of why people resist changes that may be useful.)

4. What tactics could be used to overcome potential resistance? (See Figure 14.3.) What are the benefits and drawbacks of the tactics you've identified? What incentives could be provided to reduce resistance?

Congratulations! If you've successfully completed this design audit, you have come a long way toward redesigning your organization for future success. Your challenge now is to implement the redesign and make it work.

Notes

1. Theodore Levitt, "The Innovating Organization," *Harvard Business Review* 66, no. 1 (1988): 7.

2. Larry E. Greiner, "Patterns of Organization Change," *Harvard Business Review* 45, no.3 (1967): 119–130.

3. John P. Kotter and Leonard A. Schlesinger, "Choosing Strategies for Change," *Harvard Business Review* 57, no. 2 (1979): 106–114.

4. Rino J. Patti, "Organizational Resistance and Change: The View from Below," *Social Service Review* 48 (September 1974): 371–372.

5. William Y. Rial, quoted in "The Upheaval in Health Care," *Business Week,* July 25, 1983, 48.

6. Kotter and Schlesinger, "Choosing Strategies for Change": 109–112.

7. Mary Kay Ash, *Mary Kay on People Management* (New York: Warner Books, 1984), 73.

8. Alvin Zander, "Resistance to Change—Its Analysis and Prevention," *Advanced Management* 15 (January 1950): 9–11.

9. "Roger Smith Takes on GM's Critics," *Fortune,* August 18, 1986, 27.

10. Doron P. Levin, "In a High-Tech Drive, GM Falls Below Rivals in Auto Profit Margins," *The Wall Street Journal,* July 22, 1986, 1.

11. George A. Brager and Stephen Holloway, *Changing Human Service Organizations: Politics and Practice* (New York: Free Press, 1978), 227.

12. John R. Kimberly and Warren R. Nielsen, "Assessing Organizational Change Strategies," *North-Holland/TIMS Studies in Management Sciences* 5 (1977): 143–155; Rehka Agarwala-Rogers, "Why Is Evaluation Research Not Utilized?" in *Evaluation Studies Review Annual,* vol. 2, ed. Marcia Guttentag and Shalom Saar (Beverly Hills, Calif.: Sage, 1977), 327–333; Louise Lovelady, "Evaluation of Planned Organizational Change: Issues of Knowledge, Context and Politics," *Personnel Review* 9 (1980): 3–14.

13. Quoted in David L. Kirp and Douglas S. Rice, "Fast Forward—Styles of California Management," *Harvard Business Review* 66, no. 1 (1988): 75.

14. Thomas J. Peters, "Facing Up to the Need for a Management Revolution," *California Management Review* 30, no. 2 (1988): 8.

15. Frank Friedlander, "Patterns of Individual and Organizational Learning," in *The Executive Mind,* ed. Suresh Srivastva and Associates (San Francisco: Jossey-Bass, 1983), 194.

16. "Changes in Management," *The Royal Bank Letter* 69 (January–February 1988): 1.

America's Fastest-Growing Companies

Call them the billion-dollar kids. They are the fastest-growing companies in America's fastest-growing markets. Innovative, opportunistic, above all entrepreneurial, they are romping through the ranks of the *Fortune* 500 like grade-schoolers at a Saturday afternoon picnic. The speed of their ascent is mind-boggling. At the beginning of the decade most members of this Shirley Temple set were mere startups, and a few didn't exist. Suddenly in American business, a childhood fantasy is coming true: You don't have to wait to grow big.

You do have to accomplish quite a few other things that most companies never achieve. In general, the supergrowth champs begin their rise by tapping into broad nationwide or worldwide trends, such as the spread of the personal computer or the female invasion of the work force. They follow those trends—and their market implications—wherever they lead. Then they find ways to survive the turbulence and intense competitive pressures that follow. When the rocket lifts off, a lot of companies can't hang on.

As large corporations get rapidly larger, it's hard to imagine which is tougher—achieving the growth or withstanding it. Consider:

* Sun Microsystems of Mountain View, California, after five years in existence, saw sales of its computer workstations more than double last year to $538 million. They'll do $900 million in the fiscal year that ends in June.

* In the Boston suburb of Canton, athletic shoemaker Reebok International increased sales 50% to $1.4 billion. The company was in its eighth year.

Source: "America's Fastest-Growing Companies" by Stuart Gannes. Reprinted by permission from FORTUNE Magazine, May 23, 1988, pp. 28, 30–33, 36, 40. © 1988 The Time Inc. Magazine Company. All rights reserved.

- Compaq Computer in Houston, the youngest superstar of the personal computer boom, saw orders for its most popular model double in three weeks last year. Sales for all of 1987 soared 95% to $1.2 billion.
- New York's Liz Claiborne, founded in 1976, leads all competitors in selling fashions to working women professionals, the fastest-growing segment of the labor force. Sales rose 30% last year to $1.1 billion.

More than a score of other U.S. companies have achieved comparable growth in the past five years. Many are retailers that are quickly able to implant a winning concept across the country. But the success stories encompass a wide range of industries and regions.

For many of these companies, being right has proved far more important than being first. You don't have to invent a product if you can figure out how the market will develop and position your company to take advantage of it. Consider how Compaq outdistanced its competition. When IBM unveiled its PC, Compaq was among dozens of startups that jumped into the market with compatible products. The young company became a master of what management writer Peter Drucker calls "creative imitation, or entrepreneurial judo." The advantage of the strategy, says Drucker, is that "by the time the creative imitator moves, the market has been established and the new venture has been accepted. Indeed, there is usually more demand for it than the original innovator can supply."

Compaq's founders quickly hit upon two key tactics to differentiate themselves from the crowd. One was their now famous portable computer, which was an instant hit. Sales of the luggable machines topped $111 million in 12 months. Less known but just as crucial was Compaq's decision to develop strong relationships with computer retailers, then a new and unproven part of the industry. From the start Compaq realized that the retailers were key and that store shelf space would become scarce real estate. Unlike many of its competitors, including Apple and IBM, Compaq never tried to compete with retailers by selling its machines directly to large customers. Compaq offered key dealers exclusive franchises and attractive margins and won the distribution battle. Today one of every six personal computers sold by dealers is a Compaq. At 25%, its share of market revenues is second only to IBM's 30%.

Businessland, the fast-growing six-year-old computer retailer based in San Jose, California, was also a latecomer. Like dozens of other entrepreneurs, Businessland cofounder Dave Norman looked at the proliferation of personal computer products and concluded that customers would never be content to shop directly with just one manufacturer. They would want to pick and choose and would want unbiased advice. The insight was hardly unique and Norman knew he would have to offer something more. His answer was to create service-oriented stores geared to small business customers.

While that approach seems obvious now, it was not so clear at the dawn of the personal computer era, when the home market was thought to be king. Even Norman didn't fully understand that his concept was just as appealing to large companies as to small ones. This year, with some 70% of its business coming from *Fortune* 500 customers, Businessland expects revenues to approach $1 billion.

In the booming market for technical workstations, Sun Microsystems executed a brilliant strategy to seize the industry lead. Sun not only started late, in 1982, but it also faced a prosperous and entrenched competitor: Apollo Computer of Chelmsford, Massachusetts. Apollo pioneered workstations—desktop machines connected to a powerful central unit and to each other—and the company made no secret of its intention to dominate the business. Moreover, Sun's founders were well aware that workstation customers were leery of doing business with a startup. The solution: Design and build muscular but inexpensive computers that were compatible with the competition's products. That way a customer could fit Sun's computers into existing installations with virtually no risk.

But the real secret to Sun's astonishing performance lay in its founders' ability to convert what appeared to be a glaring weakness into a strategic asset. The young company was so financially strapped that it could not afford to design the specialized electronic circuitry considered essential in building a high-performance workstation. Sun's founders realized that in the fast-paced computer industry, custom-built components were becoming obsolete in months. By using off-the-shelf parts, Sun could take advantage of technological breakthroughs as soon as they reached the market. The approach has enabled the company to double the computing speed of its workstations every year.

Sun is an example of what Raymond Miles, dean of the University of California business school at Berkeley, calls the "designer company," in which the presiding genius concentrates on key innovations and contracts out for all sorts of parts and services a more mature company would supply in-house. The designer approach worked for real-life designer Liz Claiborne. She and the three other founders of Liz Claiborne Inc. are all garment industry veterans. They spotted the opportunity in 1976. Says co-founder and vice chairman Jerry Chazen: "We knew we wanted to clothe women in the work force. We saw a niche where no pure player existed. What we didn't know was how many customers were out there." Clothes designers had not fully exploited one of the most profound demographic changes in the postwar era: Women baby-boomers were flooding the labor market.

Liz Claiborne's founders made two other instinctive decisions that stimulated the company's rapid growth. They decided not to build their own manufacturing plants or to field a traveling sales force. Both moves disregarded conventional industry wisdom, yet turned out to be pivotal. Lack of factories increased costs but gave the company more production flexibility than any competitor. The absence of a road force impelled the company to focus on winning orders from large department stores and specialty retailers, whose buyers were accustomed to traveling to New York. With practically no overhead, Liz Claiborne was perfectly positioned for rapid growth when sales took off.

Charles Lazarus saw the same social phenomenon, the working woman, but a different opportunity. He founded Toys "R" Us on the premise that "when Mamma went back to work, department stores were dead." He reasoned that working women wanted a store where they could shop for their children quickly, easily, and cheaply. Unlike department stores, which count on the rapid turnover of a limited number of items, Toys "R" Us offers a warehouse full of playthings. Says Lazarus: "We don't want to decide which toys you should buy. We offer everything. And we make it easy for you to toss some crayons and coloring books into your cart." Toys "R" Us operates 350 stores, and sales last year topped $3.1 billion.

Reebok co-founder Paul Fireman experienced a different revelation. "There was a social change going on that nobody had noticed," he says. "We realized that the aerobics craze was for real and that there was a huge untapped market of women seeking both comfort and style. The industry was only focused on jogging shoes. It wasn't growing with the customer." That realization brought Reebok 20 million customers that its competitors had overlooked. And what customers—instead of one set of sneakers, they often bought four or more colorful pairs of Reeboks. Sales jumped from $13 million in 1983 to $1.4 billion by the end of 1987.

A confluence of social forces turned Sol Price's warehouse club idea into a winner. By the late Seventies mass marketing had made consumers more selective; for many familiar items they didn't want advice, they just wanted a bargain. Then steep inflation made that desire urgent, and the California entrepreneur's Price Club took off.

Its strategy is brutally simple: Provide incredibly low prices, low enough to undersell not only other discounters like Kmart and Wal-Mart, but even many wholesale distributors. At huge, no-frills, cash-and-carry warehouses, Price sells cases, cartons, and pallets of products. The aisles are wide enough for stock boys to replenish inventory with forklifts and for shoppers to load their purchases onto flatbed carts. Last year some two million individuals and small businesses paid $25 just for the privilege of shopping at a Price Club. Total sales: $3.3 billion.

Supergrowing companies almost inevitably face a challenge that threatens to drag them under: transforming themselves in a few months or years from exuberant startups to corporate giants that need procedures and structure to stay efficient. Unfettered entrepreneurialism was probably crucial to the early success, but channeling it in an organized way eventually becomes just as important. Otherwise, says Richard Cavanagh, dean of Harvard's Kennedy School of Government, these companies "essentially become day-care centers for adults. People Express is a good example. They had great esprit but they never got it under control."

The opposing risk is that organization and control will crush the unique attributes that propelled the company. In the worst cases, writes Cavanagh in a book he coauthored, *The Winning Performance*, "Opportunities for breakdowns and malfunction multiply. Layers of organization can add drastically to response time. Functional specialization can lead to major problems of coordination and control: Is manufacturing really providing what sales is selling at the time it was promised? Systems may fail to monitor costs that get out of line. Leaders may lose their in-depth understanding of business dynamics or even their fundamental zeal. People throughout the company may lose their motivation and morale, adopting a nine-to-five mentality."

To avoid creeping bureaucracy, the founders of fast-growing companies try to push decision-making down to line managers. That's no problem for retailers like Toys "R" Us, Businessland, and Price, which regard each store as a business unto itself. Says Lazarus of Toys "R" Us: "No matter how big we get, the key unit in this company is the store. We want our store managers to take the business home in their stomach. We want them to think that their store is the only store in the world. We reward them with bonuses and stock options, and we've made a lot of millionaires."

Reebok dealt with its unwieldy size by creating five separate product divisions. The moves came just in time to avert chaos. When the company expanded to market eight different lines of shoes, most of its 2,200 employees had less than two years' experience at Reebok. They needed better supervision—and so did veterans of the freewheeling early days who never worried about anything except what the competition was up to. Co-founder Fireman recalls, "We had to teach our Roman legions how to operate in a time of peace."

Lack of organization nearly led to disaster in 1986, when Reebok jumped into the sportswear business. Practically overnight clothing sales reached $39 million. Says company president C. Joseph LaBonte: "The brand was so damn hot that anything we put on the racks just blew out of there. But we didn't know what we were doing. The product quality was not high. The good news was that our distribution was so bad that we didn't ruin ourselves. Most of the clothes never reached the shelves in time for the holiday sales. We eventually destroyed the rest." LaBonte, who was brought in to clean up the mess, slashed the size of the apparel group by 50%. "Now we are setting up an infrastructure so we don't have to panic all the time," he says.

How much structure does a growing giant need? The contrasting examples of Compaq and Sun make that question hard to answer. Most of the billion-dollar kids have navigated on the fly, imposing organization only when forced by circumstance. Compaq is the remarkable exception. If IBM is the Zeus of the personal computer industry, Compaq is the Pallas Athena, springing to life full-blown in a suit of armor. From the beginning, Compaq's founders—all Texas Instruments veterans—have tried to leave nothing to chance.

Even at the enterprise's birth, says senior vice president of finance John Gribi, Compaq was "a large company in its formative stages, not a small company trying to grow big. We had all our systems in place before day one. You have a clean slate, but you only get one shot at writing on it. Any startup has that advantage. It's just a question of whether you make good use of it. When our market took off, we were positioned to grow with it." Originally called Gateway Technology, the startup hired a San Francisco firm called NameLab to come up with a catchier name. Consultants also designed a corporate logo for all the company's products, literature, and advertising, with colors selected from an international color standard to ensure consistency each time a corporate trademark was printed. With sales running at an annual rate of $1.8 billion, Compaq still uses the accounting system it started with and has not fiddled with its management structure.

When Compaq executives talk about how they do things, one hears caution, earnestness, relentless rationality. "Once you announce a product, you're committed," says co-founder and chief executive Rod Canion, 43. "You don't want to make any mistakes, so it justifies putting the time and resources into making the best decision possible." Before giving the green light to a new product design, Compaq executives hammer out a consensus on everything from its design and manufacturing requirements to its price and marketing strategies. In the process, says Canion, "you always have disagreements. But at Compaq, instead of just arguing over who is right, we tear down positions to reasons. And when you get to reasons you find facts and assumptions. Then you try to eliminate the assumptions and come to agreement on the facts. Almost always, when you get your team to agree on the facts, you agree on the solutions." Canion says the approach depends on not having big egos. "In companies you usually hear slogans," he says. "From the very beginning at Compaq, what you heard was, 'Doing what makes sense.'"

Surely Compaq's alter ego is hard-charging Sun. Past policies exert no hold over its present. Though the company prospered by using off-the-shelf chips, last year it surprised the computer industry by commissioning its own microprocessor—the heart of all desktop computers. The gamble paid off almost immediately. Sun's new computers are a huge success, and competitors were so impressed with the new microprocessor that a number of them, including AT&T, Xerox, and Unisys, have decided to license it.

Sun co-founder and Chief Executive Scott McNealy is an admirer of Compaq, but he disdains the company's measured approach to decision-making. At Sun, he says, "We're more emotional. We get all fired up. Our adrenaline gets going and we start knocking against walls. Our new microprocessor's success was 90% assumption and 10% fact. It was an emotionally charged issue. How much courage do we have vs. what do the facts say? Facts are available to everybody else, but intuition is proprietary." At times Sun seems incapable of backing away from an opportunity, no matter how risky. In just the past year the company has committed itself to major development projects at the top and bottom of its product line. First the company introduced a high-performance "super-computing" workstation, and then it unveiled a high-powered personal computer that will compete with Compaq models.

Sometimes Sun even tries to recreate that little-company feeling. When the initiative of the startup days began to slacken, McNealy would break up the growing mass of employees. Last year, for example, after a key development project got bogged down, he ordered a team of engineers to clear out of headquarters and finish the job off site. The project got back on schedule. Another division, formed to design a new line of low-cost computers, was set up on the East Coast. Says McNealy: "You have to fire-wall product development groups and give them enough autonomy to do their jobs."

Aware that their progress is exceptional, the founders of fast-growing companies are obsessed with keeping it going. They fret about losing their entrepreneurial magic, losing touch with their markets, or not being able to hire ambitious go-getters like themselves. Most act like owners of small businesses rather than managers of large public corporations. At Businessland, for example, Norman still makes frequent sales calls. "I let all our store managers know I'm available if they need me," he says. Toys "R" Us's Lazarus frequently monitors sale statistics for individual stores on computer screens installed in his office, his home, and his beach house. "I don't ask people how they are doing, I look at the tube. I can see all kinds of things. I look for items not sold. Nine times out of ten it means they are not stocked on the shelves," he explains.

Even the slightest stumble provokes endless agitation and self-doubt. When Liz Claiborne laid an egg with high hemline dresses last fall, Chazen put the blame on himself. "I should have known better," he says. "We didn't recognize conflicting social phenomena. The working woman wants to be stylish, but she also wants to be dignified. It was the biggest boo-boo that I know of in my 35 years in the business." In Compaq's business, new models replace old ones about every nine months. As Canion says, "Your last successful product doesn't mean olive oil. One success is gone almost before it even happened. We never even consider slacking off. You've got to keep running."

Why the obsession with momentum? Most of the billion-dollar kids are in fast-growing industries where eventual shakeouts seem inevitable. Says Businessland's Norman: "There will always be two or three companies that will have a major share of any market. If you don't grow, you'll die." Adds Sun's McNealy: "There are only going to be a few major computer companies. A billion dollars in sales isn't big enough. We have to get bigger."

Another reason to keep up the growth is that Wall Street loves it. Security analysts are infatuated with the supergrowing companies. Smith Barney's Ilene Goldman rates Sun a top pick because "the company will outpace the industry's growth rate," which she figures at 25% per year. Salomon Brothers' Jack Seibald thinks Price Co. will also grow at a 25% rate. Montgomery Securities and Drexel Burnham are bullish on Reebok. Analysts at Prudential-Bache Securities issued "aggressive purchase" or "accumulate" recommendations in April for Sun, Toys "R" Us, and Businessland. First Boston's Charlie Wolf says that Businessland's stock "is significantly undervalued." Morgan Stanley pushes Compaq. When the growth stops, often the rave reviews do too.

There's apparently another reason to press the chase for supergrowth: It just feels good. Is growth a narcotic? "My wife asked me that same question," says Toys "R" Us President Norman Ricken, who pauses, then blurts, "The market is just out there and it belongs to us." His boss, Charles Lazarus, looks at a map of the U.S. studded with bright red pushpins for each Toys "R" Us location, then adds, "Growth creates problems, yes, but it also eliminates them. The only thing I know how to manage is growth. We're in the growth business. What we sell is toys."

The parents of the other billion-dollar kids could make similar statements, for down deep they all seem to be empire builders. They have developed compelling visions of the future of their industries, and they aim to exploit their leadership positions. Nearly all are convinced that their markets are still largely untapped. Retail chains like Businessland, Toys "R" Us, and Price Club can open stores in new locations. As Compaq and Sun computers get more powerful and easy to use, they become more attractive to larger groups of customers. The hotter the Reebok and Liz Claiborne brand names become, the more kinds of products they can sell.

The supergrowing companies have several other strategies for maintaining their pace. Many are expanding overseas. More than 35% of Sun's revenues already come from exports. Compaq makes its personal computers in Scotland as well as in Houston. Reebok shoes and Liz Claiborne dresses are best sellers in Tokyo. By the end of the year, four Price Clubs will be open in Canada. Toys "R" Us, long established in Canada, now operates in Britain, West Germany, Hong Kong, and Singapore. France is next. Exults Lazarus: "We're getting terrific store sales volumes. It's what the U.S. was like ten years ago."

Companies with plenty of cash look for strategic acquisitions. Reebok is the most active so far. Over the past two years it spent almost $300 million to buy Rockport and Avia, two fast-growing competitors. Fireman says both companies exemplify what he calls the "sense of aliveness" that the Reebok brand stands for. "Reebok is two companies," Fireman explains. "Reebok the brand, and Reebok the corporation, which acquires younger companies that can connect with our image. One of the things Reebok the corporation can't get caught up in is becoming the product. That's what happened to Cadillac. They built the same product, but the customers moved on. Reebok the brand will compete with Avia the brand. I figure that between the two of them, one will win."

Businessland also acquired two smaller competitors, but for much more straightforward reasons. Explains Norman: "Our biggest suppliers, IBM and Apple, were putting moratoriums on the numbers of dealers they were licensing. We needed to make these acquisitions to get authorized IBM and Apple locations. We were buying medallions."

The most popular growth strategy is to diversify into related product lines and services. Liz Claiborne expanded from its initial base of sportswear into dresses and knitwear. The company has also started a surprisingly successful menswear division. Says Chazen: "We discovered that 70% of our women customers also bought clothes for their husbands." Price Clubs will soon be opening pharmacies, as well as photo-processing, optical, and automotive service centers. New from Reebok: golf and bicycling shoes, plus Weeboks for children.

In addition to its stores, Businessland now sells its products through a mail-order catalog. The company is also beefing up its service operation. In the future, says vice chairman and co-founder Enzo Torresi, "We will help you tie your personal computers into your mainframes. The potential for revenues is three times bigger in service than in product sales." Adds Norman: "We'll try anything if it fits our basic strategy." Compaq, the most tightly focused company in the group, is looking into building such peripheral products as printers.

Many of the billion-dollar kids are also committing themselves to ambitious and risky ventures outside their proven lines of expertise. Price Co. is getting into real estate development with plans to build shopping centers in Connecticut, California, and Arizona. Liz Claiborne moved into retailing. "It's a huge opportunity," says Chazen. "We saw retailers like the Limited and the Gap move into manufacturing, and we said, 'We can manufacture better than these guys. Why don't we get into retailing?'" Five new Liz Claiborne stores, called First Issue, are already open, with eight more planned by the end of the year. Toys "R" Us bred Kids "R" Us, a new chain devoted to children's clothes. Says the ever ebullient Lazarus: "We planned the store for Mama. She's our customer. All the things she needs in one place. This will be a billion-dollar business in two years. You can go in with confidence. If you look at it that way, business is very easy."

No company's supergrowth can continue for long. If Sun were to grow as fast in the next five years as it did in the past five, it would be bigger than Du Pont. Five years after that it would be half the current size of the U.S. economy. In a more realistic scenario, these companies that have weathered the strains of exceptional growth must soon face a new challenge: surviving the slowdown. For them as for all prodigies, adjusting will be difficult, and as adults some may not fulfill the promise of their adolescence. Win or lose, they are teaching lessons in a new business phenomenon—and inspiring entrepreneurial fantasies that no caveats can diminish.

FUN DAYS AT THE SUN FRAT HOUSE

Last April Fool's Day, Scott McNealy, the 33-year-old founder and chief executive of Sun Microsystems, drove to work and found his office transformed into a miniature golf course. The night before, a band of engineer pranksters had torn out the wall behind McNealy's desk, removed the furniture, and covered the floor with fresh sod. The one-hole course they built was a tricky par 4. From an elevated tee, the fairway took a wicked dogleg to the right. Extra hazards included two sand traps and a birdbath, not to mention the glass picture window. Total distance: 12 yards.

McNealy was so flabbergasted that he bogeyed the hole. "I went into the trap, and it took me two shots to reach the green," he explains.

Such outrageous stunts are not only tolerated by Sun's exuberant leader, they are savored. In fact, with his buckteeth and boyish looks, McNealy seems more like the head of a college fraternity than the chief of a FORTUNE 500 company. And freewheeling Sun, nestled in the heart of Silicon Valley, does nothing to dispel the image. In addition to its tradition of yearly April Fool's shenanigans, the company stages weekly dress-down days and throws monthly beer bashes. On Halloween, employees show up for work in gorilla suits. Says McNealy: "We're trying hard to be different from other companies. One of our goals is to provide an environment that people have a blast working in. We like to think of Sun as a billion-dollar startup."

Fair enough. At the age of six, Sun can hardly be called mature. Nor can McNealy, who came to Sun just two years out of business school. But the young chairman's personality is a perfect match for Sun's wide-open culture. Under McNealy's leadership, Sun raced ahead of its competitors to become the leading manufacturer of high-performance technical workstations—the current rage among engineers, scientists, and financial analysts, who crave the extra horsepower these desktop computers offer. For Sun's fiscal 1987, which ended last June, revenues increased 156% to $538 million. And sales in its most recent quarter set a $1-billion-per-year pace.

Sun's growth astonishes McNealy as much as anyone else. Raised in Detroit, he is the son of an American Motors vice chairman. McNealy studied economics at Harvard and earned a business degree at Stanford in 1980. One of only three members of his class who sought manufacturing jobs, he joined FMC in Chicago. Within ten months he quit to work for Onyx Systems, a Silicon Valley computer maker. "FMC put me on a strategy team, and I wanted to be a plant manager. I wanted to make something," he recalls. McNealy left Onyx in early 1982 when a business school buddy, the brilliant India-born Vinod Khosla, asked him to help start Sun. Khosla was Sun's first chief executive. McNealy was head of manufacturing.

"That meant I built the first 25 Suns by hand," he recalls, "and I had the skinned knuckles to show for it."

McNealy was named Sun's interim president in 1984; the man the company's board of directors had recruited for the job, a veteran executive from Digital Equipment Corp., never fit in with Sun's rambunctious troops, and resigned. A few months later the 30-year-old Khosla decided to retire, and McNealy was appointed interim chairman as well. "At some point, I guess I became more than interim," he says.

With 6,500 employees, Sun is no longer a mere startup, and McNealy is growing with his job. Over the past year he has proved himself a tough and forceful executive as he hammered out major deals with such industry giants as AT&T, Xerox, and Unisys. Yet McNealy still relishes his role as Sun's most enthusiastic cheerleader. "I'm not a strategizer at heart," he says. "I'm more focused on cohesion and pulling everybody together. Goals only limit you. We have let the market and our ability to have fun set the company's goals."

McNealy's business heroes come from the computer and car industries. They include Kenneth Olsen, founder and chief executive of Digital Equipment, as well as William Hewlett and David Packard, the pair of billionaires who inspired thousands of Silicon Valley entrepreneurs by starting their company with $538 in a garage. "These are guys who stuck with their strategies for a long, long time, all the while protecting the cultures of their corporations," says McNealy. He reserves a special affection for Henry Ford. "By bringing automobiles down the cost curve, Ford really changed the way we live our lives," he says. "The same thing is going to happen with computers."

Still a bachelor, McNealy plays hockey at an indoor rink in San Jose and golf on any course he can find. "My real dream is to play enough golf to make it to the Masters," he jokes. Give his engineers the word and they just might decide to stage that hoax, come next April.

Questions

1. The case notes that Compaq and Sun are studies in structural contrasts. How do the structures of these two organizations differ? Are their design choices consistent with their strategies?

2. What designs have Liz Claiborne and Toys "R" Us used to manage their rapid growth? What are the advantages of these designs?

3. What strategies do these companies pursue to keep growing? What are the design implications of these strategies for the organizations adopting them?

Bankruptcy at Frontier Airlines

Organization History. Frontier Airlines was formed in 1950 through the merger of Monarch Airlines of Denver, Challenger Airlines of Salt Lake City, and Arizona Airways of Phoenix. In 1967 Frontier bought Central Airlines of Fort Worth, Texas, and merged both operations, extending its route system to 14 states. The year 1974 saw Frontier Airlines become an international carrier with the addition of service to Winnipeg, Canada. Two Mexico destinations were added in 1978 after the passage of the Airline Deregulation Act. In 1982, Frontier became the major subsidiary of a new holding company, Frontier Holdings. In addition to the airline, other subsidiaries included Frontier Services and Frontier Development. The holding company added two additional subsidiaries in 1983 with the creation of Frontier Leasco and Frontier Horizon Airline.

Until 1983, when an additional 1.5 million shares of common stock were issued, RKO General, a subsidiary of General Tire, held the majority of Frontier's stock. After the stock sale, RKO's share was diluted to 45.2 percent, but it remained the dominant shareholder in the firm. RKO was controlled by the O'Neil family, and the O'Neil brothers, Thomas and Shane, were very active players in the operations of Frontier, as board members and major stockholders.

With the 1967 acquisition of Central Airlines, Frontier's market area expanded considerably, but its market strategy remained consistent: small to medium-size cities within approximately 45 minutes flying time from the Denver hub. Until the Airline Deregulation Act of 1978, Frontier's longest flight segment was Denver to St. Louis, almost two hours. Frontier's other large cities were Dallas-Ft. Worth, where it had the most daily nonstop flights from Denver; Kansas City; Las Vegas; and Salt Lake City. In addition, it had

Source: © 1988 Timothy P. Bunger. Used with permission.

daily flights to Omaha, Tulsa, and Memphis, with the remainder of its service going to small cities and towns primarily in the western United States.

Frontier centered its operations in Denver, using the hub and spoke concept it helped pioneer. By bringing passengers to a central point and connecting them with other flights to their final destination, this system provided economies of scale; it was more likely that a flight to a certain destination would carry more passengers when connected through the hub. It also gave the passenger more options than would have been available with nonstop service from each city.

Before the deregulation act Frontier's competition was limited, as was that of the entire airline industry, by the Civil Aeronautics Board (CAB). The CAB controlled routes and fares and allowed only a limited number of carriers into a given market, virtually guaranteeing each carrier at least a small profit.

Frontier did in fact report annual profits from 1972, when A. L. Feldman became president, until 1982 (see Table 1). Feldman was responsible for several cost saving measures, including the sale of the high-operating-cost B-727s originally purchased in 1966, the implementation of a Management by Commitment Program (MBC) at Frontier, and an increased emphasis on the hub and spoke concept. Feldman was one of the first airline executives to support industry deregulation and actively lobbied Congress and the CAB to that effect. He believed that Frontier's hub and spoke system in Denver would place it in a very strong competitive position in a deregulated environment.

By the late 1970s Frontier had achieved an enviable reputation with the traveling public for friendly and superior inflight service in an all-coach seating configuration. This reputation was based on a combination of high quality meals and more leg room than that in the average coach section. Complimentary wine was served on all dinner flights, and meal service used china plates, stemmed glassware, and linen napkins. During this time, the meal service on Frontier was rated superior to many domestic airlines' first class service.

Feldman was a very popular leader at Frontier, because employees perceived him as a very straightforward and honest person. He left Frontier in 1979 for a position with a larger airline, yet even after his untimely death in 1980, his legacy was very evident at Frontier. In fact as late as 1984 he was described by employee consultant Philip Clapp as a "real hero to the members of the [employee] coalition."[1] His departure left some large shoes to fill for his successor, Glen L. Ryland, who had come to Frontier with him in 1972 as vice-president of finance. Unfortunately, Ryland did not have the same leadership style as Feldman, and would never have equally close relations with employee groups.

Causes of Decline. For the first few years, the Airline Deregulation Act of 1978 brought new challenges and increased profits to Frontier. Several factors combined to produce these profits. First, Frontier was the dominant carrier at Denver, with approximately 33 percent of the total business. Second,

Table 1
Frontier Airlines: Selected Financial Statistics

	1984	1983	1982	1981	1980	1979
Total Operating Revenues	$674,639	$584,654	$539,839	$577,430	$468,865	$389,655
Total Operating Expenses	$690,308	$603,462	$530,871	$526,483	$432,478	$357,346
Operating Income (Loss)	($15,669)	($18,808)	$8,968	$50,947	$36,387	$32,309
Pre-Tax Income (Loss)	($51,247)	($31,487)	$16,341	$52,191	$33,839	$26,173
Net Income (Loss)	($31,108)	($13,772)	$17,150	$31,961	$23,214	$21,165
Current Assets	$90,525	$96,473	$101,197	$102,259	$93,933	$72,143
Current Liabilities	$148,862	$136,577	$119,425	$102,181	$100,839	$81,130
Revenue Passenger Miles (RPM) (000)	5,079,988	3,931,190	3,570,547	3,502,488	2,971,592	3,012,253
Available Seat Miles (ASM) (000)	8,007,823	6,561,734	5,852,084	5,641,852	5,009,239	4,943,631
Load Factor— Percent	63.40	59.90	61.00	62.10	59.30	60.90
Operating Expenses: Per Available Seat Mile—Cents	8.41	8.86	9.07	9.33	8.63	7.23
Per Revenue Passenger Mile—Cents	13.26	14.79	14.87	15.03	14.55	11.86
Yield per RPM—Cents	11.88	13.18	13.71	14.78	13.91	11.32
Employees at Year End	5,704	5,605	5,359	5,887	5,622	5,577

Due to the sale of Frontier to People Express, no separate financial data is available for 1985–1986.

Frontier's operating costs were lower than those of the major carriers such as United and Continental, its primary competitors in Denver. Finally, the Rocky Mountain area was growing rapidly with the oil and gas business, and Frontier flew to all of the major oil centers in Wyoming, Montana, Oklahoma, and Texas. Frontier's profits climbed to nearly $32 million in 1981 before they began to decline.

During this period from 1978 to 1980, Frontier grew considerably and initiated routes that made it a national rather than a regional carrier—routes that included major cities such as Atlanta, Los Angeles, Seattle, Houston, San

Diego, and Oakland. These new routes placed Frontier in direct competition for the first time with United and Continental, in those carriers' prime markets.

To support this growth Frontier purchased new Boeing 737 and McDonnell-Douglas Super 80 aircraft. During this time airlines were reporting record profits and the stock market was eager to sell airline issues. Several officers at Frontier proposed raising capital for aircraft purchases through the sale of equity securities, but the conservatism of both Ryland and RKO made the company decide to finance the majority of these purchases with bank loans instead, a move that it would later regret as interest rates rose and bank funds became scarce. Because these loans were callable at any time Frontier was basically being held hostage by the banks.

After the record profits of 1981, several competing airlines attempted to lure Ryland away from Frontier. To retain him as CEO at Frontier, the Board of Directors gave him a new contract that included an annual salary of $350,000 plus stock options and stock appreciation rights, a guaranteed position as a paid consultant after retirement, and a $500,000 interest-free loan to be repaid upon his retirement. In addition, the company increased the amount it paid into a generous retirement annuity.

Frontier's decline in profitability can be attributed to several factors, but the primary cause was intense new competition. Deregulation had opened the industry to the forces of the free market system and produced turmoil for the industry while offering the traveler new choices and lower fares. Competition abounded in all areas of fares, routes, and service. Deregulation had changed the rules; now any carrier could fly to any city, at any time. This new freedom, combined with economic growth in Denver, caused a significant number of new carriers to enter the Denver market. The increased competition drove down ticket prices and was evident in the fact that in 1984 92 percent of Frontier's passengers traveled on a discount fare, up from 86 percent in 1983, 73.3 percent in 1982, and only 56 percent in 1981 (see Figure 1). In addition to these new carriers, the previously established carriers increased service at Denver. By 1984 United Airlines, the largest carrier in the U.S., had increased its presence in Denver, where it now controlled 40 percent of the market, reducing Frontier's share to 27 percent. In addition, by 1984 Frontier was competing with other carriers in 95 percent of its markets from Denver.

The final blow to Frontier's Denver dominance was the Continental's Chapter 11 filing in late 1983. Continental discontinued operations for three days and in that time it financially reorganized the company so that, after having had one of the highest operating costs in the industry, it now had the lowest costs of any major carrier. Continental's costs were now significantly lower than those of Frontier.

It was at this time that Frontier's plight truly became serious and that mistakes made over the past few years began to become more evident. Frontier was no longer the master of its own fate, since Continental had returned with both considerably lower costs and the court protection of Chapter 11. In addition, Frontier was forced to match the new lower fares of

Figure 1
Percentage of Discount Fares

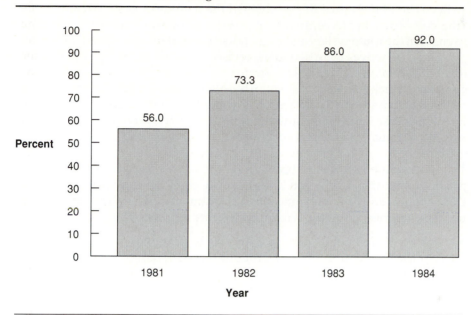

Continental in order to preserve the market share which it had in Denver, while United, with a much broader base of operations and greater financial resources, elected not to match the new fares. In retrospect many former Frontier officials believe that Frank Lorenzo, CEO at Continental's parent corporation Texas Air, was gambling on just this turn of events—that Richard J. Ferris at United would not feel compelled to match Continental's fares. It is now generally believed by many in the airline industry that had United matched the fares, Continental would have been unable to draw enough passengers to provide cash flow and thus might not have been able to exit successfully from Chapter 11.

Frontier would have had a much better chance of survival without Continental in Denver. Continental's competitive presence was probably one of the most important factors in the next three years (1983 to 1986) leading up to Frontier's bankruptcy. This factor is especially significant in light of reports that Ryland did not believe that Continental would survive three months after the Chapter 11 filing.

Responses to Decline

Strategic Responses. With the forecast of significantly lower profits in 1982 than in 1981 (down to $17.2 million), Frontier began a strategic response by creating a holding company. At the same time it embarked on new organizational objectives which would permanently change the structure of the airline. The 1982 Annual Report defined the new strategy as being to lower "the cost structure, to competitively price the product, to restructure and strengthen the route system and to continue the marketing support programs."

These objectives were tied to the revised strategy of vertically integrated diversification and growth. This strategy led to the creation of the holding company, which centered on aviation but also included a development group charged with finding acquisitions that would level out the cyclical profitability swings that were inherent in the airline industry. Frontier's plan was to use the various subsidiaries to lower its operating costs while achieving greater city-to-city convenience for its passengers through the hub in Denver. The Denver hub had always been crucial to Frontier, and at one point, in an effort to strengthen this hub, Frontier had even offered to purchase the Denver operation of Continental (before Continental's Chapter 11 filing). The new subsidiaries of Frontier Holdings were as follows:

• *Frontier Airlines:* The principal operating subsidiary of Frontier Holdings. At the height of its growth, Frontier served 78 cities in 27 states in the United States, Canada, and Mexico, accounting for nearly 96 percent of the total revenues earned by Frontier Holdings.

• *Frontier Horizon:* A new airline unit formed in August 1983, Frontier Horizon began service on January 9, 1984, from Denver to San Francisco, Chicago, and Washington, D.C., and on March 1 to New York City. Horizon operated a fleet of seven Boeing 727-100s. Horizon's objective was to provide low-cost, quality service in high density markets out of Denver where the higher cost Frontier could not compete economically. Scheduling was coordinated so that traffic was fed to and from each airline at Denver to strengthen passenger loads.

• *Frontier Development:* This group was responsible for new business acquisitions and development to expand Frontier Holdings' nonairline business activities. Russells, a wholly owned mail order catalog company based in San Francisco, was acquired in 1982 and expanded in 1983. Russells sold a variety of upscale merchandise, and a retail store was opened in late 1984 in downtown San Francisco. In addition to mailings to approximately two million households, Russells' catalog was distributed in the seat pockets of Frontier and Horizon Airlines.

• *Frontier Services:* This group, charged with providing support services related to aviation travel, concentrated on three areas: training, ground handling, and aircraft maintenance. Five schools provided training for pilots, aircraft mechanics, and customer service personnel in the travel and transportation industry. The group also included a division certified for the repair of most commercial prop jet aircraft and a division that performed airline ground handling services in 26 cities. In addition, Frontier Services managed a shuttle service for Frontier passengers traveling between the Denver airport and the surrounding Colorado communities of Boulder, Ft. Collins, and the major ski areas during the season.

• *Frontier Leasco:* This group was an asset management subsidiary that focused on the acquisition, financing, leasing, and sale of aircraft and other related equipment. By early 1984 Frontier Leasco had over $70 million in net assets, including 18 aircraft.

Operative Responses. In addition to the competitive pressures from outside the firm, there was a competitive situation building within the firm. The creation of Horizon had fostered considerable animosity at Frontier Airlines, whose employees perceived the two subsidiaries as competing for diminished resources.

The initial step to reduce Frontier's overall operating costs was taken in June 1983, when the local members of the Airline Pilots Association agreed to wage and work rule changes that would amount to a 20 percent labor cost savings. Later that year the other labor groups, except for the mechanics, agreed to similar reductions. Management personnel, however, took salary cuts totaling only 10 percent. Unfortunately, instead of being a positive step, the pay cut and this inequality created considerable mistrust and animosity among the employees.

A positive step was taken with the formation of marketing alliances with small commuter carriers in 1983. These alliances were negotiated in order to feed passengers to Frontier and Horizon from very small communities that it was uneconomical for Frontier or Horizon to serve. One of these was a new carrier that began service with some of the surplus Convair 580s that Frontier had discontinued flying earlier that year. Unfortunately this carrier was undercapitalized and unable to continue service and went bankrupt only months after it began operation, owing Frontier Leasco several million dollars in start-up loans and operating costs. In retrospect it appears that these loans were based more on the personal relationships between the principals at both firms than on good common business practices.

Another positive step was the creation of new passenger services. Frontier used the Services subsidiary to begin free shuttle service for its passengers between Ft. Collins and Boulder and Denver's Stapleton Airport. In addition, in 1983, it offered transportation to eight major ski areas in Colorado for a minimal additional fee, and initiated private membership clubs at six airports, including Denver. In conjunction with a marketing agreement with American Airlines Advantage™ Frequent Flyer Program, these moves combined to offer increased incentives to business travelers on Frontier.

But while Frontier was attempting to improve its position with the programs mentioned above, it was failing to compete in other areas. Frontier had not been updating its fleet of Boeing 737s by installing enclosed overhead luggage compartments on the older aircraft. As the fleet approached a 50/50 mix of aircraft with and without the overhead compartments, passengers resented the inconsistency. This became an even more important factor as increasing numbers of passengers had to share limited storage space on the aircraft. Another example of Frontier's reluctance to spend for capital improvements was the fact that the majority of the gates at Denver, and many elsewhere, did not have covered loading bridges. This lack forced passengers to walk outside during inclement weather and became a negative factor as all competitors installed bridges. Finally, in an effort to reduce costs, Frontier reduced its once renowned food service and began offering cold snacks in place of the once full hot meals. At the same time more seats were added to each aircraft. These changes did reduce costs but also destroyed the few competitive distinctions that Frontier had enjoyed. In fact, excellent meal service had been so important a part of Frontier's image that when it was cut one disgruntled passenger said, "If you have to fly Frontier's 737's instead of bigger [planes], you ought to get strawberry parfaits."[2] These changes were made at a time when Frontier probably most needed to differentiate its product.

Further stress had been created in December 1983 when Merrill-Lynch was retained to analyze RKO's investment in Frontier and to contact potential buyers for the firm. This arrangement generated one offer to purchase Frontier's assets through liquidation, but the offer was rejected as inadequate by the Board of Directors. Conversations with former executives indicate that this offer was unacceptable to Ryland, who would have lost control and his generous contract. In addition, it appears that several other possible suitors were rebuffed by Ryland's demands for continued control and protection of his contract.

The overwhelming consensus among other top executives was that Frontier could not survive as an independent carrier. From late 1982 through 1984 the other officers of the company recommended several options to Ryland. In an April 8, 1985, article[3] sources said that these options had included the following:

- Sale to a third party with stronger financial resources.

- Scaling back to a feeder operation in which Frontier would feed passengers from the smaller cities into Denver for connections on larger carriers such as United or Continental. This retrenchment would be followed by growth once again to a larger operation.

- Liquidation of the carrier's assets. Other airlines were interested in the leased gate space at airports served by Frontier and in the Boeing 737 aircraft, but not in the carrier's stock. This option would have resulted in the loss of over 5,700 jobs.

Unfortunately, Ryland did not seem willing to face the difficult choices that needed to be made and instead personally "shopped" the firm on Wall Street, looking for a potential buyer that would allow him to remain in control, as well as honor his contract.

As we have already seen, Ryland did not share the same good employee rapport that Feldman had enjoyed. Ryland's increased salary and perks, combined with his apparent unwillingness to listen to and communicate with employees, only furthered ill-will between the two sides. In fact, one source close to the company was quoted as saying, "Employee morale is the pitsville."[4] Frontier needed additional cost reductions, but its employees were unconvinced of the seriousness of the situation; they were still seeing the profit of 1982. Unfortunately, costs were rising while the yield per passenger was falling (see Figure 2). One source estimated, "It will take 40% hard dollar reductions to make Frontier cost competitive."[5] On October 12, 1984, Ryland took his campaign for lower costs to the press. In the October 29 issue of *Business Week* he was quoted as saying that Frontier would stay in business only if it got "substantial . . . reductions . . . in labor costs. Failing that, the company will be liquidated."[6] These statements not only increased the tension with the employees, but more importantly created a crisis of confidence on the part of Frontier's customers—passengers and travel agents. Finally, in late 1984, at the urging of several senior officers, Ryland was asked by the O'Neils to leave, his "Golden Parachute" very much intact.

RKO then brought in M. C. Lund, a veteran Frontier officer, who like Feldman, had an excellent rapport with the employees. His first move was to guarantee the sale of Horizon, in an effort to get the labor unions to agree to further wage and work rule reductions. In December 1984 Horizon was sold to a group of investors which included some of its current managers. Lund also raised cash by selling five aircraft to United Airlines for $96 million and then leased them back.

Lund was also instrumental in assisting the employee union groups in their efforts to purchase Frontier through an employee stock option plan (ESOP). In October 1984 the unions had joined in retaining a consultant, and they were working toward a leveraged ESOP buyout. In retrospect, it seems that more effort was expended both by the rank and file employees and by management in trying to complete the ESOP agreement than was spent in trying to solve the firm's fundamental problems.

Within three months the situation at Frontier had deteriorated further. In April 1985 Lund was replaced with a CEO from outside the firm, Joseph O'Gorman. Remaining upper management members were replaced by executives from O'Gorman's former carrier. The new managers immediately implemented a turnaround plan. They took control of cash, running weekly, sometimes daily cash flow projections. They opened new communication channels, including a 24 hour information line, and instituted programs to improve customer service, both on the ground and in the air. Employees were given additional customer service training, and aircraft were scheduled for interior renovations, including new seat covers and enclosed overhead compartments. A first class section was added to the fleet, and jet bridges were installed at all of the gates in Denver. Various units of the holding company, such as Russells and the training schools, were sold off. Finally, an additional 25 aircraft were sold to United Airlines for approximately $265 million in order to provide a cash cushion and assist with the ESOP plan.[7] The sale of

Figure 2
Cost versus Yield

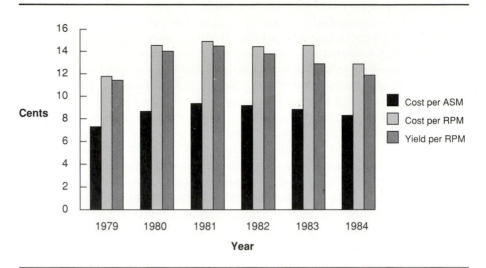

these aircraft forced Frontier to adjust flight and ground schedules to use the remaining aircraft more efficiently. In October 1984, as part of the continuing restructuring, Frontier discontinued service to 20 cities across the United States and Mexico.

Results. Unfortunately, these actions were taken too late, as Continental was now well on its way to financial health, still under the protection of Chapter 11, and was continuing to outperform Frontier in market share at Denver. In August 1985, as Frontier's financial situation deteriorated, Lorenzo of Texas Air made an offer to purchase Frontier Holdings. The prospect of having a "union buster" as owner sent shock waves through the employee group and spurred furious action to complete the ESOP or to find an alternative buyer. One was found in Donald C. Burr, founder and president of People Express Airlines, based in Newark, New Jersey. Burr was a former employee of Lorenzo, an executive at Texas International Airlines who had left to start People Express. Reportedly, a serious rivalry between Burr and Lorenzo had increased the bidding for Frontier to a point which RKO could not refuse. The $300 million deal was completed in October 1984. Burr used the cash remaining from the aircraft sales to United to finance the sale and basically bought the company for no money down.

In completing the sale of Frontier to People Express, Burr promised that there would be no layoffs for three years and that he would not sell former Frontier assets without the approval of the Frontier employees. In addition, he agreed to allow the Frontier operation to remain autonomous. "We'll be our own little Frontier," said one Frontier official.[8] However, reality soon set in and all involved realized that autonomy was not possible. Within four months Frontier was being operated like People Express—selling soft drinks and meals on board flights, and cutting fares to unprofitable levels. In January 1986, O'Gorman resigned in protest as president and CEO of Frontier and was replaced by Larry Martin from People Express.

Within a few more months Frontier was becoming a serious cash drain on People Express. Frontier still had some very valuable assets in Denver: two maintenance hangers and 20 gates at the terminal worth approximately $1 million each. Burr was now looking to sell Frontier, and even some People Express assets, in order to keep People Express operating. United Airlines, which was especially interested in the Denver real estate, made a tentative offer to buy Frontier for $146 million. But talks between the two airlines which centered on reaching an agreement with the pilots' union, broke off on August 18, after each side rejected the other's last proposal.[9] Finally, on August 24, 1986, Frontier, completely out of cash and with the United talks at an impasse, ceased operation. Three days later Frontier entered Chapter 11 proceedings. The final irony came on September 16, when Lorenzo and Texas Air purchased both People Express and Frontier for $298 million and merged their operations with Continental.

Notes

1. "People Express' Bid for Frontier Preempts Texas Air Takeover Attempt," *Aviation Week and Space Technology*, October 14, 1985, p. 31.

2. "How Frontier Airlines Is Getting Outgunned," *Business Week,* August 6, 1984, p. 66.

3. "People Express' Bid for Frontier Preempts Texas Air Takeover Attempt," p. 31.

4. "How Frontier Airlines Is Getting Outgunned," p. 66.

5. "How Frontier Airlines Is Getting Outgunned," p. 66

6. "A Game of Brinkmanship at Frontier," *Business Week*, October 29, 1984, p. 43.

7. "Frontier Airlines Future Linked to Outcome of Employee Buyout Plan," *Aviation Week and Space Technology*, April 8, 1985, p. 66.

8. "People Express' Bid for Frontier Preempts Texas Air Takeover Attempt," p. 31.

9. "Will Frontier's Fall Ground People Express, Too?" *Business Week*, September 8, 1986, p. 22–23.

Questions

1. Characterize the airline industry environment prior to and after deregulation.

2. What was Frontier's market position within the airline industry prior to deregulation? How did it change after deregulation?

3. How did changes in Frontier's strategy after deregulation contribute to its demise?

4. How did management's actions during Ryland's tenure as Frontier's president contribute to the decline?

5. Frontier's demise came about as a cumulation of a number of poor decisions. What are some of the points at which different decisions might have increased Frontier's chances for survival?

The Turnaround at StorageTek

StorageTek (STK) is a manufacturer of high-performance computer information-storage and -retrieval subsystems that are used primarily with IBM and IBM-compatible mainframe computers. Located in Louisville, CO, STK was founded in 1969 by Jesse I. Aweida, a former IBM employee, and three other engineers. As president and CEO, Aweida was the architect of the STK's early successes.

Known for his aggressiveness, impatience and openness to new ideas, Aweida stated "I believe that making a decision, even a bad decision, is better than making no decision at all . . ." He was also noted for having a "knack for quick correction." And, while his ability to change course quickly averted a number of potential crises, it did not ultimately save STK from bankruptcy.

A Bit of History. For much of the 1970s, IBM, the computer-industry monolith, was embroiled in a series of private and federal anti-trust suits. Because IBM's management was occupied with legal issues, it assumed a low-profile in relation to small competitors, permitting them to gain a foothold in its markets by offering equipment incorporating the latest technology at a price lower than its own. In the tape-drive market, one of STK's key areas, IBM did not introduce any new products for almost seven years. And, IBM did not reduce the price of its existing products in this line, even when competitors created technology that made its existing drives obsolete.

Tape drives for large-scale mainframe computers are classified as peripherals. And, peripheral products for large-scale IBM mainframes have very short life cycles, even by fast-changing computer industry standards. Once IBM introduces a new generation of computer technology, old products are obsolete.

Source: © 1989 Patrick Ertel, Gordon Koury, Jill Sokol. Used with permission of the authors.

STK's original product was a tape drive that automatically adjusted to variations in computer tapes. Prior to the introduction of STK's drive, all drives, including IBM's, needed to be manually calibrated to handle tape variations. Therefore, STK's product represented a major advancement in tape-drive technology because it increased data processing efficiency and accuracy. To capitalize on this innovative product feature, STK developed a hands-on demonstration to market its drive.

STK's market strategy was to invite potential customers to test drives in action. To illustrate the capabilities of its drives, potential customers were asked to select tapes from their own libraries that could not be read by their existing equipment. Most often, if the "unreadable" tape was not damaged, it could be read by STK's self-adjusting drives. This unique capacity, along with low cost and reliability, quickly gained loyal customers for STK's IBM-compatible tape and disk drives.

Initially, STK did not try to enter the mainframe computer market or other product areas dominated by established firms. Instead, STK concentrated on becoming the principal manufacturer in its own specialized industry niche by quickly developing and responding to technological advances in information-storage and -retrieval equipment. By pursuing this very specific product strategy, STK saw its first profitable year in 1972, when sales reached $26 million. It was now the second leading supplier of IBM-compatible disk-storage equipment and tape-storage subsystems, bested only by IBM.

STK's market and product strategies served it well. It was enormously successful throughout the 1970s, averaging a whopping 47 percent annual growth rate. The basis of this success was a very simple concept: provide high-quality, IBM-compatible disk and tape drives priced 15 percent lower than IBM's comparable products.

Expanding Horizon. By 1979, Jesse Aweida created ambitious plans for STK's operations, stating that he felt his personal management mission was "to work on key issues and the future." He intended to make significant changes in STK's historic product mix by developing peripherals for small- and medium-sized computers, as well as by selling more solid-state disk drives. To round out product offerings, Aweida envisioned the introduction of STK-built telecommunications, data-processing and data-management equipment in the foreseeable future.

By the end of 1979, Aweida felt he, personally, had successfully made the transition from small entrepreneur to the leader of a large organization. Overall, STK's sales surged from $4 million in 1971 to $922 million in 1981, making it the ninth largest competitor in the computer industry. At that time, STK held 55 percent of the market for IBM-compatible high-performance tape drives.

However, the limited competition enjoyed by STK and other firms manufacturing IBM-compatible products changed drastically by the end of the 1970s. After the federal government—carrying out the Reagan

Administration's mission to decrease business regulation—halted court proceedings against IBM, it spent hundreds of millions of dollars to regain control of the markets that STK and other competitors had nibbled away. Almost immediately, IBM introduced new products and aggressively cut prices, creating havoc for smaller competitors.

In spite of a quickly changing competitive environment, STK continued to pursue expansion. For example, in 1980, Aweida developed still another new vision; he wanted STK "to become the first full-line, plug-compatible, high-end supplier" of computer equipment. In other words, he envisioned STK selling a complete range of large-scale computers and peripheral equipment at a lower cost than IBM. This meant that STK, in a marked departure from previous product strategy, would now compete head-to-head with industry leaders.

Aweida pushed STK away from its original focus into various new product arenas. The development of a mainframe computer, optical disk drives and other new technology consumed much of STK's attention and cash. As a consequence, its less glamorous, but profitable, tape and disk-drive manufacturing operations were neglected.

Shopping Spree.   Consistent with his new vision for STK in the '80s, Aweida also began actively seeking mergers. Memorex, Amdahl, Exxon and other lesser known firms were all considered merger or acquisition candidates. However, STK had little success in its attempts to grow by adding other companies' capabilities and assets to its own.

Typical of the ventures considered was the proposed merger between STK and Amdahl Corp., a U.S. maker of IBM-compatible mainframe computers. Had the merger taken place, it would have created a new entity capable of supplying complete computer systems and generating more than $1 billion in annual sales. However, Amdahl's major shareholder, Fujitsu, asked STK to sign a letter of intent to rely on Fujitsu for many big computer components. Aweida refused to agree, so, Fujitsu, concerned about the consequences of a merger and Aweida's "freewheeling style," backed out of the deal. Later, the consequences of the attempted merger became painfully clear: Amdahl, marketing Fujitsu's products, became one of STK's direct competitors.

Despite such setbacks, Aweida continued to pursue rapid expansion. Under his direction, STK initiated research in areas such as micro-technology, personal computing, telecommunications and optical storage devices. To fund these various projects, STK used several financing methods: it formed partnerships, issued new debt and sold stock.

One of STK's large projects involved the creation of a research subsidiary to develop a mainframe computer. To assemble a top-notch research team, Aweida lured 14 specialists away from Amdahl with attractive stock, salary and bonus packages. Financing for the greater part of this $50-million project was raised through private investors who became limited partners in the new venture. The mainframe, however, never made it to market because manufacturing problems created fatal delays. Sadly, the product was obsolete before it was introduced. STK, formerly setting its sight to be first-to-market with storage and retrieval innovations, was left in the dust of quicker-moving competitors.

In 1982, the effects of such mistakes and miscalculations began to overwhelm STK. When it missed more deadlines on new-product deliveries, it started to cut corners to get products to market as quickly as possible. The most visible example of these problems occurred in late 1982, when, in an attempt to hastily meet delivery commitments, quality control measures received short shrift. As a result, one disk-drive model experienced a failure rate in excess of 10 percent. This further compounded STK's problems because the defective drives cost it more than $6 million in repair expenses.

But, just as harmful as the cash drain created by repair expenses was the damage inflicted on STK's reputation. Formerly known for quality and reliability, STK began to lose credibility with customers. An additional effect of quality-control problems came in the wake of negative customer reaction to defective units. The salesforce, bearing the brunt of customer's hostility, became disgruntled, and quit at an alarming rate.

Financial Reaction. STK's difficulties were now attracting industry attention, and financial markets began to react to stories of its problems. As a result, STK's stock price fell and its debt ratings were revised downward. In 1983, STK's sales collapsed, its profits disappeared and it operated at a loss for the first time since 1972.

One cause of STK's woes was a severe change in the product life cycle for data-storage devices. Essentially, while STK was developing a new thin-film disk drive, the 8380, to compete with IBM's new 3380 orders for its existing drives stopped. During this time, IBM solved some of the manufacturing problems it had been experiencing with its drives, was able to produce more units and cut prices. Thus, IBM captured a large market share when it sold 20,000 units of its new thin-film drive in 1983, and 40,000 units in 1984. In contrast, STK's competing drive did not even reach the market until late 1983, and it sold only 4,000 units in 1984.

Other product development fiascoes compounded STK's problems. An expensive undertaking, the long-touted plug-compatible mainframe-computer project, was scrapped, causing a write-off of $31.5 million of STK's cash and $50 million invested by its outside limited partners. Such incidents further eroded STK's credibility and reputation.

However, STK wasn't the only computer manufacturer experiencing problems. An industry-wide shakeout—produced when IBM, finally free from anti-trust actions flexed its long-unused muscle—occurred, forcing weaker competitors out of the marketplace. When the dust settled, IBM's only remaining competitor in the IBM-compatible mainframe market filed for bankruptcy. Then, in September 1984, Control Data Corporation pulled out of the IBM-compatible disk-drive market, leaving STK and Memorex as the only other U.S. companies making IBM-compatible disk drives.

Damage Control. STK finally reacted to its growing problems in 1984. It cut back several more product-development projects and laid off 10 percent of the workforce in early October. Also, to improve its cash position, STK tried unsuccessfully to renegotiate $265 million in bank debt. These actions, however, were too little and too late.

By this time, STK had stretched itself too thin by simultaneously investing in several major technology-development programs. Overall, STK's 8380, a poorly engineered and unreliable product that was expected to generate substantial revenues, was unable to compete with IBM's plug-compatible version 3380 disk drive. Instead of providing STK with capital, the 8380 simply drained funds needed for operations and research and development. Essentially, STK had expanded too fast without a supporting increase in revenues. Thus, STK lost $505 million in 1984 and, in 1985, its stock sold for as low as $1.50 a share, down from a high of $40.38 in 1981 when STK was in its glory days.

Faced with a crushing debt load, reliability problems and slumping sales, STK was forced to file for Chapter 11 bankruptcy on October 31, 1984. The filing was a last-ditch desperate effort, illustrated by the fact that STK didn't bring insolvency counsel on-site until the day before filing. As evidence of STK's dire straights, it was discovered during an 11-hour all-night meeting that it did not have enough cash to pay the $400 bankruptcy filing fee. This forced STK's top managers to make withdrawals from an automatic teller machine to come up with the needed money. Furthermore, paperwork had to be processed at a drive-up bank window in order to meet a 7:30 A.M. filing deadline.

Filing for Chapter 11 created two main benefits. It relieved STK's immediate debt burden, giving it both cash and time to regroup. The bankruptcy filing also provided an opportunity for drastic changes within STK and sent a powerful message to employees, customers, creditors and management that "business as usual" could not continue.

Shortly after the bankruptcy, Aweida resigned as CEO, and STK began the search for a new President and CEO. The choice of new leadership, like the bankruptcy filing, had to be carefully considered because it, too, was a signal to creditors, customers and employees. Clearly, by seeking a "turnaround artist," STK communicated that it intended to emerge from Chapter 11 and return to profitability. So, in January 1985, Ryal Poppa, with the blessing of STK founder Jesse Aweida, took over the giant task of righting the foundering 16 year-old computer manufacturer.

In addition to Poppa, Stephen Jerritts, runner-up in the selection for the number one position, was invited to take the reins as Chief Operating Officer, while Robert Costain, who had worked with Poppa at Pertec Computer, was appointed Vice President for Strategic Planning. Chief Financial Officer, Bill

Mansfield, the only STK pre-bankruptcy officer to remain, rounded out the foursome charged with the daunting task of reorganizing STK under Chapter 11 and returning it to profitability. Mansfield staunchly insisted that bankruptcy be put into proper perspective, a message which he communicated to shell-shocked employees, customers, and creditors. He reassured STK's stakeholders that, despite bankruptcy, its core values were intact.

Poppa, a former IBM salesman and marketing wizard, earned his reputation as a turnaround artist based on his success in revitalizing several smaller computer firms, notably Pertec Computer in Los Angeles, CA, and BMC Industries in St. Paul. Because of his role in turning BMC into a $350 million high-growth company via acquisitions, Poppa was named as one of *Business Week*'s 50 "Corporate Elite" in 1985.

Poppa, however, was dogged by critics who claimed that his turnaround mastery was more smoke-and-mirrors than substance. And, his legacy at Pertec tended to support detractors claims. After 8 years, Poppa sold Pertec and departed with a "golden parachute," and, within a year of exiting, Pertec began to flounder. Pertec's sales and revenues declined, reinforcing claims that Poppa bailed out when Pertec ran out of operating strength. As further evidence, critics point that after three years at BMC, Poppa left it with a 15-1 debt-to-equity ratio. To survive, BMC struggled to sell Poppa's purchases.

In contrast to Aweida's amiable and participative management style, Poppa brought a highly directive, delegating style to STK. Although hard-nosed, Poppa gained employee support in face-to-face meetings and through a well-crafted campaign designed to boost morale and to sell the notion that Chapter 11 did not spell STK's death. Poppa truly excelled in the role of corporate communicator. So, while he delegated much of the day-to-day authority for operations, finance, and Chapter 11 proceedings to others, he remained personally involved in clarifying STK's problems and appropriate solutions. And, although critics claim many of these communication efforts were merely self-promotional, his gift of persuasion produced some tangible benefits for STK.

As part of Poppa's communication program, he instituted regular meetings, open-door policies, videos and suggestion forms to ensure two-way communication with STK employees. In his first meeting with employees, held four days after he started with STK, he expressed several very clear messages.

1.   He acknowledged the cause of STK's problems—management errors, competition, reliability problems, unfocused efforts and excessive research and development expenses;

2.   He stated the pressing need for cuts, citing STK's bankruptcy as evidence;

3.   He defined his vision of STK as a computer firm providing information storage and retrieval solutions;

4.   He defined a common goal for all employees—get STK out of bankruptcy.

Poppa repeated these themes to employees at all levels of STK. And, he also employed videos to describe Chapter 11 in the most favorable terms possible. Bankruptcy, he explained, was intended to allow a firm to rebound from financial problems. It was not necessarily a precursor of organizational death.

Over a span of 18 months, Poppa personally made 287 customer calls, delivered 42 speeches to industry groups and made 61 speeches to chambers of commerce. Throughout his first months with STK, Poppa spent two days each week calling on customers. In addition to visiting customers, top managers shared the task of meeting with customers—at least three each day—who came to STK for in-plant visits. In these meetings, Poppa and the rest of the STK management team reiterated their commitment to turn STK around.

Also, Poppa and Jerritts met extensively with STK's various creditors, selling the idea of a "new" STK. Because all creditors had to agree on the Chapter 11 reorganization plan before it could be enacted, these meetings were a key to STK's turnaround. As an added benefit, the meetings may have led to the unique secondary market that developed for STK's debt.

Getting Down to Business. Once STK's new management team was in place it began to formulate turnaround strategies. According to Mansfield, several hundred reorganization scenarios were proposed, of which 78 were considered. Ultimately, STK reorganized around a scenario that identified three core operational areas: manufacturing, service, and leasing operations. STK was returning to its roots.

Strategically, STK management redefined itself as an information storage and retrieval firm and listed its strengths as service, research and development and marketing. This meant STK would manufacture disk drives, tape drives, and printers. To become competitive again, STK formulated a strategic plan to manufacture, on a timely basis, innovative, reliable, high-quality products comparable to or better than those of its competitors. And, the products would be priced *below* those of its principal competitor, IBM. Product development, which was continued even though STK was struggling to emerge from Chapter 11, was consolidated around STK's disk, tape and printer product lines.

Simplification and Funds Generation. STK quickly enacted programs to stem the hemorrhaging of its funds. Operationally, cash was freed up via three major layoffs, which took place during November 1984, January 1985, and the summer of 1985, and trimming employment levels from 16,500 to 8,500.

STK first pursued alternatives to layoffs, shifting personnel internally as much as possible. Even employment levels in core areas were reduced to increase efficiency. However, layoffs in STK's core areas were based on performance, not seniority. Each layoff was handled in a slightly different way, but in spite of STK's serious cash shortage all departing employees received outplacement services, including help preparing resumes and counseling.

As another part of its restructuring, STK sold its communication and computer subsidiaries; discontinued semiconductor research; and dumped a $100 million optical disk project. Throughout 1985, STK divested a number of assets, including those of its Microtechnology Division; majority interest in Global-Ultimacc Systems, a software firm; tangible and intangible assets comprising its Image Processing Systems Division, which was engaged in the research and development of a digital-image device; an investment in the metal fabrication operations of Documentation; and a weeks-old $6 million corporate jet.

Cost reduction and cash management efforts included an increased emphasis on accounting, collecting receivables, and principal and interest payments on unsecured debt. In addition, stringent inventory controls were introduced and four management levels eliminated, reflecting STK's reorganization among functional lines. These efforts soon paid off: by the end of 1985, a cash balance of $200 million was generated.

Returning to Proven Expertise. To compete with IBM's high-performance 3380 disk subsystem, which was being marketed at a discount, STK introduced a comparable product, the re-engineered 8380E, in April 1985. On another front, STK was being challenged by IBM which introduced a new generation of cartridge tape subsystems, the 3480. However, STK was able to counter by introducing a new generation of high-speed printers, intended to challenge both IBM and Hitachi.

Although STK ended 1985 with losses of $57.4 million on sales of $673.4 million, fourth quarter numbers revealed income of $2.2 million, its first profit in two and a half years. Furthermore, STK amassed a cash balance of $170 million, enabling it to fund a $60-million product-development program. And, orders for the 8380E and 8380 storage devices looked promising.

The project on which STK's future hinged was the successful development of the ACS 4400, a cassette drive with a mechanical robot arm. The ACS 4400 was revolutionary because it could store and retrieve entire tape libraries without human assistance. Each library could hold 6,000 tapes and 16 libraries could be configured together. Code named "Cimarron," the automated tape library allowed STK to lead the industry into a new kind of storage medium and a new level of storage hierarchy termed "Nearline." The ACS 4400 was introduced in the fall of 1986.

The Plan Comes Together. Poppa, speaking a few years later, admitted that, in late 1986, he initially believed STK could not be salvaged. But, as the year progressed, he became convinced of STK's intrinsic value and communicated that to corporate stakeholders. Through Poppa's efforts, an esprit de corps focusing on survival and communicating the "new STK" emerged.

STK's cash position looked promising by mid-1986, but the possibility of class action suits on behalf of creditors and shareholders threatened to sink frantic reorganization efforts. However, at an employee function dedicating the STK flag in early July 1986, Poppa made a surprise announcement. As employees munched on hot dogs and apple pie, he revealed that an agreement had been reached with STK's 8,500 creditors. According to the terms of the agreement, STK would repay $800 million in debt with $190 million in cash, and with about $300 million in notes and newly issued common stock to cover the balance of creditor claims. The crowd erupted in applause, spirits raised by signs that STK would indeed survive.

The announcement's timing was chosen because Poppa realized that one of STK's inherent strengths was the pride and success that drove it in the '70s. He drew on this aspect of STK's culture, implying "we were winners before, we'll be winners again."

According to Mansfield, the successful resolution of creditor claims was due to a high level of trading activity in STK debt by high-risk investors interested in "taking equity." In particular, Michael Price, manager of Mutual Shares Fund (MSF), which invests in "special situations," became a major player as MSF acquired $200 million in STK debt. This active market in STK debt is unique among bankruptcies and proved to be a major factor in resolving creditor claims.

In late 1986, the IRS brought a claim against STK for $640 million in back taxes. STK, however, employed an innovative legal procedure, made possible by Poppa's efforts in Washington, D.C. In 1986, he successfully lobbied Congress to obtain a tax provision allowing STK to realize a net loss carryforward. This elicited a favorable ruling from the judge presiding over STK's bankruptcy. And, although the IRS appealed the ruling, an April 1987 settlement was reached through the intervention of the U.S. Attorney General's office. According to the terms of the settlement, STK paid $37.1 million in back taxes, allowing it to emerge from Chapter 11 on July 28, 1987, two and a half years after filing.

Life after Bankruptcy. After earning profits of $35.4 million on sales of $698.1 million for 1986, STK introduced 1987 with the theme "Flying Free Again" and announced the forthcoming ACS 4400 to customers and reporters around the globe via satellite. And, although IBM had earlier abandoned a project similar to the ACS 4400, STK projected $5 billion in net sales from the product over the next five years.

STK now claimed 7 percent of the disk drive market; 11 percent for printers; and 30 percent for tape drives. In addition, the ACS was expected to enhance its position by gaining a further share of IBM's information-storage and -retrieval device market. On the downside, however, tape drives had been dropping in their contribution to revenue by nearly 10 percent annually since 1985.

With its successful emergence from Chapter 11, STK secured a $50 million line of credit from a consortium of six banks. And, although STK was falling short of revenue and profit predictions, it continued to introduce new products, models, features, and enhancements. Product introductions included an

18-track cartridge tape drive, a triple-capacity disk subsystem, and a new impact printer. Furthermore, STK began forging alliances with U.S., Asian, and European companies to develop new technologies.

At year's end, final STK figures for 1987 showed that revenues and sales were up 7.8 percent and 25 percent, respectively, while profits were down 28.2 percent. Nonetheless, STK moved ahead, finalizing a 1988 agreement with Sterling Software and a multi-year deal with International Computers, Ltd., valued at $100 million. And, in May 1988, STK outsold IBM and Memorex to garner a $150-million contract to produce an 18 track cartridge drive for use on Xerox high-speed printers.

As STK's fourth quarter of 1988 closed, product orders had increased by 10 percent over the previous year, but ACS demand remained lower than expected. In contrast, 18-track-cartridge drive demand was significantly higher than anticipated, given a predicted continued decline for disk drives.

On February 28 and March 1, 1989, STK was one of the most actively traded stock on the New York Stock Exchange, with investors purchasing million-share blocks of stock. On Thursday, March 3, 1989, STK reported a $44 million profit for 1988 reflecting a favorable Security and Exchange Commission review of its accounting practices. On volume of 4,839,600 shares, STK stock closed at 2⅛ up from 1⅜ at the beginning of the week.

By early 1989, STK had achieved a semblance of operational stability, its strategic plan calling for decentralization of the decision-making process. In a January 1988 top management restructuring, Poppa assumed all of COO Jerritts' duties. Jerritts' contract was bought out in a reduced settlement three years before expiration. He subsequently moved to NBI, a troubled word-processor manufacturer, as CEO. In early 1989, Robert Costain, Vice President for Strategic Planning, was named Vice President of Engineering, a low-profile management slot. Shortly thereafter, STK acquired Aspen Peripherals, founded in 1985 by none other than an entrepreneurial wizard named Jesse Aweida.

Bibliography

"100 Company Profiles," *Datamation* (June 15, 1988): 118.

Sandra D. Atchison et. al., "Has Storage Technology Found Its Iacocca? *Business Week* (February 4, 1985): 36.

"Back-to-Basics Plan Saves Storage Tech," *New York Times* (June 18, 1987): 1.

Adriel Bettelheim, "StorageTek Reports $44 Million Profit," Denver Post (March 3, 1989): 1C.

Daniel A. Beucke, "StorageTek's Bottom Line: Quick Healing," *Denver Post* (May 24, 1985): 1C–7C.

"Court Backs Plan for Storage Tech," *New York Times* (June 19, 1987): 4.

Jim Hendon, "StorageTek Names Planning Executive," *Rocky Mountain News* (February 15, 1985): 100.

Jim Hendon, "StorageTek Gets a New Top Officer," *Rocky Mountain News* (February 18, 1985): 68.

Jim Hendon, "Rebuilder Gets Nod at StorageTek," *Rocky Mountain News* (January 19, 1985): 88.

Mark Ivey, "Storage Technology Could Be One of Price's Longer Shots," *Business Week* (December 8, 1986): 86.

Mark Ivey, "Storage Technology Is Turning Around—But Where's It Headed?" *Information Processing* (February 24, 1986): 106–107.

Lee Keough, "The Resurgence of StorageTek," *Computer Decisions* (April 6, 1987).

Don Lyle, "Poor Strategy Cited in STK Woes," *Rocky Mountain News* (March 7, 1985).

Kimberly Mayer, "StorageTek: After System 'Crash,' Financial Repairs Under Way," *Rocky Mountain News* (July 13, 1986): 68.

Kimberly Mayer, "StorageTek Clears Major Hurdle," *Rocky Mountain News* (July 8, 1986): 1B.

Stephen T. McClellan, *The Coming Computer Industry Shakeout.* (John Wiley & Sons, Inc., 1984).

Patricia McShane, "Optical Disk Delay," *Computer Decisions* (April 9, 1985): 26.

Jeff Moad, "A Troubleshooter Learns to Ski," *Datamation* (April 1, 1987): 106.

Jeff Moad, "Pinning Hopes on a Vision of Storage," *Datamation* (February 1, 1987): 17–19.

William Olsen, "Key Exec Departs from StorageTek," *Rocky Mountain News* (March 8, 1988): 3B.

Thomas Schilling, "Turnarounds Make Their Careers," *Rocky Mountain News* (July 27, 1986): 62–71.

"Software Girl Weds Hardware Boy," *Forbes* (June 9, 1980): 108–110.

Barry Stavro, "Back From the Dead," *Forbes* (July 28, 1986): 41–43.

"Storage Technology Looks to Reload," *Computer Decisions* (July 15, 1985): 70–75.

"Storage Tech's Survival Strategy," *Financial World* (October 15, 1979): 33–34.

"Trick or Treat," *Economist* (November 10, 1984): 76–78.

Bro Uttal, "Storage Technology Goes for the Gold," *Fortune* (April 6, 1981): 54–61.

Michael A. Verespej, "Ryal Poppa's New Chess Game," *Industry Week* (May 13, 1985): 80.

Hesh Weiner, "Picking up the Pieces," *Datamation*, (January 15, 1985): 38–41.

Kathleen K. Weigner, "Uphill Racer," *Forbes* (April 21, 1986): 144.

Steve Wing, "Blue-Ribbon Beauties," *Denver Business* (April 1988): 9.

Questions

1. What caused STK's slide into bankruptcy?

2. How well did STK's turnaround fit the model presented in Chapter 12? Provide examples of how Poppa's top management team developed and implemented STK's turnaround.

3. How did Poppa's communication skills help STK regain credibility with its various stakeholders? Provide examples to support your answer.

Early History of Organization Design

The first recognized attempts at systematically studying the development and design of organization structures occurred in the last two decades of the nineteenth century. At that time, increased interest in organizations was paralleled by the growing economic and industrial development of the United States and Western Europe. The forces of expanding technology and commerce, paired with new advances in transportation and communication, dramatically increased the scope and complexity of business undertakings. For the first time in history, problems of managing large-scale organizations became widespread as industrial and commercial enterprises began to replace individual proprietors and partnerships as the usual forms of business. An unprecedented increase in the size of production facilities created previously unexperienced problems of waste and inefficiency. As a result, new concepts for designing organizations had to be investigated. The problems encountered were beyond the capacity of single individuals to solve. A detailed history of organization design would require a separate volume,[1] so the primary focus of this module is on the evolution of organization design since the late 1800s.

THE INDUSTRIAL REVOLUTION

The seeds of the modern industrial corporation—the forerunner of today's *Fortune* 500 company—were sown in Great Britain in the late 1700s.[2] At about the time of the American Revolution, another revolution was taking place in the practice and management of work. This **Industrial Revolution**, as we call it today, resulted from a series of events that occurred in a relatively short

607

period of time. It is perhaps best dated with the year 1776, a time that marks the birth of American democracy and publication of Adam Smith's *The Wealth of Nations.*

The basic change was the transfer of work skills from craftworkers to machines. These craftworkers, aided by relatively simple tools, would produce an entire good, such as a watch, a pair of shoes, or a gun, and then sell it directly to individual consumers. The Industrial Revolution changed this pattern, which had endured for centuries. New inventions—James Watt's steam engine (1765), Richard and Arkwright's "water frame" (1769), which automated textile manufacturing, and Edmund Cartwright's power loom (1785), among others—required only an unskilled operator to feed them material and remove finished parts. Eventually, automated machines were developed that made even an operator unnecessary. An enormous increase in productivity resulted, and subsequently, lower prices. As prices dropped, consumption grew, and the cycle of modern capitalism was soon underway.

The outcome was phenomenal growth in the size of organizations. In the United States, the railroads were the first industry to feel the need for improved management as a result. Between 1860 and 1910, the number of miles of railroad track in use jumped from 30,626 to 266,185—an increase of 769 percent. By 1890 railroads employed some 750,000 workers.

As the railroads moved west, the nation was soon bound coast-to-coast by a web of steel rails and a network of telegraph lines. By 1866, an underwater telegraph cable brought Europe and the United States minutes rather than months apart. These and other developments in transportation and communication opened new world markets, and together with new production processes, prompted further economic growth. As industrial and commercial undertakings expanded in order to capitalize upon the new markets and production processes, it became evident that their size and complexity would require more knowledgeable management.

Many of today's industrial giants can trace their origins to this period. In 1873 Andrew Carnegie began what was to become U.S. Steel. In 1879 John D. Rockefeller, Sr., established the Standard Oil Company. Henry Ford, Sr., formed Ford Motor Company in 1903, and William C. Durant combined Buick, Oldsmobile, and Cadillac with some 20 other automobile companies to form General Motors between 1908 and 1910. As these and other industrial empires developed, the nature of modern organizations was further changed.

HENRY R. TOWNE: A MILESTONE

Truly revolutionary ideas often sound surprisingly self-evident a few decades after they are proposed. We laugh today to think that people once found such ideas as washing one's hands before surgery a major breakthrough. The thought that management (and hence organization design) could be learned in a classroom or from a textbook was also considered revolutionary in the late 1800s. It was commonly understood that management could be learned only by observation and practice—if it could be learned at all. Management was assumed by many to be an art, and by even more to be a divinely bestowed gift or talent, rather than an acquired accomplishment. According to this last group, no one could hope to really succeed as a manager who had not "the knack born in him."

The person who first challenged these ideas was Henry R. Towne, cofounder and president of Yale & Towne Manufacturing Company. In 1886 he presented a paper called "The Engineer as an Economist" at a meeting of the American Society of Mechanical Engineers (ASME) arguing that management as a field of study was equal in importance to engineering.[3] He observed that the management of work was often wholly unorganized, had no medium for the exchange of experience, and was without professional association. He urged the ASME to "remedy" this situation. Towne's paper is the milestone most frequently referred to as the beginning of a search for a science of management.

Towne's "remedy" involved five sequential and overlapping stages:[4]

1. Accumulation of all knowledge pertaining to machines and human work.
2. Distillation of this knowledge into applicable laws and formulas.
3. "Scientific" establishment of optimum performance standards for machines and workers.
4. Transfer of this information through a reorganization of human and mechanical production processes.
5. Establishment of cooperation between labor and management.

As ASME president in 1889 and 1890 and cofounder of the Chamber of Commerce of the United States, Towne's influence was far-reaching. He possessed a rare combination of engineering ability and managerial capacity that made more significant his appeal for the acknowledgment and nurturing of management as a science. In the years after the presentation of his paper, the ASME was a central forum for the discussion of managerial challenges.

FREDERICK W. TAYLOR: "FATHER OF SCIENTIFIC MANAGEMENT"

While Towne's presentation is recognized as marking the beginning of the search for a science of management, the birth of **scientific management** is generally credited to Frederick W. Taylor (1856–1915). Taylor had been present at Towne's address and was impressed with his insights regarding management. As an engineer, Taylor saw that a business is a system of human cooperation that will be successful only if all concerned work toward a common objective.[5] To this end, Taylor called for a "mental revolution" where "both sides take their eyes off the division of the surplus . . . and together turn their attention toward increasing the size of the surplus."[6] Thus, as envisioned by Taylor, the concerns of labor and management should be based on a "mutuality of interests." In brief, he advocated a congruency between the goals of employee and employer. In his words: "It is safe to say that no system or scheme of management should be considered which does not in the long run give satisfaction to both employer and employee, which does not make it apparent that their best interests are mutual, and which does not bring about such thorough and hearty cooperation that they can pull together instead of apart."[7]

Taylor was committed to eliminating the inefficient and wasteful practices of the past and to transcending what at the time appeared to be insolvable conflicts of interest between labor and management. He believed that the interests of employers and employees could be made to coincide. According to Taylor's doctrine, increased productivity and expansion of output resulting from improved methods of organization were to be shared so that there would be both an increase in wages for labor and an increase in profits for investors. Scientific management was to be a tool for greater productivity, greater purchasing power, and a higher standard of living. Taylor summarized his work in what has become known as the *four principles of scientific management:*

1. Development of a true science of managing, complete with clearly stated laws, rules, and principles to replace old rule-of-thumb methods.
2. Scientific selection, training, and development of workers, whereas in the past workers were randomly chosen and often untrained.
3. Enthusiastic cooperation with workers to ensure that all work is performed in accordance with scientific principles.
4. Equal division of tasks and responsibilities between workers and management.

Although the groundwork of Taylor's system had been laid for several years, it was not until 1910 that it began to receive widespread publicity. At that time, rate hearings were being held to determine whether a number of Eastern railroads should be allowed to raise their freight charges. Louis D. Brandeis, counsel for the opposition (later a Supreme Court Justice), coined the term *scientific management* to describe the principles and philosophy of Taylor's work.[8]

It was Brandeis's strategy to prove by expert testimony that the railroads, by adopting the methods of scientific management, could not only considerably reduce their costs, but could also increase wages without increasing rates.[9] To this end, Brandeis presented 11 expert witnesses, including Henry R. Towne, Henry L. Gantt, Carl G. Barth, Frank B. Gilbreth, and Harrington Emerson, who testified for almost three days. The high point of the hearings was reached with Emerson's testimony that the railroads could save $300 million a year (equivalent to over $11 million a day in today's dollars) through the application of scientific management.[10]

Within 24 hours, scientific management, previously an obscure technology developed by a relatively unknown engineer, became international news. Although Taylor had not testified, most of Brandeis's witnesses acknowledged him as their teacher. Taylor became a national hero overnight. Newspapers and magazines published dozens of articles about his work. This publicity and the publication of Taylor's book, *The Principles of Scientific Management,* in 1911, gave a new impetus to the campaign for efficiency.

Conferences were held and societies formed to study Taylor's work. His book became known throughout the world, and even Vladimir Lenin urged the Russians to put scientific management into effect.[11]

HENRI FAYOL: EMERGENCE OF ADMINISTRATIVE THEORY

Like those of Taylor, the ideas of Henri Fayol (1841–1925) have had a lasting impact on the development of organization theory as a science. Fayol is generally recognized as the greatest European management pioneer.

Although aware of Taylor's theories, Fayol worked independently in France during the same period that scientific management was developing in the United States. Whereas Taylor approached the study of management from the workshop or technical level, Fayol approached it from the viewpoint of upper-level administration.

An engineer by training, Fayol served as general director of the Commentry-Fourchambault Collieries. Drawing on more than 50 years of industrial experience, he formulated 14 principles of management, shown in Table M1.1 Many of these principles, such as "division of labor," "unity of command," and "scalar chain," are also principles of organization.

Fayol's ideas drew widespread attention with the publication of his paper, "Administration Industrielle et Generale," in 1916. Before long, *Fayolism* became as firmly entrenched in French management thinking as *Taylorism* had become in the United States.[12] In fact, his paper published as a separate book soon became known as "a catechism for the chief executive's education."[13] American managers were largely unaware of Fayol's work, however, until his book was translated into English in 1930.

The familiar ring of Fayol's ideas suggest how thoroughly they have penetrated current organization theory and practice. While many of them may seem relatively self-evident today, they were revolutionary when first advanced. The continuing validity of Fayol's ideas has earned him the title of "Father of Modern Management."

Table M1.1
Fayol's 14 Principles of Management

1. *Division of Labor.* Work should be divided to permit specialization.
2. *Authority.* Authority and responsibility should be equal.
3. *Discipline.* Discipline is necessary to develop obedience, diligence, energy, and respect.
4. *Unity of Command.* No subordinate should report to more than one superior.
5. *Unity of Direction.* All operations with the same objective should have one manager and one plan.
6. *Subordination of Individual Interest to General Interest.* The interest of one individual or group should not take precedence over the interest of an enterprise as a whole.
7. *Remuneration.* Rewards for work should be fair.
8. *Centralization.* The proper degree of centralization-decentralization for each undertaking is a matter of proportion.
9. *Scalar Chain.* A clear line of authority should extend from the highest to the lowest level of an enterprise.
10. *Order.* "A place for everything and everything in its place."
11. *Equity.* Employees shoud be treated with kindness and justice.
12. *Stability of Tenure of Personnel.* Turnover should be minimized to assure successful goal accomplishment.
13. *Initiative.* Subordinates should be allowed the freedom to conceive and execute plans in order to develop their capacity to the fullest.
14. *Esprit de Corps.* Harmony and union build enterprise strength.

MAX WEBER: BUREAUCRACY AS THE IDEAL

Whereas Taylor's and Fayol's primary attention had been directed toward practical problems of managing for effective goal accomplishment, the concern of Max Weber (1864–1920) was with the more fundamental issue of how organizations are structured. Although Weber (pronounced *Vayber*), a German sociologist, published most of his work at the turn of the century, his ideas remained virtually unknown to English-speaking theorists until they began to be translated in the late 1920s.[14] Primarily prescriptive in nature, Weber's writings strike an interesting contrast to the practitioner-oriented recommendations of Taylor and Fayol. Weber's major contribution was an outline of the characteristics of what he termed **bureaucracy**.

Four points about Weber's work deserve emphasis:

1. To Weber, *bureaucracy* was an ideal that did not exist in reality. It was a standard, or model, to be used not only in constructing enterprises, but also in assessing, through comparison, their relative performance. In this regard, his basic model is hypothetical, rather than factual. It is meant to be a working model, not to correspond to reality.

2. Weber did not use the term *bureaucracy* in the disparaging, emotionally tinged sense of red tape, endless lines, and rule-encumbered inefficiency. Rather, he used it as a noncritical label for what he regarded as the most modern and efficient method of organizing yet developed.

3. Weber's ideal bureaucracy is based on *legal* authority as contrasted with that which rests on either *tradition* (custom) or *charisma* ("the gift of grace"). As developed by Weber, legal authority stems from rules and other controls that govern an organization in the pursuit of specific goals. Managers are given the authority to interpret and enforce these rules and other controls by virtue of their position. Obedience is not owed to a person but to the impersonal authority of an office. This is necessary if authority is to outlast the tenure of individual officeholders. Familiar examples of legal authority structures are the military, politically elected offices, government bureaus, colleges or universities, and business firms (especially those above a certain size).

4. The need Weber identified for efficient organizing is culture-free. The increasing size of organizations, advanced technology, and modern legal demands combine to make bureaucracy inevitable. Bureaucracy in government has been followed by an increase in the bureaucracy of business corporations, trade unions, churches, service groups, and voluntary associations. What is not often understood is that bureaucracy developed as a reaction against the personal subjugation, nepotism, even cruelty of the capricious and subjective judgments of earlier administrative systems (such as monarchies and dictatorships). To see the benefits Weber attributed to bureaucracy, one should consider what it replaced. Today, all organizations in any culture are bureaucratic to some degree.

Advantages of Bureaucracy

The essential characteristics of Weber's ideal bureaucracy are outlined in Table M1.2. Weber claimed certain advantages would accrue to organizations that embodied these characteristics, as follows:

- *Division of labor.* A division of labor will lead to increased efficiency through specialization.

- *Authority hierarchy.* A clear chain of command will develop from the highest to the lowest level of an enterprise (Fayol's scalar principle), defining different levels of authority, and thus individual discretion, as well as enabling better communication.

- *Formal selection.* Employees will be hired and promoted based on merit and expertise, thus benefiting both them and their organization.

- *Career orientation.* Although a measure of flexibility is attained by electing higher-level officials who presumably express the will of an

Table M1.2
Characteristics of Weber's Ideal Bureaucracy

1. *Division of Labor.* Labor is divided so that authority and responsibility are clearly defined.
2. *Authority Hierarchy.* Offices or positions are organized in a hierarchy of authority.
3. *Formal Selection.* All employees are selected on the basis of technical qualifications demonstrated by formal examination, education, or training.
4. *Career Orientation.* Managers are professionals rather than owners of the units they administer. They work for fixed salaries and pursue "careers" within their respective fields.
5. *Formal Rules and Other Controls.* All employees are subject to formal rules and other controls regarding the performance of their duties.
6. *Impersonality.* Rules and other controls are impersonal and uniformly applied in all cases.

electorate (for example, a body of citizens or a board of directors), the employment of career-oriented officials will assure the performance of assigned duties without regard for extraneous pressures.

• *Formal rules and other controls.* Organization efficiency will increase as formal rules and other controls relating to employee performance are enforced.

• *Impersonality.* By applying rules and other controls impersonally and uniformly, involvement with personalities and personal preferences will be avoided. Subordinates will thereby be protected from arbitrary actions of their superiors.

Disadvantages of Bureaucracy

While Weber considered bureaucracy to be the most efficient means of organizing, both his own experience and subsequent research have shown that it often results in certain disadvantages:

• Rules and other controls may take on a significance of their own and, as a consequence, become ends in themselves. A favorite saying of bureaucratic managers is: "I must follow official rules; nothing personal."

• Extreme devotion to rules and other controls may lead to situations in which past decisions are blindly repeated without an appreciation of changed conditions. Such "bureaucratic rigidity" results in managers being compensated for doing what they are told—not for thinking.

• While delegation of authority to lower levels may increase organization effectiveness, it may also encourage an emphasis on subunit rather than overall organization goals, thereby prompting subunit conflict and decreased effectiveness.

- Although rules and other controls are intended to counteract apathy, they may actually contribute to it by defining unacceptable behavior and thus specifying a *minimum* level of acceptable performance. That is, it is possible, once rules have been defined, for employees to remain apathetic, for they now know just how little they can do and still remain secure. This is commonly known as **working to the rules**, meaning that what is not covered by rules is by definition not an employee's responsibility. Unless care is taken, such a situation may result in a "vicious circle of bureaucracy," since once employees discover the appeasing effect of rules, they may push for even more controls in order to further restrict management's power.

Despite these and other criticisms, bureaucracy is a central feature of modern societies. Remember, as envisioned by Weber, bureaucracy is both rational and efficient. To gain its benefits, however, requires learning enough about its characteristics to avoid being controlled by them.

In sum, Weber's ideas have stood the test of time remarkably well. His pioneering work, like those of Taylor and Fayol, has stimulated a wealth of research into the nature and intricacies of organizations. In this respect, it remains a landmark in the early history of organization design.

Notes

1. For example, see Daniel A. Wren, *The Evolution of Management Thought,* 3d ed. (New York: Wiley, 1987).

2. The following section is based on Ralph M. Barnes, *Motion and Time Study Design and Measurement of Work,* 7th ed. (New York: Wiley, 1980), 570–571; Alfred D. Chandler, Jr., "Rise and Evolution of Big Business," in *Encyclopedia of American Economic History,* vol. 2, ed. Glenn Porter (New York: Scribner's, 1980), 619–638; and Alfred D. Chandler, Jr., "The American System and Modern Management," in *Yankee Enterprise,* eds. Otto Mays and Robert C. Post (Washington: Smithsonian Institution Press, 1981), 153–170.

3. Henry R. Towne, "The Engineer as an Economist," *Transactions, American Society of Mechanical Engineers* 7 (1886): 428–432. Also see Harlow S. Person, "The Origin and Nature of Scientific Management," in *Scientific Management in American Industry,* ed. Harlow S. Person (New York: Harper, 1929), 6.

4. David F. Noble, *America By Design: Science, Technology, and the Rise of Corporate Capitalism* (New York: Knopf, 1977), 167.

5. Lyndall F. Urwick, *The Life and Work of Frederick Winslow Taylor* (London: Urwick, Orr & Partners, 1957), 7.

6. Testimony of Frederick W. Taylor, Hearings before the Special Committee of the House of Representatives to Investigate the Taylor and Other Systems of Shop Management under Authority of House Resolution 90, 62nd Cong., 1st sess., October 4, 1911, to February 12, 1912 (Washington: Government Printing Office, 1912), 1388.

7. Frederick W. Taylor, *Shop Management* (New York: Harper, 1903), 21.

8. Horace B. Drury, *Scientific Management: A History and Criticism* (New York: Columbia University Press, 1922), 38; Henry V. R. Scheel, "Some Recollections of Henry Laurence Gantt," *Journal of Industrial Engineering* 12 (May–June 1961): 221.

9. Oscar Kraines, "Brandeis and Scientific Management," *Publication of the American Jewish Historical Society* 41 (September 1951): 41–60.

10. Testimony of Harrington Emerson, U.S. Congress, Senate, *Evidence Taken by the Interstate Commerce Commission in the Matter of Proposed Advances in Freight Rates by Carriers*, 61st Cong., 3d sess., August to December 1910 (Washington: Government Printing Office), S. Doc., 725, Ser. Set 5, 908, 2829.

11. Vladimir I. Lenin, "The Urgent Problems of the Soviet Rule," *Bulletin of the Taylor Society* 4 (June 1919): 35–38. Reprinted from *Pravda, April 28, 1918.*

12. John D. Breeze and Arthur G. Bedeian, *The Administrative Writings of Henri Fayol: A Bibliographic Investigation,* 2d ed. (Monticello, Ill.: Vance Bibliographies, 1988), 3.

13. Charles de Freminville, "Henri Fayol: A Great Engineer, A Great Scientist, and a Great Management Leader," *Bulletin of the Taylor Society* 12 (February 1927): 304.

14. Max Weber, *The Theory of Social and Economic Organization,* ed. and trans. Alexander M. Henderson and Talcott Parsons (New York: Oxford University Press, 1922–1947); Max Weber, *The Methodology of the Social Sciences,* ed. and trans. Edward A. Shils and Henry H. Finch (Glencoe, Ill.: Free Press, 1904–1917/1949); Max Weber, *From Max Weber: Essays in Sociology,* ed. and trans. Hans H. Gerth and C. Wright Mills (New York: Oxford University Press, 1906–1924/1946).

MODULE 2

Strategies for Studying Organizations

Over the past half century, and particularly since 1970, there has been a virtual explosion in research on organizations, with a multiplicity of disciplinary approaches, substantive interests, settings, and fundamental conceptions emerging of how and why organizations behave.[1] Diversity has become a dominant feature of research on organizations.

This diversity has had both positive and negative effects on the development of organization theory as an established field of study. On the plus side, cross-fertilization of ideas among disciplines has safeguarded against academic isolationism and conceptual stagnation. The various disciplines have ensured a wide range of issues being studied and have led to the development of differing methods of research. Boundaries once clearly labeled organizational sociology, industrial/organizational psychology, strategic management, public administration, and so on, are now quite vague, prompting a proliferation of new knowledge in all areas.

On the negative side, diversity has also produced irreconcilable differences in concepts, terminology, and measurement. As a result, much organization research is noncumulative and noncommunicable across disciplines. Confusion and controversy are traditionally characteristic of a new and growing area of study, and organization theory has been no exception.

The aim of this module is to familiarize readers with the more common strategies (that is, methods) of organization research so that they can critically appraise the results of such investigations. As will soon be apparent, each of the methods to be discussed has certain limitations as well as certain strong points. Selection of research methodology is therefore a matter of strategy not morals. As recognized by Homans, "There are neither good nor bad methods but only methods that are more or less effective under particular circumstances."[2]

THE RELATIONSHIP BETWEEN
THEORY AND RESEARCH

Before discussing strategies for studying organizations, it may prove helpful to examine the relationship between theory and research. Our ability to analyze phenomena of various kinds depends on the adequacy of the theoretical schemes we employ. Such theoretical schemes not only help us select the facts that are significant (from among the endless number of facts that exist in an organizational setting), but also help us understand their meaning.

As a consequence, research efforts in any field are greatly aided by development of a substantive body of theory. The two—theory and research—work together. Theory can suggest new ways to design organizations, whereas research can be used to determine the efficacy of new and old patterns of organization design. In this regard, theory serves both as a tool and a goal. The tool function of theory "is evident in the generally accepted proposition that theories guide research by generating *new* predictions not otherwise likely to occur." As a goal, theory is often an end in itself, providing "an economical and efficient means of abstracting, codifying, summarizing, integrating, and storing information."[3] Although the field of organization study is still in an early stage of development, both the tool and the goal functions of its theory are evident throughout the preceding chapters.

The Purpose of Theory

In studying organizations, as in any scientific pursuit, the purpose of theory is to devise simplified explanations of reality. Derived from the Greek word, θεωρια, meaning "contemplation," theory may be more generally defined as the "knowledge of principles."[4] The word **principle**, meaning a statement of fundamental truth, is derived from the Latin word *principium* for "beginning." The great mathematician and philosopher Rene Descartes referred to principles as the "first causes [or source] of all that can be in the world."[5] Being such, principles are often phrased in the form of causal relationships that attempt to explain phenomena. In reference to organization theory, if certain conditions prevail and new phenomena are in accordance with those which a principle covers, then knowledge of the principle should make it possible to more accurately predict behavior in each new situation.

Principles, or "first causes," are derived from **hypotheses**. Regarded as essential to the scientific method, hypotheses are propositions regarding relationships that *possibly* exist among various phenomena. Thus, a group of interrelated principles derived from hypotheses and dealing simultaneously with the same theme is said to comprise a **theory**. Vital to the continued evolution of knowledge in all disciplines, theories are a basic requirement for the ultimate development of organization theory as a science. Figure M2.1 depicts the relationship between theory, hypotheses, and principles.

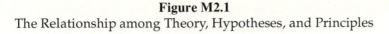

Figure M2.1
The Relationship among Theory, Hypotheses, and Principles

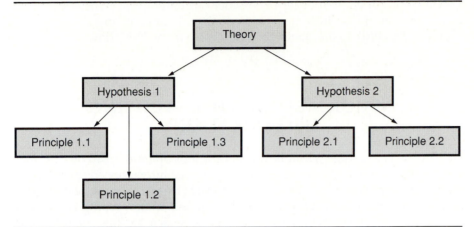

PRESCRIPTIVE VERSUS DESCRIPTIVE THEORY

Organization theory may be characterized as either prescriptive or descriptive. **Prescriptive theory**, also known as **normative theory**, is evaluative in form. It seeks to enhance one's ability to predict and control and thus to specify how things should be done—that is, what works and what does not. Because prescriptive theory involves value judgments, it is often moralistic in nature.

Descriptive theory, on the other hand, is intended to describe and explain what is rather than what should be. Also known as **positive theory**, it seeks to explain why specific things occur, leaving individual theorists to make inferences about how things should be done.

In the past, a certain measure of dissension has centered around the prescriptive role of organization theory. However, it now appears evident that future organization theory will be both prescriptive and descriptive. Organization theory will not only be required to explain why something occurs (descriptive), but it will also be called upon to specify the best ways for it to happen (prescriptive).

The Practicality of Theory

Most of us belong to numerous organizations and will undoubtedly join others in the future. Organizations are a fundamental part of our existence. As a result, each of us has ideas about how organizations operate based on our personal experiences. It may not always be obvious, but we use theories of organization daily.[6] We may have tried to cash a check on an out-of-town bank or tried to register at a hotel that had no record of our reservation or tried to identify a medical specialist familiar with a unique health problem. In such instances, we are literally forced to use some "theory" about how organizations operate in order to conduct our daily lives. Considering this fact, there should be little question whether theories of organization are useful or practical. In a modern society, we use them every day.

MAJOR METHODS FOR STUDYING ORGANIZATIONS

While we all have ideas about how organizations operate based on our own experiences, knowledge drawn solely on personal interactions is necessarily limited. To overcome this limitation, methods of research (or methodologies) used in studying organizations range from broad and sweeping surveys to tightly controlled laboratory experiments. Research studies include field analyses of single or multiple organizations, surveys employing highly structured, self-administered questionnaires on which respondents simply check off appropriate answers, anecdotal accounts of organizational experiences, intensive in-depth interviews, systematic forms of direct observation, and more. At first glance, it would seem that the only feature these approaches have in common is that they are, or are meant to be, of value in the study of organizations.

With additional thought, however, certain commonalities do emerge. This is particularly so if, following McGrath's suggestion, "we consider each of them in terms of the nature of the setting within which data-collection takes place and in terms of the extent to which activities of the investigator intrude upon, or are responsible for, the nature of the setting."[7] Viewed from this perspective, four major strategies for studying organizations can be identified: (1) field studies, (2) interviews and questionnaire surveys, (3) laboratory experiments, and (4) use of secondary source materials.

INTERNAL AND EXTERNAL VALIDITY

Before entering into a discussion of strategies for studying organizations, it would seem wise to touch upon two fundamental questions that are of paramount concern *irrespective* of the research approach taken. These questions relate to the concepts of internal validity and external validity. Both concepts are vital for a complete understanding of research methodology. In general, *validity* refers to the technical soundness of a study. As researchers plan their studies, they must attend to both internal and external validity to safeguard against difficulties that may prohibit meaningful implications being drawn from their finished work.

Internal validity is the basic minimum for making a research effort interpretable. It refers to the extent to which the results of a study can be attributed to a single explanation. Internal validity asks the question, "Has the research strategy in question controlled the influence of extraneous variables that could serve as plausible alternative explanations for why the results of a study turned out the way they did?" Internal validity underlines the necessity, central to any research, of making certain that the influence of all variables that might account for observed changes be taken into consideration both in the design of a study and in the interpretation of its findings. If, when compared to the reported findings, there are no other equally likely interpretations of a study's results, it is said to possess internal validity. Any inferences advanced on the basis of the study in question would seem warranted.

Thus, a study that is internally valid has successfully accounted for all potential influences *except* for the one under study. If, for example, we were comparing the communication effectiveness of two organizations, then it would be desirable for communication structure to be the only systematic difference between the organizations. Figure M2.2 illustrates a research strategy that might be employed. As indicated by the double arrow, the research question involves the effectiveness of Communication Structure 1 as compared with the effectiveness of Communication Structure 2. To design an internally valid study, a researcher must control (or eliminate) all differences between organizations 1 and 2 *except* differences in communication structure. Any other differences between the organizations (for example, size, goals, age) may result in performance differences that appear to be due to communication structure, but in reality are not.

External validity concerns the generalizability of an investigation's results. It asks the question, "To what extent can a study's findings be generalized?" That is, are the findings applicable to or across, persons, settings, and times not represented in its sample? The concern of external validity is whether the results of a study are specific to factors such as the nature of the setting in which the study was conducted and the nature of the persons participating. If not, and its results can be shown to be representative of other realms (populations, situations, times, or settings), the study is said to possess external validity.

In a basic way, external validity addresses the issue of how unusual is the particular organization(s) being studied. Is it sufficiently representative that accurate inferences can be drawn to other organizations? Figure M2.3 illustrates the nature of external validity. As in Figure M2.2, the arrows represent the questions being asked. To what populations, situations, times, or settings can the results of a study be generalized?

Our attention now turns to a discussion of the four major research strategies identified earlier as being among the most commonly used by organization theorists: (1) field studies, (2) interviews and questionnaire surveys, (3) laboratory experiments, and (4) use of secondary source materials.

Figure M2.2
Research Strategy for Comparing Communication
Effectiveness of Two Organizations

——— Comparison Question ———

Communication Structure 1	Communication Structure 2
Organization 1	Organization 2

Source: Adapted from Drew, Clifford J.: *Introduction to Designing and Conducting Research*, 2nd ed., St. Louis, 1980, The C.V. Mosby Co.

Figure M2.3
External Validity Questions Generalizability of
Results to Other Realms

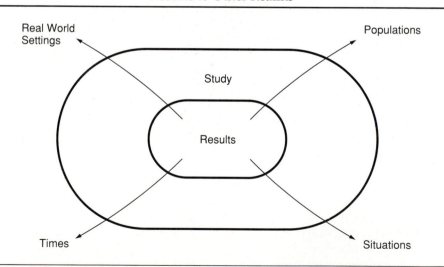

Source: Adapted from Drew, Clifford J.: *Introduction to Designing and Conducting Research*, 2nd ed., St. Louis, 1980, The C.V. Mosby Co.

Field Studies

Numerous research procedures can be classified under the heading *field study:* participant observation, clinical field research, ethnography, qualitative research, naturalistic field observation, and so on.[8] The field study of organizations was pioneered in the early 1950s by investigators who, taking an almost anthropological approach, literally lived and worked in the organizations they studied.

When utilizing the field-study method, one or more researchers or their agents enter an organization, either openly, in the role of investigators, or covertly in some disguised role, for the express purpose of learning more about its activities. Field researchers generally hold that for studying the dynamics of social interaction there is no substitute for participating in the activities of the organization being considered. Thus, data are collected through the use of *field notes* describing those events that seem to have meaning, checklists of specific activities, coding schemes for detailing daily experiences, and ratings of organizational properties judged important based on events and activities observed.

The field-study method is particularly valuable for exploratory analyses of organizations or groups that are not well enough known for investigators to be precise and systematic about the variables they wish to investigate. In such circumstances, the field method is useful for generating hypotheses that can subsequently be tested. This flexibility is of particular value in allowing researchers to modify their data-collection techniques when new insights emerge as a study progresses. In this regard, the depth of penetration and understanding the field method allows is unmatched by any other approach, often leading to the discovery of significant facts that a researcher from "outside" would not find. Some of the richest and most descriptive data on the nature of organizations have come through studies utilizing the field method. Many of these studies are considered classics in the organization theory field.

An outstanding example is Melville Dalton's ten-year, four-firm investigation of conflict between line and staff officials.[9] Dalton was in the unique position of being both a concealed observer (gathering information for his Ph.D. dissertation at the University of Chicago) and a legitimate employee (working his way through school) in two of the firms analyzed in his study. He served as a checker in a steel mill, measuring work output and computing the pay of over 100 employees in a large maintenance department. He recorded events, biographical information, gossip, and initial hypotheses in looseleaf notebooks. Of particular significance was the fact that his job allowed him to circulate freely and at times to have access to personnel files. On occasion, he even had the opportunity to interview various members of the mill's management staff and to socialize with them after regular working hours.

The field-study method has its limitations, though. Ironically, its major strength, intimacy and detail of input, is also one of its principal weaknesses. There is a very real possibility that a researcher who lives and works in an organization over an extended period of time will lose his or her objectivity. In such circumstances, the role of field researcher requires both detachment and personal involvement. Because the internal validity of this type of study depends entirely on the special talents and observational accuracy of the field analyst, the necessity of maintaining a proper perspective cannot be minimized. In the instance of the known observer, this problem is further complicated by the tendency of people who are aware that they are being studied to modify their behavior—a phenomenon known as **subject reactivity**. It is also clear that through the course of data collection, observer accuracy is likely to decline because of forgetting, new learning, fatigue, decreased motivation, and other factors. Such difficulties make replication, usually considered to be a necessary step in scientific progress, virtually impossible.

An additional limitation exists with respect to the concealed observer role. Namely, "the role can only be assumed when the researcher possesses or can acquire the attributes of a subject group member."[10] Toward this end, researchers have pretended to religious beliefs they did not have in order to join a Pentecostal sect; have undergone plastic surgery, lost weight, fabricated their age, and adopted a "new personality" in order to study Air Force recruits during a nine-month training program; and have manufactured symptoms of mental illness in order to enter a mental hospital disguised as a patient.

Given the extremes that some researchers are apparently willing to go to in order to gain access to data, a final problem emerges—the question of ethics. Field studies involving illegal behavior, covert entry into a firm, and deception by researchers regarding their true role are especially open to charges of ethical impropriety. Potential invasion of participant privacy and their possible embarrassment if confidential attitudes or actions are made public must be considered. When commenting about researchers who are in a situation under false pretenses, claiming to be something they are not, Scott points out that "most groups take a dim view of people who tell lies to insiders and reveal secrets to outsiders."[11] In this sense, field researchers operating in concealed observer roles are inevitably spies, double agents, who (to paraphrase Hughes) will ultimately betray their subjects, but with the hope that in the end, the truth will help us all.[12]

Field studies have also been criticized for their lack of measurability. Because the data gathered are generally based on the inevitably biased perceptions and subjective interpretations of individual researchers, quantification is very difficult. Field studies provide no independent check on a researcher's use of ill-defined, idiosyncratic, and unsystematic constructs for selecting, collecting, and aggregating data. Further, since they are presented in narrative form, field studies generally require a great deal of time and space for results to be adequately covered. Where used, quantification is primarily an illustration of patterns of worker interaction. Information pertaining to such factors as an organization's structural properties is usually presented in an almost entirely descriptive fashion. Perhaps of even greater concern is that since statistical techniques do not apply, there is an absence of generally accepted rules for drawing conclusions from field-study data.

There is also substance in the criticism that "generalizations about organizations . . . [can]not be justified on the basis of one or a handful of cases."[13] Having each been conducted by different researchers, in unique social situations, and during specific periods of time, field studies can rarely be duplicated. Hence, generalizations are difficult to make and apply, and external validity is exceedingly difficult to establish. Perhaps Lijphart says it simplest and best: "A single case can constitute neither the basis for a valid generalization nor the ground for disproving an established generalization."[14]

Another shortcoming of the field method is that such studies are often both very time-consuming and very expensive. As previously mentioned, field analyses involve tedious collection of specific data and careful observation over a considerable period of time. Such activities require a trained researcher and, simply put, are hard work. Costs associated with field studies include time, money, and psychological demands. To cite one example, the first sentence of Scheflen's preface to his book, *Communicational Structure,* is particularly telling: "The major effort of ten years of my career has been the analysis of this thirty-minute transaction and the publication of the method and results."[15] Although benefits gained from field studies have been impressive, the costs have been great.

Interviews/Questionnaire Surveys

Given its various limitations, the field-study method is often combined with other research strategies such as surveying or interviewing persons whom the case researcher cannot observe directly. The *interview* and what has been called its "stepbrother," the *questionnaire,* capitalize on language, our most powerful form of communication.[16] Both are especially suited for gathering data on the values, attitudes, and beliefs of individuals as well as information pertaining to the characteristics of the organizations of which they are a part. Moreover, both methods have several special advantages. Most notably, they each allow researchers to exercise considerable control over selection of their subjects. They may choose to study an entire population, or simply some portion of it deemed to be representative of the whole. In the case of the questionnaire, great quantities of comparable data can be collected from large numbers of people (from several hundred into the thousands) by mail or through group administrations in a relatively short time and at minimal cost. Interviews, by comparison, are typically more costly (at least three to five times as much per respondent) and more time-consuming.[17] The collection of comparable data in either case gives the questionnaire/interview approach its chief advantage of restating findings in quantitative terms so that they can be aggregated and subsequently analyzed using computerized statistical techniques.

Although it employed few statistical analyses, an outstanding example of the interview approach to organization research was Gouldner's three-year investigation of a gypsum factory that employed 225 people.[18] One of the first studies of its kind, it described in extensive detail the process of bureaucratization, its causes and its consequences. Of particular interest to our present topic is that the data forming the basis for this study were largely obtained through 174 formal interviews, each lasting an average of an hour-and-a-half to two hours. Of this total, 132 interviewees were drawn from a representative cross-section of employees stratified to take into account seniority, rank, and department affiliation. This database was then supplemented with information gathered through simple observation (for example, walks around the plant) and thousands of pages of documentary material (for example, company reports, memoranda, private correspondence, and newspaper clippings).

A good illustration of the questionnaire approach is Lawrence and Lorsch's investigation of the relationship between environmental differences and effective organization design.[19] Utilizing data from questionnaires augmented on occasion by interviews, Lawrence and Lorsch surveyed key personnel representing the middle- and upper-level management of ten firms in three divergent industrial environments. Data were collected on the assumption that such incumbents have the best vantage point for viewing an entire organizational system, as well as access to information about how a total system operates, by virtue of their managerial positions.

Sources of Error. Before proceeding further, it is important to raise a troublesome issue suggested by both the Gouldner and the Lawrence and Lorsch studies. This concerns the *reliability* of data received from respondents. The very nature of self-reported data is somewhat suspect, because when individuals talk or write about themselves, events they took part in, or the actions of others, their statements have often been shown to more accurately reflect their own wishes and their relationship to those inquiring than the reality of a situation. All too often this type of error goes unacknowledged, and, as suggested by Rubenstein and Haberstroh, it is implicitly assumed "that reports of events by informants or subjects correspond closely or exactly with the actual way in which the events occurred."[20] Rubenstein and Haberstroh give insight into the sources of error that may contaminate a researcher's data and thus prevent determining what "really happened." The following is taken from their discussion:

> 1. One general source of error is the informant's perceptual slant—his
> **Einstellung**, or perceptual set. The effect of perceptual set or slant has been investigated by many students of intergroup prejudice by such means as attitude tests. Perceptual ability is also known to vary and much has been said about it.

Reports of a given event from several witnesses without training in careful observation have often been found to bear little resemblance to each other.

2. A second general source of error is the informant's failure to remember just what did happen. Assuming that he received a fairly reliable impression of an event at the time that it happened, it has been indicated by experiments in recall and by the experience of all of us that it generally becomes more difficult with passage of time to describe the details of an event as we originally perceived it. A great deal has been said on this matter in relation to the reliability of witness reports weeks or months after the occurrence of the event.

3. A third general source of error may be the reluctance of the subject, for whatever reason, to report his "true" impression of what occurred. This condition has been encountered often in organizational studies where subjects may distort descriptions of events or interpersonal relationships for fear of retaliation, desire not to upset others, or a general reluctance to verbalize a particular type of situation or event.

4. Assuming that all of these sources of error have been acknowledged and accounted for, there is a fourth and overriding source of error which is usually explicit in rigorously designed and executed investigations—the inability of the subject to communicate his or her report; or conversely, the inability of the investigator to get from the subject through whatever techniques (interview, questionnaire, observation) the information that the subject is willing and able to give.

One last difficulty involves the true representativeness of samples included in interviews and questionnaire surveys. A systematic theory of organizations should be based on data from a representative sample of all organizations of all types. As Meyer has noted, "It is hard to know what constitutes a representative sample of organizations . . . and we can never be sure that any sample is representative of all extant organizations, as in public opinion polls.[21] Whereas conventional interview/questionnaire research primarily relies on the use of probability samples drawn from a defined population to minimize the likely margin of error, organizational studies seldom draw random samples and no claim of representativeness can be made. For the most part, organizational researchers have relied on two sampling strategies: (1) sampling from lists of specific types of organizations, and (2) sampling by "aegis" (that is, conducting research in one or more organizations to which access has been granted under the sponsorship of an upper-level manager). External validity of results in either circumstance is, of course, quite suspect.

As preceding comments suggest, both the development of a list of items for a questionnaire and the development of a line of questioning to be pursued in an interview require a great deal of work and, in some instances, are part art and part science. Moreover, given the scarceness in most research settings of support staff, time, and resources it is essential that a study's population sample be chosen wisely.

Laboratory Experiments

The problems associated with the interview and questionnaire approaches have led to the development of a third research strategy—*laboratory experiments*. Within the context of organization theory, the term **laboratory** refers to *any* setting that allows an investigator to rigorously control conditions under which observations are made. It is thus simply an analytic concept and does not necessarily denote test tubes, white coats, one-way mirrors, or any other paraphernalia typical of many experimental settings. An office, a factory, or a government bureau may function as a laboratory.

The most important feature of laboratory experiments is the possibility of experimental manipulation and control. In a laboratory experiment, the conditions under which an event occurs are deliberately varied to assess the effect of one or more independent (manipulated) variables on one or more dependent (observed) variables, while other influences which are not of interest are held constant. Of course, this requires establishment of highly precise and controlled conditions. Figure M2.4 presents this idea pictorially.

Such control allows the systematic variation of dependent-variable measures as well as the systematic modification of the independent variables whose influence is being investigated. As a result of this greater control, conclusive answers can often be obtained and relatively precise and subtle theoretical points tested. Laboratory experiments are thus excellent when honing concepts and refining measurement techniques. They are even more valuable when the conditions necessary to test a hypothesis are uneconomical, difficult, or even impossible to obtain using other research strategies.

The prime criticism of the laboratory approach concerns the issue of realism versus artificiality—that is, whether laboratory experiments truly reflect realities of organizational life. Both sides in this debate have their vocal advocates, and at times their exchange of views has become quite heated. Barnes, for one, argues that laboratory experiments are seldom representative of real-world organizational conditions. In pursuing this point, he offers the following observations:

> The laboratory involves a temporary system; the organization is a quasi-permanent system that exists beyond the lives of its members. The laboratory sets up temporary human relationships which all too often have a pretend-like quality. Organizations require relationships that are, so the slang expression goes, "for real." The laboratory builds an ambiguous hierarchy in which subjects report to an experimenter most often as volunteer or nonvolunteer enrollees taking his college course. An organization has several complex hierarchical systems which depend upon both formal authority and colleague influence over a period of time.[22]

To this Barnes adds, "To change and study a single variable in a laboratory may be relatively easy compared with isolating, changing, and studying the variable within an organization."

Figure M2.4
Simple Laboratory Experiment Model

a. Relationship between Independent and Dependent Variables

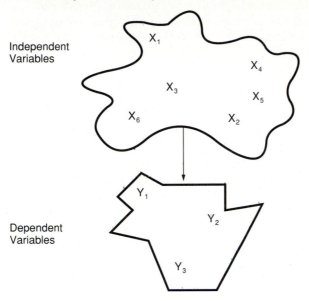

Independent
Variables

Dependent
Variables

b. Experimental Manipulation and Control

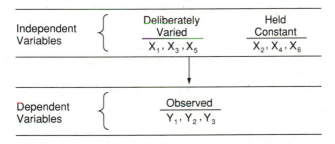

Independent Variables	Deliberately Varied	Held Constant
	X_1, X_3, X_5	X_2, X_4, X_6

Dependent Variables	Observed
	Y_1, Y_2, Y_3

Source: Adapted from Alphonse Chapanis, "The Relevance of Laboratory Studies to Practical Situations," *Ergonomics* 10 (1970): 562–563.

In response to such criticisms, defenders of the laboratory approach turn the argument around and reply that this is precisely the pupose of taking an issue into the laboratory—to "see the phenomenon for what it actually is, not as we ordinarily find it camouflaged in the natural element. In the laboratory, the only reality that counts is the reality of the variable we are looking at, and it is just as real there as it is anywhere else."[23] Hence, it is the defender's position that, to the extent laboratory experiment artificiality stems from control over irrelevant variables, the artificiality is a strength and not a weakness.

In further defense of the laboratory experiment, Weick contends that "one of the ironies of laboratory experimentation is that presumed liabilities turn out to be conceptual assets for organizational researchers."[24] To support his contention, he notes numerous similarities (as opposed to Barnes' contrasts) between laboratory experiments and conditions that prevail in many organizations.

> To illustrate, participants in experiments are apprehensive about being evalu-ated, but so are ambitious employees. Laboratory tasks require limited skills, ignoring the "rest" of what the person brings to the laboratory, but the same holds true with a division of labor and partial inclusion. Relationships be-tween experimenter and subject involve asymmetrical power, but the same holds true for superiors and subordinates. Subjects seldom know why they are doing the things they do in laboratories but employees often operate under similar conditions of ignorance and faith. Participants in laboratory groups sel-dom know one another intimately, but the same is true in organizations where personnel transfers are common, where temporary problem solving units are the rule, and where impression management is abundant. People participate in experiments for a variety of reasons, but the decision to participate in an or-ganization is similarly overdetermined. Finally, people are suspicious of what happens to them in laboratories, but so are employees suspicious as they be-come alerted to the reality of hidden agendas and internal politics.[25]

The significance of these competing views leads us directly to consider-ing the degree or extent to which the results of laboratory experiments may be generalized to real-life organizational settings. This, of course, involves the crucial question of external validity. If, indeed, the purpose of taking an issue into the laboratory is to avoid dealing with the "camouflage" common to field conditions, it should be clearly realized that, when conditions in an experiment are hard to find in everyday life, external validity (that is, the generalizability of results) is severely restricted. Nevertheless, it should not be automatically assumed that results of other research strategies are more generalizable.

The generalizability of laboratory findings in comparison with the results of other types of investigations is an empirical matter requiring careful attention to the populations, situations, settings, and times sampled in a study relative to the populations, situations, settings, and times to which one wishes to generalize. Research conducted under supposedly artificial condi-tions need not be less externally valid than research performed in a more natural situation.[26]

As one might suspect, given the controversy surrounding the laboratory approach, it is the least used of the research strategies employed by organi-zation theorists. One example, however, is Huber, O'Connell, and Cummings' study of the effects of environmental information and group structure (independent variable) on an individual's judgment of perceived uncertainty (dependent variable).[27] To tightly control the objective environment and test the hypotheses in question, a laboratory simulation in which three-person decision-making teams (students) played a military game was employed. Information concerning the state of the objective environment was varied on two dimensions, load (low, medium, or high number of messages) and specificity (low or high content). Team structure was controlled at two levels, loose and tight. Significant relationships were found between perceived environmental uncertainty and both information load (amount) and team structure.

Secondary Source Materials

A fourth and final major strategy for studying organizations is the use of archival data that others have compiled; these constitute *secondary materials*. An important and relatively inexpensive source of information about organizations, secondary materials are especially useful for obtaining background information otherwise unavailable. Secondary sources are virtually unlimited. Materials included in this category vary from raw files, such as transcripts of meetings, correspondence, organization charts, personnel files, and policy manuals, to already prepared statistics, such as departmental budgets and operating costs. Some organizations even publish employee-directed newsletters, newspapers, and periodicals. In many cases, data can also be found in directories like the *Encyclopedia of Associations* or in reports compiled by various government agencies.

A great many organization theory studies make use of secondary-source materials. Some rely upon them almost exclusively, while others use them as a supplementary aid to gain insight into various facets of a research problem. For instance, Miles and Cameron primarily relied on published firm and industry sources (for example, annual reports, *Moody's Industrial Manual*, special reports submitted to public agencies, and in-house reports), reports of government agencies (for example, Federal Trade Commission, Center for Disease Control, Department of Agriculture, Federal Communications Commission), press releases of special interest groups (for example, Action on Smoking and Health, American Cancer Society, American Heart Association), and reports of tobacco industry lobbies (for example, Tobacco Tax Council, Tobacco Institute, Tobacco Research Council), to analyze attempts of the U.S. tobacco industry to cope with environmental threats emanating from the smoking and health controversy.[28] These sources were supplemented by articles appearing in popular and professional publications.

A principal advantage in using such material is that it can be relatively inexpensive to collect. However, the cost benefit is not always as great as first might be assumed. For example, the expense associated with selecting and separating desired information from available administrative records can be quite high, especially if it must be done by hand. An amazing number of organizations do not maintain their administrative files in usable or retrievable form. "It is not uncommon to find that whereas absenteeism data are kept for individuals for pay purposes, no summaries are ever made, and thus obtaining absenteeism rates for units or departments requires a great deal of work (e.g., going through the individual absenteeism records, one by one, to get the needed data)."[29] While possibilities for substantial economies do exist, they are not always realized.

A second issue concerns the accessibility of secondary-source materials. Since 1966 access to government records has been facilitated by the Freedom of Information Act. However, availability of information on individuals has been complicated by the 1974 Privacy Act. Acquisition of data falling within the jurisdiction of both acts can be quite involved.

Without going into detail, there are other concerns associated with using secondary-source materials.

1. Available secondary-source materials are often dated or otherwise unsuitable for a research problem's specific purpose.

2. Different units of measurement may have been used by different organizations or sources. Consequently, combining several data sources may lead to erroneous conclusions.

3. If previously unreleased information is not kept confidential, the subject(s) of a study could be publicly embarrassed.

Multiple Research Methods

No single research method is wholly satisfactory. Field studies and laboratory experiments can be relatively accurate but may not be generalizable. Interviews and questionnaire surveys may be generalizable but lose a certain measure of richness and accuracy by aggregating different frames of reference. In some instances, secondary-source materials may be more objective than data obtained by other means, but then again, this is not always so. Documents and records can seldom be taken at face value, since they typically reflect the biases and interests of those who compile them. Often they are obsolete or sloppily maintained, and there is always the chance that they have been fudged in order to look good to higher executives and funding sources or to prevent lawsuits.

For these reasons, the use of multiple research methods is generally advocated. Known as **triangulation**, this practice is believed to counter-balance the weaknesses of different methodologies by the strengths of others. The triangulation metaphor is taken from the surveying technique for accurately fixing (establishing) the position of an unknown point from the bearings of two or more known points. In organization research, it can be exceedingly difficult to fix the degree to which a measure actually reflects the phenomenon it is intended to gauge. Relating it to other measures helps. Hence, it has become a standard research rule of thumb that all important variables should be measured by at least two methods.[30]

Perhaps more importantly, results obtained from one method are not only useful in confirming the results produced by another method, but when combined, can be essential in accurately interpreting research outcomes. As Nadler advises,

> One can avoid misinterpreting information or jumping to false conclusions by cross checking important pieces of information through other methods of data collection. For example, if a questionnaire indicates major problems around supervision in one department, it may be useful to interview some supervisors and nonsupervisory personnel in the specific department for more detailed information. It also may be valuable to spend some time in the department observing the interactions between supervisors and subordinates. The most effective data collection strategy, therefore, is one that uses multiple measures and multiple methods of data collection. It is by combining data from interviews, questionnaires, observations, and archival sources that the consultant is able to triangulate and thus discard the data that may be distorted or biased.[31]

Bourgeois' study of the relationship between top-management perceptions of environmental uncertainty, strategic goals, and industry volatility in explaining economic performance in 20 firms is a fine example of triangulation. In addition to interviews with chief executive officers, data from questionnaire surveys, and secondary-source materials (industry statistics and annual reports) were combined to measure the study's focal variables.[32]

On balance, the research strategies reviewed are more powerful when used in coordination than when used separately. Field studies, laboratory experiments, interviews/questionnaire surveys, and secondary-source materials should be viewed as complementary rather than conflicting methodologies. Suitability of each depends in large part on the nature of the problem, how much is known about the variables involved, the extent to which these variables can be manipulated and observed, and the quality and accessibility of additional information relating to the problem. All the research strategies discussed have strengths and weaknesses that must be carefully weighed against one another. These are summarized in Table M2.1.

Notes

1. John R. Kimberly, "The Study of Organizations: Toward a Biographical Perspective," in *Handbook of Organizational Behavior,* ed. Jay W. Lorsch (Englewood Cliffs, N.J.: Prentice-Hall, 1987), 226.

2. George C. Homans, "The Strategy of Industrial Sociology," *American Journal of Sociology* 54 (1949): 330.

3. Melvin H. Marx, "The General Nature of Theory Construction," in *Theories in Contemporary Psychology*, ed. Melvin H. Marx (New York: Macmillan, 1963), 6.

4. W. Stanley Jevons, *Elementary Lessons in Logic* (New York: Macmillan, 1882), 340.

Table M2.1

Summary of Strengths and Weaknesses of the Most Common
Strategies for Studying Organizations

Strengths	Weaknesses
Field Studies	
1. Useful for exploratory analyses	1. Based on the perceptions and subjective interpretations of the researcher(s)
2. Useful for gaining insights and generating propositions	2. Causes problem of reactivity
3. Flexibility to capitalize on new insights that emerge as a study develops	3. Lacks measurability
4. Depth of penetration and understanding	4. Requires a great deal of time and space for presentation of results
	5. Difficult to draw generalizations and establish external validity
	6. Time-consuming and expensive
	7. Requires careful observation and tedious collection of specific details
	8. Limits to the concealed observer role
Interview/Questionnaire Studies	
1. Especially suited for the collection of data describing employee values, attitudes, and beliefs, as well as organizational characteristics	1. Reliability of data collected (i.e., self-report bias)
2. Control over selection of subjects	2. Problem of perceptual slant
3. Capable of generating large amounts of comparable data	3. Subjects' failure to remember what happened
4. Relatively fast and inexpensive	4. Reluctance of subjects to tell the truth
5. Suited to the quantification of findings	5. Inability of subjects/researchers to communicate
6. Allow statistical data analysis	6. Questionable representativeness of samples and questionable external validity of results
	7. Difficulty of establishing external validity

5. Rene Descartes, *Discourse on Method*, trans. John Vietch (Chicago: Open Court Publishing, 1899), 68. Originally published 1637.

6. This paragraph paraphrases Ronald G. Corwin and Roy Edfelt, *Perspectives on Organization* (Washington: American Association of Colleges for Teacher Education, 1976), 14.

Table M2.1

(continued)

Strengths	Weaknesses
Laboratory Experiments	
1. Possibility of control and manipulation of variables	1. Artificiality—questionable realism
2. Allow for the creation of conditions that may be uneconomical, difficult, or even impossible to establish in the field	2. Requires highly controlled conditions
3. Excellent for sharpening concepts and refining measurements	3. Difficult to generalize results to real-life situations and to establish external validity
4. Allow a researcher to examine phenomena in an uncamouflaged state	
Secondary-Source Materials	
1. Relatively inexpensive	1. Truthworthiness unknown
2. Typically plentiful	2. Possible problem of accessibility
3. Helpful in providing background material	3. Often unsuitable for a research problem's specific purpose
	4. Units of measurement may not be comparable between sources
	5. Privacy of subjects may be infringed upon

7. Joseph E. McGrath, "Toward a 'Theory of Method' for Research on Organizations," in *New Perspectives in Organization Research,* ed. William W. Cooper, Harold J. Leavitt, and Maynard W. Shelly, II (New York: Wiley, 1964), 536.

8. The field study literature is voluminous. For a representative sampling, see Karl E. Weick, "Systematic Observational Methods," in *Handbook of Social Psychology,* vol. 1, 3d ed., eds. Gardner Lindzey and Elliot Aronson (New York: Random House, 1986), 567–634; Robert B. Bechtel and John Zeisel, "Observation—The World Under a Glass," in *Methods in Environmental and Behavioral Research,* ed. Robert B. Bechtel, Robert W. Marans, and William Michelson (New York: Van Nostrand Reinhold, 1987), 11–40.

9. O. Melville Dalton, *Men Who Manage: Fusions of Feeling and Theory in Administration* (New York: Wiley, 1959).

10. W. Richard Scott, "Field Methods in the Study of Organizations," in *Handbook of Organizations,* ed. James G. March (Chicago: Rand McNally, 1965), 272.

11. Ibid., 274.

12. Everett C. Hughes, quoted in John Van Maanen and Deborah Kolb, "The Professional Apprentice: Observations on Field Work Roles in Two Organizational Settings," *Research in the Sociology of Organizations* 4 (1985): 24.

13. Marshall W. Meyer, *Theory of Organizational Structure* (Indianapolis: Bobbs-Merrill, 1977), 70.

14. Arend Lijphart, "Comparative Policies and the Comparative Method," *American Political Science Review* 65 (1971): 691.

15. Albert E. Scheflen, *Communicational Structure* (Bloomington: Indiana University Press, 1973), xi.

16. Thomas J. Bouchard, "Field Research Methods: Interviewing, Questionnaires, Participant Observation, Systematic Observation, Unobtrusive Measures," in *Handbook of Industrial and Organizational Psychology,* ed. Marvin D. Dunnette (Chicago: Rand McNally, 1976), 368.

17. Edward E. Lawler III, David A. Nadler, and Cortlandt Cammann, eds., *Organizational Assessment: Perspectives on the Measurement of Organizational Behavior and the Quality of Worklife* (New York: Wiley, 1980), 332.

18. Alvin W. Gouldner, *Patterns of Industrial Bureaucracy* (Glencoe, Ill.: Free Press, 1954).

19. Paul R. Lawrence and Jay W. Lorsch, *Organizations and Environment: Managing Differentiation and Integration* (Boston: Division of Research, Graduate School of Business Administration, Harvard University, 1967).

20. Albert H. Rubenstein and Chadwick J. Haberstroh, *Some Theories of Organization,* rev. ed. (Homewood, Ill: Irwin, 1966), 699.

21. Meyer, *Theory,* 66, 75.

22. Louis B. Barnes, "Organizational Change and Field Experiment Methods," in *Methods of Organizational Research,* ed. Victor H. Vroom (Pittsburgh: University of Pittsburgh Press, 1967), 77.

23. Dennis W. Organ and Thomas Bateman, *Organizational Behavior: An Applied Psychological Approach,* 3d ed. (Plano, Tex.: Business Publications, 1986), 53.

24. Karl E. Weick, "Laboratory Experimentation with Organizations: A Reappraisal," *Academy of Management Review* 2 (1977): 124.

25. Robert J. Swieringa and Karl E. Weick, "An Assessment of Laboratory Experiments in Accounting," *Journal of Accounting Research* 20 (Supplement 1982): 74.

26. Edwin A. Locke, ed., *Generalizing from Laboratory to Field Settings* (Lexington, MA: Lexington Books, 1986).

27. George P. Huber, Michael J. O'Connell, and Larry L. Cummings, "Perceived Environmental Uncertainty: Effects of Information and Structure," *Academy of Management Journal* 18 (1975): 725–740.

28. Robert H. Miles and Kim S. Cameron, *Coffin Nails and Corporate Strategies* (Englewood Cliffs, N.J.: Prentice-Hall, 1982).

29. Lawler et al., eds., *Organizational Assessment,* 344.

30. Ibid., 342.

31. David A. Nadler, *Feedback and Organizational Development: Using Data-Based Methods* (Reading, Mass.: Addison-Wesley, 1977), 140.

32. L. Jay Bourgeois III, "Strategic Goals, Perceived Uncertainty, and Economic Performance in Volatile Environments," *Academy of Management Journal* 28 (1985): 548–573.

GLOSSARY

Administrative Man Term for a decision maker who is subject to bounded rationality.

Advanced Information Technologies Information management software using databases on distributed computer networks.

Analyzer Organization that has a relatively broad domain of operation and competes on the basis of efficiency. *See* Defender and Prospector.

Aspiration Level A subjectively defined goal for organizational performance.

Autonomy A core job design characteristic referring to the extent to which an individual has discretion in job performance.

Bounded Rationality Term meaning that decisions are not completely rational but rather are bounded by the limited mental capacity and emotions of the individuals involved, as well as by environmental factors over which they may have no control.

Bureaucracy A system of management pioneered by Max Weber.

Carrying Capacity Term from population ecology referring to the maximum number of organizations a population niche can support at equilibrium.

Centrality (Group) A group's importance and degree of connectivity of its assigned tasks.

Centralization/Decentralization The extent that decision-making authority is delegated within an organization.

Certainty Condition of decision making in which the available alternatives and the benefits (or costs) associated with each are known.

Coalition An alliance of individuals or groups who believe they can attain something they value through an organization.

Computer-Integrated Manufacturing An automated production system of people, machines, and tools linked electronically for the planning and control of the production process, which includes the acquisition of raw materials, parts, and components and the shipment and service of finished goods.

Consortia An interorganizational design where a number of organizations join forces to collectively pursue a common interest, such as research and development.

Contingency Theory Approach to the study of organization-environment relations postulating that effective organization design is contingent on prevailing environmental conditions.

Continuous Change Changes in niche shape and size that occur gradually so that conditions within a niche are not noticeably different over relatively short periods of time. *See* Discontinuous Change.

Continuous-Process Technology An automated production system that manufactures high volumes of liquids, gases, or crystalline substances.

Cooptation Absorption of key resisters or various influential people into an enterprise's decision-making structure.

Decentralization *See* Centralization.

Decision Making The act of choosing between two or more alternatives. *See* Certainty, Risk, and Uncertainty.

Dedicated Automation Devices that perform their functions with little human intervention but are dedicated to a single or a few functions.

Defender Organization that has a relatively narrow domain of operation and competes on the basis of efficiency. *See* Analyzer and Prospector.

Descriptive (Positive) Theory Theory that seeks to describe and explain what is rather than what should be.

Deutero-Learning The capacity of learning to learn.

Differentiation Segmentation of an organization into distinct subunits, resulting from environmental complexity and dynamism. *See* Integration.

Discontinuous Change Changes in niche shape and size that occur rapidly so that conditions within a niche are noticeably different over relatively short periods of time. *See* Continuous Change.

Domain Abandonment Exiting an industry niche, usually through divestiture or by closing a division's operations.

Domain Consolidation Consolidation of an existing domain to the organization's areas of core expertise.

Domain Continuity Maintaining an existing organizational domain while focusing on operational issues within it.

Domain Creation Development of new performance opportunities through the creation of new operational domains, usually through research and development or by acquisition. *See* Domain Defense and Domain Offense.

Domain Defense Domain tactic undertaken to protect the legitimacy of an organization's domain through the creation and control of information, and through political action. *See* Domain Creation and Domain Offense.

Domain Offense Domain tactic focusing on increasing an organization's economic performance by expanding its domain of operation into adjacent product or market areas. *See* Domain Creation and Domain Defense.

Domain Strategy Refers to the breadth of an organization's domain and how it exploits opportunities within it. *See* Defender, Analyzer, Prospector.

Domain Substitution Substitution of one operational domain for another through research and development, acquisition, or other interorganizational arrangements.

Domain Tactic Action taken to modify or protect an organization's domain of operation. *See* Domain Creation, Domain Defense, and Domain Offense.

Dynamic Networks A vertically disaggregated interorganizational design where two or more organizations specialize in the design, production, distribution, and marketing of a good or service. This form is typically contract-based and is coordinated through the "primary" or "broker" organization.

Economic Man Term for hypothetical decision maker who is completely rational and seeks to maximize benefits.

Economies of Scale Low unit cost associated with the high-volume production of a standardized good.

Economies of Scope Increased flexibility and relatively low unit costs gained in the high-volume production of a set of goods.

Effectiveness *See* Goal Approach, System-Resource Approach, and Stakeholder Approach.

Efficiency The ratio of some output (goods or services) to some input (e.g., labor, capital, raw materials).

Einstellung An informant's perceptual set or slant

Enacted Environment The parts of an organization's general environment that its managers perceive and act upon.

Entropy The tendency for a system, without the continual infusion of new resources, to deteriorate until it eventually fades.

External Validity The generalizability of an investigation's results.

Formalization The use of rules, policies, and procedures, training, and socialization to standardize behavior in an organization. *Also see* Socialization.

Functional Interdependence The interdependence among functional specialists charged with completing a common project.

Functional Unit Grouping Unit grouping in which individuals performing similar jobs or tasks are placed within the same unit.

Garbage-Can Model Model that emphasizes the impact of chance and timing in determining organizational decisions.

General Environment The sum of factors outside an organization's boundaries that influence, or may influence, its structure, goals, and effectiveness.

Generalist Organization Term from population ecology referring to an organization with a relatively broad domain of operation. *See* Specialist Organization.

Globally Integrated Designs Interdependent networks of geographically dispersed divisions coordinated through a global headquarters.

Goal Approach An approach to assessing organization effectiveness that views organizations as principally concerned with the attainment of specific end states or goals.

Goal Displacement One of two types of goal transformation in which an organization substitutes some other goal for its original goal.

Goal Succession The deliberate replacement of an organization's primary goal, once it has been achieved, with a new goal.

Horizontal Job Specialization The extent to which a complete job is divided into smaller, component tasks.

Hybrid Structure A structure comprising a mix of design strategies. Some parts of a mixed structure may conform to a functional design, others to a market-based design, and yet others may represent a compromise.

Hypothesis A proposition regarding relationships that *possibly* exist among various phenomena.

Incomplete Divisionalization Partially divisionalized structure where some staff units report directly to corporate headquarters instead of to the divisions.

Incrementalism Term meaning that, rather than consider all options, decision makers limit their search to a few alternatives differing only slightly (that is, incrementally) from the status quo.

Industrial Revolution A rapid major economic change occurring around 1776, marking the transfer of work skills from craftworkers to machines.

Industry Niche A resource space that defines the performance opportunities available to an industry's member organizations. *See* Niche Size and Niche Shape.

Innovation The implementation of new ideas; a principal process by which change occurs.

Integrating Manager Integrating mechanism wherein one manager is responsible for coordinating efforts of all units working on some aspect of producing a good or service.

Integrating Mechanisms Design options that enhance horizontal communication to increase coordination across unit boundaries. *See* Liaison Position, Task Forces and Standing Committees, Integrating Manager, Matrix Unit Grouping.

Integration Process of unifying the efforts of differentiated subunits through the use of coordinating and integrating mechanisms. *See* Differentiation.

Intensive Technology Characterized by the use of a variety of different techniques and skills to transform an object into a finished good or service, accompanied by reciprocal interdependence among units. *See* Reciprocal Interdependence.

Interdependence The relationship created whenever one person or unit does not entirely control all the tasks, information, or resources necessary for completing a project.

Internal Validity The extent to which the results of a study can be attributed to a single explanation.

Interorganizational Designs Created when two or more organizations choose to cooperate by combining their strengths to overcome individual weaknesses.

Job Enlargement The job design practice of adding tasks to a job to increase job scope, or range, decreasing horizontal job specialization.

Job Enrichment The job design practice of adding responsibilities to a job to increase employee discretion in job performance, decreasing vertical job specialization.

Joint Ventures An interorganizational design where two or more organizations jointly invest in a project of mutual interest.

Key Result Area A result area vital to an organization's existence.

K-Strategist Term from population ecology referring to an organization that competes on the basis of efficiency. *See r*-strategist.

Laboratory Any setting that allows an investigator to rigorously control conditions under which observations are made.

Legitimacy A global or summary belief that an organization is good or has a legitimate right to continue its operations.

Liaison Position Integrating mechanism in which a position is created as a common point of contact to facilitate horizontal communication between two units.

Licensing Arrangements An interorganizational design where one organization licenses its brand name to another.

Long-Linked Technology Characterized by the mass-production assembly line and accompanied by sequential interdependence among units. *See* Sequential Interdependence.

Market-Based Unit Grouping Unit grouping practice in which all individuals involved in a workflow are placed together in a unit regardless of their function.

Marketing and Distribution Agreements An interorganizational design where two or more organizations agree to market and distribute the other's goods or services.

Mass-Production Technology A production system that produces large volumes of a standardized good.

Matrix Unit Grouping Unit grouping that uses both functional and project lines of authority within an organization.

Means-Ends Inversion The substitution of means (the methods for doing work) for ends (outputs).

Mechanistic Systems Term referring to organizations with rigid structures, distinct functional specialities, precisely defined tasks and responsibilities, and a well-defined chain of command. *See* Organic Systems.

Mediating Technology A technology that entails the joining together of independent clients and customers, accompanied by pooled interdependence among units. *See* Pooled Interdependence.

Minority Equity Investments An interorganizational design where one organization purchases a minority equity position in another organization.

Niche Collapse A discontinuous change in niche shape that eliminates previous performance opportunities and replaces them with others.

Niche Contraction A discontinuous decrease in niche size that leads to industry decline.

Niche Creation The initial appearance of an industry niche where member organizations attempt to establish the legitimacy of goods or services produced.

Niche Dissolution A continuous change in niche shape that eliminates some performance opportunities while opening others.

Niche Erosion A continuous decrease in niche size conducive to industry decline.

Niche Eruption A discontinuous increase in niche size conducive to industry growth.

Niche Evolution A continuous evolution in the shape of an industry niche that expands the range of performance opportunities.

Niche Expansion A continuous increase in niche size conducive to industry growth.

Niche Shape Defines the *ranges or types* of activities that an industry's niche will support. A variety of factors shape niches, such as consumer preferences, technological development, and government regulations and policies, by determining what is possible and what is not.

Niche Size The size of an industry niche defines the *level or amount* of performance a niche will support. A niche's size is determined by several factors, including consumer demand, the availability of raw materials, economic conditions, and so on.

Nonsubstitutability (Group) The replaceability of a group's activities.

Normative Theory *See* Prescriptive Theory.

Number Magic *See* Over-Measurement.

Official Goals The general aims of an organization as expressed in its corporate charter, annual reports, and the public statements of its top managers.

Open System A system that depends on other systems for its inputs.

Operative Goals The actual intentions of an organization as disclosed by its operating policies.

Optimum Decision Best possible decision.

Organic Systems Term referring to organizations with flexible structures, loosely defined tasks, and communication that resembles consultation rather than order-giving. *See* Mechanistic Systems.

Organization Chart Schematic device showing the formal hierarchy of authority among positions and jobs within an organization.

Organization Design The managerial activity of creating and modifying an organization's structure. *See* Organization Structure.

Organization Structure The patterns of coordination and control, workflows, authority, and communication that channel the activity of an organization's members.

Organizational Domain An organization's domain of operation is defined by the goods and services it produces, and by the customers or clients it serves.

Organizational Form An organization's form is defined by its goals, technologies, structures, and markets. *See* Organizational Population and Population Ecology.

Organizational Goals Those ends that an organization seeks to achieve by its existence and operation.

Organizational Learning The process by which an organization develops knowledge about the relationship of its actions to environmental outcomes.

Organizational Population Term from population ecology referring to a group of organizations with a similar organizational form. *See* Organizational Form.

Organizational Slack The difference between the total resources available to an organization and the total side payments necessary to maintain participant contributions.

Organized Anarchy An organization with no clear or consistent idea of what it is trying to do, how it is supposed to do it, or who should make decisions.

Over-Measurement The tendency to attach an artificial importance to goals that are easy to quantify and hence readily measurable. Also known as number magic.

Performance Feedback A core job design characteristic referring to the extent to which employees receive information about the quality of their task performance.

Pooled Interdependence A condition where units within an organization may not directly interact but are interdependent because unless each performs adequately, the survival of the whole organization is threatened. *See* Mediating Technology.

Population Density Term from population ecology referring to the extent that a population niche is filled by organizations.

Population Ecology An approach to the study of organization-environment relations that focuses on organizational adaptation through environmental changes that favor the creation of new organizational forms and the demise of old ones.

Population Niche Term from population ecology referring to the resource and constraint space within which a population of organizations can exist.

Positive Theory *See* Descriptive Theory.

Prescriptive (Normative) Theory Theory that seeks to enhance one's ability to predict and control and thus to specify how things should be done.

Principle A statement of fundamental truth.

Productivity A measure of an enterprise's ability to produce more goods/services with less inputs (people, materials, money, information) and thus for less cost.

Programmable Automation Devices that perform a significant number of their functions without human intervention and can be changed from one task to another by reprogramming their software.

Prospector Organization that has a relatively broad domain of operation and competes on the basis of being first-to-market. *See* Analyzer and Defender.

Rational Decision A decision that is fully objective and logical.

Reciprocal Interdependence A condition where units involved in the production of a good or service rely on feedback from the object being transformed and on mutual adjustment among units to coordinate their efforts. *See* Intensive Technology.

Research Grants and R&D Partnerships An interorganizational design where one organization enters into an agreement to fund or participate in research with another organization.

Resource-Dependence Model Model of organization-environment relations that emphasizes the dependence of an organization on other organizations to obtain necessary resources, and on the subsequent actions managers take to reduce the uncertainty caused by dependence.

Risk Condition of decision making in which the available alternatives, the likelihood of their occurrence, and the potential benefits (or costs) associated with each are known.

r-**Strategist** Term from population ecology referring to organizations that compete on the basis of moving quickly to exploit resource opportunities and being first-to-market. *See* K-Strategist.

Satisficing Settling for a "satisfactory," or "good enough," alternative rather than searching for the optimum choice.

Scientific Management An approach to management pioneered by Frederick W. Taylor.

Sequential Interdependence A condition where units within an organization are serially dependent on each other to produce a good or service. *See* Long-Linked Technology.

Side Payment The price participants (for example, investors, employees, customers) require for their cooperation with the demands of other participants or groups of participants.

Simple Structure The structure of usually small organizations where tasks are not highly specialized among employees or between employees and an owner/manager. Simple structures also tend to be highly centralized.

Skill Variety A core job design characteristic referring to the extent to which an employee uses a variety of skills in job performance.

Socialization The process through which individuals learn what behaviors are and are not acceptable within an organization.

Specialist Organization Term from population ecology referring to an organization with a relatively narrow domain of operation. *See* Generalist Organization.

Stakeholder (or Multiple-Constituency) Approach An approach that defines organizational effectiveness as the extent to which an organization's stakeholders (e.g., customers, employees, shareholders, government agencies, creditors) are satisfied with an organization's performance.

Strategic Choice Theoretical approach to organization-environment relations that focuses on managers' perceptions and enactment of an organization's environment.

Subject Reactivity The tendency of people who are aware that they are being studied to modify their behavior.

Suboptimize Function at less than an optimum level.

System A set of interdependent parts that relate in the accomplishment of some purpose.

System-Resource Approach An approach that defines organizational effectiveness as the degree to which an organization is successful in acquiring scarce and valued resources.

Task Environment Aspects of the general environment relevant to an organization's goal setting and goal attainment.

Task Forces and Standing Committees Integrating mechanism used to facilitate communication among representatives of units having a common interest or problem by assembling them together as a working group.

Task Identity A core job design characteristic referring to the extent to which employees can clearly identify with the outcome of their effort.

Task Significance A core job design dimension referring to the extent to which an employee perceives that the performance of his or her job makes a significant contribution to others, inside or outside the organization.

Technological Complexity The degree of control and predictability of the production process.

Technological Interdependence The pattern of interactions among units within an organization.

Technology The techniques and processes used by an organization in the transformation of material or informational inputs (for example, labor, knowledge, capital, or raw materials) into various outputs (either goods or services).

Theory A group of interrelated principles derived from hypotheses and dealing simultaneously with the same theme.

Triangulation The use of multiple research methods.

Uncertainty Condition of decision making in which the available alternatives, the likelihood of their occurrence, and their potential outcomes are unknown.

Unit/Small-Batch Technology A production system that manufactures only one or a few of a particular item.

Value-Adding Partnerships A vertically disaggregated interorganizational design where two or more organizations specialize in different areas of the production of a good or service.

Vertical Job Specialization Refers to a low degree of employee discretion in how a job will be performed, usually as a result of horizontal job specialization.

Workflow Interdependence The interdependence among individuals in different functional areas who are producing a common good or service.

Working to the Rules Performing exactly what is required by prevailing work rules and nothing more.

NAME INDEX

SUBJECT INDEX

Note: A boldface entry indicates a key term that can be found in the Glossary.